CASEBOOK SERIES ON EUROPEAN POLITICS AND SOCIETY NO. 1
Director, Stanley Hoffmann

The Communist Parties of Italy, France and Spain: Postwar Change and Continuity

CASEBOOK SERIES ON EUROPEAN POLITICS AND SOCIETY

2 CULTURE AND SOCIETY IN CONTEMPORARY EUROPE
Edited by Stanley Hoffmann and Paschalis Kitromilides

The Communist Parties of Italy, France and Spain:
Postwar Change and Continuity

A Casebook

Edited by
PETER LANGE
MAURIZIO VANNICELLI
Center for European Studies, Harvard University

With a Foreword by
STANLEY HOFFMANN,
Chairman of the Center for European Studies, Harvard University and Director of the Casebook Series on European Politics and Society

GEORGE ALLEN & UNWIN
Center for European Studies, Harvard University

First published in 1981

GEORGE ALLEN & UNWIN LTD
40 Museum Street, London WC1A 1LU

© Selection and compilation, The President and Fellows of Harvard College, 1981; © Editorial matter, Peter Lange and Maurizio Vannicelli, 1981; © Foreword, Stanley Hoffmann, 1981.

British Library Cataloguing in Publication Data

The Communist parties of Italy, France and Spain. –
(Casebook series on European politics and
society; vol. 1).
1. Communist parties – Europe – History
I. Lange, Peter   II. Vannicelli, Maurizio
III. Series
324.24'075'09   JN94.A979   80-41833

ISBN 0-04-329033-7
ISBN 0-04-329034-5 Pbk

Set in 10 on 11 point Plantin by Typesetters (Birmingham) Ltd
and printed in Great Britain
by Hazell Watson & Viney Ltd, Aylesbury, Bucks.

LK 7-29-82

Contents

To Abbey

Foreword

Students of European affairs and of communist movements may greet another volume on what is generally called eurocommunism with a mix of exasperation and incredulity. Has not enough been said already about a phenomenon that was treated far too seriously while it lasted, and that now deserves to be buried?

However, the mass of documents painstakingly selected by Messrs Lange and Vannicelli have a great and original merit: they allow the readers to judge for themselves rather than having to rely on the speculations and categorical opinions of innumerable commentators. And the subtle introductory essays written by Lange and Vannicelli constitute neither special pleading nor attempts at prophecy, they neither point with pleasure nor denounce with alarm. They put in historical and national perspective something that has never been a single movement, and even less a wave sweeping Western Europe (which it would be in America's national interest either to break by building a barrage, or to greet by splashing happily in it). They are dealing, on the one hand, with a common problem: the situation of three major West European communist parties, linked to Moscow since the beginning of the Third International by ideological and institutional bonds, yet out of the government (which it is the objective of any revolutionary party to conquer, or at least to share), and operating within rapidly industrializing (some might say even post-industrializing) Western societies, in which the industrial proletariat has grown along lines far more complex than those forecast by Marxist dogma, in which the political systems, through various tribulations, have led not to single-party 'socialism' but to varieties of representative and pluralist democracy, and which all belong to what the Soviet Union considers to be the American camp. But Lange and Vannicelli, on the other hand, are looking at a complex process: trying to define a communist way adapted to the specific realities of their country has been, for the three parties in question, anything but simple and clear; it has never taken them on a single straight road; they have followed separate, winding paths, which have converged at times and diverged at other moments. This is precisely why the term 'eurocommunism' has always been misleading.

All that it should suggest is an attempt to find a road that is not necessarily and constantly that of Moscow – either in the realm of ideology, or in that of policy, or in organization, or with respect to the issue of Moscow's control of the apparatus. But even in so far as relations with Moscow are concerned, it is always necessary to ask three distinct questions. In which of these areas does the party try to assert its originality or autonomy? Since when, and for how long? And who initiated the quest (after all, Moscow's control is not incompatible with the definition of separate national strategies) or, to put it somewhat differently, to what extent did Moscow incite, or merely accept, or actually oppose which search? Moreover, the party's relation to Moscow is not the only interesting problem. There is also the relationship of the party to the other national political forces, and to the national society: how radical a transformation of it does the party seek, with whom, at what price? And there is the relation of each of these parties to the other communist parties of Western Europe, and to the developing European Community.

It is clear that different answers have been given to these questions at different moments by all three parties. Even though there have been some (not many) joint meetings between their leaders, they have remained divided, in the first place, by their very different pasts: their organization, ideology and strategies had never been the same – and the contrast was particularly sharp between the French, with their attempt to control membership, their *ouvriérisme*, their defensiveness, and the Italians with their mass party and Gramsci's hegemonic idea. They have also been separated by contemporary divergences in three areas: the effect of recent national experiences (with the Spanish and Italian parties, after the traumatic experiences of prolonged dictatorship, giving priority to anti-fascism, while the French party sometimes behaved as if bourgeois democracy was the main enemy), the effect of recent foreign experiences (the French and the Italian parties drew opposite lessons from the turmoil and tragedy of Allende in Chile), the effect of the national situation – both that of the party (which, in France, controls the largest share of the working class, whereas the PCI still shares it with the Christian Democrats) and that of the country (in which the general stability of the regime, and the role and importance of the socialist parties, are of course key factors).

Precisely because of national differences, and because of the twists and turns of each national strategy (twists and turns that can only be understood by reference to the international situation – in turn, appraised differently in each country – and to the domestic political constellation of the moment), it never made any sense for American policy-makers to respond to the so-called phenomenon of eurocommunism in a monolithic way. We were not dealing with a monolith traveling on a pre-programmed trajectory. There exists, indeed, a double problem – the integration, or lack of integration, of the working class in the society and polity of Western European countries (and the formidable tensions that result from the lack of integration), and the costs which American foreign policy and strategic positions would suffer if the communist parties of Western Europe came to power (an expression which is itself far too vague, since there are degrees of power, as the Italian case demonstrates). But the answers are different in different times and places, and it can never be assumed as a matter of principle that the costs would always necessarily be so high as to offset the advantages which both Western European nations and Washington itself might find in a less imperfect relationship between that part of the working class that keeps supporting the communist parties, and the rest of the national society.

This volume documents the common questions and the multiple responses – for instance, the different attitudes toward the EEC, toward the superpowers' contest, toward political alliances, or the different responses to demands for greater freedom of expression within each party and for a loosening of 'democratic centralism.' Published at a time when the divergences seem greater than ever and when the contrast between the French party's abrupt zigzags and 180-degree turns, and the sinuous, almost baroque set of Italian variations and arabesques is at its most obvious, this volume is useful not because it is the documented balance sheet of a failed and dead experiment, but because it allows one to understand the continuing process and drama that result from the multiple reactions which ever-changing events suggest to three parties faced both with a common predicament and with different national situations.

STANLEY HOFFMANN

Acknowledgements

The preparation of this casebook, the first in the Center for European Studies series on European politics and society to be published by George Allen & Unwin, became, in tritest terms, a learning experience for all involved. When the idea of this casebook first emerged, it seemed a relatively simple and useful task: the collection, translation, editing and assembling of Italian, French and Spanish communist party documents within a framework designed to show the development of the three parties and their domestic and international roots. As with all 'simple' projects, the reality turned out to be something quite different. The voluminous output of documents by the French and Italian parties kept several Harvard students, notably Liz Sherwood, Mary Jo Connelly and Giovanella Cingano, busy during the summer of 1978 reading, collecting, xeroxing and analyzing materials. On the other hand, even the crevices of the extraordinary Harvard library system did not hold the Spanish documents which we needed − the PCE had too recently come 'above ground' to have created a broad distribution system for its materials. So, with minimal funds available, we prevailed upon a Harvard senior who had written his thesis on the Spanish Communist Party, Dan Rabinowitz, to take a Laker flight to London and hitch-hike to Madrid, where he spent a sleepless week xeroxing.

Financial constraints and a desire on our part to keep the casebooks an educational project in their production as well as in their usage led us to hire student translators and editors for the collected materials. Special recognition for this laborious work during the winter and summer of 1979 must go to Paul Mattick, Jr, for his elegant and efficient translations of French documents, and to David Quilter, who not only employed his sizeable language skills by translating documents in all three languages, but also organized a whole contingent of undergraduates who worked many hours on translations. As time went on, more and more students became involved in this work, many of them learning of the eurocommunism project from courses they took from professors and teaching fellows affiliated with the Center for European Studies. We will never be able to reimburse properly our translators for their work, but our great appreciation goes to Lisa Doneghy, Frank Gellardin, Dominique Ghossein, Kate Gitlow, Susan Heard, David Low, Edith Scott, Nicole Sinek, Kerry Sorenson, Sandro Tombesi, Janet Towse, Vicente Valle and Fernando Vidal.

The difficult task of editing the documents for consistency, coherence and readability, while maintaining the particular style and flavor of each party and each language, was assumed by Neal Johnson, a Harvard senior, during the summer of 1979. It was at this point that the particular human resources of the Center for European Studies became invaluable: resident country experts or natives could be called upon for evaluation and analysis of phrases, shades of meaning, and so on. In this category, very special appreciation is extended to Antonio Bar, a research associate of the Center from the University of Zaragoza in Spain, and Paul Friedrich, a Harvard German Kennedy Memorial Fellow, who gave freely of their time and knowledge.

The final organization and assemblage of the casebook was done in the fall and winter of 1979−80. The preparation of the essays was the product of much discussion, debate and drafting among the editors in trying to take account of the shifting fortunes and policies of the three parties. The final version of the introductory essay was prepared by Peter Lange, the section essays by Maurizio Vannicelli and Peter Lange. Harvard students Suzanne Marilley, Carlos Navaez and Liz Sherwood researched the glossary. Throughout the lengthy process of production, the staff of the Center for European Studies tolerated innumerable pressures and disruptions. Marilyn Arsem, Peggy Coulson-Graceffa, Bob Allen, Jeanne Finning, Emily Odza, Donna Isaac-Gelfand and Jill Singer all gave many extra hours to type, xerox, proof-read and edit. We would also like to thank Hilde Stempel, Kenji Ogata and Barbara Talhouni who managed to type the final manuscript from heavily edited material.

Although any casebook of this type is mainly the product of a lot of hard work and much drudgery, we feel that the inclusion of undergraduates (American and European), Center Associates and staff make it a uniquely special expression of the Center's approach to the training and teaching of European politics. This approach, however, would have been impossible without the incomparable day-to-day oversight of the project by Abby Collins. Her administrative skills and unflagging attention to detail were combined with a spirit of the project as a whole which enabled her to enthuse all those who became involved and to give the good-spirited nudge when things began to drag. Without her this casebook and the larger project of which it is a part would never have seen the light of day.

Dilemmas of Change: Eurocommunism and National Parties in Postwar Perspective

Only a few short years ago, examinations of contemporary political trends in Western Europe had to come to terms with eurocommunism. The political gains of the southern European communist parties and the apparent, and self-declared, similarity of their doctrinal and strategic evolution seemed sufficiently important to warrant sometimes dire warnings from leaders of the major Western democracies, sharp criticism from high levels of the Soviet Union and inclusion in textbooks on comparative European politics. A vast number of scholarly articles analyzed the nature and future of eurocommunism and of the nations in which the eurocommunist parties were playing an increasing role. Whether hailed as a new, more advanced form of Marxism or denounced as another chameleon-like reincarnation of the communism of old, whether welcomed as a long overdue adaptation of Western European communism to Western traditions or decried as a chimera which, if successful, would signal another step in the decline of the West, eurocommunism was the subject of endless debate. The nature, purpose and future of NATO and of the European Economic Community, the possible evolution of relations between the superpowers, the prospects for democratic life in Italy, France and Spain, all these and other momentous issues seemed to hinge in important respects on the real significance of the emerging eurocommunist movement.

Today, not only the sense of urgency which attended the discussion of eurocommunism but the theme itself have largely disappeared. Even before the splits among the parties which emerged over critical questions such as the Soviet invasion of Afghanistan, eurocommunism seemed in decline. The political losses suffered by the parties, their drawing back from the eurocommunist self-characterization and from the public encounters among party leaders which were so much a part of its symbolism, the revival of forms of party behavior which some had judged to be surpassed, the general sense that there was a conservative trend in Europe which would once more isolate the parties, drove eurocommunism from the pages of the press, the columns of the pundits and the research of scholars. If, only a short while ago, the predominant questions had been 'What is eurocommunism?' and 'What are its likely consequences?,' today many would seem inclined to ask, should they even think it worth doing so, 'Did eurocommunism ever exist?' Others would simply conclude that the concept of eurocommunism was never more than an artifice imposed by ideologues, trendy journalists, naïve academics and overanxious policy analysts on an unchanging and perhaps unchangeable communist reality.

It has been an assumption in the preparation of this casebook that these latter views, like the initial analyses of eurocommunism to which they were a reaction, have been based on a flawed approach to the issues raised by the development of the southern

European communist parties. The approach had tended to treat eurocommunism as a fixed doctrine and/or as a stage of party change with specifiable traits against which the 'progress' of any particular party might be measured. In contrast, we have found it more useful to understand eurocommunism as a *process* of change. This process has been gradual, uneven, and often halting and contradictory, but it has occurred along different dimensions which are identifiable, as are the features of party life which are undergoing transformation, and some of the critical turning points and causal factors. The final outcomes of the process remain uncertain and not wholly defined. We know more about where the parties have come from, what they have been reacting against and how they have reached their present positions than about where they might go and what they are striving for. The documents reflect clearly the degree to which the parties have changed in the postwar years, as well as the often fitful and uneven character of the process of change. They also show the extent to which the process of change seems more the product of an uncertain groping for new positions in the face of pressures beyond the parties' control than the result of a calculated movement toward clearly defined goals.

If the first feature of our approach is that we treat eurocommunism as an open-ended process, the second is that we view this process as one of gradual and mediated adaptation of the parties to the domestic and international contexts in which they have operated. Highlighting this interdependence of the parties with their national and international environments is a departure from the analytical standpoint which treated communist parties as almost wholly self-contained, ideologically driven agents of a foreign power, 'organizational weapons' entirely alien to the societies in which they functioned. This latter standpoint led analysts to concentrate on factors entirely internal to the parties – their ideology, their system of discipline – and on their linkages with the Communist Party of the Soviet Union and its goals. Sensitivity to the parties' interdependence with their domestic and international contexts, in contrast, requires that in analyzing change one pay heed not only to those factors which have affected all three parties similarly and to those which have been peculiar to individual parties, but also to the ways in which even experiences common to all the parties have been filtered by national settings and party traditions, sometimes leading to very different responses on the part of the individual parties.

The interplay between the general and the specific, between what is shared and what is peculiar, has been extremely important in guiding the selection of documents. We have sought to provide the student or scholar with a clear sense of the development of each of the national parties. At the same time, we have assured that there are sufficient common points of reference – events to which all the parties have reacted, issues they have all faced, problems they have all had to manage – to allow for comparison. Thus, the reader should be able to observe and judge, over time, how much, in what way and, to some extent, why each party has changed or not changed along a variety of dimensions.

In the remainder of this introductory essay we will present the outline for the analysis of the parties which guided preparation of the casebook and which we think useful in understanding eurocommunism. Before turning to this schema, however, a few obvious questions raised by the organization of the casebook should be answered.

Why these parties?

Eurocommunism, as we define it, is not confined to the Italian, French and Spanish communist parties, nor is it a uniquely European phenomenon. Other communist parties in Europe have been subject to the same process of change in recent years: and some, such as the Swedish, have been transformed in a more substantial and coherent fashion than any of the southern European parties. The Japanese Communist Party has developed its doctrine, strategy and specific policies in ways which parallel the southern Europeans. Eurocommunism, then, is a widespread process and is associated not so much with Europe as with advanced industrial democracy.

There are, of course, obvious exceptions: the communist parties of Portugal and the United States, to cite two prominent examples. The exceptions would suggest that eurocommunism is less likely to emerge in societies which are less developed and more peripheral to the advanced industrial political economy and/or in communist parties which are politically and socially isolated within their societies and can hope to achieve national power only on the heels of major social upheaval. Why these two conditions should make eurocommunism less probable will become clear below as we discuss the factors which have promoted its development in other countries.

Within the range of cases in which eurocommunist developments are present, the selection of the southern European parties was based on three intersecting criteria. The first was practical. Our intention to provide a historical panorama of party development along a number of policy dimensions required the presentation of a large number of documents for each party, thus limiting the number of parties which could be covered. On a more substantive basis, we decided that, given the limitation on the number of parties to be examined, we should concentrate on those which were both relatively large in membership and electoral terms and which have played and continue to play a major role in the political development of their respective societies. Finally, we also wanted parties which have played a prominent role in international politics, both within the communist movement and, due to their presence, strength and policies, in relations among the major Western powers. On these bases, the Italian, French and Spanish communist parties (PCI, PCF and PCE) are by far the most appropriate cases.

Why begin with the end of the Second World War?

Eurocommunism is a concept of the 1970s. Its origins, while somewhat contested, date from the middle of the decade when the parties of Italy, France and Spain appeared both to be making major gains in domestic politics and to be moving rapidly toward revision of most of their traditional Marxist–Leninist doctrines and practices. The PCI's (Italian Communist Party's) acceptance of NATO, the PCF's (French Communist Party's) abandonment of the dogma of dictatorship of the proletariat, the PCE's (Spanish Communist Party's) of the acceptance of the Spanish monarchy all came at about the same time and, tied to a number of other changes, appeared to signal the emergence of a new movement. Some went so far as to think that a possible third great schism was developing within international communism. Whether or not that was the case, to all but the experts on European communism, something wholly new seemed to be emerging, a notion both symbolized and reinforced by the coinage of a new term, eurocommunism.

Both the suggestion of novelty and the expectations which accompanied it were exaggerated, exaggeration which explains in considerable part the speed with which the term has been abandoned subsequently. There were a number of novel revisions of doctrine undertaken by the parties in the mid-1970s, some of them of considerable importance, especially for the parties' relations with other parties and social forces within their countries and for their ability to achieve legitimacy in a broader international setting. None the less, with a few notable exceptions, the parties had been laying the ground for these revisions for a number of years as they gradually responded to changing conditions in the national and international context in which they operated.

The timing of the dramatic new stances at mid-decade was undoubtedly related to the particular conjuncture of international and domestic developments: the springtime of détente, the severe strains of stagflation, the decay of conservative regimes too long in power. All these presented the parties with new opportunities for national power. The timing was also a product of a kind of implicit co-operation/competition among the parties as they sought to benefit from the image of innovation and strength projected by any one of them and to avoid being seen as a laggard, out of step with the revisionist march. The parties' eventual acceptance of the 'bourgeois' term, Eurocommunism, to characterize their new, common front was part and parcel of the process. Of course, in such a situation the room for tactical maneuver was considerable. It is not surprising, therefore, that one of the parties, the PCF, often seemed more a free rider than an innovator, less a convinced eurocommunist than a seconder of the initiatives of others. The French party, the documents clearly show, was more willing than the others to try to capitalize on the conjuncture without developing broader analyses or drawing more general theoretical and strategic conclusions. None the less, even for the PCF, and certainly for the others, most of the new positions which were subsumed under the term eurocommunism had foundations in longer processes of change and adaptation; and when they did not, only a long retrospective view could show this to be the case.

This, then, suggests why we have felt that an analysis of eurocommunism as a process of party change must be historical. Only thereby can one identify its roots and causes, its coherence and contradictions, the degree to which it is common to several parties or peculiar to one or another. It appeared important to provide sufficient documentation to allow the reader to see to what extent any of the parties has taken the lead and been consistent in its revisionism, and under what conditions change has occurred and has been more or less rapid, or even reversed.

But how far back should one go? The PCI traces the roots of its postwar strategy and of many of the positions which it has assumed in recent years to the heritage of Antonio Gramsci, one of the party's founders, its second general secretary and a major Marxist, and Italian, theoretician, who died in 1937, after eleven years in fascist prisons. The Spanish and French parties make lesser historical claims, in part because they have less eminent national theoretical traditions. For these parties' changes, which eventually led to some of the positions of the 1970s, appear to date from the traumas of 1956, or even later developments. Thus, the problem of starting point, always an issue in historical analyses, is complex.

The decision to begin with documents from the immediate post-Second World War years was based on two considerations, First, the development of the parties since 1945 can be interpreted as evolving attempts to find doctrines and strategies for influence and power within structural constraints which challenge Marxist–Leninist dogmas and traditional communist strategies. These constraints, and the problems they posed for the parties, can be traced to the years immediately following the end of the Second World War. In the international arena, the *division of Europe* harshly posed for the parties the problem of what balance to strike between their loyalty to the Soviet Union and the fact that they would have to operate in countries under the United States' strategic, political and economic umbrella. The fact that the Soviets basically accepted the division while at the same time making clear (after 1947) that they intended to use the Western parties as instruments in the Cold War struggle with the United States only aggravated the problem. In domestic politics, the immediate postwar years were marked by the re-establishment and consolidation of democratic regimes in France and Italy, and the survival and reinforcement of Francoism in Spain. For the Spanish party, this meant merely that the clandestine struggle would continue, a prospect for which a Leninist party was well suited. For the French and Italian parties, however, the problem was how to seek power in a democratic context while at the same time remaining true to the parties' Leninist and internationalist identity. In the domestic political economies, the immediate postwar years signalled the firm rooting of processes of advanced capitalist development which were increasingly to confound the communists' catastrophic economic predictions and the social and political consequences they drew from them. Even in the first years after the war, the parties had to recognize that the immediate socialization of their domestic economies was improbable. The problem, which became more intense as capitalist reconstruction (in France and Italy) took hold and as the Spanish economy became successfully industrialized, was how to analyze the emerging political economy of an advanced industrial welfare system and how to devise a strategy which might win support both within a more affluent and socially differentiated working class and among other social strata. This problem, and the constraint to which it was linked, was closely related to the preceding two. Together, they meant that the parties were, from the immediate postwar years, faced with a profound tension between their traditional analyses and ways of doing things and the realities of the postwar Western European world.

This brings us to the second consideration in choosing the immediate postwar period as a starting point. The three parties did not immediately respond to the new constraints and the problems posed by them. After an initial period of moderation, corresponding to the time of their participation in broad national coalition governments and a relatively relaxed international atmosphere, the parties returned to more rigid, traditional and pro-Soviet positions. There were differences. The PCI much more than the PCF sought to maintain some of the policy lines which it had developed at the end of the war. None the less, both parties basically pursued policies which reflected their traditions and their linkages to the Soviet Union. The start of their gradual adjustment to the international and domestic constraints which they already faced was to await events in the 1950s. The documents from this earlier period, therefore, establish a base line against which later developments can be judged, as well as, in a few cases, showing some of the ways the parties responded to the peculiar conditions immediately after the war.

The preceding remarks should enable the user of this volume to identify the major features of its organization and the major premises on which that organization is based. In addition, we have begun to indicate some of the factors which we feel can explain the development of the eurocommunism process. In the pages which follow, we want more systematically to offer an interpretation of eurocommunism, indicating some of its basic dimensions and postwar determinants.

Eurocommunism is, for us, a process. Such an interpretation may seem obvious to many, but it is worthwhile spelling out its several implications. The accuracy of this interpretation can thereby be better judged in light of the documents.

To consider eurocommunism as a process implies, first of all, rejection of the view that the development of the post-Second World War parties has been simply the product of rational, instrumental calculation on the part of party leaders in pursuit of ideologically derived goals. This instrumentalist interpretation has been common, and often justified, in the past. It is consistent with the Leninist doctrine of the vanguard party of professional revolutionaries. It is also consistent with much of communist practice in the period between the wars when the parties were relatively small, their internal discipline rigid and when the political climate was polarized and highly charged. Goals, strategies and tactics determined in Moscow could be, and were, imposed on the national party organizations and were implemented with discipline, regardless of their appropriateness to the national circumstances in which any individual party found itself or of the preferences of national party leaders or members. The parties then were truly 'sections of the Third International.' The most dramatic example is, perhaps, the acceptance of the consequences of the Hitler–Stalin pact in 1939, which required a sharp break with the policies and alliances which the national European parties had been pursuing since the equally centralized and abrupt shift to the policy of the Popular Front in 1934.

In the postwar period this instrumentalist interpretation seems increasingly less appropriate. The reasons for this will be sketched below: they have to do with the kinds of changes in the parties' environments which were indicated earlier as characterizing the postwar period. They have to do as well with the changing role and character of the parties' electorates and with modifications in their organizations. On the one hand, the parties have assigned increasing importance to electoral politics. The size of the party vote, both in absolute terms and relative to preceding elections, has become a measure of the success of party policies, a sign of the extent of their national legitimacy and a criterion by which to judge the strength of their position with respect to other parties, particularly other parties on the left. The shifting policies of the PCF in the 1970s, for instance, cannot be understood without paying heed to the party's battle with the French Socialist Party for electoral dominance of the left. At the same time, the salience of electoral politics has led the parties to broaden their electoral appeals. As the parties' electorates have become more heterogeneous, however, party policy, especially at election time, has increasingly reflected this heterogeneity. It has, therefore, shifted to adjust to the pressures coming from different sectors of voters and/or has had the effect of obscuring potential contradictions and inconsistencies. On the other hand, the parties' organizations have also become less wieldy. Larger memberships, less strict criteria of membership, the erosion of old revolutionary models and myths, the increasing involvement of the parties in electoral and institutional politics have been coupled with a declining capacity to encapsulate, indoctrinate and discipline members. Supporters have become less communist, more Italian, French, or Spanish. This change has not been of equal extent or speed in the parties. It has gone farthest and fastest in the PCI. The French and Spanish parties have been slower to change the way they make and implement policies, even when the policies themselves have been similar to those of the Italians. None the less, none of the parties is any longer an 'organizational weapon' in the hands of party leaders, much less of the leaders of the Soviet party. They have become societally embedded institutions. Thus, their policies are today the product of a mix of goal-oriented behavior determined by party leadership (influenced by the national, international and party contexts) and adaptive behavior reflecting the interaction of party members and cadres with the societies in which they live and work. It is out of this crucible of intention and adaptation that the process of eurocommunism has developed.

A second implication of the interpretation of eurocommunism as a process is that it is to be understood historically and not just as the product of the contemporary conditions in which the parties operate. Such a historical perspective does not simply mean paying heed to the long development of each party's strategy, although this is certainly part of what is intended. It also means taking note of the ways the past conditions the present. This conditioning takes several forms. First, it appears as the conscious rejection of past values, strategic orientations and tactics by leaders and members, either because these have fallen into general disrepute (for example, Stalinism) or because they have been judged inappropriate to promotion of the parties' goals in the postwar world and in their specific national contexts. Secondly, it appears as a response to the experiences of the parties themselves, to the policies that have succeeded or failed and to the ways party members have reacted to policy innovation or stagnation. Finally, and at a less conscious level, the historical conditioning of party policy appears as the response to the larger national and international processes of stability and change with which the parties interact and to which they adapt.

The third implication of viewing eurocommunism as a process is that change in the parties' ideological positions, strategies and policies need not be uniform and consistent but may instead appear in some arenas and not in others. Whether change is the product of intention or adaptation, there is no reason to assume that it will occur uniformly in all areas of party life. From the standpoint of the leaders, even if they wish to revise party values or policy, they are unlikely to do so in one dramatic shift, for the risks both in terms of the support of members and the reactions of those outside the party are indeterminate, and so too are the advantages. Thus change is likely to be incremental and often disguised in small changes in nuance. Furthermore, leaders may feel that change in one area of party policy, let us say toward greater moderation in domestic affairs, requires stability or even change in the opposite direction in another area of party affairs – foreign policy, for instance. In this sense, the European communist parties are increasingly like other political parties and large institutions. Since the transmission of directives from top to bottom can no longer occur with the discipline of the past, and since members and supporters have multiple ways of expressing their discontent with policies, ways which may damage the ability of the party to implement any policy, leaders are likely to search out the mix of tradition and innovation which they feel most likely to maintain effective party performance in the short run while promoting long-run change toward stances they prefer. Uneven change, therefore, is not just the expression of the weight of tradition or of a lack of clarity of purpose, although it may be both of these; it is also often a counsel of wisdom.

To the extent that change is the product of adaptation, unevenness and inconsistency are even more likely. The world does not, except in occasional abstractions of social scientists, change in consistent and uniform ways. Contradictory processes are often at work. Institutions, including European communist parties, which are adapting and responsive to these processes are also likely to be changing unevenly and in sometimes contradictory fashion. Party leaders, seeking to behave strategically, may seek to impose coherence where adaptation, if left alone, would be even more incoherent. None the less, as we have already noted, it is unlikely that even leadership's intentional intervention will bring uniformity and consistency to party behavior.

The fourth implication of viewing eurocommunism as a process is that its development is unlikely to be linear: reverses are possible. This is the case for two reasons. First, we have already suggested that change in the parties is the product of adjustment, both intentional and adaptive, to changes in the national and international environments in which the parties operate. There is, however, no reason that these external conditions develop in any linear way. To take but two examples, neither steady untroubled Western economic growth nor international détente have proven irreversible characteristics of the post-Second World War world. To the degree that the communist parties have been adjusting their ideologies, strategies and policies to come to terms with these external conditions, it should not come as a surprise if sharp changes or even reverses in direction were to take place in party policy. This need not suggest that all change in the parties is contingent, subject to rapid abandonment in the face of environmental change. If this were the case, the process of eurocommunism would itself lose most of its significance. Rather, what is intended, on the one hand, is that one should not expect change in the parties to occur without reversals, and, on the other hand, that the process of eurocommunism can be identified precisely in those features of party change which, over an extended period of time, resist even reverses in the pattern of external change to which the party changes were initially a response.

The second reason why the process of eurocommunism may be subject to reversals is that the party leaderships which to some extent are guiding the process are not themselves certain of where they wish to carry their parties. While there may be some clarity about what positions – ideological, strategic, policy – need to be abandoned, it seems that the leaderships are far less clear about how their parties can best pursue their goals in a changed and changing world. As a result, it should not come as a surprise that positions are sometimes undertaken and subsequently abandoned. Reactions to new postures, both within the parties and from social and political forces outside the parties, may lead to rethinking and to different attempts to accomplish similar ends. In this sense, the process of eurocommunism can be viewed as the expression of political experimentation on the part of historically formed political parties seeking to adjust deeply entrenched ideological values and modes of analysis, strategic perspectives and policies to economic, social and political conditions never before encountered. That this process of experimentation and party change, especially in a world which is itself changing, should often take the form 'two steps forward, one step backward' is perhaps unsettling for those who need to make public policy toward the eurocommunist parties but should not be surprising for those who analyze them.

For the latter, the task is to identify what is enduring and what transient in the process.

The final implication of thinking of eurocommunism as a process is that the individual European communist parties cannot be expected to develop in precisely similar ways. This conclusion follows naturally from what has been discussed in the preceding pages. All of the factors which influence the process have taken somewhat different forms with respect to the national parties. The historical traditions and patterns of internal organization of the parties are different. So too are the domestic economic, social and political environments in which the parties have operated. And so too are the positions of the countries in the international system, their national traditions with respect to international politics and the ways in which events, both in the international system generally and in the international communist movement, have affected national politics and the parties themselves. To expect the process of eurocommunism to look alike in each of the three cases, therefore, is to ignore historical specificity.

Again, however, this point can be pushed too far, suggesting that eurocommunism as a general process does not exist. We would not agree, and we think the documents clearly show this is not the case. Rather, the historical specificity of the cases should alert us, on the one hand, to look for those factors which, while beneath the surface, have influenced the development of all three of the parties, pushing all three to abandon doctrines and practices which they shared in the past and to seek new positions, many of which have traits in common. These factors will be highlighted when we turn to a brief examination of the dimensions of eurocommunism. On the other hand, we need at the same time to be sensitive to the ways these general factors, and the issues and problems they pose for the parties, have been filtered through specific national traditions, experiences, institutions and processes and have been mediated by the internal traditions and organizational characteristics of the parties themselves. As we have suggested at several points, it is this interplay between the general and the specific in the parties' environments and the ways these external pressures are mediated both by the intentionality of party leaders and the less conscious processes of party adaptation which lie at the heart of the process of eurocommunism. A brief overview of the dimensions of this process should enable us more concretely to identify what is enduring and what fleeting in that process.

Dimensions of Eurocommunism

The process of eurocommunism has been uneven. The pace, regularity and consistency of change have differed from party to party. They have differed as well as one examines different aspects of doctrine, strategy and practice in any individual party. The latter requires that one identify divisions within the process which facilitate its analysis. The documents collected in this volume have been divided into five categories (general strategy, political and social alliances, internal party affairs, relations with the international communist movement, relations with the international system). This division provides the reader with a general overview of the development of the various parties' strategies and with more specific detail on issues toward which ongoing policy decisions and adjustments have been necessary. The emphasis in these divisions is on eurocommunism as a process reflected in statements about practical political policies and how these are justified (or not justified) in terms of doctrine. Our focus, then, is on the outcomes of the process and each section is preceded by an introduction which highlights features of the documents which are of particular interest from a comparative standpoint.

The process of eurocommunism, however, can be analyzed as well from the standpoint of the extent and character of the breaks which the development of the parties' policies has made with the traditions of Leninism and the Third International. The focus here is on dimensions of change, on the general factors which have influenced the process in all the parties and on the ways these have been filtered through specific national conditions and experiences. In the next few pages we will look at the process from this perspective. No extensive description will be undertaken. Rather, we want simply to lay out an overview which can be used by the reader to give some causal ordering to the general and party-specific developments.

Two general dimensions of change from traditional doctrine and practice can be identified: subordination/autonomy (with respect to the policies of the Soviet Union) and one-party rule/democratic pluralism. In turning to a brief discussion of these dimensions and of the factors which have promoted change along them, it is worthwhile restating two points previously discussed. First, it is much easier to delineate the specific content of the doctrines and policies which the parties have been abandoning than that of the positions toward which they are moving. All of the parties appear to have made a significant break with their traditional postures toward the Soviet Union and toward one-party rule. But to differing extents, none of the parties has settled on precise consistent understandings of what policies are implied by autonomy from the Soviet Union or acceptance of democratic pluralism. Nor have they entirely brought their ideological doctrines into line with their developing strategies and stated policies. In this sense, and the differences among the parties need to be stressed, change has been more a negation of the past than movement toward clearly formulated, ideologically embedded positions on which the parties have settled. Secondly, focusing on these dimensions makes clear once again both the extent to which the process of change has often been the response to events and conditions over which the parties have had little control and why this has meant that the process has often been fitful and subject to reverses.

Subordination/Autonomy

Prior to the end of the Second World War, the history of the relationship between the European communist parties and the Soviet Union was fundamentally one of subordination, a subordination expressed in the fact that during much of this period the parties called themselves 'sections of the Third International.' This should not suggest that there were no disagreements between the national party leaderships and the Soviet and International leaders. There were several important disputes. None the less, it was decisions taken at the international level which were determinant of national party doctrine and policy. Part and parcel of this relationship was the parties' acceptance of Soviet ideology, revolutionary strategy and model of development.

There were numerous factors which contributed to this relationship. The parties had been born of the Russian revolution, of Lenin's efforts to build a European communist challenge to the dominant socialist parties of the Second International and to the new Soviet state's sense that its survival depended on revolution in the West. By the late 1920s the Soviet party had been able to impose its will on the individual national parties, often through the direct selection of their national leaderships. Secondly, once the parties were formed, the Soviet party and nation became a fundamental resource in their attempts to promote revolution at home. On the one hand, the myth of the revolution was at the heart of the parties' ability to win and mobilize support. On the other hand, the parties were convinced that the Soviet Union's existence was essential to their own survival. Soviet interests, the interests of world revolution and the interests of the individual national parties were inextricably intertwined, and the final judgement of what policies best served these interests lay at the center of the movement, in Moscow.

By the end of the Second World War some of this structure had begun to break down, in part through the action of the Soviets themselves. The recognition in 1935 that the rise of fascism signalled the need to develop communist strategies which might differ from those which had been used in 1917, and the dissolution of the Comintern in 1943, began to loosen the bonds between the parties. Furthermore, the prestige which the French and Italian parties gained during their respective national resistance movements gave them autonomous resources in developing national support. There is little doubt, however, that at the end of the war even the Italian party, which seemed most inclined to develop a national strategy, and which had an independent theoretical tradition on which to draw in developing that strategy, remained fundamentally subordinate to Soviet direction. There was, for both the Italian and French parties, greater flexibility in the period of flux of the immediate postwar years, but with the onset of the Cold War and the creation, on Soviet initiative, of the Cominform, tighter subordination was restored. This is most clearly evidenced in the parties' acceptance of the Soviet-inspired criticisms of their policies at the first meeting of the Cominform in 1947, their strident rejection of the Marshall Plan, their willingness to follow the Soviet lead in condemning Yugoslavia and their mobilization against the formation of the Atlantic Alliance. In a period of intense international and domestic tension and hostility toward communism, close links to the Soviet Union and acceptance of its guidance were, for the Western communist parties, almost a necessity. The ideological and material resources which they derived from this relationship were critical to their survival and the polarized situation left little room for maneuver.

The years since 1956 have been marked by the development of more autonomous postures. On ideological issues the parties have, to varying extents, abandoned many of the precepts which have been traditional in the communist movement and which the Soviet Union continues to espouse. The parties have also become increasingly critical of the Soviet model of a socialist society and have abandoned the notion that this model is appropriate to the countries in which they operate. Again distinct differences still remain between the parties. Finally, the parties have taken foreign and domestic policy positions which are in disaccord with those of the Soviet Union. Domestically, for instance, the parties have pursued political alliances of which the Soviets publicly disapproved. In the area of foreign policy, the parties have lent varying degrees of support or acquiescence to institutions and policies of which the Soviets disapprove (the European Economic Community) or which have an anti-Soviet function (NATO), and have openly opposed Soviet foreign policy behavior (Czechoslovakia, and, more recently, PCI and PCE condemnation of the Soviet invasion of Afghanistan). The specific details of how the development of greater autonomy has proceeded can be followed in the documents. In general, one can say that change has come first in strategy and on specific policy issues and only later, and much more slowly, in ideology and in general conclusions about the USSR. It has been most difficult when the adoption of new positions required not just quiet and subtle differentiation from tradition or from the Soviets, but open and explicit confrontation with them.

The development of greater autonomy has also not proceeded as far, as fast, nor as coherently in all three parties. The PCI began earlier, has sought autonomous positions on a wider scale of issues and has been more consistent in its positions on these issues. The PCE, although operating in clandestinity for much of the postwar period, has also had a fairly long and consistent pattern of autonomous positions. Its relations with the Soviet Union, in fact, have been worse than those of the Italian party, and the PCE's (or, at least, Santiago Carrillo's) criticism of the Soviet model of socialism has been more systematic and thoroughgoing than that of even the PCI. The French party has been later and less consistent in the development of autonomy. Its positions have seemed more contingent, both because they have often come as the result of sudden shifts in policy and because they have, for the most part, been poorly integrated into a changing ideological posture. None the less, even the French party, at least until Afghanistan, appeared somewhat more autonomous from the Soviet Union than in the past.

This raises a final point about the dimension of autonomy. To say that the parties have developed a more autonomous relationship to the Soviet Union does not mean that their positions, especially with respect to foreign policy issues, are never, or even only rarely, consistent with those adopted by the Soviets. The parties have not become, and cannot be expected to become, anti-Soviet and/or pro-American. Nor have they abandoned many of the traditional values which would lead them to support movements and regimes, especially in the Third World, which they view as revolutionary and which the USSR also supports. None the less, when examining the whole range of issues, ideological, strategic, domestic and international, which traditionally have been of concern to the USSR, which affect Soviet interests (as a world power and as a state whose legitimation is strongly tied to ideology) and on which the Soviets express views and criticize the European parties, it is clear that the three parties with which we are concerned have greatly increased their autonomy.

Less clear is how far this process will go and how it might conclude. Particularly the Italian party seems to have reached the point at which its continued unwillingness to repudiate Soviet traditions and behavior *in toto* and to join wholeheartedly the Western camp is becoming the last major obstacle to its participation in national government. At the same time, the increasing frequency and clarity of the party's differences with the USSR make ever more glaring the failure to carry these criticisms to a more systematic level. Finally, as the party approaches governmental power, it is increasingly faced with the need to develop positions on foreign policy issues which cater less to points of principle (where the party can seek some middle ground between Soviet and Western positions) and more to the practical needs of statecraft in a divided world. The party's reluctance to continue the rapid development of its foreign policy and of its analysis of the USSR in the late 1970s may, in part, have been a product of the recognition of these difficulties and of a cautious response to them and to their potential consequences. Of course, the peculiar national and international standing of the PCI makes these problems more difficult for that party than for the others. Nevertheless, they cannot fail to influence the ways in which autonomy develops in the other parties as well. For all three, it is factors such as these which help us understand the sources of the hesitancy and experimentation which characterize this development and the process of eurocommunism as a whole. It is also worthwhile recalling that when the Soviet invasion of Afghanistan once again placed the question of autonomy at the top of the agenda, the PCI (and, more weakly, the PCE) increased their criticism of the Soviet Union and deepened their analysis of the sources of the Soviet's behavior. For these parties, autonomy was further advanced.

One Party/Democratic Pluralism

The orthodox posture of the communist movement to the liberal democracy of the West was disdain or, at most, highly instrumental and tactical support. The communists viewed Western democratic institutions as 'bourgeois democracy,' the expression of the class power of the bourgeoisie. Behind the institutions of fictive political participation and power embodied in the electoral and legislative process lay the invisible, but for that more powerful, exercise of class power. Democratic procedures might at times offer a useful terrain on which to carry forward the fight for socialism in the present, but they were wholly without importance for the socialist state of the future. In the latter, the dictatorship of the proletariat was the appropriate expression of state power.

Underlying this analysis was a fundamental tenet of the classical communist (and also socialist) interpretation of Marxism: that the economic dimension of society, its modes of production and exchange, deterministically shape the political dimension. Politics and political institutions did not have an independent determinative role but rather were nothing but the expression of the relations of class power expressed in the mode of production. Thus, the political institutions of any historical period were (and could be) nothing more than the most appropriate means by which the economically dominant class could exercise political rule and buttress its economic power. It followed, in this interpretation, that the institutions of one historical epoch (defined in terms of class relations) would be wholly outmoded and inappropriate in another epoch. More concretely, the institutions of the era of the ascendancy of the bourgeoisie would be abandoned after the revolution and the ascendancy of the proletariat and the establishment of socialism. The 'dictatorship' (in 'real' if not in formal terms) of the bourgeoisie would be replaced by the dictatorship of the proletariat which would, in the course of the revolution, destroy the bourgeois state, replacing it with institutions which would allow the attainment of a true democracy, possible because of the change in class relations in the economic structure of society.

This conception of the revolutionary process and of liberal democratic institutions had, as its complement, a conception of the role of the communist party which stressed its 'vanguard' function, its privileged access to the correct interpretation of both doctrine and strategic and tactical insight and its need to pursue disciplined action. Such a party would be small and difficult to enter, made up of 'professional revolutionaries,' of the 'few but good,' who would submit to the disciplines of democratic centralism and would commit their lives to revolutionary activity. The party was to be separate from the masses, for its function was to help them create a revolution which they would be unable to achieve, or even aspire to, without the guidance of the vanguard. It would be in close contact with the masses, would seek to organize and mobilize them, sometimes even with clandestine or disguised leadership through 'front' organizations, but it would always be sensitive to the dangers of 'tailism,' of falling victim to the limited, non-revolutionary consciousness of the masses. Furthermore, even in the 'construction of socialism' (i.e. a transitional phase to communism in the orthodox view), this party would have to continue to exercise leadership. It would have to be the agent of the proletariat's dictatorship for a period, assuring that the new socialist society under construction would not succumb to reactionary attempts. Thus, whatever the original intention in Leninist theory, the tendency toward one-party dictatorial rule received legitimation in the thinking of the Third International, in the acceptance of the Soviet Union as a socialist model and in the ideological and practical dependence of the Third International parties on the Soviet Union.

These interrelated doctrines began to erode during the 1930s under the impact of the rise of fascism. The Western parties and the Soviet Union, after first treating fascism as simply a different institutional manifestation of the bourgeoisie's dictatorship, came to realize that there had been advantages for the working class in the liberal democratic institutions and in the pluralistic political process. The new approach was legitimized in the policy of the Popular Front adopted at the Seventh Congress of the Third International in 1935. It was, however, a policy which remained very instrumental or tactical in character: the political alliances with socialist parties which were sought by the communists often were very contingent and much of the purpose was better to protect the Soviet Union from the threat posed by a spread of fascism in the West. This instrumental character was underlined by the fact that the decisions of the mid-1930s were only very limitedly integrated into communist ideology: concepts like the dictatorship of the proletariat with all its implications remained fundamentally untouched. None the less, the innovations of the Seventh Congress have been used by the Western parties in the post-Second World War period as a starting point for their doctrinal revisions.

The process of theoretical and strategic revisionism of the eurocommunist parties in the years since the Second World War has proceeded along several fronts. First, as already discussed, the parties have abandoned the Soviet model as appropriate for the West. In this area, as in the others we shall discuss, the Italian and Spanish parties began earlier, have gone farther and have been more thoroughgoing in their theoretical rethinking than the French party. Secondly, the parties' analyses of modern capitalism, as well as their practice, increasingly suggest to varying extents that there does indeed exist a degree of autonomy for politics. Liberal democracy, with its affirmation of basic civil and political rights and freedoms for *all* members of the community, has been a fundamental achievement which the working class has a stake in and which must form the basis for socialist society in Western Europe. The French party has been more equivocal about whether these rights will be part and parcel of a fully socialist society than the other two parties, but all agree that they must be preserved in the process of building socialism. This does not mean that the parties view these institutional guarantees and procedures as all that is required in order to build and maintain socialist society and 'real' equality. The economic bases of society and the failure to provide individuals with opportunities for participation other than through the electoral and legislative process continue to restrain full liberty. Thus, the parties wish to extend the opportunities for participation, to create participatory mechanisms beyond (but including) those of the classical liberal institutions, as the economic bases of the society are transformed.

In practical terms, this revised theory of the socializing and socialist state has led the parties to declare themselves favorable to pluralism of political parties, arguing that even under socialism parties other than that (or those) of the working class will be allowed to exist and operate freely. Free elections will be conducted and the parties will be willing to leave office should they fail to win an electoral mandate to rule alone or in coalition. Individuals will be free to practice their religious beliefs, to organize themselves politically and to express dissent within the limits of legality. The independence of the judiciary and the existence of free and autonomous trade unions have also been guaranteed.

As all of the preceding suggests, the parties have abandoned the doctrine of the dictatorship of the proletariat. The Italians abandoned this concept early in the postwar period and their creation of a 'new' mass party with membership criteria very different from the classical Leninist party was the embodiment of a different approach, first at the practical level and later at the doctrinal one, to the issues of the party and of political struggle for socialism in Western democratic societies. The French party, by contrast, only abandoned the doctrine of the dictatorship of the proletariat in 1974, and with such brusqueness, discipline and lack of developed theoretical justification that doubts about its commitment to the new approach remain. In the case of all three parties, nevertheless, their practice from the mid-1950s to the 1970s has increasingly been to seek widespread alliances in which the working class would win a 'hegemonic' position through competitive struggle. Again, however, the French party has gone less far and has moved with less consistency and commitment than the other two parties. Its contribution to the rupture of the Common Program alliance with the Socialist Party when it appeared that the PCF might emerge as the junior partner in that alliance suggests the extent to which the PCF is still torn between the old and the new, unable to make a firm commitment at the practical level to the implications of revised theoretical and strategic positions. Even with the recent developments, however, the PCF, and of course the other parties to a far greater extent, have broken with the theoretical and strategic dogmas of their past on the questions of the relationship between democracy and socialism.

What are the general factors which have contributed to the development of the process of eurocommunism along the two dimensions just discussed? Without entering into a lengthy discussion, four major factors can be cited. The first factor of importance has been the decline – one is almost tempted to say collapse – of the Soviet myth. This began dramatically in 1956 with Khrushchev's denunciation of Stalinism. It has been furthered and accelerated by the increasingly apparent difficulties encountered by the Soviet model of domestic political-economic development both in the USSR and in Eastern Europe, by the continuously repeated repression of dissent in the Soviet bloc nations and by the need for the Soviet Union to intervene militarily to secure its control and block internal evolution in a democratic direction in its satellites. Together, these events have highlighted the lack of relevance of the Soviet model for the Western European parties. More important, they have made the Western parties' identification with the Soviet Union ever less a resource which can be used to build and mobilize support domestically. Old party members may retain an attachment to the myth, however tarnished, but the young generations of communists are increasingly less attracted to the contemporary Soviet model, even when they continue to be attached to the revolutionary heritage of Leninism and of the Russian revolution. Thus, over the course of the last twenty-five years, revelations about the Soviet Union's past and present internal regime and Soviet international behavior have greatly increased the domestic political advantages to the parties to weaken their ties to the Soviets and to develop independent positions on the relationship between democracy and socialism. At the same time the constraints on the parties' ability to seek to exploit these advantages represented by the commitments of members have declined.

A second factor working in much the same direction has been the break-up of the international communist movement, particularly the split between the Soviet Union and China. Here again the effect has been to destroy old models and to undermine traditional principles. The Sino-Soviet split and the more general decay of unity among the communist parties has led to a gradual re-evaluation among the French, Italian and Spanish parties of the concept of proletarian internationalism, with its traditional meaning of placing defense of the Soviet Union's interests (as defined by the Soviets) above all national party interests or international values. With the PCI in the forefront, the parties have gradually sought to redefine proletarian internationalism – rechristened 'internationalist solidarity' at the 1976 Conference of European Communist Parties in Berlin – diluting its traditional content. This change has been enhanced by the Soviet Union's altered status in the international system. As the USSR has become a superpower, has been increasingly unable to present itself as an embattled national threatened by capitalist encirclement and has itself operated in the international system to promote its national rather than revolutionary interests, the European parties have been able to distance themselves from the Soviet conception of appropriate international behavior. In this regard, the partial unity among the three parties achieved in the 1970s (the narrow conception of eurocommunism) was of major importance. It enabled the parties to escape the charge of the Soviets and their allies that they were placing national interests above the interests of the international movement. Furthermore, it allowed them to operate in international communist conferences to assure that their more autonomous postures would attain international recognition and could not be isolated. The 1976 Berlin Conference of European Communist Parties was exemplary in this regard, for by working together the euro-communist parties and their allies such as Yugoslavia were able to win agreement to a reinterpretation of proletarian internationalism, to the idea that international conferences should not be binding on national parties and to the more general principle that parties could assume dissenting positions within such conferences and within the movement.

A third factor working to increase the parties' development of greater autonomy has been their growing recognition that their close attachment to the USSR was an insurmountable obstacle to their efforts to win national power. With the waning of the Cold War and the opening of new domestic opportunities for political and social alliances and electoral gains, the incentives to develop autonomous domestic and foreign policy stances which would create the possible terrain for compromise with other domestic forces have grown.

Here domestic and international economic, social and political developments within the West have come to play a crucial role. The consolidation of the domestic political regimes (in Spain, the promise of and then the transition to democracy), the relative successes of the domestic political economies and the increasing economic and political-military interdependence of these societies have become facts which the parties could no longer ignore. The traditional catastrophic interpretations by the parties of their respective domestic societies were no longer theoretically or practically credible, even to much of their membership, much less to potential voters for the left. Furthermore, both domestic economic success and economic interdependence increasingly constrained the credible options which the parties could pursue. To propose policies which would promote the isolation of their countries from the West or which would lead to severe economic costs for even their own − now better off − working- and middle-class supporters, was likely to be counter-productive. Thus, to varying extents, the parties had developed a stake in their domestic political economies. Finally, the parties also had to come to terms with the political-military commitments of their countries. The Atlantic Alliance, like the Warsaw Pact, had become a fundamental fact of European life and the behavior of the USA and USSR gave no reason to presume that this was likely to change in the near future. Even the economic difficulties and political-military strains among the Western nations in the later part of the 1970s did little fundamentally to change the situation. While opening new political opportunities, these strains did nothing to alter the basic structural linkages which had been built up over the preceding decades.

The parties responded to these evolving conditions at different rates and with diverse specific policies. The different characteristics of the national party systems and of the particular national political problems of highest priority were important in this regard. So too were the peculiar features of each national economy and the foreign policy traditions of each nation. None the less, all of them adjusted first their strategies and then their ideological doctrines to the incentives inherent in the new situations. These incentives might not, in themselves, have been sufficient to wean the parties away from the Soviets and from their traditional dogmas. After all, for all three parties, and especially for the French, adjustment lagged behind change in the parties' environments. In the context of the other factors cited, however, these incentives became increasingly important.

This suggests the final factor which has created both the opportunity and the necessity for the parties to develop greater autonomy and revised positions of the relationship between socialism and democracy: the relaxation of international tensions, or, in its more recent formulation, the détente process. The importance of the détente process to the parties' willingness and ability to adjust to the changing conditions in which they are operating cannot be overemphasized. On the one hand, relaxation of tensions between the superpowers created the possibility for greater domestic maneuver, especially in France and Italy where it contributed to a depolarization of domestic politics and the opening of new opportunities for alliance-building. It is worthwhile remembering in this regard that in his speech at the Twentieth Congress of the Soviet Communist Party in 1956, Khrushchev not only announced the possibility of peaceful coexistence with the West but also declared the legitimacy of different (from the Soviet's) and parliamentary paths to socialism. Thus, even from the Soviet standpoint, there has been a linkage between better superpower relations and greater strategic autonomy for the national parties.

On the other hand, détente has reduced the degree to which the parties' international and domestic policy choices had to be evaluated in the light of a harsh zero-sum calculus: anything not pro-Soviet was pro-American, and vice versa. With the decline of tensions and increase of co-operation between the Soviet Union and the United States, the Italian, French and Spanish parties could at one and the same time accept their nations' alignment with the West and the European Economic Community and seek to promote more 'progressive' foreign policies within their own nations and the Western alliance. This, in turn, allowed the parties to maintain legitimacy in the eyes of even more traditional supporters while also appealing to other sectors of the population and to potential domestic allies. Finally, especially in the case of the PCI, it enabled the parties to seek to extend their international ties to socialist and social democratic parties in the rest of Europe and even to try to find some *modus vivendi* with the United States. The specific ways that détente has made itself felt have depended on the specific national circumstances in which each of the parties operated, but in all cases the relaxation of international tension enabled the parties to develop their autonomy from the USSR and to increase their theoretical and strategic accommodation of pluralistic democracy.

These, then, are the factors which have contributed to the development of the process of eurocommunism along the two dimensions outlined. The specific ways these factors have made their influence felt in each of the parties can be followed in the documents and the introductory notes. In concluding this essay, however, we need briefly to reflect on how the process has proceeded in order to offer, if ever so tentatively, some thoughts on the possible future of eurocommunism.

As this volume was going to press the eurocommunism which was such a fashionable topic of conversation and analysis in the 1970s appeared to have met its demise. The French Communist Party had made a major contribution to the collapse of the Common Program by becoming intransigent just as the left seemed within reach of electoral victory in 1978. It had then retrenched on many of the more open positions, in both domestic and international politics, which it had been developing in the 1970s. The retrenchment culminated in the party's strong and vociferous support for the Soviet Union's invasion of Afghanistan, a position not supported by either the PCI or the PCE. While the PCF did not abandon all the terrain across which it had advanced since the early 1960s, there was little question that the process of euro-communism as it applied to the French party had undergone a sharp reversal.

Such a reversal did not take place in the Italian and Spanish parties. Their condemnation of the Afghan invasion, quicker and stronger in the case of the PCI, represented a further growth of autonomy. Nor did either party abandon the alliance policies which they had been pursuing domestically, despite the fact that the prospects that such alliances would be soon achieved and national power attained seemed dimmer than a few years before. Nevertheless, even in these two parties there was evidence that the process of eurocommunism had slowed, that the parties had become more sensitive to the dangers inherent in advancing change further, and less certain about the direction in which they should be moving.

The slowdown and hesitancy, and even the partial reversal of the PCF, are understandable when the process of eurocommunism is viewed from the perspective suggested in this essay and supported in the documents. If conditions from 1968 to the late 1970s promoted the rapid development of the process, subsequent developments have worked in the opposite direction. Since the late 1960s all of the causal factors we have cited promoted autonomy and democratic revisionism. To cite but a few important developments: the invasion of Czechoslovakia, the decay of the ruling parties in all three countries, the acceleration of interdependence, the flowering of détente. By the middle of the decade all three parties seemed convinced that events were working to their benefit. Subsequent developments proved this optimism unfounded. Domestic factors showed that the path to power might require even greater change if an approach to national government was to be likely. Reactions set in within the parties themselves. And, perhaps most important, détente decayed and then collapsed, shrinking the parties' room for maneuver, raising the internal potential party costs of moving too fast and reducing the probability that those possible allies on whom the success of the parties' policies depended would respond in the desired fashion. In this light, the fact that the Italian and Spanish parties have largely persisted in advancing, if more slowly, along the dimensions of the eurocommunism process is noteworthy. It would seem to signal that the commitment of these parties to their eurocommunist postures – a commitment developed over a lengthy period of years and with considerable, if lagged, theoretical backing – is relatively firm even if there are hesitations and doubts about where, how and when to proceed.

But what of the PCF? Can it still be considered a eurocommunist party? How does its recent reversal of policy reflect on the analysis of the process as a whole? And can it be expected once again to progress along the dimensions of the eurocommunism process? The answer to the first question can be no more than 'perhaps.' The party has undertaken a marked retrenchment in recent years which has led to sharp polemics with its former *confrères* in Italy and Spain and to its isolation in French politics and, increasingly on the French left. At the same time, the PCF has not abandoned some of the significant revisions of doctrine, strategy and policy which it undertook from the early 1960s onwards. This is most evident, but perhaps least significant, at the level of doctrine where the party has not reverted to the traditional dogmas of the communist movement. At the strategic and policy levels principles have been maintained, but behavior has generally reverted toward past patterns. Even here, however, exceptions are to be noted: even at the height of its support of the Soviet invasion of Afghanistan, the PCF continued its criticism of the Soviet treatment of dissent and its exiling of Andrei Sakharov. On the whole, the reversals in PCF policy raise serious doubts about the extent to which its commitments are, or ever were, solid rather than opportunistic. Until further evidence emerges, however, the future path of French communism is uncertain. Present evidence points in the direction of an end to French euro-communism, but the bases remain for future shifts, perhaps on more solid ground back to the eurocommunist process of development.

The recent reversals of French policy also allow us to reflect a bit further on the character of the process of eurocommunism as a whole. As we have indicated at several points, the PCF has always been the laggard. It undertook serious policy and strategic change later than the other parties and it never developed the theoretical backing for its new positions that the Spanish and Italian parties did. The differences in the rhetoric of the parties, and especially the contrasts between the PCI and PCF as reflected in the documents, are striking in this regard. Furthermore, the PCF remained much more a party of cadres rather than becoming a mass party like the PCI. The result was that the adaptive pressures from below (restraining pressures from below were present in both), as contrasted to the adjustments of policy imposed from above, were never as strong. The relative weight of traditionalists in the core constituencies of the PCF seems likely to be much higher than in the PCI. In the case of the PCE, the Soviet attempt to promote a split of the party in 1969, under the direction of Enrique Lister, allowed the party to expel many of the traditionalists; and many of the party's leaders and core members entered after the party had adopted distinctly eurocommunist positions. Finally, for historical reasons the PCF has always been more sectarian than either of the other parties. Fundamental to this are two factors, one historical, the other contemporary. First, unlike the other two parties, the PCF did not spend a major portion of its history fighting dictatorship in its country. The latter experience in the PCI and PCE appears to have made them peculiarly sensitive to the advantages of democracy and its fragility in their countries, to have encouraged them to try to develop a wide net of social and political alliances and, more generally, to the need to develop strategies and policies adjusted to the national peculiarities of their systems. Secondly, the dynamics of conflict within the left in France have been different from those in the other two countries. The PCF in the 1970s, as well as in earlier periods, had to contest for dominance of the left with a Socialist Party (PS) which was often electorally stronger and more dynamic. When, in the last decade, the party sought to reach some compromise with the socialists, it found itself increasingly the loser in the bargain. This outcome served to confirm its more traditional posture of hostility and open conflict within the left. The PCI did not face this problem, for it has for most of the postwar period been both the larger and the more dynamic of the left parties. In the 1960s, during the first years of socialist participation in national government, the PCI was, in fact, somewhat more hostile to the PSI than was its usual practice. The PCE is also the smaller party on the left and may in the future face problems – although not necessarily adopt solutions – similar to those of the PCF. In the present period, however, the lengthy process of consolidation of the democratic regime and the necessity for the two left parties to co-operate in local government and in the face of a large and heterogeneous center–right coalition have encouraged co-operation tempered by electoral and policy competition.

Taken together, these contrasts between the PCF and the other two parties highlight once again the extent to which the process of eurocommunism cannot be understood simply as the adjustment of all the parties to a general set of factors but must also be seen in light of the ways these factors have been mediated by the particular experiences of the parties.

The question of whether the PCF is likely once again to take up the process of euro-communism raises the issue of whether the process as a whole is likely to continue. On the one hand, it seems unlikely that the three parties will in the near future move in tandem as they did in the mid-1970s. To the extent that the co-operation of this period encouraged development in all the parties, this spur to revision is unlikely to reappear. On the other hand, the underlying factors which encouraged the process of euro-communism over the course of the postwar period have not disappeared, nor do they seem likely to. From this longer perspective – the one advanced in this essay and inherent in the selection of documents – it seems improbable that the process has come to an end, even for the French party. Such predictions, however, are clearly hazardous, for they make assumptions not only about the future development of the factors which have promoted eurocommunism, but also about the decisions taken within the parties themselves. It is, perhaps, more judicious to put this hypothesis another way: to the extent that the parties, including and especially the French, fail further to respond to the factors which have led them to become more autonomous and more pro-democratic over the course of the postwar period, they will probably consign themselves to political ghettos, within their political systems. In the case of the PCF, acceptance of such a position would be consistent with recent behavior, but not with much of that of the last twenty years. For the PCI and PCE, it would be a major reversal of perspective, one which is consistent neither with their recent behavior nor with the development which is amply documented in the pages which follow. From this standpoint, then, the process of eurocommunism seems likely to continue, with many of the twists and turns that have been inherent in it from its beginnings.

PETER LANGE

PART ONE

National Roads to Socialism

Introduction to Part One

The strategy of a national, democratic and peaceful road to socialism is at the core of eurocommunism: it is, indeed, the fulcrum from which all other aspects of eurocommunism derive. The search for strategic and ideological autonomy from the Soviet Union, the acceptance of the democratic 'rules of the game,' a gradualist approach to change, the adoption of the characteristics of a mass party, are manifestations of the strategy of the national, peaceful road to socialism; they are inter-dependent and mutually reinforcing expressions of the factors shaping the euro-communist position.

The intuition of a national, peaceful road to socialism is neither new nor original. The debate between proponents of revolutionary means of struggle and advocates of peaceful transition has been an integral part of the evolution of Marxist–Leninist doctrine. The entire history of the working-class movement has been marked by this debate. With regard to the eurocommunist parties, in the immediate post-Second World War period the leaders of the French and Italian communist parties publicly committed themselves to a peaceful road to socialism. This commitment, however, was undeveloped; and to differing degrees it was attentuated during the Cold War. It has only been since 1956 – at different rates and with differing degrees of coherence and conviction – that the parties have reaffirmed and elaborated such a strategy. As it is presented today, this strategy is regarded not only as an expedient to attain power but also as a program of government and the basis on which socialist society is to be built in the West.

By assigning ideological legitimacy to the concept of national roads to socialism, the Twentieth Congress of the CPSU represented a turning point in the parties' ability to elaborate such a strategy. The Soviet Union's acceptance of the principle of diverse roads to socialism opened the way to the parties' development of strategic postures better adopted to the national contexts in which they operated. The Twentieth Congress of the CPSU was significant in another respect: Khruschev's revelations about Stalinism promoted and eventually impelled the development of domestically rooted models of political struggle and of 'indigenous' visions of socialist society. In the years after 1956 the domestic structures (meaning the historical conditions, patterns of socioeconomic development, institutional arrangements, and so on) facing the parties became even more important points of reference for their strategic choices.

The peculiar characteristic of a strategy of a peaceful road to socialism lies in its search for a synthesis of traditional communist goals and strategic principles, and the constraints and opportunities stemming from the domestic and international conditions of a given country. Such a strategy, to the extent it is fully elaborated, enables the parties to respond to societal and international change. It therefore represents an explicit rejection of the rigid ideological dogmatism of the Third International period, of the old tendency to act politically according to preconceived blueprints.

The realization that the Bolshevik experience is unrepeatable has been central to the parties' adoption of strategies of peaceful, national roads to socialism. Basic to this realization is the conviction that the methods of struggle used by the Bolsheviks for acquiring political power are inappropriate to the West, that the domestic and international conditions of 1917 Russia differ fundamentally from those in contemporary Western Europe. For the eurocommunist parties, the 'storming of the Winter Palace' formula is a thing of the past. This is why they argue that each communist party should have its own original model of socialism, one in which the characteristics and requirements of the national context predominate over pre-existing models and previous experiences.

In more concrete terms, the adoption of nationally rooted roads to socialism means, above all, that the eurocommunist parties have come to accept democratic rules of political behavior. Parliament and state institutions have become the channels through which the eurocommunist parties seek to bring about changes in society. Social mobilization and the use of the pressure on political institutions which it can generate remain part of the strategic vision; but respect for parliamentary and democratic legality shapes the use made of mobilization and the parties' more general operational code of behavior. The anti-system posture of old has been largely abandoned; the eurocommunists have committed themselves to working within and through the system in the pursuit of their goals.

Gradualism is another factor basic to the strategy of the peaceful road. As envisioned by the eurocommunist parties, transformative changes in society can occur in a gradual fashion. The strategy of the (violent) overthrow of the existing system and its replacement by a new (socialist) system has given way to one of gradual change, of step-by-step structural reform of capitalism. It should be stressed, however, that the parties emphasize that their gradualism differs, both in content and in kind, from that of social democratic parties. While for the latter, they argue, the goal is to make the existing system of liberal democracy more just through reforms of some of its features, the ultimate, long-range goal of the eurocommunists is said by them to be the transformation of the *entire* system, its evolution into a socialist society in which elements of liberal democracy and of socialism would coexist.

If gradualism is the method by which eurocommunist parties act politically, reforms are the means they advocate for bringing about far-reaching changes in society. Indeed, policies of reform have become the basis on which the platforms of the parties rest. On the one hand, the immediate reforms demanded by the PCF are more sweeping than those of the others. On the other hand, the content of reforms increasingly diverges. Whereas, for instance, extensive nationalizations were common to the platforms of all the parties until the mid-1960s, they remain central only in the program of the PCF. Experience with nationalized industry has contributed much to the PCI's skepticism about such a policy.

Differences of a similar nature emerge in the parties' posture toward the economic crisis of the 1970s. While the PCI and PCE moved significantly toward establishing priorities among and generally moderating their reform demands, the PCF was insistent in pressing for the full program of very extensive reforms formulated at the beginning of the decade. These differences reflected diverse views on the responses the parties should adopt to the crisis of the national economy. The Italian and Spanish communists, arguing that it would be counter-productive to try to build socialism out of the debris of capitalism, were determined to contribute to the resolution of their respective countries' economic difficulties, while at the same time introducing structural change. The French communists, in contrast, showed no intention to adopt such a stance, explicitly rejecting the proposition that they should in any way contribute to the 'management' of capitalism's crisis.

In the evolution of the eurocommunist outlook, the strategy of the national, democratic and peaceful road to socialism has increasingly come to incorporate principles of political, economic, ideological and cultural pluralism. These principles, furthermore, are to varying degrees becoming recognized as integral to the socialist society they wish to construct. Non-communist parties will be allowed to operate freely. Alternation of power will continue to be the accepted rule of behavior and Euro-communist parties have committed themselves to leave power if the electoral verdict should be unfavorable to them. Organized opposition will be tolerated. In the economic realm, private property will be permitted to exist; small- and medium-sized enterprises will not be nationalized. Finally, those personal and collective rights commonly associated with liberal democracy will be maintained both during the transition from capitalism to socialism and in the socialist society.

It is evident that such a conception of socialism involves the abandonment of many traditional Marxist–Leninist dogmas. The parties have revised their doctrines at different rates. They have also made differing efforts to justify their revisions in theoretical terms and to confront them with ideological traditions. This is illustrated by the manner with which they have treated the concept of the dictatorship of the proletariat. Common to all three parties is a recognition that this notion is incompatible with the strategy of a peaceful and democratic road to socialism. The PCI, immediately after the war and much more forcefully after 1956, critically re-examined this dogma and it disappears from its rhetoric in the mid-1960s. In fact, by the end of that decade even the vanguard role of the party is abandoned. The PCE too shows a lengthy history of critical re-evaluation of the concept and abandoned it entirely in the final stages of Francoism. In contrast, the PCF displayed little inclination to reappraisal until the mid-1970s when the party leadership summarily, but not unambiguously, banished the concept. All three parties now recognize that in the West dictatorial power need not be pursued by any class. The building of a socialist society will result from a set of alliances in which the working class is increasingly to acquire predominance due to its capacity to exercise hegemony. Here again the Italian and Spanish parties have gone much farther in their elaboration of this set of ideas. The differences in the patterns and timing of ideological and strategic development and in analytical style reflected in this illustration appear consistently throughout the documents.

When viewed chronologically, the documents in this section on the national road to socialism show significant continuities. Abandonment of revolutionary means of struggle, legality, parliamentarism, the need for alliances and policy gradualism, are the most conspicuous examples. None the less, for each of the parties there are evident points of acceleration of strategic development. The immediate postwar period, when the French and Italian communist parties were part of national coalitions and participated in the rebuilding of the constitutional order, represents one such phase. During the Cold War, however, the growth of the strategy of the national road to socialism was stalled, and in some cases reversed. The year 1956 marks another watershed. The initial signs of a relaxation of international tension, the denunciation of Stalinism and the Soviet acceptance of the possibility of national and peaceful roads to socialism created more favorable conditions for the parties' strategic evolution. The Italian and Spanish parties, the latter after a change in leadership, significantly elaborated the principles of their national strategies. The French party adjusted to the new conditions more slowly. It was only after the establishment of the Fifth Republic, with its dramatic consequences of the communists' prospects for influence on national politics, that the PCF shifted noticeably toward a more positive stand on the peaceful and democratic road to socialism. The PCF's contemporary elaboration of such a strategy, with its emphasis on alliance with the socialist party and its acceptance of many principles of liberal democracy, has its roots in this phase. A third phase of rapid acceleration followed the Soviet invasion of Czechoslovakia in 1968. Thereafter, the elaboration of the strategy of the peaceful road to socialism took on increasingly those strategic and ideological connotations which are at the core of eurocommunism. It is in this last phase that the parties become identified with those particular strategic formulations which marked their behavior in the 1970s: historic compromise, common program and national reconciliation.

When compared with the revolutionary tactics and aspiration of the Third International, the present strategy of the three parties appears to be a momentous break with the past. The transition from capitalism to socialism is no longer seen as the result of the activity of a handful of committed revolutionaries, of a vanguard leading the working class to power; rather it is perceived more and more as the outcome of the struggle resulting from the alliance of all non-monopolistic forces in society. In the eurocommunist vision of things, socialism will emerge from within advanced capitalism, peacefully, legally and gradually; its alliances will be born of mass mobilization as well as of parliamentary activity, but without violent breaks. To many observers the credibility of the parties' commitment to this vision remains questionable. They raise doubts both about the compatibility of democracy and socialism and about the degree to which the parties, once in a position of power, would retain their eurocommunist principles. A conclusive answer to both doubts can be only provided by the events. But the documents show that the strategies of national, peaceful and democratic roads to socialism have a long history of development.

MAURIZIO VANNICELLI

DOCUMENTS FOR PART ONE

ITALIAN Communist Party:
From National Unity to Historic Compromise

FRENCH Communist Party:
Socialism with French Colors

SPANISH Communist Party:
From Illegality to the Peaceful Road

ITALIAN Communist Party: From National Unity to Historic Compromise

1 Palmiro Togliatti's speech to the Neapolitan communist cadres, April 11, 1944

. . . This work, comrades, aimed at extending and organizing the contact between the popular masses and the communist vanguard, is all the more necessary in Italy today, after twenty years of fascist dictatorship. In these twenty years the people have not only been exploited and oppressed. They have been excluded from all participation in political life, cut out of all fertile ideological debate and violently forced to submit to the stupidest of propaganda . . . The spectre of Bolshevism has been the screen behind which reactionary forces have come together for the ill of the people, bringing our country to military defeat and catastrophe . . .

What we communists have been accused of! They have accused us of being the enemies of property. But those who thus accused us were themselves a band of thieves who sacked the whole of Italy . . .

They have accused us of promoting violence. But who made violence the rule and the basis for government, the fundamental law of national life, if not fascism and its men?

They have called us subverters, wreckers. Walk through the streets of Naples, see the piles of squalid ruins and then tell me who the destroyers have been. Go look at the great cities of the South, Sicily, Reggio, Messina, Catania, all reduced to heaps of ruins. All those ruins bear a signature; they are signed, fascism.

They have accused us of being enemies of the family. But if you look into the bosom of most Italian families today, you will find disintegration, laceration and worse, all from the national disaster brought by fascism.

They have accused us of being defeatists. But who brought the Italian army to a defeat without precedent in our history, in its gravity or its magnitude?

. . . Finally, they have accused us of being anti-national and, moreover, this term has practically become a euphemism meaning us. Comrades, I challenge anyone, after the severest political and historical examination, to find a single act by our party contrasting with, or damaging to, the interest of the nation. But where was the Italian nation brought by the men and by the regime that banished us and that called us anti-national? It has been brought to catastrophe, not through a few accidental errors – as one still hears said from time to time – but because the entire fascist policy, from first to last, has been contrary to the nation's interests . . .

We communists have the merit – which we declare – of having always fought against the anti-national policy of fascism, from start to finish, without hesitation or doubt. I know our party has committed some grave errors in the past. But in rejecting fascist policy, and above all its criminal war policy, we have never been mistaken. Our errors were in the way we realized our policy; we did not tie ourselves closely enough to the popular masses, and therefore we were unable to block the development of fascism and the triumph of reaction.

. . . The nation cannot limit itself to taking note of the catastrophe and singling out those who are responsible. It seeks a road of salvation, a way out of the abyss it is caught in. Our duty is to indicate this way concretely and to direct the people to it and along it, step by step, beginning with our immediate circumstances. If we refuse, or are incapable of doing this, if we reduce ourselves once more to the status of an association of propagandists who speak ill of the past and dream of a distant future, unable to advise or to do anything about the present, we would not only be condemning the party itself to a difficult and miserable life, without rapid or sure development. If we behaved this way – and this is rather more serious – the working class, the people, and the whole nation would be deprived of the guide they need, a vanguard organization to coolly and calmly examine every situation and show the way out of each. The vanguard must direct the people toward these roads, and yet never lose sight of the final objectives of national rebirth of the country and realization of the people's deepest aspiration.

We are the party of the working class and we do not deny, nor will we ever deny, this character. But the working class has never been isolated from the interests of the nation . . . We claim the traditions of Italian socialism, of that great mass movement of workers and the people, that erupted on the political scene, demanded recognition for the interests and rights of the workers, and asked that the people be assured their due place in directing the country. It is a movement that has performed the great tasks of healing, reviving and renovating Italian national life.

Today the problem of unity, of liberty and of Italian independence is once again in question . . .

When we defend the interests of the nation, when we put ourselves at the head of the fight to liberate Italy from the German invasion, we are in line with the true and great traditions of the proletarian movement . . .

Comrades, we want a democratic Italy, but we want a strong democracy, which will eliminate every trace of fascism and will prevent the re-emergence of anything that reproduces or resembles it . . . Therefore, comrades, our policy is a national policy and a policy of unity . . .

However, we have posed three conditions for the constitution of a new democratic war government of national unity. The first is that the unity of democratic and liberal anti-fascist forces is not broken, but rather extended and reinforced, since it is the greatest conquest realized by the Italian people in the struggle for its own liberation since the fall of Mussolini's regime . . .

In the second place, the Italian people should be given as solemn a guarantee as possible that, when the country is liberated, a national constituent assembly, elected through universal, free, direct and secret suffrage by all citizens, will decide the fate of the country and the form of its institutions. This position is democratically the most correct. It does violence to no one and excludes no one from national life, except the fascist traitors . . .

The third condition that we pose is that the democratic government, formed on the basis of the mass parties, should have a clear, precise program for war and for relieving the misery of the people and should commit all its efforts for its realization.

For these three conditions we are ready to ignore all other problems, or to postpone them. On the basis of these conditions, in fact, it seems to us that a greater unity of national forces can be realized: for the war, for crushing the invaders, for liquidating fascism, for liberation and for victory, that is, for the fulfilment of those tasks to which all the positive forces in the country aspire . . .

But there is still one point on which we must give a clear and exhaustive answer, dispersing any possible doubt. What will we do tomorrow? What is our program? Are we not speaking one way today so that tomorrow we can take another course?

On this point we want to dissipate any uncertainty that might still survive. We have a program for Italy's future. For now it is sufficient to mention its rough lines, waiting to specify them more clearly in the future. The objective that we propose for the Italian people will be to create a democratic and progressive regime in Italy. We will call the workers, peasants, intellectuals and the young to fight for this goal. We want Italy to be reconstructed, and reconstructed quickly, in the interest of the people. We know the depth of the damage to the Italian social fabric, and therefore we know that if we posed any other objective we could not fulfill our duties to the nation, which looks for a guide in us. If a national constituent assembly were called tomorrow we would propose that the people make Italy into a democratic republic, with a constitution guaranteeing all Italians their rights: the freedom of thought and of speech; freedom of the press; association and gather; freedom of religion and creed; and freedom for the small and medium owner to develop himself without being crushed by the greedy and egoistic groups of the plutocracy, that is, large monopoly capital. That is to say that we do not in fact propose a regime based on the existence or predominance of a single party. In a democratic and progressive Italy there will have to be, and there will be, different parties corresponding to the different currents of ideas and interests that exist in the Italian population; we propose, however, that these parties, or at least those among them with a basis in the people and a democratic and national program, maintain their unity to confront every attempt to revive fascism. We do not want to banish the democrats or the liberals, but the fascists. The democratic, progressive regime that we propose, and in whose building we want to, and will, co-operate in every way, must be a strong regime. It must defend itself against any attempt to revive fascism and reaction, and any attempt to suppress or crush popular liberties. This new democracy must outlaw each and every trace of fascism, and must take measures to pull out the roots from which fascism arose in the past, and from which it could reappear in the future. Therefore we propose that after the war the Italian constituent assembly should initiate a profound agrarian reform, which would create a new situation in the countryside favoring the small and medium peasant; it would destroy every vestige of feudalism; it would give the land and the means to cultivate it to the peasants who lack them today; and it would no longer permit the large landholder and the speculator to oppress agricultural workers and the rural classes, and use their economic position to dominate political life and push the country on to a reactionary track . . .

Yet the very structures and social forces which pushed the social democrats to the left made it extremely difficult to translate that radicalism into practice. The limits of trade union and political success radicalized the movement but weakened it as well. The social democrats' isolation from the surrounding society increased their class-consciousness but not necessarily their ability to wage class struggle. The isolation from Berlin provided the critical distance necessary to develop dissenting left-wing views, but lessened their influence on the national party or contacts with other radicals. Despite their dissatisfaction with the center and right, the Düsseldorf radicals were too weak to implement radical tactics alone, too sensible to continue the suffrage struggle without them and too committed to party unity to leave. After 1910 they turned back to the parliamentary arena once again. Their experiences in national and municipal politics were to erase any lingering doubts about the limits of parliamentarism and reformism.

Palmiro Togliatti, *La politica di Salerno* (Rome: Editori Riuniti, 1969), pp. 3–41.

2 Palmiro Togliatti's report to the Eighth Congress of the PCI, December 1956

Some have wanted to call our many-sided political action a matter of tactics, of simple cunning. They are simply demonstrating that they do not understand the substance of what they are talking about, and even within the party we must respond with serious arguments to those who claim that the search for an Italian road is a pure expedient to make it easier to win a majority and develop the movement. It is the very way the problem of socialist revolution is posed in reality. The need to destroy the capitalist order and create a socialist order does not come from the decisions, nor the capability, nor the strength of a political party. It does not even come out of the strength of a class-based union movement. It comes from the development of the real and subjective forces from which today's society is woven, and their conflicts. This development and these conflicts are what make the passage to socialism historically necessary; one can even say that socialism objectively matures in the very bosom of capitalism. Therefore it is evident that the conditions and forms of its maturation must differ from place to place and from one moment in history to another.

The diversity of the roads to socialism springs from history, the economy, the development of the workers' movement, and often comes from the very spontaneity of this movement. It is the duty of the leadership of the working class to inform the entire vanguard of the proletariat of this and therefore not to break from the political directions and the methods of work that in their very diversity from one country to another are the only ones that can assure the fundamental unity and the success of the whole movement.

The overall picture is of an economic system that cannot assure a rational and continual development of productive forces, that is unable to give all its citizens work, that cannot overcome its inveterate contradictions and backwardness. Transforming the very structures of this system is a necessity not only for the workers, but also in different ways for the great majority of the population. Realizing this transformation of the economic structure in a radical and definitive way is the task of the socialist revolution. However, there are other changes, of a partial nature, that are absolutely required today and that cannot be avoided if we want to assure better conditions for existence for whole groups of the population. Above all, there must be a general agrarian reform, realized through the general introduction of a limitation on landed property. Equally urgent are measures to reduce the power of the great monopolistic groups.

Conducting an effective struggle against the great private monopolies is in the immediate interest, or rather today it is a necessity, for the defense of the productive activities of the greater part of the population, including vast strata of small and medium producers, whose earnings are reduced, in favor of the great monopolies, by the way the latter dominate the market. The great monopolies are the leading force in current capitalism. They are the most reactionary force and the most aggressive. They are the defenders of those international ties that threaten the independence of the nation. To concentrate our blows against the great monopolies, to put them on the defensive, to isolate them, and to propose and adopt measures that limit their power and tend to destroy them, is the task of everyone who wants to fight effectively against capitalism and for socialism today, along with the ever larger and more determined popular masses; it is the task for everyone who does not just want to sit and wait for the 'great day when we will change everything.'

This is the general justification for our struggle for structural reforms, one of the principal points in the search for our own road of development toward socialism in current conditions. It would be mistaken to confuse the demand for these reforms with what were once called transitional demands, that is, the marching orders for the moment of an acute revolutionary crisis, and simply designed to lead the popular masses in the struggle for power, catchwords, meant to be consummated rapidly in the very course of this struggle. Structural reforms are a positive objective which we want to realize, and which is realizable in the current conditions of the political struggle.

Structural reforms are not socialism. They are, however, a transformation of the economic structures which opens the road for advancing toward socialism. They are measures of struggle against today's principal enemy of the working class and of socialism. They are in the interest of the people, of progress and of peace.

We hear objections that with this action we tend to reform and not to destroy capitalism and, on the other hand, that there have already been structural reforms, for example, nationalizations, without the countries where they were effected advancing towards socialism. The first objection does not hold, since, if it were valid, it would have to be true for every other kind of claim, whether economic or political, other than pure wage increases. The second, instead, poses the entire question of the struggle that the working class and the popular masses, guided by their parties, should pursue under the current conditions, to assert themselves as the dominant factor in national politics and the economy. By itself, a nationalization may not mean much. When made in a certain manner it can

even give some advantages to particular capitalist groups, or to non-progressive political groups. But things change when this or other measures of struggle against large monopoly capital are an integral part of continual and determined action by great political and mass organizations with the support of a substantial share of public opinion, to impose, even in current conditions, an economic policy that favors the workers and the middle classes, and commits the government itself, through parliament, to take anti-monopolistic action. Then things change. Then the state's intervention can also assure a rather different meaning from that when the government acts as a pure board of directors for monopolistic groups and the forms of state capitalism are nothing but forms of subordination of the state apparatus to the will and the interests of large capital. The problem, therefore, cannot be resolved with formulas, but only through action, organizing and leading a broad mass movement, to impose radical changes in the general directions of economics and politics. Everything lies in recognizing that today there are conditions that allow us to conduct such an activity, and to conduct it successfully. The problem then becomes one of political conditions in which the class struggle takes place, of the degree of maturity of the working class, the peasant masses and the middle class; of the position that these social forces occupy in civil society and in the political struggle; of their degree of consciousness; of the general loss of prestige both of capitalism and of the ruling classes that express it; and of the ever-growing prestige and attractiveness of socialist ideas among the great human masses.

Objective analysis furnishes us, for our country, with the outlines of a convergence, in the struggle against contemporary capitalism in a broad front of social forces. This coming together is the objective basis for a vast multiple and original system of class alliances.

The questions of liberty, democracy, parliamentarism and socialism are therefore always posed, here, in relation to the way class conflict takes place, the struggle conducted by the working class and by the popular forces it leads, and the successes of this struggle against the capitalist ruling classes. Here lies the most profound point of divergence between our conception, which is revolutionary, and the reformist conception of the social democrats. From the assertion, which is scientifically correct, that the objective conditions of socialism mature within capitalist society itself, reformism deduces that all one has to do is to wait for socialism to flow out of the breast of capitalism, by itself, by a miracle. From here it deduces the tendency to consider the development of capitalism as something that is, in itself, a march toward socialism. From this conception the socialist leaders have derived the doctrine that their duty is to administer capitalism and capitalist society well, since socialism will arrive for us anyway.

We are democratic because we act within the area of the constitution, of democratic customs and the legality it determines, and we demand that everyone respect this legality and apply every constitutional norm, above all those who govern. We have conquered the terrain of democracy in order to proceed beyond it, toward socialism. It would therefore be absurd for us to deny it. On the contrary, we defend it. On the contrary, the urgency of socialist renewal, the fact that it is in the interest of the great majority of the people, the spreading of this consciousness and its translation into an ever larger and more powerful movement of organized and united masses, allow us to see the norms of democratic and constitutional life not as an obstacle but as an aid to building socialism with a minimum of hardships and sacrifices for the working masses themselves and for the country.

There is no revision of our principles in these assertions. The dictatorship of the proletariat, that is, political leadership by party of the working class in the construction of socialist society, is a historical necessity. But even Lenin, after having confirmed that it is inevitable that all nations would come to socialism, added that 'they will not all come the same way. Each will have its particularities in the forms of democracy, in the variety of the forms of dictatorship of the proletariat, and in the speed of reorganization of the various aspects of social life.'

Establishing the prospect of democratic development toward socialism does not mean negating the need for a tenacious struggle. Struggle is indispensable, within the forms required by the situation; the working class, guided by its revolutionary vanguard, must be at the head of this struggle; in the course of the struggle itself the front of advance toward socialism must gradually be extended to new social groups and from this an ever stronger socialist consciousness must emerge, in the working class and in the whole people. If all of this is not there, there will be the risk of simply spinning phrases.

Palmiro Togliatti, *Nella democrazia e nella pace verso il socialismo* (Rome: Editori Riuniti, 1966), cf pp. 9–80.

3 Elements for a programmatic declaration, approved by the Eighth Congress of the PCI, December 1956

The Italian Communist Party's positions and program are derived from:

(1) the development of capitalism and its internal contradictions in the period of imperialism,
(2) the economic and political structure of Italian society, and the concrete historical conditions of the socialist revolution in Italy,
(3) the new conditions, favorable to the advance of socialism, created by the socialist revolution of October 1917 and by the further great victories won by the working class and the peoples in the struggle against capitalism and imperialism,
(4) and the conditions created in Italy itself by the victory of the resistance and by the collapse of fascism, which came about under the leadership of the advanced forces of the working class and of the people.

From these elements, which have been formulated according to the principle of Marxist–Leninist doctrine and in the light of the national and international communist workers' movement's experience, there arises the possibility and necessity of attaining socialism by following an Italian path, by means of the movement and struggle in our country's working classes, and the proletariat's alliances to free itself from capitalist exploitation, to make Italy rise once more, and to create a society of free and equal men.

Capitalism and Socialism
(1) Capitalism is founded on private ownership of the means of production and of exchange, which are administered in the interests of capitalists, in order to create and increase continually their own profit. Labor, considered as goods, is exploited for this end.

This society is threatened by profound objective contradictions and is lacerated by class antagonisms.

It is a precondition for the economic struggle itself that the proletariat should conquer for itself full equality of civil and political rights, and exercise the fundamental democratic liberties: freedom of thought, freedom of speech, right to vote, freedom of the press and of propaganda, association for trade union, co-operative and political purposes, the right to strike, the right to hold public demonstrations, and freedom and respect for their dignity in their place of work. The proletariat's class struggle is, therefore, right from the beginning, a struggle for freedom, and the working class is opposed to the bourgeoisie not only in its refusal to put limits to the extension and exercise of democratic liberties, but in its insistence that a substantial social equality should correspond to them.

Socialism puts an end to private appropriation of the means of production and exchange, and replaces this by collective ownership and management, in the interests of the whole of society. It suppresses exploitation of man by man, and the division of society into classes of exploiters and exploited. It organizes production, not according to the law of maximum private profit, but in order to guarantee the maximum prosperity to all the workers. It overcomes the internal contradictions of capitalism, eliminates the periodic crises, unemployment, the hardships and poverty of the working masses, and the imbalances that cause this poverty and hinder economic development. It is based on the principle of payment of every man according to his labor.

An indispensable condition for economic and social relations being profoundly transformed and for the transition from capitalism to socialism is that the problem of political power should be solved. In capitalist society political power is in the hands of bourgeois ruling groups, and the government is an instrument at their disposal (that is, the dictatorship of the bourgeoisie). Democratic liberties are always subject to limits, and there is always a danger of their being destroyed. Never is there any corresponding real equality between men who are divided into exploiters and exploited. *Democracy becomes effective only when the working class conquers political powers and uses it to transform the economic structure of society*, just as the bourgeoisie, in the past, used democratic institutions to destroy the feudal order, and is today preventing their full development, and is also prepared to suppress them in order to defend and preserve the economic relationships on which its dominance is based. Only with the implementation of socialism do liberty and the equality of men become fully effective, because there is a corresponding equality in economic opportunities, and the end of any kind of exploitation.

The Progress of Socialism in the World
The first, definitive overthrow of capitalist domination and of the chain with which imperialism kept the world subject came about with the October Revolution in 1917.

The special character of the October Revolution and the forms assumed by the working-class government in the Soviet Union were the product of the historical conditions in which these great events took place. Revolutionary violence and the temporary restriction of some democratic rights were a necessity joined by the need to overthrow the resistance of the reactionary classes and their parties, to emerge from the imperialist war and give the whole people liberty and peace, to be triumphant in the civil war and repel foreign invasion – which was organized by imperialist governments and fomented by internal enemies – to guide economic reconstruction in the towns and in the countryside, and in this way to achieve a new real unity among all the forces of the people. The building of the socialist economy was conditioned by the situation of the country, where capitalism was not yet highly developed and feudal and colonial institutions still had great importance, and which was for more than thirty years isolated in a world still dominated by imperialism.

The democratic, socialist character of this state was not damaged either by the indispensable measures taken to overcome the resistance and aggression of internal and external enemies, or by the consequences of the grave errors that restricted the bounds of democracy for some periods. The Soviet Union remains the first great model of a socialist society, the center and the most powerful mainspring of the great movement which aims at transforming the economic and political structures of the entire world.

The victory of the October Revolution and the construction of socialism in the Soviet Union brought about radical progress in the socialist awareness of the working class and popular masses throughout the world. The center of gravity of the working class and the people's revolutionary movement was displaced. This came about also because social democracy, after the failure and collapse of the Second International at the outbreak of the First World War, did not manage in the period between the wars to do anything leading to changes in the foundations of social institutions.

The communists have always emphasized that the decisive question in the struggle for socialism is the question of *political power*, because the construction of a socialist society is impossible if political power is not removed from the ruling castes of monopolistic capitalism and if it does not pass to the proletariat and to other working classes in alliance with the proletariat.

The course of the political struggles showed, even

in the period between the two wars, that new situations might arise, different from the one that had faced the Russian proletariat in 1917, and that therefore the problem of power would be posed and resolved in a different way, in relation to the disposition of the class forces, and to the objectives of the struggle to be waged for democracy and peace.

It has proved to be a mistaken and dangerous policy to imitate slavishly or to transpose mechanically the measures adopted during the construction of socialism in the Soviet Union, even though the fundamental objectives to be reached are the same. Correction of the errors denounced at the Twentieth Congress, which had led to unjustifiable restrictions of democracy, to grave violations of legality and to various errors in the relations between socialist states, concerned this topic as well. Where this correction was not made in time, as in Hungary, the working-class government and all the conquests of the people's regime were seriously threatened, and the way was opened for aggression by the forces of counter-revolution, organized and stimulated by imperialism.

The struggle for socialism is entering a new phase, in which there is a possibility of new forms of transition to socialism, new methods of organizing the dictatorship of the proletariat, and new ways of exercising power in favor of the construction of a socialist society.

With the end of the worst period of the Cold War, which imposed a close unity in policy and action on all the forces of democracy and socialism, and particularly on the communists, the communists are adapting their conduct to the new conditions of the whole movement's development. The paths that face them, and which must be followed in the different countries, do not coincide. The forms in which power is organized in the countries which are already socialist are different; the content and the means of implementation of the class alliances for the construction of socialism are different; the pace of this construction, both in industry and in agriculture, is necessarily different. All this confirms that as the advance towards socialism makes progress, and especially as it embraces countries where capitalism is highly developed and the political structure highly differentiated, there will be a great increase in the multiplicity of the movement's forms, of its economic and political aspects, and of its objectives and tasks. Fidelity to the principles and methods of Marxism–Leninism, of the class struggle and of proletarian internationalism, the critical analysis of new experiences and continuous contact with reality and with the movement of the working masses will enable the communists to cope easily with the new situations that already exist or are arising.

The communists know that an adequate transformation of the structure of society in a socialist direction, and the solution of the fundamental contractions inherent in our society, can only be carried out by the conquest of political power on the part of the working class and its allies. But with the present balance of power between the forces of the proletariat, of the people and of progress, and those of exploitation and reaction, and faced with the urgent problems of unemployment, land and poverty, the communists declare that the tasks of dismantling a most backward and burdensome structure of Italian society, and the first steps toward transforming them in a democratic socialist way, cannot and must not be postponed to the moment of the conquest of power by the working class and its allies, but can and must be pursued as concrete, attainable objectives, to be reached by means of the workers' economic and political struggle.

This is the Italian path toward socialism; and this struggle ensures it broader support and guarantees its advance positions, so as to storm the breaches of the fortress of privilege and capitalist exploitation.

The concrete Italian path to socialism is, therefore, derived from the experience of the whole nation; it has been opened up by a victorious struggle of the workers; it is recognized by the most progressive sections of the people; it corresponds to the aspirations of the great majority of the citizens; and it contains objectives that can be attained in practice by applying the democratic method, and by means of a consistent struggle against the forces of conservatism and of reaction.

As the expression of this vast movement of renovation, the republican Italian society and the Italian state, it is an important victory on the Italian path to socialism.

The republican constitution does not limit itself to a mere formal recognition of the democratic rights of citizens, but ratifies the principle that it is necessary to remove 'the obstacles of an economic or social order which, by limiting *de facto* the liberty and equality of the citizens, prevents the complete development of the human personality and the effective participation of all the workers in the political, economic and social organization of the state.'

It is not unreasonable to state that the republican constitution, although it is distinct from constitutions of a socialist type both in its social contents and because it does not provide for a direct democracy on the basis of production, does nevertheless recognize in a concrete way the right of the workers to attain rulership of the state and sets up some of the conditions which may, when they are put into effect, encourage this process and allow some remarkable progress to be made by the nation's society on the road toward its transformation in a socialist direction.

For this reason the Communist Party has declared from the beginning that it does not regard the republican constitution as an expedient to use the instruments of bourgeois democracy until the time comes for armed insurrection to conquer the state and transform it into a socialist state, but as a pact of unity drawn up by the great majority of the Italian people and set up by them as the basis for the organic development of the nation's life for a whole period of history. Within the framework of this pact, it will be possible to carry out in full constitutional legality the necessary structural reforms to undermine the power of the monopolistic groups, to defend the interests of all the workers against economic and financial oligarchies, to exclude these oligarchies from power and to allow the working classes to attain power.

The communists declare once more that they have never been and are not now in favor of violence for violence's sake. Absurd and ridiculous, too, is the idea of a revolution imposed by foreign armies. Armed insurrection is an action into which the working class and the people may be forced by open violation of legality and recourse to violence on the part of the capitalist ruling classes, in obstinate defense of their privileges and in order to destroy democracy. Present-day conditions are such that violence by these classes may be prevented by active adherence of the overwhelming majority of the population to democratic institutions by reform of the economic structure, and by the workers' mass struggle. Democratic institutions can be developed as the effective basis of a regime which may advance toward socialism by opposing the attempts of the monopolistic groups by subversion and by removing the bases of their power.

The Italian working class and people are now beginning to be faced with the historic task of proceeding to the construction of socialism along a new path compared with the way in which the dictatorship of the proletariat has been carried out in other countries, by fulfilling their indispensable role of leadership through new alliances and new kinds of collaboration, respecting democratic methods, and overcoming resistance and conspiracies and the enemies of liberty and social progress with the irresistible force of an entire people of workers on the march toward their complete emancipation and redemption.

Il Partito communista italiano e il movimento operaio internazionale (Rome: Editori Riuniti, 1968), cf pp. 103–27.

4 Palmiro Togliatti, 'On socialism and democracy,' *Rinascita*, April 1961

It is our action to lead society towards socialism that lends new content and effectiveness to our struggle for democracy and to the whole democratic life of the country.

We must make this point clear to all, not only by stressing the existence of an insuppressible link between the struggle for democracy and the struggle for socialism, but proving by words and deeds that democracy is something quite new and real for us. We are not satisfied with forms only. It is not enough to hold an electoral consultation now and then to create the basis of a democratic regime . . .

Here lies the great difference characterizing the 'democracy' of those who fight for socialism.

This line is not doctrinarian but corresponds to a practical policy, which our party has realized in Italy. It contains the implicit and explicit answer to the question of what the forces fighting for socialism today will do 'afterwards,' that is to say, whether they will respect democracy when they exercise power and lead society. The 'future' will correspond to what is being done now; it will correspond to the democratic content of our present struggle.

The conquest of power by the working people is the beginning of a true democratic regime, in the economic and political field and in the whole society . . .

The dictatorship we refer to is something quite different. It is, as a matter of principle, an extension of democracy. It means the advent to the leadership of the state of a new ruling class — the working class and the masses of working people — having the task of organizing the exploitation of social wealth for the good of all instead of a handful of privileged. It entails, therefore, the end of exploitation of man, and it will ensure to all a worthy life and the necessary development of human personality. Owing to its very nature, this advent to power of a new class is the beginning of a true democratic renewal of the whole society.

Foreign Bulletin (April 1961), pp. 34–5.

5 Palmiro Togliatti's report to the Tenth Congress of the PCI, 1962

The advance to socialism, in fact, must take place and is bound to take place strictly in harmony with the real conditions existing in each country. This has been and still is the starting point of our efforts to find a national road to advance socialism. Therefore, it is necessary to take into account the economic development and economic structure and national peculiarities, features and conditions of political struggle, the extent and forms of democratic life, the organization, strength, traditions and orientation of the popular and working-class movement; all this, of course, in the framework of international relations . . .

To advance to socialism, it is necessary to act and not to confine oneself to propaganda only, or to mere protest against present-day conditions, waiting for the 'great day' . . .

Neither can we limit ourselves only to the action and struggle – although necessary and indispensable – for economic improvements and for the defense of political rights. The former can be annulled by the developments of economy, the latter by reactionary attacks. To avoid both, the working class must succeed in intervening actively and autonomously, with its own initiative and aims, in the sphere of politics and economics. When they are compelled to do so by the very strength of the working-class movement, the bourgeois ruling classes accept this intervention, but they endeavor by all means to weaken it, turning it towards aims of a merely partial and paternalistic nature, which leave unaltered the essence of political and social relations. If the working class accepts this position, it condemns itself ultimately to play a merely subordinate role *vis-à-vis* the bourgeoisie and forgets its main aim, that is, socialism . . .

Any improvements, even of partial nature, in the workers' living standard, any blow dealt to the system of privilege and exploitation, is a positive element.

Nothing is more foolish and dangerous than a policy of 'so much the worse, so much the better.' We always rejected such a policy . . .

Beyond temporary measures, there are two basic issues over which the claims of the workers and of the masses must be focused, that is, the problem of economic structures and that of the political leadership of society, with the aim of weakening and if possible breaking down the absolute domination by the bourgeois ruling groups. To this end, reforms of structure, nationalizations and a plan for democratic economic development must be considered.

Here we meet with the most serious objection. The struggle for these aims takes place within the present state, which maintains its nature of a bourgeois state until a qualitative change is made. We know the class nature of the state, nor does it change because one or two nationalizations are approved. Our constitution itself, which is not a socialist constitution, has not changed the nature of the state. This argument remains abstract, however. To make it become concrete it is necessary to study how the present power bloc of ruling classes formed and organized itself as well as the possibility and way of transforming it by means of a progress of political nature . . .

The point is to see whether it is possible, starting from the present state structure, on the ground of the democratic organization in which the masses participate today and imposing deep reforms of structure, to develop such a movement and to reach such results as to modify the present power bloc and create the conditions for the formation of another bloc, in which the working people participate and in which they play the part they are entitled to. Obviously in accepting such a perspective, namely, the perspective of advancing to socialism in democracy and peace, we introduce the concept of a gradual development, and it is very hard to say exactly when the qualitative change will take place. In the capitalistically advanced countries having a deeply rooted democratic organization, we foresee a struggle, which might be a long one, by which the working people will thrive to become the ruling classes and thus to pave the way for the transformation of the entire social structure. It would be naïve and useless to confine this struggle to electoral competitions, waiting to conquer 51 per cent of the votes. The ruling bourgeois classes are always in a position to prevent this. Equally or even more naïve is the proposal of those who would like us to organize straight away, from above, so-called 'power committees' and then go forward.

In this way the conception of the conquest of power becomes commonplace. When it has reached the numerical and organizational strength it has today in a country such as Italy, the working class aims at imposing its power in forms that are much more complex and articulate, but also much more effective. It does so in defending democratic institutions and parliamentary democracy, claiming local and regional government autonomy, fighting for substantial reforms, putting forward new proposals for democratic control and forms of direct democracy. Can the working class find in a capitalistically advanced society the mass power which stems from the entente, co-operation and alliance with non-proletarian strata of the people, such as were, in other countries, the mass of landless and poor peasants? . . .

At present not all the political and social groups which might agree on the need to fight against monopoly capital are on socialist positions. We are aware of this. There exist, however, increasingly favorable conditions for the creation of a socialist consciousness in the masses and it is our task to work to stimulate it. Even in the camp of Catholic organizations and among representatives of the religious world, the acceptance of principles of socialist nature is beginning to emerge . . .

Today a socialist consciousness cannot be separated by a national consciousness. The most pressing problems that confront us today – the problems of employment, the agrarian question and that of the South – cannot be solved locally but only on a national scale. Only in a socialist society can national solidarity develop fully.

Foreign Bulletin (December 1962), pp. 8–56, *passim*.

6   Political resolution of the Tenth Congress of the PCI, September 1962

Concerning the strategy of the socialist revolution and the problem of the state, two mistaken conceptions have taken shape in the Italian working-class movement in recent times. They must be fought. The first of these mistaken conceptions stems from an abstract vision of the state as a force that can become 'independent' and place itself above the classes, or at any rate on a possible neutral ground, detached from the actual class structure and relations. In this way

one forgets that the state, though in the diverse political forms it assumes and in the changeable internal balance, is always an expression of the dominant power bloc; and therefore the building of a new democratic regime advancing towards socialism is closely connected with the formation of a new historical bloc that, under the leadership of the working class, fights to change the structure of the society and bring about an intellectual and moral revolution, besides a political one. The ideological autonomy of the working class, its political unity, the development of its class organizations and of the mass organizations that unite it with other social groups, its bonds with all the forces of the world that fight against imperialism, are decisive elements for the formation of this new historical bloc and to make a political action directed to change the class basis of the state stem from the struggles for immediate aims, to modify progressively the internal balances and structures, to impose in this way the advent of new classes to its leadership. Otherwise the social struggle and the very partial conquests lose their character of progressive struggle for power, fall back on reformism and remain necessarily condemned to a subordinate place within the dominant system.

Equally mistaken is, however, the attitude of sectarian extremism that holds it necessary to fight such opportunistic degeneration by calling upon the working class to confine its actions to the factory, denying the value of the struggle for democracy, placing the advance to socialism outside the democratic texture of the society, challenging the significance of transitory objectives and conquests and therefore denying the policy of the working-class alliance. It is indeed because of the extension and the forms that the rule of the monopoly system has assumed that it is not possible to break it down without trying one's strength in the field of state, without opposing and fighting in this framework against the choices of the ruling classes, without utilizing and developing the democratic conquests that the working class has managed to gain for the achievement of the real goal of the forces that inspire it to socialism.

The revolutionary working-class struggle must develop within the state, as it has historically formed through the battles of these years, to claim and impose its transformation in the light of the constitution, to conquer in its framework new positions of force, to carry forward the socialist transformation of the society. This is all the more valid today when the weight and the intervention of the state in every sphere of national life and economy is extending and more evident, and the bond between the economic struggle and the political struggle becomes closer.

The construction of an Italian road to socialism in this way appears as a process of mass struggle, around positive objectives that introduce modifications into the economic structure and in the political set-up, that shift gradually the balance of power in favor of the working class and its allies and stimulate the formation of a social and political bloc, capable of carrying out – in constitutional legality – the socialist transformation of Italy.

Foreign Bulletin (September 1962), pp. 54–6.

7   Enrico Berlinguer's closing address to the Twelfth Congress of the PCI, February 1962

Comrade Longo has reconfirmed with great clarity our choice for a democratic road to socialism; he has reconfirmed, that is, that we see the access to power of the working classes as a process which must take place within the framework of democracy and its consistent development, through an inseparable interplay of mass social struggles and political and parliamentary battles, through a movement that aims at achieving, even before the conquest of power, ever new positions of working-class power in all spheres of civil life, thus increasing the workers' direct and indirect influence over the direction of national policy, through a movement that simultaneously stimulates a continual extension of freedom and a general advance of political democracy.

This choice of ours arises from historical reasons and principles that are deeply rooted and that today take on new meaning.

It arises, first of all, from the fact that, as a result of the changes produced in the structures of capitalism when it enters its imperialist monopoly and authoritarian phase, the problem of freedom and democracy 'changes aspect,' as Togliatti put it.

The fate of freedom, its extension to those extreme confines where democracy overcomes all class limitations and becomes socialist democracy, is essentially entrusted to the positions of power which the working classes succeed in winning . . .

But having thus recalled the essential basis of our

choice, the problem arises, and it is a problem that today takes on new aspects, of how the defense and development of democratic freedom must be used not only to increasingly better guarantee the satisfaction of the interests of the working masses, but also to transform the structures of our economy and renew the democratic institutions themselves, to introduce into all our political and social life new forms of direct democracy and thus ensure a real participation of the workers in the management of the economy and public life . . .

As has been underlined by many comrades, with a wealth of arguments and examples, the most important fact in the processes that have developed in our country in this recent period lies precisely in the new, closer interrelationship that has been established between all the aspects of the action of the working masses, between the various aspects of the struggle in the social sphere and those in the political sphere.

This interrelationship is becoming increasingly evident in almost all the working-class movements. It is visible in other movements as well, the student movement above all; and it is also reflected in one way or another in other phenomena which do not concern only or principally the social sphere, but rather express the existence of new tensions in cultural life, social practice and even in the field of religion.

We can say that there is no struggle, even the most immediate and elementary, that through its breadth, its content and goals and also through a process of maturation of consciousness does not objectively, and increasingly subjectively, give rise to problems of a political nature; that is, problems of freedom, democracy, participation, control and power . . .

The central problem lying before us in the coming months is to succeed in winning important gains for the working masses, on the social level, that is, in their living and working conditions, and on the level of democracy and participation, that is, on the level of new forms of control and power for the working classes.

In all this lies the substance of our strategy of reforms. But it is my opinion that this expression is perhaps not in itself capable of fully expressing our policy, because it does not give a complete vision of the process through which we intend to advance towards socialism, since it may lead to neglecting other essential elements, especially with regard to the decisive questions of political leadership and power.

In substance, I feel that this expression – strategy of reforms – must be integrated with other concepts and incorporated with the expression 'historical bloc,' which is also part of our tradition. We have often said, for that matter, that in our conception it is not the party that wins power, but a bloc of various social forces, of which the party is a part, and that we must begin now, step by step, to create this historical bloc, establishing within it the hegemony of the working class. The strategy of reforms is therefore essentially a strategy of alliances, which, in the last analysis, has always been and remains the central problem in any revolutionary process. The important, pre-eminent thing is the real, overall process; it is conceiving of the struggle for socialism as a non-linear, complex, bitter and diversified advance of the progressive social groups and their unity, of society as a whole and of a consistent development of democracy.

Within this framework, the connections between goals of an economic nature and goals of a political nature, between social and organizational successes, between the construction of a unifying fabric at the grass-roots level and initiative for the construction of new political blocs, are increasingly evident. This vision is not, for that matter, an intellectual invention, but something derived from the consequences of state monopoly capitalism, as far as concerns the relationship between the economic and the political and the contrast between new forms of authoritarianism and, increasingly, pressures for freedom.

We place all this within the framework of what we call a democratic road, that is, a road of great, broad class and political struggles and a consistent defense and application of the principles and political system outlined in the republican constitution.

Foreign Bulletin (January–February–March 1969), pp. 101–11.

8 Enrico Berlinguer's speech to the Central Committee in preparation for the Thirteenth Congress of the PCI, December 1971

From the development of the social and political struggle over the past few years – with its interweaving of working-class and popular gains and reactionary counter-attacks and threats – there emerges a basic problem, which we must place at the center of our congress debate. The present terms of this problem can be stated as follows.

How can we continue to move forward along the road opened up by the struggles and gains of the last few years, at the same time avoiding a backlash of reaction of such magnitude that it throws the whole situation to the right, outside the democratic process? . . .

Italy is a country in which the possibilities of advance towards radical transformations of the economic, social and political structures are perhaps greater than in all or almost all the other advanced capitalist countries, but it is also a country in which dangers of involution or reactionary turnabouts are always present . . .

Our initiatives, together with the responsible positions of other political forces, have made it possible to obtain a turnabout in the trend that seemed to make the referendum inevitable. And if today there is hope that the country will be spared a conflict of religious nature, with all the connected dangers of lacerations among the popular masses and damage to the sovereignty of the state and the principle of the separation of church and state, this hope is due, to a decisive extent, to the line of national and democratic responsibility that has guided us throughout. We intend to follow this line as far as possible . . .

When the proletariat's alliances shrink, and the social base of the ruling groups correspondingly broadens, sooner or later the whole political situation tends to move backwards and even the prospects for a successful policy of reforms begin to crumble. Therefore (although this statement is undoubtedly somewhat schematic), in the relationship between reforms and alliances, the primary factor in measuring the validity of a line must remain the question of alliances. On this point, our recent experiences can offer a number of lessons and occasions for critical reflection.

Steps forward have been accompanied by errors and defects which have weighed negatively on the whole political situation . . .

The accent must thus be placed on the subjective factor, that is, on the need for a correct orientation and initiative on the social, political and ideological level, if these *potential* alliances are to become *real* . . .

With regard to the content and forms of the struggles, certain elements seem to particularly deserve critical analysis: the degree of unity realized around demands among the workers, technicians and white-collar workers, and among the workers themselves, and the breadth of consensus around these demands it has been possible to arouse in public opinion. Propaganda and informative activity, popularization of the reasons for agitation, demonstrations and strikes and contact with public opinion have become increasingly decisive conditions for the success of every struggle and a means for checking and correcting corporative content and forms of struggle that lead to isolation. But there is more to it than just propaganda. The essential thing is that our demands both within the factory and for reforms be such as to offer positive and advanced outlets to the objective contrasts existing among the different social strata, thus laying the groundwork for a new collocation of the middle classes within a common framework of renewal . . .

The question of relations between the workers and their trade unions, on the one hand, and the merchants, artisans and small and middle-sized manufacturers, on the other, has become more difficult and delicate. Nor can the problem be solved by sacrificing the workers' interests. But, in the same way that something has been obtained in the rural areas in relations between the paid farm laborers and the other peasant classes, this question must become the object of more careful study and political initiative . . .

In general, the greater or lesser breadth of the working-class alliances depends to a large extent on whether the working-class movement, in all its manifestations, increasingly succeeds in presenting itself as the bearer of the most deeply felt popular and national needs. This is not a matter of tactics, but rather of principle and historical choice: the working class fulfills its revolutionary function to the extent that it asserts itself as the liberating and leading force of the whole national society . . .

As far as we are concerned, we are not impatient: our strength (I should almost like to say our power) is quite large, even on the opposition, with the added advantage, among other things, of a certain detachment; and our real weight in national political life is also great, although not such as to determine its general direction.

The real problem is another: it is that the necessity of creating a democratic government alternative is today increasingly urgent; it is a national and democratic necessity which no responsible political force can ignore.

Enrico Berlinguer, *For the Renewal of Italy, Peace and the Liberation of the Oppressed Peoples of Imperialism* (Rome: PCI Publication, 1972), pp. 43–69.

9   Enrico Berlinguer, 'Reflections after events in Chile,' *Rinascita*, nos 38, 39, 40, September–October 1973

Events in Chile extend an awareness, against all illusions, that the characteristics of imperialism, and North American imperialism in particular, remain abuse and economic and political strangulation, a spirit of aggression and conquest, and the tendency to oppress peoples and deprive them of their independence, freedom and unity every time the concrete circumstances and balance of forces give it the chance . . .

The policy of détente and the prospect of peaceful coexistence are, first of all, the only way to guarantee a primary goal of vital interest to all humanity and to every people: the goal of avoiding atomic and thermonuclear war, of ensuring world peace and asserting the principle of negotiations as the only means of solving controversies among the states . . .

Détente and coexistence do not, in themselves, automatically and in the short run, imply an overcoming of the division of the world into blocs and zones of influence. Therefore, they do not prevent the United States from intervening in various ways, including the most brazen, in those zones and countries it would like to keep permanently within its direct or indirect sphere of domination . . .

But it is also obvious that the progress of détente and coexistence is an indispensable condition for overcoming the division of the world into blocs or spheres of influence, for establishing the right of every nation to independence and therefore, in the last analysis, for reducing the possibility of imperialist intervention in the life of other countries. At the same time, moving resolutely down the road of détente and coexistence means stimulating the processes of development of democracy and freedom in all countries, whatever their social system . . .

In all our action, we have always given due importance to the basic fact represented by Italy's membership in the political-military bloc dominated by the United States and to the ways this fact inevitably conditions the Italian situation . . . The first problem is to modify the internal balance of forces in such a way as to discourage or thwart all attempts by internal and international reactionary forces to subvert the democratic and constitutional system, to undermine the gains our people have won, to break their unity and halt their advance towards the transformation of society . . .

Events in Chile require careful thought not only

concerning the international framework and problems of foreign policy, but also concerning problems related to the prospect of democratic and socialist transformation in our own country . . .

But together with the differences, there are also similarities, and in particular the fact that the Chilean communists and socialists had also set out to pursue a democratic road to socialism.

This mixture of differences and similarities must therefore prompt us to define more deeply and better exactly what the Italian road to socialism is and how it can advance . . .

The essential task lying before us – and it is a task we can fulfill – is to extend this fabric of unity, to rally the vast majority of the people around a program of struggle for the democratic renewal of our whole society and the state and to build a coalition of political forces that corresponds to this majority and this program and is capable of realizing it. Only this line, and no other, can isolate and defeat the conservative and reactionary groups, only this line can give democracy solidity and invincible strength, only this line can advance the transformation of society. And, at the same time, only by following this road can we begin to create today the conditions for building a socialist society and state that guarantee the full exercise and development of all the freedoms . . .

We have also always considered it mistaken to see the democratic road simply as a parliamentary road. We do not suffer from parliamentary cretinism, whereas there are some people who suffer from anti-parliamentary cretinism. We see parliament as an essential institution in Italian political life, and not only for today, but also in the phase of transition to socialism and in building socialism itself. This is all the more true given the fact that in Italy the rebirth and renewal of parliament was won primarily with the struggles of the working class and the working masses. Therefore, parliament cannot be conceived and used, as in Lenin's times and as may occur in other countries, as nothing more than a place to denounce the evils of capitalism and the bourgeois governments and to make socialist propaganda . . .

But parliament can fulfill its role, as Togliatti said, only if it increasingly becomes a 'mirror of the country' and if the parliamentary initiative of the parties of the working-class movement is tightly linked to the mass struggle, to the growth of democratic power in society and to the establishment of democratic and constitutional principles in all the sectors and organs of the state . . .

But there is also another very important aspect of our democratic strategy. The working-class movement's decision to maintain its struggle on the terrain of democratic legality does not mean falling prey to any sort of legalistic illusion, abandoning that essential part of our work, whether in the government or in the opposition, that lies in promoting a constant initiative for far-reaching democratic renewal of the laws, structures and organs of the state . . .

In the last analysis, the chances of success for a democratic road to socialism depend on the working-class movement's capacity to make its decisions and assess its initiatives not only on the international yardstick, but also in relation to the concrete relationship of forces in every situation and at every moment, and on its capacity to deal with the reactions and counter-reactions transformation sets off in all aspects of society: in the economy, in the structures and organs of the state, in the positions and orientations of the various social and political forces and in their mutual relationships . . .

The democratic road to socialism is a progressive transformation of the entire economic and social structure, of the underlying values and ideas of the nation, of the power system and the bloc of social forces in which this system finds expression. In Italy this transformation can be achieved within the framework of the anti-fascist constitution. What is certain is that this general transformation we want to achieve in Italy by the democratic road needs both force and consensus in all its phases.

The element of *force* must find expression in unceasing vigilance, in the combativeness of the working masses, in our determination in quickly thwarting maneuvers and attacks on freedom, democratic rights and constitutional legality. Being fully aware of this absolute necessity, we have always warned the working and popular masses against all forms of illusion and naïvety, against all tendencies to underestimate the aggressive intentions of the right-wing forces. At the same time, we have warned the enemies of democracy against every illusion . . .

A far-reaching transformation of society by the democratic road requires *consensus* in a very specific sense: in Italy such a transformation can only come about as a revolution of the great majority of the people, and it is only on this condition that *consensus* and *force* complete one another and can become an invincible reality . . .

The problem of alliances is thus the decisive problem of every revolution and every revolutionary policy, and it is therefore also decisive for the success of the democratic road . . .

The strategy of reforms can succeed only if it rests on a strategy of alliances. Indeed, we have stressed that in the relationship between reforms and alliances the latter are the decisive factor, because if the alliances of the working class shrink and the social base of the ruling classes expands, sooner or later the possibility of realizing any reforms at all will cease to exist and the whole political situation will move backwards.

Naturally, the point of departure for an alliance policy lies in the search for convergence between the immediate economic interests and prospects of the working class and those of other social groups and forces. But this search must not be conceived and put into practice in a schematic or static manner . . .

We do not, then, limit ourselves to seeking and establishing convergence with already defined social figures and economic categories. We rather aim at winning over and incorporating in a diversified grouping of alliances entire groups, social forces not classifiable as classes, such as women, young people, the popular masses of the South, cultural forces, movements of opinion, and so on. We propose goals that are not only economic and social but involve such areas as civil development, democratic progress, personal dignity and the expansion of the many human freedoms. This is how we understand and carry out the concrete work to build and prepare the bases, the conditions and guarantees for what has been called a new 'model' of socialism . . .

If it is true that a policy of democratic renewal can succeed only if it has the support of the vast majority of the population, it follows that a policy of broad social alliances is not in itself sufficient. What is also needed is a particular system of political relations capable of favoring convergence and collaboration among all the democratic and popular forces, with the aim of achieving a political alliance among them.

For that matter, a contraposition and head-on clash between the parties that have a popular base and through which important masses of the population feel themselves represented would lead to a split down the middle of the country which would be fatal for democracy, overwhelming the very foundations on which the survival of the democratic state rest.

With this in mind, we have always thought – and today the Chilean experience strengthens our conviction – that unity among the workers' parties and left-wing forces is not enough to guarantee the defense and progress of democracy in situations where this unity finds itself confronted with a bloc of parties extending from the center to the extreme right. The central political problem in Italy has been, and more than ever remains, the problem of how to avoid the welding of a solid and organic bond between the center and the right, the formation of a broad front of clerico-fascist stamp, and instead succeed in drawing the social and political forces in the center on to consistently democratic positions.

Obviously the unity, the political and electoral strength of the left-wing forces, and an increasingly solid understanding among their various and autonomous expressions are an indispensable condition for maintaining a growing pressure for change in the country and for bringing such change about. But it would be illusory to think that even if the left-wing parties and forces succeeded in gaining 51 per cent of the vote and seats in parliament (something which would in itself mark a big step forward in the relationship of forces among the parties in Italy), this fact would guarantee the survival and work of a government representing this 51 per cent.

This is why we talk not about a 'left-wing alternative,' but a 'democratic alternative,' that is, a political prospect of collaboration and agreement among the popular forces of communist and socialist inspiration and the popular forces of Catholic inspiration, together with formations of other democratic orientation . . .

Our policy of dialogue and debate with the Catholic world necessarily develops on different levels and with different interlocutors.

There is, first of all, the problem posed by the presence in Italy of the Catholic Church and its relations with the state and civil society; on this problem our principled position and political line are well known. Then there is the problem of the search for a broader mutual understanding and working agreement with those movements of Catholic orientation which are, in growing numbers, taking their stand within the workers' movement and adopting clearly anti-capitalist and anti-imperialist attitudes.

But it is impossible to escape the other big problem represented by the existence and strength of a political party like the Christian Democratic Party which, quite aside from the fact that it calls itself 'Christian,' gathers in its ranks, or under its influence, a large part of the working and popular masses of Catholic orientation . . .

We have always kept firmly in mind the ties existing between the Christian Democratic Party and the ruling groups of the bourgeoisie and the important, and at times decisive, influence these groups exert on Christian Democratic policy. But other forces and economic and social interests are also present within and around the party – forces and interests that go from various middle-class categories to sizable segments of the popular strata, particularly in certain regions and zones, peasants, young people, women, and even workers. The weight and pressures arising from the interests and aspirations of these forces have also made themselves felt to a greater or lesser extent in the course of the life and policy of the Christian Democratic Party and can be made to count more.

Alongside this varied and contradictory social composition, we must also consider its origins, its history, its traditions and the different political and ideological trends that have been and are at work within it: from reactionary to conservative and moderate, to democratic and even progressive . . .

This being the reality of the Christian Democratic Party and the point it has reached today, it is clear that the duty of a party such as ours can only be to isolate and drastically defeat those tendencies that aim, or may be tempted to aim, at contraposition and splitting the country in two, or that in any event refuse to budge from a position of preconceived ideological anti-communist preclusion, which in Italy implies in itself an impending danger of splitting the nation. On the contrary, we must work constantly to increase the weight and ensure the eventual predominance of those tendencies that with a sense of historical and political realism recognize the necessity and maturity of a constructive dialogue and agreement among all the popular forces, without this implying confusion or renunciation of the ideological and political differences proper to each of these forces.

Certainly we are the first to realize that the march towards this prospect is not easy and cannot be hurried. We also know how many difficult battles will have to be waged, with determination and patience, on the most varied levels and not by our party alone, to ensure the success of this prospect. But neither must we think that the time at our disposal is infinite. The gravity of the country's problems, the still-impending threats of reactionary adventures, and the necessity to open at long last a sure road of economic development, social renewal and democratic progress for the country make it increasingly urgent and appropriate to arrive at what we can call the great new 'historical compromise' among the forces that represent the vast majority of the Italian people.

PCI translation in special issue of *The Italian Communists* (1973), pp. 4–30.

10 Political resolution of the Fourteenth Congress of the PCI, March 18–23, 1975

A far-reaching democratic change of course is a national necessity. It is a possible goal, but at the same time a difficult one. To achieve it, political maneuvers, even the most adroit and intelligent, are not sufficient. What is needed is a further shift in real forces, in the orientation of broad masses, a change in political relationships. We must therefore broaden and expand the struggle movement, raising its political level, militancy and cohesion. We are fully aware that we are moving towards a phase of important bitter contests. The outcome of these battles will be victorious, if we succeed in uniting tenacious, intransigent defense of working-class gains and the living standards of the broad masses with a strengthening and expansion of the country's democratic fabric, defense of our democratic institutions and a clean-up and renewal of all national life . . .

With their united struggle, vigilance and mass mobilization, the working class and the democratic movement have clearly demonstrated their will to bar the road to any fascist comeback and to move forward along the road of democracy. In this struggle, vigilance and mobilization, of which the communists are an essential part, lies the most solid guarantee for our constitution and the institutions born out of the resistance. This struggle, vigilance and mobilization represent the decisive force to cut the neo-fascist phenomenon at the roots and eliminate this reactionary presence and threat.

But the fight against fascism is also an immediate constitutional obligation for the state powers: it is the first and most urgent problem in the sphere of public order. The republic must enforce its laws unequivocally and without hesitation, revising them, where necessary, in order to deny the right to political citizenship to those who do not and must not have this right. This today is the foremost yardstick for measuring the authority of the democratic state . . .

Defense of the democratic state requires a broader development of democracy. For this reason, we stress that the democratic state can be strong and vital if it rests on the confidence and initiative of the broad masses of citizens and their organizations, if it avails itself of the will to participate that is emerging with increasing vigor in all sectors of society; if it works to strengthen the country's democratic fabric, encouraging both original forms of participation and organization and an organic relationship between these forms and the representative institutions; if it grants the regions and local authorities all the powers due them, according to a vision of the state that is not reduced to its central organs, but diversified and decentralized, as dictated by the constitution; if, in this framework, civil, political rights and those of national minorities are fully guaranteed and respected . . .

Today, more than ever before, to achieve the great goals the communists propose . . . agreements and convergence among the political and popular forces and different social strata. A policy of renewal of such great scope will require the backing of a vast grouping of forces; it will require a whole new commitment to rally the support of the broadest possible majority of the people. For this reason, the communists will fight to defeat all policies based on contraposition, division and preclusion and to establish in all fields the principles, methods and practice of unity . . .

In these questions, as elsewhere, we can grasp the full gravity of an essential aspect of the Italian political crisis, which is not simply a crisis of government formulas and party coalitions, but also, and more basically, the outcome of an incapacity on the part of the ruling forces to grasp the new factors in the situation, establish a correct relationship with them, express an adequate political synthesis and exercise real leadership. What we are witnessing is therefore the crisis of a system of power, of a way of governing, in which the center-left experience, as others before it, has worn itself out. It is also a crisis of the Christian Democratic Party.

Naturally, particularly in Italy, it would be mistaken to reduce the Catholic question to the Christian Democrat question alone. A number of developments are opening up new fruitful possibilities for initiative on this terrain by the working-class movement, and the communists in particular, and for constructive dialogue with the Catholic world . . .

This is not to deny that in immediate political terms the central question is the crisis in the Christian Democratic Party and in its relationship with society and the state. The present Secretariat of the Christian Democratic Party seeks to answer this crisis with a policy that not only deepens it, but at the same time aggravates the country's problems: a backward-looking policy that retraces the old road of contraposition and discrimination; a policy that offers no prospects for renewal and increasingly encounters the open opposition, reservations and doubts of those, including many Christian Democrats, who sense the responsibilities this party derives from the quantity and quality of support it has long enjoyed in the country. A rigorous struggle against present Christian Democratic policy and orientations and to win this party as a whole over to consistently democratic anti-fascist policies, favorable to reform, can only be based on a line of broad democratic, popular unity.

A fundamental axis of our prospect is a higher level of political and ideological unity in the working class and between its parties. Precisely because they are convinced of the essential role of the Italian Socialist Party in the national political framework, the communists stress that in the common struggles of the working masses, as in debate between the two parties, unity-oriented relations between the PCI and the PSI must grow and find new strength, together with a common effort to take the standpoint of the general interests of the working-class movement and the country and favor the establishment of the broadest possible democratic agreements . . .

Thus the question of what we communists have called the 'historical compromise' returns to the center of the issue of the country's political crisis. This is without doubt the political proposal most suited to interpreting the increasingly widespread aspiration to real, prompt change in all fields. Nevertheless, this proposal cannot be reduced to the problem – however decisive – of the PCI's presence in the majority and in the government; it must instead be seen as a strategy, which we hold valid for the whole country, and as a method, which in practice has already shown itself to be the only one permitting real progress and solutions to the country's problems. At the same time, the historical compromise line must not be seen as a crystallized formula that immobilizes political relationships and closes the field to other democratic parties, but rather as a process committing all forces, in autonomy and each with its own peculiar characteristics, to an effort to expand and renew democracy and come to grips with the great questions of our country: it must be seen as a more advanced terrain of struggle and a challenge, whose goals are the salvation and rebirth of Italy.

The Italian Communists, nos 2–3 (March–May 1975), pp. 121–40.

11 Enrico Berlinguer's report to the Central Committee of the PCI, October 30, 1975

The events and changes of these last two years confirm that the goal the workers' movement and communists must set for themselves is that of a full development of democratic life, capable of eliminating not only existing authoritarian regimes and pressures, but also their roots, with the introduction of deep-reaching democratic transformations, including some of a socialist nature. This goal, which is particularly pressing in southern Europe, is also present, in different ways, in the other countries of Western Europe.

To achieve these goals of democratic progress, two conditions are necessary. First, that the process of international détente move ahead; and in this sense, the Helsinki Conference is to be welcomed as a great positive event that operates the road to new steps forward along the road to a system of security and co-operation in Europe. As everyone knows, we see détente as a process that, without altering the equilibrium between the United States and the Soviet Union, between the Atlantic Alliance and the Warsaw Pact, and between these two blocs and the area of non-aligned European countries (among which we ascribe particular importance to Yugoslavia), must lead to a simultaneous reduction of military potentials and arms procurement on both sides, as well as, naturally, to a development of co-operation in all fields of economic, political and civil life, going beyond the nevertheless useful and positive bilateral agreements already in existence or planned . . .

The second condition, if we are to achieve real democratic progress and economic and social renewal in Western Europe, is that in all the individual countries – and as far as possible in the European West as a whole – we arrive at a rapprochement and collaboration among the parties that have their base in the working class, the working people and the popular strata and therefore, first and foremost, between the communist and socialist parties, but also with the social democratic parties in general, the parties and organizations of Christian inspiration and other democratic forces of different ideological orientation . . .

We are not boasting when we say that few parties in Europe and none in Italy have worked as hard as ours in studying the issues involved in revolution and building socialism in the West, from both the ideological and political standpoint. Our assessment of the existing socialist societies unquestionably differs from that of certain Christian Democrats, Social Democrats, and even some socialists, who seem to think that the essential characteristic of these societies is that they are 'bureacratic,' 'police' regimes . . .

Nevertheless, these assessments and feelings do not overshadow our full independence of judgement on the set-ups in those societies, particularly in certain of their legal and political aspects, which restrict freedoms, and on other aspects concerning relations among the socialist states, and also on the political strategy of other communist parties working in the capitalist countries (as happened recently for Portugal).

The most important fact remains, however, that for a long time now we have concretely developed our political action in full awareness of the substantial diversity of the roads to socialism and to the building of socialism in our country and in the countries of the European West in general.

It is our profound conviction that, whatever the differences among the various countries of Western Europe, there is not one of them in which the policy of the workers' movement can diverge from certain common characteristics of a strategy of effective advance towards socialism for the whole of the European West. These characteristics can be summed up in conceiving the transformation of the foundations and ends of society and its development as a process capable of guaranteeing, in every phase, full respect of all the individual and collective freedoms and their concrete development.

In the light of this conviction, which is rooted in us on the basis of a long political experience, hard struggles and a deepened theoretical and cultural elaboration, we consider mistaken those positions that present the revolutionary process as a process that can, in certain cases and moments, be something different from, or even in conflict with, the process of development of democracy. In the same way, we consider mistaken those positions that present things in terms of a cut-and-dried dilemma: either immediate advance towards the socialist transformation of society or retreat towards reaction and fascism . . .

We can avoid falling into this dilemma only if we fully understand that there can be no real advance towards socialism that is not the product, at one and the same time, of a consistent development of democracy and of the fact that the proletariat has taken the leadership of this development firmly in its own hands.

Outside this strategy, the working class itself splits and loses its capacity to become the leading force: a force capable of rallying in a diversified system of alliances all those social and political forces of different inspiration that are interested in a deep-reaching renewal of society carried out in freedom and in democracy.

One of the major reasons for our strength and advance in Italy and the prestige that our party enjoys in Europe and the world lies, along with its unfailing internationalism, in the consistence and enthusiasm with which it has mastered these principles, developing them according to a consistent strategy . . .

It would have been disastrous if our party, if other democratic forces, if the decisive part of the workers' movement and the workers' unions, had not worked – each with its own autonomy and specific characteristics – to prevent a sectional fragmentation of the workers' movement, the outbreak of a generalized brawl among the political forces and growing chaos in all aspects of social and civil life. These are precisely the cards that the right-wing reactionary groups were betting on and will continue to bet on, because they are the only cards they have . . .

It is for this reason that anyone who tries to divert the workers' movement from this path, even if motivated by ideas that are supposedly 'farther to the left,' is actually playing into the hands of those forces that are aiming at adventurous, authoritarian, right-wing solutions.

The Italian Communists, nos 5–6 (September–December 1975), pp. 43–57.

12   Enrico Berlinguer's speech to the Conference of the Communist and Workers' Parties of Europe, Berlin, June 29–30, 1976

Today, in the face of a new international situation and the increasingly evident inability of capitalism to give a positive answer to the big problems of economic and social development, the task not only of reflecting on the socialist experiences hitherto achieved but also of seeking new roads towards socialism in the countries of Western Europe is once more on the agenda.

What roads and what socialism? The roads followed in the countries of Eastern Europe do not correspond to the peculiar conditions and orientations of the broad working class and popular masses in the countries of the West.

Some of our adversaries claim that socialism and communism are and will be the same everywhere. This is not true, nor was it true for the bourgeois revolutions nor for the societies they gave rise to. There already exists in the world today a variety of

experiences in the building of new, no longer capitalist, societies. And it is logical that other varieties can and must develop, among which the substantially new varieties that will be built in the countries where capitalism has reached the highest points of its development and where deeply rooted democratic traditions and particular forms of organization and political expression by the working people exist.

In Italy, where the working class and our party have been and are protagonists in the fight to restore, defend and develop democracy, we are fighting for a socialist society that has at its foundation the affirmation of the value of the individual and collective freedoms and their guarantee, the principles of the secular, non-ideological nature of the state and its democratic organization, the plurality of political parties and the possibility of alternation of government majorities, the autonomy of the trade unions, religious freedom, freedom of expression, of culture and the arts and sciences. In the economic sphere a high level of productive development must be ensured by means of a democratic form of planning that makes use of the existence and positive function of various forms of enterprise and management, both public and private, all aimed at satisfaction of the big needs of man and the national collectivity. It is highly significant that some other communist and workers' parties in Western Europe have arrived, on the basis of autonomous research of their own, at similar conceptions concerning the road to follow to reach socialism and the characteristics of the socialist society to be built in their countries. This convergence and these common features were recently expressed in the declarations we signed with our comrades of the Communist Party of Spain, the French Communist Party and the Communist Party of Great Britain. It is this new type of elaboration and searching that some people have referred to as 'Eurocommunism.' Obviously we were not the ones to coin this term, but the very fact that it has gained such wide circulation indicates the depth and extent of an aspiration to see solutions of a new type in the transformation of society in the socialist direction take root and advance in the countries of Western Europe . . .

We think it is very important that in the course of the debates in preparation for this conference it has been possible to arrive at formulations concerning relations among our parties which to us seem proper and correct.

The solidarity among our parties is based on recognition that each party elaborates autonomously and decides in full independence its own political line, both internal and international; it is based on strict observance of parity of rights and non-interference in each other's internal affairs and on respect for the right to choose freely different roads in the struggle for the transformation of society and the building of socialism.

Respect for these principles does not conflict with the need, which we strongly feel, for broader and less formal debate around the big theoretical and political problems facing the movement for socialism all over the world. It seems evident to us, for example, that development in the elaboration of Marxism has not kept pace with the great transformations taking place in the reality of today's world, with the different experiences in struggle and in the building of socialism and with political practice. Often things have been limited to the use of stereotyped formulations, to battles of quotations or to arbitrarily labelling as revisionist in one sense or the other every position that differs from one's own.

The truth is that, just as there is not and cannot be any leading party or leading state, on the theoretical level as well, the development of Marxism requires the concurrence of many different contributions from both parties and individuals . . .

It is our opinion that respect for the principle of non-interference can not exclude freedom of judgement on theoretical or political positions taken by other parties, as well as on particular events in international life and in the workers' movement. Everyone knows, for example, that while we have always stressed the great advances made by the socialist countries, we Italian communists have more than once expressed critical judgements both on certain events and situations (for example, for Czechoslovakia) and on more general problems relative to the relationship between democracy and socialism in various socialist countries.

The Italian Communists, nos 2–3 (April–June 1976), pp. 59–63.

13 Enrico Berlinguer's speech to the PCI Conference of Intellectuals, Rome, January 1, 1977

We are living, I believe, in one of those moments described in the *Communist Manifesto*, when some

countries, and in any case ours, must either embark on 'a revolutionary transformation of society' or risk 'the common ruin of the contending classes': that is, the decadence of a civilization, the ruin of a country.

But in the present conditions a revolutionary transformation can be undertaken only if it successfully tackles the new problems raised for the West by the push for liberation of the Third World peoples. And, as we communists see it, this involves two fundamental consequences for the West: first, opening our minds to a full understanding of the legitimate demands of these countries for development and justice and establishing relations of co-operation with them on an equal footing; and, secondly, abandoning the illusion that it is possible to perpetuate a type of development based on an artificial expansion of individual consumption that is a source of waste, parasitism, privilege, dissipation of resources and financial disarray.

This is why a policy of austerity, of rigor and war on waste, has become an unavoidable necessity for everyone and, at the same time, a lever that can be used to advance the battle to transform society in its underlying structures and ideas.

A policy of austerity is not a policy that tends to level everyone towards indigence, nor can it be pursued with the aim of enabling an economic and social system now in crisis to survive. A policy of austerity must instead have as its aim the establishment of justice, efficiency, order and, I would add, a new morality; and it is precisely for this reason that it can and must be adopted by the workers' movement.

Seen in this way, while it does involve giving up certain things and making certain sacrifices, a policy of austerity acquires meaning as renewal and becomes, in effect, a liberating act for broad masses long kept in positions of subjection and pushed to the sidelines of society: it creates new forms of solidarity and, thus rallying growing consensus, becomes a broad democratic movement, at the service of social transformation . . .

But what stands out above all is the narrowness of prospects characterizing the austerity policy urged and carried out to date by the government. This is the point of greatest differentiation between ourselves, on the one hand, and the government leadership and the dominant economic groups, on the other. Basically, their state of mind is one of surrender, which is just the opposite of what is needed if the people are to accept with conviction certain necessary sacrifices. To make the effort necessary, the country must be able to see clearly what lies ahead or at least some basic elements of a new prospect. Instead, the representatives of the old dominant classes and many government officials point at most to the goal of putting Italy's economic development back on the same track as before the crisis — as if *those* roads and ways of development could still represent an ideal of society to be pursued today, and, above all, as if the crisis of these years and today were not the crisis of precisely *that* model of society (a crisis not limited to Italy, but also affecting, in various forms, other European nations).

For us, the reason for this lack of vigor, courage, scope and prospect in the austerity now being conducted is clear. In this lack we can see evidence of a historical process marked by irreversible decline of the leading role of the bourgeoisie and confirmation that this leading role has already begun to pass to the workers' movement, to the united popular forces: naturally, to a working class and popular masses that show the necessary maturity to prove to the entire country that they are a force that can democratically lead society as a whole to salvation and resurgence. And this means that the workers' movement itself must exercise, within its own ranks and in its economic and political organizations, a broader, more responsible self-critical spirit, in order to overcome those negative, misleading, subordinate or extremist attitudes that are still present to a not indifferent degree and that, in the concrete, hinder the positive solution of such crucial problems as the economic, productive and financial overhaul of society and the state . . .

The principal reason why we see the crisis as an opportunity is that goals for transformation and renewal of the sort I have mentioned are not only compatible with an austerity policy, but can and must be an integral part of such a policy, which is indispensable if we are to overcome the crisis, but overcome it by moving ahead, not by returning to the past.

The Italian Communists, no. 1 (January—March 1977), pp. 40–6.

14 Draft theses for the Fifteenth Congress of the PCI, December 1978

The PCI fights for a profound renewal of the country and to save and advance democracy, according to the guidelines of the Republican Constitution, in such a way as to begin the transformation of Italy into a socialist society founded on political democracy; and it works to make its contribution to the advance of the ideals of peace and socialism in Europe and in the world.

These goals become increasingly relevant and impelling in the face of a world situation charged with dramatic risks, but also containing new possibilities for mankind's liberation and progress. The deep crisis gripping Italian society also requires radical democratic transformations in the direction of socialism . . .

In today's situation there is critical rethinking on various aspects in all the progressive and revolutionary forces: advanced democrats, social democrats, socialists, communists, Christians. New possibilities are opening up for constructive dialogue and agreements: for mankind, Europe and Italy.

The common historical task facing us is that of opening new roads to progress and renewal in Western Europe, towards socialist transformations. A coming together of great importance can be achieved between the forces inspired by the ideals of socialism and those forces in the Christian and Catholic world that have begun to seek roads for far-reaching renewal . . .

This is a vision of the transition to socialism and the characteristics of a socialist society that has deep roots in the history of Western Europe, in the century-long struggles for political, cultural and religious freedom that have characterized it and, above all, in the great battles for democracy, freedom and social progress fought and won by its workers' movement . . .

In recent years the Italian communists' thinking has met with similar but autonomous reasoning on the part of other communist parties in Western Europe and in countries such as Japan. Despite the historical differences and diversities in orientation under which they operate, these parties have arrived at the common conviction that the fight for socialism and the building of socialism must take place within the context of a full expansion of democracy and all the freedoms. This is the option of Eurocommunism . . .

To overcome the contradictions inherent in capitalism, a development of the productive forces must be assured by means of a democratic planning of the economy. This goal can and must be pursued through mass political battles. To be successful, planning requires a democratic political power, characterized by the participation of the entire movement of the working people and the consensus of the majority of citizens.

To achieve the ends and values of socialism, total state ownership of the means of production is not necessary. There must be public sectors of the economy and sectors in which private enterprise operates. Democratic political power must set the major goals of development, working out – in collaboration with the various social forces and the various democratic institutions and organizations – a plan that constitutes a clear-cut frame of reference for all public and private economic interests . . .

This conception of the process of transformation of society in the socialist direction implies a diversified organization of the economic system ensuring integration between planning and market, between public and private enterprise, among national, regional and company levels of economic co-ordination, and participation by the workers in deciding and overseeing the policies governing the productive process . . .

A policy of austerity that serves as an instrument for social transformation and civil and cultural progress is today a prerequisite for planned development. This requires a democratic political power endowed with a high capacity for leadership and founded on a basis of consensus broader than a simple majority. Only in this way will it be possible to overcome the obstacles and defeat the resistance of the economic and financial oligarchies and the vast, tangled undergrowth of corporative interests and parasitic strata and groups.

In the pursuit of such a task, the central role of the working class emerges: the working class as the antagonist of capitalism, not only for its objective position in the productive progress, but also for the level of maturity of its political conceptions and ideals and the positions and political power it has won in Italian life. This hegemony cannot be exercised without unity of the broadest strata of urban and rural workers and without a vast system of alliances. These alliances must be based on a convergence of concrete interests and on the need to find solutions to the big problems, historical and modern, facing Italian society. Hence the policy of alliance between the working class and the peasants, the popular masses of the South, the intellectuals and the working middle classes. Of particular relevance and importance today is the alliance between the employed working class in the North and South and the vast youth and women's masses and other strata of the population that the present type of development and the crisis in society tend to push to the sidelines and exclude . . .

Historical experience confirms the validity of the Marxist conception that sees the mode of production – and the class relations and conflicts that develop within it – as underlying juridical and political systems and organizations and ways of thinking; however, the relationship is not one of mechanical dependence, but rather of dialectical reciprocity.

The parties are linked to particular class interests, but they are not a pure, mechanical expression of these interests. In the Italian situation they are the fundamental, although not exclusive, instruments in the organizations of democracy. Even when society has been transformed in its economic bases and the division into antagonistic classes has been eliminated, different interests will continue to exist and various ways of thinking and political, cultural and religious orientations and traditions will retain their importance and value.

Hence the possibility for existence and the function of various parties – and their alternation in government – in the phase of democratic and socialist renewal of society as well, and in the work of building and governing a new society.

The leading role of the working class itself in the process of overcoming capitalism and building a new society can and must be exercised through collaboration and agreements among various parties and currents that aspire to socialism, and within the framework of a democratic system in which all the constitutional parties enjoy full rights, including those that do not want the transformation of society in a socialist direction and oppose such a transformation, naturally within the confines of democratic constitutional rules.

Finally, in socialist society, the freedom and autonomy of the social organizations, and particularly of the trade unions, must be guaranteed.

This pluralistic vision is not a tactical expedient, nor a sudden discovery made today, but the result of a long maturation of ideas and policy. It is the product of that current of culture and experiences that freed the Italian socialist movement from mechanistic and dogmatic distortions and permitted the development of an original Marxist thought – from Labriola to Gramsci and Togliatti – in the analysis of Italian reality and in a fruitful relationship with the highest points of world Marxist thinking. And it is also the product of the democratic struggle waged over the decades by the working class and popular masses, with the essential contribution of the PCI . . .

On this basis the PCI reconfirms its political positions and its principled stands on freedom of culture, the arts and science, which must be fully guaranteed in a truly secular socialist society and state. Only in this way can the cultural forces effectively exercise their role in innovation and criticism.

Particularly significant is the development of our party's political and theoretical positions on religion. The PCI reaffirms for today and tomorrow the principle of respect for religion and all the religious freedoms and the central importance of the preservation of religious peace for the purposes of democratic community life and growth and for the success of a policy for unity among the popular masses . . .

The goals and ideals of solidarity, justice and fraternity, freedom and democracy that will characterize the new society are and must be reflected in the internal life of the PCI and in the moral climate and behavior reigning within it. But we have long abandoned the conception of the Communist Party as a 'foreshadowing' of the socialist state and society.

It must be clear that the party is a *part* of society and the state. It strives to be, in the first place, the direct and organized expression of the working class and all the popular strata, a mass party and a party of struggle, an autonomous force for the transformation of society, capable of fulfilling a conscious role in its government. In such a pluralist vision, the party is destined to remain a part of, not to become, the state . . .

The PCI has long affirmed and sanctioned in its statutes the principle of its own secularity, establishing that party membership is based on acceptance of its political program.

Nevertheless, the Communist Party has a definite point of reference in a tradition of culture, ideas and ideals that, starting from the fundamental Marxist inspiration, has historically developed and must proceed in continual and fruitful contact and dialogue with the most vital currents of Italian and world culture, with the developments of modern thought and science and with the various elaborations and interpretations of Marxism.

We do not conceive the thought of Marx, Engels and Lenin as a doctrinaire system. For this reason we have long felt that the formula 'Marxism–Leninism' fails to express all the wealth of our theoretical patrimony and thinking. For the Italian communists the thought of the founders of scientific socialism, together with that of Lenin and other theoreticians and leaders of the workers' movement, among whom Gramsci and Togliatti with their particular contribu-

tion occupy a prominent position, stands as a source of orientation for analysis and political elaboration, as an instrument for investigation and a basis for orientations to be put to use and critically verified and renewed in contact with reality, experience and other currents of thought. In this sense, the wording of the party statute must also stress the wealth of this patrimony and the need to know and study it more deeply, and this implies revision of the restrictive formula now used in Article 5 . . .

The policy of unity is a strategic option for the PCI. It was not only the decision in an exceptional moment of national life, during the fight to free Italy from fascism, but also the pivot of a long-range prospect for the construction of a new, progressive democracy in Italy and for advance towards socialism with democracy . . .

Essential elements in our unity-oriented policy are relations of unity with the PSI and the search for collaboration and agreement with the popular and progressive forces of Catholic inspiration. This is the line expressed in the formulation of the historical compromise.

The policy of unity today finds new motivation and force in the crisis gripping the country and the dramatic nature of the political situation. Over the past decade, both in the movements, struggles and consciousness of the broad working class and popular masses and in political relations, unity has increasingly come to be seen as an essential condition if we are to tackle the crisis and renew the country . . .

Thus the situation is at a crucial point. The policy of democratic solidarity and unity is facing a decisive test. It is essential to move ahead. We must defeat the resistance of the conservative forces and corporative drives, ensure firm defense of order and the democratic system and give new impetus and scope to a united effort to solve the problems facing the country through renewal and reforms. This requires that unity policy take root more deeply in the minds of the people, becoming will and commitment in struggle. The PCI reaffirms that it will not be possible to break out of the dramatic grip of the crisis nor to tackle organically the necessary task of far-reaching transformation of society and the state, unless the policy of democratic solidarity finds full and consistent application on the government level as well, with the participation of the PCI overcoming all residual discrimination.

The Italian Communists, special issue (1978), pp. 5–20.

FRENCH Communist Party: Socialism with French Colors

1 Maurice Thorez, interview with the London *Times*, 1946

One can imagine other routes for the march to socialism than the one followed by the Russian communists.

. . . The progress of democracy around the world, in spite of rare exceptions that confirm the rule, allows us to envision routes for the march toward socialism other than the one followed by the Russian communists. In any case the route is necessarily different for each country. We have always thought and stated that the people of France, rich with glorious tradition, would by themselves find their way toward more democracy, progress and social justice. However, history shows that there is no progress without struggle. There is no already laid-out route upon which men can advance effortlessly. They must always surmount obstacles. This is the very meaning of life.

Reprinted in *Cahiers du Communisme* (November 1946), p. 1016.

2 Maurice Thorez, 'The economic situation in France,' 1955

The Reinforced Pauperization of the Working Class
A consequence of the development of state monopoly capitalism is the aggravation of the relative and absolute pauperization of the proletariat.

This pauperization is denied by the social democratic 'theorists.' Seeking to justify their policy of class collaboration, the social democratic 'theorists' want to create the belief that an amelioration of the workers' situation can be achieved within the framework of the capitalist regime . . .

Hit by a declining real salary and by the high cost of living, exhausted by the intensification of work and in danger of unemployment, the working class has witnessed an increase in its tax burden. It is on working-class families that the weight of indirect taxes, which are crushing in France, first falls. The proletarians, the employees and the civil servants are paying the direct tax on salaries and wages without resorting to tax fraud . . .

In our country we are facing the aggravation of all the characteristic contradictions of capitalism: contradictions between capital and labor, between city and country, between the oppressed peoples of the colonies and imperialist France.

State monopoly capitalism shows itself incapable of 'renewing' the national economy or 'nursing it back to health.' Far from being a directing force in the economy and impressing upon it a methodical or planned direction, the bourgeois state is impotent in the face of the economic laws of capitalism, which act like untamed forces of nature. The dominance of monopolies seeking maximum profit carries the chaotic nature of the national economy to an extreme degree.

Productive forces – particularly the working class – are wasted and destroyed. To fight against the exploitation of the proletariat, against the despoliation of working masses, is the only way to ensure the future of France, most importantly on the basic level of struggle against pauperization and mortality, for the health and normal life of the people . . .

Cahiers du Communisme (March 1955), pp. 259–79.

3 Maurice Thorez' report to the Fourteenth Congress of the PCF, July 1956 (I)

Economic Situation in France
The signs of obsolescence and decline are particularly visible on the face of French capitalism.

The concentration of production continues. The power of the monopolies grows unceasingly. More than 48 per cent of all wages paid to our working class come from one-half of 1 per cent of the firms.

In such a situation national industrial production inevitably follows two contradictory trends: on the one hand, the tendency — as a result of the predominance of the monopolies — is to stagnate and rot; on the other hand, the tendency is to exploit scientific and technical advances, provoked by the intensification of competition in the market.

It is true that a relative growth of industrial production has occurred in France in the last few years. But this phenomenon has developed on an unhealthy and unstable economic base. It was brought about by the following principal factors:

(1) the militarization of the economy and the arms race, which alone created an appearance of prosperity;
(2) the growth of merchandise exports, due in part to the temporary decline of German, Japanese and Italian competition, and also to the practice of dumping;
(3) the temporary renewal of military conscription after a long and ruinous war, a renewal profitable above all for the monopolies, but carried out for the most part at the expense of the state, that is of the taxpayers.
(4) the brutal aggravation of the exploitation of the working class and decline in the standard of living of the workers.

The growth of the proletariat's misery accompanies the increase in the capitalists' wealth. The factions opposed to pauperization and the organized struggle of the working class against capital's encroachments can only slow down the basic trend; the partial improvements won by force of arms by the proletariat have not reversed this general law of pauperization.

Pauperization is spreading to the countryside as well. Agricultural workers, the rural semi-proletariat, sharecroppers, small farmers and small landowners face ever more difficult living conditions.

Craftsmen and small businessmen are subjected to the effects of an unjust tax policy, of unbridled competition by large firms and of the insufficient buying power of the laboring masses.

Just as we are fighting for the future of our peoples, for our success and greatness, for a socialist France, we call on the working class to resist, step by step, the monopolists' attack . . .

'XIVᵉ Congrès du Parti Communiste Français,' *Cahiers du Communisme* (July–August 1956), pp. 28–31.

4 Maurice Thorez' report to the Fourteenth Congress of the PCF, July 1956 (II)

Some Theoretical Givens

Marxism–Leninism never presented the transition to socialism in different countries as having to be carried out in a uniform way. It invariably recognized the necessity of a revolution by which the working class conquered power, destroyed the apparatus of the capitalist state and established a proletarian state apparatus.

Marxism is opposed to reformism, which preaches the imperceptible evolution of capitalism to socialism, without conquest of political power by the proletariat, but with the help of small reforms.

In order to excuse themselves for having turned their backs on the socialist revolution, the reformists usually say that they prefer the salvation of 'fundamental liberties' and respect for the 'development of the human person.'

From the liberal bourgeois who have always affirmed that parliamentarianism abolishes classes and class struggle, to the socialists of the right who do not wish that any state, even a democratic one, should have a class content, and the so-called 'personalists,' along the way a noisy chorus is coming, especially today, to exact from socialism 'the guarantees against the abuse of power that must be given to men' in order to defend 'the institutions that must be saved at all cost' and to accuse the communists of themselves being 'deprived of their liberty.'

Let us therefore recall some elementary theoretical givens.

The first is that 'pure,' classless democracy does not exist and never has existed. Being a form of the state's power, democracy can be nothing but a mode of organization for the domination of one class, or of one group of classes, over the others.

The socialist revolution invariably retains the content of the dictatorship of the proletariat during the transition period.

The question of the forms, the paths and the means of revolution is not, however, resolved.

The *Communist Manifesto* speaks of the overthrow

of the bourgeois regime by violence. However, Marx and Engels only meant by this formula to express the fundamental tendency, the general line of the proletarian revolution. They always simultaneously affirmed that the methods of revolutionary transformation would vary according to the countries; they admitted, in certain cases, the possibility of the proletariat arriving at its goals by peaceful means.

Lenin, in turn, emphasized the difference in paths of transition in different countries . . .

In our time the structure of the world has been transformed to the advantage of socialism, facilitating the transition to the new regime in the countries where this has not yet been accomplished.

Lenin explained in his time that the struggle to build socialism would for a long time remain harsh and difficult, even after the conquest of power. As a matter of fact the overthrown bourgeoisie would not only keep for some time its superiority in many areas of national life, but it would retain the powerful support of the exterior. Things have changed a lot since then. The French bourgeoisie, which would confront the proletariat in the struggle for power, is no longer able to count on such solid support from the foreign counter-revolution, even though the latter has, in documents like the Atlantic Pact, registered its right to intervene.

'XIVe Congrès du Parti Communiste Français,' *Cahiers du Communisme* (July–August 1956), pp. 40–3.

5 Roger Garaudy, 'About the "Italian road" to socialism,' 1957

The bourgeois press, in France as in Italy, was disappointed by the Eighth Congress of the Italian Communist Party: it hoped to be able to oppose the Italian Communist Party to the French Communist Party, to dissociate the two largest communist parties of the capitalist world, to throw doubt on the final goal of our struggle, and confusion on our methods and means.

It then hoped, and again in vain, that there would arise serious disagreements about the appraisal of the Hungarian events, and that the Soviet Union would be arraigned for trial . . .

The Eighth Congress of the Italian Communist Party is richly instructive for us and leads us to ask ourselves a number of fundamental tactical questions. These questions can be summarized as follows:

(1) A great number of the elements of what our Italian comrades call 'the Italian road to socialism' appear to us rather to constitute elements of a short-term (or 'immediate') program, for example, with regard to the constitution of a Popular Front government. If, in France, we do not give such elements the title of 'French road to socialism,' this is not only a matter of terminology: evidently short-term objectives, even the most elementary and immediate, when they are valid, lie on the road to socialism: a wage demand or a strike, even a trivial one, also lie on this road. But does it not create illusions to present one particular step or another as defining 'the road' towards socialism?

(2) Does not the stress put on the constitution and on structural reforms risk pushing other objectives to the background, in particular bread-and-butter struggles, and even risk blurring perspectives? For instance, on the parliamentary angle, which is certainly not negligible, we can present several inconvenient aspects:

(a) Is it not risky, as a vulgarization of the idea, to assimilate the Italian road purely and simply to the parliamentary road? This is in no way the spirit of the party's leadership, but several speakers at the Congress give this impression.

(b) This insistence on the constitution and structural reforms opens up a prospect of peaceful development, but does it not thus risk creating the illusion that we alone choose our road? Whether the road to socialism will be a peaceful one does not depend on us alone: the existence of monopolies and their allies can force us to make use of other roads and perhaps it will be necessary not to be content with a rapid look at this eventuality, but to examine concretely how the problems can be posed. This puts into question the possibility of a unilateral definition of the road to socialism . . . Up to now there has not been a single historical example of such a peaceful development. Not only did the October Revolution occur otherwise, but the People's Democracies were born after the war, out of the victorious struggle of the Soviet army and the armed popular resistance, and the Chinese republic was born of long years of armed struggle. Without a doubt we will be told that there is a peaceful passage from the democratic revolution to the socialist revolution, but the problems were posed very differently for Lenin in April 1917, or for today's China, since the bourgeois democratic revolution was carried out under the direction of the working class, and for Italy or France where the revolution of 1789 and the first Risorgimento were carried out under the direction of the bourgeoisie.

(c) A certain number of measures proposed by our Italian comrades, notably 'structural reforms' and 'nationalizations,' do not appear to us necessarily to serve either the interests of the working class or those of the middle classes, but (since the monopolies control the state) can rather serve the interests of capital. They can thus, in certain cases, constitute a democratic objective. But does it not create illusions to make this one of the essential elements of a road to socialism? . . .

Cahiers du Communisme (January–February 1957), pp. 33, 54–5.

6   Theses of the Fifteenth Congress of the PCF, June 1959

No. 29

Democracy will be renewed if it shows itself capable of satisfying the fundamental interests of the people and of the nation. To achieve that it will have to recognize the place of the working class in political life and guarantee its due role in the functioning of representative institutions and the government of the country. It will have to struggle to isolate the trusts and the monopolies and to shelter the institutions of the state from their usurpations.

Nationalization may be one aspect of this democratic struggle.

Nationalization in itself is not socialist in character. It does not change the nature of an economy founded on capitalist exploitation; it does not change the relations of production . . .

However, nationalization may be a national restoration in as much as it aims to prevent the seizure of the country's riches by foreign capital (for example, to take back the petroleum reserves in France which were ceded to an American trust). It may be a legitimate democratic claim in as much as it facilitates the struggle of the working class against its capitalist exploiters and the monopolies.

Without sharing reformist illusions about the pre-tended 'socialist' character of nationalization or management councils, the communists participate in all bodies where it is possible for them to defend the interests of the working class and to develop its influence.

The French Communist Party proposes:

The nationalization of *de facto* monopolies, that is, the nuclear industry, the petroleum and natural gas industry, the big steel and chemical enterprises, the large shipping companies, as well as the commercial banks and the insurance companies.

Institutions

Today in France the essential condition of all progress is the elimination of the regime of personal power imposed by the monopolies. The struggle for socialism, the struggle in which the question of the power of the working class and its allies is of prime importance, is therefore directly linked to the action for democracy.

It is in this light that the problems relative to the functioning of democracy, to the roles of representative institutions and of the state, to economic organization, and to the control of the masses of the political and social orientation of government, must be posed.

The main task to be accomplished is the restoration and renovation of democracy in France.

In our country, with its old tradition of democracy, the parliament can play a great role.

Since the present national assembly is unrepresentative and essentially powerless, the French Communist Party strives for the election, with the help of a ballot which truly reflects the views of the country, of a constituent assembly, charged with the drafting of a democratic constitution, founded upon the following principles:

– that supreme power be held, in the republican state, by representatives of the people, elected through universal suffrage, direct and proportional, and who form a single national assembly;

– that government should originate in this assembly and should be responsible to it;

– that proportional representation be applied to all elections; that those elected are responsible to those who elect them, and can be removed by them;

– that the rights and liberties of all men be guaranteed by law;

– that the professional army be abolished.

'XVᵉ Congrès du Parti Communiste Français,' *Cahiers du Communisme* (July–August 1959), pp. 537–9.

7   Maurice Thorez' report to the Fifteenth Congress of the PCF, June 1959 (I)

'XVᵉ Congrès du Parti Communiste Français,' *Cahiers du Communisme* (July–August 1959), pp. 30–3.

The new regime is striving to break the resistance that its reactionary policy has provoked.

The constitution, which in fact abolishes national sovereignty and concentrates all authority in the hands of one man, leaves not one power to the assembly, which an iniquitous electoral law has turned into a caricature of popular representation. This assembly has so stripped itself of power – however it was already reduced – that it has yet to come to a vote.

In every field, authoritarian administration and the cult of the chief are substituted for democratic control. The ministers, themselves simple clerks chosen for the most part outside parliament, follow the dictatorial path. The tendency is to centralize ever more strongly the power of the state and to extend the scope of its authority over individual initiative and over the activities of private associations . . .

The draconian prohibitions against criticism of the courts by the press reveal the true character of the judicial reform. This 'reform' takes great care to break all links between the judges and the people, effectively licensing attacks on liberty and all enterprises of repression.

The creation of 'urban districts,' when needed, by simple administrative decision, and the possibility of transferring to them the prerogatives of the community in any field, constitutes a direct threat to community liberties. These measures aim in particular to paralyze the creative activity of the working-class municipalities.

The repeated seizure of democratic newspapers and the incessant and damaging lawsuits against them prove the intention of the government to reduce the freedom of the press to nothing . . .

We have always said that all today depends upon the will of one man. But such a substitution of the parliaments and of the ministers themselves by one fortunate man, one chief who decides all and who alone formulates policy, is this not the negation of democracy? Is this not in fact the definition of a regime oriented towards fascism?

We have heard the same formulas before; they were current a quarter of a century ago in our neighboring countries. Unhappily, we know only too well where they led the people of Italy and Germany, and also, alas! where they have led our own.

8   Maurice Thorez' report to the Fifteenth Congress of the PCF, June 1959 (II)

The Forms of the Transition to Socialism

The transition to socialism is a general historical necessity. But the forms of this transition may and must vary, because of the national particularities of each people and, as a function of the changing conditions of history, of the changing relations between class forces on the international scale.

From 1946 on we have been indicating that 'the people of France, rich in glorious tradition, would find their way themselves' and that a peaceful transition to socialism was not precluded. Since the end of the Second World War, the general crisis of capitalism has only been aggravated. The base of the socialist revolution has spread over the surface of the globe. The influence and the prestige of socialism are more noticeable than ever. The probability of its establishment has grown for the countries which still suffer the yoke of capitalism. Thus, it is becoming possible for the revolution to adopt peaceful ways.

Revolutionary violence is not a goal in itself for the communists. In fact, the working class is interested in the accomplishment of the socialist revolution by peaceful ways which permit us to avoid the trouble and the disorganization of the productive forces. The use of violence is never the result of workers' preference: the form of struggle of which they make use depends upon the degree of the exploiters' resistance to the will of the people.

In the countries that have a strong parliamentary tradition, such as ours, it is possible to use a democratic assembly of those chosen by the people, for the accomplishment of the socialist revolution's tasks . . . This would naturally be a parliament elected by direct suffrage, and proportionally, under the new rules fixed by a constituent assembly, convoked by the mass movement.

The parliamentary path presents itself as a particular case among the peaceful paths toward socialism. On the condition of associating the parliamentary struggle with a powerful popular movement directed by the working class and its party, the possibility, in our time, of converting the parliament from an instrument of bourgeois domination to a tool for the socialist transformation of the country is not precluded.

This eventuality assumes, let us repeat, a well-deployed struggle of the working class, the peasant masses and the urban middle classes against huge monopolist capital, against reaction. It assumes a broad union of the popular forces.

As the common declaration by the representatives of the Communist and Workers' Parties meeting for the fortieth anniversary of the October Revolution, has emphasized, the peaceful transition of power to the hands of the working class necessarily remains a revolutionary upheaval. One does not imperceptibly evolve from capitalism, as the reformists and revisionists would have us believe. The transition always represents a revolutionary leap.

This leap is in every case the result of an acute class struggle. Revolution necessarily entails the destruction of the old state machine – military and police apparatus, upper administration, and so on – and its replacement with another apparatus, one formed with the popular forces and capable of serving the dictatorship of the proletariat invoking a veritable democracy for all workers and establishing social ownership of the principal means of production.

'XV⋅ Congrès du Parti Communiste Français,' *Cahiers du Communisme* (July–August 1959), pp. 60–1.

common masses, holding them apart from political life, preventing them from exerting their pressure on the course of public affairs.

Certain people feign astonishment at our defense of the right of parties to exist.

But in contemporary society, the parties express the interests and aspirations of the different working and social classes.

And we do not lose sight of the fact that, if the capitalist monopolies continue the campaigns to discredit the parties, it is above all with a view to destroying the party of the working class, which is their principal enemy, and also the other parties which articulate, more or less plainly, the demands and aspirations of the social classes affected by the monopolies.

Even while combating the politics of the parties which are in the service of the capitalist class, we communists defend the right of parties to exist because, on the one hand, we believe that, along with the working class, all the social classes which are not monopolistic should be able to express themselves; and, on the other hand, because we have enough confidence in the judgement of the masses to accept competition between our party and the other democratic parties.

'XVI⋅ Congrès du Parti Communiste Français,' *Cahiers du Communisme* (June 1961), pp. 67–8.

9 Waldeck Rochet's report to the Sixteenth Congress of the PCF, May 1961

The Role of Parties and of Elected Assemblies
To attain their ends, the propagandists of the presidential regime have conducted for the last several years a systematic campaign, not only against the parliament and the elected assemblies, but also against the parties.

This campaign, like the one aimed against our parliamentary institutions, seeks to discredit the parties and must cause workers and democrats to think, as it incontestably aids reactionary schemings and arms enemies of democracy.

To disband the parties – as was repeatedly suggested by de Gaulle – is one of the methods used by big capital to weaken the democratic spirit in the

10 Political resolution of the Seventeenth Congress of the PFC, May 1964 (I)

True democracy, which is propounded by the communists, cannot be achieved by an act of man, or of a party.

It cannot be achieved through the present authoritarian constitution or by a return to the past practices which permitted the success of the *coup de force* of May 1958.

In order to build a true democracy, and in order to protect it from the forces of reaction and division, experience has shown that one must:
– rid France of personal power, establish a strong and stable republican government, dependent upon the people and upon the judgement of democratic parties and organizations for the formulation of an all-encompassing plan;

– favor the active participation of millions of French men and women in public affairs, by giving them their due representation in the elected assemblies and by giving the workers and their organizations the power of control and administration in the economic and social domains.

This necessitates a democratic constitution and profound reforms in the fields of economy, society and culture.

The French Communist Party believes that with regard to the political structure such a constitution must include:
– a national assembly elected through universal suffrage, having as its primary task the making of laws and the controlling of the government.
– a strong and stable government, responsible to the national assembly, whose role is to govern by applying the plan wanted by the majority of the people.

In order to realize the twofold condition of governmental stability and the blooming of democracy, the French Communist Party proposes the proportional election of a constituent assembly which would adopt the new democratic constitution, clearly defining the respective jurisdictions of the government and of the national assembly.

This democratic constitution must, at the same time, assure the effective guarantee of the fundamental rights of men and of citizens; and notably provide for the application of proportional representation in all elections, the right to vote at 18 years of age, the free activity of democratic syndicates and parties, the extension of local and regional liberties, the democratization of the apparatus of the state, the purging of the police, the suppressing of the professional army, the separation of church and state, of church and school, the democratic control of radio and television, the democratic regulation of the civil service, guaranteeing the rights of agents of the state and those associated with the administration of services . . .

'XVIIᵉ Congrès du Parti Communiste Français,' *Cahiers du Communisme* (June–July 1964), pp. 517–18.

11 Political resolution of the Seventeenth Congress of the PCF, May 1964 (II)

Anxious to put an end to domination by large capitalist enterprises, the French Communist Party proposes a program of nationalization, notably the nationalization of the big steel and iron mining companies, the nuclear industry, the petroleum and gas industry, electronics, aeronautic construction, air transport, the large commercial banks and the insurance companies.

It concurrently supposes the democratization of the nationalized sector, which assumes the participation of the unions in the direction of the administration of the large public establishments and national enterprises.

It demands the institution, at all levels of economic life, of a power of control by the workers, the extension of the functions of the company councils, and the free operation of unions inside companies.

'XVIIᵉ Congrès du Parti Communiste Français,' *Cahiers du Communisme* (June–July 1964), p. 518.

12 Waldeck Rochet's report to the Seventeenth Congress of the PCF, May 1964

Attempting to mask the deeply reactionary character of their policies, the Gaullists and their supporters maintain that modern capitalism brings about an increase in wealth, to the profit of all, and that technological progress leads to the deproletarization of the working class.

But the official statistics belie this unbelievable theory and, on the contrary, confirm that the concentration of capital brings about the proletarization of larger segments of the peasantry and the urban middle class, as well as an increase in the number of salaried workers.

According to the last census issued by the National Statistical Institute, in eight years – from 1954 to 1962 – the active agricultural population went from 5,127,000 to 3,841,000, amounting to a decrease of 1,286,000.

Most of the peasants who had to leave the lands for another profession became proletarians.

And this process of proletarization is linked to capitalist concentration and touches the non-peasant middle class as well. In eight years the number of independent, non-agricultural businesses has decreased a total of 14 per cent, with a 36 per cent decrease in the number of family members employed in such businesses.

At the same time, if those employees whose number has grown by 17 per cent since 1954 cannot be identified purely and simply as proletarian, the fact remains that they are wage-earners subject to capitalist exploitation, and who, further, participate more and more in the working-class struggle.

Finally, engineers involved in production, in research institutes and laboratories, along with those in other sectors of the economy, make up a part of the salaried workers who belong to the middle class.

Without a doubt, the position of this social stratum is complicated by the fact that certain of its members exercise some of the authoritative functions of employers; on the other hand, their circumstances, their mentality, and often their origins, draw them into bourgeois circles.

Nonetheless, more and more engineers and trained personnel take part in and support working-class actions, and are becoming more aware that their interest as wage-earners and their futures as workers give them solidarity with the working class.

Obviously this does not mean that French society is divided exclusively into two classes, the capitalist class and the working class.

In truth, even while the working class is growing, we are experiencing a shrinking of the old middle class as well as expansion of the new middle classes.

But, for society as a whole, this means that the number of workers whose fate and whose future is intertwined with that of the working class is growing and that, far from disappearing, the working class is becoming even stronger, as its weight and its role in society grows . . .

'XVIIᵉ Congrès du Parti Communiste Français,' *Cahiers du Communisme* (June–July 1964), pp. 24–7.

13 Waldeck Rochet's report to the Eighteenth Congress of the PCF, January 1967

The 'one-party' question is no longer an obstacle
For a long time the socialists have maintained that it was impossible for them to envision unity with the communists because in the Soviet Union and in other socialist countries there is only one party.

But we know that our party has delivered the appropriate response to this question by indicating that, for France, we reject the proposition of a single party as an obligatory condition for socialist revolution and we declare ourselves for the plurality of parties . . .

We know that if in the Soviet Union there is only one party, the Communist Party of the Soviet Union, that is a result of the historical conditions under which the first socialist revolution, the October Revolution, was played out . . .

It was during this struggle, when the existence of the socialist revolution was decided, that the Communist Party of the Soviet Union became the sole party of the revolution to enjoy the confidence of the working class and the people . . .

Not only may the existence of a single party not correspond to all situations and not be appropriate for all countries, but in certain cases the fact of imposing such a condition must even retard the advent of socialism by hindering the union of all socialist and progressive forces.

This is the case, for example, in a country like our own where alongside the Communist Party there is a prominent Socialist Party and where the achievement of unity of action between the communists and the socialists is a prime condition, indispensable for the hastening of the achievement of unity of the working class and the assembly of all the democratic and progressive forces around it.

. . . By rejecting the single-party theory as an obligatory condition for the socialist revolution, and by prescribing a lasting co-operation between socialists and communists, our Communist Party contributes to removing an obstacle to the achievement of working-class unity . . .

To acknowledge the possibility of a peaceful transition to socialism within a plurality of parties in no way means that socialism may be realized without class struggle, without mobilization of all the forces of the working class and its allies.

Under the risk of entertaining dangerous illusions among the workers, on the contrary, it is necessary to take as our point of departure the Marxist idea that the upper class will never willingly renounce power.

The transition to socialism, peaceful or non-peaceful, demands, at any rate, the unity of struggle of the working class and the assembly around it and at its side of all the democratic, progressive and national forces; in other words, the conquest of the majority of the people so that the isolated upper class is no longer in a position to resort to civil war.

As the resolution draft submitted to the Congress indicates:

Whatever its form, the transition to socialism implies the conquest of political power by the working class in close alliance with the hard-working peasantry and the urban middle classes.

This means that the peaceful transition to socialism within the plurality of parties does not depend only on the wishes of the Communist Party. It assumes certain conditions concerning the other parties. Notably, the Socialist Party must turn away from the policy of class collaboration with the bourgeoisie in order to practice a policy of actual struggle for democracy and for socialism . . .

With the transition to socialism, the objective is to reinforce, to democratize all those institutions which presuppose the exercise of freedom of thought, freedom of assembly and association, the right to strike and the entirety of the rights of man and of citizens. The rights of the minority must be exercised within the framework of the new democratic legality established by the majority . . .

'XVIIIᵉ Congrès du Parti Communiste Français,' *Cahiers du Communisme* (February–March 1967), pp. 64–6.

14   Waldeck Rochet's speech to the Central Committee of the PCF, 1968

It is not a question of restraining, but of extending the democratic liberties.

The interests that we hold in the defense of immediate demands should not, however, lead us to underestimate political action.

We know that the daily struggle for demands must find its conclusion in the political struggle to prepare for the replacement of the Gaullist power, to establish a true democracy and, beyond that, advance toward socialism.

We must, at the same time, defend the February 24 unity accord against its detractors and continue to develop the great ideas of our party's program for democracy and socialism.

For, if the February 24 accord offers a perspective on the future to workers and democrats, it also has led to anxiety and harassment for the possessors of Gaullist power, for whom the essential preoccupation is the retention of their power by any means.

Pompidou pretended to have discovered a short sentence in the text signifying that the victory of the left would be dictatorship, the end of liberty.

In reality, the sentence in question had no relation to democratic liberties. It only indicated the possible measures to take in the instance that the financial fiefdoms who hold the command levers of the economy sabotage the economic work of the leftist government.

But, like all patent defenders of capitalism, when Mr Pompidou speaks of liberty, he dreams above all of the liberty of big capital to exploit the working class and blackmail the governments which do not please it.

This is why, interpreting the February 24 accord in his way, he was not afraid to liken crudely the defense of capitalist privileges to the defense of democratic liberties, while attempting to give credence to the notion that the latter would be threatened by the February 24 accord.

Democratic liberties are expressly guaranteed in the February 24 accord.

Likewise in the Communist Party program in which this is an essential passage:

True democracy carries within itself respect for the rights of man and of citizens, the free activity of parties and unions, the safeguard of community and local rights, the separation of church and state, the secularism of the schools, the democratic administration of radio and television.

This, as is perfectly clear, is not only not a question of restraining, but it is a question of extending democratic liberties.

L'Humanité, April 20, 1968, p. 5.

15   Georges Marchais, 'False revolutionaries to unmask,' 1968

As always, when the union between the working class and democrats progresses, the leftist groups become agitated in all spheres. They are particularly active among the students. At the University of Nanterre, for example, one finds the 'Maoists,' the 'Young Revolutionary Communists,' which are composed in part of Trotskyites, the 'Liaison Committee of Revolutionary Students,' the majority of whose members are also Trotskyites, the anarchists, and various other more or less folkloric groups.

Their contradictions notwithstanding, these groups – some hundreds of students – are unified in something they call 'the Movement of March 22 of Nanterre,' formed by the German anarchist Cohn-Bendit.

Not satisfied with the agitation that they conduct in the student circles – agitation which goes against the interests of the masses of students and favors fascist provocations – these pseudo-revolutionaries now pretend to give lessons to the working-class movement. More and more one finds them at the doors of factories or in the centers for immigrant laborers distributing tracts and other propaganda material.

These false revolutionaries must be energetically unmasked because, objectively, they served the interests of the Gaullist government and the huge capitalist monopolies.

One of the master thinkers of these leftists is the German philosopher, Herbert Marcuse, who lives in the United States. His theses are known. They can be summarized in the following way: the communist parties 'have failed,' the bourgeoisie has 'integrated the working class, which is no longer revolutionary'; youth, especially in the universities, 'is a new force, full of revolutionary possibilities, and must organize itself for a violent struggle.'

The followers of Marcuse must understand where we live, must take into account the force, the influence of the French Communist Party and of the combativeness of the working class. While maintaining appearances, they direct their attacks against our party – and the CGT – and try to challenge the fundamental role of the working class in the struggle for progress, democracy and socialism.

The theses and activity of these 'revolutionaries' are laughable. One sees that these are, generally, sons of the high bourgeois – repulsive to students of working-class origin – who will quickly set aside the 'revolutionary banner' to take up the direction of Dad's firm and so exploit workers in the best capitalist tradition.

Therefore, we cannot underestimate their harmful work which causes worry, doubt and skepticism among the workers, and in particular among youth. Evidently their activity falls in line with the anti-communist campaign of the Gaullist government and other reactionary forces. Moreover, some newspapers, magazines and weeklies – some claiming to be of the left – lend importance to these groups and through their columns spread their lucu-brations. Most importantly, it must be recognized that leftist adventurism inspires the greatest bias against the revolutionary movement.

By developing anti-communist sentiment, these small groups of the left in fact serve the interests of the bourgeoisie and big capital . . .

L'Humanité, May 3, 1968, pp. 1, 4.

16   Waldeck Rochet's report to the Central Committee of the PCF (Champigny Manifesto), 1968 (I)

The peaceful path is the path of class struggle in all its forms
The document draft submitted to the Central Committee pays much attention to the question of the different forms of transition to socialism.

The Twentieth Congress of the Communist Party of the Soviet Union (CPUSSR), the declaration of eighty-one parties of 1960 and our own congresses have shed light on this problem.

They have emphasized that, as a result of profound historical modifications and radical changes in favor of socialism, we have seen more favorable conditions created for the victory of socialism.

In the document submitted to the Central Committee there are clearly set forth the conditions which permit us to envision as possible in a country like ours the transition to socialism by a peaceful path, which is to say, without civil war, but which does not mean without relentless class struggle.

As our document indicates, the peaceful path to socialism must not be confused with the 'parliamentary path.'

Our Communist Party does not at all underestimate the activity in the elected assemblies or the role which a parliament composed of a majority favorable to democracy and socialism could play.

But it believes that for the transition to socialism it is, above all, by multiple mass actions of the working class and the broad social classes opposed to the domination of the monopolies that the relation of social and political forces can be modified in favor of democracy and socialism.

The peaceful path to socialism is the path of class struggle in all its forms, without civil war. For if revolution by a peaceful path becomes possible, it will not be because the bourgeois ruling class has changed its nature and is disposed to willingly renounce power, but because new conditions may permit the working class to win over the majority of the people, that is, to assemble such superior forces in action that the isolated bourgeoisie will not be in a position to resort to civil war . . .

L'Humanité, December 7, 1968, p. 6.

17   Waldeck Rochet's report to the Central Committee of the PCF, 1968 (II)

It is not a question here of constructing in advance a system, achieved through co-operation and alliance, for the transition to socialism in France, for that will depend on national circumstances and on the positions then occupied by the parties and organization fighting in the class struggle.

At any rate, such co-operation assumes that one essential condition is filled by our prospective allies: the abandonment of class collaboration with the bourgeoisie. We hope that the Socialist Party takes a lesson from so many deceiving experiences and, in accord with the Communist Party, takes the road which really leads to socialism.

They sometimes also say that, for communists in power, the supreme value would be the state, that the socialist state, such as we conceive it, would be totalitarian, that, for us, democracy would only come afterwards and would be long in coming.

The socialist state which we propose to establish bears no likeness to this description.

The document draft which we are submitting to the Central Committee clearly shows the double function of the new political power.

On the one hand, it must guarantee the broadest democracy for all workers and for the entire people by having them participate in the direction and administration of public affairs in all areas and on all levels.

On the other hand, and at the same time, it must assure the defense of the new social regime against the sabotage operations of the former exploiting classes and the enemies of socialism looking to seize power again and restore capitalism.

As to the rights of the minority, they must be and they will be exercised within the framework of the new laws, democratically established by the majority.

It is this double aspect of socialist power – continued development of democracy and defense of socialist conquests – which characterizes what in Marxist terms is called 'the temporary dictatorship of the proletariat.'

Such a state is the opposite of a totalitarian state because it exercised power not only in the name of the great majority of citizens, but with their direct participation and because, essentially, the activities of the socialist state will consist, in addition to the tasks of creation and construction, in the organization of the new economy, of the highest cultural life.

L'Humanité, December 7, 1968, p. 16.

18   Theses of the Nineteenth Congress of the PCF, February 1970

II Big Capital's Policy in France
(5) In France, as at the international level, the crisis of state monopoly capitalism is worsening.

As our party demonstrated in 1958, an authoritarian, personal regime was installed to strengthen the monopolies' domination of the nation's life.

This policy was carried out by engaging all of the state's resources in an effort to accelerate the accumulation of capital and to strengthen monopolist groups by overexploiting the working class and by means of a generalized attack against the workers' buying power, against social security, and against the quality of both life and employment as well as by the plunder of the urban and rural middle classes. Accordingly, the 1959 Gaullist decisions, Giscard d'Estaing's 1963 stabilization program, his 1967 moves, and the current Gaullist-centrist government's 'recovery' plan all bear witness to the continuation of this detrimental policy sponsored by big capital.

The monopolist concentration, based solely on the search for maximum profit and systematically encouraged by the regimes – notably by means of taxation subsidies and policies of public control and credit, as well as by the use of the public and nationalized sectors for the profit of big capital – continues to intensify. A dozen monopolist groups currently dominate the nation's major sectors and manage them according to their own individual interests. Small and middle-sized industrial enterprises are more and more dependent on these large financial groups. It is the same in the commercial and agricultural sectors, and among the artisans.

The growing militarization of the economy has brought considerable profit to the monopolies. State military investments surpass civil expenditures. The establishment of the nuclear strike force has derailed and slowed the rise of those sectors crucial for the nation's future. At the same time, non-military scientific research, especially basic research, is in danger of asphyxiation – which would at least do great harm to economic progress, if not to national independence.

The use of the defensive forces is regulated solely by the law of monopolist profit, scorning the needs for national and social development. It brings about marked regional disequilibria, backwardness and neglect in certain sectors, double shifts and over-manning in others, a growing deficit in external trade, and in all cases a waste of the wealth generated by the laborers.

Speculation against the franc, leading to the flight of a considerable amount of capital from France, has revealed the parasitic nature of monopolist capital, which freezes enormous amounts of resources and deprives the nation of opportunities for useful investments.

This policy has severe consequences for the national economy . . .

(10) The spread of state monopoly capitalism has broadened and deepened the antagonism between the monopolist bourgeoisie and the entire laboring stratum. The basis of this antagonism is the marked contradiction between the demands of modern large-scale production, spread more and more throughout society, and the maintenance of social relations based on capitalist appropriation.

In this setting, the basic conflict in society is and will continue to be the discrepancy between capital and labor, between the monopolist bourgeoisie and the working class.

At the same time, new contradictions arise. By setting as its goal the reinforcement of the privileges of the monopolist group, the attempts at monopoly planning lead to the aggravation of economic disequilibria and social antagonisms. Monopolist capital is confronted with the demands of the scientific and technical revolution. This crucially important change is characterized by the growing involvement of science in the production process, up against the basic anarchy of capitalist production and the monopolies' desire to make the highest possible level of profits in the short run.

Within the framework of monopolist relations, the trend towards the internationalization of production also gives rise to new contradictions. The growing interdependence of the economies of the six Common Market nations (and especially of France and the German Federal Republic) subjects them more to the effects of the intensifying competition among the most powerful capitalist groups. Far from promoting harmony among its members and creating a barrier against American imperialism, the economic 'integration' of the Little Europe of the monopolies is accompanied by a massive penetration of American capital in decisive sectors of the economy, while it promotes the predominance of West Germany in the industrial and financial areas . . .

Under the guise of 'recovery' and 'balancing the budget,' the regime has undertaken to accelerate the monopolist concentration on the national and 'multi-national' level, brutally cutting social welfare programs, subsidized housing and public health, teaching and research, and in this way gravely compromising the national future.

By promoting the investment of foreign capital, especially American and West German capital, and the establishment of sophisticated monopolist groups which seize control of production, distribution and credit, it is endangering the material technical and economic bases of national independence . . .

'XIXᵉ Congrès du Parti Communiste Français,' *Cahiers du Communisme* (February–March 1970), pp. 420–5.

19   Georges Marchais' report to the Nineteenth Congress of the PCF, February 1970

Nationalization
The nationalization of the principal branches of industry, banking and credit is the first key to our program.

The upper class affirms that in our time, when immense means are necessary to satisfy the requirements of modern production, as much from the technical viewpoint as from the viewpoint of profitability, the establishment of large units of production is indispensable. What they hesitate to add is that concentration of the monopolist type has as its sole law the law of profit, and that this fact in itself inevitably brings about profoundly negative consequences for workers and for the nation.

What is inadmissible is not the concentration of productive forces as such, but rather their concentration in the hands of a few private owners who dictate the entire economic life of the country. It is all the more inadmissible that, at present, the activity of the great monopoly enterprises depends heavily upon the utilization of public monies.

To allocate the property of these large industrial and financial enterprises to the entire nation is to permit it to co-ordinate the powerful financial and technological means necessary for the growth of the economy, to undertake necessary investment and research, and to orient production in a coherent manner adequate to national and social needs. This is why nationalization is the democratic and modern form of concentration. Proof is provided by the incontestable technical superiority of the few branches already nationalized, the French National Railroads and Renault, for example.

Nationalization is also the necessary condition for the actual planning of economic and social development. Rendered necessary by the interdependence of the different aspects of modern life, this planning will have as an object the growing satisfaction of the individual and collective needs of the population.

In short, nationalization would assure the material bases of the nation's independence and would protect our economy from the dominance of foreign capital, all while promoting the development of our international co-operation with all countries with respect to our national interest . . .

'XIXᵉ Congrès du Parti Communiste Français,' *Cahiers du Communisme* (February–March 1970), pp. 62–3.

20 Lucien Mathey, 'National road to revolution,' 1971

The conditions of the struggle for socialism in the France of 1971 are very different from those which marked the era of the Commune. The productive forces have undergone a prodigious development. The capitalism of free competition has been transformed into the capitalism of monopolies, it has attained its 'supreme stage': imperialism; today, state monopoly capitalism unites big financial capital and state power in one single mechanism. The acceleration of capitalist concentration has reduced and is unceasingly reducing the number of powerful companies that dominate the economy. By this it leads to the assembly of the working class in giant enterprises, favors its organization, elevates its level of consciousness and increases its abilities to struggle.

The transition to socialism will always be a revolutionary transformation, effected by the conquest of political power by the working class and its allies, and a radical change in the system of ownership of the means of production and exchange.

But the paths to this revolutionary change will be necessarily different from one country to another, adapted to the conditions of the struggle for socialism in each country, and also in relation to the evolution of the class struggle on the international scale.

In the France of today the working class can achieve a solid and lasting alliance with the intellectual workers, the working peasantry and the urban middle classes. This is to say that it can create a relationship of forces depriving the dominant bourgeoisie of the possibility of violently opposing the progress of democracy and the march to socialism; it can open the path for a peaceful transition from capitalism to socialism.

But we at no point confuse this possibility with the abandonment of class struggle. Without underestimating the role of the elected assemblies and the parliamentary struggle, we nevertheless consider the mass actions of the working class and the other social classes opposed to the domination of the monopolies to be decisive.

'The peaceful path to socialism is the path of class struggle in all its forms, without civil war.'

The thesis that we support on the forms of the march to socialism orients our action toward the creation of the conditions which would permit the peaceful transition to socialism. This is why we put every effort into winning over the majority of the people to this idea.

Cahiers du Communisme (March 1971), cf. pp. 82–91.

21 Georges Marchais' interview with *La Croix*, November 1971

Socialist democracy, for us, is the intense participation of the greatest masses of our people in the direction and the administration of the country, at all levels and in all areas.

The rights of the minority will be fully respected in so far as they are exercised within the framework of the law.

Concerning religious freedoms, we will not give way to philosophical divisions over the common interests of the whole of the working population. This would be to turn our back on our principles, to weaken the popular movement's adherence to the building of socialism. On the philosophical plane, we are resolutely in favor of respecting the convictions of each and in support of the freedom of confrontation between world views and cultural currents without the state or the administration being obliged to interfere, unlike the way they do today when they temper the secularism of the schools.

In a socialist France the state, naturally, will have to be secular. The separation of church and state must be scrupulously respected.

The freedom of belief, the freedom of sect, the freedom of religious training and of public expression of these will be guaranteed in law and in practice. Whatever the case, socialist law will guarantee religious freedoms against all persecution, against all administrative repression.

We are the party of the working class, that is to say, of a class which does not aspire to exploit anyone else, of a class which can liberate itself by liberating all of society. This is the theoretical foundation of our support of democratic liberties.

But the first and the best of the guarantees which we give in this matter are the efforts we are making from now on to realize the co-operation of all forces interested in social change and to assure a real participation in public affairs by the popular masses.

The guarantee is the fact that all of our policy rests on the following idea: socialism in France will be the result of a democratic movement by the immense majority of the people.

. . . all the forces engaged in this fight, including innumerable Christians, will be the beneficiaries of these guarantees. The result of this fight will also be up to them, since we do not intend to do things *for* them, but *with* them.

As for religious liberties, their respect is dictated to us by the same principles of our theory. For us, the real borderline does not run between believers and atheists, but between exploiters and the exploited. All persecution, harassment or anti-religious sectarianism is, for us, scientifically absurd.

Today, Christians and communists can act together to transform society, to establish a real, entirely new democracy, and to install and edify socialism. It is possible, it is what we want, it is why we act.

La Croix (November 1971), pp. 127–33.

22   Georges Marchais' report to the Twentieth Congress of the PCF, December 13–17, 1972

(1) The leftist government will substantially increase salaries and treatments, particularly those which are the lowest.

(2) The length of the working week will be brought back to 40 hours in 5 days without a drop in salary.

(3) With regard to social security, the leftist government will support free medical care. National education will be thoroughly democratized and the state will assure free studies, books and furniture.

(4) In the country, a policy favorable to the growth of agriculture will guarantee the increase of the great majority of the peasantry, and the improvement of social protection and rural machinery. The policy will catalyze the modernization of the conditions of production, notably by encouraging and helping co-operation . . .

(1) The individual and collective liberties to which our people are profoundly attached will be guaranteed and some will be restored in full.

(2) Political parties and groups, including opposing parties, will be able to freely pursue their activities.

(3) Our country's institutions will be democratized.

(4) The common program will form the content of a real legislative contract binding the left-wing majority and its electors on the one hand, and the government and the left-wing majority on the other . . .

France does not lack resources. What is happening today is that they are hoarded, monopolized, diverted, blocked, wasted by some financial and industrial feudalities. The realization of the common program will put an end to this tremendous waste.

(1) The decisive financial and economical levers will be at the disposal of the nation. The leftist government will proceed, on the one hand, with the nationalization of the business bank, of the large financial holdings, of the savings banks, of the large

private insurance companies, and, on the other hand, with the nationalization of the monopolies holding key positions in industry.

(2) A national plan, democratically drawn up, will ensure the growth of the national economy and will make the satisfaction of the people its goal.

(3) The fiscal belongings and other fiscal privileges which the big capitalists have will be abolished. The taxes on real corporate profits will be augmented and a new tax will hit the large fortunes.

(4) As measures of social and democratic progress, the nationalizations will result in the increased output of the machinery of production, in the progressive elimination of the wastes and imbalances of capitalist management, and will increase the rate of growth of the national economy.

As economic efficiency, superior to the capitalism of monopolies, will thus create immense supplementary resources whose greatest part will go to the satisfaction of individual and collective needs.

'XXᵉ Congrès du Parti Communiste Français,' *Cahiers du Communisme* (January–February 1973), pp. 52–7.

23 Political resolution of the Twentieth Congress of the PCF, December 13–17, 1972

A permanent crisis now pervades all aspects of national life. It is a crisis of capitalist society, the depth of which springs from the system itself. A new world, brought about by the success of socialism, by the growth of the workers' movement, through the reinforcement of democratic and national battles, and through the beginnings of the scientific and technical revolution, knocks at the door of the old world . . .

The root cause of the crisis lies in the capitalist demands for development, capital accumulation and profits. All public resources at the government's disposal are put at the service of private monopolies to ensure their profits. Capital accumulated over the years in the hands of several giant monopolist groups has been solely destined for the investments necessary for production. The pursuit of profit has provoked, simultaneously:

– the excessive exploitation of labor in production and in other activity;

– the trend towards more widespread and more diversified unemployment;

– the limitation of expenditures for the collective welfare;

– the acceleration of inflation;

– speculation of all sorts, notably on currency. This pursuit of profit is at the root of the depletion of national, natural, material and human resources.

Under-utilization lies alongside over-use of our material capacities. Research is sacrificed; technical progress is slowed. Instead of freeing the laborers, it is a pretext to exploit them and to deepen their alienation.

Speculation, the growing militarization of the economy and the consequent creation of the strike force and the budget for repression have absorbed, either directly or indirectly, tens of millions.

Inflation damages the buying power of the laborers, retired workers and pensioners. It saps the currency and threatens to bring ever more grave consequences for our nation . . .

National production is becoming more unstable. Vital sectors of the economy are disorganized. National and public enterprises are diverted from their primary tasks and deliberately put at the service of the monopolies.

Regional disequilibria are becoming more pronounced while some regions waste away.

The maneuvers of speculative capital prove that the national interest gives way to the interests of their urban and multinational corporations.

National independence is jeopardized. Big capital seeks to put 'supranational' institutions in place, in order to integrate the nation in Little Europe and in the Atlantic policy, exacerbating the exploitation of workers, and maintaining its political and ideological domination.

Big capital is wasting the nation's greatest resource: its people.

The stagnation of wages, the soaring of prices, unemployment, tax increases, job insecurity, downward mobility, the decline of buying power and of social benefits weigh more and more heavily upon the workers.

Working conditions, shifts and hours, work accidents, and physical and nervous fatigue, on the one hand, lack of collective benefits, pollution and the destruction of the environment, and noise, on the other hand, undermine health and impoverish life. Shortages of public housing at moderate rents, the vast problems of urban life, transportation, of rest and leisure continue to become worse.

... Unemployment touches women and young people in particular. The situation of unskilled workers, the most exploited category of workers, in which most of the immigrant workers can be found, is intolerable. The number of especially disadvantaged persons – those with all sorts of hardships – is growing, and their condition is deplorable ...

'XXe Congrès du Parti Communiste Français,' *Cahiers du Communisme* (January–February 1973), pp. 415–16.

24   Georges Marchais, 'Liberty is indivisible,' 1973

Someone said to me one day: 'You communists, you're more for bread than for liberty.' Without knowing it, a *L'Humanité-Dimanche* reader responded to this by writing in the newspaper: 'What good is my liberty, me, who sees twelve francs a day old-age pension?' There is no liberty for those who have no bread.

Liberty is the liberty to work and to choose one's work, it is the liberty to learn and to improve oneself, the liberty to shelter oneself, to pass leisure time, and to enjoy a happy old age, the liberty to raise decently the number of children that one wishes, the liberty of opinion, of expression, of meeting and of association, the liberty to participate in the administration of one's business and the direction of the affairs of one's village, of one's city, of the country ... liberty is all of this and for everyone. It comes through a social organization which liberates man from material worries and anxieties of the next day, gives satisfaction to his material and cultural needs, assures him of the appropriate conditions for multilateral development, permitting his personality to blossom. It implies the disappearance of the exploitation of man by man which is the foundation of the capitalist system, and which is translated today by the domination of the larger part of the population by a tiny privileged minority. It calls for socialism.

In our eyes, socialism and liberty are inseparable, socialism being one degree higher than liberty. Thus, we intend to march toward a new society without sacrificing or altering any rights, any personal or collective liberties which the French people have acquired over the course of the centuries. Much to the contrary, we intend continually to widen and develop democracy, for it is the first condition for the victorious building of socialism in our country. We do not fear competition in this field. This is exactly why the communists' action, their presence in the union of the left, their force, constitutes the best guarantee for the future of liberty in our country. They have shown it from the moment of the elaboration of the common program of leftist government by including in it the necessary guarantees for the respect and extension of liberties, of the installation of a true democracy. This democracy we intend to enrich unceasingly, to lead 'all the way,' that is, to socialism.

A little while ago I said, 'Democracy demands respecting the popular verdict by all, and in all circumstances.' This clearly answers the question of 'succession.'

When someone asks us this question, he has this in mind: if tomorrow we declare ourselves to be for the policy of the left and consequently the experience deceives us, can we go back to a rightist policy?

If we start out on the road to socialism and suddenly we miss the beautiful days of capitalist exploitation, can we go back to the regime of Mr Marcellin and Mr Chirac? In short, if the majority of the people withdraws its confidence after having given it to you, will you give up power? I respond: we will in every case respect the verdict expressed by direct, secret and proportional, universal suffrage, whether it is favorable or unfavorable. How, for example, could we envision undertaking or pursuing the construction of a socialist society in France without the support of the majority of the French people?

In *Le Défi Démocratique* (Paris: Grasset, 1973), cf. pp. 96–118.

25   Georges Marchais, 'The debate on *autogestion*,' 1973

Some to the left are convinced that we would create a 'centralizing and bureaucratic' form of socialism. We would be, in their eyes, proponents of a centralized and authoritarian state and economy of which the workers would be no real part; they would only change masters, the bosses ceding their places to the bureaucrats. Having thus caricatured the economic and social organization that we support, our censors present themselves naturally and with little cost as the champions of the participation of the workers in the decision-making process at all levels, the pioneers of self-management.

Systematic centralization and invading bureaucratization have developed considerably with the monopolistic capitalism of state. They are the negation of progressive democracy. As the great industrial and financial capital is concentrated, its state power is more and more centralized and its authoritarianism is accentuated. The 'center' is that unique mechanism which binds monopolies to the state and which grips the country. And since its politics are deeply contrary to the interests of the large masses of the population, this center recedes more and more from its citizens, hides itself from their gazes, their control, their intervention. It becomes more and more distant, foreign, inaccessible. The elected representatives of the people see themselves supplanted by the hierarchies of power. These are the bureaucrats and technocrats against whom the wishes, the interests and the aspirations of our simple people collide . . .

Really, this is not our ideal. The ultimate goal of the communists is a society whose members will govern themselves, for they will be in the position to regulate the whole of their relations and social problems without dealing with the constraints of a government.

In *Le Défi Démocratique* (Paris: Grasset, 1973), pp. 99–102.

26 Georges Marchais, 'Socialist diversity,' 1973

If the principles of socialism have a universal value, the conditions under which they are applied considerably influence the forms in which they are realized.

The communists of the whole world have a common ideal, great common objectives, common fundamental principles. They none the less are not ignorant of the diversity of situations among countries. The traditions, starting points, concrete problems to resolve are not the same in every country; the solutions can therefore not be the same.

This is why, within the socialist world, there exists a certain diversity among its constituent countries, and only a superficial or tendentious mind could present this socialist world as a monolithic, uniform, standardized bloc. Perhaps we ourselves bear part of the responsibility for the fact that such a schematic and false image is widely accepted. Perhaps we have not always sufficiently brought out the diversity of socialist countries. It is correct and necessary to emphasize what they have in common, in order to consider the essence of socialism . . .

Socialism does not depend on decal-transfers. It possesses different features in the USSR and in Cuba, in the German Democratic Republic and in Korea, in Rumania and in Vietnam. It could not be otherwise; socialism in effect does not appear, ready and made to measure, from the thigh of who knows what revolutionary Jupiter. It is the work of men in definite conditions. How could it ignore differing traditions, climates, natural resources, modes of life, national temperaments?

For example, there is only one party in Hungary, the Hungarian Socialist Party. But in the German Democratic Republic there are five different parties and the chairman of the people's chamber is a Christian-Democratic deputy.

For example, agriculture in the Soviet Union is totally collectivized. But in Poland, the collective sector includes only a small part of agriculture.

For example, while the Czech regions and Slovakia each have their own institutions, Czechoslovakia constitutes a single republic. But Yugoslavia is a federation of several national republics.

What will the future be? One could think that since the socialist countries are aiming for equivalent levels of development, the result will be a general uniformization of their characteristics. This is to imagine that there is a mechanical link between mode of production and level of economic development, on the one hand, and institutions and way of life, on the other. But it is not like this at all. The mode of production does determine certain general features of a society, a given level of economic development involves certain very general consequences – but no more. There exists *one* capitalist system, but what differences between situations, institutions, life-styles exist in the various capitalist countries! In truth, the diversity of the socialist societies can only increase. Just as socialism is born in effect from the real movement of the social life of each nation, each people is and will be led to generate original solutions to the problems, however similar, which the very growth of socialism ceaselessly poses, solutions which without a doubt will go beyond our present-day imagination and will enrich our common theoretical patrimony.

This diversity will be even more accentuated as new countries pass to socialism, at different stages of development, with different traditions.

A Socialism with the Colors of France

It is with this common-sense observation as our starting point that we say: *the socialism we wish for ourselves will have the colors of France*. Now it is twenty-seven years since Maurice Thorez declared to *The Times*, 'We have always thought and said that the people of France, rich with a glorious tradition, will itself find its road toward greater democracy, progress, and social justice.' The socialist France, which the French will build when the majority of our people has decided to, will take its place in our history. It will not go hither or yon to look for a model of socialism, for there exists no such model. It will not be a copy of any other experiments, for history does not repeat and each nation has its original personality. It will be the crowning of the efforts, obscure or illustrious, of all those who have toiled, thought, struggled through the centuries for the good of our country.

Of course, in France as in every other socialist society, the principal means of production and exchange will be collective property and political power will be exercised by the workers and by the whole people. But, given that, it appears here and now that socialism in France will present many features of its own.

For example, to take the road of decisive economic and political transformations does not necessarily require passage through the seizure of the Winter Palace. The France of today is not the Russia of 1917. And thanks, among other things, to the successes already achieved by the Soviet people and by the peoples of the other socialist countries, and thanks also to the unity of left forces if it is preserved, we can today envisage a *peaceful* passage to socialism so seriously that our whole policy is henceforth founded on this perspective.

For example, the traditions of our country lead us to rule out the idea that socialism in France could take the form of a one-party regime. Not only will there be, in a socialist France, several democratic parties, governing together, but there could also be opposition parties, freely using all the means of legal activity.

For example, in no way do we imagine the expropriation, the collectivization of the hundreds of thousands of family farms which are the wealth of French agriculture. And if it would be advisable to favor the development of co-operation, this is perfectly compatible in a very large sector with the maintenance of personal property and responsibility.

For example, in a socialist France it would be absurd to nationalize the small shopkeepers and those artisans who render the greatest service to the consumer and who are today dramatically threatened by the competition of large-scale capitalist commerce.

In *Le Défi Démocratique* (Paris: Grasset, 1973), cf. pp. 177–83.

27   Georges Marchais' report to the Central Committee, 1974

II   The Economic Objectives
As the document published on the first of January by our economic section indicates, the monopoly capitalists concentrate their efforts essentially in four areas:

(1) to slow down wage increases and possibly freeze salaries; to reduce the laborers' incomes and their families' consumption;
(2) to reduce the people's buying power by raising prices, so that they bear the brunt of the primary economic difficulties;
(3) under the pretext of adapting themselves, to bring about a new transformation of the structures of industry, which will result in the closing of certain firms considered not to be profitable enough;
(4) rapidly to obtain high speculative profits

It is precisely in order to permit the monopolies to attain their objectives that the government is submitting to the enormous and scandalous 'scarcity' blackmail. It dares to demand new, so-called inevitable sacrifices of the laborers and of women, agricultural workers and the retired.

But such a policy of austerity, of high cost of living, of restrictions, of overproduction, can only aggravate, as the very same policy did fifteen years ago! It can only further impoverish France, further aggravate unemployment, further increase the risks of a slow-down of production . . .

In truth, far from being outdated, the common program goes to the heart of the current problem. It is more valuable than ever.

Numerous examples serve to confirm this.

The problem is to relaunch economic activity, making production more responsive to needs, while saving raw materials and industrial products.

Thanks to nationalizations and democratic planning, it will be possible to put an end to the parasitic and excessive production currently undertaken for profit, to double shifts and to the wastefulness which currently leads, for example, to diverting enormous sums to speculation. Putting an end to the production of the strike force, reconversion of the military nuclear industry, and energy economies will require the co-operation of national enterprises releasing vast amounts of energy reserves for other uses.

In this way it would be possible to develop, throughout the whole national territory, production useful to the nation, in an effective and co-ordinated manner; it would be possible, for example, to exploit fully our coal reserves, develop the different forms of energy production, foster collective benefits, organize mass transit adapted to current needs and build socially financed housing. Civil research will uncover new ways of doing these.

The administration of the state budget could become more rigorous and more favorable for the working population, due to the resources extracted through tax reform which will hit the big corporations hard; to the abolishment of subsidies and exorbitant gifts of all kinds which they receive; to the resolute struggle against speculation; to the reduction of military expenses.

The completion of these initial social measures will increase domestic compensation by providing a stable and healthy base for economic development. And this does not at all contradict the preservation of a favorable balance of payments. For, as I said, certain imports can be limited if national production is developed, along with new outlets for exports such as the socialist and developing nations.

In addition to the rise of democracy, the laborers' acquisition of new powers and responsibilities within the firm and at all levels of national life will constitute a powerful factor of development and renewal for the nation.

L'Humanité, January 22, 1974, pp. 5–6.

28 Georges Marchais' report to the Twenty-First Congress of the PCF, October 1974 (I)

Change is only possible by implementing profound democratic reforms which attack the domination of big capital. This is why the Common Program of the left incorporates reforms: that is its fundamental trait.

As an anti-monopolistic program, a program for the democratization of economic, social and political life, it is limited in the sense that it is not a program concerned with the institutions of socialism. When we state that it is in no way for us a question of 'reassuring,' we are simply anxious not to generate confusion: to equate the common program with socialism would be to diminish, to water down, the idea of socialism and its revolutionary content.

But, because the democratization initiated by the common program will go beyond what our country has ever known, we have labeled this political change as 'advanced democracy.'

By restraining the domination of big capital, the nationalizations that we propose will permit the promotion of an innovative economic policy to serve the workers and the national interest. It is an indispensable base for the coherent implementation of the aggregate of democratic reforms prescribed by the common program.

It is in this way that nationalization will permit planning which is both modern and democratic, making possible the development of key sectors of national activity, creating more stable and more favorable operating conditions for small urban and rural producers as well as for commerce.

This economic policy will give a new dynamism to the country's economy. It will create the conditions needed to bring about real and lasting solutions to the problems which assail France . . .

Nationalization will also contribute to the moralization of economic life.

Nationalization must be accompanied by real measures of democratization. In the nationalized and public sector enterprises, administration will be decentralized, autonomous and founded on the actual participation of personnel in all decisions concerning the life and development of the enterprise. Beyond that, in all sectors union rights and the prerogatives of the company councils will have to be broadened . . .

'XXIe Congrès extraordinaire du PCF,' *Cahiers du Communisme* (November 1974), pp. 34–6.

29 Georges Marchais' report to the Twenty-First Congress of the PCF, October 1974 (II)

Economic Situation

The policy of big capital's power is plunging the nation into crisis.

The growth of class struggle and popular movements – or to speak in more electoral terms, the 'push to the left' – springs, in part, from the economic and social situation in France.

It is now clear that our country is in crisis.

But although the representatives of the regime and of big business are today forced to admit this, they still try to hide its real causes, its true nature . . .

In 1969–70, drawing notably on the lessons of the great movement of May–June 1968 and sharpening its analyses of present-day capitalism, our party confirmed that we see the present crisis, not as a mere transition crisis, but as a profound crisis.

In an article which appeared in *L'Humanité* in June 1971 we asserted that the general definition which Lenin gave when writing on what he saw as 'a period in which symptoms that the situation cannot continue as before appear . . . in which a system's problems reach the point where they must find a new response,' could be applied to the period of crisis into which French society is entering . . .

The crisis is not only economic. It is political, moral and ideological. It is also cultural. The bankruptcy, the authoritarianism, the incredible destruction of talent, of energies, of devotion, as well as the proliferation of commercial production dictated only by the seeking of profit are bringing indignity to France and to the glory of her culture. In brief, the crisis is all-pervasive.

Mr Giscard d'Estaing's policy . . . His basic goal . . . is that a handful of large corporate capitalists will retain their places in the bitter struggle of world capitalism to which the potentates of industry and finance are giving way. His means are the increased exploitation of the laborers, the decelerated concentration of the economy, the marked drainage of national resources to benefit the large corporations, the rendering of all the state's means to the big capitalists, notably in an effort to promote exports, and the trend toward a more forceful collaboration with the other capitalist powers. As a consequence of this policy entire sectors of our economy are neglected and the domination of foreign capital is strengthened.

Far from remedying the crisis, it has only seemed to aggravate it . . .

'XXIᵉ Congrès du Parti Communiste Français,' *Cahiers du Communisme* (November 1974), pp. 14–23.

30 Article, 'What the communists want for France,' *L'Humanité*, 1975

The harsh living and working conditions which the people have always known have been dramatically aggravated by the crisis which now confronts our nation.

The present crisis, contrary to what the big capitalists and their political representatives claim, is not a simple, passing crisis. This is a serious, lasting, global crisis, which affects all aspects of national life – economic and monetary, social, cultural, political and moral.

The crisis originated in the big capitalist bourgeoisie's hoarding of our nation's resources and the labor of its people. For this purpose, the people endured an even more intense concentration of the national economy at the hands of industrial and financial groups which dominated and directed all aspects of economic life. For this purpose, they used all the state's political and financial means. They further exploited the laborers, extended their exploitation to other social classes as well, deliberately co-ordinating price increases and unemployment, and imposing austerity on most of the population. In this they accumulated and over-accumulated an enormous reserve of private capital. But in their eyes that no longer provided them with a sufficiently high level of profit. In an unbridled race for the highest possible profits, in the shortest period of time, and greatly indifferent to the needs of the nation, they sought to increase these gigantic reserves of capital by way of speculation, foreign investments and parasitic manufacturing, even as they wasted the investments.

Ultimately, while a tiny fraction of the population depleted such enormous wealth, firms closed or passed under the control of multinational companies, workers were laid off, harvests were doomed to destruction, the nation's scientific and technical potential were sold off, social benefits were neglected, the natural environment was degraded, pollution accumulated and the people's needs were ignored. It was this contemptible squandering of resources and energies which provoked the crisis.

A similar crisis afflicted the whole capitalist world. It was manifested in the disorganization of the monetary system, in trade disputes and in merciless competition among the different national, monopolist groups. These results further aggravated the other consequences of the crisis in each capitalist nation. Concurrently, the capitalist powers had to face up to the world socialist competition and face the Third World's increasing desire to control its own national resources.

All along in the service of the big bourgeoisie, the Giscardian regime's policy plunged the nation ever deeper into the crisis. While it received unprecedented support from some large capitalist corporations, it instituted ever more severe austerity for the people, struck serious blows to freedom and democracy, and entrenched our nation more firmly in the Atlantic bloc.

L'Humanité, November 12, 1975, p. 7.

31   Georges Marchais' report to the Twenty-Second Congress of the PCF, February 1976

Who are the leaders of France today?
To be a capitalist 'who counts' in 1976, it is no longer enough to own one or even several factories, employ several hundred or even several thousand wage-earners. For forty years we spoke of the 'two hundred families' which dominated France. That day is over. Our era is the era of the giants of banking and the large multinational industrial groups, who exploit tens of thousands of workers, who integrate a considerable number of diverse enterprises, and who make use of enormous reserves of capital. These groups know only one end, only one religion: profit. Few in number, they constitute the heart of the capitalist system, its hardest core. They exert a world hegemony over the whole society, including all other factions of the bourgeoisie . . .

The Deeper Cause
The character of the recent evolution is the result of the giant trusts' unbridled search for the highest level of profit in the shortest periods of time; it has become more and more brutal and detrimental to the needs of the economy as well as of the nation's people. The system's contradictions have sharpened to the point where they have destroyed its organization, impeding its functioning. The nation's leaders endeavored to accumulate investments in the sectors that interested them, even when the existing potential was partially under-utilized, but solely with the hope of a place in the race for profits. They seek to compound their capital in parasitic production, speculation and foreign investment. This is why, although most Frenchmen work hard and live poorly, factories are closed, workers and young graduates are thrown into unemployment, the progress of the sciences has slowed and technology is destroyed or sold off. Hundreds of thousands of very expensive apartments built at the taxpayers' expense in other cities lie empty and the intelligence and talents of millions of children are left to waste.

The crisis, then, had its source in the big bourgeoisie's hoarding of the nation's resources and the labor of its people, sacrificed to the profit motives of the financial and industrial fiefdoms.

A Global Crisis
It is because of this that it is possible to understand why the crisis is not only economic, but also social, political, ideological and moral.

The crisis is social because the working class, and now millions of other workers, are rising up against a trend which so badly damages their interests, and because, as a consequence, the class struggle is becoming more acute.

The crisis is political because the state in the service of big capital is today implicated in each problem and because, owing to this, the masses in struggle are turning more and more against it; because men and women who seek to serve the general interest, who work for the state bureaucracy, the courts and even the police, ask themselves about the meaning of their activity and sometimes refuse to continue to serve the big private interests; because a desire for change is growing in all strata, and because the privileged minority resorts more and more to arbitrary, violent, illegal and authoritarian means in order to maintain its domination.

The crisis is ideological and moral, because the law of profit, the strongest law governing the behavior of those at the top of the scale, spares no aspect of social life and nourishes the development of criminality, corruption, pornography and evil; because the class in power cultivates immorality and perversion; because all thought, all brave and innovative ideals can only be revolutionary; and because the heads of our government, like the nobles before 1789, guard their privileges and their fiefs, having nothing other to offer than the aggressive defense of a decadent regime.

Hence the crisis that France is undergoing is caused by the functioning of the system itself; the system alone – capitalism in its current state, characterized by the all-powerful domination of the economy and the state by a small caste of millionaires, otherwise known as state monopoly capitalism – is the cause.

Giscard d'Estaing: A Disastrous Balance Sheet
The false battle against inflation consisted in reducing the buying power and consumption of the workers and the buying power of the peasant class, while the large businesses raised their prices with the state setting an example.

Under the pretext of 'refreezing the economy,' Giscard deliberately organized the development of unemployment. He favored the ruin of millions of little and middle-sized businesses to clear the way for the trusts. He scrupulously handed them the national enterprises. He approved the dismantling of the essential sectors of our industry sold to foreigners. He reduced even more of the social and cultural services . . .

As to the rest, it suffices to consult the preparatory work for the Seventh Plan which extends over the period 1975–80 to know what future the Giscardian authority is preparing for the French. This future is defined this way: accentuation of the drainage of national resources to the benefit of multinational capitalist companies and permanent inflation, the reduction of popular consumption and permanent austerity, the slowing of economic growth and the establishment of permanent unemployment.

'XXIIe Congrès du Parti Communiste Français,' *Cahiers du communisme* (February–March 1976), pp. 20–6.

32 'What the communists want for France,' Twenty-Second Congress of the PCF, February 1976

The right of all citizens to conduct and control public affairs will be guaranteed by the regular organizing of elections in the various councils and assemblies, guaranteeing the various political currents a proportional representation. This participation will be one of the essential aspects of an intense democratic life which will emerge in the economic as well as in the political domain.

In that spirit, each worker – whatever his function – will . . . be able to participate directly or through a representative, in the choices and decisions at all levels of the enterprise as well as outside it, in the relations which will be established between the units of production and the local collectives . . .

In nationalized firms, which will be granted the greatest autonomy in management, workers will be represented at all levels and will participate in managing. In private enterprises the rights and authority of the action committees will be increased, notably in matters of working conditions.

Trade unions – which will not be confused with the different organs of management and control – will possess the means to develop their activity. Their independence from the state, employers and political parties will be guaranteed. The right to strike will be respected without restriction. All limits upon the right to strike, as well as those which hinder the free functioning of union locals, will be abolished. The political parties will be able to organize themselves and express themselves freely on the shop floor.

Each worker will be able to exercise equally his control and initiative in the affairs of his neighborhood, his region. Counties, provinces and regions will be administered by councils elected by universal suffrage, direct and proportional. These assemblies will rely on permanent organs of participation, representing the different aspects of society.

The county will constitute a fundamental step in the democratic system. Within the sphere of its increased authority, it will possess full administrative and financial authority and it will possess full administrative and financial autonomy. The state will no longer act as a guardian, but will make an effort to help localities to achieve efficient management through non-compulsory and flexible plans to stimulate local initiative. The state will be relieved of the unnecessary burdens that it carries today. Local financial resources, thus increased, will come from local taxes and from additional state aid, allocated to achieve a just balance among all counties. The population will be greatly involved, in many different ways, with the running of the country and with determining choices and means. The municipalities, particularly the big cities, will be able to lean on structures of resident participation established in neighborhoods and larger communities . . .

Because the citizen does not possess a real freedom of decision if he is not fully informed, the right to information must be guaranteed for all. Freedom of the press will be guaranteed. Radio and television will be a public service, belonging to the nation. They will guarantee the expression and confrontation of currents of thought, both philosophical and political.

Democratic choices will be made on the basis of real information and in a climate of free exchange of ideas which will give weight and validity to the decisions taken by the majority and will guarantee the respect of the minority.

In their contact with the administration, the citizens will be protected from arbitrary decisions. The members of a political party will not possess any special privileges. The state will be secular. The national education, a public service, secular and free, will not teach an official philosophy.

Put in the exclusive service of the people, the police will protect freedoms, the people's safety and goods – the courts of justice will guarantee to all a real equality in the eyes of the law, respecting individual liberties and all rights of defense; they will contribute in securing to all the full use of their rights . . .

The army, placed in the service of the entire nation, will in no case be used against the liberty of any people or against the liberties of the French people. The military will be able to exercise their rights as citizens. Democratic status will guarantee them the freedom of information, expression and association. They will have the right to belong to the political party of their choice.

The French Communist Party has drafted a declaration of liberties, which would guarantee all the freedoms already acquired as well as the new freedoms necessary to our people . . .

We want a free and sovereign France, refusing all foreign rule, pressure or reprisals, independent of any politico-military bloc, as well as of any global strategy, whatever they may be. We want this independence tomorrow and are fighting for it today.

Master of its decisions, our country will recover its full freedom of action and will multiply its political and economic relations with all countries, whether they are capitalist, socialist or part of the new world of countries which have freed themselves from colonial oppression and which fight to escape from the imperialists who pillage their resources. Our country will co-operate with all on a basis of independence, non-interference, equality of rights and mutual advantage. It will contribute in this spirit to the establishment of a new global economic order, more equitable and profitable to the people.

France will be inspired by these principles in its dealing with the West European countries to which it is economically bound. While the big capitalist bourgeoisie makes Western Europe a 'region' of the American empire, we want our country to work hard toward constructing a democratic Europe, peaceful and independent, a Europe of workers . . .

Because it possesses its own traditions and temperament, and because the conditions in which it lives, works and fights are always particular, each people makes its own history. Each must find its own way towards a greater democracy, progress and social justice, and follow it in all freedom. The French Communist Party learns from its experiments, its successes and errors. It puts into perspective the great help their work and actions have been to the people of the world's struggles. The party, however, uses none as a model. It concentrates on providing solutions to the problems of our country which are based on the scientific principles of socialism and which adhere closely to the national reality and historical moment. Socialist France will follow the correct path of our history and will reveal a profoundly original character. The progress of détente and the long tradition of our people's defense of freedom will particularly favor the blossoming of the democratic character of the socialism which we want, a socialism resolutely bearing the colors of France.

'XXIIe Congrès du Parti Communiste Français,' *Cahiers du Communisme* (February–March 1976), pp. 370–80.

33 Paul Laurent, 'Pluralism and the influence of the Communist Party,' 1976

The Twenty-Second Congress of the French Communist Party confirmed it with total clarity: the

French communists are supporters of pluralism in the nation's life. Of a true, democratic pluralism; one which does not crush one current of opinion to the advantage of others; one which does not consider the domination of the state and all the decisive branches of the economy by a tiny group of big capitalists as the normal expression of economic pluralism.

The conception of the communists is different. The pluralism for which we fight assumes a real right of expression and information for all currents of thought and opinion. It assumes a true democratization of economic and political life which finally assures the working class, the salaried workers, the peasants, all the levels of power, of a role in proportion to the place they hold in national activity. Today, it is the monopolies which exercise a real dictatorship over economic life, it is with the present regime that a technocratic bureaucracy which claims the right to dictate all aspects of national life is developing.

As Georges Marchais has emphasized to the Twenty-Second Congress: 'Nothing is possible on the road to democracy until the domination of the economy by big capital is ended. Democracy and liberty today are the principal battlefields of class conflict, of revolutionary struggle.'

Therefore, in order to assure social progress, the progress of democracy, and the success of socialism, the problem is not to deprive the liberties of the minority that the reactionary forces constitute, it is to give many more liberties to the workers who constitute the great majority of the nation. It is to give the people mastery of the control levers of the economy.

At the same time, the Twenty-Second Congress has clearly shown that a pluralist conception of French political life naturally complements the idea of the struggle for a guiding influence by the Communist Party over the popular movement.

First of all, because all political parties look to exercise a guiding influence, it is the normal law of democracy that each political body may endeavor to show the value of its point of view through action. One wonders why the Communist Party alone would not be motivated by this ambition; and not at all, as certain people claim, by the goal of eliminating its adversaries and allies. We are the only party to demand proportional representation, that is, representation of all the population. Our attitude is valid for today and for tomorrow. We look to exercise a guiding influence over the political movement without any spirit of monopoly or domination, because we are profoundly convinced that this corresponds to the interests of the working class, of all the exploited, of the people, of the country.

L'Humanité, October 22, 1976, p. 1.

34 Pierre Juquin, 'Freedom is indivisible,' 1976

Our Twenty-Second Congress, held in February of this year, clearly defined the objectives of our action. It determined the principal nature of our original path for the nation and for French socialism.

Our independent orientation and independence of action do not at all weaken our solidarity with the other communist parties, and in particular with those which have already started their people on the road to socialism.

Conversely, this solidarity does not keep us from expressing our point of view on what appear to us to be errors in the policies of one socialist nation or another.

Some violently denounce the human rights violations committed in these nations, while refusing to act when freedom is jeered at in nations in which our friends are in power. We, because our policy is based on principles, believe that the fight for freedom allows for no discrimination. This is a point on which we never compromise.

How, then, can we admit that communist ideals, whose objective is the liberation of mankind and for which we are calling France to battle, are tainted by acts of injustice? We cannot just accept the fact that there are, in the Soviet Union and Czechoslovakia, citizens hunted and imprisoned for having expressed their opinions. We will never accept the existence of practices in some nations which violate the rights of human beings in the name of socialism.

In acting on this we are very conscious of acting to further the spread of socialism and its influence and authority in the world. We seriously think that the Soviet Union – which has offered so many sacrifices and done so many great things to promote freedom – can only emerge greater, and strengthen the universal communist following, by putting an end to these repressive measures.

For we cannot, in judging its commitment to the cause of freedom, put the Soviet Union on the same level as Uruguay!

Democrats cannot confuse the sort of violence used by exploiters, colonizers and fascists to oppose the cause of freedom in the world with the problems which arise in the course of that advancement which may appear to thwart it, as serious and sorry as they are.

Hence we will make known our criticism of one aspect or another of the Soviet situation each time that it is necessary. But we will not be party to the lies and systematic slander, denigration and global discrediting involved in anti-Sovietism. We are and will always be anti-fascist, but never anti-Soviet.

For us, socialism and freedom are synonymous . . . Freedom cannot be divided, either in terms of time or of space. We have a passion for freedom.

L'Humanité, October 22, 1976, p. 6.

35 Georges Marchais' report to the Twenty-Third Congress of the PCF, February 1977

An Original Independent Path

Our path towards socialism is an original path. As we have written in *Le Défi Démocratique*, the policy of the French Communist Party defines a French path towards socialism, a socialism 'à la française.'

How could it be otherwise? The national originality of our policy has reasons of principle. Socialism is a social formation which appears and develops as a necessary response to the objective needs of a country. These needs are concrete and particular, and the responses which socialism brings to them are, and must be, concrete and particular. Socialism in France, thus, will found itself on the reality of France in all its aspects.

This does not contradict the fact that general laws and universal principles of socialism exist. The collective ownership of the major means of production and exchange, planning, the power of the worker, the democratization of national life, the directing influence of a vanguard party inspired by scientific socialism – these are the laws of socialism. Their translation into life may assume, inevitably assumes, varied forms. The conditions and the traditions of each country necessarily endow it with specific traits in all areas, whether they concern institutions and political life, the economic structures and organization, social life or culture. Already a certain diversity of socialist reality exists, and only the bad faith of the anti-communist propaganda would tamper with it. Socialism possesses different traits in the Soviet Union and in Vietnam, in Hungary and in Cuba, in East Germany and in Yugoslavia. And the more numerous the socialist countries are, the greater the diversity of socialist reality will become. Thus, there does not exist and cannot exist, one 'model' of socialism which would be transferable from one country to another.

It is the same for the paths which lead to socialism, the methods of struggle. We have often said, to illustrate that the France of today is neither the Russia of 1917 nor the Czechoslovakia of 1948, that the national and historical conditions of class combat are profoundly different. No party or groups of parties may legislate to others, propose universal recipes, define a model strategy. Thus it is inevitable, it is good, that we follow an independent path of struggle for socialism . . .

'XXIIIᵉ Congrès du Parti Communiste Français,' *Cahiers du Communisme* (March–April 1977), cf. pp. 62–4.

SPANISH Communist Party: From Illegality to the Peaceful Road

1 Declaration of the PCE, 'For national reconciliation, for a democratic and peaceful solution to the Spanish problem,' June 1956

The need for profound changes in Spain's political direction has as one of its principal causes the economic situation in which the country finds itself after seventeen years of dictatorship . . .

The monopolistic development of capitalism, by virtue of its own objective laws, invariably carries within itself – in Spain as in the entire capitalist world – the accelerated accumulation of wealth at one extreme, and privation and misery at the other.

But in Spain the consequences of the development of monopolistic capitalism are aggravated for two reasons.

First, because the industrial development of the country enters into ever-sharpening contradiction with the feudal remnants in the Spanish economy, whose most important exponent is the great latifundial proprietor, the principal cause of, among other evils, the seasonal suspension of work suffered by the great mass of day-laborers, and of the poverty of the internal market.

Despite its promises of agrarian reform, the Franco dictatorship has not only done nothing practical to resolve the problem but the monopolistic groups which operate in the shade of the dictatorship have extended their tentacles to the countryside, and the secular oppression of the large landowner over the peasant has come to equal that of finance capital.

Secondly, through the economic policies of the government, directed toward forcing such developments to the benefit of the financial oligarchy, Franco proclaimed his goal to be the industrialization of Spain. All industrialization demands the accumulation and the investment of large amounts of capital. When industrialization policy is initiated by a state which represents the national interest, resources are extracted primarily from those social groups in the most privileged economic situations. But when the state finds itself in the power of such groups, and the

'industrialization' is carried through with the sole, egoistic aim of increasing the benefits of the previous classes, resources are extracted from the working masses and from the weakest strata of the bourgeoisie. This is the case in Spain. Such is the essence of the so-called industrialization policy which General Franco has pursued since his rise to power . . .

The Franco dictatorship claims to 'industrialize' the country on the base of an interior market which is increasingly narrow and insolvent. Such an economic policy carries within itself the seeds of its own negation. How can industrialization be encouraged if one boards up the natural well of all economic expansion: the market . . .?

The Franco dictatorship's militarization of the economy has definitely reduced, rather than enlarged, the internal and external markets. The market which militarization has opened in selected sectors is ingenuous and precarious. The Spanish economy, instead of freeing itself from its traditional economic and political dependency on foreign capital, has fallen into a dependency even greater than the most rapacious of contemporary imperialisms . . .

Franco, under the flag of industrialization, with which he hoped to acquire a national image, actually served the narrow interests of a group of the Spanish financial oligarchs and of foreign capitalists. One and the other exploit Spain as if it were a colony.

Franco's economic policy has presented itself as anti-monopolist, but under his dictatorship monopolies have grown like mushrooms after rain . . .

Serving such interests, General Franco's economic policy has led to the chaotic forcing of industrial development in some sectors at the expense of stagnation and recession in others, and the impoverishment of the population. This has sharpened the contradictions between the interests of a reduced group of oligarchs and those of the immense majority of the Spanish.

It is clear that, although official statistics may speak of certain advances in industrial production, the dictatorship has not strengthened itself; on the contrary, it is much weaker today, and its social base has diminished considerably.

Spanish Communist Party document, 1956, pp. 16–25.

2   Dolores Ibarruri's speech to the Central Committee, 1958

When we speak of the principal group in power, it would perhaps be more correct not to continue speaking of one faction, because by now it is more accurate to speak of several factions fighting for power and for the legacy of the dictatorship.

The Opus Dei faction is small; however, its men occupy excellent positions within the state and the financial oligarchy; it is disciplined and insatiable in its desire to assume the direction of the country and eventually to restore a medieval monarchy where it can settle down for ever.

At the same time the monarchist-Francoist faction, a minor associate of the Opus Dei, is active in political acrobatics, trying to make its support of Franco compatible with its loyalty to the pretender. Its members are sometimes left in an awkward situation, since it does not satisfy either of their two lords when they try to serve both at the same time.

There is also a faction formed by the chiefs of the army who alternate their military duties with the sessions and meetings of the administrative councils.

These different factions, all related somehow to the monopolist oligarchy and all agreeing in principle to try to maintain the power of the oligarchy, are engaged in a power struggle which sometimes is evident in the official press. This struggle is evidence of the weakness of the dictatorship's position.

Among them, Franco is no longer supreme arbiter, the common denominator. Franco is now the man whose replacement is inevitable, and each faction wants to fulfill this replacement or, at least, secure its privileges in it.

The unstable balance of the competition among these factions, so precarious that any unexpected event, any popular uprising, can demolish it, is the foundation of the power existing today in Spain; such a foundation is utterly decayed and would fall very quickly, if it were not for its American support.

Behind all the factions fighting around General Franco for power, there is not true social force. Its

whole structure would collapse as soon as left- and right-wing anti-Francoist Spaniards decide to co-ordinate their forces in an action directed towards imposing the political changes which Spain needs.

Spanish Communist Party document, 1958, pp. 32–3.

3   Emilio M.'s speech to the Central Committee, 1958

The financial oligarchy, the monopolist capital, has carried out in recent years a redistribution of the national income and wealth which favors only itself. Not only has it strengthened its position within the basic industries, but it also has created an extremely large number of enterprises which produce for consumption, the traditional market of small enterprises and modest industries. This unfair competition weakens the position of the small bourgeoisie and the non-monopolist industrialists just when the national situation reflects the first symptoms of the crisis which has already begun in the United States of America.

Under these conditions, governmental policy has become oriented towards the elimination of the so-called 'unproductive' enterprises, towards clearing the ground for the action of the financial oligarchs and the monopolies. A fundamental tool of this policy is the recent tax reform ...

The *small individual businessmen* who constitute a group numerically more important than the small industrialists, have similar problems. They suffer, on the one hand, from the ruthless competition of the big enterprises and, on the other hand, from state intervention. Monthly statistics of the chambers of commerce show a large decrease in their sales, as compared to those of the big enterprises who benefit from superior economic power, and state aid as well as tax exemptions ...

As a social group, the individual businessmen have carried out positive efforts towards raising the tone of their political opposition to Francoism. Their direct contact with the people, and the latter's perspicacity, have prevented a clash from taking place between the businessmen and the popular masses in our country ...

The situation of the professional groups also offers important experiences of struggle for the party.

Many of the professionals are educated in the universities and special schools; therefore they have personally experienced the problems of students and intellectuals which will be referred to by other comrades. Their way of living makes them fit perfectly into the middle class, in any of its three groups. Their aspirations are those of the petite bourgeoisie and their economic opportunities are so limited that they are sometimes less than those of qualified workers and specialists . . .

The term 'liberal profession' today lacks the implication of autonomy and independence that it had in the past. In Spain the monopolist power of the grande bourgeoisie and the gradual impoverishment of the country have destroyed any possibility of independent professional and economic advancement for these professionals . . .

The Francoist dictatorship has damaged this group's professional development in an extraordinary fashion. Because, from a political viewpoint, they have been traditionally democratic, the liberal professions have been the favorite target of repression; a systematic official opposition to anything that means progress, innovation or a revolutionary sense of living has eliminated the possibility of its cultural development . . .

It is evident in the treatment suffered recently by state officials. The state machine has been purged, and the men and women who most strongly support democracy have been hunted out, fired and put in jail. Now that they have been replaced by nationalist veterans of the civil war, the Francoist state believes it has a solid pillar upon which it can rely for the development of its policies. However, it has hurt the interests and even the feelings of these functionaries; it has identified them with popular needs and complaints and has brought them to the people who are, ultimately, their origin. Our policy of national reconciliation has been the fundamental motor of this development. The attitudes of those officials who, because of their duty to maintain the public order, could have been better employed by the dictatorship to carry out its plans for a civil war, are sufficiently revealing . . .

The political and economic decomposition of a system which, at the same time that it allows the limitless enrichment of its highest officials, abandons to miserable salaries its most immediate collaborators, highlights in these latter groups the need for not being silent any longer, the need for claiming what the Francoist state systematically denies them: the right to a better standard of living . . .

In spite of the considerable differences among the various levels of the middle class, the policies of our party completely include what is essential to their economic aspirations and are capable of moving those groups together with the masses of workers and peasants of our country . . .

The program of the party presents these forces with a clear choice of solutions: a secure and hopeful future. Their class interests, however antagonistic to those of the working class, can become compatible within the framework of a democratic solution to the crisis of the dictatorship. Today its major enemy is the same as that of the working class: the monopolies, those who maintain the civil war and Francoism . . .

This position is based on the Marxist–Leninist science, which points out the inevitable movement towards the uniting of proletarians, peasants, middle class, small national bourgeoisie, against the monopolies and big financial capitalists, towards the democratic development of Spain's future . . .

The middle class must behave energetically to impose its solutions; it must break the obstacles opposing it. To achieve this goal, it has to begin by making use of all the legal forms of struggle, taking them away from the hands of the representatives of its major enemy . . .

We communists have the task of making sure that the conditions which have been created for the struggle of the middle class will be the same as those of, and will be directed by, the proletariat.

Spanish Communist Party document, 1958, pp. 258–71.

4 'Spain twenty years after the Civil War,' Santiago Carrillo's report to the Central Committee, 1959

The Communist Party reiterates that the task put forth today before the Spanish people is the abolition of the Francoist dictatorship and the restoration of democratic bourgeois liberties. This and no other is the character of the struggle at the present time. Upon making this affirmation, the Communist Party does not conceal its determination to achieve for Spain, in the future, a socialist system . . .

The Spanish democratic future will coincide with an international situation which is much more favorable to its strengthening than in other periods of history. Spanish democracy will flourish in a time period in which socialism influences, and will influence even more decisively, all historic evolution. This international situation cannot help but shape the democratic future of our country . . .

The strengthening of the international role of the Soviet Union and of the socialist camp represents, and will represent even more in the years to come, an ideological, political and moral support of enormous importance for the struggle of the working class and the progressive Spanish forces for the strengthening of democracy and socialism.

In Spain an additional factor which may turn out to be of great importance in coming years is the working class which, comprised of industrial and agricultural workers, represents, together with their families, approximately half of the population of the country. Added to the diverse groups of workers who live on a modest wage and the poor and middle-level peasants, it constitutes the vast majority. That is to say, the forces which in favorable conditions may rise in insurrection for socialism represent the vast majority of the Spanish population.

The attitude of that great majority will be influenced on the one hand by the rich revolutionary traditions of the proletariat and the working masses of our country, while, on the other hand, it will be inspired by the example of the success of the Soviet Union and the socialist camp. Through the aggregation of all these factors, the revolutionary politics of the party of the working class, the Communist Party of Spain, may find the decided support of wide popular strata.

All of this means that the necessary conditions may occur in Spain so that in the future the socialist revolution, that is, the acquisition of political power by the working class and the passage from bourgeois democracy to socialist democracy, will be achieved along a peaceful and parliamentary route.

The Communist Party affirms its determination to do everything it possibly can in order to follow this peaceful and parliamentary course to the victory of socialism in our country, so that the inevitable socialist future of Spain may be accomplished in a bloodless manner, without insurrection or civil war.

History shows that changes in social systems have not always and in all countries been accomplished in the same manner. When the Russian proletariat, under the leadership of the great Lenin and the Communist Party, acquired power and initiated the first socialist revolution in history, it had to overcome terrible opposition . . .

The violent opposition encountered by the first socialist revolution could only be overcome by equally violent methods. One of the greatest glories of the communists and of the Soviet people is the establishing of socialism in their country and the opening of the road for the triumph of the new social system in the entire world under the most difficult and adverse conditions . . .

The victory of socialism in Spain can take place along a peaceful and parliamentary route, in the historic circumstances of this time, if, when the moment arrives, the forces which consider themselves to be progressive decide to march forward, toward socialism, together with the Communist Party, instead of allying themselves with the reactionary groups of capitalism which pull backwards.

By this route the development of socialist democracy in Spain can witness a plurality of parties, representative of the diverse social classes and strata won over to the fulfillment of socialism, in which the divergences originating in the differences of interests of those classes and strata would be amicably resolved, without violence or imposition, on the basis of mutual understanding and a common interest in building and strengthening the socialist system . . .

Spanish Communist Party document, 1959, pp. 79–83.

5   Political resolution of the Sixth Congress of the PCE, 1960

The political crisis of the Francoist regime reaches a gravity never seen before, and the country finds itself in the worst economic circumstances yet experienced under the dictatorship.

The so-called 'Stabilization Plan' comes to beat on a sick economy. This plan is a set of measures designed by the international monopolist capital; its aim is to prevent the virtual bankruptcy of the dictatorship's economic policy from becoming an open and visible bankruptcy. By means of the plan, the financial oligarchy wants to burden the people's shoulders with the consequences of the chaos that it has itself produced.

The 'Stabilization Plan' is not only a plan of misery and suffering for the working masses but also the realization of an unprecedented economic catastrophe, a mad squandering of energy and resources that would leave our country subjected to the foreign monopolies.

How can we prevent the catastrophe from happening? There is only one way: to turn the energies of the working class and of all the people to the struggle against the Plan . . .

The Congress urges all party organizations and all militants to stimulate and organize the action of the peasants, the petite bourgeoisie and the non-monopolist bourgeoisie against the attack of the dictatorship and the monopolies.

We communists say to all the peasants and even to all the landowners who have no links with the monopolist capital: unite in order to obtain fair prices for your products, to fight for a reduction in taxes and against the arbitrariness of the interventionist organs, against the abuses of the banks and the monopolies! Unite to prevent the Stabilization Plan from converting most of Spanish soil into waste lands and from pushing its inhabitants into forced emigration!

We communists say to thermodorian merchants and industrialists: struggle together against the taxes which burden you, for cheap and abundant credit, against the integration into the European market which would condemn you to destruction, against the dictatorship of the big monopolies and the absenteeist aristocracy!

In the struggle against the Stabilization Plan all those who are interested, from the proletariat to the non-monopolist bourgeoisie, should take part. This convergence of interests constitutes the basis for the concordance of all the left- and right-wing opposition forces in their struggle against the dictatorship to bring about a peaceful change, opening the way for democratic development.

Mundo Obrero, February 15, 1960, pp. 2–3.

6   Santiago Carrillo's speech at the Sixth Congress of the PCE, 1960 (I)

It is fitting to add that the dictatorship of the proletariat, in proportion to the strengthening of socialism as a decisive force in the world, maintaining the general features appropriate to any socialist revolution – as specified in the declaration of the twelve parties of socialist countries in Moscow, 1957 – can have forms which are sensibly different from those which it had in the USSR. The dictatorship of the proletariat can take, and certainly will take in other countries, the form of parliamentary democracy.

Under a given set of circumstances, the world weight of socialism and the renovation of democracy in specific countries can allow the working class, allied with other progressive forces of society, to attain power, basing itself on a parliamentary majority and an active and powerful movement of the masses. With the government in their hands and the masses' active support, the representatives of the working class and other progressive forces can change, through parliamentary decisions, the character and the tenor of the instruments of state power, converting these [instruments] into faithful agencies of the socialist revolution. In this way the working class and other progressive forces can place themselves in full possession of state power and can continue to achieve the socialization of the means of production through parliamentary measures. By this road the socialist forces can isolate and reduce the reactionary elements, without the necessity of resorting to extreme measures of violence.

In this case power could be exercised by the working class, in alliance with other socialist and progressive parties and groups. Within this coalition there could exist different points of view. Such differences should be resolved by negotiation, in the greater interests of the socialist transformation, taking into account the opinions of the working class and the people.

This form of dictatorship of the proletariat does not exclude the possibility of legal existence of an opposition . . .

The question of whether the forms of socialist transformation, of the dictatorship of the proletariat, are to be violent or parliamentarian depends upon the degree of resistance offered by the capitalist and reactionary forces. And the character of that resistance is closely tied to the greater or lesser respective weight of socialist and capitalist systems in the world.

VI Congreso del PCE, Spanish Communist Party document, 1960, pp. 88–9.

7   Santiago Carrillo's speech at the Sixth Congress of the PCE, 1960 (II)

The Democratic Program of the Party
The speculation of the Francoists and some members of the opposition that the communists intend to 'subvert the social order' and to restore a 'party dictatorship' after the fall of fascism, is a vulgar lie, an invention without foundation. Our party program specifies in great detail what policy we understand the communists will fulfill once Spain has extricated itself from the dictatorship.

The content of the next program fits within the framework of bourgeois society; it does not represent any threat to the bourgeoisie as a class; on the contrary, its application would facilitate the development of the bourgeoisie, would widen the domestic market and would facilitate the export of national products, as well as the acquisition of raw materials and machinery.

The fundamental change of structure which we communists propose is agrarian reform, through the expropriation, with compensation, of the aristocratic absentee landlord. Properties exploited rationally by the owners themselves, regardless of their size, would remain exempt from this measure of expropriation.

What does this structural change attempt to accomplish? It involves, naturally, giving ownership of the land to those agricultural workers and to those country-dwellers who lack it; ending the extreme misery reigning in the countryside; breaking the feudal ties which exist in agriculture and introducing more modern and productive methods of working the land. Initially, this structural reform is of interest to the country-dwellers and agricultural workers. But it is of equal interest to the whole country, save a few exceptions. It is a measure without which it is impossible to resolve the acute problems which the backward national economic structure poses. Agrarian reform will represent a considerable extension of the interior market and an increase in the productivity of the countryside. For the same reason, it is of interest to the industrialists, who need a market for their products, and to the populace in general. In all other modern countries the agrarian reform which we propose for Spain took place many years ago. It is a democratic bourgeois measure.

An additional proposal seeks to limit the power of the monopolies. But all Spain clamors for that! Such a limitation is of interest not only to the workers and peasants, but to the petite bourgeoisie and the non-monopolistic bourgeoisie. Either the power of the monopolies will be limited, or the living conditions of the masses will worsen and non-monopolistic enterprises will sink, one after another. It involves a democratic measure, of national interest, which suits the needs of the people and wide sectors of the bourgeoisie.

We also propose a series of reforms to better the living conditions of the workers in diverse sectors and, in general, of all those who live from their work. There is nothing in these measures which affects the social order. They are, in various respects, more modest than those already proclaimed in other capitalist countries.

Our program includes political reforms. We propose the establishment of a parliamentary system in which political parties, without discrimination, are represented in proportion to their real strength in the country. Does this have anything to do with a claim to a 'party dictatorship'?

We also propose that the local, provincial or regional administrative organs enjoy a true functional autonomy, protected from the bureaucratic arbitrariness of the central power. We propose that the Spanish, Catalonian, Basque and Galician nationalities enjoy the right to self-determination and that they have within the state, if they wish, a statute of autonomy which guarantees their right to direct their own affairs . . .

One can agree with this program or one can be against it, or part of it. What is not possible is to say, without provoking laughter, that it involves a socialist program or program which tends toward the re-establishment of a 'party dictatorship.'

It involves a democratic and peaceful policy. Those are our immediate goals.

VI Congreso del PCE, Spanish Communist Party document, 1960, pp. 82–3.

8   'The duties of the people,' Santiago Carrillo's report to the Central Committee, 1961

The Peaceful Route and the Route of Armed Struggle
For us the peaceful route is not a transfer of powers from Franco to Don Juan, it is not a permutation of

one political team of the oligarch to another, although let us not dismiss the fact that if the populace is prepared politically and the party is capable of mobilizing it, an attempt of this kind would allow the masses to take to the streets to establish a democratic government, thus precluding the fulfillment of the oligarch and imperialist ambitions without need of engaging in civil war . . .

What we understand to be the peaceful route are mass strikes and street demonstrations culminating in a national strike. We have defined a national strike as a general political strike of the workers with the support and active co-operation of the masses of the petite and middle-level bourgeoisie and, naturally, of the peasantry; and as the taking of the masses to the streets in order to effect a change of regime, fraternization with part of the armed forces and the neutralization of the rest. That is to say, we conceive the national strike to be a national popular uprising against the dictatorship.

Therefore, it is unlike classic armed insurrection and civil war because armed struggle is not the principal form of action, although it is possible that in the course of the national strike there might be skirmishes between the popular masses and re-calcitrant defenders of the regime and the party will be prepared to lead any necessary combative action of the masses. In any case, in order to create conditions favorable to the national strike, it is necessary to raise the struggle of the masses to a much higher level than the present one. In order to lead the masses to the streets to demand a change of regime it is indispensable to promote a series of fights which are much more combative than those of the present.

This peaceful route is possible even if the official bourgeois and social democratic leaders continue to resist, on the condition that there be developed a vast network of organs of unity and struggle in factories and mills, in the universities and the countryside, among professionals and the middle strata, wherever the masses are . . .

Certainly, it is possible that determinate factors could block the peaceful route. If the current situation goes on too much longer it is logical that the most advanced sectors of the working class and the wide peasant masses, whose living conditions already border on the intolerable, could see no alternative to armed struggle . . .

And if, in spite of our efforts to follow a peaceful route, there were to arrive a moment in which armed struggle would constitute the only alternative, the communists would lead the struggle with the decisiveness, the firmness and the spirit of sacrifice which has always characterized our party . . .

Spanish Communist Party document, 1961, pp. 72–5.

9 Santiago Carrillo, *Despuēs de Franco Que?*, 1965

In Favor of Pluralism
Our conception of parliament presupposes, naturally, a multi-party system. The official propaganda in our country hurls menacing and wrathful words against pluralism of parties. It is almost not worth the trouble to initiate a direct polemic with that propaganda; its motivations are obvious. We have carefully investigated the hateful experience of what is meant in the Spanish context by the destruction of multi-partisanism. In this sense it can be said that we have come full circle. Any regime with free parties, no matter how many defects it may have, would be a thousand times preferable to the present one.

Our criticism of bourgeois parties and social democracy is well known. But when faced with a fascist dictatorship, it is not essential to insist upon it. It is more important to see the other side of the question. This side shows that parties, even with their inherent defects, are a democratic element in the political life of a country, in as much as they reflect the diverse interests and positions of different socal classes and strata. Even those parties whose leadership is most submissive to the dictates of monopolist capital find themselves forced, when there are great movements of opinion among the masses of a country or among their members, to take into account the popular will, in one way or another. The existence of parties and political propaganda are means of interesting the wide masses in the life of the country and participating in it, on a greater or lesser scale, that is, to counteract what we could call 'popular political absenteeism' which is of interest to monopolist money, which spreads it.

It is true that the parties will be more efficient, more faithful to their programs and more democratic in a regime of political and economic democracy than they are under the system of state monopoly capital. The parties will be more authentic, more democratic, more representative of the interests which they claim to embody. What makes the multi-party system unclear, what sometimes erases the boundaries between parties which claim to be leftist, rightist or centrist, what often leads to the Communist Party being the only one which is faithful to its program, is that the other parties, from the top, are decisively controlled not by the members of their ranks and committees, but by the monopolistic group . . .

Santiago Carrillo, *Despuēs de Franco Que?* (Buenos Aires: Editorial Impulso, 1965), pp. 97–9.

10   Editorial, 'Foreign capital in Spain,' *Mundo Obrero*, 1966

The role of foreign capital in Spain is currently a subject of profound concern and controversy . . .

Of all the Francoist legislation, the only 'regulations' governing the investment of foreign capital in Spain can be summarized in just one phrase: the foreign capitalist can set up any business he would prefer, when and how he wants to do it; Francoism guarantees a high rentability. Under such conditions, an inevitable process has taken place in Spain. The large international trusts have, at wholesale prices, taken control of most (in some cases, all) of a series of existing industries and, at minimal expense, they have created a range of new industries which, in many cases, yield profits even before they begin to function. Consequently, existing industries which feel themselves threatened by the new ones find themselves compelled to beg for foreign 'help' or 'association' in order to be able to survive.

What situation do we find ourselves in? Foreign capital has not only recovered its traditional position within the Spanish economy (and here it is sufficient to point to the reappearance of German capital in companies which supposedly had been nationalized at the end of the Second World War), but it has also extended its tentacles over all branches of services of industry.

Mundo Obrero, no. 8 (1966), p. 1.

11   Political declaration of the Central Committee of the PCE, 'Political situation in Spain,' 1967

Francoism, far from being in better shape after the referendum operation, finds itself in an even more critical political and economic situation.

On the street, in free assemblies, in professional meetings, many groups of Spanish citizens reject the dictatorship and demand freedom. This is the irrefutable rejection of the results of the farce of December 14.

The contradictions among the dominant groups have worsened since the referendum. The struggle between the 'ultras' (Alonso Vega, Solis, Fraga, led by Franco) and the advocates of a progressive ('evolucionista'), more open polity who regard as noxious the present fascist structures, is being aggravated even in the core of the government itself.

Fascist legal measures are appearing in rapid succession: effective annulment of the press law through a reform of the penal code; the decision to take to the military courts any case relating to participation in workers' or students' struggles; the persecution against workers' commissions and their leaders, against students, professors and intellectuals; confiscations and suspension of newspapers; the increasing pressure against the foreign press; the restrictive modifications imposed upon the project for the law on religious liberty; and, as a culmination, the projects for the electoral law and the law of the movement.

This new attack of the 'ultras' is not directed exclusively against the opposition, but also against the progressive, 'evolucionist' sector. The regime is beginning to turn upon itself.

In reality, the 'ultras'' aim of returning to 'iron hand' politics originates in the fact that their positions are already so weak that just one more step backwards might mean their definitive collapse.

The masses' worker and democratic movement has already attained such a degree of unity, organization and militancy that the presence of the 'ultras' in power is becoming more and more difficult.

On the other hand, the hegemony of the 'ultra' group within the ruling coalition no longer corresponds fully to the interests of the grande bourgeoisie, nor is it supported by the intermediate bourgeoisie.

When Spain seems to be drifting towards an economic crisis (within a capitalist Europe where the signs of recession continue to appear) and when the failure of the regime's economic policies is evident, the continuation of the dictatorship and the nefarious policies and the repressive attacks of the 'ultras' will undoubtedly lead to an aggravation of the socio-political tensions.

The most immediate task is to defeat the plan for the reinstatement of fascist forms of repression, and at the same time to strongly demand AMNESTY for all the political exiles and prisoners.

Today it is a national necessity to eliminate the 'ultras' and the bureaucrats of the movement from the key positions of the national government. Most social groups would gladly welcome such an action.

The new workers' movement must not relinquish any of the conquered legal positions. A firm resistance, together with local or sectorial counter-attacks and an exposition of the real problems of the workers, must be our answer to the efforts of the vertical hierarchies to get rid of the authentic workers' representatives.

The struggle for the liberty of the unions, against the effort of Solis and his gang to legally maintain the monopoly of the 'verticalists,' offers itself as a broad basis for the convergence and the participation of large masses of workers. These masses are already taking in their hands the task of elaborating their new union structures. When the masses continue advancing decisively along this way, the hierarchy will be defeated and progress will take place, through assemblies and free congresses, towards the unitary, independent and democratic workers' central union.

Mundo Obrero, no. 10 (1967), p. 4.

12 Santiago Carrillo's interview with *Le Figaro*, 'On the re-establishment of the monarchy,' 1967

I am not sure that the present regime should necessarily lead to a monarchy. As long as he lives, Franco has not the slightest intention of being replaced as head of the state. And the monarchists do not have the strength or the will to get rid of the Caudillo. If Franco is not ousted from power before his death – which is something no one can claim will happen – there are so many things that could occur after his death that it does not seem obvious to me

that the monarchy will take over. On the other hand, I believe that the monarchists have, on this issue, the same opinion I have; that is precisely the reason for their claim that Franco re-establishes the monarchy in himself while he is still in power.

On the other hand, we would not accept a monarchy or any other regime imposed from above on to the people. We believe that the first step towards attaining a true political change must be the re-establishment of political liberty. Afterwards the people should freely choose a republic or a monarchy. This is a matter for a constitutional convention. We communists support a republic. However, if the majority would prefer the establishment of a monarchy, we would conform to the democratically expressed will of the majority.

Mundo Obrero, no. 7 (1967), p. 5.

13 'Domestic situation, call for pact of unity,' resolution of the Executive Committee of the PCE, 1969

In leaving the state of exception, the situation of our country is not the same as before. We are not coming back to the starting point. The labor and democratic forces have shown that even when confronted with many obstacles, advances can be made in their organizations and capacity for struggle. The Communist Party has tested its maturity. The preparations for post-Francoism have been accelerated. In effect, the negative consequences of the state of exception have not disappeared as if by a miracle. The press has not returned to the point at which it was when the state of exception was declared. The university, occupied by the police, is still under it. Hundreds of democrats are the objects of brutal prosecution. Detentions and arbitrary rulings are still going on in other provinces. But in spite of objective difficulties, the positive factors have gained more importance. Without failing to take the obstacles into account, we can responsibly claim that the two tense months of the state of exception have represented a true *qualitative change* in the behavior of our party and of the mass movement. Only by such a qualitative appreciation is it possible to perceive the full dimensions of the strength gained by the regime's opponents and of the weakness of Francoism itself. It is important that the masses (through their own experience and through propaganda) begin to understand the new and great opportunities that they have of further weakening the dictatorship in order to prepare for the general strike and the national strike.

Gradually the 5·9 per cent limit imposed on wage increases has collapsed. The workers' commissions and their leading structures have been active.

In the university, where the departments are occupied by the police, the students have not taken down the flag of the democratic and revolutionary struggle.

In the countryside the movement of peasant commissions has developed. They are supported by the CC.OO.

The progressive Catholic movement, against which the state of exception was also directed, has reached a new level. In the Basque Country, Catalonia, Madrid, Galicia, and so on, such a generalized attitude of protest had never before been seen among the priests. This protest has sometimes been supported by bishops as well.

The progressive intellectuals and lawyers, who have been the victims of prosecution and deportations, have courageously denounced torture and have demanded the cessation of special jurisdictions. Unhappiness and dissatisfaction have been manifested among wide sectors of the middle classes.

For a Democratic Alternative

In the new situation there is a certain conviction in the atmosphere, which for others is just a feeling, that 'this is about to end.' THE PREPARATIONS FOR THE REPLACEMENT OF FRANCOISM HAVE BEEN ACCELERATED. There is intense political activity; the problem of change, the search for solutions is what is in the foreground of all political forces.

During this period important changes have taken place in the attitude of the Spanish church. The attempt at converting the Episcopal Conference into a mere tool of the politics of the 'ultras' produced an energetic reaction within very broad sectors of the church hierarchy who expressed a desire to separate the destinies of the church and the regime.

As during all revolutionary crises, there is in our country a convergence of the most distinct contradictions. As a function of such contradictions, diverse alliances and tactics come into play.

Some speculate about a monarchic solution. As a reply to such speculations the Communist Party reaffirms that it considers a republic to be the political regime most suited to Spain's needs. Only

the people have the right to decide, under conditions of true democracy, what the future regime will be!

We see, in the present Spanish crisis, a uniqueness which has to be taken into account. The strength of the democratic mass movement and the role of our party in it leads even the right-wing forces to the conclusion that it is not possible to replace an anti-communist dictatorship with an equally anti-communist solution. Hence the real possibility of a convergence, of a certain compromise between these forces and the democratic ones. It is necessary to emphasize that, for us, what is fundamental is the development of the mass movement in a direction that will necessarily arrive at a democratic solution . . .

Mundo Obrero, no. 10 (May 24, 1969), pp. 1–3.

14   'The position of the communists with respect to the national and regional problem,' political resolution of the Central Committee of the PCE, 1970

The struggle for democracy and socialism includes the realization of the national liberties of Catalonia, Euzkadi and Galicia.

The actions and mass movements which each nation has developed to recover those liberties are an active part of the general struggle for democracy and socialism which is led by the working class.

The latter can only carry out its leading role if it assumes with resolution the defense of these nations' language and national liberties and right to self-determination.

The right to self-determination implies the freedom of peoples and nations to rule themselves freely, including even the creation of their own state. It also implies freedom to decide to remain within the same state through some formula of voluntary association, federation, autonomy, and so on.

The PCE believes that the unity of the many people of Spain, so long as it is established freely and democratically, is most convenient to the people's interests, to the proletariat's class interests and to those of the democratic and socialist revolution.

The communists understand that the democratic liberties for which we are fighting include the fulfillment of the aspirations of the peoples of

Catalonia, Euzkadi and Galicia to gain autonomy in order to create provisional governments which would be expressions of the forces which, within each of these nationalities, are opposed to the dictatorship . . .

The new structure of the democratic Spanish state will be decentralized and broadly regionalized, economically and politically, which is the only way of tackling the very serious problem of regional inequalities which today constitute an enormous obstacle to the authentic development of Spain.

Mundo Obrero, no. 15 (September 30, 1970).

15   'The reactionary Opus Dei,' *Mundo Obrero*, 1971

The major political goal of the Opus Dei group is to impose the monarchy of Juan Carlos upon Spain as a reaction to the physical decline and degradation of General Franco.

Through this action, the 'Sacred Mafia' intends to perpetuate its power monopoly. The facts confirm our February declaration: Franco's dictatorship is potentially dead but there exists the threat of a neo-Francoist monarchy.

It is now essential to vindicate freedom, to be against any intentions of succession, to require that, regardless of what political regime Spain may have, it must be determined and structured according to the freely expressed will of the Spanish people.

The Opus Dei presented itself with a renovating European and liberalizing program. Facts have demolished such a hypocritical appearance. Surrounded by the hatred of the masses, without even prestige because of its incompetence and robberies even of the capitalists who were formerly impressed by the Opus Dei's technocracy, the Opus Dei lacks a political basis and uses police repression as its essential tool of government.

Immobilism no longer characterizes the Opus Dei; now it is a significant regression, whose clearest symptoms are the six-month-long suspension of Article 18, the unleashing of the criminal elements of the socio-politico brigade, the reform of the Public Order Law to emphasize its fascist features, the strengthening of censorship and the efforts to monopolize the press and all information, and the inability to allow a minimum of 'association' even within the rigid framework of the movement.

Against the Monarchy of Juan Carlos

The present policies of the Opus Dei neatly sketch what Juan Carlos' monarchy would be. It would be the continuation of the Francoist dictatorship with all its defects, aggravated by the degradation of the present power system.

Such a monarchy would imply a greater domination by American imperialists over Spain, since the prospective king, lacking the authority that Franco won among the Spanish right after his military victory of 1939, would have to depend more heavily upon the help of the USA. It is not by chance that Nixon and the CIA are pushing for the succession to take place . . .

The most distinctive feature of the Opus Dei plan is its almost exclusive reliance upon repressive methods; the government has not been able to create any political instruments to support the new monarchy. The latter is thus condemned, even before it is born, to be the monarchy of neo-Francoism, of police and repression. To place Juan Carlos on the throne would be to push Spain to crisis, perhaps to a civil war. All this should be cause for reflection among the bourgeois groups and within the sectors of the army who wish Spain's development to be peaceful.

The present political moment requires that all the opposition forces unambiguously declare themselves to be against the succession maneuver. Only the people of Spain, through the exercise of their sovereignty, have the right to decide Spain's future regime.

The Communist Party, determined partisan of the republic, will accept the people's decision, at the same time maintaining its position if it does not predominate.

The Democratic Alternative

During recent months important progress has been made in our effort to unite labor, democratic and anti-Francoist forces.

In spite of a certain slowing of progress and still existing problems and predictable complications, we believe that important steps have been taken toward the Pact for Liberty. This process is, in itself, a political factor which has an influence on the life of the country.

Among the new facts which have emerged in the opposition camp, we must mention the rupture of Carlism with the regime; the program it approved in Montejurra, which presents clearly democratic positions helps to weaken the regime and to deepen its crisis, and creates favorable conditions for the opposition.

Happily the Communist Party sees an improvement in its relationship with the Socialist Party of Spain, in spite of some remaining disagreements. The establishment of good relations between the two workers' parties is today essential for the struggle for democracy; tomorrow it will be essential for the defense of the working class and the advance towards socialism.

The achievement of an anti-Francoist unity between Euzkadi and Galicia is crucial if the two nationalities are to participate strongly and effectively in the struggle for the democratic alternative.

The conditions which would permit a convergence of a broad spectrum of political forces in support of that alternative are maturing; it includes Carlists and communists, socialists, Christian democrats of several orientations, liberals, the forces from Catalonia, Euzkadi and Galicia, and representative sectors from the church and the army . . .

Liberal and Democratic Tendencies within the Armed Forces

During these trying six months, some fundamental changes have begun to take place within the army. An example is the public confrontation between the 'ultra' generals and those who, in spite of having been appointed by Franco, adopt liberal positions . . .

The Burgos trial abruptly put in evidence the tensions which exist within the armed forces and confirmed our party's predictions about the changes which were taking place. Some military personalities have publicly expressed the need for political parties, workers' unions, a parliament and a government chosen and controlled democratically. Those liberal currents, which reflect the changes of present-day Spain, have antecedents in our country's history.

It is necessary to continue along the path we are already on, with respect to all levels of officers within the army; we must deepen our party's understanding of this important problem; we have to fight simplistic anti-militarism and try to eliminate the prejudices which hinder this fundamental aspect of our task. Any armed forces officer who is loyal to the national interest has a place within the pact for freedom, together with the forces struggling to achieve a democratic alternative and to turn the nefarious page of fascism.

Mundo Obrero, no. 15 (September 4, 1971), pp. 1–3.

16 'Domestic situation, Franco's move toward centrism,' Santiago Carrillo's report to the Eighth Congress of the PCE, 1972

To more deeply involve Spanish capitalist development with the European, thus protecting its own development, the oligarchy must organize itself politically into groups, and inaugurate a new political game with 'democratic' airs, broadening its popular base to maintain its power and promote at least the appearance of minimum formal liberties.

This is all the more necessary as the regrouping of the democratic and popular forces, in spite of repression, has reached such a considerable level that the possibility of such forces drawing in broad sectors of the middle bourgeoisie and perhaps even some of the more dynamic grande bourgeoisie, and the consolidation of the Pact for Liberty have become facts, threatening oligarchic interests . . .

The oligarchy is interested in a sort of change which would not endanger its dominant position. It has in mind a process which would put into its hands all the controls necessary to guide the course of events without risk. Hence 'centrism.' 'Centrism,' as it is being defined, is a concept of political development which uses Franco's decline and his mechanism of succession, not to prolong the power of the 'ultras' – as is the intention of the Caudillo and naturally of his secret counsellor, Carrero Blanco – but rather to establish a representative system, legalizing some hand-led political associations, organizing some mockery of union liberty, vaguely liberalizing the present Cortes and the national council, along with some other additions to the same court, all crowned with the installation of Juan Carlos as monarch.

Certainly the attitude of the 'political class' is not an expression of 'centrism' but rather its caricature, absurdly confirming the real nature of the oligarchy's interest in political change.

Nevertheless, when the possibility arises, even if it be problematic, that such changes will shortly be initiated, beginning with continuist solutions, simple developments of the so-called 'organic democracy,' with infinite brakes and controls designed to control the rhythm from above, the oligarchs will feel tempted since, if such a possibility were to be confirmed, they anticipate that in the process they will find the time and material to set up bourgeois political parties with powerful electoral machines which would guarantee that the change would not fundamentally alter the balance of social forces. The same calculation is made by some who call themselves 'social democrats' and who hope to prosper by being the bail of the 'left' in a rightist combination, although it would be well to ask them: and who bails *you* out?

Definitely 'centrism' is the policy of the social right, which in the face of the exhaustion of the Francoist dictatorship was forced to seek a new political equilibrium, one closer to those who, following the defeat of fascism in Western Europe, have tried to assure the development and social predominance of capitalism.

It follows that the working class, the peasants and the forces of culture who aspire to an authentic democratic and social transformation can entertain no illusions about 'centrism' and its promises. One of the political tasks of the communists is energetically to battle against such illusions and the vacillation, passivity and expectancy – or exasperation – which 'centrism' can engender.

At the same time we must not lose sight of the fact that this policy is developing in a country dominated by fascist laws and institutions; that if its perspective is social conservatism, then the objective, on the condition that the working and democratic forces maintain their critical positions, their independence and their own political action since 'centrism may contribute to undermine those institutions and laws,' is to open certain gaps in the 'bunker' and to use 'its very appearance as a debilitation of the regime,' a strike against the partisans of the dictatorship, driving it towards its death . . .

'Centrism' does not respond to the political needs of Spanish society. 'Centrism' only answers to the fears of the oligarchy. 'Centrism' seeks to remedy with hot towels a social illness which requires the scalpel of the surgeon.

VIII Congreso del PCE, Spanish Communist Party document, 1972, pp. 24–30.

17   'Tactical problems in the movement of masses,' Santiago Carrillo's report to the Eighth Congress of the PCE, 1972

The role of CC.OO and of the mass movements comprising the rest of the social sectors has until now been decisive in reshaping the political forces at work in Spain today.

But now we must be concerned with giving these movements much more breadth and combativeness so that they will be able to impose an authentic democratic alternative.

This confers an enormous practical importance on the tactical problems of the mass movements, because the solution of these problems is going to determine the greater or lesser role of those movements in the unfolding of events; that is to say, of *who* reaches a hegemonic role, the working class and the popular masses, or the right.

Between the political forces linked to the workers' movement and other movements there have existed and still exist important tactical differences.

Before the last trade union elections, for example, a coalition of all the reformist and leftist groups united against the tactic of utilizing legal means to elect true workers' representatives, a tactic defended by the Communist Party . . .

These groups argued that to utilize legal means was to 'integrate oneself' into the 'vertical syndicates,' almost 'to collaborate,' while others insisted that to present workers' candidates was to designate them as propitiatory victims of repression.

Still others argued that this tactic was justified in other times but that it would be inappropriate in the current situation . . .

The important thing is to elucidate a problem of principle of the working class and of the movements of the masses in a period of oppression, when these movements are illegal and persecuted. And this problem does not limit itself to the trade unions, to the utilization of elective offices and the local trade unions, but extends to many forms which exist in each sector and which may be developed to facilitate contact with the vanguard of the masses . . .

The practice of utilizing legal means in combination with extra-legal forms of struggle has isolated the political line of verticalist functionaries of the working masses and has delivered a blow to the vertical trade unions from which they have not been able to recover.

All the progress made by CC.OO has been made precisely through the combination of legal and illegal forms . . .

The just leadership of the workers' movement and the mass movements requires an assimilation of Lenin's tactical principles which, enunciated many years ago, continue to be completely valid, as has been demonstrated by the experience of these movements in our country. As we defend them we know that we invent nothing, as those who fight them from pseudo-leftist positions have invented nothing. It is the repetition of a traditional polemic between Marxist–Leninist revolutionaries and the petit or middle-level bourgeois or reformist revolutionaries. But in this our party must maintain its position firmly in order to propel the growing evolution of the class struggle. It is an option between the actual class struggle and the revolutionary phase.

Meanwhile the range of legal means, or better yet, of the means that practice – although not the laws – has *legalized*, becomes wider every day. They are what we have called the zones of freedom, conquered by the movement of the masses in a bitter struggle. Will these zones become larger or smaller? In spite of the obstinacy of the group currently in power, and although it involves a process of advances and setbacks, everything leads us to believe that in the future, even before the regime changes radically, that group will give way to another – or others – who will find themselves forced to concede certain openings. It seems beyond doubt that events will go in this direction, notwithstanding their present immobility. Our party and the other of the opposition, along with the mass movements, have to be prepared to utilize boldly any new legal opportunity which may present itself to reinforce their ties to the masses, to extend and widen the struggle, and to *occupy* any new position which is favorable to the preparation of the definitive assault on the dictatorship. Not only is it not the time to renounce the use of legal means, but it is necessary to increase the pressure to widen them and it is necessary to be prepared boldly and intelligently to use all such means which may be open to us in the near future . . .

The experience of the present revolutionary and democratic movement, without speaking of the past, has confirmed that elitism and individual terrorism cannot assure the determining role of the revolutionary forces in the current process of change. Such actions awaken at the most a passive sympathy on the part of the masses; they do not drive the masses themselves to be the protagonists of the political-social struggle.

We do not renounce revolutionary violence; but it must be violence of the masses, based in the masses, which in specific moments may be necessary, even indispensable. Men inured to war, prepared for that sort of violence, are molded in demonstrations and commando attacks, in confrontations with the repressive forces, in the daily actions of struggle.

They acquire a knowledge of weapons which one day might be useful to them in the army, into which they go with the intention, not of killing time, but of learning to be good combatants . . .

VIII Congreso del PCE, Spanish Communist Party document, 1972, pp. 59–64.

18 'The party fights for socialism,' Santiago Carrillo's report to the Eighth Congress of the PCE, 1972

The Communist Party fights for the victory of the socialist revolution, for communism . . .

The struggle against the dictatorship, for political liberties, for anti-feudal and anti-monopolist democracy, is, until its culmination in socialism, an uninterrupted process, in which all phases are bound together and conditional upon each other. No phase is for us a goal in itself; rather it is a step toward the final goal.

In each one of their initiatives, no matter how partial and occasional they are, the communists always are aware of their fundamental goal: the conquest of political power by the working class, in alliance with the working peasants and with the forces of culture which propose a classless society.

The communists must always be politically and ideologically prepared to work toward the achievement of these goals. This goal the communists do not conceal.

On the contrary, they openly proclaim it at every proper moment, unlike all the parties which enclose their objectives within the framework of capitalist society, even though the communists may temporarily establish alliance with such parties.

The Communist Party, inspired by Marxism and Leninism, reaffirms that the passage from capitalism to socialism is impossible without a deep political-social revolution.

Hence our party also differs from those political parties and groups which, while declaring themselves to be socialists, reduce their action to a policy of gradual reforms. Without underestimating such reforms, without renouncing the struggle for such reforms – which can better the living conditions of men of both labor and culture and spur social progress, without minimizing the importance which the struggle for reforms can have in the expansion of consciousness and the organization of a revolutionary platform from which to launch the struggle for power, the Communist Party proclaims that simple reforms will never be sufficient to transform capitalist society into socialist society . . .

The revolution is, without a doubt, an act of violence, regardless of the degree and forms which it takes.

It is an act of violence because without imposition and coercion it is impossible to depose the dominant classes and socialize the ownership of the fundamental means of production; it is impossible to change. No dominant class abandons its position without resistance.

The Communist Party conceives a 'dictatorship of the proletariat' to be a period of transition from capitalism to socialism, a period which has not been obviated by modern historic development. But it has been transformed, as a consequence of the wide and revolutionary development of the productive forces, in so far as a dictatorship can no longer be conceived of as only the power of laborers, but as the *power of all workers*, including the forces of culture, who have a direct role in modern production and who stand in opposition to capitalism . . .

However, the notion of dictatorship, in this case, cannot be identified with the vulgar notion of dictatorship, considered as the *totalitarian power* of a minority imposing, through the state apparatus, its arbitrary will upon the majority of the population . . .

Even the forms of the dictatorship of the proletariat in economically backward countries, where the proletariat was a minority and the majority of the forces of culture were on the side of the overthrown classes, are not models which necessarily have to repeat themselves in the most developed countries, and under modern historic circumstances, when socialism is already a great world force − thanks to the Russian October and other revolutions; and in the rich Russian experience there are both positive and negative lessons from which it is necessary to learn.

The Marxist concept of the dictatorship of the revolutionary socialist forces in the period of transition is identified, dialectically, with the broadest democracy. It does not necessarily mean a sole dominant party or the bureaucratic deformities which sometimes have made it appear to be the exercise of power by one man, or one group of men.

In the developed capitalist countries under the most democratic forms, the dictatorship of capitalism legally exists because all the institutions and laws of the state affirm the inviolability of private ownership of the means of production. In this lies the *capitalist dictatorship* characteristic of the most prominent modern *bourgeois democracies* . . .

Although with a radically different foundation, the dictatorship of the socialist revolutionary forces can, through laws and institutions designed to defend collective social ownership, and to spur the development of socialist forms (increasingly moving toward communism), act by guaranteeing formal democratic liberties to the bourgeois opposition until, having become an antique monument, it extinguishes itself through an exhausted economic, social and ideological base.

The workers in power will not need to impose any official philosophy and will respect freedom of thought and freedom of intellectual and artistic creation. The Marxist−Leninist concept of the world will win minds, and at the same time will evolve and enrich itself through a free and open dialogue with other ideologies.

Within such a context, socialist democracy can adopt the most effective forms of pluralism which, when combined with other forms of worker democracy, will have even less in common with traditional, class-antagonist politics.

VIII Congreso del PCE, Spanish Communist Party document, 1972, pp. 80−3.

19   Communiqué of the Central Committee of the PCE, 1973

The Central Committee believes that the formation of the Carrero Blanco government testifies to the decline of General Franco's role as dictator. A historic period, born with the triumph of fascism over democracy following the bloody war of 1936−9, is on the verge of closing. The physical exhaustion of the dictator coincides with the political exhaustion of a regime which has maintained itself through terror and which is in open contradiction with the reality of Spanish society today and of the world which surrounds us.

Broad strata of the petite and middle bourgeoisie, and even part of the monopolist bourgeoisie, understand that fascism has become a brake to its own development. Currents in favor of political change are strengthening within these strata.

Nevertheless, the Francoist bureaucracy of the movement, which in the last three decades of its power monopoly has become accustomed to considering the country a non-transferable property, is maneuvering to assure that Francoism will survive Franco.

The government of Carrero Blanco, the shadow of the Caudillo who claimed to prefer the atomic bomb to socialism, who has covered up the 'Matesa' scandal and others and who covertly launched the 'ultra' mutiny of last May, seeks, as he himself has declared in a speech before the Cortes, 'to leave him well tied and completely tied.' That is to say, to make sure that Juan Carlos will be the docile instrument of the Francoist bureaucracy, that monarchy will simply mean the continuation of the *movimiento*'s political monopoly.

The maneuvers of Franco and his successor show the emptiness of every attempt at political change initiated by the regime. The Spanish people cannot expect that the fascists who govern today will present them with a gift of political liberty. To win it, there is no other way than to do away with the present political system . . .

Mundo Obrero, no. 15 (September 1973), p. 2.

20   'Francoism or monopoly capitalism,' manifesto program of the PCE, 1975

Under the influence of monopoly capital, the power of the state has been considerably modified. In other times, when the bourgeoisie was still a revolutionary class, its power stood for that of all citizens. Slowly, however, the growth and the power of the state appeared ever more clearly as the power of the bourgeois class.

Today the state is the power of the highest level of the bourgeoisie, the monopolists; the power of these true modern feudalists is not of the whole bourgeoisie.

Using the power of the state, the monopolistic groups not only allow themselves to repress and exploit the working class and the salaried masses, but by means of monopoly control of basic products, of credit, taxation, dominant positions in foreign commerce, drain the petite and middle bourgeoisie of a considerable part of the surplus value they have accumulated and of an even larger fraction of the emoluments of the liberal professions.

The power of monopoly capital methodically organizes the destruction of a small and medium property; it provokes the ruin of countless firms. And all that not to the benefit of society and progress, as it claims, but to the advantage of a group of financial feudalists.

More precisely, the net domination of the capitalist state by the capitalist minority warrants that that state be ever more opposed, not only by its radical enemy, the working class, but also by broad sectors of the same bourgeoisie, who have not attained the level of the monopolists.

The confrontations between the agrarian sectors and the apparatus of the state, which robs them and openly aims for their destruction, are the 'plat du jour' in the advanced capitalist nations of Europe, a phenomenon also manifested in our country.

The organization of small- and medium-sized merchants, relentlessly pursued by supermarkets, also sustain a more or less confused struggle against that kind of state.

A sector of the bourgeoisie itself thus confronts a type of state which has become the exclusive instrument of the monopolist class.

In this way there develops in modern capitalist society a socio-political contradiction between the vast majority of the population, including the salaried workers, middle classes, and the petite and middle bourgeoisie of the city and country, on the one hand, and, on the other, an oligarchic monopolist minority. In Spain that contradiction is aggravated even more by the dual monopolistic and landholding character of the oligarchy.

The objective existence of this contradiction does not mean that all those affected social forces are aware of it. It is the duty of the Communist Party and other progressive forces in the country to make it known, and to put it in the open to create a broad *anti-monopolist* and *anti-latifundist* front capable of resolving it in favor of the popular forces.

Manifesto program of the PCE, cf. pp. 34–6.

21 'Socialism in developed countries, socialism in democracy,' manifesto program of the PCE, 1975

No great Marxist theorist has argued for the notion of a single party, not even a *Communist Party legally favored over other parties.* Nor for the consecration of Marxism as the *official state ideology; nor the subjection of culture and art to administrative canons; nor the monopoly of information by the state; nor the existence of one sole model of socialism* . . .

The reality is that the socialism which would triumph in the developed countries differs from that which triumphed in more backward countries. In the developed countries, for the victory of the revolution, it will suffice to have adequate utilization of modern means of production and of existing services to guarantee an immediate redistribution which would satisfy the needs of the populace, creating the conditions needed to put an end to social inequalities. This high level of material development, together with democratic traditions, cultural development and the exercise of customary individual freedoms, will be the basis of its consolidation . . .

The Spanish Route to Socialism

The Communist Party of Spain believes that in the present conditions of the world, as the struggle for socialism in developed countries is entering a phase of concretion, it is its duty to formulate theoretically and practically the forms and appropriate routes for the revolution in our country; to find what is new, what is specific in our development, in order to win the great masses of the working class and the populace for the cause of socialism.

The Communist Party of Spain believes that the route, the form and the appropriate model of socialism for our country will differ in many respects from those which are known today. National peculiarities, worldview and historical experience will determine those forms, together with our revolutionary ability and the determination of the masses.

The Communist Party of Spain rejects the dogma which alleges that the forms which socialism has had in other countries are universally valid.

It is clear — and Lenin had already foreseen it — *that the triumph of socialism in one or several countries of developed capitalism will logically carry within itself more developed forms of socialism, and will*

help all socialism to raise itself to a higher, more evolved level . . .

Spanish Communist Party document, 1975, pp. 17–19.

22 'Political situation in Spain,' press conference by Santiago Carrillo in Paris, 1976

We find ourselves before a government that obstinately pursues Spanish democrats – not only the communists – and that obstinately carries on a repressive policy which closely resembles that applied by the regime during Franco's lifetime; a government that does not take a single step towards democratization; and I will go as far as saying it has only one policy: with repression and immobilism, it is a policy of trying to divide the forces of Spanish democratic opposition, tolerating one part of those forces, and persecuting the other; saying clearly: we are willing to accept those members of the opposition who give their consent to what in Spain are called the 'constitution' and the 'laws,' but which in fact continue to be the constitution and the laws of fascism.

This policy has not prevented the opposition from unifying and, as you know, a Commission of Coordination has been created from the old Junta Democratica and the old Plataforma de Convergencia Democratica.

In such conditions we consider it inevitable that the workers' movement, the popular movement and the youth movement will continue to develop and grow, exerting political pressure in favor of democracy. This is not a policy of impatient men. It is the only means which remain today for the democratic forces in our country to influence Spanish political life, and to try to arrive at a real democratic change.

The ultra-right is not so strong in Spain; the ultra-right is weak. And to demystify for once and for all that government that we have today in Spain, it must be said that it is not a government of the center. The centrists are in the democratic opposition. In the present government are the right, the extreme right and the slightly less right. But the centrists are out of the government; they are with the democratic opposition.

The problem is: how to find the exit? How to

overcome this situation without provoking the conditions of a confrontation, of bloodshed in our country? We believe that there still exists a way: the way of concerted, negotiated democratic rupture.

This does mean, at least in our judgement – and I do not want to compromise the opinions of all the opposition on this question – in our judgement, the united opposition could negotiate with the army; it could negotiate with the church; it could negotiate with the economic powers; it could even negotiate – but only united into a single bloc, not divided – with elements in the present government who call themselves reformists, and who in private let it be known that they are convinced of the failure of politics in this government. A negotiation of this type could lead to a democratic rupture without the shedding of blood in our country . . .

The truth is that we have a monarchy. This monarchy is heir to the Francoist regime. This, in principle, in my view, compromises the opportunities of the monarchy, and at the same time greatly conditions the politics of the king. I do not have great hope that the king will be able to open the way to democracy in Spain. I will also say that from the moment that the re-establishment of democracy means that it is necessary to give to the people the opportunity [to take a stand] concerning the form of the state, I have no hope.

But if by a miracle – I do not believe much in miracles, but rather in the power of the people and the power of democratic opposition – if by a miracle produced by the power of the people, and by the power of democratic opposition, the king accepted the creation of a government of broad democratic coalition, the king agreed to consult with the people, and to convoke constituent elections so that the people could decide the form of government, the form of the state, we would pose no obstacle to such a possibility . . .

Nuestra Bandera, no. 84 (March–April, 1976), pp. 3–8.

23 Press conference by Santiago Carrillo and Felipe Gonzalez (PSOE), 1977

CARRILLO: There is a series of questions on which the wide democratic movement in this country is not in complete agreement and on which we must continue our discussions, if our two parties are to agree.

GONZALEZ: When one analyzes a situation like the one our country is passing through, the points of convergence are, fortunately, greater than those of divergence. To cite some themes: everyone in this country is aware that early municipal elections are necessary soon; one cannot prolong that theme; it is a point of similarity, including the criteria which should be maintained, of proportionality in the representation, and so on.

CARRILLO: It is a dialogue which we have initiated and which we are going to continue, because it is in the interests of the PSOE and the PCE to contribute in this way to the solution of the political and economic problems facing Spain today.

We have declared our support, not to an alliance of a general character, but to an agreement in those places where the municipal elections are stated in terms of struggle against the traditional apparatus of political bosses. There are certain differences on this problem. What is important, I think, is that we have agreed to examine that question more concretely when the municipal law comes out, and above all, that we have agreed upon the necessity of leaving the road open, whatever the electoral tactic may be, so that after the elections it will be possible to establish municipal government councils in those places where they are stipulated.

Mundo Obrero, no. 49 (December 8–14, 1977), p. 3.

24 Thesis of the Ninth Congress of the PCE, 1978

Thesis I The Process of Change
The democratic rupture has not occurred all at one time; instead, it operates through successive phases, accumulating reforms attendant upon the installation of a system of democratic liberties.

The radical political rupture realized all at once, with the installation of a provisional government, as was publicly recommended by the Communist Party and the Junta Democratica, was impossible because of several factors, among which we can single out the reformist orientation taken by some forces of the opposition and that springing from the Franco regime itself, as well as by international pressure, fundamentally European and American, fearful of the hegemony of the working class and the forces of the left. These factors influenced the failure of the mass movement to achieve the strength necessary to cause a radical political rupture, despite the movement's size and importance.

The absence of a provisional government, based on a broad coalition, which would decree measures of authentic democratization before convoking elections, has not only influenced electoral results, but has also obliged the country to live in an ambiguous situation in which a popularly elected Cortes coexists with dictatorial deputations and municipal governments, in which the new class syndicates still cross paths with the substance of the old vertical apparatus, and so on. All this gives some the distorted impression that nothing has changed, and others, if they perceive the reality of the changes, an impression of the extreme fragility of the changes.

Despite the fact that political change is developing in ways other than those proposed by the PCE, it is correct to affirm that its course is testimony to the correctness of the policy of national reconciliation and the Pact for Liberty. The policy of national reconciliation was established by the PCE in 1956 as a *totally new factor in Spanish politics*. It was no more and no less than a proposal to all political and social forces to accept a common civic framework; a new legal, democratic framework to free political struggles from the cloaks of intolerance and fanaticism in which they had been wrapped until then; in order to move them to a new level of patriotism and citizenship in which opposing ideologies and class conflicts would not acquire the dramatic contours which frequently bloodied the history of the country, especially during the twenty years of fascism. These battles must be fought within the parliament, the municipalities, the social organizations, the press, and so on, and *not on the battleground of civil war*. It was not a matter of confusing classes or ideologies, which would be unacceptable to a party like the PCE which will never renounce being the party of the working class and of the progressive forces of the country, nor its aims of putting an end to the regime of the exploitation of man by man, by means of the implementation of socialism and communism. It is a matter of these struggles flowing through the channels of liberty and tolerance.

The desire of the PCE is to banish from our country the climate of intolerance, of fanaticism and of political irrationality; this desire has been proven by its known stands on the monarchy, the national flag and the church.

The PCE has amply contributed to the creation of this new socio-political climate, just as much by these positions as by those adopted toward the remaining political forces. The PCE has treated the political parties of the right as political adversaries, not as enemies. The climate thus achieved reduces the danger of civil confrontations, and creates the conditions for the disappearance of the viscerally anti-communist ideology, so habitual in the Spanish right.

To situate the working class in a hegemonic position, representing the general interests of the country, leaning on liberty and democracy, such has been the guiding principle of the policies of the PCE throughout the last forty years.

One of the fundamental preoccupations of the PCE has been to obtain a greater political role for the workers, through the presence in one way or another of the working class in the government. This has brought the party to formulate the policy of democratic concentration. This is a policy which includes the fundamental aspects of the content of the Pact for Liberty, established in the concrete conditions of the past electoral period.

The agreements of Moncloa represent a success of the policy of democratic national concentration pushed forward by the Communist Party, and have begun to give a greater place to the representative forces of the working class in the elaboration of governmental solutions.

Every pact is the result of a transaction in which the parties have to yield something in order to reach a common end. In that which concerns the workers, the sacrifice of not improving the conditions of life in 1978 has been accepted, because the workers are conscious of the fact that the most important thing today is the conservation and widening of the stands of labor if one wishes to avoid in the short run even greater sacrifices. In addition, among the workers the idea that the class struggle must today adopt forms other than those which it had under the dictatorship is taking root. The strategy of labor today, in addition to bettering living and working conditions, will have to pay greater attention each day to the conquest of political, economic and social power.

The Communist Party proclaims its end to be the socialist transformation of society. The consolidation of democratic liberties should open the way to political and social democracy, which represents the first steps of the march towards socialism, and, subsequently, towards a truly communist society, in which man reaches his fullest freedom. Political and social democracy is not a type of third road between capitalism and socialism; it is the transitional stage between capitalism and socialism, carried ahead by the alliance between the forces of labor and of culture, on the basis of the consensus of the great majority of society.

The hegemony of those forces will not be achieved by electoral victory alone and access to power, but rather by a series of political and social transformations which will involve, by their own dialectic, changes among the correlations of political, economic, cultural and ideological forces. The new power of the alliance of the forces of labor and culture will have to secure itself by leaning on the majority will of the people, of the electors, and will have to weaken the positions of the oligarchic minorities which are today dominant.

We communists favor the unity of all the Spanish peoples into a federal state, whose goal will be to achieve the effective self-government of each nationality, territorial unity, region, in accordance with the will of the people. Federalism would be a superior form of unity in Spain, combining diversity and cohesion, assuring in the matters reserved to the competence of the Spanish state the homogeneity indispensable to modern development.

These aspects, as well as the democratic transformation of agriculture with the defense of peasant family property, the encouragement of democratic co-operativism in production and distribution, or worker participation in the management of public enterprises, and many others, give this march towards political and social democracy the character of a *new model of growth, leading to a new model of society.*

Mundo Obrero (February 2–8, 1978), pp. 1–3.

25 Article in *Nuestra Bandera,* 1978

The conception of the democratic route to socialism logically leads to the conclusion that the theory of the dictatorship of the proletariat is no longer valid as a definition of the type of state necessary for the transition to socialism. If we were to enclose ourselves within a Leninist framework, we, in 'applying' what Lenin has written, would find ourselves in a dead-end alley in the face of today's fundamental problem of finding the political forms needed to achieve the socialist transformation of the industrially advanced societies.

Because of this, we, and some other communist parties, have formulated the conception of the democratic route to socialism. This means, in sum, that the advance to socialism will be achieved through a widening and deepening of democracy; with complete respect for all political and individual freedoms, and with a plurality of parties, and so on. Elections, parliament and representative democracy will undertake a fundamental role. And at the same time forms of direct democracy will appear, which, in the educational system, health, local life, and so on, will allow an even larger role for the masses in the solution of their problems. The advance to socialism will be the democratization of society and the democratization of the state.

In reference to the party, we, although maintaining the conception of democratic centralism, do not think that Lenin's writings, which were written when the Communist Party was a clandestine, illegal party, can be followed literally. Lenin's concept of the party, outlined in *What Is To Be Done?* in 1903, argues for a party formed principally by a group of professional revolutionaries, with very strict discipline and organization. But even Lenin, in the period of 1905 and afterwards, modified that concept. In some of his works he even refers to the possibility that nuclei of revolutionary workers, without strict adhesion, would collectively enter the party, then called the Social Democratic Party . . .

What is the implementation of democratic centralism going to mean for us today? Something very different from what it was under conditions of secrecy. It is going to mean the election of all agencies by the militants, with democratic forms and with secret votes. At the same time, a truly democratic centralism seems to me to be indispensable if the party is to have political cohesion and the ability to act as a party. For example, the 'legalization' of factions which is practiced in some socialist parties, as in the Italian one, does not contribute, in my opinion, to a raising of the level of the democratic life of a party. Perhaps the opposite happens. What we need is to reach a free and true discussion of ideas, resolving differences by the law of the majority. In fact, many of those who criticize us for applying democratic centralism are more centralist than we. Now, in order to apply that democratic centralism which we need, it would be absurd to refer to Lenin's *What Is To Be Done?*

Nuestra Bandera, no. 90 (1978), pp. 40–1.

26 S. Sanchez Montero, 'In preparation for the Ninth Congress. A new communist party for a new communist policy,' 1978

The Party as an Instrument

The organizational problems of the party cannot be posed in an abstract form, beginning with immutable principles and methods, but must take a concrete form, in accord with the party's situation and policy. For it is in this way that the means are part of the ends, the party organization, its forms and principles, are part of its policy.

The policy of the Communist Party of Spain is 'Eurocommunism.' That is to say, a policy whose goal is to arrive at the construction of socialist society in Spain as the first phase of communist society, through a democratic route, of the unfolding of democracy in all aspects of the life of the society – political, economic, cultural, and so on; a democratic and pluralistic socialism which would guarantee the widest development of freedom for *all* men and women, and with the independence of each communist party which will not depend on any leading center, although it will be imbued with the spirit of international solidarity toward all peoples in their struggle for democracy and socialism; a Eurocommunist policy which arises from a situation in which growing freedom coexists with the remains of the dictatorial apparatus, still very powerful, and whose dismantling is a fundamental task for the consolidation of democracy.

The organization of the party must be in line with that policy, it must be the instrument capable of fulfilling it . . .

We need a mass party. A party whose social composition will be a reflection of its policy and in which, together with the majority of working militants of industry and agriculture, there will be a high percentage of women, peasants, professionals, intellectuals, technicians, small businessmen and artisans. A party composed of activists, militants and adherents in which each member fulfills the voluntary contribution dictated by his revolutionary consciousness and his opportunities, in which one can militate and occupy leadership offices of the highest level without abdicating religious beliefs and practices – if one is a believer – in which there exists a deep respect for the intimacy and conscience of its members, of whom it only demands the fulfilling of their duties as such. A party which is democratic in its internal functioning and life, more democratic than any other, in which each militant can express and defend his opinions with complete freedom and in which decisions will be made by the majority. A party barren of any messianic spirit, which does not aspire to be the dominant party or the only Marxist and revolutionary party, but which aspires to construct socialism together with the others. But a party which cannot be confused with the others and whose objective necessity for the success of the struggle for socialism is as important or even more so than yesterday, whose task is less heroic than in the past, but more difficult and complex.

But 'Eurocommunism' has nothing to do with reformist social democracy. The goal of social democracy is not the construction of socialist society which would make capitalism and all its results disappear, but the reform of capitalism in order to file down its most wounding raw edges, to have it work better, and more definitively, to perpetuate itself. 'Eurocommunism' is the revolutionary, Marxist policy which would be achieved today in a country like Spain by the creators of Marxism and the great Marxist revolutionaries if they were to live here . . .

The Communist Party of Spain is, should be and has to be a new communist party for a new communist policy.

Nuestra Bandera, no. 90 (1978), pp. 43–5.

PART TWO

Alliance Policy

Introduction to Part Two

The realization that in Western Europe societies, because of their characteristics and structures, the working class is not in a position to acquire and manage power without the support of other social strata is one of the fundamental principles of the euro-communist position. In particular, it implies that in order to pursue and bring about the far-reaching changes they advocate, eurocommunist parties have to seek alliances with classes and groups which are beyond the traditional 'constituency' of Marxist–Leninist parties. All eurocommunist leaders seem to agree that the complexity and magnitude of the tasks implicit in the transformation of society in a socialist direction require broad popular consent. For the French communists, an electoral majority backed by popular mobilization would be sufficient. For the Spanish and Italians, any attempt to transform society with only 51 per cent of the vote would run the risk of igniting counter-revolution. For these parties the experience of Allende in Chile is an oft-cited example.

In both its theoretical and its strategic underpinnings, the eurocommunist search for allies cannot be fully understood unless it is placed in the broader context of the strategy of the national, peaceful road to socialism. Indeed, it is almost inconceivable to think of one without thinking of the other. The pursuit and eventual success of the strategy of the peaceful, national road to socialism requires the formation of a broad consensus on the modality, content and direction of change.

With regard to French and Italian communists, the quest for new allies was articulated as early as the immediate post-Second World War period. Basic to the PCI's and PCF's position was the argument that the alliance among diverse political and social forces which had been molded by the struggle against Nazi Germany should continue in the postwar period, that it should form the basis on which their respective countries should be reconstructed and, in the long run, the socialist society built. The PCI went farthest in this direction, with its appeal to the middle strata and to Catholics.

After an attenuation of this approach in the Cold War period, the PCI re-launched the alliance policy, in both its political and its social aspects, after 1956. The PCF, on the contrary, did not again undertake an approach to the Socialist Party until the 1960s, and the attempt to build support among the middle classes was poorly developed until the early 1970s. After a prolonged period of isolation, the PCE launched an alliance policy not dissimilar to that of the Italians; the initial justification and goal for the PCE's search for alliances was to bring about the collapse of the Francoist regime, but the policy has been maintained subsequently.

Irrespective of their national differences, the extent to which social alliances have become a cardinal element of the parties' strategies has been reflected in the increasing heterogeneity of their electorates and of their membership. This has required a trans-formation of the parties' traditional organizational structure, internal dynamics and electoral behavior. In the case of the PCI, this transformation occurred in the immediate postwar period, when the party began to assume the features of a mass party with very large membership, few restrictions on member recruitment and few if any required activities of those already in the party ranks. In the 1970s, the PCI has also increasingly used catch-all electoral techniques. The PCF has been much slower to abandon the restrictive membership criteria, attention to intensive socialization of members and rigorous requirements for participation of those who wish to belong characteristic of a cadre party, despite recent and sporadic appeals to a heterogeneous electorate. Even after the breakdown of the Francoist regime, the PCE has found it quite difficult to become a mass party and to extend its electoral ties into middle-class and Catholic electorates.

The alliance policy pursued by the parties can also be understood in terms of the parties' attempts to become representatives of all productive forces in society. As traditional definitions of the working class became more and more blurred following the economic and technological development of post-Second World War Europe, the parties found themselves forced to go 'beyond the working class,' or at least to expand their definition of the working class to include the new classes 'produced' by techno-logical progress and by the reshuffling of society's class composition caused by the evolution of monopoly capitalism. Clearly the parties could no longer remain anchored to the *ouvrièrisme* of old, ignoring the far-reaching transformations of Western European labor markets and patterns of socioeconomic stratification. The expansion of monopoly capitalism, interpreted as a tendency towards economic and financial concentration and as a trend towards the centralization of the economic system, came to be seen as the overriding source of social and economic injustice in society, and thus the target against which all productive forces, and not simply the working class, should be rallied. The lines of societal cleavages at the basis of the eurocommunist parties' vision of capitalist society have, consequently, undergone a transformation; society is still basically divided into two blocs, but substantial segments of the middle class are also negatively affected by the evolution of monopoly capitalism, thus becoming potential allies of the working class. New strata produced by the technological revolution have also become available as allies of the proletariat. Even independent workers, whether professionals or artisans, are victimized by monopoly capitalism.

The problem posed for the parties has not only been to extend their class alliances. Operating as they do in countries in which Catholicism and the Catholic Church exercise great influence, the parties have been compelled to overcome their old hostility towards religion, to abandon old dogmas about the inherent incompatibility between Catholicism and Marxism–Leninism. This effort has been most conspicuous and of longest standing in the case of the PCI. As early as the immediate postwar period, the party sought to accommodate Catholic values and to open its organization to Catholics. The PCE also has given great attention to this issue. Like the Italians, it has confronted a Catholic Church closely allied with its major opposition, in both the Francoist and post-Franco periods. Thus, as with the PCI, reducing the salience of the religious issue has been seen as crucial to strategic success. Given the different role of the religious issue in France, the Catholic question has played a much less prominent role in the PCF's alliance policy.

A third factor has combined with the two preceding ones to make the policy of alliances a possibility as much as a choice: the lowering of domestic political barriers. Throughout the period in which the parties were ghettoized or relegated to the margins of the political system, or, as in the case of the PCE, forced into clandestinity, the search for political and electoral alliances with non-working-class strata and

Catholics had little hope of success, despite the parties' rhetoric. As anti-communist domestic barriers broke down, the new possibilities created an incentive for the parties to elaborate a full-fledged policy intended to gain the support of strata which had been encapsulated in the anti-communist camp. In the case of the PCI this required less of a departure from existing social alliance policy than was the case with the other two parties. This can perhaps be explained by the fact that for a variety of reasons, including the PCI's own efforts, it had never been as socially and politically isolated as were the PCF and PCE. With regard to political alliances, the emergence of a less Manichean domestic scenario has permitted the search for agreements and compromises with government and other non-communist political forces. In this respect, the PCI and PCE have reached out farther than has the French party.

The issue of the nature of the relations that should develop between the working class, its parties, and the strata, social groups and political parties towards which the policy of alliances is addressed remains the source of much confusion. It would be misleading to conceive of the policy of alliances as if the eurocommunists were attempting to become catch-all parties, willing to garner the support of all strata of society at the complete expense of ideology and program. While their short-term conception of alliances does envision equality among all allies and, especially in the cases of the PCI and PCE, allows for a softening of programmatic goals in order to build linkages, the long-term conception implies the acquisition of a leading role by the working class in this bloc of alliances: that is, the assumption by the working class of a hegemonic role. The ideological and political justifications given by Eurocommunist parties for the concept of hegemony are too complex to be analyzed here. Suffice it to say that for eurocommunist parties the working class's claim to a hegemonic position, both in the alliance which should act as a vehicle for the transformation of society and in the socialist society itself, is ultimately justified by the argument that only the working class can genuinely represent the interests of all social strata and laboring forces. Yet how such hegemony is to be attained, on the basis of what program, and with what specific compromises, is often unclear. In the case of the PCI, for instance, there is a repeated tension between two schools of thought: one which stresses the role of alliances among the organized representatives of various strata and groups (an emphasis on alliances 'from above'), and one which advocates alliances built directly between the working class and other strata, circumventing the social and political representatives of the latter (alliances 'from below'). Paralleling this difference is one over the appropriate balance between social mobilization, on the one hand, and parliamentary and electoral maneuver, on the other, as both the means to acquire allies and the uses to which they should be put.

In addition to differing viewpoints towards social alliances within and between the parties, there are also marked differences among the parties with respect to the types of political alliances to be pursued. These differences are largely a consequence of different opportunities for alliance-building that the three countries offer.

The divergence between French and Italian communists is particularly striking here. While the former have oriented their policy towards the realization of a programmatic agreement with the Socialist Party and other forces of the left (the Common Program), the latter have developed the strategy of the 'historic compromise,' meaning the search for a convergence among all democratic, change-oriented parties and forces. The policy of national reconciliation pursued by the Spanish Communists is undoubtedly more similar to the strategic posture of Italians than to that of their French counterparts, especially in its underlying goal of achieving an alliance among all 'forces of labor and culture.'

To explain these divergencies one need begin by observing that the French political system makes an alliance with non-leftist forces difficult to achieve and victory by a left alliance possible. Throughout the Fifth Republic the trend has been towards the emergence of a bi-polar system, one pole revolving around a moderate force and the other consisting of the leftist parties and forces; the division between these two blocs has sharpened rather than attenuated in the post-de Gaulle years. The greater fragmentation of the Italian political system, the different nature of the major non-leftist party, the DC, the nature of the relations between socialists and communists and the seeming impossibility of a significant leftist majority – these are some of the factors which make it possible and necessary, in the PCI's view, to broaden the horizon of its alliance policy. In Spain, the policy of national reconciliation finds its legitimacy in the unity-in-action which has characterized the behavior of all democratic forces in their struggle against the Francoist regime. Of course, the historical and ideological heritage and traditions of eurocommunist parties are also instrumental in causing differences among their respective alliance policies. The PCF has, for instance, been traditionally less inclined to abandon *ouvrièriste* tendencies, to open up to new classes and strata; while already in the period of anti-fascist opposition the PCI has sought to develop an extensive policy of alliances, one drawing on its Gramscian heritage.

In the pluralist vision of a socialist society coloring eurocommunist parties' strategies and behavior, the policy of alliances is indeed more than a means for the acquisition of power. It is supposed to serve as the instrument through which changes will be brought about, the driving force of the march towards the socialist society. The pluralism inherent in a strategy for building socialism based on the convergence and consensus among different classes and strata is to become the *Leitmotif* of the brand of socialism envisioned by the eurocommunist parties.

MAURIZIO VANNICELLI

DOCUMENTS FOR PART TWO

ITALIAN Communist Party:
Varieties of the Historic Bloc

FRENCH Communist Party:
The Heritage of Frontism

SPANISH Communist Party:
The Search for National Reconciliation

ITALIAN Communist Party: Varieties of the Historic Bloc

1 Palmiro Togliatti's speech in Reggio Emilia, September 24, 1946

'Middle class,' as the words imply, should be a social level that finds itself between two extremes of the scale and should include those between the salaried employee and the land and business proprietors, yet include neither the one nor the other. The idea of the 'middle class,' explained in such a way, should be clear enough; it is, however, a rich group containing solid components. Between the employee and the capitalist there exists a vast range of social groups. The sharecropper and the tenant both belong to the middle class, neither one a landowner, both paying rent to have land, yet at the same time neither one is salaried. Also belonging to this class are the small landowners, who do indeed possess the land which they cultivate, but cannot be classified with the capitalists and great landowners who belong to the upper echelons of society. There are also varied groups consisting of the small businessmen, retailers, craftsmen and small contractors. Finally, there are the intellectuals who range from schoolteachers, priests, freelance professionals, to men of great culture, poets, artists, scientists and writers. If all these groups can be considered to belong to the so-called 'middle class,' it is absurd to maintain that they represent a uniform body which would be of the same political philosophy and ideology. It is wrong, therefore, to assert that such a body, composed of such numerous and varied groups, would not by definition be compatible with the Communist Party.

We are a party in which the middle class is represented to a great extent by those who live in the country, but also, although not in the same measure, by those of the city. Our greatest successes have been achieved in those zones where we have had the greatest number of members and supporters from among the middle class; furthermore, among the more than 4 million voters who support us, the middle class is well represented. Even more can be said: for example, thanks to our party and its political actions, the misunderstandings between the proletarians of the country and the city as well as of intermediate rural groups were overcome – misunderstandings which were created and propagated by those reformist leaders who, with regard to these intermediate groups, could do nothing but cry for their 'proletarianization,' which was and is an economic, political and historical mistake.

If we enter into a discussion of interests, we will be able to ascertain that there is no contrast between the interests which we defend and those of the intermediate social groups. The best proof of this is furnished by the fact that these groups have found in us, the communists, their most reliable protector. We desire an explanation of these facts by those who babble on about the incompatibility between us and the middle class, and pretend to monopolize the latter.

The contrasts and incompatibilities, they tell us, are not of interests but of ideas. Workers and laborers would adhere to the Communist Party and follow it willingly because they find in its propaganda ideas with which they are familiar, such as solidarity, social progress, emancipation from work, while members of the middle class would cling to other ideas, those of liberty, for example, or of the autonomous development of the human being, ideas to which we would not be capable of ascribing enough importance.

Therefore, according to these new prophets, the idea of liberty is completely alien to us. But how does one explain, then, that where a barricade is raised behind which a battle for liberty is fought, everywhere and always the workers of the vanguard have shed their blood; there, everywhere and always, the communist flag has been raised and men and women of the poorest classes of society have entered into the battle.

Only in a society founded upon non-compulsory work, emancipation from slavery and its associated freedoms, will a human being be truly free and will mankind be in a position to live an existence worthy of itself. Why should this, which is our ideal, be inaccessible to the middle class, and why should we, who live and fight for this ideal, be considered the enemies of the human development?

It seems to me that those who talk of a supposed incompatibility between the communists and the middle class have in mind something quite different from what they say, and that their real intentions are far from that of being attentive and objective in their analysis of political currents and social tendencies. I have the impression that their intentions are none other than to introduce a division within the nation of Italy, a division which could be disastrous to the future of democracy. Italy abounds in intermediate groups, both in rural and in urban areas. If an artificial division were created between these groups and parties like our own, which are decisively democratic and anti-fascist, or if the impression could be generated that there exists between these parties and human culture a certain incompatibility, without a doubt very important political results could be obtained, but in whose favor? Certainly not in favor of the people – their unity would be threatened; certainly not in favor of democracy – it could not triumph without the necessary unity of the popular forces; but rather in favor of those reactionary groups which seek to destroy the unity of the people, because in the unity of the people they see their privileges permanently threatened . . .

If Italy wishes to guarantee a better future for itself, it must introduce into its social structure and into its political and economic life modifications such that reconstruction can soon be realized in the interest of all the working classes, and that the inevitable costs fall upon the wealthy, and not upon the poor, upon those responsible for this national catastrophe and not upon its victims.

It should be clear that we are not proposing a reconstruction based upon communist or socialist principles. The country as a whole is not ready for such a transformation, even though certain sectors have matured enough, and even though as we all know that across Europe, with few exceptions, economic development is heading in the direction of socialism. What is ready to be done, however, is the necessary rebuilding of the economy, keeping in mind the general interests of the nation and not the exclusive interests of a few privileged groups, a reconstruction which does not permit these old reactionary groups to once again take over the domination and direction of Italian life. This is why we say that a 'new course' of economics and economic policies is needed.

When we speak of this 'new course' we are accused of wishing to suppress private initiative. This is not true. We desire that room be reserved for the development of private concerns, especially those of the small businessman. Now, however, we insist that the state direct the entire work of reconstruction, in order to co-ordinate and direct these private concerns, encouraging the development of free enterprise . . .

With things being as they are, it seems evident to me that the adoption of a 'new course' for our economy should generate interest not only among the workers and laborers, but among also many other groups within the 'middle class.' The workers and laborers, that is, the proletarians, can always resort to a strike as a means of defense, but the middle class does not have this possibility. The day in which the old plutocratic groups could return to power marks the moment when the 'middle class' will find itself economically crushed and seeing its ideals trampled by criminals and rogues. Therefore, collaboration between the workers with the more advanced ideas and the members of the middle class is indispensable, not only for the welfare of the country, but for the best defense of the interests of the middle class.

Palmiro Togliatti, *Opere Scelte* (Rome: Editori Riuniti, 1974), cf. pp. 456–84.

2 Palmiro Togliatti's speech to the Constituent Assembly on Article 7 of the constitution, March 25, 1947

And now on to the second part [of the Constitutional Article 7], the one about which there has been much debate and on which the most important voting split in this hall will happen. Here we touch the bottom line of the relationship between the Italian state and the Catholic Church. Now, we have not involved ourselves in this problem just today or just during the discussions in the first subcommittee and in the committee of seventy-five. Since the beginning of 1946, when the Fifth Congress of our party was held in Rome, we have dedicated a far from minor part of our debates to the examining of this problem, and our position was then defined as follows in my relation to the Congress. Let me quote from it.

'Since the church organization' – I said then – 'will keep on having its center in our country, and since a conflict with it would disturb the conscience of many citizens, we must regulate with care our position towards the Catholic Church and the religious problem. Our position is also in this regard consequently democratic. We request and want that there be in the Italian Constitution the assurance of freedom of conscience, faith, cult, religious propaganda and organization. We consider these freedoms as the very basic democratic freedoms, that must be reinstituted and defended against any threat from wherever it may come. Beside this there are other questions that involve the church and have been regulated by the Lateran Pacts. For us the solution given to the Roman question is something final, which has closed and done away for ever with one problem. To the Lateran Treaty there is indissolubly tied the Concordat. This is in our opinion an instrument of an international kind, beside being of a national one, and we understand very well that it could not be revised other than by a bilateral agreement, save for violations that might lead either side to denounce it ...'

As you can see, there are here some fundamental points, to which we have a duty to keep faithful, to which we have tried to keep faithful, to which I believe we have kept faithful so far.

First fundamental point: the request for freedom of conscience, of faith, of cult, of religious propaganda and organization. The first draft of the Constitution, as for this, satisfies us. We will endorse all those proposals tending to pacify more and more the conscience of all believers of all faiths, by guaranteeing to them all the liberty they are used to to carry out their cult and propaganda.

Second point: we consider as final the solution to the Roman question, and we do not want to reopen it in any way.

Third point: we think that the Concordat is a bilateral pact, and that it can be changed only bilaterally ...

The colleagues of DC allegiance sometimes talk as if considering themselves the only defenders of the freedom of religious conscience of the Catholic masses. I do not think that any left-wing party would want to leave them the exclusive right to this function.

In our party too there exist, and I think they are the majority of the members, Catholic citizens, and we are asserters and defenders of the freedom of religious conscience. It is true we defend this freedom in the manner of a democratic, modern progressive, communist party, if you wish; but, at any rate, we defend it. We do not leave you the exclusive right to this function ...

And now we are facing the future and new difficulties for our country: we are facing political and economic problems that are accumulating and getting tangled with each other. In this situation we need religious peace, and we cannot let it be disturbed by any means.

Now the opposite of 'peace' is 'war.' It is true that to wage war there must be two sides and that one of them can always declare – as you are doing, comrade Nenni – 'we don't want war;' but to declare war only one side is needed. We must take this into account.

This is the real factual situation nowadays. We, the Communist Party, who from the moment we started to behave legally in the country have always had among our principal objectives that of maintaining the religious peace, cannot overlook this situation, but we rather have to take it into account and change according to it our position and, consequently, our vote.

And at this point my declaration of vote could change into an appeal: I could address myself to our socialist colleagues, to the colleagues from other sides, inviting them to vote with us, to vote as we will vote. But essentially we vote taking our responsibility into account; and we understand very well that our responsibility is maybe heavier than that of any other member of this assembly ... Our responsibility is greater, in substance, also than that of our socialist colleagues', because we are not only a working-class party, but we are considered that workers' most advanced party, and in substance the majority of the working class orients its action according to how our party is moving.

This is why it is not only to our personal, individual conscience and convictions that we appeal, as do other colleagues, when deciding how to vote. Essentially we appeal to this political responsibility of ours, and to the way we realize the political line we have drawn for ourselves in the present situation of the country.

The working class does not desire a division for religious reasons, just as it does not want a division between us and the socialists. We are therefore glad, even if we shall vote in disaccord with the Socialist Party, that this fact does not open a confrontation between us. But at the same time we feel that it is our duty to make all efforts so that a division and a confrontation will not open up between the communist and socialist masses on one side and the Catholic workers on the other ...

This, DC colleagues, is the point I wanted to reach, because from it I derive two lessons: the first is that there is no confrontation between the socialist regime and the religious conscience of a people; the second is that there is not a confrontation even between a socialist regime and the religious freedom of the church, and particularly the Catholic one.

This is the deepest position of principle, which does not only justify, but explains, the side we take in this voting. We want to make this truth clearer and clearer for the Italian people. It is therefore useless for you to ask yourselves superfluous questions: it is useless for you to wonder what is behind it. There is nothing else behind it but this: our vote will be given according to (a) persuasion and by discipline: by discipline to a political line, according to (b) persuasion that this policy is the one that best reflects the interests of the Italian nation . . .

Our fight is a fight for the rebirth of our country, for its political, economic and social renewal. In this fight we want the workers' unity, first of all, and around it we want to make the political and moral unity of the whole nation become a reality. Let us disperse the shadows which are preventing the realization of this unity! By giving the vote we give, we are sacrificing, therefore, nothing from ourselves to the end. We are today what we have been throughout the fight for liberation and throughout the period of deep crisis and reconstruction, begun after the end of the war. We are today what we shall be tomorrow, in the struggle we shall lead along with you, next to you – if you wish – or in a confrontation with you, for reconstruction, renewal, rebirth in Italy . . .

Luciano Gruppi (ed.), *Il compromesso storico* (Rome: Editori Riuniti, 1977), pp. 131–47.

3   Theses of the Ninth Congress of the PCI, January 30 to February 4, 1960

The activities of the monopolies and clerical groups have met powerful resistance from the movements led by the workers' vanguard, which – if they have not yet been able to break the clerical monopoly – have noticeably modified the political picture of the country and brought about the present crisis of the Christian democrats and its system of alliances...

It was the failure of the integralistic experiment which brought about the crisis of the Christian democrats.

The origin of this crisis lies in the opposing pressures that the monopolies, on one hand, and the organized masses on the other, exert on the Catholic party. The great monopolies press to have a political force at their disposal which expresses and realizes perfectly its interests; this pressure is increasingly reflected by the DC as the governing party, and to a certain extent by the other bourgeois parties.

But the experience has demonstrated that where a strong democratic movement exists, one which is united, guided by a revolutionary vanguard, an inter-class Catholic party of the masses can identify itself with the interests of the great monopolies only at the price of losing many ties with the masses of workers and with the lower and middle levels of the middle class.

The present crisis of the DC is, therefore, an aspect of the more general crisis which is beginning to shake the whole of Italian society . . .

The collaboration between the PCI and the PSI is not an obstacle to greater unity between the democratic forces, but rather it provides the circumstances for an effective intervention in the crisis of the middle-class political alliance, and for uniting the forces of the Catholics, republicans and social democrats – in which opposition against the present domination by reactionary groups is growing – in the fight for democracy.

The communists look with favor upon the fact that at the heart of the DC Party, of the present directing body, which is shielded by its conservative position and by the Cold War, there now exists an opposing faction which, when confronted by the imbalance of Italian society and the current changes in the world, admits the need for a different foreign policy, asks for a planned intervention of the state in the economy, and would like a more independent policy toward the great privileged groups . . .

The crisis of the DC is the crisis of the interclass movement. In order to push it to a definite end, it is essential to intensify the battle for a democratic renewal of the country, prohibiting conservative groups from putting, by means of a co-operative policy, a brake on the contradictions within the Catholic movement; increasing the contradictions between these groups and the Catholic masses; attempting – by means of contact with the various forces of the Catholic world – to establish a solid ground of understanding with the workers' movement. The communists maintain that if the democratic Catholic forces want to contribute actively to the work of democratic renewal, and combat the resistance of the monopolistic groups which they denounce, they must confront the problem of overcoming anti-communism, liberate themselves from subjection to clericalism, demand political autonomy for the Catholic movement, participate in the battles for the unity of the masses. These conditions seek to prevent their manipulation by groups of clerical leaders.

The communists refute the false interpretations of the influential character that the policies of the PCI would have on an agreement with the Catholic world; they emphasize the historical reasons which stand at the origins of these policies.

The key to an agreement with the Catholic world is not for the PCI to work out a variation of the traditional communist tactic of a front from the bottom, which was applied between the two wars toward the base of social democracy. It is peculiar to this country, and it is founded upon the analysis of the driving forces of the Italian revolution begun by Gramsci, or, in other words, upon the recognition that the Catholic Church and the Catholic movement not only influence the nuclei of the working class in Italy, but also influence a large part of the farming population and the middle classes which today can and must participate as such in the construction of a new society.

Therefore, since the victory of socialism in Italy is tied to the formation of a broader and more articulate bloc of forces than the alliance between the poor farmers and workers, an agreement with the Catholic world is an aspect of the Italian road to socialism, as a prospect of united battles and of alliances not only with the Catholic masses, but also with their organizations.

PCI party publication, Rome, 1960.

4   Draft theses for the Eleventh Congress of the PCI, October 1965

The failure of the center-left's projected reforms has opened up a deep political crisis within the socialist forces and the more democratic Catholic forces. We cannot, however, foster the hope that they will spontaneously flow back to the left. If there is to be a new majority we must wage a vigorous political and ideological struggle . . . A new majority cannot therefore be formed simply from a convergence of political forces as they are; the existing political forces must be led into new positions; this will involve ramified action which takes account of the objective causes of their involution and stimulates them to change, aiding united action in all fields. What we need is a new, wider and more solid unity of all democratic forces.

The argument of the socialist right and part of the Christian Democratic left that there is no alternative to the center-left, as there is no majority except the present one, is false. This different majority does not exist if one considers the problem in purely static and parliamentary terms. The center-left, too, with its contradictory aims, would never have been born without all the joint struggles which led to the downfall of centrism.

It is therefore all the more absurd to think that a real shift to the left can be carried out without mobilizing the masses, without struggles, without the rupture of the present class and political equilibrium.

The first step in this direction is, therefore, the struggle to bring down the present government. The Italian conservative forces today have no alternative solutions which can ensure a stable mass basis for their power; the rupture of the present government formula would put the Christian Democrats with their back to the wall. It would be rather difficult for the Christian Democrats to form an alliance with the forces to their right. While the collapse of the center-left would not only facilitate unity among the left, it would also allow the Christian Democrat left to regain its freedom of action. The survival of this government, even on the present precarious basis, worsens the situation, harms the relationship between the left-wing forces and strengthens the conservative ranks . . .

The failure of the center-left is also the failure of a conception of an alliance between the socialist working-class movement and the Catholic movement, limited to the search for an agreement with the Christian Democratic Party and based on abandoning the fight against its interclass nature and its conservative tendencies. This has reduced the encounter between the DC and the PSI to a compromise for the division of power; it has helped the *dorotei* [right-wing ruling clique] to establish their hegemony and has deprived this alliance of both the breadth and the content with which communists have always conceived the dialogue with the Catholics.

Since the DC has governed for long years in the interests of the bourgeoisie, it is deeply interwoven with the capitalist structure and with the ruling economic forces. It is only the long united struggle of the left against it which has managed to make it show any willingness to change. By weakening its attack on the DC's interclass role, the PCI was bound to help the conservative forces in the DC seriously damage the DC left and allow the party to abandon the 'democratic challenge' it had been forced to throw down; the PSI was thus also bound to strengthen the tendency to consider the alliance with the PSI merely as a means to split the working-class movement.

The Christian Democratic Party, with its conservative position and the predominant weight it exercises on the political life of Italian Catholics, is today the principal obstacle to wider consciousness among the Catholic workers of the need to attack the strong points of capitalistic power. This is yet another reason why dialogue must be carried on without mitigating the attack against the DC, trying to ensure all Catholics are politically independent . . .

L'Unità, November 7, 1965.

5   Luigi Longo's speech to the Central Committee, October 13–17, 1969

We hold that a new government, oriented to the left and capable of dealing concretely with the questions raised by the masses, heeding their needs and aspirations and giving a valid, solid foundation to Italian democracy, is necessary and urgent. This does not mean raising the question of communist participation in government today. But we must say that no government can consider itself oriented to the left if it is based on the prejudicial preclusion of the Communist Party from all participation in basic decisions concerning national life. Such a preclusion underlay the orientation of the center-left, and it inevitably led to a policy contrary to the demands and aspirations of the popular masses, which in our representative assemblies are to a large extent represented by the Communist Party and identify with it. Such a preclusion in itself robs all good intentions of their credibility, if for no other reason than the fact that, without the contribution of the Communist Party the Italian left today is not strong enough to overcome the conservative opposition of the right and thus carry through the necessary political and social reforms . . .

In my opinion, it is evident that today, within the line of struggle for the conquest of new positions of power and decision, the question cannot be raised as an immediate problem on the government level, but rather in terms of the future, in relation to the mass struggle. But it must be raised in terms of a not too distant future, because the rapid development of these struggles and the unifying processes at work must permit us to concentrate our efforts on a rapid development in the evolution and orientation of the left-wing forces. To continue with the absurd and out-dated preclusions that have already brought on the failure of the center-left, the crisis of the left-wing bloc, and even the crisis of the Christian Democratic power system, means to abandon all hope of finding a valid solution to the present political situation and to the many problems now on the agenda . . .

The possibility of bringing about a radical shift in the center-left policy of stagnation and impotence concretely emerged after the May 1968 elections. The outcome of these elections created the possibility of opposing the Christian Democratic Party with a bloc of forces capable of representing a valid alternative to the center-left. We said then that the moment had come to develop a unity-oriented relationship between the left-wing forces within the government coalition parties and the parties of the left-wing opposition. And we committed ourselves to doing everything possible to contribute to the creation of a united left-wing grouping based on a plurality of positions and contributions and on the autonomy of the various forces participating . . .

We must say that during the past year considerable progress has been made in this direction, although still not enough in relation to existing needs and possibilities. The powerful development of the united trade union and popular movement, the isolation of the social democratic sector, which has now set up as a separate party, and the greater combativeness of the Socialist Party, of the left wings of the Catholic Workers' Association and the Christian Democratic Party show that we have been moving in the right direction and that not only we, but all the forces of the left, must continue along this line. It is in the struggles themselves and around concrete problems that we must day by day build the great new left-wing bloc, whose task it is to give positive outlets to the struggles of the democratic working masses and to indicate those goals that can unite all our efforts behind a real policy of renewal and social progress, capable of offering a clear alternative to the center-left. For this reason, we raise the question of a radical change in the policy hitherto followed by the center-left coalition. It is within the framework of this need that the problem of relations with the communists, so widely discussed these days, must be seen; but we must repeat what we have already said many times before: these discussions on relations with the communists are purely academic or simply attempts to avoid the real problems of the moment unless they are conceived in terms of our party as it really is, with its political positions and its organization.

It must be clear that we are available only for a radical shift in Italian politics, a shift that cannot take place within the framework and on the basis of the center-left, but only through its elimination. We are therefore available, as we have said many times, for convergence and even momentary and partial collaboration with all the left-wing forces, lay and Catholic, with all movements and groups interested in the goals and struggles of the working masses. We have never conceived our policy in relation to government posts and patronage to be won, but rather in relation to problems to be solved and our participation in political and social decisions that concern the workers.

For this reason we have never favored the 'so much the worse, so much the better' philosophy, and we have always accompanied our opposition and criticism in parliament and in the country with constructive proposals aimed at satisfying the basic needs of the popular masses, promoting democratic progress and safeguarding freedom and peace.

For this reason, we are willing to establish relations of collaboration and understanding with the democratic and left-wing forces at all political and organizational levels ... The problem for all democrats is to unite in a common effort to open a new road that promises substantial transformations in the present social system, that gives political expression to the democratic battles of the working class and prepares the conditions for a left-wing alternative.

L'Unità, October 17, 1969.

6   Enrico Berlinguer, 'Working class and social bloc,' 1971

The revolutions which have been successful have been those which have seen a combination of different social forces on the battlefield, which have been able to realize systems of alliances which have made the working class and the other more advanced groups of the society strong enough to combat and overwhelm the resistance of the dominating classes.

It was in this way that Russia won the first great proletarian revolution in October of 1917, founded on the alliance between the workers and the peasants. And thus was won the Chinese Revolution. But even other revolutions – such as the Vietnamese and Cuban – were initially peasant revolutions on a national scale, but developed into and succeeded as revolutions with social characteristics and contents only in as much as they were founded upon sufficiently large social blocs, at the head of which were placed proletarian nuclei and other advanced groups which knew how to inspire themselves with the principles of Marxism and the ideals of socialism, which knew how correctly to take advantage, before and after the conquest of power, of the new conditions, of the worldwide power ratios determined by the existence of a state like the Soviet Union, by the role it had in the defeat of Nazism, by its power and by its politics, besides or in addition to the influence exerted today by other socialist states...

It is true that the revolutions which have thus far been victorious have not been in developed capitalist countries, in countries from which could come the affirmation of a 'model' and of a new idea of socialism. It would be absurd to conclude from that that in these countries the revolution must assume the characteristics of purely a workers' revolution. On the contrary: if the workers' dream has been fatal to the bourgeoisie where it has been manifested, it is one hundred times more so in countries where capitalism is developed, in countries like Italy – rich in social stratification within the working class itself and in which the middle class is strong enough to maintain a system of alliances with and support from the masses. Especially in these cases it is necessary that the proletariat succeeds in introducing a social force which is capable of upsetting the middle-class domination. It is true that a social force comparable to that which is found in Russia in the form of the alliance between workers and peasants has not yet been found in the countries of developed capitalism, where the alliance itself between the workers and farmers does not represent a huge majority of the people and therefore is as such insufficient to win. But precisely this makes it even more evident that the problem here rests in overcoming the social democratic and corporate tendencies which lie at the heart of the workers' movement itself.

There exist new conditions and opportunities for new advancements. But because of this, the reactionary forces, ranging from right political groups, internal and external, to left-center, far from lowering their weapons and giving up, are ready to take advantage of every occasion to recuperate lost territory and to drive back the workers' movement. We observe the symptoms of this every day. The situation could therefore develop in a direction of great new advancements or in a direction of regression.

Under these conditions the major problem, which has yet to be resolved, is that of the quality and size of the social and political coalitions which can be developed with regard to the different prospects in Italy today: this is the problem on which we are working together with the other forces of the workers' movement, on which the moderate forces are working, as well as the conservative and reformist forces, and on which the reactionary groups and forces are working as well.

Until now, the adversary has not been able to create around itself a coalition strong enough to permit a victorious offensive or to stabilize its present political assets: on the contrary, at the heart of the conservative-reactionary front there exist sharp contrasts and signs of crisis, while the array of the progressive and democratic forces marches forward substantially united. There are, however, vast areas and social forces which are not yet clear about the directions toward which they could turn: for this reason the party remains open.

Rinascita, January 15, 1971, pp. 1–3.

7   Enrico Berlinguer's report to the Central Committee in preparation for the Fourteenth Congress of the PCI, March 10, 1974

Relations with the Catholic world and the crisis in the Christian Democratic Party
The fate of the democratic system and the chances for achieving a new political leadership for the country depend to a large extent on how relations among the left forces, and particularly between communists and socialists, develop, and on the direction Christian Democratic policy takes.

We have always considered a correct policy towards the Catholic world as essential. Naturally this policy cannot be reduced to a policy towards the Christian Democratic Party alone. The Catholic movement is a worldwide reality, and the working-class movement must have a policy on this scale as well . . .

We look to the whole of the social and political movements of Italian Catholics, in a constant effort to establish a climate of understanding, convergence and agreement with the broad Catholic masses: an effort that has already produced beneficial effects for the struggles of the working masses and the cause of democracy and has avoided irreparable lacerations in the people and the country. Over the past few years important Catholic forces and organizations have moved to the left, in some cases taking openly anti-capitalist and anti-imperialist stands and action. Another effect of this shift to the left has been a fall in the Christian Democratic electorate and stronger pressure from the popular forces within the Christian Democratic Party.

Broader working-class alliances with the middle classes and in action on the great national questions
The problem today is to develop further a unity-oriented process extending into all social environments, promoting initiatives and struggles that strengthen the workers' unity, raise the level of organization of the popular masses and broaden and consolidate the alliances of the working class.

The general goal is clear: prevent the right-wing forces from expanding their social base and following, and indeed increasingly reduce this following, at the same time winning new parts of the population over to democratic and left positions . . .

A positive development has occurred in the positions and orientations of the artisans, first and foremost, but also among certain strata of small farmers, merchants and small and medium-sized industrialists. In all these directions there are many possibilities for further important progress, in demanding and obtaining measures to promote the activities and initiatives of these strata, in increasing the size and influence of their associations and in expanding and strengthening points of convergence with the working class and its battles for renewal. Serious imbalances in the party's action in this field have emerged and must be overcome by our organizations.

As we have often said, the alliance policy of the working class does not lie solely in the search for points of convergence with intermediate categories occupying more or less well-defined positions in the economic and social structure. This aspect is certainly essential, but it is not the only one that counts. The alliance policy of the working class must also express its national capacity to tackle the country's big problems – problems which interest and bring together whole areas of society – and to fight for their solution: its capacity, that is, to point to goals that are not only economic and social, but directly concern our civil and democratic development and that answer the needs and aspirations of the vast majority of our citizens.

It is therefore clear that we look and appeal to all the forces and expressions of the Catholic world. And it is also clear that we shall continue to work to win new and increasingly broad support for our party and the other left parties among Catholic voters.

But while conducting this manifold political and ideological action towards the Catholic world as a whole, we have never ceased working on the problem of establishing a positive relationship with the Christian Democratic Party . . .

The need to fight for a far-reaching change in Christian Democratic positions and orientations has always been clear to us. What we have denied and continue to deny is the seriousness, much less the Marxist basis, of a line based on the idea that the 'nature' of the Christian Democratic Party is somehow immutable.

The Christian Democratic Party is a party containing deep contradictions. It is a party tied to the interests of big economic concentrations, to renter interests and parasitic groups; but it is also a party that, because of its origins, certain of its traditions and the presence within its ranks and electorate of masses of middle-class citizens, peasants, women and also workers, must take popular needs and aspirations into account.

Our initiative must use these contradictions to increase the weight of the popular, anti-fascist, democratic and unity-oriented components within and around the Christian Democratic Party and reduce that of the more conservative, narrow-minded and sectarian groups. To abandon this action to transform one of the basic elements in Italian political reality in favor of intoxicating slogans that can produce no result, save dimming the critical capacities and judgement of a few groups of young people, is pure infantilism . . .

The need for frank discussion between the PCI and the PSI to attain a higher level of unity within the workers' movement
The development of effective, non-divergent action by the two great parties of the Italian left, the development of unity-oriented relations between the PCI and the PSI, is an essential condition for pushing forward all the processes of renewal, including those that are necessary and possible in the Catholic world and within the Christian Democratic Party itself. This is an essential question, as is the common commitment of socialists and communists to open the road to a transformation of society in the socialist direction. Nor did we in any way underrate this question when we said that it was illusory to think that all our problems would be solved if the left were to gain 51 per cent of the popular vote. We repeat, a shift in the correlation of forces between the Christian Democrats and the left-wing parties in favor of the latter – and there are already concrete signs of such a shift – constitutes one of the most important conditions for bringing about the necessary change in the orientations and position of the Christian Democrats themselves.

The great role of the united trade union and the fight against moderate, sectorial and extremist trends
The progress made over the past years by the trade union movement along the road to unity and autonomy and in elaboration and struggle for general goals of economic development and social reform is a decisive factor for the solidity of the Italian democratic system and stands as one of the most important guarantees for the future of this system. A united trade union movement that intervenes not only in matters of wage demands for the employed but also on questions concerning the great goals of democracy and the economic and social progress of the whole country is a strong-point for republican democracy and in line with the historic traditions of Italian trade unionism. We therefore welcome, with great satisfaction, the important progress made as concerns the line now guiding the trade union movement as a whole: a line that defends the interests of the workers, peasants, technicians and all the working people, both employed and unemployed, in the North and South, and at the same time looks to the general interests of the nation. Over the past years this line has produced results of great importance.

As far as we are concerned as a party, we do not intend to intervene or interfere in the specific questions of trade union life. But it is obvious that when questions concerning the future of the Italian working-class movement are being debated among the workers, the communists are called on to make their own contribution to this debate, with a sense of responsibility, but also with a firm, clear political and ideological orientation.

The Italian Communists, nos 5–6 (special issue), 1974, pp. 104–21.

8   Enrico Berlinguer's report to the Fourteenth Congress of the PCI, March 1975

Many people see the 'historic compromise' as essentially a proposal for a new government alliance and formula including the PCI. This interpretation undoubtedly grasps one essential aspect of our proposal, since today the creation of a parliamentary and government majority, including the great force for renewal represented by the PCI, would certainly be an innovation of no small account. But this interpretation does not entirely grasp the scope or express all the aspects of the 'historic compromise.' The question of the PCI's entrance into the government area is undoubtedly decisive, but while confirming that we are ready at all times to shoulder our responsibilities, we must also point out that the moment in which this will take place does not depend on us alone. We are not, nor will we ever be, beggars, and we are not in any hurry. If anything, the urgency is objective; it lies in the state of the country, in the seriousness of the present crisis. We are aware of this urgency and we do not feel we are alone in this awareness, but we know that the march towards a new majority will not be easy and smooth, because we too have conditions to lay down for our entrance into such a majority.

But while the question of the PCI's direct participation in government responsibility is undoubtedly an important aspect of the 'historic compromise' strategy – since this event would in any case mean a change of course, given who we are and what we represent – it would be mistaken to reduce our whole strategy to this one aspect.

In fact, on the one hand, the strategy of the 'historic compromise' goes beyond the question of communist participation in government and, on the other, it is already today, and can increasingly become in the immediate future, a valid line for tackling and correctly and positively solving the country's most pressing problem, quite aside from the formation of a new government majority.

It is precisely in this dual sense that we have said that it is not entirely correct to talk about the 'historic compromise' only as a proposal, and much less as an 'offer,' to the other democratic parties. Naturally the 'historic compromise' is also a proposal, but in a broader, higher sense, in that it is addressed not only to the other parties, but to all citizens of democratic orientation, to the whole country. But precisely for this reason we prefer to use the term *strategy*, and to use it in the sense of a strategy to get Italy out of the crisis, to renew it and to save and develop democracy: a strategy not only for the PCI, but for the whole country. In this sense the 'historic compromise' is a more advanced level of struggle and, at the same time, a challenge that the Communist Party throws out to all the other democratic forces, and first and foremost to those who stubbornly insist on maintaining the country's political life within the confines of old formulas, more or less refurbished or dressed up in new forms, but suffering from the common, insurmountable weakness of having been tried at length again and again and having all failed.

Underlying the strategy of the 'historic compromise,' which, it must be remembered, was elaborated in more organic form after the tragic events in Chile, but in reference to the peculiarities of the Italian situation, there is a very simple concept: namely, that to save democracy and achieve a general renewal of society and public life in Italy will require great struggles, exceptional efforts and commitment by the widest variety of popular energies. Precisely because this renewal is opposed by economic groups that, while they may be narrow, are powerful and aggressive, it is essential to isolate them and prevent them from establishing a mass base: this is why we maintain that a broad majority must be created that includes all the popular and democratic forces and takes account of the different ideological origins and political traditions with which they identify and around which they are organized.

They are those who abstractly object that with such a broad majority there would hardly be any opposition forces left and thus one of the essential factors in democratic dialectics would disappear. But such arguments have more to do with exercises in formal logic than with concrete Italian reality. The day on which the democratic forces jointly undertake real action to renew society and public life there will certainly be no lack of opposition from the privileged groups. And precisely in order to deal with this opposition, at the same time maintaining a framework of democratic guarantees and full respect for all constitutional freedoms, the majority supporting the government will need the broadest possible consensus and the widest possible participation and initiative by the working masses, in a relationship of confidence between the country's political leadership and the people, in all its major social, political and ideological expressions.

But while we see the 'historic compromise' as the only prospect capable of producing and guaranteeing a democratic transformation of the country, we must remember that it also indicates the correct method to tackle and solve the country's present and most pressing problems.

L'Unità, March 19, 1975.

9   Gerardo Chiaromonte, 'The force of unity,' 1977

I do not think it is correct to speak of 'two societies.' I think it is more correct to speak of 'one society,' although characterized by deep and lacerating contradictions. Where does the difference between the two expressions lie? It lies in the emphasis (the necessary emphasis) on the historical and political (as well as social) origins of the problems so dramatically facing us today. Without this emphasis, one not only risks serious blunders on the specifically cultural level, but there is also danger of falling into a sort of impotence, failing to see that however difficult the problems emerging in our society may be they can and must be solved, tackling them for what they are, on the political and cultural level.

There is no doubt (and there is now very broad agreement on this) that the type of development that Italy experienced in the years of monopoly expansion aggravated beyond all measure existing distortions and imbalances and created new ones. The policy of the DC, its shortsightedness and improvidence, the unproductiveness and corruption of its power system, did the rest. Did shortcomings and errors on the part of the workers' movement, both political and trade union, also play a certain role? Yes, certainly, but no one can deny that the major responsibilities lie with the ruling capitalist classes and the DC. The present crisis broke over this society, already so deeply imbalanced, further aggravating the various contra-

dictions to the point where they have become lacerations and even disruption. The condition of youth (in an economic situation that offers no or almost no prospects of jobs for young people and with an education system in total disarray) is certainly one of these contradictions, perhaps the most lacerating.

The nature of the crisis that has hit Italy (in a deeper, more serious way than the other capitalist countries) is such as to exacerbate the contradictions between the employed and the unemployed, between North and South, between men and women, between the older and younger generations. The danger lies in the emergence and growth of real lacerations within the people: it is this that makes the present crisis perverse, and this is also the point of departure for our analysis of the Italian situation and our policy. A policy that aims at relieving and overcoming these contradictions, at unity of the people and working masses around a policy for reform and renewal, for expansion of the productive base, austerity and the search for new ways of living, studying and working. This, we feel, is the only line possible today for the forces that want renewal, because it is the only line that seeks to avoid the perverse effects of the crisis (which could be fatal for the democratic and socialist battle for a long period) and the only line that works to build a new society and new values, without succumbing, more or less consciously, to the myths and values that one says one wants to destroy, and without working, in practice, for division and defeat of the people. In fact, when one attacks the force that today has the greatest capacity for aggregation, the employed working class and its trade union movement, one is working for division . . .

Naturally – as we have repeatedly said over the past months – all this does not mean lessening our efforts to ensure that the policy the occupied working class in the North and South carries forward is increasingly a truly national policy, capable of embracing the aspirations and expectations of the most excluded strata of society, in substance, the general interests of the country and its economic, social, civil and political development.

Our line for unity among all the democratic and popular forces derives from this vision of things. We remain convinced that to get the country out of the crisis requires a very broad unity of quite different social and political forces. It does not depend on us if the nation does not have the government it so greatly and urgently needs. We did not choose the present political framework (as it is called). Everyone recalls the proposals we advanced after June 20 for the formation of a government capable of tackling an emergency situation. Everyone knows the proposals we advance today. Just the same, we think we did well to permit the formation of the present government last summer: first, because it has represented a step forward with respect to the previous situations (with the official, no longer masked, dropping of anti-communist discrimination, which had been the foundation of the DC's dominance and power system); secondly, because these months of work have led to positive results in various fields, and, above all, have enabled us to defend the bargaining power, both trade union and political, of the working class and other strata of workers in the storm of the crisis; thirdly, because a different arrangement (with the PCI in opposition) would have made it impossible to form any government after June 20, aggravating the crisis of Italian society without opening any prospects for a positive solution to the political crisis.

Frankly, it does not seem that there can be any other line for us, unless we want to work, in the immediate future, for a worsening of the situation (in the insane and absurd hope that this could benefit the workers' and democratic movement) or, in the longer run, to create a dangerous pole of aggregation (the whole DC) for the divisive pressures unleashed by the lacerating contradictions of the crisis (this, in our opinion, would be the prospect, if we were to abandon the policy of unity of all the democratic and popular forces for another line).

The Italian Communists, no. 1 (January–March 1977), pp. 78–82.

10 Enrico Berlinguer's speech at the conclusion of the national *L'Unità* festival, September 17, 1978

The more immediate goal is the creation of a democratic Europe of the workers, capable of making an effective autonomous contribution to the cause of international détente, peace and international co-operation. The final goal is to build, in conditions of democracy and peace, a socialist democracy, an original, new model of socialist society, according to the needs and with the features already indicated. But these are issues we shall deal with in greater depth at our coming Congress.

The term 'Eurocommunism' has been used. Actually what we are dealing with are orientations and proposals on the part of a number of West European communist parties which, despite differences in their positions, share the features and goals I have mentioned, with the aim of promoting, not a 'Eurocommunism' in opposition to a 'Euro-socialism,' but rather a common searching and collaboration among all the working-class and democratic forces of Western Europe.

Nor can we be charged with 'Eurocentrism,' since the task facing the working-class and advanced democratic forces of Europe is just the opposite; namely, to make its contribution to the solution of the problems of underdevelopment, rooting out poverty, hunger and neo-colonialism in the world, and to a worldwide revolutionary process that advances towards socialism as the highest form of democracy and freedom.

We have always desired and encouraged debate with our socialist comrades, as well as with other forces that identify with socialism: a common effort in research and deeper study on political and theoretical themes concerning both past, present and future . . .

We do not forget that an essential, peculiar characteristic of the PSI has always been its nature as a party that fights to bring society out of the capitalist mechanism, that fights for socialism, a characteristic that distinguishes it from the social democratic parties.

In Italy great common struggles, unity in the trade unions and local administrations, and the policy of national democratic unity have cemented a deep bond of unity between communists and socialists. And, in substance, developments in the field of theoretical reflection, as concerns both historiography and the analysis of today's reality, trends and prospects, have tended to bring the two parties closer together . . .

We understand and certainly do not oppose the PSI's aspiration to expand its influence and increase its role. But we believe that this must take place within the context of an expansion of the initiative and strength of the left as a whole, of the entire united workers' movement.

In addition, we believe that the left parties must develop their action and unity not in opposition to the democratic, progressive forces in the Catholic world and efforts to promote popular, democratic policies within the DC, but rather as a factor in favor of a broader democratic and popular unity, above and beyond the question of government formulas, as a factor in favor of a substantial understanding among all the Italian popular and democratic forces, which is indispensable if we are to solve the big problems facing the country. This is the strategy and method we call the 'historic compromise.'

In expanding left strength and initiative in the battle to win more advanced positions, there is a specific role for the PSI as well as for the PCI, there is room for both parties to move ahead. There is need to strengthen their unity, on the basis of rigorous respect for, and recognition of, their mutual autonomy and respective peculiar characteristics and roles . . .

What has made it possible to avoid economic and financial catastrophe, thus preserving the minimum, elementary conditions for survival of the country's social and political fabric? The major social factor lies in that maturity and sense of national responsibility shown by the working class and its united trade union organizations. The political factor lies in the at least partial success of the line we communists have always fought for, a line that has led to a closer relationship and greater solidarity – although not yet to the recognition of full equal dignity – among the popular and democratic parties.

Thanks to this solidarity, the Italian Republic has been able to avert the other great danger that has arisen in this period: the danger of capitulation to the terrorist conspiracy and attacks that have developed in a spiral of bloodshed, culminating in the kidnapping and assassination of Mr Moro.

This capitulation has not occurred. The country, the democratic forces, the public powers have held strong, rejecting the blackmail of the terrorists and those who are maneuvering them. And we claim an undeniably determinant role in this firm stand on the part of the democratic state.

What would have happened if the PCI had not thrown its weight in defense of the republic and against subversion?

How does the DC see the policy of emergency and what is it doing within its own ranks in this regard? Mr Zaccagnini has recently said (as we have been saying for a long time) that emergency policy must become an opportunity to change our society and make it more 'just.' But to reach this goal it is absolutely necessary to curtail the influence of those groups and categories I mentioned above. In short, the working class cannot bear the burden of overhaul and renewal alone, with the rest of society remaining as it is.

The DC must make up its mind
The working class can contain its wage demands within certain limits, and indeed it is already doing so. But the DC must make up its mind: big wealth, big property, the big tax evaders must finally be made to pay their part. And the manner in which those strata and categories I mentioned before live, work and earn must also be changed and modernized, although this may require a gradual process to avoid the danger that they will shift *en masse* into reactionary positions.

This problem concerns all the parties, but in particular it concerns the DC; because it is the DC that has governed the country in the manner we all know, aggravating to the utmost those distortions, inefficiencies and wastes in economic and social life and in the state that are today choking the country and make it so difficult to solve the big problems of employment, the South, the pay jungle, the schools, the public administration and the justice system. Emergency must be used for this, to begin a solution to these problems . . . .

The present Christian Democratic leadership has abandoned the line of head-on confrontation followed by the DC for a number of years and defeated first in the 1974 divorce referendum and then in the 1975 regional elections. The defeat of that line also sparked a rank and file movement for renewal within the DC. But while we recognize this new element, we are still far from being able to say that the DC appears capable of really freeing itself of its deeply rooted patronage and parasitic incrustations. And it is of vital interest to the country that the DC move in this direction. And while this is a job that falls primarily to the DC itself, there is no doubt that its success also depends on the attitude and action of the other parties and, above all, of our own party.

Hence our line, which combines the element of criticism, denunciation, struggle and competition with the element of dialogue, collaboration and agreement.

It is with this same spirit that we have entered and work within the new parliamentary majority. And we repeat that we shall remain in it only if and to the extent that implementation of the program agreed on proceeds properly and on schedule. But our role and our responsibilities before the working masses and the country do not permit us to take a passive position, simply registering the positive and the negative of what is being done. On the contrary, our role and our responsibilities compel us to intervene constantly with our criticism, proposals and initiatives toward the government and in parliament and, above all, to develop our action in the country among the masses.

At the workers' conference in Naples last March, we dealt in depth with the problem of working-class alliances at a time when the issue facing us is not just to safeguard democracy and preserve the country from economic collapse, but also to prepare and set in motion a process of renewal of society and the state.

We must build a broader social bloc. The phase reached by capitalism today – and not only by Italian capitalism – raises a problem for the alliance policy of the working class, which, if not new, is certainly of new importance and dimensions.

The Communist Party therefore says to communist workers: be in the front lines in the democratic debate in order to steer the workers' struggles in directions that will exert a real influence on economic policy orientations; be the champions of class unity and action to win new alliances; rebut the arguments of demagogues who fuel narrow corporative drives that lead the working class to forfeit its role as a national leading force.

The Italian Communists, no. 3 (July–September 1978), pp. 78–89.

11   Draft theses for the Fifteenth Congress of the PCI, December 1978

Continuity and developments of the unity-oriented strategy
The policy of democratic unity is the axis of the PCI's strategy. It may entail various options and solutions as regards the majority and the government. The strategy of unity does not contradict or jeopardize the plurality of the political forces. Nor can it be seen as dimming the historical-political identity of the individual parties in a confused, paralyzing embrace; much less can it stifle the conflictuality rising from a pluralistic society. On the contrary, unity is vigorous if each party is in a position to uphold and bring to bear its ideas, positions and proposals; if the relationship is antagonistic; if debate and struggle are freely waged on the political and cultural level and in the sphere of ideas; if each party strives to be itself, but with utmost effort, correctness and consistence in maintaining the commitments and achieving the goals underlying common agreements and programs.

The political unity of the working class and the need for unity between the PCI and the PSI have been an essential element in our policy during the entire historical phase opened by the anti-fascist resistance and the liberation struggle. And they remain so today, with all the more evidence, now that the possibility for a political change of course in Italy has emerged and, in our country and in Western Europe, the big questions of the search and struggle for a new road to democratic, socialist transformation are open and pressing.

In the advance and gains of the working people, a determinant factor has been the capacity of communists and socialists to elaborate in unity a set of social and political demands and programs that have served as an important point of reference for the workers' and people's movement, first in the resistance struggle and later under the republic.

Underlying these united platforms is a common, troubled reflection on the historical causes of the defeat suffered by the Italian workers' movement following the First World War. They are the product of the search for a strategy aimed at founding a new democracy, capable of defeating all reactionary attempts and welding together the growth of freedom and advance towards socialism. This unity-oriented inspiration, which has succeeded in overcoming differences in traditions and moments of crisis and severe tension, has been an important factor in giving an original character and stamp not only to the PCI and the PSI, but also to the trade union and mass movements.

It is these peculiarities that have made it possible in our country to achieve extensive forms of convergence and dialogue among the left forces, forms that, far from lowering the level of research on strategy, have enriched it in terms of theoretical reflection as well.

Even in the troubled center-left period, when the design of dividing the workers' movement and isolating the Communist Party was actively pursued, the fabric of unity, particularly in the trade unions, stood up under the difficult test. This solidity and persistence of unity-oriented relations within the workers' movement and the reasons for, and value of, unity which we have always sustained, even in the moments of most vigorous opposition, have stimulated critical reflection on this experience in both parties and have been a factor in prompting the innovations and developments in their orientations and policy in recent years . . .

Concerning the Catholic question, the processes under way confirm the correctness and validity of the general orientation that has guided the PCI's actions over the past thirty years. This orientation has found application in a series of important positions that have embodied sentiments deeply felt by our people, strongly influenced national life, counted in the evolution of the Catholic world and made it possible to face moments of confrontation that could otherwise have become lacerating, as in the case of the divorce referendum.

Of particular importance is the phenomenon of reaggregation under way in the Catholic area, of which one aspect is a tendency to greater involvement by Catholics, in their capacity as Catholics, in society. This is a phenomenon involving broad masses of people and particularly young people. It is not limited to Italy, but in our country acquires particular political significance.

This complex process is in any event marked by a desire to react against the disorder and break-up of society and a search for certainties and values. It is characterized by a widespread aspiration to overhaul justice and a full unfolding of the human personality. We are dealing, that is, with an involvement revealing substantial potentialities for renewal and also elements of criticism of capitalist society. There are, however, some Catholic organizations, particularly among youth, that take an attitude of contraposition to the work of transformation being promoted by the workers' movement. At the same time, movements of an integralist stamp are also emerging and developing, making certain sectors of the Italian Catholic world particularly susceptible to moderate and conservative calls.

The PCI reconfirms its conviction that the winning and building of a democratic society and state and their development in the progressive direction towards socialist-type solutions can and must proceed with the involvement and participation of broad sections of the Catholic world. This strategy of unity and agreement, which considers mistaken and dangerous attempts to found the renewal and progress of Italy and the process of democratization and secularization of society and the state on Manichean cleavages, head-on confrontations on the religious or ideological level and efforts to get back at the church for past grievances, has shown itself to be a winning one. It has armed the workers' movement in the political and cultural battle, in the most difficult tests and in the contentions that have marked our country's history . . .

We reconfirm the full value of this inspiration and line in the formulation of the historic compromise. With its elaboration and action over the past years, the PCI has sought to bring home the need and urgency for a far-reaching renewal and transformation of Italian society. To satisfy this need for salvation and progress, we have held and hold indispensable a convergence and coming-together among the broad masses of socialist, communist and catholic orientation; a coming-together of the big social and political forces, on the basis of a line of democratic, national solidarity and joint responsibility, to advance détente, disarmament and international co-operation in Europe and the world, and, in our country, to ensure a common effort for the big goals of reform and transformation of society and the state.

With the historical compromise, the PCI has proposed a strategy and method for the renewal of Italy, in concrete terms applicable to the present situation.

This line cannot in any way be reduced to, or crystallized in, a particular government formula as regards parliamentary or government solutions. The essential thing is recognition of the need for unity and agreement, which must be built around the big goals of transformation of the social and economic structures, intellectual and moral reform and a democratic organization and operation of the state; the essential thing is the commitment of all the democratic and progressive forces to work for these ends, on the basis of their respective peculiarities and autonomy, with the most open debate and on an equal footing of dignity and rights, but with a sense of the general interests and an effort for mutual understanding and solidarity.

This is the substance, not only of a line, but of the vision of political and social life and the roads and methods for rebirth, democratic development and advance towards socialism that we hold to be most valid and realistic in relation to the history and reality of our country.

The Italian Communists (1978), special issue, pp. 83–8.

FRENCH Communist Party: The Heritage of Frontism

1 Maurice Thorez' interview with the London *Times*, 1946

The unity of labor and republican forces is the sure foundation of democracy. The French Labor Party, which we propose to constitute through the fusion of communists and socialists, would be the guide of our new people's democracy. It would open wide its ranks to the Catholic workers to whom, well before the war, we extended a fraternal hand that many have grasped. Besides, many share our conception of secularity: no war against religion, absolute neutrality of education with respect to religion.

Cahiers du Communisme (November 1946), p. 1016.

2 Maurice Thorez' report to the Twelfth Congress of the PCF, April 1950

There are comrades who do not take into account the modifications of attitude which events have provoked in the midst of socialist workers. There comrades continue to repeat: 'Nothing doing with the socialist.' They do not distinguish between the traitorous leaders and the hoodwinked workers who still follow them. Sometimes the comrades who so easily resign themselves to a break with the socialist workers are themselves former socialists. They must believe that after their departure no one remains in the Socialist Party who is worthy of interest; no one who could, after their example, become a true revolutionary militant. What an error and what a spirit of conceit!

Naturally this is only a bad excuse, a pretext to try to justify the absence of any real effort around the socialist workers.

Sometimes people answer us: 'Here, the socialists don't exist.' This is not true. The Socialist Party, on account of the treasonous policy of its leaders, has lost many voters and members. However, it conserves an influence which must not be underestimated. Further, not all the workers who leave the Socialist Party become communists. They remain more or less under the influence of their former party. They remain impregnated with the social democratic ideology. We will not help them to reform their 'social democratism' if we limit ourselves to propaganda. It is action in common which will lead these workers to take the decisive step. In working for unity, one cannot neglect the workers who were members of the Socialist Party and who remain unorganized.

'XIIe Congrès du Parti Communiste Français,' *Cahiers du Communisme* (May 1950), pp. 26–7.

3 Waldeck Rochet's report to the Thirteenth Congress of the PCF, June 1954

It is necessary to emphasize, as indicated by the resolution adopted by the Central Committee in its meeting at Arcuil:

> The urgent necessity of increasing the efforts at explanation and political work directed toward united action with the socialist workers, speaking to each man, striving to create a climate of understanding.

Changes are occurring in the consciousness of the socialist workers who better understand the consequences of the policy of national betrayal pursued since 1947 and who are beginning to see the communists in another light.

In the development of our contacts with the socialist workers, we ought never to lose sight of the fact that the united front is the organization of action for concrete, clearly defined objectives, and it is, above all, the organization of action at the workplace.

Everything which tends to favor the development

of the action of the masses is favorable, and to the degree that negotiations between leaderships favor such a development they are positive.

We cannot forget, as point 17 of the proposed theses makes clear, 'that agreements reached at the top cannot remain solid or effective if they are not supported by the activity of numerous rank-and-file committees, democratically elected in assemblies open to all the workers.'

Addressing this important problem during the Central Committee session of 29–30 October 1947, the party's secretary general indicated, recalling the experience of the Popular Front, that its principal error had been the fact that it had become a simple entente at the top.

The struggle for the united front with the socialist workers demands a solidly argued denunciation of the policy of betrayal carried out by the leaders of their party.

It is beyond doubt that the policy of the Socialist Party, with Guy Mollet at its head, is at the service of the French bourgeoisie, and given that the ruling circles of the French bourgeoisie follow a policy of alienating our national independence to the profit of the American imperialists, the Socialist Party has also become a tool of American policy . . .

In response to the policy of united action of the Communist Party, the socialist leaders propose, under the name of 'Democratic and Social Front,' a new version of the famous 'third force policy,' which concretely means entente with the reactionary heads of the MRP, and entente expressed notably in the partial legislative elections of Seine-et-Oise and Pas-de-Calais, and in the election of Guy Mollet to the chairmanship of the Council of Europe.

With their democratic and social front the socialist leaders wish above all to try to block the idea of unity, striving to make it believed that it would be possible to change the current policy without the communists.

We have certainly seen how the socialist leaders of Guy Mollet's stripe, after having defined their foreign policy as inspired by the wish to maintain the 'equilibrium' between the socialist camp and the American imperialists, have been led by the force of things to present themselves as they really are, as defenders of American policy.

In all this, the dominating preoccupation of the socialist leaders is to keep the socialist workers from seeing that any change in domestic policy depends above all on changing France's foreign policy, which cannot happen without a struggle together with the communists.

The politics of united working-class action is inconceivable without great efforts to realize unity in action with Catholic workers, with respect for their beliefs.

Maurice Thorez gave a simple and clear definition of the policy of the offered hand in his radio broadcast appeal of 17 April 1946. He said, notably, 'We offer you our hand, Catholic, worker, employee, artisan, peasant, we who are lay people, because you are our brothers, and like us are oppressed by the same interests.' There is in this declaration a wish for unity with the Catholic workers and an affirmation of principle, emphasizing what differentiates us from them.

We wish to fight sincerely and loyally alongside the Catholic workers for national independence and peace, for freedom and the defense of the interests of the laboring masses.

'XIIIᵉ Congrès du Parti Communiste Français,' *Cahiers du Communisme* (June–July 1954), pp. 693–700.

4   Maurice Thorez' report to the Fourteenth Congress of the PCF, July 1956

Life itself imperiously dictates the *necessity* of contacts and organized co-operation between the communists and socialists. And in the same way life furnishes unprecedented possibilities for unity in action.

International détente, as well as being a new way of posing the problems of relations between states and the struggle against war, has a fortunate influence in this regard . . .

One of the conditions for the realization of the united front is that the communists pursue without weakness their independent works of organizing and mobilizing the masses, of educating them in the spirit of Marxism–Leninism. Ardent promoters of unity in action, they continue to explain to the masses that only Marxist–Leninist theory can supply the correct position on all problems of foreign and domestic policy, the necessary ideological foundation for the successful defense of the workers' cause.

At the same time, the Communist Party resolutely combats all manifestations of sectarianism in its ranks. It struggles against the remnants of the anarchist theory of 'active minorities,' which spawns contempt for the masses, the tendency to neglect their actual state of mind, and impatience with regard to the socialist workers.

The Communist Party proposes the Marxist–Leninist concept of the vanguard, which ought never to lose contact with the bulk of the class, but rather should keep just one step ahead of it.

We condemn every resentment, every inimical attitude towards workers who are members of socialist, Christian, or other organizations. We offer our hand to all workers, without distinction, among philosophical opinions or beliefs. We support the unity of the whole working class.

One cannot, however, forget that the steps necessary for unity must be made *from both sides*.

'XIVe Congrès du Parti Communiste Français,' *Cahiers du Communisme* (July–August 1956), pp. 45–8.

5   Address of the delegates of the Fourteenth Congress of the PCF to their socialist comrades, July 1956

We consider unity of action not only necessary but possible.

The positions of our two parties have recently moved closer on many questions: economic demands, secularism, prohibition of atomic weapons, reduction of armaments, peaceful coexistence between all countries regardless of their form of society.

We believe it to be possible because of the very fact that the socialist and communist workers have shared aspirations for socialism, even if they remain divided over the ways and means.

Communists and socialists affirm that only the collective appropriation of natural resources and the means of production and exchange will abolish social classes and, consequently, eliminate the exploitation of one class by another.

Communists and socialists affirm that it is to the working class that falls the mission of substituting collective socialist property for capitalist private property of the means of production . . .

The Communist Party believes that the transformation of capitalist society is conditional on the existence of a revolutionary party opposed to reconciliation with the bourgeoisie. On its side, the Socialist Party affirms, in the same Declaration of Principles (1946), that: 'The Socialist Party has always been and continues to be a party of class struggle based on the organization of working people.' Thus our two parties declare themselves parties of class struggle whose goal is the establishment of socialism.

Communists and socialists also affirm that whatever the means for attaining this goal, the road will pass through a social revolution which will substitute collective property for capitalist private property . . .

The Communist Party affirms that the people will strive to use parliamentary institutions for the transformation of the social system. It does not, however, forget that, as a result of the bourgeois resistance, the forms of struggle may not always be peaceful. The choice between peaceful and violent means for the abolition of the dictatorship of capital depends not on the working class, but on the desperation with which the reactionary bourgeoisie will maintain a past whose time is gone . . .

Communists and socialists declare themselves partisans of democratic freedoms . . .

Our two parties affirm their devotion to freedom of conscience, to the separation of the church from schools and the state.

Our two parties affirm that they are internationalist. The Communist Party is deeply attached to proletarian internationalism, which does not contradict but, on the contrary, presupposes a policy of national independence and greatness . . .

The interests of all workers are unified. The Communist Party has always proclaimed its profound friendship for the peoples of the Soviet Union who were first to break the power of capital, construct socialism and march cheerfully towards communism. It affirms its solidarity with the colonial and dependent peoples struggling for their right to manage their affairs democratically and in total independence; it expresses its solidarity with all the workers of the world. This is why the Communist Party has greatly rejoiced in the direct relations established between the Socialist Party and the Communist Party of the Soviet Union . . .

It is incontestable that a government based on the united front of the working class, bringing around it a broad new popular front, would make possible the realization of a vast social, democratic and peaceful program, and would prepare the way to the realization of our common aspirations: socialism.

'XIVe Congrès du Parti Communiste Français,' *Cahiers du Communisme* (July–August 1956), pp. 324–6.

6   Maurice Thorez' report to the Fifteenth Congress of the PCF, June 1959

During the crisis of May 1958, our party made a great effort to involve the mass of socialist workers in the defense of democracy.

The working-class and democratic forces were at the point of unity; they would have succeeded in barring the route to personal power except when Guy Mollet succeeded, at the last moment, in counter-manding the decisions of his own party and in maintaining the division among the workers. Inside the Socialist Party the influence of the working class has carried less weight, at the crucial moment, than that of the worst reactionaries.

The deep crisis of the Socialist Party then became apparent to all eyes.

This crisis is the result of the policy of class collaboration which it has practiced in all areas . . .

The Socialist Party has contributed to lowering the workers' living standard by favoring the spreading of the big bosses' ideology within their ranks, notably with respect to productivity. Placed in January 1956 at the head of the government, it prolonged and intensified the Algerian War and conducted the disastrous adventure of Suez. Its whole policy opened the way to de Gaulle.

This policy was accompanied, in the ideological realm, by a complete abandonment of the theory of the class struggle, under the pretext of 'rethinking' this doctrine. We are no longer dealing with an opportunist orientation, as is habitual with social democracy, but with a systematic effort to liquidate every socialist idea . . .

The 'thinkers' of the SFIO announce the end of capitalist concentration; they speak of 'dis-concentration,' with contempt for the most obvious facts. They speak of the 'innumerable owners of stocks and bonds.'

. . . To believe Jules Moch, the gap is not growing between the two poles of society, there is no pauperization. There are even no more proletarians, or very nearly. Others slander the working class, representing it as incapable and apathetic. They go in these knowing circles as far as to reverse the obvious order of things, and instead of speaking of the negative, opportunist influence of the petite bourgeoisie of the the working class, they pretend that it is the 'apathy' of the working class which

affects the intellectuals and the petite bourgeoisie.

Of course, for these pseudo-theoreticians, the state would cease to be a superstructure at the service of the bourgeoisie.

These pernicious ideas are even more widespread in the Socialist Party since workers have an even smaller place in it . . .

The non-proletarian character of the Socialist Party is ever stronger with the cadres . . . The workers have given place to employees and functionaries, as well as to purely bourgeois elements, in particular to representatives of the top state bureaucracy . . .

Last November the Pas-de-Calais elected seven socialist deputies. Among them one found an industrialist, a commercial director, a mining engineer, a doctor, a professor, a schoolteacher, an employee. Not a single worker. Only twenty years ago all the socialist deputies from Pas-de-Calais were mineworkers or former mineworkers.

The socialist workers cannot be satisfied with such a situation.

They cannot fail to draw conclusions from the bankruptcy of their party, ravaged by the split. They remember that the growth in influence and membership of the Socialist Party always coincided with the practice of unity of action.

The Necessity for Union on a Common Program
The agreement between democratic parties for a common program for joint realization is in our eyes an urgent necessity, because such an agreement is the condition for common victory over personal power and reaction, and the guarantee that after this a really democratic policy, meeting the needs of the people, will be applicable.

We must not lose sight of the fact that a popular movement of exceptional strength is necessary to finish off personal power.

The absence of a program common to the democratic parties allows the Gaullists in power to prolong their noxious reign by speculating on people's fear of the unknown and of a return to the past.

It is thus that the communists, socialists and other democrats declare themselves opposed to personal power. They call for the lowering of military expenditures and the renunciation of the strike force, much greater credits for schools and the democratization of teaching, the extension of nationalization under democratic management, democratic reform of the bureaucracy, raising of the workers' buying power, a serious housing-construction policy, defense of union and political freedoms, democratic control of radio and television, and so on.

'XVᵉ Congrès du Parti Communiste Français,' *Cahiers du Communisme* (July–August 1959), pp. 49–54.

7 Political resolution of the Sixteenth Congress of the PCF, May 1961

In all areas the practice of unity has been widely extended. The French Communist Party has continually called for the development of this unity. It has multiplied its proposals for the unification of all democratic forces. Throughout the country the communists have displayed the initiative for the collection of these forces.

The power of the monopolies strikes at broad strata of the French population: the working class, the laboring peasantry, the middle strata of the cities, certain groups of the bourgeoisie. It is the union of all these strata which will make possible the victory over personal power. The road to victory must pass by way of this union.

The Gaullist government well knows the invincible power of the union of democratic forces. This is why it multiplies its maneuvers, diversions, provocations with an eye to hindering its realization.

The French Communist Party emphasizes that the collaboration of the party of the working class with the other democratic parties is possible and necessary as much to restore and renew French democracy as to construct socialism in our country on the basis of an alliance between the proletariat, the laboring peasantry, the intellectuals and the other middle strata of the cities.

The struggle for unity consists – as always – in the fraternal efforts of the communists to win the socialist workers to common action and, at the same time, in the ideological political struggle against those who would divide them. The socialist leaders defend the capitalist system and divide the working class. Disowning Marxism, the class struggle and the traditional socialist slogans, they render a new service to the bourgeoisie.

In France, Guy Mollet and the right-wing socialist leaders openly serve the politics of the monopolies. They have even campaigned with the most reactionary forces for the last Gaullist referendum.

If the right-wing socialist leaders are the declared servants of Gaullism, they are not the only ones to spread the reformist ideas of class collaboration and to oppose, for this reason, common action with the communists. Other parties and groupings have the same attitudes . . .

Our Communist Party has made it known that it ardently desires that all the democratic parties come to agreement to place a candidate of the union of all democratic forces in opposition to the candidate of personal power, but that it could not envisage coming out, from the first round of voting on, for a non-communist candidate without a precise agreement on a common program, providing, notably, for democratizing institutions as well as for the means of achieving them . . .

If communists and socialists do not make the same judgement on the socialist October Revolution, that does not in our opinion constitute, at the present moment, an insurmountable obstacle to the realization of unity between communists and socialists.

It is a fact that the victory of the October Revolution and the building of socialism in the Soviet Union and in many other countries have created new conditions which allow countries such as ours to take roads other than that followed by the Russian communists in 1917 in their struggle for socialism. There is an easier road on which communists and socialists can embark together.

In fact, thanks to the new balance of power established in the world in favor of socialism, the working class's aspiration to socialism has grown, and other social strata are also arriving at the idea that socialism alone can resolve the social problem, definitively guarantee peace, assure the prosperity of the nation and the spread of culture.

But, to the extent that communists and socialists are equally in favor of peaceful coexistence – which is the case – they are logically led, despite the differences which remain, to move towards each other and to search for an agreement in the struggles against thermonuclear war, for controlled general disarmament, and for peaceful coexistence.

The same goes for the communist thesis on the diversity of roads to socialism and the possibility, under certain conditions, of reaching socialism peacefully.

In the past the opposition between communists and socialists has been the more pronounced as the communists' ideas were generally misinterpreted and often grossly caricatured.

In many circles the idea that the communists are

invariably for revolutionary violence has taken hold . . . But this conception of the seizure of power by an active minority has never been the communists'.

For the communists, who base themselves above all on the movement of the masses, not only has violence never been an end in itself, but they believe that the working class, the peasantry, all the workers have a profound interest in the accomplishment of the socialist revolution by peaceful ways which would avoid disturbing and disorganizing the national economy.

In fact, the use of violence has never been the result of the workers' preference, but has depended uniquely on the degree of the employers' resistance to the will of the people and on the forms of struggle that the employers have used.

Of course, when we defend the possibility of a peaceful passage to socialism, we are in no way abandoning the Marxist thesis that the bourgeoisie will never give up power of its own free will. And we do not forget Lenin's injunction that the working class ought to make use of all the means and forms of revolutionary struggle without exception. Our Central Committee has stressed on many occasions that the possibility of a peaceful development of the socialist revolution appears when there is a superiority of forces on the side of the working class and its allies such that the high bourgeoisie is no longer in a position to turn to civil war.

In all cases, including the utilization of a truly democratic parliament, the revolution is above all the result of mass popular struggle, which demands the unity of the working class, the laboring peasantry and all the social strata interested in the victory of democracy and socialism.

It is to contribute to the success of the march to socialism by the peaceful road that our party – which has rejected the idea of a single party – has proposed an entente between the Communist Party and the Socialist Party, not only for today but for tomorrow in the struggle to realize together the construction of socialism.

The question of the existence of a single or of several parties to build socialism has been controversial. Already our Sixteenth Congress has given a clear answer to this question, and the draft resolution submitted to the present Congress gives it clear and unequivocal confirmation when it states that:

The French Communist Party has rejected the idea that the existence of a single party is a necessary condition of the passage to socialism. This idea,

maintained by Stalin, was an unwarranted generalization of the specific circumstances in which the October Revolution developed.

. . . We hope that the working class will succeed in realizing its unity on the political level completely. But even if this unity is realized this still will not be the 'single party,' for, besides the party of the working class, other democratic parties could exist representing certain social strata and collaborating in the construction of socialism.

Henceforth the argument of the 'single party' can no longer be validly invoked as an obstacle to the collaboration and unity of action of the two parties.

Another equally controversial question is that of the nature of the political power which the working class ought to establish when it reaches power to realize socialism.

In their statutes and their fundamental programs, communists and socialists affirm that the goal is the abolition of social classes and the suppression of the exploitation of one class by another with the socialization of the great means of production and exchange and the transformation of capitalist society into a collectivist or communist society.

Communists and socialists affirm also that it is to the working class that this historical mission falls.

But the differences appear when it comes to defining the state system which the working class ought to establish to carry the realization of socialism to a good conclusion.

The founders of scientific socialism, Marx–Engels–Lenin, showed that to assure the transition from capitalism to socialism, the working class must of necessity build, temporarily, a proletarian government of a new type which they called the 'dictatorship of the proletariat.'

This proletarian government, by which the working class exercises its political leadership, in alliance with the working peasantry and the middle classes of the cities, has as its essential task the assurance of the socialist transformation of society. And to accomplish this great task, two notable conditions must be met:

(1) Defense of the new regime of socialist democracy against the agitations of the old exploiting classes and their agents by making use of the measures of constraint necessary to break their resistance, their attempt to restore capitalism.

(2) Securing the widest democracy for all workers and educating the broad masses so that they may

participate actively in the construction of socialism and the running of public affairs.

The dictatorship of the proletariat as conceived by the Marxists is in every way a hundred times more democratic than any bourgeois regime because the working class, who exercised power in close collaboration with its allies, rules in the interest of the immense mass of the people, who enjoy all democratic freedoms. In addition, it has a temporary character since, as soon as socialism has triumphed and society includes only friendly classes, all class constraints disappear; the state then transforms itself into a state of the whole people; socialist democracy expands fully.

Evidently the forms of dictatorship of the proletariat can vary according to historical conditions and national particularities.

We believe, for example, that in France – in the light of its democratic traditions and the conditions of our epoch – it is possible to envisage, in the case of a passage to socialism, new forms of proletarian dictatorship, less violent and more brief in duration . . .

There are other questions where our points of view are not the same. For example, it is true that the two parties are run on different principles of organization. But if such a question can present difficulties in case of a reunification of the two parties, it is not of a nature to prevent the two parties from collaborating and realizing unity of action . . .

'XVIᵉ Congrès du Parti Communiste Français,' *Cahiers du Communisme* (June 1961), pp. 575–6.

8 Waldeck Rochet's report to the Eighteenth Congress of the PCF, January 1967

The Socialist–Communist dialogue on ideological differences

It is proper to emphasize that if dialogue between the two parties is possible, it is because communist workers and socialist workers aspire equally to a more just society, to socialism.

We know that in their statutes and their fundamental program, the French communists and socialists affirm, in almost identical terms, that the goal to be reached is the abolition of social classes and the suppression of the exploitation of one class by another by socializing the main means of production and exchange and by transforming capitalist society into a collectivist or communist society.

But, if both socialists and communists aspire to socialism, it is with respect to the ways and means of passing from capitalism to the new regime that their disagreements appear.

These disagreements have their source, above all, in the fact that, as Marxists, the communists are revolutionaries, while the socialists are generally inspired by reformist ideology.

This is why, moreover, the communists and socialists have different evaluations of the socialist October Revolution and of the experiences of the other socialist countries.

The social democratic leaders of various countries criticize this great historical work, but as far as they are concerned they have no example of the realization of socialism to show, for in the countries where they have been in power they have been content to manage capitalism's affairs.

However, if communists and socialists have followed different roads since the great October Revolution, the major problem which is posed today is that of knowing if the profound changes which have taken place for fifty years to the benefit of socialism can permit our arrival at a *rapprochement* between communists and socialists.

In this regard, it appears that the argument about the past strongly risks arrival at an impasse. The debate, on the other hand, could make possible the working out of common positions, if it deals with the problems of the moment and the perspectives of the future.

And this, not because we would be inclined to throw a veil over the past – far from it – but because we believe that the great changes which have occurred since the revolution of October 1917 permit us, indeed, to grapple with the problem of the passage from capitalism to socialism under new conditions.

In the first place, it is proper to recall that as a result of the victory of the socialist October Revolution and the arrival of socialism in numerous countries – a circumstance which has considerably weakened the capitalist system in the world – new conditions exist today which permit countries like France to take a different and easier road than that followed by the Russian communists in 1917.

While Marxist theory says that the passage to socialism is in all cases a qualitative transformation of society, thus a social revolution, it does not give pre-established schemas of the forms and means which the working class and its allies must apply to pass to the new order.

For example, for a long time the socialist leaders have maintained that the opposition between socialists and communists could not be overcome because, according to them, the communists in principle and invariably favor the seizure of power by violence, by armed insurrection.

In truth, for the communists, revolutionary violence has never been an end in itself. On the contrary, the communists believe that it is in the interest of the working class to accomplish the socialist revolution by peaceful ways which permit the avoidance of trouble and the disorganization of the productive forces. The employment of violence is thus never the result of the workers' preference. It hangs on the level of the exploiters' resistance to the people's will on the forms of struggle which they utilize.

'XVIIIᵉ Congrès du Parti Communiste Français,' *Cahiers du Communisme* (February–March 1967), pp. 60–3.

9 'Champigny Manifesto,' Waldeck Rochet's report to the Central Committee of the PCF, 1968

Great changes have occurred in the economic and social structure of our country.

As our party had predicted, and as the powerful popular movements of May–June 1968 have forcefully shown, conditions are rapidly maturing for *joint action of all the strata attacked or threatened by the monopolies.*

More and more, in fact, French society is characterized by the concentration of enormous power in the hands of a small group of monopolists, at one end, and by the worsening of living and working conditions for the immense majority of the population, at the other.

Under the rule of state monopoly capitalism, a narrow financial oligarchy controls the essential levers of the economic and political activity of the country. The state is mobilized entirely for the safeguard and mobilization of the profit of big capital. It systematically favors capitalist exploitation at the level of society as a whole. Its policy, domestic and foreign, is identified with the general interests of the monopolies.

The principal victim of this policy is the working class, as monopolist concentration notably expresses itself by the intensification of work and its excessive duration, pressure on wages, rising taxes, unemployment.

Contrary to the 'theories' of big capital's apologists, the working class, with its proletarian center – whose labor is the source of the monopolies' enrichment – is constantly growing.

The situation in the countryside, dominated by capitalist concentration, the anarchy of production and the degradation of the conditions of existence of the immense majority of peasants, has led to the development of peasant struggles and to new progress of the alliance between the workers of the towns and those of the country.

Although it could be put to serve the well-being of all, the prodigious scientific and technical revolution which marks our epoch is entirely subordinated to the law of profit and takes the forms of a greater exploitation of the workers. At the same time, it provokes the massive growth and rapid change of strata of employees whose wage and working conditions are brought closer and closer to the workers'.

The number of engineers, technicians, researchers and teachers grows ceaselessly. Despite great diversity of their situations, the immense majority of these people bear the increasing weight of capitalist exploitations. The monopolists' regime refuses them any creative participation in the economic and political destiny of the country, in the elaboration of a living culture. Their role in the class struggle is increasing. Certainly their education and their social origin does not predispose them to recognize easily the decisive role of the working class. But the struggles of spring 1968 have shown that part of them, a much larger one than in the preceding period, is coming to participate actively in the fight at the sides of the workers and employees. This necessary alliance of the working class and the intellectuals is considered as a crucial question by the French Communist Party.

State monopoly capitalism accelerates the eviction of numerous artisans and shopkeepers. Together with the considerable masses of small peasants, they are coming to swell the army of wage workers, whose total number currently represents *two-thirds of the active population.*

Denied by the government and overexploited by the big bosses, while its mass never ceases to grow, youth – and at its head, working-class youth – with increased combativeness demands the right to a joy, the right to education and to leisure, and also the right to speak. The young people have played a great role in the recent events. The upcoming generation has taken a place on the front lines of the battle against Gaullism and capitalism, for demands and progress.

This has accentuated and aggravated the tension which sets in opposition, together with the working class, the immense majority of the population to the big capitalist bourgeoisie and its bagmen.

Thus are developing the foundations of a community of interests among all the social strata, victims of the monopolies and their policies, and the possibility of their assembly around the working class . . .

L'Humanité, December 7, 1968, p. 7.

10   Georges Marchais' report to the Nineteenth Congress of the PCF, February 1970

The experience of the workers' movement in France and throughout the world, both its successes and its reverses, has amply demonstrated the necessity of realizing working class unity, the unity of the political parties and other organizations which support democracy and socialism. Division among the ranks of labor and the democratic forces has always favored the enemies of democracy and socialism. And, on the other hand, every time it has been achieved their unity has permitted the winning of important gains.

In today's conditions only the unified action of the working class and its alliance with the other non-monopolist strata can make possible a deployment of a mass movement capable of forcing the regime of big capital to retreat. It is thus necessary to consider as a task of decisive importance the realization of working-class unity and the assembly around it of all salaried workers, the intermediate strata of both the cities and the country who have, as we have seen, various reasons for fighting the politics in power . . .

Unity cannot aim at putting the working class in tow to the bourgeoisie or a part of it. It cannot aim at the application of big capital's policy by people who claim to represent the world of labor, like the English Labor Party leaders, the Italian Social Democrats, or the Swedish Socialist Party for whom the UDR produces significant propaganda here in France. The unity for which we fight implies, consequently, a rejection of the policy of class collaboration.

Our party attaches particular importance to co-operation with the Socialist Party. In its statutes this party takes a position for socialism. Together with our party, the majority party within the working class, our two organizations exercise the decisive influence over the workers. This is why an agreement between the Socialist Party and the Communist Party would constitute, as the declaration adopted by our two parties last December 18 says, 'the keystone of the union of the left.'

This in no way means that we have any intention of setting the union of the left apart from other democratic forces desirous of assuming their responsibilities in the struggle for democracy and socialism . . .

A correct understanding of unity of action of the labor and democratic forces combines the development of common action at the rank-and-file level with agreements made at the leadership level of political organizations . . .

But, to rouse up a majority assembly of the labor and democratic forces which would allow us to put an end to the Gaullist-centrist regime and to assure it a democratic replacement, it is necessary for the democratic parties and organizations to propose a clear and common alternative to the workers, to the masses of people. It is equally necessary that an agreement on this alternative constitute a resolute and lasting engagement on the part of the participants . . .

A long-lasting political accord cannot be an agreement of the purely electoral type. It thus ought to find its expression in a common program for struggle and government. This program would specify the common aims decided on by the democratic organizations, as well as the means and the forms of struggle necessary to realize them together.

During the last period, the socialist workers have been able to verify the baneful consequences of the politics of class collaboration and anti-communism. These politics led to the defrauding of the working class and the people of the possibilities for change which existed in May–June 1968 and then again in May 1969. It led to a collapse of the Socialist Party's voting strength, essentially to the profit of the reaction. The future of the organizations which are dedicated to socialism does not lie in class collaboration. It lies in the class struggle against reaction in its various forms and in co-operation with the revolutionary party of the working class.

'XIXᵉ Congrès du Parti Communiste Français,' *Cahiers du Communisme* (February–March 1970), pp. 68–73.

11   Theses of the Nineteenth Congress of the PCF, February 1970

22.   Conditions are ripening for common action of all the strata victimized by the monopolies. As is evidenced by the general discontent which the 'austerity' policy of the Gaullist-centrist government provokes, the objective foundations for a new advance of the anti-monopolist assembly – alone capable of imposing advanced democracy and opening the way to socialism – have been further enlarged.

23.   The working class is the leading force of the assembly of all the non-monopolist social strata. Its numbers and its place in the active population do not cease to grow. Because it is the most directly exploited, it has the greatest interest in critical changes in the economic and social policies of the country. Linked to the most modern forms of production and unable to free itself without freeing society as a whole, it marches at the head of social progress. Its concentration, its organization and its experience, the fact that in the Communist Party it possesses an authentically revolutionary party basing its activities on a scientific doctrine of struggle, Marxism–Leninism, gives its fight an unequalled efficacy. This was confirmed during the struggles of May–June 1968 when the working class correctly oriented its class combat, put a stop to left-wing adventurism and escaped the trap offered by the bourgeoisie to destroy its living forces and thus paralyze its activity for a long period.

24.   Although its numerical significance diminishes from year to year, the small and middle peasantry still includes more than a million peasant families who wish to live on, while the policy of the government is leading to the degradation of the conditions of their existence and accelerates their expropriation. The peasantry is organizing more effectively, it expresses its anger in various forms, demands that the government stop sacrificing it for the profit of the big growers and the capitalist monopolies, and demands an improvement of its lot. Its alliance with the working class remains an essential condition for the success of democratic struggles. At the same time the unyielding activity of the communists is necessary to develop, among the small and middle agricultural cultivators, a consciousness of the fact that they can defend their future only in a close alliance with the proletariat.

25.   The intellectuals of all disciplines see the degradation of their material and moral conditions. Many among them are tending to discover the cause of this in the capitalist system whose goal is profit rather than the development of human potential. The economic struggles in which they engage and the active participation of a part of them in political combat brings them close to the working class and creates the basis of a durable alliance with the latter. The French Communist Party considers this alliance, to whose development it contributes, of capital importance for the future of the revolutionary movement.

26.   During the last years the discontent of the middle strata, notably of shopkeepers and artisans, has been realizing and expressing itself in protest movements which reactionary and adventuring elements sometimes attempt to mislead. The working class and its party defend all which is legitimate in their demands . . .

28.   The young generation, while it does not constitute a social stratum of its own, none the less plays its own role in the struggles of our time.

Its numerical significance is growing. It is, in its mass, super-exploited by the big bosses and hazed by the government. Young workers, high school students and peasants are questioning their future. With anger they compare the thrilling possibilities offered by technical and scientific progress in our epoch with the impasses into which capitalist society throws them. The young workers are on the front lines of the battles for economic demands and social progress. More students are struggling for the democratization and renovation of teaching and for the assurance of jobs, for suitable conditions of life and study . . .

29.   The role of women in economic, social and cultural life is growing. In industry a million and a half of them are an integral part of the working class. The living and working conditions of millions of working women, notably salaried employees, bring them close to the working class.

The interests of millions of workers' wives, even when they themselves have no profession, are directly tied to those of the working class.

With these laboring women and employees, and these workers' wives, other categories of manual and intellectual female workers in both the city and the country are participating more actively in political life.

Defending their legitimate demand, supporting their actions in defense of their interests, opening to them the prospect of a just and peaceful society, the French Communist Party contributes greatly to their consciousness-raising, to their participation in the general struggles of our people . . .

'XIXe Congrès du Parti Communiste Français,' *Cahiers du Communisme* (February–March 1970), pp. 435–40.

12 Georges Marchais' report to the Central Committee, 1974

Comrades,

Last Thursday our Central Committee took up the question of the presidential election.

It decided to 'do everything possible to achieve a common candidate of the left for the first round' and mandated the Political Bureau to take to this end all useful steps in relation to the other organizations which signed the Common Program for government.

This decision is based essentially on the political strategy which has been applied by our party for many years.

We struggle to replace the government of big capital with a democratic regime which will carry out far-reaching anti-monopoly reforms. These reforms will make possible the satisfaction of the most pressing demands of the workers and the laboring population as a whole. They will also open up the way for our people's march towards socialism under conditions appropriate for our country. This is our goal . . .

The ideas and objectives of the Common Program must seize upon the masses themselves. Already, in the struggle to achieve the Common Program, Waldeck Rochet has unceasingly insisted on this necessity: 'In reality,' he said, 'to achieve a common program with an advanced socialist content, *this program must become, in its very content, a need for the broad masses of our people.* In other words, the correct proposals made by the communists, with respect both to foreign and to domestic policy, must be approved and supported by a growing number of French men and women, in such a way that they will have to be taken into consideration.' This is what has happened, because we have followed this line of action . . .

Certainly the designation of a candidate from our party for the first round would not be in contradiction with our strategy. We would in any case not have hesitated to take such a decision if our partners had refused a common candidature based on the Common Program. This said, and while emphasizing the great significance of the 5 million votes cast for our comrade Jacques Duclos in 1969, it is evident that conditions are not ripe today for a majority of French people to come out in favor of the election of a communist to the presidency of the republic. Further, a double candidature of the left would have encouraged maneuvers on the right with the aim of dissociating the parties united around the Common Program. It might have led to the absence of a candidate of the popular forces at the second round.

L'Humanité, April 9, 1974, pp. 5–6.

13 Georges Marchais' report to the Twenty-First Congress of the PCF, October 1974 (I)

There are Frenchmen who are Christians and others who are materialists. There thus exist between them undeniable philosophical differences. We say this very clearly! Our party is not seeking an impossible ideological reconciliation with the believers. We do not propose to them that they deny their faith, no more than we intend to abandon our own convictions or the scientific foundations of our actions. Nor do we intend to choose for them how they should be Christians, to choose one faction among them over another. No, we say simply that workers and democrats, whether they are Christian or atheist, have interests, demands and aspirations in common.

This real and profound movement of change is reflected to a certain extent and on certain questions addressed by the church itself. It pushes a growing number of Christians to take a position for union with those who, though not sharing their philosophical convictions, are inspired by the same aspirations, and with the communists in particular. They verify more and more that the co-operation, the common struggle which we propose to them is not a trap, but a step taken on principle. They can see that this co-operation is really being established in the respect for each person's convictions, in loyalty. We intend to increase our efforts towards the acceleration of this evolution.

What do we have in mind when we say that the Gaullist democrats and patriots have their place in the union of the people of France? We have ceaselessly fought the economic and social policy constructed under the aegis of General de Gaulle. Our party – *qua* party – has denounced the personal and non-democratic character of the government installed in 1958. We think – and this is a historical fact – that in the course of the succeeding years, the big bourgeoisie has not only maintained but reinforced its domination. At the same time we have supported the positive aspects of de Gaulle's foreign policy, his wish to see France recapture its independence, his initiatives in favor not only of peaceful coexistence, but co-operation with the socialist countries, his refusal to allow the political, economic and military decisions of France to be made outside Paris. We have done this all the more, as these are objectives for which we have always fought.

'XXIᵉ Congrès du Parti Communiste Français,' *Cahiers du Communisme* (November 1974), pp. 48–9.

14 Georges Marchais' report to the Twenty-First Congress of the PCF, October 1974 (II)

For us union is not a tactic of the moment, a maneuver tied to present contingency. It is a guiding thread of all our activity. And it is so for a simple reason: union constitutes the only means to ensure the success of the struggle of the working class and the popular forces . . .

It is evident that we do not desire union for union's sake, union without content or principles.

Union, for us, is uniting to multiply the fighting capacity of the workers, to enlarge, mobilize and con-solidate the struggle of the labor, democratic and national forces against the rule of big capital. We want union in order to fight the power of the mono-polies, to install an advanced democracy and to march afterwards to socialism. We want union so that a politics may triumph which responds to the pressing needs and fundamental interests of the working class, of manual and intellectual workers, of the working peasantry, of the great mass of our people. Every other conception of union does not derive from a wish to sever the working class from the tow rope of the bourgeoisie or of a part of the bourgeoisie. They derive, when all is said and done, from the most con-temptible opportunism, indeed, from electoralist horse-trading.

The union of the people of France proceeds through the raising of the duality of the union of the left. It proceeds by the conquest of new social strata for the idea and the objectives of democratic change. It proceeds through the assembly of all the men and women concerned by this change, in the diversity of currents of thought and political families to which they belong.

Following the recent conferences organized by the Socialist Party, we are justified in saying that an ambiguity exists as to whether the Socialist Party still believes that the common objective of the left parties remains the profound democratic change defined by the Common Program.

In effect, if the Socialist Party has thought it good to give itself a socialist program today, to elaborate with others a plan for a socialist society, that is its business . . .

If one looks, for example, at the final declaration adopted by the conferences organized by the Socialist Party, one can say that it contains absolutely no reference to the Common Program while, at the same time, it presents socialism as the only 'alternative' and as the only 'new road.' Moreover, commenting on these conferences, Michel Rocard has declared for his part that these meetings lead naturally to 'modifying the nature and the technical content of the alliance.' These facts, and others like them, lead us naturally to ask whether the Socialist Party would not envisage substituting its 'plan for a socialist society' for the Common Program – a plan whose coherence is not evident, and in which the workers would not find the concrete, important measures they desire to better their lives.

Among the leadership of the Socialist Party, some people appear to be disturbed at our slogan of the union of the people of France, which seems to go too far . . .

The high bourgeoisie has not, indeed, renounced, and will never renounce, its efforts to call the union of the left into question. It renounces this even less today when, confronted with the crisis of its system, it does ignore, to escape from the current impasse, the possibility of resorting to a government of the left which would accept the 'loyal' management of its interests, in the manner of Mr Helmut Schmidt. This is confirmed by the persistent speculations on the possibility of seeing Giscard d'Estaing call François Mitterand to run the government, while, as far as one can see, it is absurd to believe that a government of the union of the left could apply the Common Program with a reactionary President of the Republic and parliamentary majority.

It is true that the men of big capital do not hope for an immediate result. But, without any doubt, they anticipate creating conditions more favorable to their plans in the future by limiting, and if possible by weakening, the relative weight of the Communist Party on the political chessboard . . .

We understand that the Socialist Party wishes to strengthen its position since we also have the desire to strengthen our party. We hope in this way to make ever more effective at its vanguard role, today to defeat the power of big capital, tomorrow in the effort of applying the politics defined by the Common Program, and then in the struggle for the building of a socialist society. Within the framework of this society, the role of our party will consist, without substituting itself for the organs of the state, in the exercise of a motivating influence, a directing political and ideological influence, so that our country can advance more rapidly and more surely towards a future of prosperity, well-being and freedom.

In this area, of the struggle for democracy and socialism, we have said many times, and we repeat it, that we do not fear rivalry. Much to the contrary, we believe it is natural and necessary, and we certainly intend to further improve our own activity on this clear and loyal basis.

But this rivalry cannot consist, for one of the partners, in choosing to strengthen itself to the detriment of the other in order then to impose its will.

Such an orientation cannot lead either the one or the other to victory. For, no more than we wish to dominate, will we be able to accept a reduction to a contributing role. This would be contrary to the interests of the workers and of our people, and to the success of the struggle for the realization of the Common Program.

According to us, the relations between our parties ought to be founded — we have often said this and we maintain this position — on equality of rights and duties in the loyal realization of engagements made in common.

'XXIᵉ Congrès du Parti Communiste Français,' *Cahiers du Communisme* (November 1974), pp. 39–49.

15 Georges Marchais' report to the Central Committee of the PCF, 1975

What is clear is that the forces of big capital will never willingly give up their dominant positions. They will never renounce the means at their disposal, in so far as they are able to use them.

For the popular movement the problem, therefore, is to give itself at every stage the means to defend democracy, to make the majority will of the nation respected, and above all to maintain and consolidate in its favor the decisive relationship of social and political forces.

This is to say that, far from finding reasons in the events of Chile or of Portugal to renounce our struggle for democracy or our democratic path, we draw from them the conviction that it is the right path for our country . . .

By its existence, by its force, by its ideas and its actions, the Communist Party opens to workers, to the majority of our people, the possibility of constructing a socialist society in liberty. Without the Communist Party there would be neither socialism nor liberty for the masses.

The path which we propose is a democratic path for another reason also. It assumes, in fact, the formation and at each stage the intervention of a powerful assembly of the working and popular forces, of the democratic majority movement of our people.

We are categorically against the conception of a power play by an 'agitating minority.' The profound transformations which are necessary radically to improve the lot of the great masses can only be achieved with the concurrence of the great masses. We are against the reformist idea that the transformation of society could be done for the price of a few simple adjustments of the 'capitalist production machine,' without class struggle. The democratic path which we propose is a revolutionary path, a path for the united struggle of the working classes, of the popular masses.

We have said that this important element of our strategy has an objective base: in effect, if it is true that it is the working class which suffers most harshly and most directly from the exploitation of big capital, today the immense majority of the population is also victim of the monopolies and their policy. The economic and political struggles have developed by involving new classes of the population. The convergence of these struggles with those of the working class, the decisive force, the moving force of this great class struggle, is happening more frequently. The parties of the left, reunited around the Common Program, have obtained the support of almost half of the voters. Consciousness of the necessity for profound change has progressed among the popular masses. The standing order of the union of the people of France for democratic change is a just order, and it is an order for combat.

We have never had any illusions as to what this union implies. When we adopted the Common Program in 1972, we did it fully conscious of the problems that this would pose for a time. In particular, we have said that the conclusion of a Common Program would give the Socialist Party 'bases in its effort to reinforce itself at our expense.' Likewise it was fair to work for a single candidate from the left in the presidential election, but this also is used by the socialist leaders toward the same goal. This said, I remind you that when evoking in June 1972 the possibility of a reinforcement of the Socialist Party to our detriment, I quickly added '. . . if we do not do what is necessary.'

To do what is necessary is to lead the action to create from the union a clear and loyal alliance for combat, without the compromise of our partners with the upper class with its policy and its power. It is to resolutely take the lead of the struggles of the working classes and the popular masses, to show ourselves to be the most active in all circumstance in the defense of their interests. It is to put it to the workers, and the democrats themselves, to compare the foresight, the devotion of the parties belonging to the left, and their determination to achieve the transformations prescribed by the Common Program. In brief, it is to illuminate their experiences, not without confusion for a time, in the new situation created by the conclusion of the Common Program.

This is the task of an entire period. We must pursue it with perseverance. It is indispensable, for everything confirms that if the Socialist Party, as its leaders openly wish, succeeds in dominating the left, it will not fail to turn its back on the Common Program and to return to a policy of class collaboration with the upper class. This does not correspond to the interests of millions of workers, of simple folk who, with reason, place their hopes in a resolute struggle against the power of big capital, in the fundamental transformation of the economic and social system.

L'Humanité, November 12, 1975, p. 11.

SPANISH Communist Party: The Search for National Reconciliation

1 Thesis No. IX of the Fifth Congress of the PCE, 1954

IX Relations between church and state
(1) Separation of church and state. But, taking into account the religious feeling of a large part of the population, the state should provide for the needs of religion.
(2) Expand and complete religious freedom: no one ought to be persecuted because of his religious beliefs or lack thereof.

V Congreso del PCE, Spanish Communist Party document, 1954.

2 PCE program, Fifth Congress, 1954

With what forces and how to fight for the realization of this program
The democratic transformation for which the Communist Party struggles corresponds to the interests of Spain, of the vast majority of the classes and strata of society.

The working class, farm workers, intellectuals, artisans, merchants, and the industrial bourgeoisie which is non-monopolistic and not infused with foreign capital, are all interested in the fulfillment of this plan. But Francoism, common enemy of all these classes and levels of society, without whose defeat the democratic development of Spain may not even be thought of, will not fall of its own accord, for all its apparent decomposition. The Francoist regime cannot be changed from above, through events hidden from the masses. To depose it and to replace it with a democratic regime is a precondition to the organized revolutionary struggle of the masses. And in this struggle victory may be obtained only on the basis of unifying the actions of all the diverse anti-Franco forces. There is no other road to Spanish democracy, to the radical betterment of the life of the people.

Toward this end the Communist Party declares itself to be prepared to collaborate with all the political groups or parties interested in ousting the regime and liberating Spain from Yankee fetters.

Once Francoism has been destroyed, the coalition of democratic political forces should be the instrument which assures, from a position of power, the fulfillment of this program. When political normalcy has been re-established in Spain, the Communist Party will fight for the maintenance of such a political coalition and for the formation of a democratic government which represents it and accomplishes this program.

The Communist Party will fight to guarantee, as much in the coalition as in the government, the leading role of the working class. Only the guidance of the working class in the coalition can guarantee the fulfillment of the program of democratic transformation needed for Spain's progress.

The Communist Party will fight tirelessly to place the proletariat in a position to play its historic leading role, to elevate its class-consciousness to attain the political and syndical unity of the working class. The Communist Party is prepared, together with other workers who belong to other parties and organizations, to adopt the practical means which would facilitate the realization of said unity, as well as the creation of united class trade unions . . .

. . . The Communist Party will fight to strengthen the alliance between the working class and the peasants, the two moving forces of the democratic revolution. To maintain this alliance it is necessary that the working class, through the organization of the mass struggle, actively helps the peasants in their fight for the land and other compensations . . .

This program will become the program of all the people in the fire of the anti-Franco struggle, through the combined efforts of the workers, peasants, intellectuals, artisans, industrialists and merchants, women and young people, against the militarization and the preparation for a new war, against the construction of Yankee military bases and sky-rocketing military costs, against the fascist terror, for peace and for the radical betterment of living conditions of the populace . . .

V Congreso del PCE, Spanish Communist Party document, 1954, pp. 29–31.

3 Declaration of the PCE for national reconciliation, for a democratic and peaceful solution to the Spanish problem, June 1956

The twentieth anniversary of a historic date draws near, July 18, 1936, when the war of Spain began . . .

In the last few years an important evolution has occurred. Considerable forces, which once made up Franco's field, have been showing their disagreement with a policy which maintains the spirit of civil war.

In the republican camp the opinions of those who believe that it is necessary to bury the hatred and bitterness of the Civil War are numerous and influential, because a spirit of revenge is not constructive.

A spirit favorable to national reconciliation of the Spaniards is winning over the political-social forces which fought in opposing camps during the Civil War . . .

Today the idea of a peaceful solution to the political, economic and social problems of Spain, based upon understanding between the forces of the left and the right, has come a long way, although there still remain serious obstacles to overcome.

In the current situation . . . the Spanish Communist Party solemnly resolves to contribute without reservation to the national reconciliation of Spain, to end the division opened by the Civil War and kept open by General Franco.

Other than national reconciliation, there is no road except violence: violence to defend the present which is tumbling down; violence in response to the brutality of those, who, knowing themselves condemned, resort to violence to maintain their domination.

The Communist Party does not want to follow that road, down which the Spanish people have so often been hurled by the wild intransigence of the ruling classes when faced with any social advance . . .

There exists in all levels of our country the desire to terminate the artificial division of the Spanish into 'reds' and 'nationalists,' to feel themselves to be citizens of Spain, their rights respected, their life and liberty guaranteed, contributing their vigor and knowledge to the national estate . . .

If the national forces which are withdrawing their support for Franco were to rise in support of national reconciliation, the understanding which was impossible among the Spanish during the Civil War could be had now, bridging the past and the present with a face to the future, on the road of Spanish continuity . . .

Spanish Communist Party document, 1956, pp. 3–6.

4 Declaration by the Politburo of the Central Committee of the PCE, May 24, 1958

Broad Catholic sectors in many countries feel that we are living in a period of transition and that Catholics cannot remain indifferent to the material and spiritual aspirations which propel the people. The current is so powerful among the Catholic masses that even Pope Pius XII has echoed them and has said that 'it is a whole world which must be remade from its foundations up,' calling upon Catholics to dedicate their labors to the construction of a better world.

Feeling the same pressure, some church hierarchs have acknowledged in recent years the necessity of structural reform and have aimed criticism at the Francoist dictatorship . . .

The dictatorship, with the acquiescence of the greater part of the ecclesiastic hierarchs, has used the authority of the church in order to shirk its responsibilities, which has unfortunately identified fascism with Catholicism.

In actuality the political and social position of the church, although limited, is becoming different from that of the regime, and its opinions on fundamental questions, such as the necessity of a redistribution of income, just wages, the right of the workers to organize, the problem of land and so many others are positive contributions to the solution of such problems which interest the majority of the people . . .

In the Catholic ranks there has grown a new generation which intervenes in the political and social life of our country, proclaiming its fidelity to the doctrine and the spiritual discipline of the church, but rejecting the historical identification with the regime which official Spain has had an interest in maintaining and prolonging . . .

We do not close our eyes to the influence of Catholicism in Spanish society and politics . . .

Spanish Communist Party document, 1958.

5 Enrique Lister's report to the Central Committee of the PCE, 1958

We communists know that there are many in the military who feel a growing sense of disillusionment and that more than a few join with the rest of the nation in protest against the dictatorship. We know that there exists a large sector of military men of liberal, democratic and modern opinions. We tell them . . . that the time has arrived for them to support the people to bring about the downfall of the dictatorship without bloody commotion.

We communists reject the suggestion of the extreme right that the army be used to substitute a new military dictatorship for the existent military dictatorship.

We know that what decides social change is not armed force, but the masses, the shapers of history, led today by the working class. We know that neither the army nor anyone else can prevent the inevitable ousting of the dictatorship and the restoration of democracy. These will be accomplished within the framework of the economic-social bourgeois system and must take place along a peaceful route. In large part, the attitude of the army will determine whether the transition is accomplished in this way, or whether the peaceful road remains closed.

We call on the military to understand that all the lying propaganda which presents the people and the communists as the enemies of the army is simply criminal . . .

The enemies of the army are those who take advantage of it in order to impose their terrorist dictatorship on the Spanish. The true enemies of the army are Franco and his advisors . . .

The enemy of the army is the dictatorship which has made many of its high officers into permanent judges, armed with a code of laws of medieval brutality, of all the people both left and right who would show their opposition to that dictatorship.

Spanish Communist Party document, 1958, pp. 174–5.

6 Dolores Ibarruri's speech to the Central Committee of the PCE, 1958

We believe that it is time to put an end to the opposition between the socialists and the communists which holds back the unfolding of the struggle and allows the opposition groups of the right to continue a policy of delaying maneuvers, reinforcing their positions and giving the impression of strength they do not yet have.

Unfortunately the Seventh Congress of the PSOE, held last August in Toulouse, has written a new disgraceful page in the already long anti-communist chronicle of certain Socialist Party leaders. The message 'To the Democratic World' approved in that Congress based itself, fundamentally, on the thesis that the Socialist Party fights not only against Francoism, but against communism and against 'Sovietism' as well. Moreover the struggle against Francoism is presented in relation to the fight against the Communist Party. The document's principal accusation against Franco's dictatorship is its inability to impede the large growth in the organization and political influence of the Communist Party, as well as the sympathy of the people toward the Soviet Union and toward other socialist countries.

Not daring to face reality, not daring to explain the real causes of the people's sympathy toward socialism elsewhere, wanting to hide the fact that if the communists are the principal leaders of the workers' strikes, and if the Day of National Reconciliation organized by the communists has had such success it is due to the correct unitary policy of the Communist Party, to its sacrifices and self-denial in the struggle against Francoism, the Seventh Congress of the Socialist Party committed a monstrous distortion of the truth by describing the successes of the Communist Party as the conveniences conceded them by Franco.

The Seventh Congress of the PSOE, instead of looking toward the people, instead of putting its faith in the strengths of the people, whose admirable awakening led to the workers' strikes and the working day of May 5, continues to look toward the Western powers. In the resolutions of the Congress there is an absence of calls for action, of direction to the people. But in order to further the anti-Francoist struggle, a call to the parties of the Socialist International to withhold recognition of any post-Franco government which is not popularly elected figures prominently.

After an experience of twenty years, during which even the least politically aware have learned that the Western powers will not lift a finger against Franco, the PSOE continues to place faith in the liberation of Spain by these powers.

The Seventh Congress has ratified a formula for the composition of a national provisional government without a defined institutional character, which would restore political liberties and would permit the people freedom of expression. This formula, taken by itself, is essentially similar to that proposed by the Communist Party, which makes the socialists' opposition to it seem even more ridiculous. But this formula is not all. What is essential is how to make it successful in practice. Experience shows that there is no road other than the struggle of the people, and a unified opposition.

We, as communists, believe that the Socialist Party should be, and perhaps will be, an important factor in Spanish politics. But its orientation, under the current circumstances, considerably reduces its role and creates within its own ranks a situation of disorder, paralyzing the action of those socialist workers who want to fight against the dictatorship . . .

The Socialist Party's repeated opposition to any agreement with our party in order to put an end to the dictatorship and re-establish democracy, and their inclination to create an anti-Francoist and anti-communist coalition at the same time, are follies which, instead of strengthening the party, weaken it, divide it, and drain it of its old popular and working core and convert it into a toy of the reactionary forces.

By fleeing from the 'communist contagion,' they become infected by reactionism, monarchism, and they estrange themselves dangerously from the working class and the people.

Spanish Communist Party documents, 1958, cf. pp. 48–52.

7 Santiago Carrillo's speech to the Central Committee of the PCE, 1958

How to continue the struggle for unity and organization of the forces of the working class

In order to give greater organization and unity to the anti-Francoist struggle, we communists must base ourselves on the initiative of the masses, developing and perfecting those forms which appear to be the most attainable by the masses, and fleeing from schemes, formalisms and routine attitudes . . .

There is no doubt that our task is to *develop and to consolidate legal and extra-legal forms of unifying* the workers, to work to raise their revolutionary tenor. In this task we are helped by the appropriate objective situation, which makes each economic struggle a clash with the regime and its authorities, contributing to the politicization of these organs.

It is true that this activity is not simple; on the contrary, it is complicated and difficult. But in such complications and difficulties lies the whole difference between a policy of collaboration with the vertical syndicates – that is, to capitulate, to submit to the dictatorship – and utilization of legal opportunities for the furthering of the revolutionary struggle, which is the tactic our party defends . . .

Both forms of unity in the working class, those which take place among the masses, in industry or on a higher plane, between representatives of both political camps, are complementary, and the action of one reverberates reciprocally and favorably to the other.

Today there is no sole standard or exclusive form for fostering unity and organizing the anti-Francoist movement.

It is necessary to devote greater interest to the possibilities of a meeting-of-the-minds and the reaching of an understanding with the groups of Catholic workers, organized in the HOACs and JOCs. We have repeatedly insisted on the fact that, in general, those workers sincerely want to defend the interest of their class.

Spanish Communist Party document, 1958, pp. 111–20.

8 Declaration of the Politburo of the PCE, 1959

The Communist Party of Spain repeatedly proposes to the forces of opposition on both the left and the right, the conclusion of a general accord, or, in its absence, of a series of bilateral accords, with the goal of co-ordinating action against the dictatorship, over-throwing it by bloodless means and constituting a provisional government . . . which would re-establish democratic liberties for all political parties, without exception, and which, in an agreed-upon time, would organize a referendum so that the Spanish can freely support the regime they prefer: monarchy or republic.

In our desire to facilitate an accord between the leftists and the monarchic opposition, we agree to the naming of a lieutenancy for that transitional period, before the referendum set up on the future regime, which must await a popular vote. We are prepared to agree, along with the rest of the forces of the opposition, to a program for that provisional govern-ment and to fulfill, with the usual rigorousness with which we communists honor our agreements, any programs which derive from that government.

We also agree to a program of action with all those forces without our participation in the transitional government.

For us the essential thing is that the Spanish, all Spanish, should have returned to them democratic liberties and that they may choose, and that they not have imposed upon them, the future constitution of Spain. Because an imposition of that nature would leave all those problems unresolved, it would irritate more than it would satisfy the Spanish who are clearly resolved to recover the ability to decide their destiny, and it would endanger public peace . . .

Spanish Communist Party document, 1959, pp. 9–10.

9 'For an authentic workers' unionism, united and independent,' *Mundo Obrero*, May 1966

No one is able to save the 'vertical trade unions.' This fact has led to the maneuvers which attempt to create a substitute for verticalism: a few unions which, with other trappings, continue to defend the interests of the wealthy.

It is unnecessary to say that in order for the unions to be authentic unions of the workers, they have to be created by the workers themselves, without meddling from the outside.

Trade unions must be fully independent of the state and of all political parties, and must devote all their strength to changing the structure of present-day society.

Trade unions must fight for the social emancipa-tion of workers and must have constitutional bases freely and democratically established by the workers' assemblies.

Our clear and decisive concurrence is one more proof that we do not have an isolated outlook. We do not lose sleep wondering about the political affilia-tions of the men who have rendered this service to the workers' movement. The only thing that counts for us is that these bases of unity correspond fully to the interests of the workers, and hence, of democracy.

A central union of the workers, grouping together in its ranks the great working masses, will have to be independent of the political parties. This means that the trade unions of tomorrow will be neither communist nor Catholic nor socialist, nor of any other political affiliation . . .

Mundo Obrero, no. 11 (May 1–15, 1966), p. 4.

10 Santiago Alvarez, 'The alliance of the forces of labor and culture,' 1967

In order to destroy the fascist forms of power, to conquer political democracy and to transform that into an economic-social democracy, it is necessary to achieve an alliance of forces which, because of their extent and weight in political-social life, may be capable of pushing the workers' popular and national struggle to the fulfillment of this historic mission.

The large movement of the masses in our country is forging an alliance which embraces the widest forces of manual and intellectual labor. The conception and form of the alliance of the forces of labor and culture demonstrate the deep meaning of that large movement of masses.

In this movement of masses and in the expression of the new alliance, there are found not only the deter-mining factors of the struggle for democratic liberties, but also the forces which 'can assure the victory of political and economic democracy.' Such forces include the working class, the peasants, the student movement, extensive intellectual, scientific, technical and professional sectors, the deep Catholic movement toward conciliation, and small contractors, artisans and merchants. It appears to be a possibility, capable of being transformed into reality, by virtue of the weight of those forces in the national life.

The importance of such an alliance lies in the fact that it finds itself led by the working class, the most homogeneous, the most numerous and, consequently, the most revolutionary class. But this importance also lies in overcoming the old concept of the worker–peasant alliance in favor of one of greater social extent. The forces of labor and culture, given the existence of the dictatorial regime, monopolistic exploitation, the dynamic of present society and the development of the class struggle within it, join the action decisively.

The alliance of the forces of labor and culture appears not through an agreement among the political parties, as happened, for example, with the Popular Front, nor through a decision expressed from above, by various ideological or political currents; but as a result of the action of masses, of their development and co-ordination, of the solidarity which blossoms from the same struggle and which raises itself with it to new levels and of the specific forms of organization created by the new movement of workers, students, professionals and intellectuals, and so on . . .

The largely heterogeneous composition of the alliance implies that in addition to the unity in its breast, there will also exist an inevitable but indispensable internal struggle; this and unity are two poles of the same dialectic process. This process will acquire specific characteristics in each one of the stages through which the alliance must pass. But the contradictions and the differences of opinion will have to be discussed and overcome on the basis of mutual respect, sincere criticism and self-criticism.

The task of the alliance, after democracy has emerged in Spain, will be to fulfill it through the achievement of 'anti-feudal and anti-monopolist democracy.' The social composition of the alliance, together with the influence which the first democratic chances will exercise, affirm this possibility. Access to power along democratic routes, based essentially on the action of masses, and the destruction of any resistance which would prevent such democracy, must be the goal of the alliance.

Mundo Obrero, no. 16 (April 1–15, 1967), p. 3.

11 J. Diz, 'Discussion of our policy of alliance,' 1970

In some student groups it has been said that the alliance of the forces of labor and culture is the same as putting the proletariat at the tail of the bourgeoisie. Such a criticism has not, in our opinion, even the slightest foundation. The leading role of the working class affirms itself precisely when, at its side, the wide popular masses begin to move, interested, for one reason or another, in achieving the democratic or socialist objectives which the course of the revolution makes the order of the day. Socialism is never reached (the founders of Marxism declared it, history confirmed it) through a 'pure' clash between the working class and the bourgeoisie. The fate of the struggle depends on the working class managing to, or not to, put together an alliance of the most extensive forces which face the domination of the exploiting oligarchy . . .

The suggestion that the alliance of the forces of labor and of culture minimizes the role of the proletariat reflects, in our opinion, a lack of knowledge about the working class and a lack of confidence in its strength . . .

Some accuse the political alliance of the labor and cultural forces of postponing an alliance with the peasants. This is a completely false interpretation.

Upon opening our policy of alliances to the cultural sectors, we found new bases and wider opportunities for the alliance with the country-dwelling masses. With a sound party policy on the rural intelligentsia, whose weight is already growing today and which will grow even more tomorrow, this policy plays a positive role in the mobilization of the peasant masses.

The alliance of the forces of labor and culture is not an 'invention,' a thing 'imagined' by the communists. It is a spontaneous, objective process now unfolding in many forms in Spain. But that spontaneous level is not sufficient. It is the historic mission of the Communist Party, as the party of the vanguard, the party of the working class, to formulate both theoretically and politically the significance and role of this alliance, to fight so that the masses can shape its formation into defensive and combative forms. This constitutes today a *sine qua non* to the fulfillment of the working class's role in the struggle.

Mundo Obrero, no. 1 (January 18, 1970), p. 7.

12   Santiago Carrillo's report to the Eighth Congress of the PCE, 1972 (I)

The People and the Armed Forces

In order to accomplish the political transformation of the country it is necessary to reckon with the armed forces. As an instrument of national defense, those forces are now incapable of countering foreign aggression. But as a repressive organ for the maintenance of the established political regime, they are very powerful. The parties and currents which seek to change the political regime must seriously attempt to neutralize the armed forces, and even to win their support. This is essential for the conquest of freedom . . .

It is true that the dictatorship has made an effort to portray the armed forces as the country's praetorian guard. If the army is looked upon with suspicion, if not hostility, by the public, it is not because of the war — since today the war is not as fundamental — but because the regime has organized the armed forces to stand vigil with their arms over the tranquil sleep of the dictator, protecting the dirty dealings and the corruption of the 'political class,' the privileges of the big bankers, industrialists, and the manorial rural properties . . .

In spite of this criticism, we communists have tried to find another image of the army, which seems to us to be closer to reality, a changing reality which can also influence our judgements and our policy.

First, its discipline and hierarchical structure notwithstanding, the army is not of a piece. There is an upper level comprised of authorities who participated in the Civil War. In addition, there are many officers who came after. And the soldiers are youth of today who have been greatly influenced by progressive and revolutionary ideas . . .

Franco and the regime have always seen the armed forces as colonial police, earlier used against the Moroccans, and later against the Spanish . . .

In order to redistribute the public expense according to just criteria, so that the powerful also pay, there must be a true political revolution in Spain. And that political revolution, which the military men should not see as lawlessness, may take place in days or in hours with less lawlessness than now occurs in a year of dictatorial government and must be the work of an understanding between the people and the army . . .

The traditional reactionaries, the oligarchic minorities, hope that the armed forces will once more expose themselves to danger for their benefit and assure them again, with Franco gone, of the continuity of their privileges.

They hope that the armed forces will help them to empower Prince Juan Carlos, without knowing beforehand whether the Spanish people will accept or reject him.

With their demagoguery, the oligarchs claim to identify their privileges with the national interest and with the armed forces . . .

Our party concludes that the army has great responsibility in the immediate future of Spain, so that indispensable political changes can occur without violence; that it will fulfill its duty to serve the nation if, instead of drawing itself up as the guardian of continuity, it understands that the moment has arrived to give the word back to the people, who should freely shape their country's political social regime.

VIII Congreso del PCE, Spanish Communist Party document, 1972, pp. 46–52.

13   Santiago Carrillo's report to the Eighth Congress of the PCE, 1972 (II)

We work for the unity of the working class in a class trade union, unitary, independent and acting with full autonomy in relation to political parties and groups. We consider the COs to be a movement, not of a party, but completely autonomous . . .

None the less, the fact that we communists have invariably supported COs and participated actively in them, together with the specific, real and undeniable weight which the party has in the working class, has given the Commission the appearance of a movement which, without being communist, concurs with the party in many of its tactical and strategic judgements of the current situation. Such concurrence is on questions such as the general strike, the accord among all the forces fighting for political liberty, the development of workers' democracy in the factories, and on the ending of the exploitation of one man by another, the foundation of socialism.

Regardless of what their critics say, such COs positions are not due to instrumentalization on the part of the communists, but to their widespread support among the workers, both communist as well as non-communist . . .

It would be fatal to consider the COs as an exclusive movement of the workers' vanguard, made up only of workers who have a well-formed revolutionary consciousness, and excluding the great mass who have not reached that level.

The COs should set for themselves the task of bringing together and mobilizing the Marxist workers and those who still suffer from the reformist influence; the most advanced ones, and the most backward, who still have not passed beyond the economic struggle; that is, the vast majority of the class, whatever its level of consciousness. Only in this way will it be possible to act by putting all the workers' weight on the scale; only in this way will it be possible for the workers of the vanguard to raise to their own level, progressively, the consciousness of the most backward levels . . .

COs could not be, consequently, a 'vanguardist,' 'activist' movement – in the sense of minoritarian, elite – but a movement which sets for itself the task of mobilizing the great masses, beginning with the most modest tasks, concerned with details on the lowest level, destined to promote a rise in the level of life. That is what is fundamental in order to begin to unite the working class, to initiate the creation of a powerful workers' front, much more than academic discussion with certain groups, although these are also useful . . .

The need for the COs to attract even the most backward masses of workers, imbued with reformism, 'legalism,' or passivity, does not mean that the COs should abandon their opposition and class struggle and that they should adapt themselves either to this regime or to any other which may represent its continuation. The COs will not be able to 'buy' their legality at the price of *adaptation*, of concessions to any political situation whatsoever, *although they might take advantage of all the legal opportunities which exist today or may exist tomorrow*. The COs are not and should not be a reformist movement, of class collaboration, under the threat of losing their credibility not only among the workers of the vanguard, but also among the wide masses. COs must maintain themselves in the democratic camp, promoting the class struggle and resisting an *evolutionist* pressure; otherwise they would also lose their international prestige . . .

The COs need not and must not situate themselves on the *front lines* of the political fight. This is the role of the parties alone. The scope of COs dialogue must remain distinct from, and even wider than, that of the parties.

The principal activity of the COs should occur in the social camp, that is their *first line*. And occupying it even more fully is how they will manage to fall into political action effectively.

VIII Congreso del PCE, Spanish Communist Party document, 1972, pp. 73–6.

14 Political resolution of the Eighth Congress of the PCE, 1972

The Pact for Liberty
The Pact for Liberty is a growing process. The democratic alternative is being formed around a basic program: *a broadly based provisional government, amnesty, political liberty without discrimination, elected constituent courts which will decide the political-social regime of the Spanish state.*

For this alternative it is necessary to win new political forces, economic interests, representatives of different estates, professionals, men of the church, functionaries of the state and members of the armed forces. And to move from our achievements to the consolidation of the pact for liberty on a state-wide scale . . .

The Political Revolution
The Eighth Congress emphasizes that the step from fascist dictatorship to democracy is impossible without a true *political revolution*. The popular masses and all our possible allies must understand this.

The political revolution in Spain need not be a civil war, or an insurrection of the classic sort. With a marshalling of forces favorable to political change, an isolation of the 'ultras,' the political revolution would require less violence than that which the regime customarily uses to remain in power.

The political revolution will be a national and democratic change, in which all forces seeking political liberty must intervene . . .

The Congress reaffirms our party's conception of an alliance of the forces of labor and culture, struggling against the dictatorship and directing itself toward the achievement of socialism in Spain . . .

We emphasize the importance of the struggle of women, who represent half of the population, who suffer discrimination in society and in the family, and whose goals and successes have been shaped demo-cratically. We communists must profoundly change our attitudes toward the feminist question, overcoming reactionary notions and adopting a position in accord with Marxist theory and with the realities of our time.

VIII Congreso del PCE, Spanish Communist Party document, 1972, cf. pp. 331–4.

15   Santiago Carrillo, 'The spirit of the Civil War,' 1974

The spirit which gives life to this government, like all those of the regime, is clear: it is the spirit of civil war, of police terror, of repression, of censorship; the spirit of the fascist bunker, of tyranny against which the immense majority rises up, more decisively each day.

It is necessary to acknowledge that fascism has far-reaching arms of influence, but at the same time its legs are flaccid. And soon they will give out. Spanish fascism will collapse loudly, as Portuguese fascism has collapsed, as fascism in Greece will collapse.

At a press conference the day before yesterday, a reporter asked me if we communists would be prepared to carry on a dialogue with the current Spanish government. That government does not attempt a dialogue; the only thing it wants is to continue the interminable monologue which has gone on for more than thirty years in Spain.

For many years we communists have declared that, for the transition from dictatorship to democracy, it is necessary to form a provisional government and to achieve national reconciliation, which would return sovereign power to the people.

A provisional government must emerge when it is ready from Spain herself; it has to spring forth from the heart of today's Spain, just as it is, and not from yesterday's Spain. And if the Communist Party participates in the government it will be not for what the party represented yesterday – even when we may be proud of our past – but for what it represents today as a spokesman for the young generations of workers, students and professionals; of the forces which march surely and decidedly toward the de-mocratic and socialist future of Spain.

Toward a Democratic Change
From here to there, there still remains a distance to travel. I am sure that we will travel it more rapidly than some think. After the recent events in Portugal there is a phantom which is already beginning to make the groups which monopolize power uneasy. Their dreams are nightmares of a provisional govern-ment; a sign that we have the wind at our backs, a sign that the victory of democracy is finally nearing in Spain!

We are not prophets. Because of today's circum-stances, tomorrow things could be different. We do not hope for democratic change as it happened in Portugal, through the officers' uprising

In Spain there is no colonial war, which elsewhere has led to a stocktaking of consciousness and up-risings by the army.

The regime has not worried about the qualitative development of the army as an instrument of national defense. And the explanation is quite simple. The regime has never thought of using the army to guarantee national integrity, which has been thrown to the foreign powers for a pittance. The regime has thought of the armed forces as a large police force, destined to protect it from popular demands for liberty and justice.

We communists have for years proposed, against all criticisms and doubt, co-operation between the people and the army. So that one day in Spain, like today in Portugal, children can place red carnations in the muzzles of rifles as symbols of the new friendship between the army and the people . . .

Mundo Obrero, no. 13 (July 2, 1974), p. 2.

16   Manifesto program of the PCE, 1975

The contradiction between the requirements of a modern development for Spain and the fascist regime. The struggle for liberty.

The Pact for Liberty
The fundamental contradiction between the pro-letariat and the bourgeoisie and the contradiction between the anti-monopolist classes and the political and economic power of the monopolies are today disguised, hidden, from the vast popular and working sectors, by the existence of Franco's fascist

dictatorship and by the total absence of democratic liberties. *So long as this restraint is not lifted, so long as the people have not regained democratic liberties,* the revolutionary perspective will remain invisible to millions of men who logically should be its protagonists . . .

The Democratic Junta

This leads the Communist Party of Spain to proclaim a democratic alternative which provides a way out of the current situation in the interest of the popular masses and facilitates, at the same time, a convergence of diverse forces interested in putting an end to the dictatorship. Such a broad alliance would prejudge neither the political regime nor future social transformation, leaving these questions to be solved in a democratic framework.

The essential points of possible convergence which the Communist Party of Spain has been making stand out as the following:

(1) A coalition-led provisional government.
(2) Total amnesty for political prisoners and exiles.
(3) Political liberties without any discrimination.
(4) Recognition of the specific national personalities of Catalonia, Euskadia and Galicia, through the provisional application of the Statutes of Autonomy, as outlined by the popular referenda of the 1930s.
(5) Freely elected constituent courts which will decide the future political regime of Spain.

The proposals of the Spanish Communist Party will permit the step from fascist dictatorship to democracy, the realization of a true political revolution, with the least possible violence, eliminating the danger of a new civil war.

The Democratic Junta of Spain voices this need. Its platform includes the measures needed to put an end to the dictatorship and to establish democratic liberties in Spain so that the people can decide their own destinies.

The Democratic Junta has launched a national offensive to co-ordinate all the forces working for an authentic democratic alternative, and to weaken and isolate the 'ultra' movements and to undo the pseudo-liberal deceits of Juan-Carlist continuism . . .

The role of the movements of masses in the struggle for liberty and for political social democracy

When we propose the Pact for Liberty, . . . as a convergence of forces, we want to underline the transitory character of the accord. Actually the diversity of the forces united in it is so wide and their class characters are so at odds that it is only possible to conceive of their alliance as a consequence of a political anachronism . . . the fascist dictatorship of Franco.

The essential task of the Pact for Liberty is to end the residual struggles of the civil war, to formulate a new democratic political framework in accordance with the general requirements of liberty . . .

The alliance of the forces of labor and culture

In our country the moving forces of the anti-Franco struggle, and the most interested in Spain's evolution towards political and social democracy and socialism, are the following.

First, the working class. In Spain the working class has been the principal carrier of progress, as much in relation to the specific tasks of the bourgeois revolution which the bourgeoisie has left undone, as to the tasks of the democratic anti-monopolist and socialist revolution.

The working class has won great prestige among the other anti-monopolist social levels . . .

By developing itself, by growing both quantitatively and qualitatively, the working class has become the largest and most decisive class in society.

It is the class which has nothing to lose with the fall of the fascist dictatorship, with the abolition of the political and economic power of the monopolies, with the abolition of capitalist private property; on the contrary, it has everything to gain . . .

Secondly, the peasants have been the traditional ally of the working class. Because of their situation, condemned to expulsion from the land by the concentration of property in the hands of the great landowners, the agrarian bourgeoisie and the capitalist enterprises, because of the plundering politics of Francoist power which reduces their income to a level of intolerable subsistence, and also because of the historic traditions of revolutionary struggle, the working peasants are the natural ally of the working class . . .

The peasants are also interested in the establishment of political and social democracy and socialism. Many signs today indicate that they are becoming conscious of their situation and increasingly frequent examples indicate that consciousness is transforming itself into action. The struggle of the peasants will be a decisive contribution to the Spanish revolution.

Thirdly, the working class and the peasants today have a powerful new ally: the forces of culture.

Among the structural changes which have taken place in our country, one of the most important is the quantitative growth of the forces of culture . . .

The growth of productive forces makes scientists and technologists participate more and more directly in the process of production. Although some of them continue to be situated socially next to the dominant classes, supplying them with technocrats, managers and high-placed functionaries, the mass of the scientific and technical workers, by intervening more directly in production, join the mass of the salaried. Even though their salaries are generally higher, they resort, like the manual laborer, to the market to sell their labor and, although it may be in diminished degree, they know capitalist exploitation and aliena- tion. This leads them to consciousness and sympathy for the anti-capitalist forces . . .

These new and developing structural character- istics are what we call *forces of culture*. During the crisis of imperialism and the ascension of socialism, wide sectors of these forces adopt a critical attitude, not only toward the Francoist dictatorship, but also toward capitalist society. Their great cultural education brings them to analyze the state of capitalist society globally, and to discover its irrationality and decadence and to opt for socialism . . .

But the phenomenon of the passage of a great part of the forces of culture to the working class camp, although it indicates how much socialism has matured within capitalist society and how close the revolution is, is a distinct phenomenon from that suggested by Marx. It is a consequence of the fact that the impetuous development of productive forces tends to erase the differences between intellectual and manual labor, and under modern capitalism it tends to integrate the majority of the intellectual workers with the manual workers into the same exploited and alienated class.

The Communist Party concludes that the old formula of the alliance of the workers and peasants no longer justly reflects the composition of the social forces behind the socialist revolution and, conse- quently, has formulated the thesis of the alliance of the forces of labor and culture, which presupposes the first and includes the new intellectual force . . .

Spanish Communist Party document, 1975, pp. 51–60.

17 Santiago Carrillo, 'Negotiate for the democratic transformation, yes! Negotiate for neo-Francoism, no!', 1976

The only centrist political program offered to the country today is the democratic alternative presented by the opposition. It is a centrist program because in essence it is a compromise among forces of the left, center and right. In order to formulate such a program of political liberty, we have all made concessions, in order to find the bases which could obtain the widest national consensus.

It simply involves formulating a democratic frame- work for all; something which does not exist today and which is indispensable for the stability of the country.

The democratic transformation is nothing more than that. Within this framework, national suffrage will continue to decide majorities and minorities.

It does not involve, then, an opposition which puts forth irresponsible positions, seeks privileges or pursues chimeras. How can they speak of *maximalisms* now when, with extremely rate exceptions, even the most leftist groups have been able to moderate their positions? I insist that the compromises at which the different forces of the opposition have arrived have created the only centrist program now offered in Spain.

The true 'maximalism' is that of the ultra-right and of neo-Francoism; the 'maximalism' of those who, when speaking of democracy, mean that everything stays the same, that the dictatorship be replaced by new authoritarianism. It is true that it is necessary to handle the situation with care. Otherwise Spain could head toward a catastrophe; to a situation in which the possibilities for reconciliation which today are real may fail. The vast majority of the Spanish desire reconciliation, they want to exorcise the demons of the Civil War and violence. But that is only possible with democracy. If the roads to democracy were to close, because of the preponderance of some and the meekness of others, because of the refusal to make a peace with neither victors nor losers – which after forty years is a reasonable demand – the democratic forces would find themselves obliged to sacrifice reconciliation for democracy . . .

Mundo Obrero, no. 19 (September 29, 1976), p. 8.

18 'United Junta and Platform to the people of Spain,' *Mundo Obrero*, March 1976

Declaration of democratic co-ordination

Prompted by the general crisis of the government and the regime, and by the absence of just and efficient solutions to the grave problems of the country, and with full consciousness of the historic responsibility carried by the democratic opposition, before the people of Spain, the Democratic Junta of Spain and the Platform of Democratic Convergence have today decided on their dissolution and the simultaneous constitution of a sole organ of opposition, the DEMOCRATIC CO-ORDINATION, as a necessary measure to offer to Spanish society a real alternative capable of transforming, through pacific means, the current state into a democratic state.

The DEMOCRATIC CO-ORDINATION *opposes* the continuity of a regime which makes impossible the democratic freedom of all its citizens, whether under the concrete form which has been established by the Fundamental Laws, or under any form of government or of the state which is imposed upon the people without consultation, with full guarantees of political liberty and impartiality and with equal access to the state means of mass communication.

Consequently the DEMOCRATIC CO-ORDINATION *denounces* as a destroyer of peaceful conviviality the intention of the so-called reformist policy of the government to perpetuate itself in power, combining democratic promises with repressive measures, and dividing the most politically responsible and trade union forces through arbitrary discrimination and exclusion. The political reforms approved by the government and sent to the courts are not acceptable to the opposition because, although they formally modify earlier criteria, they do not recognize the democratic liberties of all the citizens of the state.

The DEMOCRATIC CO-ORDINATION declares its decision to undertake the necessary political actions for the attainment of the following objectives.

The immediate liberation of all political and trade union prisoners and, without exception, the return of exiles and an amnesty which restores all the political and union rights of those who have been deprived of them.

The full and effective exercise of human rights and political liberties defined by international law, especially the freedom to organize politically, without exception.

The immediate and full recognition of the rights and political liberties of the different nationalities and regions governed by the Spanish state.

The functioning of a sole and independent judicial power according to the requirements of a democratic society. The DEMOCRATIC CO-ORDINATION invites:

The national and regional opposition to join with this organ to provide a democratic alternative to the Spanish state.

The political parties and the trade union organization which did not form a part of the platform or of the Junta, to integrate themselves into the DEMOCRATIC CO-ORDINATION.

The economic, professional and cultural sectors and the public administration, as well as ecclesiastic, military and judicial institutions, to open a dialogue at the altar of the greater patriotic interests, to work toward achievement of the peaceful alternative defined here.

All the democratic, political, trade union and social forces and all the citizens of Spain to mobilize for the effective conquest of fundamental rights and liberties, and for the establishment at the moment of the break, of coalition-led executive power organs, without exclusions or obligations, which guarantee complete democratic liberties and rights, and the opening and development of a constituent process until the transfer of power to a constitutionally elected government.

The DEMOCRATIC CO-ORDINATION concludes that the fulfillment of its political end as a democratic alternative requires its continuation until general elections are called, without detriment to the liberty of each party in the constitutional debate, and that, after the democratic break, it will reconsider the appropriateness of its continued existence.

The signers of the DEMOCRATIC CO-ORDINATION declare their profound conviction that they all concur in this act, wishing to overcome past confrontation, and that they will respect the decision of the constituent process, as well as that of the democratic elections.

The DEMOCRATIC CO-ORDINATION expresses its total conviction that this program constitutes the only peaceful route to democracy. Its attainment is not, for that reason, the exclusive task of the opposition, but a duty of all the Spanish.

Madrid, March 26, 1976

Signers:

Workers' Commissions	Independent Group
Communist Movement Party	Carlist Party

Spanish Communist Party	Popular Democratic Party (subject to ratification)
Spanish Socialist Workers' Party	Popular Socialist Party General Workers' Union
Spanish Workers' Party	Democratic Left (subject to ratification)
Spanish Social Democrat Union	

Mundo Obrero, no. 13 (March 31, 1976), p. 3.

19 'Christians in the party,' *Mundo Obrero*, 1976

We are sure that the Christians who join the party have realized, along with wide sectors of the Christian masses, that political commitment is autonomous and of a lay nature. Other than their individual reasons for supporting socialism, the Christians who join the party do it as an option of class and they do not subtract the militancy from their faith. They have overcome the confusion between the faith and the traditional politics of Christianity.

The PCE recognizes the complexity of the decision which inspires and animates the militancy of the Christians who join the party. It admits them *with their faith* and thus abandons the old policy of attempting to make the Christian communist abandon his faith upon joining the party, or, more frequently, that they maintain it at a private level, that is, without giving it any social expression. We say *with their faith*, that is, fully respecting their Christian convictions, which have not only stopped being an obstacle to the revolutionary mission, but are an impulse for their militancy and participation in the class struggle.

The Central Committee of the PCE believes that the Christian membership of the party strengthens the lay character of the party and overcomes certain currents which were attempting to maintain the identification of communism with atheism which, although not statutorily sanctioned, occurred in practice for reasons which stem from the historic confrontation between the churches and the communist parties and the majority of the populace.

The Christian militants in the party suffer no discrimination, have the same opportunities for promotion to ruling organs, and the same rights and duties as any other militant. They do not constitute, nor should they constitute in any form, a differentiated sector of the party, as has been suggested. Christian communists must join together with the mass of the party, with all their comrades, in a single collective struggle.

The presence of Christians in the party contributes to the shaping of the mass party we seek. It does not involve merely a 'legitimization' of the Christians in the party, after a long period of unyielding confrontation between the communist parties and the church, but an understanding that the presence of Christians is as important for the internal life of the party as for its social and political projection . . .

Mundo Obrero, no. 36 (October 18–24, 1976), p. 9.

20 Santiago Carrillo's speech at the Seventeenth Congress of the PSOE, 1976

Dear Comrades:

Upon your meeting legally in Spain, for the first time since the Civil War, we want to send to you the fraternal greeting of the Communist Party of Spain.

We desire for your Seventeenth Congress good work and success for the advancement of the common cause of democracy and socialism.

National and international public opinion follow your deliberations with great interest, because the PSOE is one of the key political forces in our country and one upon which depend its present and its future.

Your party, as ours, has advanced constructive proposals for peaceful transformation from the dictatorship to democracy. The feat of having defended firmly the essential principles in which transformation must base itself has meant for both of us many treacherous attacks from reactionary forces who have accused us of a 'maximalism' quite far from our true positions.

Those attacks tended, on one side, to give the impression that we were trying to resuscitate the Popular Front, when what we have both agreed upon is the need to bring together the widest consensus of those who want to re-establish political liberties, without exclusion or discrimination and without mortgaging anyone's independence; on another side, to create an atmosphere of confusion, they certainly intended to differentiate us, to maintain that which is specific to each of us, to bring us to misunderstandings and mistrust.

Their objectives will not be achieved. Respecting the particularities which distinguish the PSOE, as well as the PCE, we have faith that the one and the other, both parties, will continue to concur as long as it involves the defense of the rights of the people and we will reject any provocation which intends to obstruct this objective.

For the Central Committee of the Communist Party of Spain
Santiago Carrillo
Madrid, December 5, 1976

Mundo Obrero, no. 44 (December 13–19, 1976), p. 1.

21   S. Sanchez Montero, 'The party's policy of alliances,' 1977

To speak of the party's policy of alliances is to speak of its strategic plan for the march toward socialism, departing from the current situation and from the concrete conditions of today's society in Spain and in the world. It is to speak of *the policy* of the party as it is established in its program.

Our party's program covers three well-differentiated stages along the road from oligarchic dictatorship – which we still have not completely come out of – to socialism. Each state corresponds to and is characterized by a fundamental objective and an alliance of political forces which makes possible its achievement: establishment of a truly democratic regime and the liquidation of the dictatorship; political and economic democracy or anti-monopolist and anti-latifundist democracy; construction of a multi-party socialist society. These are the three stages to which we have referred: unity of all opposition forces in the Pact for Liberty; alliance of the anti-monopolist and anti-latifundist democratic forces; alliance of the forces of labor and of culture; and socialist formation which brings together all political forces working for socialism. These are the three political alliances corresponding to each one of the previous stages. Of course, in reality things do not occur with such bookish schematism. It involves a unique democratic and revolutionary process, and in each stage and type of alliance there are mixed elements of the others. But such a differentiation is not a theoretic abstraction; it corresponds to the foreseeable, dialectical development of the struggle for socialism in Spain.

The Pact for Liberty was, and continues to be, the alliance, or better yet, the political compromise of all the forces opposed to the dictatorship, of the left, the right and the middle, whose goal is the acquisition of political liberty, the establishment of a democratic regime and the liquidation of the dictatorship.

The viability of the Pact for Liberty was assured by the double economic and political convergence of the interests of the working class with those of an important part of the bourgeoisie in the defeat of the dictatorship; the working class, because only by acquiring liberty would it be able to organize and develop its forces, to defend itself from vicious oligarchic exploitation and to declare its commitment to socialism; the bourgeoisie, because the dictatorship had become an obstacle to its economic development and to the establishment of political liberties as well as Spain's entry into the Common Market, the establishment of full relations with socialist countries and their market, and so on.

On the basis of this objective convergence, a political compromise would be possible which would accelerate the decomposition of the dictatorship, by winning over or neutralizing important sectors of the administration, the army, the church and economic sectors of the bourgeoisie, and which would permit, without violent trauma, the destruction of the old totalitarian and fascist system and the establishment of a new democracy. The break would have to be achieved through the formation of a provisional government with the decisive participation of the popular masses, most important the working class, under whose political supremacy a true political revolution would be achieved, even if it did not at all alter the foundations of the capitalist system.

The Democratic Junta (JD), the first serious attempt at a unitary process, culminated in the creation of the Pact for Liberty. Its strategy was based on organizing and mobilizing the masses, and it assured their leading role in the change from the dictatorship to democracy. But fundamental political forces, such as the PSOE and the Christian Democrats, remained outside the Democratic Junta. One year later, the condition of the Platform of Democratic Convergence around these forces made it clear that the JD would not reach its objective all by itself. Only by joining with the Platform was the unity of the opposition made possible. From the union of the JD and the Platform there emerges the

Democratic Co-ordination (CD), which essentially changes the character and strategy of the JD. Another important step in the unitary process was the creation of the Platform of Democratic Organs (POD), which included the unitarian organs of the nationalities (with the exception of Euskadia, where none existed, although some of the most important Euskadian political forces did join in).

The democratic inroads have created an original, fluid situation in which everything continues to be legally prohibited, but everything is done more openly and publicly each day. The masses are *imposing* democratic legality. Obliged by popular pressure and, at the same time, basing itself on it, the government has taken a series of measures which have seriously weakened the position of the 'ultras' in the army and in the repressive apparatus, although they still have strength in both. Such progress, which is 90 per cent the result of popular pressure, has virtually precluded the possibility of a coup by the 'ultra' forces, making the advance toward democracy irreversible.

It must be emphasized that the democratic break, still not achieved, continues to be a fundamental political objective, necessary for the establishment of democracy. And consequently we must complete and maintain the unity needed to reach this goal . . .

Nuestra Bandera, no. 85 (1977), pp. 9–11.

22   Santiago Carrillo's statement on the meetings of the Moncloa, 1977

What is happening in the Moncloa indicates that the Communist Party was right, and the facts have come to demonstrate it very rapidly in this case. The transition from dictatorship to democracy cannot be directed, and the problems of the economic crisis cannot be confronted, by a minority government. And for that government there does not exist an alternative government, because the left is also a minority. There is the alternative of democratic concentration.

The pact of the Moncloa is not a pact of fear, but that does not mean that in this country the threats to democracy have disappeared; the threats to democracy are real . . .

Relations PCE–PSOE

I want to tell you that in all this endeavor of co-operation we give priority to relations with the comrades of the PSOE. I wonder at a recent series of declarations of socialist leaders in which we are attacked very aggressively, not only politically, but personally. It seems as though our comrades of the PSOE sometimes become nervous. We will not become nervous and, say what they will, we will always say that we communists and socialists have a long road to travel united and that we are prepared to travel it.

The same in the area of trade unions. In this period a unity among the trade union organizations is necessary: unity in action, directed toward a future unitary workers' trade organization, because the managers are not organizing themselves by political colors. They organize themselves in a single union of managers.

Some say: 'But, instead of this, why don't the communists propose a leftist alternative?' I answer them: What leftist alternative? Where in these Cortes are there votes for a leftist alternative? There aren't any. And I add, even if there were, those in power in this country, who are the same as those of yesterday, would not allow a leftist alternative. The problem is that the only leftist alternative in Spain today is the policy of democratic concentration which the Communist Party defends and fights for.

Tomorrow, when democracy is established and consolidated, then there will be other alternatives for the left. Then we will see more clearly than today where the left really is and where it is not. We communists want a socialist society, an egalitarian society, a society with neither oppressed nor oppressors. But in order to shape such a society we cannot allow the country to go backwards. We have to make it move forward, although the pace may be slow today. What is important is that it is steady and that it gives us a platform from which we can march toward the future.

Spanish Communist Party document, 1977, cf. pp. 1–2, 8–9.

23   Resolutions of the Ninth Congress of the PCE, 1978

The policy of national reconciliation

At heart, national reconciliation is a proposal to all

Spanish political-social forces, including those most opposed to the Communist Party: the proposal of accepting a common patriotic framework, a new legal and democratic model in which we can all move forward. We propose to take the political-social conflicts which confront and will continue to confront the different social forces, political parties and philosophical schools out of the atmosphere of intolerance and fanaticism in which they have evolved until now, in order to place them in a new setting, that of patriotic citizenship, in which opposing ideologies and class conflicts do not immediately acquire the dramatic forms which frequently bloodied the history of the country.

This strong desire to overcome violence and at the same time to escape from economic catastrophe by a peaceful route, to move toward a situation in which all parties can freely defend their principles and programs and seek popular support for them, is what can make all the Spanish agree today, even if their earlier ideas on the organization of Spanish politics and society were at odds and are even now opposed . . .

The strong desire of the Communist Party of Spain to rid our country of the climate of intolerance and fanaticism which so frequently has driven our history down the path of civil war has been expressed by new communist positions on issues such as the monarchy, the flag, the army, relations with the church or with the right, and so on.

On the monarchy, the Communist Party of Spain, which is republican, has reached an understanding of the issue in light of concrete conditions of the present.

If the monarchy favors the consolidation of democracy and the drafting of a constitution which would establish a parliamentary democracy, the Communist Party would consider it a serious mistake to endanger the democratic process by questioning the form of government. The problem could be posed if we were to find ourselves before an autocratic monarchy which would prevent democratic and parliamentarian rule. But as long as the monarchy is not an obstacle to the democratic decisions of the people, the Communist Party will not question the present monarchic form of government.

On the issue of the flag, the Communist Party decided in April of 1977 to adopt, along with the red flag of the Communist Party of Spain, the red and gold flag of the state, a decision which helped to create a new climate of understanding between the left and certain institutions. Without that decision, so criticized at the time, the issue probably would have become intractable and would have given birth to sterile contradictions, endangering the democracy . . .

Another key aspect of Communist Party policy which has helped to dispel irrational myths and to create new political-social relationships is the policy toward the religions and toward the church. Today Christian participation in the party is already normal. But it must not be forgotten that this is so because the Communist Party began to encourage the dialogue between Christianity and Marxism in the mid-1950s. It was the first party of the Spanish left which grasped in a new way the phenomenon of the first, timid steps toward the transformations which occurred in our country . . .

Under Franco's dictatorship the class struggle was made difficult by the burden of repression. In proportion to how this burden is being lifted, the class struggle is developing more through economic and social transformation, and through the conquest of a greater political role for the workers.

The fact that the working class has been and is today the class most interested in the defense and consolidation of democracy, and in the economic and social transformations which improve the economic situation and help to overcome the crisis, as well as to spur the advance toward socialism, places the working class in a position to represent the general interests of the country, to become the hegemonic class . . .

IX Congreso del PCE, Spanish Communist Party document, 1978, pp. 57–63.

24   Interview with Santiago Carrillo, *Nuestra Bandera*, 1978

The Moncloa Pact, 'Eurocommunism,' the party . . .
The concept of the Italian 'historic compromise' is related to the continuity of the anti-fascist struggle which culminated in 1945 with the defeat of the forces of the Axis, and which was carried out through a policy of wide democratic consensus. I do not think that the name 'historic compromise' can be applied to the Pact of the Moncloa because it does not describe what the Popular Front was or, of course, what the National Movement was. It is a compromise very much of today; I would say that it is the formation of a policy of national reconciliation.

It is clear that that Pact, if it is put into effect, will

have historic scope, but I believe that the comparison with the Italian example is not well made.

What gives this Pact a political-economic character rather than a social character is precisely its having been formulated by the political parties without exclusive reference to the problem of the distribution of income, that is, of wages, but with reference to a whole series of structural problems in politics and the economy.

If the Pact had been made among trade unions, businessmen and the government, then it would have been simply a social pact; but made among political parties and with those political-economic structural components, the Pact is what we and the trade unions, particularly workers' commissions, have been asking that it be: a political-economic pact and not a social pact.

Nuestra Bandera, no. 90 (1978), p. 30.

PART THREE

The Party

Introduction to Part Three

The organizations of the eurocommunist parties have undergone substantial re-evaluation and change in the past three decades. At the close of the Second World War all the parties were marked by the heritage of the 'bolshevized' revolutionary cadre party tradition of the Third International. In the years since, to differing degrees and with different pace and timing, the parties have generally been becoming mass parties. The PCI has even been characterized as a catch-all party, at least with respect to its electoral and recruitment behavior. The need to operate in a democratic context, to which the parties gradually adapted their strategies, required that they move to a more open structure, better able to reach the ever-wider range of social strata which they included among the allies they hoped to attract. Furthermore, changes in the societies themselves – the increasing complexity of social structure, growing urbanization, and a number of other factors associated with advanced industrialization in the West – made organizational change necessary if the parties were to avoid isolation and were to be able to implement their strategic designs. The extent to which such change has occurred, however, has varied considerably. The national contexts in which the parties operate, and the evolution of their national strategies, have differed; it is understandable that so too have their patterns of organizational change. The pressure to make the parties more open to society has also promoted occasional debates about the appropriateness of democratic centralism as the organizing principle of party life; but, to date, changes in this regard have been limited.

Several distinct traits of party change can be identified. First, all the parties have increasingly been attempting to gain the electoral support of wide strata of the population. The PCI led the way in this respect. Its electoral targets were already very heterogeneous in the immediate postwar period, and have, if anything, expanded further subsequently. Middle-class groups, peasants, Catholics, intellectuals were always desired as electoral supporters. In addition, the party was determined to seek to equalize its electoral backing throughout the nation and especially in the South where it was initially extremely weak. In these efforts it had considerable success, especially in the 1970s when it garnered much new middle-class and southern support. The 1979 elections, however, signalled at least a temporary halt to this trend.

The Spanish and French parties have been much slower to pursue the kind of heterogeneous electoral strategy undertaken by the Italians. In the case of the Spanish party, the reasons for this are obvious. In the years since the death of Franco, in fact, the PCE sought to broaden its electorate, particularly to Catholics. The PCF, in contrast, appears even today to remain partially captive of its *ouvrièriste* traditions, of its reluctance to make the changes in internal party organization which would be necessary successfully to pursue a broad electoral policy and of its preference to reinforce its support in the pockets of electoral dominance which it won immediately after the war. The changes in the social and territorial composition of its electorate have thus been less marked than those of the PCI. Even in the 1970s, despite some losses in old electoral bastions and some gains in new areas, the profile of the PCF's electorate looks much like that of the past. The size of its vote has also been more or less stagnant, showing none of the tendency toward steady growth which the PCI displayed until 1979.

Party change has also occurred with respect to organizational membership. At the close of the Second World War all the parties were relatively small and had highly restrictive criteria for membership and practices governing the acceptance of new members. This was the heritage of the bolshevized, Leninist cadre party and of the period of clandestinity. All the parties have, to differing extents, abandoned many of the features of this type of party, moving toward becoming mass parties. Here again the PCI has led the way. From the times of Togliatti's return to Italy in April 1944, the party began to revise its traditional recruitment and membership procedures. It opened its ranks to recruits from all social strata, encouraged active and widespread recruitment and, perhaps most significantly, ruled out religious belief as a bar to membership. Even a commitment to Marxism–Leninism was no longer deemed essential; adherence to the party's program was to be the sole criterion of eligibility. The party did not, however, cease to seek to teach members the official Marxist–Leninist doctrine nor to try to convince them of its correctness.

This loosening of admission criteria was combined with changes in the procedures of admission, transferring decisional control from the paid party functionaries to the grass-roots organizations. The intention of all these changes was to make the PCI a mass party which would have as large a membership, and as wide a social presence, as possible. The policy proved successful, membership growing to over 2 million in the early 1950s. While membership fell for a variety of reasons in the late 1950s and 1960s, it rose once again in the early and mid-1970s, and is today well over 1½ million.

The French party too adopted more open membership criteria and practices in the immediate postwar period, although it never abandoned functionary control. After the onset of the Cold War it returned to many of its traditional procedures, and its membership, which had rivalled that of the PCI, fell dramatically. Throughout the 1950s and 1960s membership probably did not exceed half a million and was often lower. (It is to be noted that the PCF has been far less open than the PCI in reporting the numbers and characteristics of its members.) In the last decade the PCF has once again made significant efforts to adapt its organizational rules to make more likely memberships from groups not part of the French party's traditional constituencies, especially the 'new' middle class of technical workers. The gains from this policy in some social groups, such as teachers and researchers, have been marked, but the blue-collar working class remains the predominant PCF constituency.

The PCE, not surprisingly, maintained very tight criteria and practices governing membership throughout the period of clandestinity. Since the death of Franco, and even in the period immediately preceding the collapse of the Francoist regime, however, the PCE sought to expand the targets of its membership recruitment to Catholics and the middle class. Today the party's membership criteria and methods of recruitment are increasingly coming to resemble those of the Italian party, although its size does not.

A third area of party change has been in the structure of organization. As in the preceding two areas, the PCI has led the way. Since the mid-1950s the role of the cell as the basic unit of territorial grass-roots organization has given way to the larger, more heterogeneous section. In the factories the party has sought to retain the cell as a critical organizational source of strength, but it has encountered significant difficulties in this regard, difficulties indicated by repeated campaigns to reinforce factory cell organization. The PCI has also sought to decentralize significantly the administrative control of the party organization. The party structures of the PCF and PCE are still today more reliant on the cell and on centralized administrative control. The Spanish party, however, has granted considerable autonomy to some of its regional components and, like the Italian party, seems to be moving toward some reliance on territorial organization in larger, more heterogeneous units.

Crucial to an understanding of the reasons why the eurocommunists have moved toward becoming mass parties is the fact that they are operating in a democratic context and have developed strategies intended to allow them to operate effectively within the rules of the democratic and electoral political game, while at the same time retaining some of their socialist transformative goals. The organizational patterns which have gradually evolved represent different mediations between the ideological and strategic adaptations which the parties have made to their respective national contexts and the traditions and long-standing goals specific to each party. The differences between the PCI and PCF, for instance, cannot be understood, on the one hand, without paying attention to the traditionally weak mass base for democracy in Italy as compared to France, the relatively greater permeability of the Italian state and the critical role of economic dualism and of the Catholic Church in Italian social and political life. Nor, on the other hand, are these differences comprehensible without acknowledging the role of the Gramscian tradition (itself capitalized on by postwar party leaders) in the PCI as contrasted to the powerful *ouvrièriste* tradition in the PCF and that party's lack of an indigenous party ideology.

As this contrast indicates, the European communist parties have not become catch-all parties, despite some tendencies in that direction, especially in electoral strategies and, in the case of the Italian, in the composition of the party's electorate and membership. All three parties continue to emphasize the importance of members, to stress ideological training, and to seek to be extremely active in society not only at the time of elections but between elections as well. Furthermore, all three parties, despite the sometimes inchoate and moderate nature of their short-term party programs, continue to stress the linkage of these programs to the long-term goal of a socialist, if also democratic, transformation of society. In addition, for all the parties the working class remains the core constituency and tactical and strategic reference point.

The extent to which the organizational changes described fall well short of a transformation of the eurocommunist parties into parties of the catch-all type is clearly illustrated by the tenacity with which they have sustained democratic centralism as their principle of internal organization. This principle has also provoked the greatest doubts among critics about the parties' democratic commitments. None of the parties functions in the extremely rigid, closed manner characteristic of the Third International and the Stalinist periods. None the less, neither the tendency to give overriding importance to party discipline, particularly once decisions have been taken, nor the emphasis on hierarchy and centralized decision-making, has disappeared from the parties' organizational life. Although the PCE has gone farthest of the three parties in introducing statutory guarantees for internal dissent and for free and secret votes on decisions, and although the PCI has been characterized by considerable open debate over a wide range of policy issues even among party leaders, democratic centralism remains very much the core of their operational code of behavior. There has been extensive debate in the parties about the need to improve internal democracy, and even about the appropriateness of democratic centralism as traditionally practiced in a mass party pursuing a democratic road to socialism. There have also been real changes, within the framework of democratic centralism, in the ways the parties function. None the less, the fear of the debilitating effects of factionalism, the hold of tradition and perhaps Michels' 'iron law' as well, continue to make a real break with democratic centralist principles unlikely.

In itself, of course, some considerable degree of centralized decision-making and control of debate is characteristic of most European political parties. In the eurocommunist parties, however, these tendencies are raised to principle, have been often used to stifle all forms of organized, internal opposition to the party leadership and have been marked by significant intolerance toward ideological and strategic unorthodoxy. All the parties have undertaken expulsions of members deemed to have broken the democratic centralist code of conduct. Some of these expulsions have resulted from Soviet attempts to support factions opposed to the party leadership, as in the 'Lister affair' in the PCE in the late 1960s. Even the PCI, however, which has traditionally been successful in containing liberal dissent and keeping it from becoming open rebellion on an organized basis, has had its share of expulsions and openly hostile resignations. The *Manifesto* affair remains the most famous of these.

Democratic centralism is today a major target of conservative critics of the euro-communist parties and has become increasingly debated within these parties in recent years. As their organizations evolve, moving farther and farther from the traditional Leninist cadre model, and as their strategies become more systematically linked to a peaceful and democratic road to socialism and to a vision of a socialist *and* democratic pluralist society, the debate over how to organize internal party life can be expected to take on increasing importance and fervor. The outcome of such debates, like further change in the parties' organizations more generally, however, is unlikely to be smooth or to respond solely to (the obvious) electoral advantages. While the abandonment of democratic centralism might make the parties more 'respectable' and 'legitimate,' the fear among leaders and members that such a change would destroy the parties' capacity to pursue their strategies coherently and to achieve their transformative goals makes dramatic shifts unlikely.

MAURIZIO VANNICELLI

DOCUMENTS FOR PART THREE

ITALIAN Communist Party:
Centralism, Democracy and the Policy of Presence

FRENCH Communist Party:
Cadres, the Masses and the Tradition of Discipline

SPANISH Communist Party:
From Underground to the Search for the Mass Party

ITALIAN Communist Party: Centralism, Democracy and the Policy of Presence

1 Palmiro Togliatti's speech to the Neapolitan communist cadres, April 11, 1944

From the moment we pose the tasks for the working class and its vanguard party that I have mentioned, it is clear that our party's character must change profoundly from that of its earliest period and of the period of persecution and clandestinity. We can no longer be a small, closed association of propagandists for the general ideals of communism and Marxism.

We must be a great party, a mass party, drawing its decisive forces from the working class and also drawing on the finest elements of the intellectual vanguard and of the peasant classes. It must contain all the forces and the capacities necessary to direct the great working masses in the struggle to liberate and reconstruct Italy. These two great objectives dictate the general line of the party; our tactical steps in any given situation must be subordinated to them. Our policy must be such that it allows us to always march side by side with our socialist friends and brothers, with whom we have sealed a pact for unity of action, which also foresees the future possibility of a single working-class party.

. . . Unity of action with the socialists is one of the best ways for the working class to guarantee the definitive defeat of the reactionary, fascist and semi-fascist groups and to bring together all the progressive forces of the country and march with them toward a secure economic, political and social rebirth. Our policy must assure the working class, and us, of all the alliances necessary to resolve the grave problems of national life in the present and future. We do not have to, nor do we want to, clash with the Catholic, peasant masses. Instead we must find, today and tomorrow, an area of agreement and common action against fascism; they hate fascism as much as we do and they can and must be our allies in the construction of a better Italy, a democratic Italy. Our policy must be to gather all anti-fascist and democratic forces, all clearly national forces, into a single bloc, to oppose the German invaders and the traces of fascism, crushing the former and destroying the latter, thus creating the conditions for the instatement and strengthening of a stable, truly democratic regime . . .

It is the Italian situation itself that requires us to create a communist party with the strength and the ability to conduct the unitary and positive activity I have sketched. We cannot be content with criticism and denunciation, however brilliant; we must have a solution for every national problem, we must show it to the people at the right moment and know how to direct the whole country towards its realization. Thus transforming our party, we are assured that we will not only work for ourselves, but for all Italy. The Italian nation today needs a great, a strong Communist Party, and we will create that party.

. . . I began by saying to you that no policy can be realized without a party that is capable of carrying it among the masses, into the workshops, into the streets, into the piazzas, in the houses, among the people, and can guide the whole people to realize it. Our party must acquire this capacity. But to this end it must, above all, have its own, particular character, that makes it recognizable and that opens the spirit of the masses to it, making them see that it is the guide they need. We must be, among all the Italian political formations, the most decisively, most completely anti-Nazi.

. . . Do not believe that the struggle against fascism is over. In the field of ideology, as well as in the political and organizational field, the struggle against fascism is just beginning and is becoming a true and great mass struggle. It is the communist duty to extend this struggle, to reinforce it, and to wage it intransigently in all fields and among all social strata . . .

We are the party of unity: unity of the working class, unity of the anti-fascist forces, unity of the whole nation in the war against Nazi Germany and against the traitors at its service. We are the party who must, in the first place, block any maneuvers, from whatever part they may come, to break the unity we need to save ourselves. Let us put all the parties, all the organizations, the whole country on guard against the enemies of unity.

We must be the party closest to the people. The people today suffer materially and morally. It is the communists' duty to be close to all strata of the people, to all those who suffer, to the workers who work and those who are unemployed, to the young, to working women and those at home, to the intellectuals and to the peasants. We must be able to understand all the needs of these popular strata and commit ourselves to satisfying them. He who does not have faith in the workers and in the people cannot be a communist. A communist works day by day to relieve the misery that he sees around him, always defending the interests of those who work, organizing and directing all strata of the people in their struggle for well-being, bread and life. Therefore you must organize a strong union movement everywhere and keep adventurists from infiltrating to break it apart; use every position you occupy, both in the union and in public administration, to tie yourselves ever more closely to the people and to serve their needs . . .

La Politica di Salerno (Rome: Editori Riuniti, 1969), pp. 3–41.

2   Palmiro Togliatti's report to the Eighth Congress of the PCI, December 1956

Our conviction is widespread and correct that our strength . . . is also closely tied to the character that we have tried to give the party since 1945. This character was already, as we said then, something new. It included the complete abandonment of the old sectarian positions, the criticism of the conception of the party as a restricted group of the elect, organized in a quasi-military fashion, the momentum of recruitment, and new forms of organization and work. Above all it included the continual effort to keep solid ties to all the popular strata in order to be able to confront and struggle for the solution of all the questions that interest the working population and that are essential to guiding the working class and the people in the consequent struggle for democracy and socialism on democratic terrain. This conception of the party, entirely clear to us, is plainly expressed in our fundamental documents; it has certainly been

heard by the comrades and has penetrated among them. However, we would be mistaken if we said there has been no resistance or reservations in applying it in all our fields of activity. This application has therefore had some limits, often quite serious, and these have resulted in a reduction of our political efficiency. When we spoke of a certain 'double-think' [duplicity] in the overall conduct of our party we began from the consideration of these resistances and these limits, and of the errors that are derived from them. The expression was perhaps not a happy one, as it seems to contain a criticism of a moral order. It is, however, certain that particular errors, constantly repeated in the same areas of work, could only give the impression of an unmanifested, but none the less real divergence on the orientations of the party . . .

The criterion for judging support for a political line is not words, it is working to accomplish it . . .

Everyone knows how in every assembly of ours, at both the center and the periphery, the need for us to work in leading social strata that are far from the working class and among groups of workers that are still hostile to us is emphasized. There have been many initiatives taken to satisfy this necessity, often good and full of results, toward the mountain populations for example, toward artisans, clerks, functionaries, pensioners, war veterans, and so forth. However, the fragmentedness and inconsistency of the work remains . . . Likewise regarding the Catholic working masses, among whom there are constant signs of a search for new ways to struggle against the current order: much is written and said about the need for a dialogue, but the work to approach them and to win them over has been too limited and unsustained. However, everywhere the effort has been made, the results have been important.

But also in establishing, extending, reinforcing and defending the ties between the party and the working class, which should be the main field for our work, perhaps we are not detecting serious deficiencies, that, unseen and uncorrected in time, are therefore destined to show up unpleasantly in factory votes. The labor front in the factory is the party's main front, and it is a multiple front. Union agitation and struggles do not exhaust it. These struggles are often very tough, today; and they do not always give the results hoped for. Party propaganda, agitation and organization must intervene, not only to overcome these difficulties, but to assure that from every struggle, even if it is unsuccessful, consolidation of the workers' class-consciousness can emerge. They should emerge even more determined to organize themselves, to unite and to oppose the exploiters with a more solid front and more effective action. Every party organization must know how always to be present among the workers, it must have a precise working plan for the fulfillment of this duty and for the leadership of the workers' struggles . . .

After the great success reported against the swindle law, a new situation was opened to the country and to us. One cannot say that this was not understood in the center of the party. One need only look at our deliberations in the month of October 1953. In them we asked the party, strong from its recent victory, to throw itself with impetus into multi-form, broad activity, toward every category of the working population, taking account of the generally felt necessity for a new policy, for profound reform. The party did not lack the orientation, it lacked the momentum in realizing this policy. Perhaps it also lacked, here and there in some, the deep conviction that this policy was correct. From this came an evident uncertainty that culminated in the late evaluation of changes that were then occurring in the economy and in others' political directions . . . One cannot, however, deny that after 1953 the whole of our political initiative was more limited and the party was somewhat closed off.

From this criticism it is clear what kind of renewal we are asking for today. The front of renewal of the party is essentially a front turned to the outside, permeating the political activity of the party and its operations. It would not be, then, a simple crack of the whip. It lies, above all, in the fullest elaboration of our political platform, which descends from a profound search for an Italian road to socialism. It lies in the richer analysis of the motivating forces of democratic renewal and socialist revolution. It lies in the fuller and freer search for allies for the working class in the struggle against the power of the great monopolies. It lies in the definition of the structural reforms we demand, of their value and of the way to win them . . .

At the heart of the work of renewing the party, then, lies the struggle for the party line and for an Italian road to socialism. What can keep us from going down this road? Two principal obstacles: Maximalist sectarianism and reformist revisionism. The first closes itself off, waiting for the great day. The second kneels before capitalism, waiting for it to turn into socialism by itself. Both renounce revolutionary action for the conquest of socialism. One hears of some influence of the second in some of our

comrades in the evaluation of the new things that appear in the world today. The first is more deeply rooted in our ranks, because of the past itself and because of the old traditions of our movement. The damage that reformism can do in the bosom of the working class is the more serious since it stifles revolutionary momentum and induces passivity. But a party that is closed off, and sectarian, is not fully convinced of the correctness of its political line, and does not fight to realize it, will not be able to combat reformism effectively. The struggle to remove either of these obstacles is intertwined with, and conditions, the other . . .

From everything I have said, the great importance of questions of the internal life and the functioning of the party is clear. The partial inability to realize a correct policy and a certain tendency toward sectarian closedness, which I have denounced, are expressed, in fact, within the party, with the appearance of bureaucratic rigidity, and with the restriction of democratic forms of activity and life. It is therefore clear how the fire must be concentrated in this direction if we want to increase the entire political and working capacity of the party. Therefore, this becomes the primary task within the party itself . . .

Our French comrades have addressed a friendly criticism to us for making unnecessary and incorrect concessions to those who adopt mistaken positions. We have made no such concessions. We have taken the seriousness of the problems we face into account, we have condemned any acts of fractionalism and indiscipline, and with those who disagreed we have discussed freely, to convince them, and to have them with us in a correct political position. So far the results have been positive, and the method has been correct, since it is the normal method for leading a party that is to be based on reasoned and informed consensus, and not only on the obedience, unity and solidarity of its ranks . . .

The press has raised too much fuss over secret voting of the ruling bodies. This secrecy has always been guaranteed by our statute, no sooner is it asked for there, than it will be here too. We remember, however, that it is not in this or that method of voting that the guarantee of party democracy lies, but in the entire way the party functions. In the old socialist party the line-ups among various tendencies at the congresses were always made with an open vote.

We are not a party of debaters, but a revolutionary party, created for action, for combat. We are the party of a class that is today exploited and oppressed, that needs a solid, energetic and unified guide to liberate itself. We are a party that must accomplish ever new and ever greater tasks, as the movement develops. Therefore we must have an organization that is always effective and we must keep it that way with an intelligent and capable cadre of revolutionary militants . . .

Palmiro Togliatti, *Nella democrazia e nella pace verso il socialismo* (Rome: Editori Riuniti, 1966), pp. 9–80, *passim*.

3 Theses for the Tenth Congress of the PCI, September 1962

(1) The action and the policy of the party exercised a decisive influence in the struggles and political changes that have taken place in recent years . . .

The most marked weakness in our action in recent years appears still to be the development of the battle for the reforms of structure . . . Undoubtedly important progresses have been made in comparison with past years. The party has improved and broadened its general campaign about the need, meaning and scope of an organic programme of structural reforms. It has intensified its fight for certain aims, contributing powerfully to raise problems and impose solutions, that are timely now (for instance, the nationalization of the electric industry, the reform of the educational system, the abolition of the share tenancy system, the setting up of regional governments). The development of the battle for reforms of structures suffers from delays in the elaboration, scarce co-ordination on a national and regional scale, and above all it is limited by narrow-minded 'economicist' and sectorial views, resulting from misunderstandings or passive acceptance of the basic aspects of our policy.

These limits (whose origin is twofold: on the one hand, opportunistic and petty reformist positions; on the other hand, sectarian positions which deny the value of a democratic political battle and of inter-mediate objectives) are noticeable in various spheres. They are felt in the opposition to give the necessary impulse to the action for the reform of the political set-up and for a democratic organization of the state, for the setting up of regional governments, for the defense and extension of local government autonomy. They are also felt in the difficulty met in securing a correct link and continuity among the various aspects

of the agrarian struggle (contractual struggles, the struggle for the land, the creation of new forms of association, the action for a different type of state intervention); they were felt as well in the difficulty of leading to political unity the various problems relating to the working-class condition and to give them an issue also by means of laws. The same limits were also noticeable in the scarce development of the battle to orient and control state capitalism policies, for the renewal of civil structures and in particular for a change in the system of ownership of urban soil as the central point for a new organization of the towns.

Strong sectarian opposition, shortcomings due to sectorial and provincial outlooks, contributed also to limit the scope and the strength of the struggle for peace, which was powerful but lacked continuity and was not equal to needs and possibilities. The same shortcomings led us seriously to underrate the battle for the emancipation of women; even now too many of our organizations have not engaged with sufficient determination in this action.

Generally speaking, we could say that the whole party must develop greater skill in co-ordinating and giving political unity to the single struggles, in making an organic political action, for aims of renewal (concerning the reform of the state, the changes in the economic structures and the course of our foreign policy) spring from the variety of struggles for immediate claims. . .

Marked shortcomings in the numerical and organizational development of the party were not registered only in the South, but – although to a lesser extent – in all our organizations . . .

To evaluate correctly the causes of such weaknesses in our action and organization and the problems that must be faced, it is necessary to be aware of the changes that have taken place in the life of our country and in its orientation. The social composition of the country is partly changed. Old forms of associated life in town and in the countryside are disappearing; they are being replaced by other forms, in a disorderly and confused way. The types of mass consumptions and the means of mass information are changing too. Traditional outlooks are shaken. Also the means by which the old ruling classes endeavor to mold and influence the outlooks and way of life of the masses are being modified.

In this situation it is inevitable that the process of formation of a social consciousness and the support of the revolutionary vanguard are assuming new aspects and pass through different, less elementary stages. The participation of most diverse strata of working people in trade union action and in certain stages of the democratic struggle is growing; this creates new possibilities for the development of the democratic and socialist battle of our party. It is necessary, however, to understand that the participation in trade union and democratic struggles does not entail as an immediate consequence the acceptance of socialist ideals by those citizens and social strata which today – as a result both of deeper class contrasts, and of the new more democratic political situation – join more readily in the battle for claims, even before they move on to a more progressive political position. The conscious organized and relentless action of the party to make these broader and determined struggles rouse a socialist consciousness and lead to a participation in the revolutionary battle is of the utmost importance today. We have to reckon with a number of intermediate political positions, and we must have a more varied approach to the masses, whilst our ideological and political polemics should be directed not only against frankly conservative positions but also against social democratic and petit bourgeois anarchic positions . . .

It is also necessary to keep in mind the labored process the working class and communist movement had to go through to overcome the mistakes resulting from the cult of personality. New problems and questions have been posed to the consciousness of many workers and militants. There were some misunderstandings concerning the critical research in which our party engaged. This led, on the one hand, to sectarian opposition to condemn past mistakes and to the failure to understand the renewal this entailed; on the other hand, it led to opportunist yieldings, particularly in the form of a weakening of proletarian internationalism . . .

It has been stressed already that in recent years reformist pressures have grown in the Italian working-class movement neo-capitalist ideologies (opportunistic interpretations of the centre-left policy, the shift towards the right, in a clearly revisionist sense, of the majority wing of the Socialist Party). At the same time – alongside the old expressions of sectarianism which continue to exercise a notable weight – new extremist positions have emerged; the very bases of our strategy are denied by these positions, which lead to sterile dogmatic attitudes.

Both these dangers are present not only in the working-class movement but also in our party, and they are actually more marked than hitherto. The practical expressions and the ideological roots of both these positions must be fought. It should be kept in mind that often they have a common origin of revisionist nature, and that they both lead to underrating or denying the role of the working-class party, either by trying to change it into a party of opinion and not of struggle, or by making of the proletarian vanguard a closed-in sect, divorced from reality. The party must be led to understand that to prevent the spread of opportunist and reformist positions it is essential to defeat in our own ranks and amidst the masses all sectarian positions which deprive the party of its capacity to step effectively into the new situation, lead to political apathy and stifle its creative force in the practical and ideological battle.

To understand on what grounds some sectarian positions have grown, we should bear in mind a particular political process which has taken place in some areas of our country, where proletarian masses have shifted on to more radical positions whilst groups of middle classes have moved on to more moderate positions. The gap that was thus created makes it more difficult for certain groups of workers to grasp the possibility of an alliance with intermediate forces. It is the party's task to fight against the mistaken consequences, of infantile extremist nature, that limited groups of intellectuals, in particular, draw from these phenomena. The party must show, on the contrary, the existence of new bases and motives for the creation and extension of the system of alliance of the working class today. The action to overcome mistaken positions must always be linked, therefore, to practical political initiative.

Together with the political struggle against the mistaken positions which emerge openly, we should intensify our criticism of passive oppositions to the implementation of our political platform, apathy, conservative 'parliamentarist and electoralist' positions and routine work. All this leads to passive acceptance of our strategy and to a lack of impact, which limits the scope of our action, blunts its revolutionary impetus, prevents the conquest of new forces.

Foreign Bulletin (April–June 1965), pp. 168–75.

4 Order of the day approved by the Central Committee of the PCI, 1965

Revolutionary party, not party of opinion
(11) There cannot be a revolutionary party the

actions and life of which are not guided by principles. For a revolutionary party they are essential: – a universal, unitary vision, springing from the movements, action, from the whole historical development and from the scientific examination and understanding of it, capable of connecting the immediate problems of the masses, the present problems of national progress, the problems and the big international questions to a general perspective of advance of socialism; – wide and deep links with the working class and with the people, and an action more and more adherent to all the aspects of the reality in which it operates; – a serious pledge, a daily pledge of the militants in the struggles for the immediate claims of the workers, for the aims of social and democratic renewal for future aims: – a type of organization, a regime of party life and habits on the part of the militants coherent with the tasks and democratic and socialist aims . . .

The ideal political and revolutionary ripening of the working class cannot merely be the result of an outside and summit action (this conception, carried to its extreme limit, causes authoritarian outcomes in the party–class relationship and in the very life of the party) but neither can it *merely* spring from the direct experience of the productive relationship and of the workplace (a conception which leads to a reformist, economicist and classist vision of things). The essence and vitality of the party is to be sought exactly in the dialectic relationship: party which is *part* of the working class and of the people – party which is the avant-garde of the working class and the people . . .

The party is an organization and struggling power, an instrument for the daily action of the masses for their immediate demands, for economic and political battles, for the ideal and cultural struggles. Its tasks cannot merely consist in fighting electoral battles and battles in parliament and in the elective assemblies. These are moments and aspects of great importance in the class struggle and for the socialist and democratic development of the country; but only if they are continuously linked to an ample varied, complex action and struggle of the masses in productive relations and in all the fields of daily democratic life. In this sense the adhesion to the party is a *militia*, a daily pledge. This character creates a difference and counter-opposes the nature of the revolutionary party of the working class to the party of *opinion*, to the electoralistic party, to the party of a social democratic type. To be able to carry out these struggles and tasks, which are particular to it and essential, the party must manage to link the maximum of democratic life to the maximum of unity, pledge and discipline in its struggles.

In what manner these two equally vital exigencies for the revolutionary party can be conciliated – the maximum of democratic life and the maximum of unity – is a complex question with no easy solution, which foresees practical and theoretical problems. We do not wish to deepen this question here, but only wish to state some points, to help clear the debate . . .

The principle of the so-called *monolithism* is extraneous to our conception and to the very reality of our party. However, there have been elements of this conception and practice also in our party and there may still be residues of such a mentality which must be completely overcome . . .

The Leninist principle of democratic centralism is something different from 'monolithism'. This demands the free comparison of ideas, concluding itself with a decision of policy and action, which must not preclude a further political and ideological research; and demands that, once a decision is adopted through a vote freely expressed, even the minority must respect it and pledge itself to enact it. It is proper of the leading political function to have the capacity to understand what is valid in different stands and also in a substantially mistaken stand, so as to propose a unitary line, clear, coherent, enriched by all the positive contributions, capable, therefore, of obtaining the consent of the greatest possible number of those taking part in the debate.

The authoritarian and bureaucratic degeneration starts when one pretends that dissenters should change opinion, not through a process of free research, led in a unitary and constructive spirit, but, on the contrary, owing to a moral and political pressure; it starts when the manifestation of a stand contrary to the prevailing trend becomes a motive for scandal and diffidence and suspicion towards a comrade, and is considered, as such, a sufficient motive for his removal from a leading organism or even for his dismissal from the party.

A democratic life cannot take place in confusion and anarchy. Above all, in a big proletarian party of the people which carries out struggles, the development of an effective democratic life postulates the moment of organization and direction: the two moments condition one another. Also in the phase of debate we must prevent it – once it is abandoned to spontaneity – from breaking up and dispersing without reaching any serious and useful result. The organization of the debate must, therefore, serve to promote the comparison of positions on all important points and on the line.

Debate must always aim at unity. Therefore it must promote an actual comparison of the stands and a common research and it must never exhaust itself in a comparison of votes on already crystallized stands. The decisions taken must be clear and binding for all members. This is essential if there is to be an actual democracy and if the party is to be a fighting party such as the revolutionary party of the working class should be. Democracy for us is not merely the search and choice of the right political line, but the action which aims at giving reality to just this line to make it advance and win, with the contribution and pledge of all militants.

The pledge to discipline and the contribution to the enaction of a political line will be all the stronger in as much as the free participation of every militant will be urged and guaranteed, in the seats indicated by the Statute, to the choice and elaboration of the political and organizational decisions.

Rinascita, June 12, 1965.

5 Luigi Longo's report to the Twelfth Congress of the PCI, February 1969

. . . Our party is not a party of pure propaganda, but a party of struggle, 'a party that makes politics.' Our party is not a party of cadres alone, but a 'mass party.' Ours is a party that is not interested only in indicating prospects, but in dealing with problems and solving them in the interest of the workers and the country. Ours is a party of struggle and opposition, which has, however, national, government-type leadership functions and responsibilities . . .

We are – and we want to be – an increasingly united democratic party. But we have nothing in common with the concept and practice of so-called monolithism. An essential part of our method – of our way of conceiving democratic centralism – is that reservations and misunderstandings with regard to the political decisions of the Central Committee are not considered reasons for division. We constantly seek unity through debate and the contribution of all militants. Real unity is only the unity of a living organism, deeply rooted in the reality that surrounds it.

There is absolutely no contradiction between full freedom of debate and decision, even by majority rule, on the one hand, and unity and discipline in action, which is essential for a fighting, mass revolutionary party such as ours, on the other. If these two aspects are separated and opposed, both one and the other rapidly degenerate.

We have no intention of reducing our party to the level of those parties where democracy has degenerated into power struggles between factions. The facts show that when the struggle between factions breaks out, it no longer matters what you think, what you do and what you are worth; all that matters is whether you are with me or against me. When a party degenerates to this point, democracy disappears and the tendency to fragmentation prevails.

Under these conditions, a party – and particularly a proletarian party – cannot carry out its proper function. A party exists and has reason for' existence to the degree that it has an idea to realize and a policy to carry out. A party must therefore be efficient, functional with respect to its purposes and homogeneous with its principles and ideals. Obviously we are not talking here of technical or bureaucratic or merely organizational efficiency, but of political efficiency. This requires, first of all, a precise perspective, the choice of a realistic and consistent line and firmness in political and ideal battle; it requires rigorous practices, the kind of practices that can be expected in people who are animated by the universal goals of justice, progress, freedom, equality and peace. Democracy demands the method of majority and minority, and the acceptance by the minority of the majority's decisions.

But is this enough? I do not believe so. Real democracy requires that we seek what is valid in every different and even conflicting point of view. This is the sense of our centralism, which is infinitely more democratic than those systems that lead to a division between winners and losers, giving the former exclusive rights in decision-making and leadership. In a situation such as the present, it is inevitable and it is useful that different points of view are expressed within the party. In any case, it is a fact that they exist.

Joining the party, entering the party, particularly for young people, cannot possibly mean immediate acquisition and acceptance of the party's line in its entirety. It must mean, instead, a process of continual acquisition and collective elaboration, together with a process of participation in the struggle and in the formation of our political line and leadership activity. But for such a process of free dialectics and unification to take place, a method and a practice that prevent the crystallization of dissent, a method and a practice that reject the spirit of faction and group, are necessary . . .

We must conserve and defend everything that is valid and change everything that must be changed, either because it is mistaken or because it is outdated. Nothing can be renewed if we throw out the party's patrimony. Continuity and renewal are inseparable in a robust, living organism. The decisive thing, for internal party democracy as well, is a correct political line; it is holding firm to the democratic struggle for socialism. At the same time, of essential importance is a correct conception of Marxism, not as a crystallized doctrine, not as a body of principles set down once and for all, but as a political consciousness of historical processes and real movements, as a doctrine and method of critical and historical investigation.

This doctrine and this method are proper to the working class, as a revolutionary class which has everything to lose from prejudice and dogma and everything to gain from an objective, open-minded examination of reality. Unity and discipline must therefore be a daily, free and responsible conquest, resulting from a free, dialetical exchange among honest and faithful militants . . .

Foreign Bulletin (January–March 1969), pp. 69–72.

6 Alessandro Natta, 'Report on the *Manifesto* question' to the Central Committee of the PCI, October 13–17, 1969

Last October the CC and the CCC expressed severe criticism of the political positions assumed and propagated by the *Manifesto*, considering them not only in radical contrast to the line of the Twelfth Congress, but 'different from and incompatible with the ideological political and structural orientation of the party.' They recognized in the character and goals of this magazine and in the activity that was being organized and promoted by its members an intent to split the party, accompanied by the pretense of 'reforming' it by organizing it into different homogeneous and univocal 'groups' or 'committees.' The

CC and CCC maintained that this type of initiative and activity must be repressed and condemned as damaging to the party, risking and hindering its democratic life and unity . . .

We sincerely wished not only to do everything politically and humanly possible to avoid having to resort to extreme solutions – in the interests of the party and the individuals concerned – but above all we wanted negotiation, responsible examination, open political struggle on the part of the whole party, and we chose the most democratic and coherent way offered to us by our party to obtain these . . .

It is not necessary to re-emphasize the danger of the political positions that are also brought forth and defended in this last issue. Their content is one of radical disagreement with, even attack against, the strategy, the international position of the party, its type of internationalist presence and action, even when the politics of the party itself are not called into question . . . They invite us to completely change our strategy and tactics, which they think to be those of the old 'united front' or even the 'leftovers of the united front'; they appeal to us to become promoters of the 'communist revolution' in the socialist countries. That which is important when considering these political ideas which we have already amply discussed and rejected in our preceding Central Committee meeting is to point out the progression of an effort, turned more and more toward the internal disruption of the party, which is dominating to the point of excluding and annulling the external class struggle, the struggle against our political adversaries in Italy and the world, notwithstanding all that has happened and is happening in this country. We must point out the change from criticism and protest to direct attack against the politics of the party. They do not hesitate – as in their unhappy and arrogant response to the stand the Political Bureau took on November 11 – to present a deformed, impoverished and even laughable image of our political line, which is envisioned as a race to power which necessitates getting rid of the *Manifesto* as an obstacle . . .

. . . the persons responsible for the *Manifesto*, with the publication of their new number and the positions taken therein, intended and still intend to defend and repeat a method and continue in an undertaking which would not only rupture and violate the discipline and methods of the party, but they intended and intend to defend and continue an effort and insist on a proposal of reform of the internal regime of the party, which, no matter how it is defined and no matter what instruments are recommended to carry it out − for example, 'protest as the common denominator of ideas and positions'; groups which would function on the basis of common or univocal hypotheses; autonomous channels or centers which would discuss and take action − would inevitably lead us to the disintegration of the party, to a system based on factions. This is the crux of the matter; and it is not our intention at this point to examine the slightly presumptuous and singular reasoning which argues that the gravity and urgency of international problems and problems in Italy justify those actions by members of the party who have not had time to measure 'inch by inch' the 'rules of the game' and the need for discipline, or that since in recent history we have not faced political protest such as that proposed by the *Manifesto*, it is necessary to draw the conclusion that if we do not completely 'remold' the party, we must modify its structure, principles of organization and direction, forms and methods of construction, beginning at the very least with the foundations. Neither would it be our intention to examine the attempts to accuse us of being responsible for this conflict, as if we had reached this critical point because the leadership of the party wanted to isolate the activity of the *Manifesto*, close it off from the rest of the party as if it were diseased, thus causing it to become a separate faction, whereas this could have been avoided by 'wanting a real debate' and 'not changing the discussion from a consideration of merit to a consideration of methods, giving it the air of a trial.' It is our duty, however, to insist that this is a calculated and cunning deformation of what has taken place which offends the truth and our political method.

. . . The thing which compels us to make a decision and choice − by now we must acknowledge the necessity − is the fact that the members of the *Manifesto* propose an image of the party that tends toward its decomposition into a complex of different factions, each with its own methods, and a struggle between them, leading to an overthrow of the base on which the unity of the party was founded and is possible. This is clear from their defense of the legitimacy of protest as 'the common denominator of ideas and positions' to all the other theories, so to speak, of group dialectics − various homogeneous groups which would have contrasting political platforms, all of which is found in Rossanda's letter and the editorial of the last issue. And this after their repeated affirmations that a contrast of positions, conflicting basic opinions in a revolutionary working-class party, are obstacles which must be overcome, after their repeated negation − on the basis of fundamental principle − of tending towards factionalism and the formal repulsion of such. Between the theory which would lead in the direction of pulling together ideas and positions based on criticism and dissent, perhaps different in origin and political motivation, and the method which proposes instead the analysis of phenomena of contrast and dissent to find the specific reasons for it in order to mediate it, extracting that which is valid in order to reach a higher level of unity, there is an abyss which cannot be breached: a party understood as a single organism with a high level of participation on the part of its members in elaboration and decision-making is the antithesis of a party conceived on the basis of individual groups and factions.

Foreign Bulletin (May−December 1969), pp. 101−10.

7 Ugo Pecchioli's report to the Central Committee of the PCI, January 1970

In recent years, and above all in 1968−9, the mass movement has taken on a richer and more articulated character than in the past.

The most outstanding phenomenon − which, because of its importance, is today at the center of political debate − is without doubt the new role which the large union organizations have assumed in Italian society and with respect to the political forces and the state: a role to be associated with their growing unity, their autonomy, their ability to extend − through an ever deeper and more democratic relationship to the masses − the scope of their contractual powers to larger and larger sectors of economic and social life. But other phenomena are also to be underlined. New social strata have mobilized and have sought to organize themselves into autonomous centers of initiative. New social and political forces, like the student movement, have defined themselves, if often with contradictions and obstacles which are as yet unresolved. From the factories to the neighborhoods of the large cities, from the schools to the countryside, an extremely broad and articulated constellation of organizations, associations, circles, and of political and cultural demands have expressed themselves. With respect to the past, these stand out not just for their extension but also for their autonomy.

Even if in certain sectors this process is still embryonic, in its general features it represents one of the great new facts of the period through which we are living. It represents a phenomenon of democratic growth of Italian society; it converges with the essential lines of our strategy of advance towards socialism. It is in good part marked by our presence, our unity policy, by the growing capacity of our militants to know how to link to and work with other groups and ideological and political tendencies.

But precisely because of its essential characteristics, this process brings with it new problems for our party. In the past – and especially in the immediate postwar years – the mass and democratic movement had a much more limited internal differentiation. The problem of the autonomy of organizations and of various associational forms had much less importance. In many cases it was the direct intervention of the party which guaranteed not only the birth but also the development of mass initiatives.

Today the question of the presence of the communists in all the organizations and differentiated forms of the mass movement, and of our ability to bring to each of these a direction and orientation based on unity, is dialectically linked to the necessity to defend and give value to the full autonomy of each organization, of each part of the movement.

This requires, among other things, a considerable and constant increase in the number of active comrades, of cadres, of militants capable of 'doing politics' and of taking the initiative. It requires, in many cases, a different articulation of the work of our organizations and a renewal of our methods of leadership. At the same time, it poses the problem of the need for a growing circulation of experiences and of ideas at all levels of the party in order to allow the widest knowledge and collective elaboration of ideas which emerge from the struggles and initiatives of the mass movement. Thus we return to the need for development of both components of the life of our party and of its mass character: development of internal democracy, understood as the stimulation and organization of participation and the co-responsibility of the militants in the formation and choices of the political line and in the action of the party among the masses; and the contemporaneous development of unity, capacity of synthesis, centralism, leadership.

Ugo Pecchioli, *Un partito comunista rinnovato e rafforzato per le esigenze nuove della società italiana* (Rome: PCI Publication, 1970), pp. 9–11.

8   Giorgio Amendola, 'The lay nature of the Communist Party,' 1972

Recent polemics have once again brought up the question of the nature of the PCI and its internationalism. I do not feel we should just let the matter drop; however, we must remember, first of all, how the nature of the Communist Party has been renewed and transformed in the course of its fifty years of existence . . .

The first point to underline is the lay or secular nature of the party, which is a political instrument for the achievement of certain goals of democratic and socialist transformation. A lay conception of the state, and the political party, recognizes freedom of conscience in every citizen, and therefore also in the militant engaged in conscious and disciplined party activity. Integralism, on the other hand, confuses religion and politics and attempts to subordinate every aspect of individual life, even the most inner core of conscience, to outside control . . .

Freedom of Conscience
Against integralism, as a source of intolerance and fanaticism, stands the lay conception of life, which distinguishes between politics and religion and leaves the solution of life's major problems up to the free choice and freedom of conscience of the individual . . . Naturally there has been – and still is – a socialist integralism, which expresses itself, particularly, in a dogmatic conception of the revolutionary party, omnipresent in every sphere of thought and action – from politics to culture, art, philosophy and religion. The responsibility for this conception, which for a time we shared, of a party that uses ideological criteria in evaluating artistic and cultural currents, far beyond the confines of political discipline and revolutionary commitment, cannot be placed on Stalin alone. Experience had shown, even before the Twentieth Congress, that no generous concentration of revolutionary will could save a party so conceived from the dangers of dogmatism and sectarianism. For this reason, as far back as the resistance period, Togliatti broke with the old party scheme, which claimed for the party the last word in every field, even in science, and fashioned the 'new' party as an essentially political instrument.

Article 2 of the PCI Statute states that citizens who accept the party's political program and are willing to work to implement it can join the PCI 'regardless of their race, religious faith and philosophical beliefs.'

Although the presence of an article in the Party Statute does not necessarily imply immediate and convinced application, it does indicate the existence of an experience already under way. Tendencies within the working-class movement and within the party itself to consider the party as an omnipresent and all-encompassing entity continue to exist, not only in connection with nostalgic memories of the old 'heroic' times, but also because of the religious feeling that leads so many workers to see socialism as an almost mystic 'faith,' and the party as a 'church' – and, if possible, as a church without renovating 'Councils' . . .

While fully understanding these feelings, Togliatti worked patiently to assert the lay nature of the party and a consequent respect for freedom of individual conscience. He was highly sensitive to the problem of civil coexistence within the party of atheists and believers, with full respect for personal positions; and he taught us all to overcome what remained in us of old anti-clericalism. This has created within the party a civil custom of non-interference in the private lives of militants . . . Tolerance does not mean indifference, but acceptance of a free confrontation of opinions, in which each contestant, while defending his own position, can take from the other what he thinks can be useful. Naturally no communist, and much less Togliatti, would think of denying the connection between politics, culture, philosophy, art and religion. Man's conscience is indivisible. But it is up to each militant, in the freedom of his own conscience, to grasp the connection that leads him, on the basis of his own philosophical convictions, his own religious faith and his own artistic experience, to approve the party program and commit himself to the struggle for its realization.

The Italian Communists, no. 6 (November–December 1972), pp. 12–14.

9 Enrico Berlinguer's report to the Fourteenth Congress of the PCI, March 1975

While development of the party and its action is due primarily to a correct political line, it also requires careful attention to organization and daily working methods.

The figures on organizational growth are significant.

After a period of difficulties, beginning at the end of the 1950s, which negatively affected the party's organizational development (shrinking membership and lesser activism, etc.), in the recent period – and particularly since 1972 – all figures on party strength have risen sharply. With respect to the last Congress, total membership has increased by 135,000, with almost 450,000 new members and a larger number of women comrades. At the same time, there has been greater involvement on the part of militants in party activities. On March 13, 1975, PCI membership stood at 1,601,507. Significant signs of growth can be seen in various southern provinces and in the so-called 'white zones' in the North, areas where in the past we have been only a small minority force. Circulation of the party press, and communist literature in general, is also rising rapidly.

This growth, which has also meant a conspicuous inflow of young people and new intellectual forces, has had a positive effect on the party's general composition, enhancing its variety.

The expansion and growing diversification of the communists' fields of action has meant an increase in activism, not only in terms of a quantitative increase in active cadres, but also in terms of a more complex action and a better use of individual aptitudes . . . While our debate produced no divisions or contrapositions – and this is a sign of the maturation of a unity in political consciousness – the confrontation of ideas and of what we could call 'accents' was nevertheless lively and in some cases even polemical. In what was a true exercise in democracy, there was no lack of original contributions, critical reservations and developments. But this occurred in a deep spirit of unity, with a sense of responsibility and in a search for a more complete synthesis. This is our method of debate tending towards unity; and we think it is something valuable for the party, for the workers, for democracy and for the whole people.

This is not to say that party democracy, as it is now exercised, is without limitations or defects. We must more fully develop the democratic method and habits that are proper to our party: a method based on participation by all our forces in shaping the party's choices and line and in their practical implementation. We must be careful not to become complacent and lazy at a moment when the dramatic, tense political situation instead requires severity toward ourselves, toward what is still not right and must be corrected and changed. In the first place, we must observe that a certain resistance to permanent critical examination, a certain excessive sensitivity, almost a sense of annoyance, still persists, even at the center, as if the indispensable task of critical reflection were not something that concerns everything and everyone . . .

In this connection, we must also work to raise the level of our cultural and theoretical debate, which is indispensable for us, overcoming certain elements of narrowness and abstractness and subjecting it to constant verification against the yardstick of real problems and the real movement.

The problems of party structure are in part a result of these new developments. Today, in particular, they must be seen in relation to the changes in the structure of the state, in the sense of regional decentralization, and to the need for closer ties with the working class, with the female masses, who for some time have been undergoing a great process of change in mentality and self-awareness, and with the popular youth masses, who have made a great leap forward in education and culture, arriving earlier at political consciousness and commitment, and have won the right to vote at 18, but are still facing grave problems in finding their place in production and in society. All this requires us to embark on a new phase in organizational policy, in order to adapt our organizational structures and working methods to these new developments . . .

The Italian Communists, nos 2–3 (March–May 1975), pp. 77–80.

10   Draft theses for the Fifteenth Congress of the PCI, December 1978

The political situation created after the 1975 elections, and particularly following the 1976 national poll, placed before the party a new, arduous test. The problem was to experiment, concretely and in a national dimension, with the line of democratic agreement and collaboration and the party's capacities for government, in a situation of acute emergency and on the basis of singular political solutions involving growing responsibilities for the party, but not its direct participation in the country's government.

The party has responded to these needs and tasks in a substantially positive manner, sustaining a difficult, complex experience with a vigorous effort in political

elaboration and in the development of programs, with a general improvement in its capacities for government and a notable effort in using and advancing new leading forces in public life and in the party itself.

Nevertheless, in the face of the objective difficulties and the attacks moved from many sides against the policy of unity and our party, attacks that have assumed the nature of a full-blown counter-offensive aimed at blocking and reversing the processes opened by the 1976 vote, shortcomings and weaknesses have come to light. These were evident, for that matter, in the poor results obtained in a number of off-season local elections, particularly in the South, in the referendum campaigns and in the difficulties encountered in increasing membership.

Underlying these shortcomings and weaknesses, there is, first and foremost, an insufficient understanding of the new phase of the political battle and the possibilities and needs it entails.

In addition, there has been a disparity between the efforts devoted to work in the institutions and relations among the political forces, on the one hand, and initiative to promote united movements involving broad masses around concrete goals and problems, on the other. This has led to difficulties in maintaining and strengthening the party's relations with various strata of the working population at all times and in all the phases of the struggle, in organically linking our presence and action in society with our activity in the institutions and in exercising our government functions in the most effective manner. An improper balance in the distribution of forces in the various fields of action and spheres of responsibility, together with an insufficient degree of co-ordination among them, have worked in this direction.

At times the policy of unity has been practiced in such a way as to dull the specific characteristics and autonomous initiative of the party. Not always has defense of our historical patrimony and political line against distortions and massive attacks conducted from various sides been sufficiently prompt and firm . . .

83

(b) *The Mass, Democratic Nature of the Party*
The fight to consolidate the policy of democratic unity and achieve the prospect of full participation by the working people in the country's government requires a further strengthening of the PCI according to the conception on which the 'new party' was built and grew.

Under the present circumstances, and given the new responsibilities taken on in national life, it is necessary to confirm the PCI's nature as a real political force, as a vanguard, mass organization of the working people . . .

84

The need to link the party with a society that is increasingly diversified but also exposed to disruptive pressures, to step up political initiative and concreteness and effectiveness in action, to organize the work and struggle of the largest possible number of militants and involve new forces in leadership, requires a strong new democratic development of the party. Decisive in this sense are the questions of participation in debate and decision-making, in the elaboration and implementation of the political line at all levels and in all sectors of organisation, from the section to the national level. To this end we must proceed vigorously in the direction that has already enabled the party to become and work as a great democratic and united political force: in the direction of a diversification and decentralization of leadership; the development of specific levels and areas of elaboration and decision-making, in the parliamentary field, in the regions and local government, in the labor sphere, in women's and youth work; in study and orientation on economic and cultural problems; and a broad, rapid circulation and generalization of ideas and experiences through a constant relationship between sections, federations, regional committees and the national organization. This necessary expansion of democracy requires a greater effort in leadership; it stands as the foundation for political synthesis and the real unity of the party's orientation and action. The essential thing today is that unity must be achieved not only with respect to political positions, but also with respect to the complexity and wealth of party life and organization, the multiplicity of its centers of elaboration and leadership and the decentralization of its functions and responsibilities.

When we reaffirm the value of the method of democratic centralism today, as we do, we must pay particular attention to a number of fundamental needs.

In the first place we must stimulate political debate and the circulation of ideas and proposals, giving all our organizations greater opportunities and powers to intervene not only on local questions, but also in the making of the big decisions and options. The results of discussions, votes and positions taken, which may also be expressed in the form of motions and documents, must be examined by the leading organisms, which must motivate their assessment and communicate it to the interested parties.

We must ensure a correct relationship between leading organisms and executive organisms, preventing the latter (secretariats, working commissions, the apparatus, and so on) from taking over functions that are not theirs, in practice depriving of authority the leading bodies to whom they should instead be accountable for their activity.

We must always make the maximum effort to arrive at unity through discussion, avoiding crystallizations into factions or tendencies to formal unanimity. If different or conflicting positions emerge, the proposals must be submitted to a vote, particularly when it is necessary to clearly define the decisions and orientations of the majority and the minorities that may emerge on various issues.

We must improve information on the life of the party, particularly through the communist press, which must report the debate, activities and struggles of the communists in all their wealth and complexity.

The Italian Communists (1978), special issue, pp. 109–15.

FRENCH Communist Party: Cadres, the Masses and the Tradition of Discipline

1 Maurice Thorez' report to the Twelfth Congress of the PCF, April 1950

The party must show proof of a firm revolutionary vigilance in order to search out, uncover and rid itself completely of the problem elements, the police, the informers and the agitators that the bourgeoisie attempts and will attempt to introduce into our ranks.

Respect for the principles of democratic centralism, control from the bottom, constant practice of criticism and self-criticism, and the verification of the functioning of each may permit the rapid isolation of the corruptors who try to slip into the party.

Democratic centralism means that discussion in the party will continue up to the point where obligatory decisions intervene for all; where the organizations of the party at every echelon democratically elect their leaders who must account for themselves regularly; where the decisions of the superior bodies, coming from the Congress and the Central Committee, must be implemented by all members and all organizations of the party.

The discipline to which communists freely submit themselves does not exclude, but rather assumes, discussion and the conflict of opinions. Naturally discussion must run within the framework of the party's principles of Marxism–Leninism.

... We do not grant the agents of the enemy, and those who think like the enemy, the 'liberty' of spreading their reactionary and anti-communist conceptions within the party. Rather, we take the 'liberty' of kicking these people out of the party. What could be the fate of our party, what would become of the French workers' movement, if we had let Doriot act as he pleased, within our own ranks, under the pretext of his 'liberty of expression?'

'XIIᵉ Congrès du Parti Communiste Français,' *Cahiers du Communisme* (May 1950), pp. 29–30.

2 Maurice Thorez' report to the Fourteenth Congress of the PCF, July 1956

Certain party members have demanded permanent discussion of all questions, without exception, within the party, as if we were forming a club, a debating school and not a vanguard unit of the working class, a party of action which is preparing itself for revolutionary tasks. One forgets what democratic centralism means. It means that entirely free discussions within the framework of Marxist–Leninist principles may be conducted within the party, and that, on the other hand, it will cease the moment that an obligatory decision for all intervenes. Democratic centralism requires that the decisions of superior bodies, starting with the Congress and the Central Committee, be carried out by the members and all organizations of the party.

The destructive and opportunist spirit still shows itself in those few who demanded generally proportional voting in the election of the leadership and the organization of factions within the party. Given that the material unity of the proletarian party and its unity of thought are necessary to give it the necessary strength for a difficult struggle, the constitution of factions, which would be true parties within the party, cannot be tolerated. It is not only today that the respect for these elementary principles for all communist parties has been called 'bureaucratism' or 'formalism,' a path to 'autocratization' by the unstable elements and by the people who are personally unhappy with the composition of the central bodies. We adhere to Lenin's opinion that 'absolute centralization and strict discipline of the proletariat are the essential conditions for victory over the bourgeoisie.'

It is sometimes said that our party shows signs of being dominated by workers. In reality, the communist party is, and must be, a workers' party. First of all, this is true of the goals at the heart of its policy, which aims at the conquest of power by the working class. But, this is also true of the composition of the party: the majority of its members must be workers, and the political influence of workers must be decisive within the party.

Is this to say that peasants, intellectuals, artisans, and small merchants do not have a place in the party? Everyone knows that this is not so. The party attempts to assemble within its ranks all there is of the best, not only of the proletarians but of the other levels of workers. Those who falsely accuse the party of being dominated by workers are thereby simply manifesting their disagreement with that fundamental principle of all communist parties according to which all communists coming from non-proletarian classes must align themselves, as a condition of their adherence to the party, to the theoretical and political positions of the working class.

The party itself, although it essentially has a worker composition, recruits its members in different social environments. And all do not immediately succeed in shedding their old ways.

This is why it is perfectly legitimate to speak of petit bourgeois influences that operate, here and there, on the party. It is not a question of using an offensive term in regard to such and such person; it is an objective characteristic always used in Marxist analysis . . .

'XIVᵉ Congrès du Parti Communiste Français,' *Cahiers du Communisme* (July–August 1956), pp. 62–3.

3   Political resolution to the Sixteenth Congress of the PCF, May 1961

A profound unity of thought and action based on Marxist–Leninist principles is necessary for the success of the difficult struggles which we have had and which we will continue to have.

This is why the party cannot be satisfied with a formal unity. Each organization, each member of the party, each responsible member must make an effort to assimilate the politics of the party, and apply them correctly and collectively.

The principle of collective leadership is an absolute principle for a revolutionary Marxist party. We could not tolerate a double leadership without harming both the party and the worker and democratic movement in general.

While rejecting opportunist ideas, the party remains, nevertheless, wary of the narrow-minded sectarianism which hinders relations with the masses.

Too many comrades still refuse or fear relations and work with people who do not think as they do on all points.

These tendencies must be fought and we must go with confidence to the socialist workers, the Catholic workers, to all the democrats, to all the republicans, to our allies in the resistance in order to find an understanding on common policies and actions.

The communists consider these efforts to achieve a united front and to unite the democratic forces to be of the utmost importance and that they should be a permanent task.

. . . The organizations of the party are not intended to carry out all the political work of all the organizations and popular movements. On the contrary, the militant communists belonging to these organizations and movements must try to involve the adherents in practical activities . . .

'XVIᵉ Congrès du Parti Communiste Français,' *Cahiers du Communisme* (June 1961), pp. 577–9.

4   Political resolution of the Seventeenth Congress of the PCF, May 1964

The activities of the masses must be reflected in the life of all the party's organizations and, likewise, the life of the party must be translated into the activity of the people.

The correct application of the democratic centralism which gives the party a unity of thought and action demands that a proletarian democracy bloom within the party.

The organizations of the party, from the Central Committee to the cell, will develop with different formats in order to create an environment in which many workers in big firms would participate, as well as women workers, peasants, young men and young women. These organizations will multiply the means of propaganda, the educational conversations in the cells.

The intense work of the party at the service of the working masses, and for the future of peace and of France, requires great and increasing financial resources. Subscriptions and collections must be permanently looked after with the conviction that it is in the heart of the democratic and working classes that the communist party finds the resources necessary for its work.

'XVIIᵉ Congrès du Parti Communiste Français,' *Cahiers du Communisme* (June–July 1964), cf. pp. 528–9.

5 Waldeck Rochet's report to the Central Committee of the PCF, 1968

Just as the working class is the decisive force in the large anti-monopolistic assembly which will impose an advanced democracy on France, so will the working class play the leading role in carrying out the socialist revolution and in building a socialist France in alliance with the working peasantry, the intellectuals and the small urban bourgeoisie.

Indeed, the working class is the fundamental revolutionary class of society in our times. It is the class which most directly suffers from capitalist exploitation. But it is also this class which neither exploits nor seeks to exploit any other social class . . . It makes up the living force of the modern industrial economy; its focus, its organization and its experience with class struggle give it an unequalled effectiveness in its fight. The class possesses a scientific doctrine of struggle, Marxism–Leninism, which is constantly enriched by experience and a party which is genuinely revolutionary, the communist party.

Far from diminishing . . . the role of the working class is increasing. One of the facts which bear witness to this is that the possibility of an alliance with other classes of working people is greater than ever before.

The peasantry, the major part of the middle strata, finds itself faced with a dilemma: it can succumb to the capitalist way or it can join the side of the working class in the socialist way of development.

Similarly, a growing number of intellectuals find direct involvement in production: the continued acceleration of technical progress considerably increases their role in the economic growth and in the organization of production. Science asserts itself more and more as a direct productive force. This is why an alliance of the working class with the intellectuals is, in our time, an important concern.

The construction of socialism in our country will not only be the task of the working class but that of all social strata interested in the overthrow of domination by big capital, in the socialization of the means of production and exchange, in the establishment of a social and economic system which allows for the full development of the creative faculties and initiatives of all the members of society.

It is this alliance with the working class, the governing force of this revolutionary transformation and of the other social strata whose interests can only be satisfied by socialism, which will constitute the social base of the new socialist state.

L'Humanité, December 7, 1968, p. 8.

6 Georges Marchais' interview with Europe 1, 1970

We have just held the party Congress. This Congress, as everyone knows, was convened in a completely democratic manner. Three months before the Congress we published a draft of a thesis giving the estimation of the Central Committee of the political situation, the democratic perspective and the socialist perspective. This draft was discussed for three months by our 19,000 cells. It was then discussed in section conferences and federal conferences, and then at the Congress. As a result, over 400,000 communists have participated in the elaboration of our party's policy.

Of the 19,000 cells, there are only ten or twelve that did not approve the thesis draft.

The 3,000 section conferences approved the thesis draft as did ninety-six federal conferences and all of the delegates to the Congress.

Consequently it is ludicrous to speak of one group manipulating the party when we have just had such a democratic preparation, where all the members of the party, after a very broad discussion, have themselves elaborated the policy of our party. And our party came out of this Congress more united than ever, since the Central Committee which was elected by secret ballot by the delegates was elected unanimously.

Therefore, there is no group manipulating the party, there are 400,000 party members who are completely in agreement with the policy that they themselves elaborated. There is no man who alone claims the right to impose his will.

We have ourselves criticized the cult of personality. We have approved the decisions of the Twentieth Congress of the Communist Party of the Soviet Union. You would not want, in a party as democratic as ours, for us to accept one man making the laws of the party.

Le Monde, May 12, 1970, p. 4.

7   Georges Marchais' report to the Nineteenth Congress of the PCF, February 1970

Roger Garaudy explicitly demands that the party modify its strategy, its tactics and its principles of organization. He also asks it to abandon its theory.

As the Political Bureau indicated in its communiqué on December 18, Roger Garaudy 'contests the role of the working class. He would substitute as a governing force of the political and social movement a so-called "new historic bloc".'

Garaudy's appreciation of the party line of May–June 1968 illustrates the manner in which he conceives this 'new historic bloc.' Intervening at the Central Committee's session on July 1968, Garaudy had, indeed, reproached the party for not having, in the end, subordinated its action and that of the working movement to the student movement. If we were to follow him, we would have been wrong in denouncing the methods and blind violence of the leftist groups. We would have had to use some sort of united front in order to influence the student population.

In short, we would have to criticize ourselves in front of the leftists.

'XIXᵉ Congrès du Parti Communiste Français,' *Cahiers du Communisme* (February–March 1970), p. 84.

8   Theses of the Nineteenth Congress of the PCF, February 1970

In order to attempt to oppose the ideas of scientific socialism, the bourgeoisie distorts Marxism–Leninism. It promotes revisionism: Trotskyism, Maoism and other leftist currents, reformism and right opportunism.

Ideological struggle at the heart of the revolutionary worker movement is a permanent necessity. Today, when new social classes, more susceptible to bourgeois ideology, are entering into the struggle alongside the working class, the fight against opportunism takes on an added importance . . .

Opportunism has a partial view of the situation of class struggle. It underestimates the real forces which can and must be raised to undertake the struggle. Lacking confidence in the masses and in their struggle, it looks for an issue in the abandonment of class positions or in adventurism. It leads to the disarmament of the working class, either by isolating it from the other social classes which are victims of big capital, and thus depriving it of natural allies, or by making it totally dependent on the bourgeoisie itself. In either case it plays, in the final account, the game of the bourgeoisie.

Behind their pretense of opposition, left opportunism and right opportunism feed off one another, and are united in fact.

Both of them avoid the essential question, the question of the power of the state, either by believing that the accumulation of partial reforms can spare the conquest of political power by the working class and its allies, or by substituting the restitution of partial and illusory pseudo-powers for this conquest, leaving intact the private ownership of the means of production and the domination of the bourgeoisie over the state.

Revisionism of the right or of the left, therefore, substitutes the contradictions which the scientific and technological revolution engender for the contradiction of capital-labor. At one moment it accuses the working class of conservatism, another moment it pushes the working class to the background in favor of other classes, which it claims are the true revolutionary elements of society. For the contradiction between the imperialist system and the worldwide socialist system, it substitutes the contradiction between 'rich countries' and 'poor countries.' In the final account it negates the role of the working class as principal element, motor and leader of class struggle on the national and international scales. It replaces scientific socialism either by a technocratic reformism or by the adventurism of irresponsible marginal groups.

In the same blow, right and left opportunism also negates the vanguard role of the Communist Party, the party of the working class, in the anti-monopolist alliance of workers and democratic forces in the struggle for democracy and socialism.

In the field of ideology, opportunism is characterized by an unprincipled eclecticism which turns its back on the creative development of Marxism–Leninism. It replaces the Marxist–Leninist analysis of the present problems of France and of the real conditions of the working class's struggle with a search for ready-made solutions, models which are abandoned as soon as they are adopted at the whim of passing events or fashions. It looks to import into Marxism–Leninism fragments of bourgeois ideology to which it lends so-called humanist or revolutionary virtues, depending on the case.

Right and left opportunism claim that the organizational principle of the Communist Party are outmoded. Democratic centralism and party unity, the sources of our strength, are subverted by the opportunists' demands for the right to form factions. For the truly democratic life of the party it would substitute petit bourgeois anarchism.

Finally, the opportunists from the position of proletarian internationalism, giving in under pressure from the adversary, indulge in the defamation of the achievements of the socialist countries and in anti-Sovietism.

The struggles against the distortions of Marxism–Leninism and the party's policy and, above all, against opportunism, are permanent tasks and integral parts of the fight against the domination of the bourgeoisie in France and for the triumph of advanced democracy, paving the way for a socialist France. As the influx of new forces grows, the importance and outcome of the ideological struggle grows.

One of the essential conditions to successful fulfillment of this task is the creative effort of the communists. Being careful to assimilate everything that can contribute to the enrichment of its theory and its action, apart from dogmatism and sectarianism, the Communist Party must strive to be an innovative spirit, which will permit it to bring to the problems of our time just and constructive solutions, conforming to the interests of the workers and of the nation. To this end it carefully takes account of the movement of social life, of the experiences of revolutionary struggles throughout the world, of the contribution of the living culture of our time, of the scientific discoveries and technical innovations.

'XIXᵉ Congrès du Parti Communiste Français,' *Cahiers du Communisme* (February–March 1970), cf. pp. 444–7.

9   Georges Marchais, 'Democratic centralism,' 1973

A united party is a guarantee of efficiency in the leadership of the struggles, the number and complexity of which never ceases to expand.

It is the guarantee that a limited group, a 'faction,' will not put obstacles in the way of the democratic decisions of the entire party.

It also provides the possibility of a regular and permanent circulation of information throughout the whole party, which makes it possible rapidly to verify whether what is happening in a given location is a local occurrence or is of general import . . .

The implementation by everyone of these democratically adopted decisions is what again permits the verification of the justness of decision, to specify, to modify one orientation, to reject another that is past its time and no longer corresponds to reality.

The Communist Party is not a complete and immovable whole. Like everything that is living, it is changing, it is evolving. Its theory and its political thought constantly change because of its practice and of the new problems posed to it. Its form of organization is regularly adapted to the demands of its action under new conditions. So it is that in 1964 it modified the statutes it had given itself in 1945; it has just brought them up to date, on the basis of experience, at the Twentieth Congress in December 1972; it may very well be led to do so again in the future.

However, this cannot lead it to question its fundamental principles, those of a party having as its goal the construction of socialism. For example, there can be no organized factions within the Communist Party because factions are the negation of democracy and the revolutionary spirit. The organization of factions is the crystallization of positions which petrify thought and are obstacles to the free confrontation of ideas; it is the permanent search for compromise within the party instead of the implementation of a scientific policy; it is the quest for tactical understandings to assure the control of the leadership.

This hardly means that in the Communist Party there is no discussion. There are numerous and passionate discussions . . .

The unity of the party has nothing to do with a so-called monolithism nor with conformism of thought. It is an unceasing process, a perpetual creation which results both in a commonality of views and objectives among communists and in a permanent confrontation, a mixing of ideas and experiences. It is not uniformity within the constraint of a few dead or stiff models, but continued assimilation by all communists of the diversity of situations and men. The greater this diversity is, the richer is the substance of the unity.

Internal democracy and discipline, far from opposing one another, only have meaning when linked to one another; they cannot exist without one another. It is this conception and this reality which the communists sum up with the expression democratic centralism . . .

Le Défi Démocratique (Paris: Grasset, 1973), pp. 200–3.

10   Georges Marchais' report to the Twenty-First Congress of the PCF, 1974

The Communist Party has demonstrated new proof of its capacity to place itself in the foreground of the workers' popular and national struggle. It has also demonstrated that in exercising this decisive role, it is not spurred by a domineering will or by a spirit of exclusion. In working for the unity of the French people for democratic change, the party has but one ambition: to be the best at the service of common objectives.

It is thus in the interest of the workers and the people, in the interest of the nation itself, that the Communist Party improve and strengthen its influence, its organization, its activity. The growing support which surrounds it, the tens of thousands of new members, testify to the fact that the number of Frenchmen who share this conviction is growing . . .

It is fitting to give the party the means to play its role.

This requires, first, that new forces must be boldly won. Workers, naturally, are the largest part of the Communist Party, for this party is rightfully theirs; it is the working-class party. This is the first measure of its effectiveness. To strengthen it implies, in the first place, securing the membership of many workers, employees, technicians, engineers, men and women.

The French Communist Party must considerably strengthen its effective force. As always, the party is open, without exclusion, to all who want to work for great democratic changes. Today membership in the party is the best way to participate in uniting the French people for the democratic changes that our times call for. The new members will take their places at the heart of the French Communist Party, in the forefront of the struggle to establish democratic reforms, while learning from the experience and the theory of the party. Therefore, to become a communist is to participate in the struggle for an advanced democracy. It is to work for the ultimate triumph of socialism.

This also means that the members will follow, at the rapid rate of the actual evolution of material and social reality, the development of the party's collective thought; the Communist Party possesses a scientific theory – Marxism–Leninism – which is the basis for its capacity to kindle the struggle of the working class and the people. The theory is not composed of ready-made recipes. It is a scientific conception of the world, an instrument for knowing reality, a method of reflection, a tool for battle. In order to allow the party to carry out its task well, the theory must be constantly enriched by new conclusions drawn from social reality, from the experience of struggles, from the progress of sciences and technology . . .

Finally, this signifies the development of the democratic life in all the party's organizations. In order to face the growing complexity of economic and social life, the intensity of the political battles, the party needs, more than ever, the thoughts, the ideas, the critical and creative sense, the spirit of initiative, the action of each cell, of each communist. All steps in that direction will be encouraged. The collective thought of the party and free discussion find their full fruitfulness in the carrying out by all of the decisions taken by the majority. This is democratic centralism. Without suggesting it as a model of organization of French society, the communists value it for the vanguard party which is theirs, for it is a decisive measure of effectiveness . . .

Le Parti communiste propose (PCF Publication, 1974), pp. 123–6.

11 Georges Marchais' report to the Twenty-Second Congress of the PCF, 1976

The goal of our policy is to serve the worker, the popular masses and the nation. We must always be open to their needs, have a hold on a reality, which is constantly evolving, more rapidly than in the past, we must be conscious of the changes which take place so that we can draw the necessary conclusions for action.

There is another rule which we value, and that is communal work, a collective management on all levels. Our party is guarded against this evil that is called the cult of personality. This evil, let us say in passing, is ravaging French political life. We communists do not want that because it is bad for a party, bad for a democracy. We also reject the anarchist negation of the role of the leaders. Collective work is inseparable from personal responsibility. The contribution of each communist to the improvement and application of the party's policies is necessary and desired. And the communists expect, rightfully so, that the leaders give themselves democratically at all levels, that they assume responsibilities with the spirit of initiative and the strictness necessary in the complex conditions of class struggle. They would fail in their duties if they did not.

Totally democratic principles give the Communist Party the original and valuable qualities without which it could not be a party of struggle, a revolutionary party which the workers need and to which they are legitimately attached. Today the concern which must spur our organizations, our goals, is to help each communist assimilate these principles and to actively involve a still greater number of members with the decisions of the party, in the search for the initiatives which it must make in the local undertakings and plans, and in their determined application.

'XXIIᵉ Congrès du Parti Communiste Français,' *Cahiers du Communisme* (February–March 1976), pp. 69–71.

SPANISH Communist Party: From Underground to the Search for the Mass Party

1 Santiago Carrillo's report to the Central Committee of the PCE, 1956

Our party, and in general all the communist parties, were born in the heat of the first socialist revolution, following the example of the Bolshevik Communist Party. The birth of communist parties fulfilled a historic need in the period of dying imperialist capitalism. Without a party capable of carrying out a struggle of principle against reformism, of organizing the masses and leading them in the revolutionary struggle against capitalism, capable of leading them to the fulfillment of the socialist revolution, the working class and the working masses found themselves unarmed. Without a party which would firmly defend the principles of proletarian internationalism, the working class could sink into a morass of chauvinistic nationalism, serving the plans of imperialists, as happened to social democracy in the First World War . . .

Inevitably the communist parties were inspired by the Bolshevik model. Logically in each historic period the most developed, most experienced parties will serve as an example to the socialists of other countries.

From our Soviet comrades we have learned much of what has allowed us to become a great party in our country. And while we will have to continue to learn much from them, because they are at the head of the world socialist movement, we will also learn from the experience of other countries and other parties of the socialist bloc and from the experiences of communist parties of the capitalist world, such as the French, Italian and other communist parties.

But it is not surprising that the disciple will sometimes tend to copy the master too mechanically; it is not strange that the disciple will assimilate the errors into which the master may fall . . .

The cult of personality has not existed exclusively within our party in Spain. The cult of personality has existed, in one form or another, in all parties . . .

One can say, truthfully, that these are not motivations which justify the existence of an anti-Marxist method within the Marxist–Leninist party. None the less it is not possible to forget that the communist parties evolve in the heart of bourgeois society and that they are not unaffected by the vices and effluvia of that society; only through a struggle of principles at every hour, at every minute, can it rise above them. As soon as that struggle weakens, or concentrates all its efforts on one specific point, neglecting others, the vices and effluvia of bourgeois ideology can penetrate and grow among us.

By condemning the cult of personality, by laying bare the serious errors made by Stalin – especially in the recent past – the personality of Stalin has been reduced to its true proportions. Stalin's merits in the socialist revolution of October and in the construction of socialism cannot be denied. Nor can Stalin's merits as a Marxist theorist be denied, even if some of his theses must be revised and corrected. But when Stalin moved away from the masses and placed himself above them and the party, he lost sight of the real situation and fell into conceptions which were profoundly harmful to the revolution and to the party, conceptions which led him to commit known offences. By valiantly uncovering all of this, the leaders of the CPSU have shown the communist and working movements the dangers of false appraisals of the role of individuals, the dangers of extreme arrogance and vanity, and they have warned against such dangers.

We communists can only condemn, today when we know them, certain of Stalin's attitudes, opposed to the principles of the party, opposed to Marxist–Leninist conceptions of the dictatorship of the proletariat, which is not the dictatorship of a party, much less the dictatorship of a man or group of men . . .

It is beyond question that some of the defects revealed by the Twentieth Congress, tied to the cult of personality in violation of Marxist–Leninist party practice, appear also in our party, although in different proportions and with different scope . . .

The external manifestations of the cult of personality are clear. Those external manifestations have existed around comrade Jose Diaz, during his life, and around comrade Dolores Ibarruri. They have consisted of presenting these two comrades as the exclusive, unique authors of all that the party has done; of presenting them as just short of miracle-workers, from whose brains and activities there has surged forth all of the thought and activity of thousands of communists. In such manifestations of the cult of personality we have arrived at forms which, when appraised rigorously, seem truly infantile. Logical respect and affection for them have been transformed into veneration: we have surrounded them with titles and adjectives which have been inappropriate. Frequently we presented them as the chiefs of all Spanish workers, as leaders of all the people, which, unfortunately, was not true and shocked sectors of the people and the workers who have still not come to accept our leadership. Party celebrations were transformed into occasions to dedicate to them the most impassioned and ex-aggerated praises. It was the exact imitation in our country of the methods in vogue, not only in the USSR with Stalin, but within the communist parties of other countries . . .

For the past six years the leadership of the party has again worked clandestinely. Secrecy does not favor the development of collective methods or democratic forms. This has been reflected in our work, causing some of our decisions to be made more slowly than we have wanted.

None the less, even during the years from 1945 to 1950 when we had the opportunity to work together in France, we employed methods which we can judge to be less than completely satisfactory. The Political Bureau was then working with the same defects which were soon to be accentuated by secrecy. In that period we, the members of the Secretariat who resolved the most important questions, were a much diminished nucleus. The Political Bureau played a small role. The CC, or better yet, the members who remained, did not meet even one time. We could have held a Congress of the party and we did not.

Can this be attributed solely to the customs of leadership and personal resolution, acquired in the first years of exile, when we acted without unity? No, that is not the only cause. There are other factors which have decisively influenced the irregularities in the functioning of the Political Bureau. These factors are related to the results of the cult of personality, of the use of leadership methods foreign to the principles of Marxism–Leninism, of methods of leadership which are not collective but autocratic, and were used in our party for many, many years. These methods have existed and taken root among us, as a result of the peculiarities of the evolution of our party, which throughout most of its history has acted in secrecy or semi-legality.

Marxist–Leninist principles of organization establish the Congress as the supreme agency of the party . . .

If we examine the development of our party we will see that this principle has rarely been applied. In thirty-six years of existence, one can hardly speak of true leadership coming from several Central Committees which the party has had. Leadership has instead been concentrated almost exclusively in the hands of the Political Bureau, and, moreover, at times the members of the Secretariat, which normally is an executive agency, have concentrated almost all the functions of leadership in their hands . . .

One of the indications of the influence of the cult of personality in our party – and probably in other communist parties – has been the assignment of extraordinary powers to the secretary general, greater than those of the collective leadership. The role of the secretary general of the Bolshevik Party underwent substantial changes during the period between Lenin and Stalin. Similar practice occurred in the life of our party, where the secretary general was considered to be the leader of the party, with the authority to make important decisions, with or without consulting the Political Bureau. In practice, his opinions and decisions were always definitive. To oppose this system, in other times, would have appeared to be disrespectful, insubordinate and a challenge to the leadership. This system was not imposed on our party by the will of Jose Diaz nor of Dolores Ibarruri. It was current practice in the Communist International . . .

Why has this conflict not arisen so acutely before in the life of our party?

The answer lies in the influence of anti-Leninist methods of leadership among us, but also in the conditions of secrecy in which our party has generally evolved. These conditions have imposed their seal upon our party: they have been fertile land for the growth of such methods.

A revolutionary party in secrecy cannot be broadly democratic; the illegal struggle requires great centralization, accompanied by certain restrictions on democracy. It was not within our power to avoid this situation; it has been imposed upon us by the dominant classes of our country as a part of their policy of persecution. We could do nothing but adapt ourselves to that situation or, inconceivably, renounce the struggle . . .

These unique aspects of our development explain why the conflict with the anti-Leninist methods of leadership has not arisen among us more rapidly . . .

Democratic centralism means that decisions in the party and its agencies are made by the majority and, after having been made, they are binding for all. It means that the decisions of the upper-level agencies are binding for those on lower levels.

But this presupposes discussion, a battle of opinions. Unfortunately many comrades among us have very specific conceptions of what discussion is. For them discussion is something purely formal; it consists of comrades repeating the same formulas in order to agree with what is proposed; but they do not allow, by any means, that one speaks in order to differ. And the comrade who shows doubt, who has something to propose, who does not always limit himself to saying 'amen,' is harassed until he is persuaded, or is tired and driven away. We must combat such methods energetically. Comrades must have the full opportunity to set forth and defend their opinions. If they are erroneous, it is necessary to help them out of their error, not with invective, but with arguments. And if they are correct, they must be accepted.

The cult of personality has nothing to do with democratic centralism, nor is it a result of this.

The correct implementation of democratic centralism excludes the cult of personality and concedes authority to the collective agencies of the party. The idea that we must destroy democratic centralism is inspired by the desire to strip us of our Marxist–Leninist revolutionary character, to reduce us to a petit bourgeois social democratic party, sterilized by its internal contradictions . . .

Spanish Communist Party document, 1956, pp. 9–55.

2 Santiago Carrillo's report to the Central Committee of the PCE, 1958

Our party is a unit of strong will, an organization ruled by the principles of democratic centralism. In every corner of the country, in spite of secrecy, we communists act following the same political line, fulfilling the directives of the Central Committee between Congresses . . .

This demonstrates that in a party which, like ours, is united around its program, its principles and its Central Committee, the most solid political centralization is possible even though organic contact is now less stable and regular.

What is essential is to assure political contact between the leadership and all the party organizations; what is essential is to assure that the program and the party orientations reach all remote places, even if we do not know exactly how many comrades there are in each place. What is essential is that each base organization, each nucleus of communists, considers itself responsible to the party for the implementation of the program in its place, and for mobilizing the masses in political action.

What is necessary is that the whole party moves in unison. That there exist a unity and a political centralization which are compatible with the flexibility that organic ties inevitably have under a dictatorship, such as that existing in Spain.

It is clear that that unity and that political centralization depend not only upon the timely decisions of the Central Committee, but also upon each provincial committee, each local committee, and, as far as is possible, each cell committee meeting and studying how to implement the party's program in their radius of action; that they take adequate and concrete initiatives in each place in order to mobilize the masses, to unite them and to organize them; that they apply the policy in a creative manner, accounting for the local problems and conflicts which interest the masses most, uniting them around such problems.

Spanish Communist Party documents, 1958, pp. 156–7.

3 'Spain twenty years after the Civil War,' Central Committee report, 1959

The Communist Party's leading role in an alliance . . . is determined by the fact that our party is the standard-bearer of Marxist–Leninist ideology, the ideology of the socialist revolution, as history has demonstrated convincingly; by the fact that the Communist Party is the party which fully represents the interests of the working class which, given its situation in society, is the class called upon to oversee the construction of socialism.

But the leading role of the Communist Party has nothing to do with the mechanical and brutal imposition of one group upon another. This role will be fulfilled in proportion to how well our party, inspired by Marxism–Leninism, shows its superiority as a leader in the realm of politics and ideology; in proportion to how it manifests in thought and action its greater understanding of the historical, political and social problems which the establishment of socialism poses; in proportion to how it is able to furnish at all times the most appropriate policies and measures, that it affirms with the greatest resoluteness and the most steel-like revolutionary will, its role as guide of the alliance. Our party will be able to play its leading role if it forges the most extensive and solid ties with the working class, rulers of the socialist society and the working masses. To execute this role, our party should assume and cultivate the qualities fit for the Marxist-Leninist party of the working class...

The leading role of the party of the proletariat should not alarm anyone who sincerely desires to strengthen democracy and to spur the socialist transformation of the country. On the other hand, it is not unusual for a given group or party to play a leading role. In any political alliance, whatever ends it proposes, there is always a group which acts on a practical level as a leader, by virtue of its competence as representative of the social class which supports it and because of its greater understanding of the political goal which it is called upon to accomplish...

Spanish Communist Party document, 1959, pp. 84–5.

4 Santiago Carrillo's report to the Sixth Congress of the PCE, 1960

Changes Achieved in the Party
Since its Fifth Congress, our party has strengthened organically, politically and ideologically. Our correct political program and our faithfulness to Marxist–Leninist principles are the primary reasons for this achievement.

In recent years the party has made a serious effort

to correct negative methods, products of sectarian tendencies and of the habits inherited from the war and of the implications of the cult of personality. The Central Committee has valiantly exposed such defects ... The methods of collective leadership have been re-established in the party, internal democracy has been strengthened within the limiting conditions of secrecy ...

Arbitrary sanctions and decisions against comrades, which sometimes were prolonged for years and years without reason, have been eliminated. Discussion in our leading agencies and in the base organs is more alive, much richer. The right to criticize even the leading agencies is exercised by all comrades. Criticism and self-criticism have become habitual practice.

It cannot be said that there do not appear here and there, sometimes, bitter aftertastes of the old methods; that they have been eliminated once and for all. Things like this are not definitively eliminated overnight ...

... our party has recently experienced a profound renovation. Our party has been able essentially to overcome a tendency which could be very strong in a party which has a glorious tradition and which has been in secrecy for twenty years, persecuted by fascist repression: the tendency to be diminished to the old and proven militants, to the troops experienced in the heroic struggles of the past. Overcoming that sectarian inclination, the party has opened itself to new generations, bringing new revolutionary forces into its ranks and boldly promoting hundreds of new troops. Those new forces are represented in the leading agencies of the party, including the Central Committee ...

We believe that this renovation of the leading agencies of the party is also in accord with the conditions of the new epoch of the world, distinct from those which determined the composition of the leadership of the clandestine communist parties of the past.

In this epoch the communist parties, although they may eventually find themselves in secrecy, can and must be mass parties with large followings among the masses. The influence which socialism is acquiring, the successes of the Soviet Union and the socialist camp, the progress of the democratic forces in the whole world, and the ideological and political maturation of the communist movement all favor the growth of the party's mass following ...

When we elect broadly representative leading agencies, we are demonstrating that for us secrecy, in spite of everything, is an accidental phenomenon: that we do not renounce, even now, the leadership of the large masses; and that we are preparing ourselves resolutely and decidedly for the time, not far away, in which that task of leadership will be accomplished in the light of day, before the eyes of our people in a regime of full political liberties . . .

If it is agreed that we are in a period of acute decomposition of the dictatorship and apogee of the mass movement, that this does not involve a passing phenomenon, but a process which follows its course and which will go along asserting itself with increasing resoluteness − and the whole national and international situation confirms it − the party must adapt its organization to the new situation and prepare itself to direct the apogee of the mass movement, and their offensive actions, toward ending the dictatorship.

And it does not address the people, the masses, in such actions with an organization appropriate to the earlier period of resistance and survival, but with a stronger, larger, more active organization, more visible to the masses . . .

It is clear that under the present circumstances we cannot rely upon a system of individual cells as a base organization. In the modification of the statutes which the Central Committee proposes, there are included distinct forms, such as groups of youths, women and even individual affiliations in specific cases.

In such a period as the present, the communists can gather together in mass organizations of distinct character, either semi-legal or even legal, in which other sympathizers and anti-Francoists can participate without being required to organize in cells, even though this is always done under the right circumstances.

VI Congreso del PCE, Spanish Communist Party document, 1960, pp. 93−9.

5   Resolution of the Central Committee of the PCE, 1969

For a Mass Party
. . . Under the present circumstances the communists' political life takes place not only within the party; it also unfolds in mass movements and organizations. Today there is more discussion than in other periods but, none the less, discussion in our organizations is still insufficient. It is insufficient because today one discusses also in the factories, in the streets, everywhere; among the masses there is greater anxiety, greater political sensitivity. The communist finds himself needing to argue more, to respond to many questioners, to accomplish an extensive political and ideological labor. This requires raising the political discussion in party organizations, reinforcing the study of its documents . . .

The Communist Party daily reinforces its ranks with promotions of revolutionaries from the working class and from other forces of labor and culture. None the less it is necessary to acknowledge that in this area there is need of greater initiative. We need to develop a true recruitment policy. We need to offer places in our ranks to thousands of workers, peasants, students and intellectuals. We need to go forth boldly to make our party increasingly a mass party. This is possible, in spite of suppression and all the difficulties of secrecy, on condition that the task of recruitment be the concern of all levels of the party.

This task is impeded by sectarian and narrow ideas such as that of 'few and good.' Without overcoming such ideas, through discussion, it is impossible to approach correctly those who would belong to the party. The barriers to their joining our ranks cannot be justified by the difficulties of secrecy. The party's defense is not in narrowness, but in numerical and political strengthening and in its union with the masses.

Above all, the unity of the party
In our party there has been much discussion of the Czechoslovakian question. The Central Committee made a statement at the proper time and, in the country as well as in exile, the party organizations have approved the position taken by the Central Committee.

Without a doubt this has been one of the most difficult discussions that has taken place in our party because of the nature of the problems debated. And it is necessary to underline that, in spite of the enormous difficulties of secrecy, the discussion could not have been more democratic. The militants have made use of their right, defending their opinions even when they differed with those of the Central Committee and, naturally, there may be those who are still not convinced that the adopted position is the correct one. In our party no one is denied an opinion opposed to that of the regular agencies of leadership on one question or another. But in accordance with the principles of democratic centralism, at the time of action, at the time of the fight, there is not, nor can there be, any position other than that of the party. It is necessary to say that the majority of the comrades who have disagreed with the Central Committee on such questions have honestly accepted, as communists, the discipline of the party, and have begun to work, putting party unity above all. He who, forgetting this elementary duty of a militant, works against the policy of the party and against its agencies of leadership, should consider where that road has always led. Violation of the principles of democratic centralism, voluntarily accepted when one joins the party, is incompatible with stability in its ranks. The most important weapon which our party has, together with its just policy, is its unity: a unity which we communists will defend firmly against anyone who attacks it, whatever the label with which he attempts to present himself may be.

Mundo Obrero, no. 10 (May 24, 1969), pp. 3–4.

6 Declaration by the PCE, 1969

On a factional and divisionist attempt
The Communist Party of Spain finds itself facing a factional battle. Eduardo Garcia and Agustin Gomez are sending 'emissaries' to some organizations and comrades, emissaries who slander the party leadership, denigrate its political program and end up by proposing participation in what is nothing more than a factional fight. If it only meant activities during the exile we probably would not have felt the need to publish this notice. But what is serious is that this work is going on inside Spain. Some 'emissaries' of Eduardo Garcia and Agustin Gomez have attempted to get together in specific provinces with groups of the party and with people who sympathize with our cause. And this already goes beyond endurance. The danger which this holds for our organization and comrades under the circumstances of Francoism is clear, even more so when the police try through all means to discover and strike blows against the party. That Eduardo Garcia and Agustin Gomez have gone to such extremes shows their irresponsibility and the loss of any notion of respect for the security and the

customs of a clandestine party. Spanish communists, no matter what their way of thinking inside the party on one problem or another may be, cannot tolerate such conduct, bordering on provocation.

Mundo Obrero, no. 17 (October 7, 1969), p. 4.

7 Santiago Carrillo, 'Democracy in the Leninist party,' 1970

One of the fundamental principles of the organization of the Communist Party is democratic centralism. The application of this principle, the correspondence between the two terms, centralism and democracy, varies according to the circumstances under which the party acts. The condition of a communist party in secrecy is not the same as that of another which unfolds under circumstances of political liberty and that of both are unlike that of a party which has achieved power in a socialist society. And even within these three distinct situations there may be other nuances and differences. On the other hand it is clear that a principle of synthesis, as that of democratic centralism, carries with it the risk, whatever the situation may be, of disequilibrium in the correspondence between the two factors which comprise it.

Fifty years after the founding of our party, given that it has developed in secrecy for the greater part of those [years], we Spanish Communists are aware that centralism has weighed more in our functioning than democracy, save in limited periods. At the same time, among ourselves, even before the Twentieth Congress of the CPSU there was concern over limiting the excesses of centralism, as proven by the party of documents of '51 and '52 and by the Fifth Congress's election of a large Central Committee, even under particularly difficult circumstances, in 1954. It is necessary to say that no illegal party – in the history of our movement – and I believe that no other type of party has ever had such a large leading agency under conditions of secrecy. This composition of the CC responded and responds to the strong desire that the fundamental decisions of the party be made, not by a minute group of leaders, but by a collective, directly tied to the mass movements, bringing together the greatest possible amount of knowledge and experiences and, consequently, with the greatest chances of correctness. And if our program has been confirmed by contrast with practice, it is due in large part to the characteristics of our Central Committee.

Another fundamental preoccupation has been to keep our party from becoming a party of exiles. Since the end of the war, Jose Diaz warned of this danger, greater in our case, given that for many years the organized militants in exile, because of the mass character of the emigration, was greater than that of those organized inside the country. Fortunately this proportion has radically changed in favor of the interior. But even in those years, in the party Congresses, the interior organization totally dominated that of the exiles because of their larger number of representatives.

But we are fully aware that those party Congresses, although they may reflect the efforts of a clandestine party to maintain alive in its heart the circulation of ideas, discussion and democracy, do not constitute in any way a functioning model for the Communist Party in another situation. We are convinced that tomorrow, as soon as liberties exist in Spain, our party will have to function – within the principle of democratic centralism – in *another manner,* much more democratically, that our party will have to create the conditions for an open and free discussion of all the essential questions; it will have to apply fully the elective principle on all levels. Today and while this situation lasts, Congresses will bring together, not delegates elected by all the comrades as their representatives, but the leaders of the provincial organizations and of the most important local ones, which are often unknown to the mass of comrades, as leaders, for reasons of secrecy. And it will be these men and women who were not elected, not voted for by the militants, who make the decisions. Greater democracy is impossible today if we do not want the party to succumb to the hands of the police . . .

When there is liberty in Spain our party will be able to, and should, move to much broader forms of democratic functioning. Our party will have to address more concretely a problem which is posed today to the great majority of communist parties: how to combine an increasingly real democratism capable of capturing the changing aspects of the situation, to truly enrich our policy and our theory, without weakening the unity of action or fomenting factions? How to have a party increasingly open to problems and opinions and, at the same time, better able to act with unity, discipline and revolutionary boldness, at all times?

Mundo Obrero, no. 7 (April 5, 1970), pp. 12, 10.

8 'Our reply to Enrique Lister,' *Mundo Obrero,* 1970

An inadmissible road

The first thing we notice in the writings of the faction, and in a more incriminating form in those of Enrique Lister, is their insulting and aggressive language, charged with hatred. The lack of political argument is counterbalanced by insults; above all, in the 'accusations' which Lister hurls at Santiago Carrillo, secretary general of the party, and against other comrades. We are a political party and not a policing organization. Those 'accusations' remind us of the monstrous police abuses which occurred some time ago in communist movements and we are not prepared to allow them to resurface.

Another aspect of the faction's writings is the high-sounding, ultra-revolutionary phrases, used helter-skelter as a substitute for political argumentation. But our party passed through the stage of revolutionary infantilism many years ago, in which the lack of 'correct analysis of the concrete situation' characteristic of Marxism was replaced by pseudo-revolutionary phraseology, with stereotyped formulas and mannerisms. To say that the party 'is falling into the swamp of reformism, revisionism, the most ferocious anti-Sovietism,' without any demonstrative argument of that assertion other than the assertion itself, may sound good to ears which are totally unskilled in the revolutionary struggle or to men who have remained burdened with the mentality and phraseology of previous times, but it irritates or amuses those party militants who are familiar with its political program and convinced that this [program] marks the road of the Spanish revolution . . .

Lister says that since 1956 there has been opposition, in the heart of the PCE, to the policy of Santiago Carrillo, that is, the party policy. We may ask ourselves: what happened in 1956 and since then in the international communist movement and in our party? In 1956, the Twentieth Congress of the CPSU was held, which condemned not only Stalin's crimes but also the bureaucratic and dogmatic deformities, the violations of democracy in the heart of the party and of the mass organizations and of the state, which made possible those abuses. In our party, after we analyzed the experiences of the Twentieth Congress and the manifestation in our party of the methods and errors pointed out there, the struggle against them was intensified (*intensified* because it had already been initiated by the Fifth Congress and earlier).

It was in 1956 that our party put forth the policy of national reconciliation and started a difficult theoretical and political endeavor not exempt from problems (such as the cases of Claudin, 'pro-Chinese,' etc.) – in order to formulate the strategy and tactics of the Spanish revolution in today's circumstances. Since the adoption of that program, the Sixth and Seventh Party Congresses have taken place and great inroads into the party and its leadership have been made by the young forces which did not fight in the war. The party has been profoundly rejuvenated and renovated, it has elevated its theoretical level without losing its combative character, joining together the new generations and the veterans who have been able to remain in the fight.

The results of that policy are clear: new mass movements such as the COs and others have appeared, we are seeing workers', peasants' and students' struggles of an extent *without precedent* under a fascist dictatorship which allows us to begin the task of organizing the general strike. The isolation of the party and the working class has been eliminated; the Pact for Liberty is possible in the near future. And throughout all of this process, the role of the Communist Party of Spain has been, is and will be decisive.

Mundo Obrero, no. 19 (November 7, 1970), p. 11.

9 'Internal democracy of the party,' *Mundo Obrero*, 1973

In the discussion of the agreements of the Eighth Congress, some party militants have expressed the opinion that in our ranks – and today, under the fascist dictatorship – there should be the possibility of manifesting tendencies, platforms and actions, and even the right to refuse to implement those political decisions of the leading agencies of the party with which they are not in agreement.

The method of all the factional groups consists of accusing the party of one or another *changes of direction*. For this, all do not hesitate to falsify our positions, to attribute to us attitudes which we have never had, to abridge some of our texts and ignore the others.

All, none the less, concur in 'denouncing' the 'lack of democracy' in our ranks. We have said it and repeated it a thousand and one times: we are the first to be dissatisfied today with the internal working of our party. We would like it to be much more democratic. But in order to achieve this there is only one road: implant democracy in Spain. As long as there is not democracy in our country, the clandestine revolutionary party of the working class will have to subject the extent of internal democracy to the demands of conspirative security, to combative effectiveness.

If our party were to permit itself today the luxury of engaging in a struggle among tendencies and factions, the workers would abandon us, they would lose their confidence in us and would think that we have stopped being *their* party. The police would force their way in through the break and would finish the job of dissolution which started with the internal fight, easily capturing and destroying our organizations. Because of this we have sometimes said that those who want a party with tendencies and factions today should leave ours and create another one. Let them destroy themselves if they wish, but let them not destroy the party, which must maintain its cohesiveness and its discipline in order to be a true instrument of liberation. And what we say today was said by Lenin, with the same words, before the revolution, arguing with those who held similar attitudes . . .

Even in such a situation, with all the limitations which reality imposes upon us, our party today has the most lively democratic working in our country, through discussion in its cells and committees, the breadth of its leading agencies and the close contact and exchange of ideas and experiences among them, the lower-level organizations and the base of the party, the openness in ideological questions, its fight against dogmatism and continuism, its constant renovation and its openness toward the forces of culture.

We are fully aware of the problems which a communist party may confront, formed in secrecy and armed struggle, on the day when it escapes to democratic legality; the danger of 'military' and 'clandestine' deformities; the danger of 'Stalinist' deformities which may lead to a prolonging into democracy of methods of leadership and functioning which will no longer be justified. We believe that one of the first great discussions, carried out in liberty, which the party will have to undertake when we are in democracy, will have to be precisely that one: the full unfolding of the forms of internal democracy in a new type of party. We are aware that on that theme, even theoretically, there are many problems to be cleared up.

Mundo Obrero, no. 8 (April 11, 1973), pp. 5–6.

10 *Manifesto program* of the PCE, 1975

11 Santiago Carrillo, *PCE,* 1976

The Communist Party will be a party of the vanguard, not because of constitutional or administrative privileges, but according to how it manages to have the most advanced and dynamic forces of the working class and other social sectors join its ranks, how it is able to formulate the most fitting solutions for the development of democracy and socialism . . .

The Communist Party believes that starting today it will be necessary to begin to formulate the design of a *political formation,* able to unite all the socialist tendencies without suffocating any, without annulling their ideological characteristics, without compromising their specific features, their independence, their own ranges of action.

That new political formation, including parties, groups, diverse organizations which would not sacrifice their structures, their ideology or their specific programs, could endow itself with a *common socialist program, with common organs for collective formulation of the political decisions related to the implementation of that program* and it could establish *a certain common discipline in the implementation of such decisions.* When deemed useful, it could confront partial struggles; political, electoral, or of other types, as such a formation . . .

The Communist Party of Spain has formulated the thesis of the national strike, as a form of popular uprising which can lead to the triumph of a political revolution in Spain, and to open the way to political and social democracy and socialism.

The national strike is not simply crossing one's arms and waiting for the state to come tumbling down, as in the old anarchist utopia . . .

The national strike is the mobilization and the confrontation of the most extensive anti-Franco strata led by the working class against the present power. Because of this, the natural detonator of the national strike would have to be the general political strike of the working class and, of course, it is clear that the strike would be its backbone.

Spanish Communist Party document, 1975, pp. 63–6.

Our concept of democratic centralism

It is suggested to us that we abandon the principle of democratic centralism in the internal functioning of the party. It is clear that there is a great deal of confusion about this concept. Many identify it purely and simply with Stalinism, with the nullification of democratic life inside the party, with the dictatorship of the leading groups.

Democratic centralism is another thing and its application differs greatly, according to the concrete situations. Under conditions of deep secrecy, those through which our party has passed for so many years, the principle of democratic centralism confers greater power on the leading group . . . In such situations the co-option of those responsible is decided ultimately by the leading group. The margins of error are evident, but fewer than the danger of disintegration which would be provoked by a formalist 'democratism.' In reality, when the leading group proceeds with a communist spirit, it co-opts those men who, in one way or another, have been previously exalted by the masses and by members of the party throughout the social and political struggle. That is to say, it confirms the natural selection which the very same struggle makes . . .

But democratic centralism is applied very differently under conditions of legality. Then democratic centralism means that in the party's discussion, both internal and public, the most divergent opinions may be sustained without error; moreover when the Congress, or the elected agencies which replace it between meetings, passes a resolution by majority vote, it is necessary to act on it with discipline . . .

Within this homogeneity of action, in our party there may coexist differing opinions on the models of socialism which exist today, differing theoretical foci on new and historic problems, differing cultural currents.

Santiago Carrillo, *PCE* (Barcelona: Los Avance-Mañana Editoriales, 1976), pp. 31–3.

12 Santiago Carrillo's report to the Ninth Congress of the PCE, 1978

It has been said repeatedly that our party is not democratic in its workings. None the less, in general, no one denies any longer the democracy which has characterized the preparation of the Ninth Congress, in spite of the fact that it is not at all simple to pass from the forms and methods of a long and profound secrecy to those appropriate for a situation of legality. There have probably been defects due to lack of experience, which will have to be overcome during the struggle . . .

The leadership of the party has maintained the promise which it repeatedly made during the time of secrecy and which directed that, once legality was attained, the party would decide its policy and the rules of its functioning in the most democratic manner. So it has happened during the pre-congressional debate and thus it will happen during this Congress.

And it is clear that if the party's leading group, formed through a natural selection throughout years of struggle, had wanted to create a hermetic, closed party without the possibility of dissension, instead of this open, visible and democratic party, it would have been able to do so, as other precedents indicate.

But we have opted, voluntarily and responsibly, to shape a party able to spread its influence quickly throughout wide sectors of the social fabric, regaining the historic time which the dictatorship has made us lose and playing an effective role in the political life of the country. And because of this we have neither hindered the enlisting of new militants nor have we created obstacles to internal democracy. We have opted, with all the consequences, to shape a true 'eurocommunist' party.

The option for a working, Marxist revolutionary party, neither social democratic nor Stalinist, is a real option, toward which there have been advances made in other countries as well as in Spain . . .

This does not deny our acknowledgement of Lenin as the greatest revolutionary of this time. It means only that the problems of the revolution in the developed countries of the West fifty-four years after the death of Lenin, when *the world has already changed fundamentally*, as the letter of *The International* says, we have to study methods and develop them ourselves, learning freely and without blind beliefs not only from the books of one master or another, but from the practice of the workers' movement of the West, from its successes and its failures, from its advances and its retreats.

IX Congreso del PCE, Spanish Communist Party document, 1978, pp. 43–5.

PART FOUR

The International Communist Movement

Introduction to Part Four

Probably no other position of the eurocommunist parties has changed more radically over the postwar period than that concerning the international communist movement. Within a relatively short period of time they have moved from total dependence on and subordination to the Moscow-led international communist movement to a position of significant strategic and ideological autonomy. All-out defense of the Soviet Union in foreign policy and an uncritical attitude towards the CPSU as the guiding party and infallible source of ideological purity, were the major characteristics of the European communist parties' positions in the immediate postwar period. Even then it would be erroneous to think that the parties were nothing more than extensions of the Moscow-dominated international communist movement, blind and docile supporters of Soviet policies and pronouncements. There is evidence that in the immediate postwar years some of the parties were anxious to establish more autonomous domestic strategies. The Cold War, while greatly constraining the options available to the parties, does not appear to have extinguished this inclination. It was only in the years after 1956, however, that the search for autonomy began consistently to shape the parties' behavior and choices.

Throughout their postwar history, the European parties have had to deal with a dilemma caused by their location at the intersection between their national systems and the international movement of which they have traditionally been a part. From the outbreak of the Cold War to the early 1960s, the conditions of the international system were such that the parties, when forced to make a decision about domestic or international politics, tended to choose their allegiance to the Soviet Union and to the international communist movement over domestic considerations. The fact that they were domestically isolated, even in clandestinity, reinforced the parties' tendency to seek in the international communist movement in general, and in the Soviet Union in particular, political support and the 'ideological legitimacy' which they lacked at home.

The 'Soviet connection' has been a source of continual ideological and strategic tension for the parties as they seek to achieve a workable equilibrium between their traditional international commitments and the requirements of their domestic strategy. Even today many of the eurocommunist parties' positions reflect a contradictory set of needs: to continue to be loyal to the international communist movement while, at the same time, gaining sufficient distance from the Soviet Union to legitimize their strategy at home. It is testimony to the parties' strategic flexibility, and the CPSU's desire to avoid an open rupture, that they have been able to disengage themselves, at times even taking clearly critical postures towards the Soviet Union, without falling into open conflict with Moscow. It is also evidence of their need, and ability, to adapt to changing international and domestic conditions while maintaining links to the international communist movement. This has not always been easy as the controversy between the PCE and the Soviet Union in recent years suggests.

Strategic and ideological autonomy from Moscow is a crucial component of the eurocommunist position. Specifically this involves the parties' reappraisal, to different extents, of their attitudes towards some of the classical defining aspects of the international communist movement. Eurocommunist parties no longer consider the CPSU as the infallible guiding party, the unchallenged leader of world communism to which all communist parties must subordinate their choices. The very conception of a 'leading center' in the world communist movement, a conception characteristic of the period of the Third International and of the Cold War, is now rejected by all eurocommunist parties; for them it is a thing of the past, no longer attuned to the changed and changing conditions in the international communist movement. The Bolshevik Revolution and the Soviet experience are still regarded by the parties as sources of ideological and political inspiration, as landmarks in the march towards socialism. For the parties, however, the hierarchical and rigid structure of old should be replaced by a new pattern of relations among all communist parties, one based on principles of equality, of non-interference in the internal affairs of fraternal parties. The church-like monolithism of Comintern/Cominform times, with its excommunications and condemnations, should give way to a centralized international movement. The vision of 'unity in diversity' which was sketched out by Togliatti as early as the mid-1950s has become accepted generally by the eurocommunist parties.

Likewise, while in the immediate postwar period proletarian internationalism signified above all defense of the Soviet Union because of its role as the fatherland of socialism, the essential force for the liberation of oppressed peoples, and the leader of world communism, today proletarian internationalism is interpreted as meaning the struggle for the realization of socialism at home, and solidarity with the struggles of the socialist movements abroad. In the case of the PCI, a change in language, the replacement of 'proletarian internationalism' with 'internationalist solidarity,' has been used to legitimate the search for linkages not just with other communist parties but with socialist and social democratic parties of other nations as well. The PCE, too, has promoted this new formulation.

Two realizations are behind the parties' new conception of the proper relations among communist parties. First, they have recognized that in the past the Soviet Union has often used the allegiance of the communist parties to advance the state interests of the Soviet Union rather than revolutionary goals. Carrillo has been most explicit in this regard. Secondly, they have realized that their domestic strategy could succeed only if it became the dominant criterion and frame of reference for their activity, implying a downplaying of old conceptions of proletarian internationalism.

The Soviet model of socialism is also viewed increasingly critically by the eurocommunist parties, both with regard to the methods necessary for building a socialist society and the structure of such a society. Two aspects of the parties' criticism are worth mentioning. On the one hand, the Soviet model is now considered to be neither exportable nor universally valid. The parties argue that conditions in Western Europe make the application of such a model inappropriate, perhaps even impossible. It is the search by the eurocommunist parties for a national strategy consonant with the historical, political and economic peculiarities of their respective countries which has induced them to abandon the dogmas of the Soviet model of socialism. On the other hand, the kind of socialism which has been built in the Soviet Union has also been criticized by eurocommunist parties. The absence of civil rights, suppression of all forms of dissent, bureaucratic degenerations, are only some of the aspects of the Soviet system which have been publicly criticized at various times by the leaders of the European parties.

Noticeable differences between the parties are evident with respect to the extent, coherence and frequency of such criticism. On all three counts Carrillo has gone farthest. The PCI, as early as the 1950s, began to criticize the Soviet model of socialism; but while these criticisms have become increasingly detailed, they have tended to be limited to some aspects of the Soviet system, avoiding a systematic overall judgement. The diversity between the Spanish and the Italian approaches is reflected in the latter's reluctance to question, as Carrillo has done, the socialist character of Soviet society. This is one of the areas in which Spanish and Italian parties differ most clearly, a difference indicated in the documents by the controversy raised by the Soviet critique of Carrillo's book, *Eurocommunism and the State*, in 1977. For their part the French communists have tended to downplay their critique of the Soviet model of socialism, and to be very restrained in the extent of their criticism.

Although eurocommunist criticism of the Soviet model has taken on momentum only in recent years, its roots go back to the issue of Stalinism and to the ways in which the Soviet leaders handled the issue. The revelations made by Khrushchev at the Twentieth Party Congress posed many problems for the European parties. It was not simply a matter of dealing with the consequences of the 'beheading of the hero.' The very sources of historical and ideological legitimacy of communist parties in the West were thereby called into question. Moderation and circumspection characterized the parties' response to Khrushchev's revelations. None the less, 1956 was the turning point in their attitude towards the Soviet system: its ideological purity was no longer accepted uncritically; its structural flaws became a matter of ideological concern. Already in 1956–7 Togliatti suggested that the critique of Stalinism must be extended to a critical examination of the Soviet system. This stance gradually has come to be accepted even by the French Communist Party. It should be mentioned, however, that even today the eurocommunists' critique of Stalinism and the Soviet system is almost always accompanied by a tendency to seek historically grounded explanations. Carrillo, the most vocal and systematic critic of the Soviet system, none the less stresses the historical factors which made the transition to socialism in the Soviet Union particularly arduous. This historicism, common to all three parties, serves another purpose: to demonstrate that the type of socialism to be built in Western societies can and must be of a different and higher form than the Soviet, one compatible with democratic institutions.

Two factors have most contributed to the eurocommunists' gradual disentanglement from the Soviet orbit: the break-up of the Communist monolith internationally and the process of détente. The parties' perception and appraisal of détente is discussed in great detail in this casebook's section on international politics. It should suffice here to say that the process of détente has facilitated eurocommunist moves towards autonomy in three ways: it has stimulated the weakening of the blocs; it has made the language of international politics less uncompromising, especially with regard to superpower competition; and it has contributed to the breakdown of Cold-War-caused domestic barriers. Thus many domestic and international issues no longer require a clear-cut choice between two inevitably opposed camps, a choice between two 'civilizations'; the domestic context in which the parties operate has lost many of the Manichean qualities of old; and the process of fragmentation within the two blocs has offered greater room for maneuver, greater opportunities for reconciling domestic requirements with international loyalties.

The break-up of the international communist monolith has been equally momentous. The vicissitudes of the Yugloslav–Soviet relationship, on the one hand, and the bitter and not easily resolvable Sino-Soviet dispute, on the other, have contributed to the break-up of the international communist monolith. Both events represented a direct challenge to the principles at the heart of the Third International, including the supreme leadership of the CPSU and the infallibility of the Soviet model of socialism. The growing autonomy of the PCI in the 1960s, made explicit in Togliatti's Yalta Testament and in the decision of the new PCI leadership to publish that document in the face of Soviet opposition, furthered the process.

While détente and the break-up of the international communist movement set the stage for the pursuit of independence by the eurocommunist parties, the factor which greatly accelerated the development of autonomy was the Soviet Union's reaction to the challenges, or alleged challenges, to its leadership, above all in Czechoslovakia. The sharp contrast in the parties' responses to Soviet intervention in Prague (1968), and Hungary (1956), vividly demonstrates the extent of the change which has occurred in their attitude towards the Soviet behavior. In 1956 the parties fully supported and justified Soviet intervention in Hungary, while they unambiguously condemned the military action undertaken by the Warsaw Pact countries against Dubček's new course. After 1968 all eurocommunist parties have come to view the principle of non-interference in the internal affairs of fraternal parties as the rule which should guide interparty relations among communist parties.

Prior to 1968, much of the history of the relations between the eurocommunist parties and the Soviet Union was characterized by acceptance of the CPSU's claim to leadership in the international communist movement. Their support for Moscow's excommunication of Tito's Yugoslavia in the late 1940s evidenced the degree to which the Western European communist parties were willing to follow the Soviet lead in the affairs of the international movement. By the time of the Sino-Soviet dispute, in the early 1960s, the position of the eurocommunist parties had, however, become already more nuanced. To be sure, throughout the most intense stages of the dispute they clearly sided with Moscow. On the other hand, the PCI and PCE were opposed to Soviet requests for the excommunication of the Chinese and for their expulsion from the international communist movement. These same parties are now also in the process of re-establishing normal relations with the Chinese Communist Party, to the displeasure of the Soviet Union.

The eurocommunist parties' development of autonomy has neither been smooth nor conducted by each of them with the same intensity and coherence. In a nutshell, all three parties have not become equally autonomous nor do they assign the same degree of strategic and ideological importance to autonomy from the Soviet Union. The Spanish and Italian communists display more autonomy than their French counterparts and are making greater efforts to achieve full ideological and strategic independence from the Soviet Union. Both the PCI and PCE, for instance, have been opposed for over a decade to international conferences of all communist parties which might have been used by the Soviets to reaffirm their leadership and/or to seek to excommunicate dissident parties. Only in the mid-1970s, in connection with the preparation of the Berlin Conference of European communist parties, did the PCF join with the other two parties to prevent the Soviets from imposing their views through a conference resolution. This was during the high point of tension between the PCF and the USSR. The principle of non-interference and of the right of each party to pursue its own nationally determined strategy has been emphatically stressed by the leaders of the Italian and Spanish parties. For their part, the French communists have tended to downplay their criticism of the Soviet Union as the leader of the international communist movement and of the Soviet model of socialism. During the Sino-Soviet conflict they supported, less ambiguously than the Spanish and Italian communists, Soviet demands for the excommunication of the Chinese. Their stance on Czechoslovakia since the Prague crisis of 1968 has been less critical of the reassertion of Soviet control. More generally, the Italian and Spanish parties have been anxious to raise to the level of principle the development of autonomous relations among communist parties and to seek new definitions of internationalism. The French party has been more content to confine its disagreement to individual issues.

Common to all three eurocommunist parties is the determination not to confuse autonomy with anti-Sovietism. For them, the Soviet Union remains the 'fatherland of socialism,' and the country which defeated Nazi Germany in the Second World War and which has helped the struggle of the movements of national liberation. The task which faces the parties in the years to come, particularly in the eventuality that they move closer to the threshold to power, lies precisely in the need to develop full autonomy; on the other hand, their historical and ideological heritage will continue to color many of their positions. In the end, whether the eurocommunist parties' quest for a share of political power at home will succeed or fail may well depend on how they resolve this dilemma.

MAURIZIO VANNICELLI

DOCUMENTS FOR PART FOUR

ITALIAN Communist Party:
Unity in Diversity – from Proletarian Internationalism to
Internationalist Solidarity

FRENCH Communist Party:
Diversity in Unity – Proletarian Internationalism and the
Strains of Allegiance

SPANISH Communist Party:
Diversity and Unity – the Frontiers of Internationalism

ITALIAN Communist Party: Unity in Diversity – from Proletarian Internationalism to Internationalist Solidarity

Titoism

1 Felice Platone, 'The socialist front and the case of Yugoslavia,' 1948

Upon reading the Cominform report on the question of Yugoslavia, the wise investigators of the civic committees were able to announce an astonishing discovery: the Italian communists were the 'confessed perpetrators' of harms done to the Italian people. They have sworn again and again the national character of their battles against imperialism and now, together with the other parties of Cominform, they reaffirm their loyalty to proletarian internationalism, to the international front of socialism, to the country of socialism, condemning without hesitation the errors that have taken the leaders of the Yugoslavian Communist Party along the path of betrayal of international solidarity and along the path of nationalism. They have sworn again and again that their fight for the renewal of Italy was democratic in character, that their policies were policies of alliance with all workers, especially the peasants, and now they blame and condemn the communist leaders of Yugoslavia because they wanted to make of their state a peasant state. And so forth. It is useless to say that those who are the most offended by the 'confessed offenders' are the neo-social democrats, standard-bearers of the nationalistic Marshall Plan, defenders of clericalism and the extremely democratic 'Truman Doctrine,' sowers of discord among the workers and hate among the people, by order of American imperialism. To them it is forbidden to understand, much less to admit, that, faced with the possibility of imperialistic expansion, the international working class is the watchdog of peace and of the independence of the people; that were the reactionary forces to mount an offensive, awaken, reorganize and mobilize the fascist forces, the united, international front of socialism would be the only defense of

freedom, of workers' rights; that the entire history of the last fifty years is centered on the advancement of the Soviet Union's Bolshevik Party to the head of the socialist front, the vanguard, the leader against the worldwide line-up of the forces of war and suppression. To deny the evidence is to create confusion and bewilderment in the minds of the workers, to divide their ranks, to obstruct and paralyze the battle and the *raison d'être* of the social democrats, of the 'Marxist democrats,' as they prefer to be called . . .

The fact that the fascists, the American imperialists, and the English talk of Soviet imperialism is natural, and it is even more natural that the social democrats or 'Marxist democrats' speak of it. But the fact that the leaders of a party which still calls itself communist, such as that of Yugoslavia, accredit by their behavior a similar absurdity is something which can only be explained as a desertion or a betrayal.

If the Yugoslavian people have resolved their national problems, if they have obtained for themselves national independence, they not only have their own forces and fighting to thank for it, but also the decisive political, diplomatic and military help of the Soviet Union. Without this help, their fighting, heroic as it may have been, would have been as fruitless as the less heroic battles of the Greeks and of other people. The Soviet Union, unlike the Yugoslavian leaders, has always been immovably faithful to the cause of proletarian internationalism and, consequently, to the cause of the people's national liberation . . .

The Yugoslavian leaders have ignored the most elementary suggestions of Marxism and Leninism, they have forgotten one of the earliest victories of Lenin and the Bolsheviks, the doctrine of proletarian supremacy in the national and democratic revolutions of this modern age, the doctrine of the workers' class alliances . . .

The objection is raised that in Yugoslavia, where peasants comprise a huge majority of the population and where the working class is small and unconcentrated, it is inevitable that the lower-middle class and, above all, the farmers would have the upper hand. Ostentation and a tendency towards isolation explain such reasoning, but in reality the working class of a single country is never isolated, never alone in its battle. At its side are the workers and the workers' vanguards of all countries, and with them come their vast experience and their revolutionary doctrine of Marxism–Leninism. To the extent that the Communist Party remains faithful to internationalism and to the cause of socialism, the working class has the capacity and the force to place itself at the head of the entire popular movement, to guide and direct it. The fact that the Yugoslavian leaders have deserted the socialist front, have strayed from Marxism–Leninism, and have ignored its teachings is proof not of the weakness of the Yugoslavian working class, but of their leaders' weakness, their detachment from the proletariat, their orientation towards capitalism and imperialism or, to say it in a word, their betrayal.

Rinascita, August 15, 1948, pp. 248–51.

2 Palmiro Togliatti's report to the Eighth Congress of the PCI, December 1956

It is natural that the question of the relations between the communist and workers' parties is also posed sharply and in a new form in this situation. The Communist International carried out a great task in giving a revolutionary orientation to the workers' movement and in educating more than a generation of its cadres. In its decisions there often prevailed a certain sectarianism which isolated the communists from the great mass of workers. The sectarianism was, however, liquidated with vigor when, faced with the threat of fascism and war, the unity of the workers and of the democratic forces was clearly the supreme necessity, the most important duty. Even in the brief and fragmentary life of the Information Bureau (Cominform) a certain sectarian closure was evident, as demonstrated in the incorrect decision which resulted in the rupture with the Yugoslav communist movement. The indispensable search on the part of

each party for its own path of advance toward and of struggle for socialism, not to speak of its own path of internal development, requires autonomy of research and of judgement in the application of the principles of Marxism–Leninism which are our guide to the national situations.

It is a difficult task and to be carried out well it requires the reciprocal aid of all the sectors of our movement, of all our parties. Since there was no longer a single organization and thus no single directive center, the idea of a system of groups and of multiple centers arose, but this form of organization appeared incompatible with the full autonomy of each party and seemed likely to give excessive responsibility to one or another party. The system of bilateral relations satisfies the requirement of autonomy . . . Bilateral relations must therefore include, above all, reciprocal knowledge and reciprocal understanding. They must allow, in fact encourage, friendly criticisms, posing problems and promoting analysis of them. What is inadmissible, from whatever quarter it might come, is a return to the systems which we have criticized and surpassed: the intervention in the internal questions of other parties, the transformation of criticism into an attack which discredits and promotes confusion, preconceived mistrust, the open or disguised support of a fractional struggle, the stimulation of ruptures of the unity of other parties or of our whole movement.

On the basis of these principles we have restored our relations with the League of Yugoslav Communists. We consider this a positive fact and we have been instructed by the first results of our study of the experience of the construction of socialism in Yugoslavia. We will develop these friendly relations. One must not, however, fall once more into errors which would violate the principles indicated above.

Palmiro Togliatti, *Nella democrazia e nella pace verso il socialismo* (Rome: Editori Riuniti, 1966), cf. pp. 9–80.

3 Communiqué of the Central Committee delegations of the PCI and the CLY on the talks carried on in Belgrade (January 15–21, 1964)

The League of Yugoslav Communists and the Italian Communist Party, in evaluating the past and present contrasts in the revolutionary working-class movement, start from the conviction that they reflect the inequality and variety of the advancement process towards socialism and of the construction of socialist society.

Thus the contrasts cannot but sharpen when single parties try, as the Chinese Communist Party has tried and is trying to impose their unacceptable political and ideological positions and even their state policy on other parties and movements.

The League of Yugoslav Communists and the Italian Communist Party intend to devote their efforts – above all through a deeper and more complete analysis of the ideological, economic and social processes occurring now in the world – in order to overcome the conflicts today dividing the international working class and communist movement and to reach a new unity eliminating the danger of a deep fracture and even of a split, which would lead – at least temporarily – to weaken the joint working-class struggle and that of the progressive forces.

The contrasts cannot be overcome, however, with a simple statement of goodwill and united aspirations. It is necessary to work tenaciously so as to reach new victories of democracy, socialism and peace enabling us to ascertain in the facts the correctness of the positions assumed; moreover, it is necessary to have a real comprehension of the differences manifested in the theoretical ideas and in the political and practical positions . . .

The necessity of a richer and more various co-operation among the working-class and communist parties is arising from the intensity of social and political processes going on in the world, from the complexity of problems facing today the working-class movement and other progressive movements. These problems that require a new and growing dynamism of thought and action cannot be faced by every party by their forces alone: their solution cannot be but the result of a co-operation, of a positive discussion and of an exchange of viewpoints among more parties under the widest forms. Among these, the form of bilateral co-operation has been very useful. The League of Yugoslav Communists and the Italian Communist Party intend – after having already practiced it successfully in the recent years – to develop it further between themselves also in the sense of a co-operation with initiatives for peace and coexistence that can be made in common agreement with other political movements and organisations, above all in the Adriatic and Mediterranean sectors.

These forms of co-operation must express the autonomy of single parties and at the same time their common commitment in the struggle for peace and socialism. Instead, every attempt of ranking the parties and groups to oppose the line of peaceful coexistence on the basis of dogmatic and sectarian conceptions *vis-à-vis* the development of the international revolutionary movement should be considered negative and dangerous . . .

Foreign Bulletin (January–February 1964), pp. 71–3.

The Hungarian Rebellion

4 Communiqué of the Directorate of the PCI, November 3, 1956

The Hungarian people are living through a tragic hour. Divided, cast into the abyss of a fratricidal revolt, the future which lies before the Hungarian working class and workers is dark. The bases of the popular democratic regime have been overrun and the white terror, atrocious reprisals, the danger of an open reactionary regime and of an irreparable rupture are already rising on the ruins. With the vanguard of the working class attacked and the working class deprived of its guide, the Hungarian people's prospect of the construction of a new society becomes more remote.

The first duty of every communist, of every socialist and of every democrat, in this hour is to raise the call against the reactionary wave which is sweeping Hungary, against the white massacres, in order to ward off the danger of fatal provocations which springs from the chaos into which the unfortunate Hungarian nation has been thrown. Over and above the differences which have divided the Italian workers in their judgements on the Hungarian events, it is today necessary that they unite, in demanding that the lives threatened by the white terror be defended, that the most elementary principles of civil life be not overthrown. No socialist, no democratic and honest citizen, can hope that liberty will rise where the most bestial form of reactionary class terror has broken out, threatening to restore to Hungary the darkest days of the Horthy dictatorship. Every friend of peace must be concerned to avoid the rise of a revanchist and nationalist center in Hungary, precisely at the moment when there is under way an imperialist war against Egypt and when the peace of the Mediterranean has been broken. The Directorate of the Communist Party calls these duties to the attention of workers and citizens. The Italian communists express their solidarity with their Hungarian comrades who have fought and are fighting for the defense of socialism and extend their deep-felt sentiments to all the victims of the white terror.

The workers' movement would, however, fail in one of its fundamental responsibilities were it not to examine the errors which have brought the Hungarian people to the present, terrible situation. From knowledge of the errors, from the courageous examination of the causes which have brought about defeat, the workers' movement can gain clarity in once again taking up the battle, in order to advance, in order to raise its capacity for struggle. From the crucible of today, the Hungarian workers' movement will learn how to rise again. From the events of Poland, from the events of Hungary, the entire workers' and communist movement will draw experience which will reinforce it, educate it, temper it. The victorious advance of socialism has always proceeded through defeats, failures, the most difficult of trials.

L'Unità, December 4, 1956, p. 1.

5 Palmiro Togliatti's speech at the eighth regional congress of the Bologna Federation of the PCI, November 18, 1956

The first four paragraphs of this speech of Togliatti reproduce the communiqué of the Directorate of the PCI of November 3, 1956 (see preceding document. [*Eds*]).

For us the situation in Hungary represents something grave, painful and bitter . . .

Soviet troops have intervened twice. We maintained the first time that the intervention represented a grievous action: we held it necessary that the Hungarian workers' party have the chance to deal with the situation which had arisen by itself without resorting to the intervention of foreign troops. We have said it from the beginning, always emphasizing that that intervention should have and could have been avoided, and that the responsibility for it could be traced back essentially to the break-up of the ranks of the Communist Party. With regard to the second intervention, it too being requested by the new Hungarian government, we have said openly, without any hesitation and from the very beginning, that, given the point to which things had arrived, it was by then a question of necessity, harsh necessity, from which it was impossible to escape, especially considering the possibility that the country might fall into chaos under the dominion of fascist and reactionary forces. To a large extent it was also a question of necessity, referring to the repercussions that the actions of Hungary and their predictable consequences could have had, and without a doubt would have had, on the entire situation in Europe and in the world.

In substance – and the facts of which we are aware show us to have been correct – we concluded that had there not been a clear stopping point, had an insurmountable barrier not been positioned before the precipitation of events, in Hungary there would have arisen a fatal nucleus of fascist provocation as well as provocation of war, and the danger of war would have become imminent not only for Hungary, or Western Europe, but the entire European continent. War would have been a definite prospect for Hungary, a very probable prospect for Europe. In front of this reality, the intervention was necessary, although it was harsh.

Today we hope that the presence of Soviet troops in Hungary can end as soon as possible. This desire corresponds to the spirit not only of our forces but of the larger part of the Italian people, and in particular to the will of that part of the people which approves and has approved the position which we took, that of having refused and still refusing to associate ourselves with the anti-Soviet stir brought about by the first and second Soviet interventions.

With regard to the more important reasons for the events, and, in particular, the reasons for the rebellion on the 23rd and 24th of the past month, the errors committed by the leaders of the party and of the Hungarian state in the course of the past month have been decisive. Whereas the Hungarian party leaders had not completed the actions necessary to change the political trend which they had followed until then, and it needed to be changed, there developed among the party supporters an unrestrained propaganda campaign and agitation against the leaders. The people were summoned up against the party without even considering in any way the almost certain consequences. Thus the Hungarian party collapsed and thus it was that, in the course of the rebellion, there were communists who fought on one side and communists who fought on the other, workers who moved in one direction and workers who moved in the other. From the beginning the reactionary forces have entered into this chaos, and precipitated a situation which required Soviet intervention.

Palmiro Togliatti, *Il partito comunista italiano e movimento operaio internazionale, 1956–1968* (Rome: Editori Riuniti, 1968), pp. 97–102.

Stalinism and De-Stalinization

6   Palmiro Togliatti's editorial, *Rinascita*, 1949

In the name of the working class and of all those Italians in whose hearts lives a love for progress, for democracy and for peace, in the name of more than 2 million Italian communists, I most heartily express to Comrade Stalin our best wishes, filled with devotion and affection.

For many years our party has lived under the most difficult of conditions. We have succeeded in becoming a great party of the masses, thanks to the battle that the communists have carried on, toppling the fascist regime. But we would have hoped in vain, had it not been for You – leader, enlivener, clever chieftain.

We know that without You, Comrade Stalin, the Italian people would find themselves today in much more difficult conditions. Thanks to You and your activities, in the decisive moments of this century the battle has been decided in favor of the working class, in favor of socialism.

You have taught us how to be communists, how to fight under any circumstances, how to be faithful to the very last principle of Marxism–Leninism and how to serve the cause of emancipation of the workers. We commit ourselves to be faithful to your teachings, to struggle for the unity of the workers, for the independence of our country, for peace; and against those who would provoke another war.

The Italian people will never again consent to being cast into another war against the Soviet Union, against the people who have led the way toward socialism.

We greatly admire and respect the invincible force of Marxism–Leninism in You, the invincible force of the working class, the highest realization of human ideals.

We wish You a long life of good health, for the welfare of the people of the Soviet Union, for the welfare of the working class and the people of the entire world.

Glory to You, Comrade Stalin.

Rinascita, December 21, 1949, p. 1.

7   Palmiro Togliatti's report to the Eighth Congress of the PCI, December 1956

Problems of the international workers' movement
In the international workers' and socialist movement, and above all for us communists, who represent the vanguard of this movement, the most important event of the recent past has been the Twentieth Congress of the Communist Party of the Soviet Union, because of the change of direction which was determined, justified and announced. There were two major areas of emphasis regarding the decisions of this congress; the first, the ascertainment of the existence of a system of socialist states, accompanied by the progressive collapse of colonialism; the second, the denunciation of the wrong political directions followed under Stalin, which resulted – according to the description given by the Soviets – in 'brutal violations of the Leninistic principles of leadership, and violations of socialist legalities' with consequences extending even to criminal acts. Other important results of this Congress, regarding the strategies and tactics of the communist movement, have been: the confirmation of the possibility of avoiding war as a consequence of modifications in the world organizational structure; the recognition of the possibility of an advancement towards socialism which excludes violence and is realized through democratic and legal means, making use of parliamentary institutions. The need for new directions and major corrections was made manifest.

An observation, however, must be made: emphasis, with accompanying evidence, was not given to the close ties between the new positions and policies, and the criticisms and denunciations of the wrong course followed by Stalin, during the lengthy period of time indicated by the Congress itself. A major point, both theoretical and practical, remains unclear. Those mistaken political tendencies which the Congress denounced not only were never compatible with our principles and with our programs, but they brought damage to the construction of the socialist society and they could have caused and did cause even greater damage when the transition was made from the construction and existence of socialism in a single country to the existence of a socialist world comprised of a system of states.

This defect perhaps served to emphasize the fact that the inflamed denunciation of the mistakes (which extended even to criminal acts) was not immediately accompanied by an in-depth investigation of their origins and conditions. The denunciation remained within the context of a dramatic posthumous exhibition of the deviating nature and of faults of a leader, rather than handling the question of the distortions produced and corrected by Stalin himself; what caused them and what, as a consequence, was the best way to get rid of them. To a certain extent this defect has made it more difficult to combat enemies who are committed to demonstrating that the Soviet system and the socialist system are responsible for those denounced acts and therefore are inherently defective. More serious than this, however, seems to be the fact that this defect has not led to an immediate evaluation of the consequences as well as of the corrections and modifications that must be made in all those countries where the communists are at the head of the state and society.

The delay has opened the way to serious consequences. In the Eastern European people's democracies new regimes have appeared because of the war, because of the previously existing reactionary orders, and because the presence of Soviet troops prevented them from turning back, forestalling a capitalistic and reactionary restoration . . .

For this reason we do not accept the use of the term 'Stalinism' and its derivatives, because it leads to the false conclusion that the system is wrong in and of itself, rather than encouraging the investigation of the evils which have become a part of an otherwise positive economical and political construction, of proper activities in the field of international relations and of the resultant decisive victories.

We have openly discussed with our Soviet friends the characteristics of these evils, which we see as distortions of certain parts of the organization of the socialist society; we have sought to contribute to the evaluation of these evils and their origins. We uphold our opinion that if there is dissent with regard to this proposition between us and our Soviet friends, let it

be perfectly clear that this dissent has nothing to do with the necessary criticisms and denunciations made by the Twentieth Congress, which we have approved without reservation and from which there is no turning back. The debate over the causes of the mistakes and the serious, painful and impermissible events denounced by the Twentieth Congress will certainly continue, because it interests the whole workers' movement, and the frantic attack of the enemies who would love to emphasize this point. I continue to be convinced that the investigation must be adjusted to emphasize the relations, the contrasts and the reciprocal influences between the economic developments and the political superstructures. When the evolution of the economic base had arrived at the point which allowed and exacted an extension of democracy, such did not occur, and there were instead restrictions and artificial shut-downs.

Palmiro Togliatti, *Nella democrazia e nella pace verso il socialismo* (Rome: Editori Riuniti, 1966), cf. pp. 9–80.

8 Luigi Longo's interview with *Stern*, in *L'Unità*, November 10, 1964

One cannot but agree with the opinion of Comrade Togliatti that the personality cult and the crimes of Stalin cannot be attributed to only one man and his temperament. This can only be explained upon the examination of the historical conditions under which the Communist Party of the Soviet Union was obliged to operate and by the modifications which, during the development of these conditions, became a working part of the organization and the structure of the party.

At the beginning, for three years, the October Revolution was in constant danger from the Russian bourgeoisie and the foreign imperialists. The necessity to defend themselves imposed an extreme centralization of economic and political power and an iron discipline. It was during the course of this battle that the Bolshevik Party assumed the triple function of political organization, state leadership and economic direction. Thus it became the only party, the central machine of the whole society.

The contrasts, the vacillations of the classes, were reflected in the party itself, making the unity of its leaders more necessary than ever, in order to carry forward the gigantic work of building socialism in one country only. It was because this fundamental choice, the necessity of unity and the expending of national energy, were essential to the building of socialism that Stalin battled against internal opposition and won by harsh methods which consequently weighed down upon the recent developments of the party and of the Soviet Union. It was during this conflict that the concept of party unity, understood to be a monolithic organization, vigorously defined every disagreement as an opposition to the party line, an abandonment of principles, and a manifestation of hostility towards the working class.

In this atmosphere the centralization of the organization, necessary in order to face and overcome the tremendous difficulties met in the building of socialism, lost all its democratic character, and thus a bureaucratic apparatus and methods prevailed with control from the top. At the beginning, and for a certain length of time, this centralization of power had an objective reason and it permitted great conquests. But this went on even when the progress of socialism and the maturity of Soviet society needed not a tightening but an honest development of the internal democracy of the party and, in general, of democratic socialism applied to politics, trade unions and economics on which the Soviet system is based. Instead of this development, the Stalinist theory was adopted. This theory consisted of an aggravation of the class struggle inside the socialist state. The more successful this was, the more it became a strengthening of the state apparatus of force. From here the multiplication of the errors and tragedies of the Stalinist period spread in all its manifestations to that which has been defined as the personality cult.

It should be observed, however, that in spite of all the errors and limitations that manifested themselves in the building of socialism, there was never any corrosion of the socialist and working-class base in the revolutionary process. The economic, social and political development of the Soviet Union was brought up to the level we know today, and this same Communist Party at its Twentieth Congress gave impetus for the return to the observance of Leninist rules of party organization and democratic socialism . . .

Foreign Bulletin (October–November–December 1964), pp. 75–6.

The Sino-Soviet Dispute

9 Giancarlo Pajetta, 'On the relations among communist parties,' 1962

We heard yesterday the heavy attack of the Chinese comrades on our party and its policy. They stated their willingness to meet in order to examine our mutual positions. We certainly agree over this need, but, in the meantime, we must reply to some topics which appear quite clear to us and in a certain sense preliminary.

In the first place, we firmly reject any attempt directed to weaken or refuse support and solidarity to the Soviet policy of peaceful coexistence. In recent days we too looked with deep emotion at the acts of heroism of the Cuban people, at the unshakable determination of this nation, of its revolutionary party and leader, comrade Fidel Castro. But we cannot forget that this country has been defended by the Soviet Union, which saved peace . . .

We have given evidence of considering of the utmost value the search for a national road to socialism, even when our viewpoints were misunderstood by some parties. But we cannot disown the importance of the revolutionary experience of the first socialist state and of Lenin's party. And we are not referring only to the glorious experience of the October Revolution or to the heroic and decisive contribution made by the Soviet Union to the victory against Nazism. We are referring also to the revolutionary spirit, which drove the Soviet communists in 1956 to denounce and rectify their mistakes, as well as to their will to achieve progress and renewal, which have been the basic elements and a new example for the communists and the democratic and working-class movement in every country of the world.

But we must reply to the Chinese comrades also when they say they do not agree with our own policy. The Chinese comrades stated that they do not agree with some Italian comrades over some essential aspects of our policy. We are compelled to remind them that we are a Leninist party, which admits no factions. The whole of our Congress unanimously approves the policy of the Central Committee, rejects the Chinese comrades' unacceptable attack, condemns their positions, which we consider unjust.

The Chinese comrades have underlined three points over which they disagree. First, the struggles for structural reforms. Not only our documents, however, but also those of the international communist movement, which the Chinese comrades quoted, acknowledge the revolutionary value of this struggle, which is an essential aspect of our action. It is not merely a matter of things put down in writing. The fact is that these struggles are in harmony with the interests of the Italian people, and it is precisely thanks to these struggles that we have remained a great party linked to the masses, a decisive element in the life of a country which, so far, has successfully foiled every attempt of authoritarian nature and is swept forward by a deep urge for renewal.

Secondly, the question of Albania. We are not worried on account of the fact that the Albanian leaders have suddenly proclaimed themselves teachers of Marxism–Leninism *vis-à-vis* the CPSU and all other communist parties. What worries us is what they are aiming at, why they are encouraged, why some people express their solidarity with them. Needless to say, we cannot accept the accusation of opportunism, which is thrown at us from that side . . .

Thirdly, the problem of the relations with the Yugoslav Communist League. We, too, criticized the Yugoslav communists; we were probably among the first to do so and we argued with them about the Lubljana Congress. But this criticism does not prevent us from seeing reality and we do not want criticism to become a repetition of anathemas. The Chinese communists accuse the Yugoslav leaders of having restored capitalism. When our delegations visited Yugoslavia, however, they discussed, sometimes argued and quarreled with the Yugloslav comrades over the organization of their workers' councils, their planning problems and the relationship between party and state, but they found no capitalists in the Yugoslav factories.

And since we are in favor of unity, we believe that political and ideological differences must not prevent relations and, whenever possible, common action. For this reason, we trust that the meeting between comrade Khrushchev and comrade Tito may be a further step towards the unity of all those who fight for peace and socialism, in Europe and throughout the world. On the other hand, experience has taught us that the policy of replacing arguments by insults gives no results.

Lastly, there is the question of public debates. The Chinese comrades say that no debate should be public. But one cannot advocate a certain method and then follow another one. The Chinese comrades, in fact, more than once publicly expressed their disagreement both at the Twenty-Second Congress of the CPSU and at the congresses of other communist parties. And they have done so in an increasingly explicit and heavy-handed manner in their press, in articles our papers published . . .

We believe that the unity of our movement must develop around a policy of peaceful coexistence. The growing strength of the socialist camp, the weight of the international working-class movement, the thrust of the national liberation movements can find at present a common meeting point in the fight for peace. The task of isolating the imperialist forces and foiling their aggressive plans is the element uniting the progressive forces of the whole world. This also means putting the policy of imperialism in crisis and helping the progressive, democratic and socialist forces to advance.

Foreign Bulletin (December 1962), pp. 70–3.

10 Palmiro Togliatti's memorandum, *Rinascita*, September 5, 1964

. . . *On the best way to combat the Chinese positions*
The plan we had proposed for an effective struggle against the erroneous political lines and against the splitting activity of the Chinese communists was different from that effectively followed. In substance, our plan was based on these points:
– never to interrupt the polemic against the positions of principle and the political views of the Chinese;
– to conduct the polemic, contrary to what the Chinese do, without verbal exacerbation and without generic condemnations, on concrete themes, in an objective and persuasive manner and always with a certain respect for the adversary;
– at the same time to proceed by groups of parties to a series of meetings for a profound examination and a better definition of the tasks presenting themselves today in the different sectors of our movement (Western Europe, the countries of Latin America, the countries of the Third World and their contacts with the communist movement of the capitalist countries, the countries of popular democracy, etc.). This work should have taken place taking into account that, since 1957 and since 1960, the situation in all these sectors has seriously altered and that, without a careful collective elaboration, it is not possible to arrive at a correct definition of the common tasks of our movement;
– only after this preparation, which could take a year

or more of work, could one have examined the question of an international conference that could truly be a new stage for our movement, its effective strengthening on new and correct lines. In this way we would also have been able better to isolate the Chinese communists, to face them with a more compact front, united not only through the use of common general definitions of the Chinese line, but also because of a more profound knowledge of the common tasks of the entire movement and those concretely facing each one of the sectors. Furthermore, once the tasks and our political line had been defined, sector by sector, one could also have renounced the international conference, if this were to appear necessary, in order to avoid a formal split.

A different line was pursued and I do not consider the result as altogether beneficial. Some (possibly many) parties were expecting a conference to be convened within a short period in order to pronounce an explicit and solemn condemnation, valid for the entire movement. Their expectation may also have disoriented them.

In the meantime the Chinese attack has been widely developed and thus their action to establish small splinter groups and to win some parties for their viewpoint. One has replied to their general attack through an ideological and propagandist polemic, not through a development of our policy linked to the struggle against the Chinese views. Some actions have been taken in this latter direction by the Soviet Union (signing of the Moscow Agreement on nuclear tests, the visit of comrade Khrushchev to Egypt, etc.) and they have been real and important victories over the Chinese. The Communist movement in other countries has not succeeded, however, in doing anything of this nature. To explain myself better, I am thinking, for instance, of how important would have been an international meeting, convened by some Western communist parties, with widespread representation from the democratic countries of the 'Third World' and their progressive movements, in order to elaborate a concrete line of co-operation and of help to these movements. It was a way to combat the Chinese with deeds, not just with words.

In this connection I consider to be of interest our experience as a party. In the party and on its periphery we have some small groups of comrades and sympathizers tending toward and defending the Chinese views. Some party members have had to be thrown out of our ranks because they were responsible for activity of building factions and of indiscipline. However, in general we conduct a broad discussion on all theses of the polemic with the Chinese within cell and section meetings and in town groups. One has the most success when one passes from examining general themes (the nature of imperialism and the state, driving forces of the revolution, etc.) to concrete questions of our current policy (struggle against the government, criticism of the Socialist Party, trade union unity, strikes, etc.). On these themes the Chinese polemic is completely disarmed and impotent.

From these observations I draw the conclusion that (even if today one is already working for the international conference) one must not abandon political initiatives helping to defeat the Chinese positions; that the terrain on which it is most easy to defeat them is that of the judgement of the concrete situation facing us today and the action to solve the problems arising in the individual sectors of our movement, in the individual parties and in the movement in general . . .

Foreign Bulletin (August–September 1964), pp. 67–9.

11 Luigi Longo's report to the Central Committee of the PCI, *L'Unità*, October 12, 1966

The events which are taking place in China under the sign of the 'cultural revolution' deeply concern the working class. The whole of the communist and working-class movement saluted the victory of the Chinese revolution as a great historical event. The Chinese people's entering into the socialist world gave the revolutionary movement a strength and a drive which held imperialism back, promoted the victory of the anti-colonial movement and the creation of new socialist states in Asia, Africa, and in Cuba. The Chinese Communist Party's recent trends towards the political and organizational division of the international communist movement and towards a strongly anti-Soviet campaign and the breaking of the Bandung front deeply concern the communists and all democratic forces. This concern is made deeper by the so-called 'cultural revolution' which is taking place.

Obviously this revolution is only one aspect of deep-lying political and social turmoil. We are concerned with the aspects that it has taken on, not only because they bring discredit upon socialism, but because we are convinced that they seriously damage China itself and the development of its socialist revolution.

Undoubtedly the 'cultural revolution' is the expression of considerable changes in the relations among the political and social forces on which the revolution was based. The revolution tends to put on one side the highest organizational force of the working class, its avant-garde, the Communist Party, to replace it by the 'red guards,' 'Mao's guards,' consisting mainly of young students.

The meaning of the cultural revolution
The 'cultural revolution' tends to strengthen the function of the army in the affairs of the country, to the detriment of the function of the political, administrative and party forces.

This could bear a great influence in the future on the development of the Chinese revolution. This functional change from the traditional party bodies to military organizations is not only temporary. According to the Chinese press, the committees of the cultural revolution should function permanently, in the factories, mines, plants, in the cities and the villages . . .

In foreign policy they are essentially aimed against the USSR and the socialist countries. According to the Chinese press itself, clashes are taking place between workers, peasants and party officers on one side and 'Mao's guards' on the other. These are worrying events because of the serious consequences which this policy brings about in China itself, as it tends to solve the problems of the transition from capitalism to socialism through military and administrative methods . . .

Research for unity among anti-imperialistic forces
May we ask ourselves: where are the Chinese leaders going? At what is the Chinese socialist revolution directed? Exasperated attitudes are again appearing, which experience has proved to be unsustainable and which are bound to cause renewed failures.

It is difficult to foresee where all this will lead. The ways and methods of the cultural revolution have already brought discredit upon the Chinese revolution and removed it from the socialist thought and practice.

Along this road China has arrived at an international isolation which runs the risk of leading to a system of social relations inside the country which will give negative results as to the building of socialism and will clash against the workers themselves. Although claiming to be 'Marxist–Leninist,' the Chinese line has led to exasperated demonstrations of nationalism and tends to replace the working class and its organizations by the army and the 'red guards' in the leadership of the country.

These changes indicate the Chinese leaders' lack of confidence in the Chinese working class and underestimation of the functioning of the working class in the government . . .

Foreign Bulletin (October 1966), pp. 17–20.

12   Enrico Berlinguer's speech at the national *L'Unità* festival, September 19, 1976

After the death of Mao Tse-tung
Yesterday immense China came to a halt and its entire population, in silence, paid deep homage and said goodbye to comrade Mao Tse-tung.

It is not possible to say much today – because of the truth and not because of our shortcomings – about the detailed, concrete developments of socialist construction in China: in fact, as has been noted, our repeated proposals and friendly initiatives – aimed at re-establishing relations between our party and the Communist Party of China, hoping that they would consent to sharing knowledge and discussions – have not been received favorably by our Chinese comrades; and, on the other hand, we know little from other sources. We remain without – as a serious and objectively based product of analysis – explanations of the changes and, at times, complete reversals of positions and trends in the construction of both the Chinese economy and the new Chinese society.

Nevertheless, from what we know it seems that Mao and the Chinese Communist Party have undoubtedly made an original contribution to the elaboration and realization – by way of a fierce and heroic battle – of a strategy of anti-colonial revolution and also of the advance of socialism with new and specific characteristics, drawn from in-depth knowledge of the reality of China and the desire to adhere completely to this reality. And precisely because of this the Chinese revolution represents not only an extension of socialist reality and socialist experience, but also its enrichment.

In this area there have been original and important contributions regarding relations between the workers and the farmers, and between industrial and agricultural development. Hence, it seems worthwhile to study the Chinese experience and its fight against the dangers of bureaucracy.

It is necessary to study this experience, but because it is necessary we must first combat and overcome the fashion which has prevailed for years and which is even more popular today – in some places – of a mythical vision, of an uncriticized exaltation of the events of the Chinese revolution, of the work and of the figure of Mao, of the reality of China and its politics.

Just as China's tendency not to understand sharp contradictions, the unmotivated reversals of position and direction, dramatic contrasts whose real ends are kept hidden, puzzle us with regard to the political economy of China, above all there are some aspects of Chinese foreign policy which cannot be overlooked. It is not simply a question of certain disquieting actions, like the positions taken toward Pinochet's Chile or Angola, but of its general strategy which we see as unjust with regard to such questions as peace and international détente; the necessary quest for unity and collaboration among all the socialist, democratic and anti-imperialist forces and in the rigorous respect of independence, of effective autonomy and sovereignty of each people, country and party.

Enrico Berlinguer, *La politica internazionale dei comunisti italiani* (Rome: Editori Riuniti, 1976), pp. 177–80.

The Prague Spring

13   Communiqué of the Political Bureau of the PCI (August 21, 1968), *L'Unità*, August 22, 1968

The Political Bureau of the PCI met this morning, with the members of the Directorate present in Rome, in order to discuss the grave situation which came about unexpectedly with the intervention of troops of the Soviet Union and other countries of the Warsaw Pact.

The discussions and agreements of Cierna Nad Tisou and Bratislava were welcomed by the leadership of the PCI with lively satisfaction, in full coherence with the need they had already pointed

out to find a political solution to the problems raised in Czechoslovakia, and in the relations between Czechoslovakia and other socialist countries: solutions to be achieved in respect for the autonomy of all parties and countries, in line with the development of socialist democracy and solidarity with the process of renewal under way in Czechoslovakia, in such a manner as to reinforce effectively the unity of the international communist and workers' movement.

In the presence of these facts, it is not possible to understand how, under such conditions, the grave decision of a military intervention could have been undertaken. For this reason the Political Bureau of the PCI considers such a decision unjustified, and irreconcilable with the principles of autonomy and independence of every communist party and socialist state, and with the needs for the defense of unity of the international communist and workers' movement. It is in the spirit of the most firm and convinced proletarian internationalism, and once again confirming the close, deep, and fraternal relationship that unites Italian communists with the Soviet Union and the CPSU, that the Political Bureau feels its duty immediately to express its grave dissent, leaving to the Directorate of the party a more thorough evaluation of the situation and of its subsequent developments; its duty to act as spokesman of the intense concern and emotion among the working class; and to confirm once again its solidarity with the renewal action undertaken by the Czechoslovakian Communist Party.

The Political Bureau of the PCI expresses the hope that the democratic Italian forces will assume a responsible position, avoiding every form of exasperation, and engages all the communist organizations to sustain the positions taken by the organs of party leadership and in firm vigilance against any form of anti-communist speculation and provocation.

Foreign Bulletin (August–September 1968), pp. 59–60.

14   Communiqué of the Directorate of the PCI (August 23, 1968), *L'Unità*, August 24, 1968

The PCI deems it indispensable and urgent that the communist parties and the governments of the five intervening countries accept the requests of the

Czechoslovakian government and Communist Party in order to proceed to the withdrawal of troops, to allowing the legal and democratically elected organs of the state and of the party to resume their activity, to the assurance to comrade Dubček and the other Czechoslovakian leaders the possibility of freedom in the performance of their offices. Only in that way will it be possible to reach a political solution, which would avoid further dramatic aggravations of the situation in Czechoslovakia and more serious lacerations in the communist and international democratic movement.

The PCI assumes these positions in so far as it takes an active part in the communist movement, deeming its internationalist duty a clear assumption of responsibility, in order to foster a new conception of unity and new relations among the revolutionary and communist forces, based upon the principles of complete respect of the independence of each country and the autonomy of each party, upon joint solidarity in the struggle against imperialism and for peace, on the research of the various ways for the conquest and construction of socialism, and upon the consequent development of socialist democracy.

The PCI denounces and rebuffs the campaign on the part of reactionary forces and the press in their attempts – hidden in the terms of hypocritical sympathy for the cause of socialist renewal in Czechoslovakia – to push various forces in a line of struggle against socialism, to obscure in the face of public opinion and in the consciousness of Italian workers the historical patrimony of the conquests in the Soviet Union and of the socialist world, as well as their decisive role in the struggle against fascism and imperialism. It is in the interest of all democratic and leftist forces of our country – even in the heat of this moment – to differentiate themselves from the reactionary bloc and its campaign, and to refute the tendency, that has already emerged in the Italian government, of an irresponsible speculation about the dramatic Czechoslovakian events – such as the anti-nuclear treaty and the reinforcement of the Atlantic Pact – that are menacing further aggravation of international tension and the division of Europe into opposing blocs. It is precisely the present European and international situation that shows the necessity for a policy aimed at overcoming the military blocs, and leading to a regime of European security, a new order of international relations which would guarantee the peace and emancipation of the peoples . . .

Foreign Bulletin (August–September 1968), pp. 61–2.

15 Luigi Longo's report to the Central Committee of the PCI, *L'Unità*, August 28, 1968

Our dissent and disapproval with regard to the military intervention

Actually, what happened in Czechoslovakia? With a long delay – twelve years after the Twentieth Congress of the Soviet Communist Party – the Czechoslovakian party decided to give a new shift to the country's and to the party's life, in conformity with the process of renewal started by the Twentieth Congress of the Soviet Communist Party. This shift corresponds also to the line carried on by the Italian Communist Party and expressed by comrade Togliatti in his memorandum from Yalta. The communist parties of the Soviet Union and of the other Warsaw Pact countries acknowledged – even lately – the mistakes made by the Czechoslovakian party under Novotny's and the old group's leadership. They openly admitted that those mistakes were to be corrected. Even today the Soviet Communist Party states that there is no way back in Czechoslovakia with regard to the decisions taken last January. So, this is a fast-standing point on which general agreement is found. We must go on from this. In other words, wide contradictions arose in Czechoslovakia during the old leadership. It is therefore a positive and very important fact that the forces capable of starting a new trend sprang out from the Czechoslovakian Communist Party itself; and that it was the party's leading legal body – the Central Committee elected by the previous Congress – to decide the change, and to take in its hands the difficult process of renewal which could no longer be postponed. This is the first outstanding difference between the Hungarian events in 1956 and the Czech situation. Thus the Czech Communist Party – in spite of unavoidable differences and tensions – was able not only to maintain its unity through the events from December up to now, but it has in fact increased its prestige and influence among the Czechoslovakian working class and in international democratic public opinion.

We certainly know, however – and in such a situation we believe it to be unavoidable – that contrasting centrifugal drives of different nature infiltrated into this process of renewal, tending to the complete liquidation of a past patrimony which – despite its mistakes – is still by and large made of socialist achievements and of a socialist foriegn policy . . .

These positions were also joined by positions tending to give up the socialist and class principles. On the other side, strong conservative trends objecting to the renewal and wishing to restore past methods and ideas also appeared in the party and in the Central Committee, as is unavoidable. Finally, there were some anti-socialist positions on the part of national forces tied to imperialism. All this undoubtedly aroused concern and created dangers. But it came out quite clearly that the Czechoslovakian leaders were fully aware of those dangers and were just as concerned with them as the other communist parties.

But we are not in a position – and it is not our task – to judge, criticize or defend the single decisions lately taken by the Czechoslovakian Communist Party. We must take a stand on the basis of the general lines expressed by the Czechoslovakian party and leaders. They have always stated that the purpose of the new course was to bring about a democratic renewal of the socialist society, to fully develop a *socialist democracy*, not to shake the socialist foundations and nature of the state but to consolidate and develop socialism in Czechoslovakia. At the same time, the new leadership reconfirmed the socialist lines with regard to two essential elements: (1) the state's international position and foreign policy; (2) the leading function, in such a society and in such a state, of the revolutionary party of the working class. They reconfirmed their policy of friendship and solidarity with the Soviet Union and the other socialist countries as well as the Warsaw Pact and its resulting engagements; briefly, they reconfirmed the position of Czechoslovakia on the side of socialism, against imperialism and against Bonn revanchism, in the struggle for peaceful coexistence, peace and the independence of the peoples . . .

Concerning the second point – namely, the leading function of the Communist Party, or better, how this function is to be performed – I think this was the issue on which the widest differences arose between the new leaders of the Czechoslovakian party on the one side and the communist parties of the Warsaw Pact countries on the other.

The Czechoslovakian comrades' lines tend to stress and implement a leading function of the party in excluding authoritative bureaucratic or repressive methods and by concentrating their efforts in the development of party democracy and in creating increasingly wider and deeper relations between the party and the working class.

Difficulties met by the new trend

First of all, we consider the new course of the Czechoslovakian Communist Party a positive one. It aimed at fully developing socialist and party democracy; at achieving deeper unity between the party, the working class and the people – through the active, responsible participation and consent of the greatest number of workers – at carrying out socialist democracy and communism and at the victory of socialism in the world. It aimed at consolidating the leading function of the party by conquering greater hegemony, influence and prestige, thanks to the party's capacity for solving the problems of the development of the society and, at the same time, through an ideological struggle against all anti-socialist positions . . .

The new leaders needed time, patience and work – in order to contain the possible bursting out of anarchist tendencies – we must say, however, that these tendencies appeared to exist to a very small extent.

In any case, regardless of the size of the dangers existing in the new situation, the question was to find the best way to overcome them. We must frankly say that the method adopted by the communist parties of the five socialist countries – through criticism, attacks, and pressures – could only make the difficulties and dangers greater. It could even lead to a split in the Czechoslovakian party, which fortunately did not take place. In any case, through all the information we have received also from the Soviet comrades, facts which would lead to an immediate danger for the socialist system in Czechoslovakia were never apparent to us.

We only noticed that some groups showed positions which were not right.

It was, however, our belief that it was the task of the Czechoslovakian leaders and party to face possible negative or counter-revolutionary tendencies, and to defend the fundamental choices made by socialism and its allies.

Our position was based on reasons of principle, on our trust in the determination and ability of the Czechoslovakian Communist Party to lead the country along the way of renewal and consolidation of the socialist society, within the framework of co-operation and alliance with the other socialist countries. Therefore, when strong differences began to arise openly among the parties and governments of the five Warsaw Pact countries on the one side and Czechoslovakia on the other, we were firmly convinced that those differences should be overcome through a political discussion . . .

. . . The first question of principle: the rights of autonomy and sovereignty

The position we took was very precise because the events required an immediate responsibility and initiative, as these are problems which not only concern a single country but the working-class movement as a whole.

As a result, some questions of principle arise: the first fundamental question concerns a right which cannot be waived: namely, the principle of autonomy, independence and national sovereignty of each state and of the autonomy of each communist party.

One can discuss the situation and the extent of the dangers existing in Czechoslovakia. Each communist party has the right to discuss whether the new course started by the Czechoslovakian Communist Party was right or wrong. However, this principle cannot be violated . . .

Foreign Bulletin (August–September 1968), pp. 8–15.

16 'Eight years since the intervention in Czechoslovakia,' *L'Unità*, September 7, 1976

Eight years ago, August 21, 1968, the troops of five Warsaw Pact countries intervened in Czechoslovakia, to end an experiment in socialist management which had stirred up vast interest, hopes, conflicts and ample discussion throughout the entire international workers' movement. At the time, our own party immediately expressed its great disagreement with the military intervention, disagreement confirmed over the course of these years on every occasion and at every center, and reconfirmed by the delegation of the PCI at recent conferences of the communist parties and the workers of Europe at Berlin. That remains therefore, with no misunderstandings, our position.

That which has been defined as the 'new course' of Prague was an attempt to start a different system of articulate and pluralistic relations within a socialist society, amidst the bodies of government, the party and the various social and cultural expressions of the society itself. Developed as a consequence of the grave and real problems which emerged and grew in Czechoslovakia because of previous methods of governance, the 'new course' was set in a form whose full political and institutional legitimacy has never been fully discussed. The changes which took place at the top of the party and government, the measures which were taken in the short span of months during which the new line emerged, obtained a clear consensus from within the country, produced a great democratic impetus in Czechoslovakia, especially thanks to the creation of new bodies of worker representation and thanks to the process of regional decentralization, created positive relations among the citizens, the party and the socialist state.

As is always the case when new roads are explored, there inevitably were uncertainties and even risks. But the directing role of the Communist Party was in no way marred; the important experiment needed the encouragement and the solidarity of the European socialist movement, solidarity which was in effect expressed by the leaders of the Communist Party. The PCI carried out such public and explicit gestures.

The misunderstandings and emerging differences with Russia and the other countries – like Czechoslovakia – which belonged to the Warsaw Pact led to a dramatic rupture and to military intervention. The removal of comrades Dubček and Smrkowski and many others from the positions of leadership in the party and the government opened the way for the abandoning of many of the gains of the 'new course,' as well as the revoking of the party membership of thousands of communists. Many left the country, and often were deprived of their citizenship. Others who remained in the country were forced to practice their own professional activities. There were proceedings and convictions, many of which continue to be harshly paid for.

One cannot easily be sure how the events of eight years ago have really contributed to the resolving of the problems of Czechoslovakia but they did open a wound which is far from being healed. The question of the autonomy and the independence of each party and of each country, the right of each party and of each country to choose and to follow its own course in the building of a new society, is more than ever the central problem. On every possible occasion we do not fail, nor will we fail, to confirm it: Comrade Togliatti's Memorial of Yalta which remains for us – we wish to reaffirm on the anniversary of his disappearance – a definite point of reference.

L'Unità, September 7, 1976, p. 1.

The Problem of Dissent

17   'An unacceptable measure,' *L'Unità*, November 20, 1976

Our position on the Biermann 'case' is very clear. We are supporters of the right to express one's own opinions, in newspapers, in books, in political discourses and through works of art: drawings and paintings, poems and songs. We are for the freedom to approve or to dissent. We are for the freedom of expression for all, even those with whom we may not agree. We believe not only in the right, but also in the duty, of discussion and of making the truth surge forth from the confrontation of ideas. We are against consensus brought about by coercion. This position of principle is expressed clearly in the theses discussed and approved in our latest congresses, and in the document which has been called the Declaration of Livorno which bears the signatures of comrades Enrico Berlinguer and Santiago Carrillo. The right of Biermann to express poetically his political opinion is not, therefore, for us a matter of discussion. The punitive measure with which the authorities of the German Democratic Republic have decided to bar his re-entry into the country and thus to take his words from the country is unacceptable.

L'Unità, November 20, 1976.

18   'Unresolved problems', *L'Unità*, December 20, 1976

Our first reaction to the release of comrade Corvalan, a heroic anti-fascist combatant, was one of joy and emotion: and we are satisfied with release of Bukovski. This joy and satisfaction are expressions of our feelings and judgements, and we are certain that nothing can or will diminish or mar them.

That does not mean that the events which led to these positive results do not present further aspects which must also be considered and evaluated; we refer to the questions which arise from the knowledge of the conditions which characterized the negotiations for the exchange between the USSR and Chile, which culminated in the release of Corvalan and Bukovski; questions which are disconcerting and demand answers.

It is superfluous to spend additional words denouncing the absolutely illegitimate character of the fascist dictatorship of Pinochet, in order to emphasize the necessity of the fight against the efforts to end democracy in Chile, or in order to push back every speculation which addresses and confounds problems radically different from those of either Chile or Russia. They are not the things to which we wish to address ourselves now.

It is easily understandable that Pinochet has accepted the negotiations and the exchange; the political advantages which he could hope to derive are obvious. The same cannot be said for the USSR; Pinochet has the advantage; there is the recognition – implied in the exchange – of the political motives for the detention of Bukovski. For us it is not a question of determining whether a given price should have been paid; the problem is completely another, and rests on those limitations of liberties presented in the USSR, which expose Russia to the possibility of receiving other such demands. Here is the question which now more than ever is openly discussed, confronted and resolved: the incrimination and detention for so-called crimes of opinion is inadmissible, as is any form of individual and collective limitation of liberty; it is unacceptable with regard to those who dissent and must face a choice between détente and expulsion from the country. When this happens, not only the development of the Soviet society and its international prestige suffer, but socialism in every part of the world becomes tainted.

The essence of what we have to say is all here: in this case Russia could have and should have measured the weight of the unresolved problems of liberty within. We have, however, confirmation that in order for socialism to advance, these problems must be confronted and resolved.

L'Unità, December 20, 1976.

19   'Arrested in Prague – the signatories of "Charter '77",' *L'Unità*, January 12, 1977

During the past few days a police operation has taken place in Prague with regard to the Czechoslovakians who signed the document 'Charter 77'; they are the objects of a rigorous attack against *Rude Pravo*. The official silence led to rumors which, initially, hinted that arrests had taken place. Then it was ascertained that it was a matter of detentions, interrogations and searches.

The following have been detained for questioning: the dramatist Vaclav Havel, the ex-Foreign Minister of the time of Dubcek, Jiri Rajek, the playwright Pavel Kohout, Frantisek Kriegel, former director of the National Front, the philosopher Jan Patocka, the writer Ludvik Vaculik, and others. According to the official information, until this evening there have been at least twelve persons detained, interrogated and then released. All had signed the 'Charter 77.' The document – which is an appeal to the authorities urging the opening of discussions between those in power and the citizens on the problem of respect for human rights – was signed by a total of about thirty people.

The number of inquiries in the course of a few days, and the virulence of the article by *Rude Pravo*, dedicated to the document and its signers, leaves no doubt as to the spirit and the means with which the Czechoslovakian leaders intend to confront the questions raised by the 'Charter 77'; questions which reach back to the wounds of 1968 and are still waiting to be resolved.

Beyond the questions of general importance regarding the Czechoslovakian political system as it is engaged in building socialism, and the intolerable violations of liberty which it tolerates and permits, there exists an ever-worsening problem concerning the political will of the rulers. Responding to requests for open discussions on the issue of human rights with police operations represents a choice which, rather than seeking a means of reconciliation of the unhealed fractures, provokes the deepening of the divisions, the embitterment of the wounds opened nine years ago.

It is a tendency which we solidly denounce, as it is a sign of even greater injury, and is compatible neither with the requirements of liberty nor with the ideals of socialism.

L'Unità, December 20, 1976.

Proletarian Internationalism

20   Palmiro Togliatti's interview with *Nuovi Argomenti*, May–June 1956

Is it possible that in the functioning of the Soviet system there has been a halt, an interruption, which has resulted in a limitation of Soviet democracy? It is not only possible, but at the Twentieth Congress it was openly recognized. Soviet democratic life has been limited, partially suffocated, by the dominance of methods of bureaucratic and dictatorial control and by violations of the legitimacy of the government. The socialist society is not only composed of men, but it is a developing society, in which exist objective and subjective contrasts, and which is subject to the vicissitudes of history. In fact, it is a question of seeing how and why a limitation of Soviet democratic life was achieved, but regardless of the answer given to this question, for us it is certain that returning to the forms organization of the capitalistic societies will never be deemed a necessity.

The plurality or unity of parties cannot be held, as such, to be a point of distinction between bourgeois society and socialist society, since it does not determine, by itself, the line of distinction between a democratic and a non-democratic society. In the Soviet Union two parties shared power for a certain period of time after the revolution in the Soviet regime and in the proletarian dictatorship. In today's China there exists a plurality of parties in power and the government is defined as a democratic dictatorship. Also in the popular democracies there still remain parties other than the Communist Party, although not everywhere.

The definition of 'party' in the Soviet Union is unlike our own. The party works and fights to achieve and develop socialism, but its work is essentially of a positive and constructive nature, not of a controversial nature against an imaginary internal political enemy. The 'opposition' against which the Soviet party struggles is the objective difficulty of succeeding, in contrast to working to fulfill the need to control what remains of the old in order to make way for the new, and so on. The dialectic of contrasts, essential for the development of society, is no longer expressed in the competition among different parties, of government or of opposition, because there no longer exists an objective material base, nor a subjective base in the hearts of men for such a competition.

Palmiro Togliatti, *Il Partito comunista italiano e il movimento operaio internazionale, 1956–1968* (Rome: Editori Riuniti, 1968), cf. pp. 34–62.

21 Palmiro Togliatti's report to the Central Committee in preparation for the Eighth Congress of the PCI, June 24, 1956

For us there is no doubt that the Soviet Union remains the first major historical model of the conquest of power by the working class and the utilization of that power, in a most energetic and effective way, to succeed – sweeping back the resistance of the middle class and the other reactionary classes, driving back the attempts of foreign intervention – in beginning the job of constructing a new economy and society and in accomplishing this work . . .

This experience, however, cannot provide a beautiful and ready-made solution to all the problems which present themselves today in those countries which are already governed by the working class and the communist parties, and even less can it be the ready-made solution to the questions which present themselves where the communist parties or the parties oriented towards socialism are parties of opposition, operating under conditions fundamentally different from those under which the vanguard of the working class in Russia operated before and after seizing power. The completed experience of the Soviet Union in its construction of a socialist society cannot contain directives for resolving all the questions which might present themselves today to us and to the communists of other countries, regardless of whether they are in power, and to the parties of the vanguard of the working class and of the people.

Thus different points or centers of orientation and development are created. What I have called a polycentered system is created, corresponding to the new situation, to the structural changes of the world and of the workers' movement itself, and also corresponding to new forms of relations among the communist parties themselves. The solution which, today, probably corresponds to this new situation could be that of complete autonomy of the individual movements and communist parties, and of the bilateral relations between them, with the hope of creating a complete, reciprocal understanding and a complete, reciprocal trust, conditions suitable for collaboration, and for uniting the Communist Party itself as well as the progressive movement of the working class.

It is evident that in this new situation we must work in new ways to establish contact with the other parts of the international communist movement and with the other socialist sectors of the workers' movement which we support whole-heartedly and for which we must battle so as to produce in our own ranks, in the working class and in the people, a spirit of proletarian internationalism. We will succeed much more easily, however, in achieving this aim than we will succeed in giving our proletarian internationalism a solid and precise content which corresponds to the situation before us, if we do not reduce ourselves to repeating the formulas of days gone by, but rather confront with new vigor and initiative all the problems which might present themselves today to the parties of the vanguard of the working class.

Palmiro Togliatti, *Il Partito comunista italiano e il movimento operaio internazionale, 1956–1968* (Rome: Editori Riuniti, 1968), cf. pp. 62–81.

22 Palmiro Togliatti's report to the Eighth Congress of the PCI, December 1956

Above all, the recent events in Poland and, in a quite different way, those in Hungary, have revealed difficulties, weaknesses, even serious errors, in the camp of socialism, not only in that which concerns the development of its economy, but also in the carrying out of socialist democracy and in relations among the socialist states.

The lessons of the Twentieth Congress of the Communist Party of the Soviet Union – which underlined the necessity, now that the hardest periods of capitalist encirclement, war and the Cold War have been overcome, that the socialist societies march forward with new vigor, completely eliminating the discord with the permanent democratic substance of socialist power which had been generated by these errors – must therefore be welcomed and gone into thoroughly by the whole workers' movement. This must be done by linking, to a far greater degree, the exposure of these errors with an analysis of their deep-seated causes, and establishing the correct tie between the new positions of principle and policy that were so clearly affirmed and the criticism and condemnation of these errors. This involves an examination that is necessarily broad and complex, and that ought therefore to go beyond the still-limited formula of the 'cult of the individual.'

Recent experience teaches us that wherever the orientation of the Twentieth Congress was welcomed – as in Poland – it made possible the consolidation of the unity of the party and the majority of the people round the new policy, even though difficulties and dangers yet remain in that country which are far from trifling.

Wherever this was not done, wherever the party did not know how to place itself in the lead and organically direct the process of renewal, a tragic and disastrous situation was met with, as in Hungary . . .

Considering the point the situation had reached, Soviet intervention was a painful necessity, but it could not and ought not to have been avoided if it meant failing to live up to the principles of proletarian internationalism, if it meant preventing the creation, in the heart of Europe, of a situation fraught with peril for peace: the advent of the most reactionary forces in Hungary would have again thrown the people under oppression, impeding it for a long time from being able to take up once more the construction of a socialist society . . .

The events in Poland and Hungary reveal that a system of socialist states, which has as its base the acknowledgement of the principle of diverse ways of development towards socialism, ought to be a system of independent states, in which the sovereignty of the smaller countries cannot be limited or placed in doubt by intervention and pressure from the stronger ones . . .

The indispensable elaboration, on the part of each communist party, of its own way of advancing and struggling towards socialism requires autonomy of inquiry and judgement in the application of the principles of Marxism–Leninism to each national situation. Therefore, the return to a centralized organization for relations among communist parties, as they existed in different forms in the past, no longer corresponds to the situation. The system of bilateral relations presents itself today as the most efficacious to satisfy these requirements. Bilateral relations require knowledge of each other and reciprocal respect; and they must allow for and bring about friendly criticism which raises problems and provides stimulation for a thorough examination of them. Such relations must absolutely exclude interference in the internal questions of the parties of other countries . . .

With regard to the Soviet Union – toward whom there are profound and imperishable reasons for gratitude on the part of all peoples – and in regard to the party, the Italian Communist Party holds that it is necessary, always, to start from the fact that the Soviet Union is the first country where the socialist revolution was carried out and the most advanced on the road toward communism; hence the need for a constant and careful study of its experiences.

Therefore, in affirming that rather than talk of a leader state or party we ought instead to talk of the guidance that comes from our principles and from the interests of the working class and the Italian people, the Italian Communist Party reaffirms, at the same time, the indestructible function that the Soviet Union – as well as the party that governs it – exercises in the socialist world, of which it constitutes the axis and the greatest force . . .

Palmiro Togliatti, *Nella democrazia e nella pace verso il socialismo* (Rome: Editori Riuniti, 1966), pp. 31–4.

23 Palmiro Togliatti's report to the Tenth Congress of the PCI, December 1962

For the unity of the international communist movement . . . The main problem confronting us now is that of the unity of our movement. We need it because of the exacting tasks we have to tackle and also because of the bitter struggle of our enemies who are always ready to resort to speculations and provocations whenever there is evidence of disagreement among ourselves. We must understand, however, that today unity can be reached and preserved very differently than in other situations. The scope itself of our movement, and the diversity in the conditions for the advance to socialism call for an articulation based, not on centralization, nor on the existence of impossible international or regional centers, but on the autonomy of decision of each party. This increases the responsibility of each of us in the face of the working class of its own country and in the face of the other communist parties. Our autonomy, in fact, although leaving us free to judge and to make fraternal criticism, will never prevent any of us from being judged also on the strength of what communists do in other countries.

Unity must stem from loyalty to the principles of our doctrine, as formulated in the documents issued by the last international meetings, in 1957 and 1960, and from the strengthening of proletarian international solidarity. No fight for socialism is possible unless it is based on such a solidarity which is and must be an unshakable principle for anyone calling himself communist and socialist. In the framework of such a solidarity and on the basis of these principles, we should debate controversial problems, but the debate should be carried out with a sense of responsibility . . .

Foreign Bulletin (December 1962), pp. 36–7.

24 Palmiro Togliatti's memorandum, *Rinascita*, September 5, 1964

It is not correct to refer to the socialist countries (including the Soviet Union) as if everything were always going well in them. This is the mistake, for instance, in that section of the 1960 Declaration dealing with these countries. In fact, there continually arise in all the socialist countries difficulties, contradictions and new problems that must be presented in their effective reality. There is nothing worse than to have given the impression that everything is always going well when suddenly we find ourselves faced with the necessity of confronting difficult situations and explaining them . . .

The criticism of Stalin, there is no need to hide this, has left rather deep traces. The most serious thing is a certain degree of skepticism with which also some of those close to us greet reports of new economic and political successes. Beyond this must be considered in general terms the unresolved problem of the origin of the cult of Stalin and how this became possible. To explain this solely through Stalin's serious personal defects is not completely accepted. There is an attempt to investigate what could have been the political errors that contributed to giving rise to the cult. This debate is taking place among historians and qualified cadres of the party. We do not discourage it because it helps towards a more profound awareness of the history of the revolution and its difficulties. However, we advise prudence in coming to conclusions and the taking into account of the publications and research in the Soviet Union.

The problem which claims greater attention, one affecting the Soviet Union as much as the other socialist countries, however, is today, especially, that of overcoming the regime of restrictions and suppression of democratic and personal freedom introduced by Stalin. Not all the socialist countries present the same picture. The general impression is that of a slowness and resistance in returning to the Leninist norms that ensured, within the party and outside of it, a wide liberty of expression and debate on culture, art and also on politics. This slowness and resistance is difficult for us to explain, above all in consideration of the present conditions when there is no longer capitalist encirclement and economic construction has had tremendous successes. We always start from the idea that socialism is the regime in which there is the widest freedom for the workers, that they in fact participate in an organized manner in the direction of the entire social life. Therefore we greet all positions of principle and all facts showing us that this is the reality in all the socialist countries and not only in the Soviet Union. On the other hand, events that sometimes disclose the contrary to us damage the entire movement.

Foreign Bulletin (August–September 1964), pp. 79–80.

25 Luigi Longo's interview with *Stern*, in *L'Unità*, November 10, 1964

My personal reactions on learning the news of comrade Khrushchev's substitution as head of the party and of the government of the Soviet Union were surprise at the sudden decision to change the leadership of the two largest organizations governing Soviet society; concern for the significance that this change could have regarding the basic principles of the policy which was initiated and carried out by comrade Khrushchev (peaceful coexistence, opening the paths towards socialism, modifications and autonomy of the communist parties, etc.); criticism of the way in which this change was brought about, which revealed the persistence within the Soviet Union of limitation of information, public debate and democracy, all of which have already been mentioned by comrade Togliatti in his Yalta Memorandum . . .

Foreign Bulletin (October–November–December 1964), p. 71.

26 Order of the day approved by the Central Committee of the PCI, *Rinascita*, June 12, 1965

The wide spreading of a new, more ample and articulated conception of the problem of inter-nationalism and world solidarity is of essential importance to solve the central problem today facing the working-class, socialist and communist movement of our country and of the countries of Western Europe, which is that of ensuring, also in this part of the world, in which capitalism has reached, or aims at reaching, the highest points of its development, the renewal and progress of democratic and socialist transformation of the social and political dispositions, the overcoming of the existing divisions in the working-class and socialist movement and the opening up of a path leading the working classes to the leadership of society . . .

In these conditions the necessity for unity and solidarity in the international working-class move-ment, in an active and effective internationalism, not only remains and must remain an integrating part of the ideal vision of every working-class movement and the essential condition of its revolutionary trend, but springs imperiously from the immediate and prospective tasks of the anti-imperialist struggle, for peace and peaceful coexistence, for the freedom of people, for the emancipation of workers, for democracy and socialism.

But, in the present conditions, to achieve unity, to increase it, to strengthen it and render it more sub-stantial and effective, we must start off, realistically, from the recognition of the diversity and of the contrasts existing if we wish to carry out an efficacious action to overcome them and to achieve a richer, more ample and real unity. But this action is to be considered as a long-respite action which must involve not only the communist parties but the whole of the revolutionary and working-class movement. For this reason we must be able to separate the differences which spring from the objective conditions and from the very advance of the movement from those which are the result of errors: tactical or strategic errors, errors made in the enaction of a just political line . . .

It is exactly starting off from these motives and from the necessity of solving these big problems that we have always considered that, given the present conditions, we must abandon every sectarian and schematic conception of the question of unity. The communist movement must not be considered as a movement closed up in itself. It must be considered and it must act as a part of the whole international working-class and revolutionary movement. And the object for which we must aim is exactly that of creating within all the sectors of this movement a deeper understanding and solidarity in the course of struggles, abandoning every attempt at uniformity and recognizing, instead, that the unity and the always greater autonomy, in judgement and action, of each party, not only are inevitable but may be useful to the cause for the advance of peace, democracy and socialism in the whole world . . .

Europe in unity, democracy, and peace

We must, however, admit also that the answer which the communist movement and the communist parties have given to the solution of the problem of a socialist revolution in the West has, until the present, on the whole, been insufficient, not adequate to the conditions in which the struggle for socialism is to develop in highly developed capitalist countries in a historical period characterized by deep and rapid modifications in the objective structure of the world, in relationship with classes, peoples, continents. The recognition of these insufficiencies does not mean diminishing the great contribution which the com-munist movement has given and gives, also in the West, to the struggle in favor of the interests of the working classes, the struggle against reaction in favor of democracy and peace, and the effort for elaboration and renewal carried out by many communist parties. This means, however, that to make the cause of democracy and socialism advance and win in the highly capitalistically advanced countries, it is essential to carry out new and original research considering all the experiences of the past and all the critical research, but being free from every precon-ceived scheme.

This search must have its indispensable starting point in the effort and in the struggle of the working-class movement of every single country. But to proceed on this path it is necessary today to find always more ample forms of connection and collaboration amongst the working-class and democratic forces of all European countries which must take it upon themselves to build a united, democratic peaceful Europe, deeply renovated in its social and political structures.

This is, in fact, the European and international value of the unification process of the socialist forces of our country, which must be set in the more ample picture of a process of unitary renewal and advance of all the democratic and left-wing forces of the European West and must become the stimulus for the development of this process. Here is the basis of a policy aiming at the creation of a dialogue with the more aware forces of the Catholic world, permitting a positive intervention in the crises and ferments manifesting themselves in the social democratic parties; carrying on, also in this direction, the unity of action of all democratic and working-class forces . . .

Foreign Bulletin (April–May–June 1965), pp. 162–6.

27 Luigi Longo's speech to the Central Committee of the PCI, February 25, 1967

Three years ago we made some reservations concerning the calling of a world conference under the particular conditions existing at that time. Our position was clearly stated by comrade Togliatti in his Yalta Memorandum. His reservations were based on the fact that the world conference would not have been attended 'by a fairly large number of parties beside the Chinese party.' He immediately added, however, that 'we shall attend it and shall participate in the preparatory meeting in which we shall certainly be given the opportunity to clarify our stand, in as much as it is connected with a series of problems of the international communist movement.'

Now, as to the Chinese party, the situation is deeply changed. At that time we did not want to compromise even the few chances existing to overcome the contrast with the Chinese comrades who regarded the conference as a mere provocation.

Now the Chinese leaders have broken all possibilities for a relationship with those communist parties which do not agree with their stands and reject their splitting activities. On the other side, we have the right to examine together the ways to oppose their segregating tendencies and to re-establish unity.

The calling of a world conference remains, however, a difficult problem. How shall we overcome these difficulties? The fact that we might have some doubts about the conference must not prevent us from participating in the meetings in which the opportunity to call such a conference is discussed. We must explain our viewpoints in fraternal meetings and

be ready to consider the viewpoints of the others and the possibility of a reconciliation of views . . .

We cannot just discuss whether to say yes or no to the conference, in an abstract sense. First of all because there are no formal proposals for a conference, and secondly because we do not know the precise contents of it. Only when these questions are clarified will we be able to say yes or no . . .

Under the present conditions, when the very necessity for internationalism is being discussed, the statement that an international collaboration and agreement is necessary is already important in itself. The existing situation in this concern is intolerable. Internationalism has always been a characteristic feature of the working-class movement, socialist and communist. Instead, the communist movement for some years has not succeeded in bringing internationalism to a high level, whilst centrifugal forces are increasing. These difficulties cannot be overcome unless we define a new kind of international unity capable of strictly securing the autonomy of each party and of not implying a hostile attitude towards those parties which do not agree with some issues of common decision.

Our view is well known: unity in diversity. It is the only way to put an end to the centrifugal tendencies existing today in the working-class movement. The alternative to these tendencies is not to return to a monolithic structure but to create a new unity for which we must find the proper forms . . .

Foreign Bulletin (February–March 1967), pp. 32–6.

28 Draft theses for the Twelfth Congress of the PCI, October 1968

New roads and forms of unity in the international working-class movement
We feel that the situation created by the presence of Warsaw Pact troops in Czechoslovakia must be overcome rapidly and that only this can restore the authority of the legal organs of the state and the party and their autonomous action for the consolidation and development of socialist society.

In particular, we consider contrary to Marxist–Leninist conceptions and to positions of principle so often affirmed in the most solemn documents of the international working-class and communist movement all positions such as those which have appeared in the press of certain communist parties, according to which respect for the principle of the autonomy of each party and the sovereignty of each state is subordinate to an evaluation of the international situation and the internal situation of the country in question, an evaluation of which it is impossible to say who is to be the judge and with what right.

Positions of this sort are all the more unacceptable in that they ignore the particular conditions and the bloc of political and social forces that in other European countries can, when united, lead to socialism.

No contradiction exists between our disagreement on the military intervention in Czechoslovakia and our commitment to work within the worldwide camp of the communist and working-class movement; and it is in this commitment that we express our basic and real solidarity with the USSR, the socialist countries and the revolutionary movements. Independent judgement and open debate on the various problems of the working-class movement are for us one of the conditions for the reassertion of the critical and creative nature of Marxism and Leninism, for their development and for the realization of a new, real unity in the revolutionary struggle for peace and socialism.

Our conception of unity in diversity does not mean agnosticism; we do not affirm the legitimacy of various roads to socialism with the intention of shutting ourselves up in our own national field. It means a commitment for the party to seek, together with the other forces of the communist and working-class movement, the necessary strategic and political unification, by waging an ideological and political battle against positions which we hold to be mistaken and inspired by a unilateral vision of the class struggle.

This ideological and political battle has not prevented and need not prevent our party from maintaining and developing its collaboration with all the revolutionary movements, including those with whom we do not agree even on essential questions, but which constitute important elements in the anti-capitalist and anti-imperialist struggle. This collaboration must move in the direction of unity in action against imperialism.

In the light of these principles, we have waged an open polemic against positions which within the working-class and communist movement itself lead to a mistaken vision of the historical tasks facing us at the present moment, such as the denial of the possibility of avoiding war and the destructive implications of thermonuclear arms for human civilization, the underestimation of the role of the working class in the advanced capitalist countries, and the hypothesis that the decisive clash will be between the 'city' and the 'country,' between the rich and poor peoples . . .

More generally, the PCI rejects any rigid opposition between peaceful and non-peaceful development of the revolutionary struggle . . .

The PCI has tried to make its contribution to a new vision of internationalism and the relationship between unity and autonomy in the working-class movement, starting from the affirmation, many times repeated in the documents of the international working-class and communist movement, that there is no leading party or leading state.

A conception of internationalism that corresponds to growth of the forces and ideas of socialism, to the various experiences it has produced in the world, to the goals of further expansion of socialism, requires that we recognize not only the legitimacy, but also the necessity, of diversity in the roads to socialism, understood not as national variants of a universal model, but as the concrete and specific forms the revolutionary process takes and as elements in the development of the Marxist–Leninist theory of revolution and socialism itself . . .

All these diversities do not overshadow what there is in common: the Marxist–Leninist matrix and ideal inspiration; the social forces on which these various movements are based; the goals of social justice they pursue; the struggle against imperialism; solidarity with the peoples who have won their independence and with the revolutionary movements; the structural revolutions they have carried out or intend to carry out in economic and social life. All this creates the possibility and the necessity for collaboration and unity, even in diversity. But this collaboration and unity must be founded on relations of equality, of mutual respect, of autonomy, on the most open confrontation of positions and experiences, 'on reciprocal criticism on points of disagreement, without this provoking resentment, questions of prestige, much less fractures at the level of parties and states,' as we stated in the theses for our Eleventh Congress. The safeguarding of the autonomy of the PCI corresponds, in effect, to this vision of proletarian internationalism and the unity of the working-class and communist movement.

This is the historically real way of being an internationalist force and of working for unity. This means that the autonomy of every party cannot be understood as shutting ourselves up within our own national fields, nor as a denial of the importance and role of the countries that are building a socialist society, foremost among them the Soviet Union; on the contrary, it requires an active presence, an elaboration and a consistent battle along the general line of the anti-imperialist and revolutionary struggle, and the affirmation of a correct conception of relations within the communist movement.

The building of this unity requires concerted efforts for political elaboration and co-ordination of action among parties and movements operating in the different sectors and areas. Within this framework the PCI has a special commitment to such elaboration and co-ordination among the parties operating in the capitalist countries of Europe and the Mediterranean . . .

Foreign Bulletin (October–November–December 1968), pp. 74–80.

29 Luigi Longo's report to the Twelfth Congress of the PCI, February 1969

In this world divided by bitter class conflicts, we communists are on the side of socialism, against hunger, against the dramatic imbalances that capitalism and colonialism have created in the modern world; we are and we will always be on the side of the great worldwide movement of the peoples struggling for peace, freedom and progress. We are on the side of the October Revolution, of the USSR and all the socialist countries, whose function has been and is fundamental in safeguarding the peace, freedom and future of the world. We are with the newly independent countries, with the national liberation movements, with all those who struggle for freedom and progress, anywhere and in any way. We are with the American blacks who want to put an end to the evils of race discrimination. We are with all those who take a stand to contest the capitalist system. We are with the young people who want a different future.

This is our internationalism. Let us look to the whole and the future of the movement and work – apart from the differences in our situations and positions – for the unity of all the working-class, popular and progressive forces in a great worldwide

movement of revolutionary renewal. We know that the frontiers of socialism do not coincide with the borders of the socialist countries, but are much broader. They include all the forces in the world that are fighting against capitalism and imperialism. We are aware of the historical function of the working classes in the capitalist countries, not only in the advancement of socialism, but also in its enrichment with new content, in the promotion of the very development of our doctrine and therefore also the basic principles of Leninism. It is an undeniable fact that today this movement develops under the most varied objective and subjective conditions. It is easy to predict that the more extensive and revolutionary the movement becomes, the greater these diversities will be. Recognizing these differences is a fundamental premise for working for unity and for promoting, in action and in struggle, a convergence and a common political will. We are not and must not be so presumptuous as to consider that the international communist movement of which we are a part, and not a negligible part, is the *whole* revolutionary movement. We make no claims to exclusiveness, and we have no mistaken restrictive conceptions. And precisely for this reason we feel that the communist movement must maintain an open attitude towards all the other revolutionary, progressive and democratic forces . . .

Foreign Bulletin (January–February–March 1969), pp. 57–8.

30 Enrico Berlinguer, 'Internationalism and autonomy,' 1971

For a revolutionary party there does not exist a contradiction between internationalism and national autonomy: these two moments are inherent in both its doctrine and its political action. This essential fact is by now deeply rooted in the minds of all the militants of our party. This surges forth from all of our history, in which the moment of active presence in the internationalist battles is continually interlaced with the search and fight to assume the supremacy of the working class and its vanguard party in our national life.

The results of this uninterrupted continuity of our politics prove wrong those who maintain that international bonds constitute a restraint and an obstacle to the advancement of a workers' party on national terrain. Due to the concept which we have developed of the link between autonomy and internationalism, we Italian communists have through time rediscovered and restated, in new forms and with new content, the vitality and the full significance of national autonomy as well as the internationalism and international solidarity.

The Relationship of the PCI with the CPSU Yesterday and Today: a correct choice

In Russia there arose and existed the first proletarian state, and that alone represented the great rallying point and the hope of revolutionaries throughout the world. The role assumed by the Soviet Union was, as it seemed to us, a decisive one — first in the life-and-death battle which had begun in Europe in order to block the road to the triumph of the barbaric Nazis; and then, after the overthrow of fascism, as the principal opponent of the politics of war and of the worldwide domination of American imperialism and as the mainstay of support for the fights for liberation which had begun to develop with ever greater passion in vast areas of the world.

It was in the midst of these conditions that the Italian communists established and long maintained a bond with the Soviet Union and its Communist Party, a bond which Togliatti called a 'bond of iron.' As we have since recognized, such a relationship has had its difficulties. It at times involved, for example, an uncriticized vision and an indiscriminate exaltation of a reality and of a politics in which, although the Soviet Union was described as the most advanced force of humanity, elements of vast contradiction were present. In addition, this relationship contributed to the retarding of a more explicit theoretical systematization of the new and more original aspects of policies like those which we have pursued from the anti-fascist war until today, in a free and autonomous manner, and with results which have reached the eyes of all.

Since our Eighth Congress, which took place under the reforming impetus of the Twentieth Congress of the CPSU, we have attempted to work our a critical and rational conception of the problems facing the socialist societies to give a more solid theoretical foundation to our policies. But in the course of this process, which involved much work for the party and its militants, we have always suppressed suggestions that we renounce the great decisions made in the past, that we criticize myths which are at odds with reality and with the decisive force of the worldwide revolution.

We have not lost our conviction that the choice made during our party's first ten years was a correct choice. The bond with the Soviet Union and with the Communist International contributed in a decisive way to inspire our anti-fascist battle for democracy, national independence and peace, and to link our battle with that of the people of Europe and of the other continents . . .

We have long recognized that the conditions under which we operate and under which our movement now operates have greatly changed and require an updating and an elaboration of the content and the form of internationalism. The most important new fact consists in the opening of a new phase of the crisis of imperialism, which corresponds to the vigorous growth of the revolutionary movement. Different countries, in Europe and in Asia, and among these great China, have embarked upon the road of socialist construction. New peoples, social forces, political trends and ideals have broken loose or seek to liberate themselves from imperialistic domination, and are entering the arena of the worldwide battle. To this must be added another fact of which we are ever more aware: the fact represented by the often sharp contradictions which emerge in the day-to-day activities of socialist countries and in their mutual relations.

From these facts we have noted some specific consequences. We regard the phase during which our movement was directed by a single center and an acknowledged guiding party as having ended. Consequently we are advocates of the necessity of unconditional respect and complete affirmation of the independence of all parties and states. Secondly, we not only maintain that there neither are nor can there be 'models' of socialist construction which are valid for all, but we strive to examine critically the true situation in each of the socialist countries, to understand and comprehend them, together with the elements of development, the objective contradictions and the limits and errors which seem to us to be avoidable and which we therefore do not wish to repeat.

This new view of the relations between the communist parties and the revolutionary movements has not caused us, and in no way causes us, to attentuate our internationalistic commitment. Rather, we hold that on this base our party has succeeded in declaring and practicing a richer and broader internationalism. Relations with the Soviet Union and with the other socialist countries, on the one hand, lose their exclusive character, and, on the other hand, we now require complete freedom to judge the internal life and political acts of these countries. There remains none the less a relationship of great solidarity, which is not the residue of a past from which we will not be able to liberate ourselves: in reality that relationship is based upon recognition of the forever essential role which the Soviet Union and the other socialist countries fulfill in the worldwide battle against imperialism. At the same time we have sought and continue to seek to expand our contacts with the revolutionary movement, including those not inspired by communism.

In essence, therefore, we maintain that the ways of expressing internationalism which were legitimate yesterday are unrepeatable. Our very own growth in the last half-century drives us to submit new, unresolved problems to ourselves and to our sister parties.

L'Unità, January 24, 1971.

31   Giancarlo Pajetta, interview with *L'Unità*, **November 23, 1975**

Q. The Berlin talks have not yet brought about an agreement on the basic document for the international conference, and a new round of talks has been fixed for January. The achievement of unity within diversity seems to be a more and more complex and contradictory problem. Is this the hurdle still facing us?

A. The autonomy of the individual communist parties is not some sort of 'isolationist' claim, in a world where processes of integration are under way and the need for international collaboration is becoming more and more evident. The need for autonomy stems from the growth of the parties themselves, from the fact that they have put down roots in the countries where they work and from the developments of the national situations which they themselves are helping to change. *Unity* remains an essential aim for the international workers' movement; the *diversities* are an existing reality that must be taken into account. The alternative cannot be to try to work as if some sort of monolithic bloc were possible nor as if it were more effective to have strategies and tactics the same for everyone, nor as if it were possible to propose a uniform model. The era of the *International*, explicitly defined as a single world party, is not only long past, it has been superseded . . .

Q. But in that case, how can the problem of internationalism be seen today?

A. A 'national road,' tactics or a strategy based on a party's own experience and autonomous decision do not, however, contradict what we see as real and necessary internationalism. On the contrary, only those parties which have a solid base in their own countries are able to make an effective contribution to the general process of liberation and collaboration, and this base is possible if it is founded on a wide and growing popular consensus, made up of participation and democratic life.

Q. It is known that one of the points under discussion at the moment in the workers' movement is the policy of alliances and unity-oriented relationships between communists and other popular and workers' forces.

A. Their ideological foundation, their multiform experiences in struggle and their link with vanguard workers' forces make the communist parties a reality, without which it is impossible to confront the problems of deep-reaching social changes and progress. Past experience, precious in itself, but fraught with difficulties, should have taught all the parties that to be a real vanguard force it is necessary to be a unity-oriented force. This has been an international experience, and for us one that has become part and parcel of the history of our party. It is for this reason that we see the building of unity in diversity among the communist parties as a basis for recognition that a broader unity of the workers' movement must take into account the existence of other socialist and social democratic parties and popular movements of Christian inspiration. Here, then, are other *diversities* to understand and work on, but not as elements in opposition to the unity-oriented processes at work . . .

Q. Are we then dealing with a new type of unity, wholly different from past experiences? We ourselves have seen in our own party that the problems of renewal and the search for new solutions involve debate and even political struggle.

A. The problem is not one of seeking a sort of unity that claims we are all identical. Nor can there be any question of trying to establish external guidelines that are binding on each party, much less of returning to organizational constraints or calls for some sort of common discipline. This is not what we are after: it would not be desirable or even realistic . . .

The Italian Communists, nos 5–6 (September–December 1975), pp. 65–7.

32 Enrico Berlinguer's speech at the Twenty-Fifth Congress of the CPSU, February 27, 1976

The Soviet Union: A Great Power for the Cause of Socialism and Peace

The period that has elapsed since your last Congress has been marked by important changes in international life. On the whole, the course of events has been favorable to the cause of peace and to the forces battling against imperialism. We Italian communists particularly appreciate the advances which have been made – thanks also to the contribution which you have made toward implementing the program of peace approved by your Twenty-Fourth Congress – for the liquidation of the Cold War, for the improvement of relations between the USSR and the United States and the other Western states (including Italy), for the consolidation of détente and for the construction of relations founded upon peaceful coexistence.

Much is owed to the tenacious initiative of the Soviet Union in making it possible to hold, with success, the Conference for Security and Co-operation in Europe. There has also been an important contribution to the construction of new international relations by the other socialist countries, non-aligned countries, those in the process of development, the popular forces, and the realistic tendencies of the political forces in capitalistic countries.

It is our firm conviction – and the experience of these years has confirmed it – that progress toward détente creates favorable conditions regarding the confirmation of the right of every people to decide their own future, the solution of the great problem of freeing humanity from imperialism, from colonialism, from neo-colonialism, and the opening of new paths to progress and democracy. Under present world conditions, the reasons and the possibilities for internationalism are alive and operating more than ever. Looking at the experiences of our country and our party, we can say that great new masses of workers and youth are taking an increasingly active part in the battle for international solidarity.

With regard to the relations between the communist parties and the workers, it seems to us that there should be a marked spirit of friendliness and unity; at the same time we are in favor of an open and frank comparison of different experiences and positions. It is known that in the Communist Party there exist different points of view, even on important questions, and we agree that the problems which develop need to be discussed in a climate of friendliness, within the bounds of the inalienable right of equality and respect for every party. The autonomous development of parties constitutes a decisive factor for the advancement of the movement towards socialism and for the development of our theory.

All the developed capitalistic societies, particularly in Europe, are facing a crisis which affects not only the economy but also the political and moral aspects of society. We have not forgotten the experience of the 1920s, nor that of the 1930s, when, by taking advantage of opportunistic yieldings and of sectarian errors made by workers' parties, the capitalistic, reactionary forces manipulated the alignment of forces in their favor and established, in different countries, fascist regimes.

Dangerous analogies can present themselves even today and we always take that into account in all of our political undertakings. Under the present conditions, however, a series of positive phenomena present themselves: the troubles and problems of society are being criticized on all levels of society; there is a growing desire for a new order in society that tends towards socialism; the workers' battles become more vigorous and at the same time more unitary and vast. It should be emphasized also that in the socialist and social democratic parties there has been a marked movement to the left and barriers have been removed to understandings with the communists. It is also of great interest to note the shifts in an anti-capitalistic and anti-imperialistic direction which have developed in certain Christian movements.

And thus new possibilities are provided for advancing the dialogues and the convergence between the different workers' forces, both within individual countries as well as throughout the whole of Western Europe, both for immediate goals as well as for exploring and covering novel ways and paths of building a new society.

Enrico Berlinguer, *La politica internazionale dei comunisti italiani* (Rome: Editori Riuniti, 1976), cf. pp. 110–16.

33 Editorial comment, *L'Unità*, June 28, 1977

We should like to start from a review, necessarily a summary for obvious reasons of space, of the contents of the long article that the Soviet weekly *New Times* has devoted to comrade Santiago Carrillo's book on 'eurocommunism,' in order to explain the reasons for our profound dissent, as regards both the tone the author has given to his remarks and some of his statements. The passages that have received the most attention are, as everyone knows, those connected with international and European problems, with the PCE's position with regard to the two military blocs existing on the old continent and with the negative repercussions that this position is said to have on the 'unity and solidity of the communist movement' and on the prospects for détente and co-operation in Europe . . .

In actual fact, after the obvious observation that the area of developed capitalism goes beyond Europe and that the situations in the European countries themselves are not identical, the author goes on to reiterate that 'there is only one communism (if we are talking about genuine, scientific communism): this is the communism of which Marx, Engels and Lenin laid the foundations and whose principles are observed by the contemporary communist movement.' And, citing social democratic interpretations, he lets it be understood that so-called eurocommunism is an instrument of division of the movement and involves an abandoning of internationalism.

It is not our intention here to go into the substance of Carrillo's book (we shall do that elsewhere), which we consider (as, we believe, Carrillo himself does) as a contribution to reflection and discussion on the problem, rather than a finished exposition of a 'doctrine' of eurocommunism: a doctrine which does not exist, so much so that there is no organizational center nor any comprehensive codification, although very significant documents have been underwritten by the interested parties on a bilateral basis . . .

For us, taking a non-existent monolithism as the point of departure and demanding an alignment on this basis does not mean working for unity: on the contrary, it means exacerbating the divisions. We must instead start from a recognition of the differences, if we want to work to overcome them.

From this standpoint there is unquestionably a contradiction in the fact that *New Times* stresses the need for internationalist solidarity and recalls in this regard the great significance of the ideas and conclusions of the Berlin Conference of the European Communist and Workers' Parties, and yet omits all reference to the fact that the vision of internationalism affirmed in that conference is the only one possible in the present historical situation: a vision that lies in feeling ourselves participants and protagonists, in our own country and in the world, of the broader movement that is fighting for social and political emancipation, national independence, peace and the progress of mankind: a movement that now tends to extend beyond the communist parties and embrace other political and social forces, with their different inspirations and their own positions. The fight for socialist transformation, it was said in Berlin, involves dialogue and understanding with the working class and popular forces of socialist, social democratic and Christian inspiration, within individual countries and on the European scale. The search for this dialogue obviously requires recognition of the legitimacy of different positions and attitudes and debate with them . . .

The Italian Communists, no. 2 (April–June, 1977), pp. 129–31.

FRENCH Communist Party: Diversity in Unity – Proletarian Internationalism and the Strains of Allegiance

Titoism

1 Maurice Thorez, 'Homage to Stalin,' 1950

The party must display a firm revolutionary vigilance in order to detect disorderly elements, police, informers and investigators, and dismiss them from its ranks. The cases of the traitors Rajk and Kostov revealed the scandalous crimes of these spies and their ringleader, Tito. Their trial disclosed that all these scoundrels had been employed for a long while by Anglo-American intelligence services. Some, said to be our friends, pretend to doubt this, as if we had not known, here in France, the treason of a Doriot, who went over to serve the police, then Hitler. Some persist in considering the traitor Tito a 'communist,' a 'revolutionary,' who will build socialism in his country! With American dollars! As if Mussolini had not been a 'socialist,' Hitler had not called himself a 'national socialist,' as if these forerunners of Tito had not also claimed to be battling against capitalism and building socialism!

... For our part, we declare that we could not call someone who parrots the worst reactionary lies and slander against us, against the Soviet Union, and against our leader, Stalin, a friend of the communists. We declare that peace and freedom cannot be effectively defended without or in opposition to the Soviet Union, outside of or against the international communist movement.

We are more devoted than ever to the ideas of Lenin and Stalin. We are more loyal than ever to the cause of the October Socialist Revolution, to the cause of communism. We are more convinced than ever that 'it is impossible to put an end to social democratism in the workers' movement,' as Stalin wrote twenty years ago.

... We are, likewise, more loyal than ever to the principles of proletarian internationalism ...

To break with proletarian internationalism, to founder in bourgeois nationalism, is to inevitably turn one's back on the working class, on socialism – to slip into the abyss. That is what happened to the traitor, Tito, and his gang of adventurers – defecting to serve the imperialist warmongers, becoming the worst enemies of their people, of the international workers' movement and of the Soviet Union.

Cahiers du Communisme (January 1950), pp. 32–3.

2 Theses of the Fourteenth Congress of the PCF, July 1956

In 1948 serious disputes arose with the Yugoslavian Communist Party, leading to inadmissible interference on our part in that party's internal affairs.

We deeply regret our errors and accusations, which created a difficult situation for our Yugoslav comrades, for the whole socialist camp, and for the entire international workers' movement.

The party's central committee was right to undertake steps to resume normal relations with the League of Yugoslavian Communists; the French Communist Party was prompted by the determination to establish contacts and relations with Yugoslavia's communist organization – contacts which are in the interest of the international workers' movement and of peace.

The only practical course for relations among communist and workers' parties is that of comparing experiences and exchanging opinions, of mutual understanding without interference in internal party affairs. In this way French communists will deepen their knowledge of the rich socialist reality existing in the world, and will broaden their horizons.

'XIVe Congrès du Parti Communiste Français,' *Cahiers du Communisme* (July–August 1956), p. 387.

3   Maurice Thorez' report to the Fifteenth Congress of the PCF, June 1959

The international communist movement has been strengthened since 1956. It has been given a new charter: the Declaration adopted in Moscow by the Conference of Communist and Workers' Parties of the Socialist Nations. All the communist parties, including those from the capitalist nations, approved the text.

The Declaration restates the principal laws guiding the spread of the socialist revolution and the building of socialism in all nations, taking into consideration the possibility of different nations' varying forms of transition to socialism, as well as particular local conditions.

After signing the Manifesto of Reconciliation, the leaders of the League of Yugoslavian Communists strayed from the family of communist parties. The League Congress elaborated a revisionist platform, in open opposition to the Declaration of Communist and Workers' Parties.

The Yugoslavians were imbued with revisionist conceptions of the character and development of capitalism. They denied the necessity of international class solidarity, and substituted, for analysis of the development of the class struggle between the socialist and imperialist camps, the idea of a confrontation of military blocs, between which they claimed to remain neutral, even while accepting subsidies from American capitalists.

This attitude gave rise to serious obstacles to the establishment of fraternal relations between the League and all other communist parties. None the less we have increased our initiatives to improve relations with the Yugoslavian communists' organization since the Fourteenth Congress.

'XVe Congrès du Parti Communiste Français,' *Cahiers du Communisme*, special issue (July–August, 1959), cf. pp. 80–1.

4   Marcel Veyrier, 'Yugoslavia: the Tenth Congress of the Communists' League,' 1974

The Tenth Congress of the League of Communists, held at Belgrade from 27 to 30 May, marks a major step in the construction of socialism in Yugoslavia . . .

This set of documents had been published after long discussions . . . which went on without interruption for at least three years, in the course of which Tito – whose personal interventions were frequent and decisive – and the great majority of the militants of the League and of the other social and political organizations proceeded to a complete examination of the experience of self-management.

They arrived at the following conclusion: after two decades this experiment made some great success possible, but opposition to it, either open or hidden, and serious deviations from it, had affected its unfolding and finally threatened the foundations of socialism.

The Communist Party, directed by Tito, called for a national insurrection and led it to the victorious conclusions of a long and glorious war of liberation. It was the only party capable of realizing this historic task, with a slogan capable of mobilizing the people: unity and fraternity. The bourgeois parties responsible for the defeat of Yugoslavia had been active only over a part of the territory; they expressed the interests of only a fraction of the population and, more precisely, of one nationality to the detriment of others, whose rights they contested or denied . . .

It was not easy to build a socialist society in such conditions, especially if one takes account of the great economic and cultural inequalities inherited from an eventful history, which initially compounded the difficulty of implementing the equality of rights inscribed in the first constitutional documents. Moreover Stalin, who in 1948 completely broke relations with the Yugoslav Communist Party and state, had them excommunicated by the whole international communist movement, an event which had disastrous consequences whose traces still exist today.

One of Tito's historical merits was his perseverance . . . He always thought that socialism was the only way to resolve the problems of his country and to overcome the inevitable crises and contradictions; and that self-management, that is to say, a great degree of workers' democracy and a real participation of the mass of people in the management of public affairs, constituted 'a tremendous factor of national cohesion' . . .

The Tenth Congress was the high point of this effort at rectification

The principal idea of the constitutional amendments adopted in 1970–1, and of the new constitution, is that the ruling class, the motive element of the socialist revolution, ought really to participate in the direction of the enterprises, throughout the processes of production and management, and in the elaboration of policy in the communes, the republics and the federation.

The role of the League of Communists is specified in black and white in the articles of the constitution. It is a revolutionary vanguard at the service of the working class and the people. Democratic centralism will be applied in such a way that the central organs elected by the Congress (the Central Committee, the presidency, and the Executive Committee) effectively direct the activity of all the communists, who will deploy in all places and circumstances.

The federal assembly has elected Tito president of the republic *in perpetuo*. The Congress re-elected him chairman of the League of Communists, under the same conditions. It is sometimes difficult for a foreign observer to understand this. But in Yugoslavia Tito is not merely a national hero; he is also, like the party which he consolidated and has directed for forty years, a factor of national unity. It is as a function of this that his comrades have given him this supreme honor. However, with the state consolidated and with the unity of the League rediscovered, in all the other social and political organizations the communists will henceforth cease to be mere empty figures. With the workers participating in generalized people's defense and the perceptible improvement of relations with the socialist countries, the non-alignment policy, whose goal is the forbidding of any foreign interference in national affairs, constitutes a coherent totality more solid than ever. And it is in these collective directions, which Tito has contributed to setting up, that his successors will find themselves moving . . .

Cahiers du Communisme (July 1974), cf. pp. 94–8.

The Hungarian Rebellion

5 Etienne Fajon's report to the Central Committee, 1956

The Events in Hungary

In Hungary the situation has taken on a new character and another dimension. The events in progress for the past ten days in that nation certainly create a very confusing scenario. It can be said that Hungary has been saved from a lengthy and scrupulously prepared counter-revolutionary campaign. The fact that deceived laborers – in truth, justifiably discontented – participated in the riot did not modify its class content, which clearly determined the riot's avowed objectives, its orientation and the support it received.

It is also apparent that there is an illegal counter-revolutionary movement in Hungary, aided from without, heavily armed, trained by experienced cadres of the former fascist army.

. . . The counter-revolutionaries' demands essentially amount to the following: the re-establishment of the bourgeois parties; the liquidation of the agricultural co-operatives and the ending of agrarian reform; the restoration of the church's feudal privileges and the transfer of Hungary to Cardinal Mindzenty's political jurisdiction; the denunciation of the Treaty of Warsaw and particularly of those clauses which call for the maintenance of Soviet troops in Hungary; finally, a change of orientation in Hungary's foreign policy, to move closer to the imperialist camp.

A distressing situation has come about in Hungary, where revolutionary workers, peasants and vanguard intellectuals must wage an arduous struggle to restore and to defend their republic's socialist conquests, and to respect the peace treaty, in which Hungary 'pledged not to tolerate on her territory any organization whose objective is to deprive the people of their democratic rights.'

As the events in Hungary draw to a close, let us bring an end to the fantastic anti-Soviet campaign which these events have triggered among our bourgeoisie and government leaders. According to this campaign, it is not the people's democracy and the reaction which have been at odds in Hungary, but the Soviet army and the Hungarian laborers . . .

The truth is simple. In accordance with the Warsaw Treaty, several Soviet units were stationed in Hungary. When the Hungarian government requested that the Soviet government dispatch a certain number of soldiers to Budapest to help the army and the Hungarian authorities re-establish order there, the Soviet government complied with that demand. Meanwhile it directed its forces to retire as soon as the Hungarian government thought it prudent, and the Soviet units have since limited themselves to ensuring Hungarian security and Hungarian respect for treaties. In an official declaration the Soviet government restated the principles governing relations among socialist states: common ideals; proletarian internationalism; close collaboration and mutual assistance; equal rights and reciprocal non-interference in internal affairs. The Soviet Union declared that it was ready to examine with the other nations which signed the Warsaw Treaty the question of Soviet troops found on the territory of certain among them.

The behavior of the different communist and workers' parties, particularly the Unified Polish Workers' Party and the Hungarian Laborers' Party, regarding events in Poland and Hungary, has provoked many reflections and discussions among French communists. These debates ought not to interfere with the proven principles stating that the internal life of each party is its own affair. I will, therefore, abstain from commenting on the recently instituted modifications to the composition of the governing bodies of the parties involved.

On the other hand, we have both the right and the duty to formulate opinions on political positions which have international repercussions and acts with generally applicable lessons.

We approve of all that the brother parties did and say so with an eye to maintaining and reinforcing Marxist–Leninist principles, international workers' solidarity and the cohesion of the peaceful socialist camp.

We particularly approve of those passages of the Central Committee of the Unified Polish Workers' Party's recent resolution dealing with the need to 'overcome the false tendencies to bourgeois liberation which exist among hesitant members, particularly in certain intellectual circles'; the need to 'isolate and disarm the reactionary forces which are resuming their activity, seeking to aggravate the class struggle and to raise the democratization of the nation's political life as a tool to fight against socialism, hence against democracy'; the need to 'oppose all manifestations of anti-Soviet agitation' . . .

How have the events in Poland and Hungary been received within the ranks of our party? They raised here a legitimate call for information and explanations. The events aroused a certain amount of excitement and, at least in the Hungarian case, concern. They did not, even so, diminish our party's confidence and its certainty of victory. Fully united around its Central Committee, the party carries on its sure advance, to which last Sunday's elections – whose results exceeded the expectations of bourgeois commentators – strongly attest.

Certain of our discussions of Warsaw and Budapest were viewed by a minute segment of opportunistic petit bourgeois as evidence of a weakening of principles within the party, justification for a slackening of proletarian internationalism and class positions – an invitation to call our Fourteenth Congress's legitimate decisions into question.

On the other hand, a different reaction was registered among a certain number of proletarian revolutionaries. It so happens that they are wondering if the events in Hungary did not have their source in the critique of the cult of personality and of Stalin's errors and if, consequently, that criticism was not inopportune. At least a few comrades go farther and challenge the perspectives illuminated by the Twentieth Congress of the Communist Party of the Soviet Union: the advance to socialism by ever more diverse roads; the possibility of preserving the peace; new aspects of the united front problem.

We must eradicate this interpretation. If we could only clear up the confusion between party democracy – which must be strengthened – and the rotten liberalism, which must be banished; the confusion between the diversity of means of transition to socialism in different nations and the petit-bourgeois belief in socialism without struggle; the confusion between effective action to stave off war and bleating pacifism; the confusion between the united front and capitulation in the face of the social democratic ideology . . .

L'Humanité, November 3, 1956, pp. 7–8.

6   Declaration of the Politburo of the PCF, 1956

After two weeks of political confusion, the cause of socialism is triumphing in Hungary.

The Hungarian proletariat – which has a rich and glorious revolutionary tradition and which victoriously set about building socialism in its homeland after the victory of the Soviet armies over fascism – understood that it was counter-revolutionary and fascist forces which, in the guise of setting forth legitimate demands, were on the verge of regaining power and restoring capitalism in Hungary.

Barricading the route of advance for the allies of Hitler and representatives of the reaction and the Vatican whom Nagy installed in government positions, a workers' and peasants' government took charge of the nation's affairs. Fully aware of the stakes in their struggle for the socialist cause, for the independence and future of their homeland and for world peace, the proletarian government requested that the Soviet army contribute to restoring internal order and carrying out the Potsdam Agreements, the 1947 Peace Treaty, and the collective international agreements which Hungary signed.

The French Communist Party fully approves of the conduct of the Hungarian workers' government.

The cause of the Hungarian proletariat is the cause of the whole international proletariat – hence, the cause of the French proletariat . . .

Faced with the disparate and brutish offensive of fascists, feudalists and their allies, the princes of the church – an attempt to restore Horthy's terrorist regime in Hungary – it was inconceivable that the USSR's army of workers and peasants would not respond to the appeal addressed to them, when the best sons of the Hungarian working class were being massacred, hanged and wretchedly tortured.

The laborers of France unhesitatingly align themselves on the side of the Hungarian proletariat and Soviet soldiers who are struggling to prevent the installation of fascism in that nation, struggling to consolidate socialist power.

The working class knows, along with all French democrats and patriots, that the re-establishment of a regime opening the way for fascism – thus making the nation vulnerable to the intervention of foreign forces – would constitute a serious threat not only to the Soviet Union and the nations of the socialist camp, but also to world peace, which is already gravely threatened by the rearmament of a vengeful West Germany, the principal weapon of the Atlantic Pact . . .

The proletariat is concerned about preserving the gains of socialism . . .

Those patriots who do not intend to see Hitler's Gestapo returned to power – endangering world peace – side with the Hungarian laborers who, with the help of the Soviet Union, are struggling for the defense of their socialist gains and, at the same time, for freedom and peace.

L'Humanité, November 4, 1956, p. 1.

7 Jacques Duclos, 'Long live socialist Hungary,' 1956

The reactionaries and fascists have uttered one final rumor regarding events in Hungary. Assisted in this by socialist leaders, they strove to the last moment, in their press and with the co-operation of state radio, to have it believed that the Hungarian counter-revolution still controls important military positions. Their goal is, in this way, to create a favorable climate for foreign intervention in Hungary's internal affairs.

Disciples of the criminal Horthy and other imperialist agents are furious to see that their schemes to restore capitalism in Hungary were thwarted. They are furious to see that a government dedicated to the defense of the People's Democracy, the defense of socialist gains and advance on the way of building socialism, had been established in Hungary.

When the Kadar government was organized to succeed the Nagy government, which voluntarily resigned, the fascist peril was at its height. Because of its arrangements with the outgoing government, the successor regime made concessions on top of concessions, having neither the possibility nor the will to battle against the counter-revolution . . .

You can be sure that, had the Soviet army not responded to the appeal to defend the People's Democracy, socialist leaders would later have reproached it for allowing the re-establishment of fascism in Hungary.

But what matters is that the Hungarian working class, assisted by the Soviet army, defeated those who dreamed of remaking Hungary as a fascist nation, a formidable hotbed of war in the heart of Europe.

The outbreak of the counter-revolutionary offensive occurred at a point when popular dissatisfaction, resulting from gross errors committed in the course of the past few years appeared in Hungary; yet those errors were not at the time made the object of much-needed correction . . .

In such an atmosphere it was possible to deceive some workers, to set them on a path which they failed to see was the way of counter-revolution.

The truth is that, despite all the lies spread by radio and by the press, the counter-revolution was crushed in Hungary and the Hungarian laborers resumed or are in the process of resuming their work.

But it is beyond doubt that the destruction resulting from riots organized by the counter-revolutionaries plunged Hungary into a very difficult situation.

That is why we must come to its aid. The Soviet Union, the People's Republic of China, and the People's Democracies showed their solidarity with Hungary, victim of an odious counter-revolutionary venture.

In the light of the failure of their schemes for civil war within Hungary, the counter-revolutionaries now seek to act from without.

They are depending on certain politicians at the UN who intend to shuffle the cards by attempting to put the Egyptian and the Hungarian situations on the same plane.

The Hungarian government appealed to the Soviet Union for help in crushing the counter-revolution on the basis of the Warsaw Treaty, as well as of the declaration issued by the Soviet government last October 30; the Hungarian government will be able to negotiate and regulate the matter of Soviet troops' presence in Hungary in the spirit of maintaining fraternal unity and mutual assistance among the socialist nations.

The help that the Soviet Union gave the Hungarian people in crushing the counter-revolution prevented what was a powder keg in the midst of Europe from exploding into a third world war.

L'Humanité, November 12, 1956, p. 1.

The Prague Spring

8 Declaration of the Politburo of the PCF, 1948

The Politburo of the French Communist Party hails Czechoslovakian democracy's magnificent victory over the reactionary forces acting on the orders of foreign instigators.

The Czech and Slovak peoples, under the leadership of the Czechoslovakian Communist Party and President Gottwald, prevented the reactionaries from transforming Czechoslovakia into a base for the operations of the imperialist camp. They brought about the union of the laborers and of all democrats and patriots, under the authority of the acting Central Committee, where communists, socialists, national socialists, democrats, Catholics and representatives of all sectors of the laboring masses are found assembled with the CGT.

The Politburo congratulates the Central Committee of the Czechoslovakian Communist Party on the establishment of the new Gottwald government, approved by President Benes, and on democracy's victory over reaction.

L'Humanité, February 27, 1948, p. 1.

9 Waldeck Rochet's speech to the Central Committee of the PCF, April 18, 1968

The events which have taken place in Czechoslovakia have set off loud echoes in our country.

It is advisable, first of all, to emphasize that these changes are the business of the Communist Party of Czechoslovakia itself, and that the Central Committee of that party has acted, in taking the measures it has, within the framework of democratic centralism.

I remind you, in fact, that in what concerns the relations between communist and workers' parties we must begin with the thesis − today accepted by all the parties − that each communist party has the right to determine its own policy as a function of the situation and the concrete conditions of the country in question.

This clear recognition of the independence of every communist party does not exclude the possibility of one party's having an opinion about one or another aspect of another party's activity, in particular if it is a matter of questions about the objectives common to all the communist parties, that is, the international communist movement . . .

The Czechoslovak communists − in their search for better methods, for more democratic practices − are inspired with concern to prevent the very foundations of socialist society from being in any way called into question.

Nouvelle Communiste (September 1968).

10 Declaration of the Central Committee of the PCF, 1968

Very serious events are taking place in Czechoslovakia. Soviet, Bulgarian, Polish, Hungarian and East German troops tonight entered the whole Czechoslovakian territory.

The Politburo of the French Communist Party, which affirmed its great satisfaction at the conclusion of the Cierna and Bratislava meetings, expresses its surprise and its reprobation following the military intervention in Czechoslovakia.

Recently the Central Committee of the French Communist Party specified that it believed the problems arising among the communist parties must be examined and resolved by fraternal discussions during bilateral and multilateral encounters, while respecting each nation's sovereignty, each party's freedom of decision, in the spirit of proletarian internationalism.

Our party, which has expressed its concern with certain aspects of the Czechoslovakian situation, has asserted, as well, that it was the Czechoslovakian Communist Party's prerogative to act against antisocialist elements in order to preserve and extend socialist victories.

The French Communist Party has never ceased its efforts in this struggle, making known its opposition to all foreign military intervention, and in its Politburo and Central Committee's decision, as well as in its secretary general's actions regarding the CPSU and the CPC . . .

L'Humanité, August 22, 1968, p. 1.

11 PCF Central Committee resolution, 1968

. . . The Central Committee of the French Communist Party, gathered in special session this 22nd day of August 1968, has studied the situation created by the military intervention of the Soviet Union, Bulgaria, Poland, Hungary and the German Democratic Republic in Czechoslovakia . . .

Our party has not concealed its recent concern over certain aspects of the situation in Czechoslovakia. By means of the Czechoslovakian Communist Party's legitimate efforts to develop socialist democracy, to better the style and the methods of the party and of the state, forces hostile to socialism displayed their activities. The exploits of those elements did not meet the necessary political and ideological opposition. The world reaction, particularly that of the revanchist and expansionist West German leaders, does not hide the fact that they anticipate a weakening of the alliance uniting Czechoslovakia to the other nations of the socialist community, an alliance which constitutes a security pledge for the Czechoslovakian people, for socialist nations and for peace in Europe.

. . . Our party welcomed with real satisfaction the positive conclusions of the Cierna and Bratislava meetings. It hailed the understanding brought about among the communist parties of the Soviet Union, Czechoslovakia, Bulgaria, Hungary and the German Democratic Republic on the real problems of the struggle against imperialism and for socialism. The Bratislava encounter created favorable conditions for strengthening the co-operation of the socialist nations on the basis of equality, of national independence, of mutual aid and of solidarity, as well as for further success in building a new, prosperous and democratic society in those nations.

Our party believes that the problem arising among the communist parties must be examined and resolved by fraternal discussion during bilateral and multilateral encounters, in the spirit of proletarian internationalism, respecting each nation's sovereignty and each party's freedom of decision.

Our party is resolutely dedicated to the principle according to which each communist party should have complete independence in determining its policy, its forms of action, its methods of struggle, of course based on Marxism–Leninism, but, at the same time, considering the actual conditions under which it is waging its struggle, the interests of the working class and of its people, and the interests of the worldwide democratic and revolutionary movement.

Consequently the PCF declares that it is opposed to all interference in the internal affairs of a brother party.

. . . This is why the Central Committee, in making the Politburo's August 21, 1968, declaration, disapproved of the military intervention in Czechoslovakia. It is up to the Czechoslovakian Communist Party, taking into account its international obligations, to find by itself, within the working class and the Czechoslovakian people, the forces necessary to safeguard and to develop socialism in Czechoslovakia with the support of the socialist nations and all brother parties . . .

The French Communist Party calls all communists, all laborers and democrats, to fight against the anti-communist speculations and provocations which the enemies of socialism in France and in the world never cease to disseminate in the course of events.

L'Humanité, August 23, 1968, p. 1.

12 Georges Marchais' interview with Europe 1, 1968

FIRST QUESTION: In the space of forty-eight hours the French Communist Party published two texts.

In the first, the Politburo expressed its surprise and its condemnation of the Soviet military intervention in Czechoslovakia.

In the second, the Central Committee recorded its disapproval. It seems to me that the second text is less forceful than the first.

GEORGES MARCHAIS: In our eyes there is absolutely no difference between the judgement rendered by the Politburo declaration and that implicit in the Central Committee resolution.

I will, first, point out that the Central Committee resolution declares that it makes the Politburo declaration its own. Further, our Central Committee clearly and sharply confirmed that it disapproved of the military intervention in Czechoslovakia.

Consequently we reject or we disapprove as you like – the military intervention.

SECOND QUESTION: In the Politburo text there was a brief allusion to 'certain worrisome aspects of the Czechoslovakian situation.'

The Central Committee dwells much longer on the fact that there were anti-socialist elements in Czechoslovakia. It informs us that the security of the communist nations could have been endangered. That gives the impression that you recognize that the Soviets had reasons to be concerned with the development of the situation in Czechoslovakia.

Don't you believe that that will lead people to believe that, in fact, you at least partially justify the Soviet intervention?

GEORGES MARCHAIS: Absolutely not. It is perfectly normal that the Central Committee resolution be devoted to a more detailed analysis of all aspects of the situation, just as it was perfectly normal that the

Politburo declaration contended itself with taking a position on the fact of the military intervention.

That the Central Committee makes mention of the activity of elements hostile to socialism in Czechoslovakia is no novelty.

Since April 19 our Central Committee has publicly stated its concern with certain negative phenomena which could obstruct the Czechoslovakian Communist Party leaders' legitimate efforts to spread socialist democracy and to improve the methods and style of party and state work.

We also communicated these concerns to Czechoslovakian comrades themselves. Indeed, we believe that it was with the Czechoslovakian Communist Party itself, with the support of the socialist nations and of all the communist parties, that the responsibility for battling these negative phenomena rested – as it was a battle for them.

That is why we persist in thinking that military intervention was unjustified.

THIRD QUESTION: The Central Committee reaffirmed its desire to maintain its special bond with the Communist Party of the Soviet Union.

Does this mean that these bonds will be maintained no matter what happens, even if events should take a dramatic turn?

GEORGES MARCHAIS: A deep friendship and solidarity has always tied the French communists to the Soviet communists. Indeed, it was the Communist Party of the Soviet Union which brought about the first socialist revolution in history, which built the first socialist society.

The Soviet Union played a determinant role in the victory over Nazism.

The Soviet Union made a supremely important contribution to the people's struggle against imperialism, and in protecting world peace.

This friendship has been subjected to great difficulties.

Our Central Committee confirmed its desire to maintain and to do all that is possible to strengthen it for the reasons I have just mentioned.

We should not be counted on to take part in the anti-Soviet chorus which these events provoked, just because of the position that our Central Committee took in opposing the military intervention in Czechoslovakia.

FIFTH QUESTION: To what extent have French domestic policy concerns influenced the positions taken by the French Communist Party?

GEORGES MARCHAIS: We have our policy. It is defined, in complete independence, by our Congress and by our Central Committee. This policy forms one whole. It has national and international aspects, which are indissociable.

Each of our actions is dictated by our sense of our national responsibilities, as much as by the interests of the people and laborers of France as by the interests of the world workers' democratic and peace movement.

It is a profoundly national policy and, at the same time, inspired by proletarian internationalism.

It is this policy which determines all positions taken by the French Communist Party, including those touching on the Czechoslovakian situation.

SIXTH QUESTION: But aren't you afraid that this Czechoslovakian affair will create new difficulties for you in your relations with the other French leftist parties? Certain of them have already accused you of having condemned the Soviet military intervention for tactical reasons.

GEORGES MARCHAIS: I just explained that we did not condemn the military intervention for tactical reasons, but as a duty defined by our national and international policy.

And I do not think that this could complicate our relations with the other leftist parties. Further, I note with satisfaction that the politicians of the left have correctly appraised our party's position.

L'Humanité, August 24, 1968, p. 2.

13 Editorial, 'Blows to freedom in Czechoslovakia,' *L'Humanité,* January 25, 1977

The Czechoslovakian authorities' behavior toward politicians and intellectuals expressing views different from those held by those in power seriously concerns French communists.

Very recently Czechoslovakian citizens raised questions touching on conditions affecting the exercise of human rights and freedom in their nation, in a document entitled 'Charter '77.' They expressed their discontent with the policy followed by authorities in this matter. They asked to hold a dialogue on the subject with those authorities. They have been answered with police pursuits and abuse, portraying them as tainted, corrupt men seeking to foment 'counter-revolution,' hired by 'foreigners.'

We cannot suppress our shock at the Czechoslovakian authorities' accusations of the signatories of 'Charter '77,' who were said in *Rude Pravo* to be 'acting on the orders of anti-communist and Zionist forces.' The use of such procedures unavoidably evokes memories of past arbitrariness. The French communists condemn, straight out, all resurgence of this.

It is not in this way that the inevitable problem of political debate will be resolved, but by realizing the necessity of allowing dissenters to play a full role in the different organizations and institutions of socialist society, in attempts to permit the expression of diverse opinions, proposals, criticisms, and also the specific policy disagreement implicit in the clash.

We cannot view the exercise of the right to petition, to distribute pamphlets, and to call for dialogue and discussions as crimes, and particularly not in a socialist society, which calls for wide democratic discussion. We cannot acknowledge the legitimacy of practices which imply that, with socialism, all dissenting voices will be condemned to silence and repression. The French communists categorically exclude all these blows to individual and collective rights and liberties from their range of possible policy. They are foreign to the ideal of socialism. French communists judge these rights and freedoms not only desirable but indispensable for the spread of socialism and the development of democracy in all areas – which presumes clashes of contradictory opinions, confrontations and the battle of ideas.

L'Humanité, January 25, 1977, p. 1.

The Sino-Soviet Dispute

14 Waldeck Rochet's report to the Central Committee of the PCF, October 6, 1963

Fourteen years ago, when the People's Republic of China was founded, we joyously welcomed the victory of the Chinese revolution, achieved under the leadership of the Chinese Communist Party.

And our party has always considered the unity of the international communist movement and the cohesion of the socialist camp the essential conditions for the further progress of socialism in the world and the preservation of peace.

Their divergencies are on major problems like war

and peace; the role of the international working class and the world socialist system; questions on the world workers' movement strategy and tactics and the struggle for national liberation; the battle against the ideology behind the cult of personality; finally, even on the principles governing relations among the socialist nations and among the communist parties.

If we first examine the most burning problem of our age – the problem of war and peace – it is clear that the Chinese leaders' line diverges sharply from the line defined in the 1957 and 1960 declarations . . .

The 1960 declaration, after enumerating all the forces in the world which would allow peaceful coexistence to be upheld among states with different social orders, named the struggle for peace and to prevent thermonuclear war the prime objective of communists of all nations.

This double affirmation of the possibility and the necessity of struggling to avoid a new thermonuclear war is based on both the changes in the relation of international forces and the qualitative changes in the means of waging war which have resulted from the appearance of nuclear weapons.

The second factor, the unprecedented destructive power of nuclear weapons, imperatively demands that all forces hostile to war make the maximum effort to prevent war for, if we wait for it to break out, it will be too late for many of the world's regimes and their peoples, who would be annihilated.

Further, peaceful coexistence among states with different social orders is the only acceptable alternative, in the face of the danger of thermonuclear war . . .

These are fundamental theses about the problems of war and peace, approved by the eighty-one parties represented at the 1960 Moscow conference; these ideas which the Chinese leaders have decided to question in their declarations and their activities.

To be sure – since it is difficult openly to present oneself as an opponent of the struggle for peaceful coexistence – under penalty of being exposed before the communists and the people of all nations – the Chinese leaders are careful to camouflage their disagreement with the 1957 and 1960 declarations . . .

The declaration by Chinese government representatives last September reiterated Mao's belief that only two possibilities exist: the possibility that war would not occur, and the possibility that it would. In reality, this ambiguous theory of the existence of two opposite and equally valid possibilities serves mainly to camouflage their hypotheses about the inevitability of world war.

The Chinese leaders confirmed that when they asserted in their June 14 letter that 'peaceful coexistence does not need to be the general rule of conduct for a socialist nation'; when they proclaimed that 'the main thing is to do away with imperialism, despite the inevitable sacrifices'; when they systematically slandered the Soviet Union's peace policy, declaring that it consisted of 'surrendering the peace to the imperialists,' and that it 'hampered the revolutionary struggle.'

What do all these proposals and accusations signify?

They mean that the Chinese leaders doubt that it is possible to avert another war because they underestimate the strength of the forces for peace and socialism and overestimate the imperialists,' leading them to launch an extremely dangerous, adventurist policy.

Their 'leftist' line tends to demobilize the masses even as it leads them to passivity – for no one battles against an illness judged incurable.

The Chinese leaders question the crucial concept of fighting for disarmament, as well, by asserting that it is 'unrealizable,' simply a matter of 'illusions.'

To be sure, it is true that imperialists do not favor disarmament, but the problem is precisely one of leading the people against the imperialists in order to compel them to retreat – to enforce the people's will . . .

We French communists, members of a party born in the struggle against an imperialist war, cannot understand how the communist leaders of a large, powerful nation can speak so lightly of the eventuality of nuclear catastrophe resulting in the death of hundreds of millions of men and the destruction of entire nations.

This adventurist line has even more serious consequences because the Chinese leaders do not limit themselves to formulating 'theories' – erroneous ones, at that – but actually use these theories to justify a policy which aggravates international tensions.

Such an attitude on their part was revealed with special clarity during the Cuban missile crisis, again, in connection with a possible Sino–Indian clash, and especially after the signing of the Nuclear Test Ban Treaty.

Despite the highly favorable evaluation of the Soviet Union's policy by the principal leaders of the Cuban revolution, representatives of the Chinese Communist Party continue to slander the Soviet Union and comrade Khrushchev, accusing them of leaning to 'adventurism,' and of 'capitulationism,' since they regret the Soviet Union's success in averting a world war . . .

The facts have since shown that China gained nothing by engaging in armed conflict on the Sino–Soviet border, but Chinese leaders did do great damage to the unity of the anti-imperialist forces in Asia.

Their policy encouraged reactionary forces in India – allowing the imperialist powers to strengthen their influence in that nation – and created a more difficult situation for the Communist Party and for progressives in India. China dealt a blow to international détente . . .

L'Humanité, October 8, 1963, p. 7.

15 Waldeck Rochet's report to the Eighteenth Congress of the PCF, January 1967

The French Communist Party defines and conducts its policy taking into account current conditions in France as well as the international situation, but it is solidly based on the principles of Marxism–Leninism. We are staunchly faithful to the principle of the independence of communist parties, of their equal rights, and of non-interference in the affairs of brother parties.

At the same time, the French Communist Party is strongly attached to the principles of proletarian internationalism . . .

Unfortunately the present Chinese communist leaders have abandoned that general line to take up a jingoistic, adventuristic and divisive policy, which provokes anxiety and reprobation.

Since 1960 Maurice Thorez has shown that the theories developed by that party do not merely reflect differences with all the other communist parties on one point or another; rather, they constitute a theoretical and political line opposed to the general line of the international communist movement.

Today it is no longer enough for the Chinese leaders to claim that the struggle for peaceful coexistence among states with different social orders will slow down the working-class struggle and the oppressed peoples' struggle for emancipation; it can

be said that Peking sees world war as the only possible means of annihilating American imperialism . . .

Loyal to the humanist ideal of our doctrine's founders, we affirm that, on the contrary, the struggle for socialism and the struggle for peace cannot be dissociated. In addition, we are convinced that it has become possible, in our age, to prevent the imperialists – especially American imperialists – from setting off another world war . . .

Rather than acknowledge that actual conditions of time and place determine whether a socialist revolution will be peaceful or non-peaceful, the Chinese automatically preclude the first possibility and predict violence. With Mao Tse-tung, they reiterate that 'the conquest of power by armed struggle is the central task – solving problems by way of civil war . . .' 'The principle,' Lin Piao declared in 1965, restating one of Mao Tse-tung's tenets, 'is as valid everywhere, in all nations, as it is in China!'

The current Chinese leaders claim, in this way, to be formulating a blueprint of lone struggle for all communist parties and all revolutionary movements, whatever their actual conditions or their strategic positions.

The Chinese leaders are propagating the erroneous theory that socialist revolution necessarily involves civil war, which tends, in certain circumstances, to divert the mass struggle to the support of adventurist platforms . . .

Our party, which has always fought the denaturation of Marxism – whether by the 'left' or the 'right' – completely rejects the Chinese leaders' current theory.

The French communists can no longer hide their concern about certain aspects of the events taking place in China in the name of 'the great proletarian cultural revolution.' These events do have international repercussions, and involve serious attacks on key principles of the communist doctrine.

This cultural nihilism is foreign to Marxism–Leninism. The true cultural revolution brought about by socialism consists, as Lenin emphasized, in putting all the cultural treasures – to which they were previously forbidden access by the exploiting classes – at the disposal of the laboring masses of the factories and fields. This assumes that all the best of the cultural heritage will be assimilated.

It can be determined, as well, that party life is inspired by a militaristic concept foreign to Leninism, and that Mao Tse-tung's cult has grown to extraordinary proportions and has an almost religious nature, whose manifestations provide fodder for the bourgeois press.

The Chinese leaders are, at the same time, giving communism a caricatured image contrary to the Marxist–Leninist image of a communist society called on to satisfy all the material and spiritual needs of all men, permitting them free, harmonious and diversified developments.

Finally, current Chinese leaders are systematically violating the principle of proletarian internationalism and the rules governing relations among brother parties and among socialist nations.

They seek to impose their nationalistic, adventuristic and sectarian line on all the world's communist parties, by devoting a considerable portion of their means to fighting not imperialism, but the strongest opponents of imperialism – those communist parties which refuse to adopt their positions . . .

They assert that capitalism is being restored in the USSR, a lie and an absurdity. They accuse all communist parties loyal to the international communist and workers' movement's principle of revisionism, when they are the ones turning their back on Marxism–Leninism, substituting 'Maoism.'

The main part of their political attack is directed, then, at the Soviet Union – at the principal power in the socialist camp, the surest ally of people attacked or menaced by imperialism. A campaign has been initiated to make the Chinese people detest the Soviet Union . . .

Experience has shown that international conferences of communist and workers' parties constitute one of the most effective means for jointly studying the problems which life poses for them, and for uniting their efforts in the struggle against imperialism and for peace, national independence, democracy and socialism.

We support a new conference which would allow communist and workers' parties to reaffirm together the great principles of the 1960 declaration; to analyze the vast changes which have occurred since 1960; to elaborate jointly a general line for the future on that basis; finally, to take measures likely to defend and consolidate the unity of the international communist and workers' movement.

'XVIIIᵉ Congrès du Parti Communiste Français,' *Cahiers du Communisme* (February–March 1967), pp. 84–9.

16 Georges Marchais' report to the Central Committee of the PCF, June 28, 1969

The Chinese leaders break with Leninism
We must clearly perceive that the international communist movement's situation also has certain negative aspects. On the one hand, there is the matter of the activities of the Chinese Communist Party leaders and, on the other, of certain opportunistic tendencies on the part of the right, which have been demonstrated in the conference preparations and in the course of the conference itself.

As is well known, Mao Tse-tung and his supporters undertook, ten years ago, systematically to revise scientific socialism and communist policy to follow a leftist, adventurist, jingoist and anti-Soviet course. They later began to intensify their struggle against the international communist movement. At the Chinese Communist Party's recent Ninth Congress, Maoism was officially substituted for Marxism–Leninism. The new statutes adopted by that Congress placed the American imperialists and the Soviet Union on the same plane. The congress issued a directive ordering a 'merciless' struggle against what Maoists call 'modern revisionists' – in the Chinese leaders' view, the overwhelming majority of socialist nations and communist parties, our own included.

At the same time Maoist leaders have passed from controversy with the communist parties to divisive activity within their ranks, refusal to be part of united action, supporting the Vietnamese people's struggle, organizing serious military provocations on the Sino–Soviet border and declaring territorial claims with regard to the Soviet Union. These claims, devoid of all basis, were inspired by unbridled nationalism. The responsibility for the border incidents rests entirely with the Chinese authorities who, it has been proven, deliberately arranged them.

The Soviet Union showed exemplary patience and restraint in the face of these provocations. That nation has sought to solve these differences by negotiation for a mutually advantageous co-operation based on equal rights.

None the less the Chinese leaders' attitude continues to cause concern . . .

How could the party be expected to ignore this question?

Because it is one of the targets of the Chinese leaders' slanderous attack, our party finds it necessary to air the problem.

Because it considers the Chinese party's assertion at the Congress that the enemy is both American imperialism and the Soviet Union simply monstrous – a sign of a total rupture with Leninism.

Because the Chinese leaders' adventurist anti-Soviet and sectarian activity plays right along with the imperialists' game, doing serious damage to the struggle against imperialism, this should be the object of the conference.

Because the Chinese leaders are pursuing their divisive dealings and spreading their anti-communist propaganda within our own nation – even though they find more and more sparse audience.

Finally, because as comrade Waldeck Rochet declared in his address, 'our party, the great authentically revolutionary Marxist–Leninist party in France, will continue to battle against left opportunism and adventurism, which can only lead to tragic failures.'

L'Humanité, June 30, 1969, pp. 3–4.

17   Central Committee of the PCF, 1976

After the disappearance of Mao Tse-tung:
message of the PCF to the Chinese Communist Party
The Central Committee of the French Communist Party salutes, with emotion and respect, the memory of Chairman Mao Tse-tung. It offers its deepest condolences to the Chinese Communist Party and the Chinese people.

With Mao Tse-tung disappeared one of the great men of our epoch, one characterized by liberation struggles and revolutionary transformations. In a time when China lived under feudal oppression and the imperialist yoke, Mao Tse-tung was one of the founders of the Chinese Communist Party. He played a determining role in the long struggle waged, under difficult conditions, by the Chinese communists for the dignity of their people, for national and social liberation. He led the resistance to Japanese militarism, he directed the combat of the popular forces to their historic victory in 1949.

His name is thus linked to one of the greatest events of our times: the triumph of the socialist revolution in China.

The expulsion of imperialism, China's passage to socialism, considerably modified the balance of power

in the world. At the same time the epic of the Chinese people contributed to the rise of revolutionary and democratic forces on all the continents.

Since then profound economic and social transformations have been achieved. China no longer experiences famines and epidemics, ignorance and humiliation. Socialism has brought China into the modern world and has radically improved the fate of its hundreds of millions of inhabitants. Before its working and creating people it has opened up immense possibilities of development. New China – for whose recognition by our country the French Communist Party was the only one to act from the start – has made a great contribution to the worldwide struggle against imperialism. For a long time and often, our communist parties and our peoples have found themselves side by side in the same struggle for peace, liberty and justice.

Certainly serious differences have since developed between our two parties, both on international problems and on the conception of socialism itself. We have deeply regretted that these differences have affected our relations. This was not our deed, and it is not our wish . . .

Cahiers du Communisme (October 1976), pp. 138–40.

Stalinism and De-Stalinization

18   Declaration of the Politburo of the PCF, 1956

The bourgeois press is publishing a report attributed to comrade Khrushchev. This report, releasing a statement which adds some very serious mistakes to Stalin's previously known errors, is understandably arousing anxieties among French Communist Party members.

French communists, with the communists of all nations, condemn the arbitrary acts attributed to Stalin – acts contrary to Marxist–Leninist principles.

The leaders of the Communist Party of the Soviet Union must be given credit for assuming the task of correcting errors and offenses related to the cult of personality by emphasizing the strength and unity of Lenin's great party and the support that it enjoys among the Soviet peoples, and its influence in the international workers' movement.

The Politburo regrets that, because of the

conditions in which comrade Khrushchev's report was presented and disclosed, the bourgeois press was in a position to publish facts of which the French communists were still unaware. Such a progression of events does not favor normal discussion of problems within the party. On the contrary, it facilitates speculation and intrigue by the enemies of communism.

The explanation given so far for Stalin's offenses, their origins and the conditions in which they occurred, is unsatisfactory. A careful Marxist analysis is essential to determine the circumstances in which Stalin was able to exercise such personal power.

It was wrong to have offered such wildly enthusiastic tributes to Stalin during his lifetime and to have given him sole credit for all the success that the Soviet Union achieved, thanks to a general party line which was truly invaluable for building socialism. Our attitude contributed to developing the cult of personality and the negative influence it brought to bear on the international workers' movement. Today it is no longer fair to attribute to Stalin alone all negative aspects of the activity of the Soviet Union's Communist Party.

Stalin played a positive role throughout a historic period. With the other party leaders, he took an active part in the October Socialist Revolution and later in the victorious struggle against foreign intervention and the counter-revolution. After Lenin's death he battled with the adversaries of Marxism–Leninism and struggled to apply the Leninist plan for building socialism. He greatly contributed to the formation of all the communist parties.

Stalin acquired a well-deserved prestige which he allowed to be transformed into a cult of personality. The development of this cult was facilitated by the Soviet Union's position – long alone, exposed to the ventures of a world of enemies – which necessitated an extreme construction of the popular forces, an iron discipline and a rigorous centralization of the power of the proletarian state. These circumstances help us understand the enormous difficulties the Soviet Union faced without, however, justifying Stalin's dealings. He committed numerous violations of Soviet law; he engaged in arbitrary repression of communist militants; he transgressed party principles; and, using reprehensible methods, he caused serious damage to the Soviet Union and the international communist movement.

The Twentieth Congress of the Soviet Union's Communist Party, during which Stalin's offenses were justly denounced, was the Congress which confirmed that the Soviet Union – having completed the building of socialism – had set out on the road to a communist society. It was the Congress of great victories for the nations of the socialist camp. It emphasized the possibility of avoiding wars in our time, and of proceeding by new paths to socialism. It illustrated the prospects for the working class's march to unity.

So that all militants, in preparing for the Fourteenth Congress of the French Communist Party, can effectively discuss problems raised by comrade Khrushchev's report, the Politburo has asked the Central Committee of the Soviet Union's Communist Party for the text, already familiar to members of certain communist and workers' parties . . .

L'Humanité, June 19, 1956, p. 1.

19   Maurice Thorez' report to the Fourteenth Congress of the PCF, July 1956

Regarding the cult of personality

. . . The cult of personality had the effect of diminishing the activity of communists and of the popular masses, of reducing the role of collective leadership within the party, and of sanctioning serious flaws in their labors and glaring violations of socialist law.

The condemnation of the cult of personality is based on:

(1) Marxist–Leninist theory, which does not oppose the concept of individual heroes, as agents of history for masses excluded from historic activity, as idealistic philosophies do;
(2) the deeply democratic nature of the Soviet system, characterized by the creative participation of tens of millions of laborers in political life, in the building of communism.

The open and courageous self-criticism practiced in this instance has provided further testimony to the strength of the Soviet Union's Communist Party and the solidarity of the socialist regime.

No bourgeois government, no bourgeois politicians, have ever dared carry out an act of this sort. Have we ever heard of self-criticism from those responsible for the non-intervention in Spain and its evil consequences? Have we ever heard self-criticism from the authors of the Munich policy, which led to world war? Have we ever heard self-criticism from the men of Dien-Bien-Phu?

But the Communist Party of the Soviet Union, trained in the revolutionary principles of Marxism–Leninism, revealed the whole truth, distasteful as it was.

In the USSR, as in the international workers' movement, the Communist Party of the Soviet Union's revelation of Stalin's offenses naturally provoked strong emotions and profound regrets . . .

In its June 18 declaration, our party's Politburo expressed its confidence and solidarity. At the same time it found that the explanations given so far by the Soviet leaders of the conditions and origins of Stalin's crimes have not been satisfactory, and it called for a thorough Marxist analysis of the circumstances in which Stalin was able to exercise his personal power.

This analysis is contained in the resolution published on July 2 by the Central Committee of the Communist Party of the Soviet Union. It took into consideration not only the subjective factor of Stalin's character, but also the objective conditions in the historical situation in which socialism was activated in the USSR.

In the conditions of capitalist encirclement, the Soviets' country was, for more than a quarter-century, a besieged fortress.

Within the nation a cruel class struggle to decide the question 'Who will prevail?' long persisted. Trotskyites, right-wing opportunists and bourgeois nationalists actually encouraged the restoration of capitalism.

These domestic and foreign circumstances called for iron discipline, constant vigilance and rigorous centralization of leadership. Thanks to the methods employed, the building of socialism was brought to a successful conclusion. And the whole international workers' movement was galvanized by it . . .

In the course of that titanic struggle, Stalin showed exceptional merit, and consequently acquired great authority and great popularity. But, little by little, he began to attribute to himself all the success of the Communist Party and the people of the Soviet Union. Further, certain negative aspects of his character which had already been pointed out by Lenin in 1922 contributed to promoting the emergence of a veritable cult of Stalin's personality. The principle of collective leadership was violated. Arbitrariness and unwarranted repression were in-flicted upon honest citizens, communists included.

Such are the circumstances which historically explain the birth and propagation of Stalin's cult of personality.

That cult did cause serious damage, but it would be wrong to believe, on the one hand, that it diverted Soviet society from its march to communism or, on the other hand, to look for the source of the cult of personality in the nature of the socialist regime.

To attribute to one personality, however eminent, the incredible strength needed single-handedly to modify the social order, is to distort history, in the idealist fashion.

As for the assertion that the cult of personality is the consequence of the Soviet system, of the allegedly anti-democratic character of the system itself – it is contrary to all fact. It is a pure and simple slander on the part of the forces of formal democracy active in the capitalist world; they would like to forget that proletarian democracy is a thousand times more democratic than their own system, given that it reflects the will and serves the interests of the vast mass of the population . . .

'XIVᵉ Congrès du Parti Communiste Français,' *Cahiers du Communisme* (July–August 1956), pp. 49–52.

Proletarian Internationalism

20 Maurice Thorez' report to the Twelfth Congress of the PCF, April 1950

There are some party members reluctant to affirm our feelings of friendship and trust for the Soviet Union, who do not recognize that nation's essential role in the battle for peace . . .

Can anyone who does not feel a strong devotion to the October Socialist Revolution, the founding of the proletarian revolution, be a communist? Can anyone who does not have boundless affection for Stalin, the friend and leader whose seventieth birthday we enthusiastically celebrated, be a communist? Those who doubt, who hesitate with regard to the Soviet Union, are foundering in nationalism and chauvinism. They are breaking with precisely those principles of proletarian internationalism which Stalin defined on August 1, 1927:

An internationalist is the man who is unreservedly, unhesitantly and unconditionally prepared to defend the USSR, because the USSR is the basis for the world revolutionary movement, and it is impossible to defend or advance the revolutionary movement without defending the USSR. For anyone who seeks to defend the world revolutionary movement without and against the Soviet Union goes against that revolution and inevitably slips into the camp of the enemies of the revolution.

Yes, to break with proletarian internationalism, to founder in nationalism, to show the least hesitancy about the Soviet Union by speaking of it as just 'another nation,' is to fail to distinguish between the socialist state and the imperialist powers, is to turn one's back on the working class and socialism. Is not that what happened to Tito and his gang of adventurers, who have gone over to serve the imperialist warmongers and who have become the worst enemies of their people, of the international workers' movement, and the worst enemies of the Soviet Union? . . .

'Documents du XIIᵉ Congrès du Parti Communiste Français,' *Cahiers du Communisme* (May 1950), pp. 23–4.

21   Resolution of the Central Committee of the PCF, October 10, 1964

In our time a greater diversity of roads is offered to the [world's] peoples for their march towards liberation and socialism.

We think that there can be no question of creating a new centralized international organization. Our party is equally opposed to the organization of parties by geographical zones, continents or social systems. Life has shown that the independence of every party is an element of strength and an invitation to creative research, benefiting the whole movement . . .

In the world communist movement there are no 'leading parties' and 'subordinate parties,' as the 1960 declaration has recalled; all parties are independent and have equal rights and they develop their policies by applying the principles of Marxism–Leninism within the concrete conditions of their countries.

Our party's mixing into the affairs of another is a violation of these rules and cannot be allowed . . .

Proletarian internationalism cannot be limited to declarations of intent. It requires solidary action. A

common line. Each party is responsible to its own people and to the movement as a whole.

It is only in taking our stand on the collective experience of the international communist movement, respecting the principles of our doctrine and its analytical method, that it is possible to develop a correct general line on the fundamental questions common to the whole movement and concerning all of humanity.

The French communists are convinced that the international conference of all communists and workers' parties is the most effective means to permit the communist parties to reaffirm together the principles of the 1957 and 1960 declarations, to analyze the important changes since then and to work out the implications for common action, finally, to defend the unity of the movement.

Far from signifying a split, or taking on the goal of excluding anyone, the conference will be the best means of reinforcing the unity of the movement, of fighting against the disaggregation of the international communist and labor movement. Refusal to meet and to discuss with the aim of overcoming differences would lead most surely to the *de facto* legalization of the split . . .

Cahiers du Communisme (November 1964), pp. 119–20.

22   Waldeck Rochet's report to the Central Committee of the PCF, October 20–1, 1968

With regard to proletarian internationalism, it was stressed that, for communists, it is class position and the interests of socialism that are the determinants.

We are in full agreement. Still, it is important not to underestimate, under threat of harming class action, the intervention of both national and international factors in the class struggle on an international scale.

It is undeniable, for example, that the national factor, with its notions of sovereignty and national independence, plays a very important role, even in the class struggles.

As far as the states which belong to the socialist community are concerned, we must stress the fact that their relations are governed by the principles of proletarian internationalism.

But this does not mean that the principles of equality of rights and of each party's free self-determination are contradictory . . .

It has been correctly noted that we must not invoke the principle of non-interference to conceal nationalist tendencies . . .

Our party has always viewed proletarian internationalism as the manifestation of the common struggle of French laborers and the laborers of all other nations . . .

As a matter of fact there are, in the whole activity of each party, both tasks which are essentially internal and national and those which relate to international solidarity, which each party must carry out with all the other parties.

For we know that the policy of each communist party depends not only on its success within its own nation, but also on the success of its brother parties on a worldwide scale and on the degree of co-operation among them.

This is why proletarian internationalism calls for the reciprocal support and solidarity of all national branches of the working class.

The problem is to know how workers' parties can intervene when certain important facts, which interest all the communist parties, come to the forefront in one way or another.

It is clear that the situation today has, on an international scale, become even more complex, and there is no thought of restoring a world center to direct the workers' and international communist movements.

Yet, it cannot be denied that there are many socialist states and that the workers' and communist international movement has grown considerably stronger, and that these developments have served to increase the responsibility of all communist and workers' parties and to demand of them that they make some serious attempts to contribute to bringing about the unity of the international communist movement.

Acknowledgement of our disagreement with the CPSU on this point has deeply affected us all.

For more than fifty years we have been on the side of the Soviet Union and its communist party in the struggle against imperialism and for social progress, peoples' liberation and socialism.

This is why there is not, why there could not be, any anti-Sovietism on our part.

We are all friends of the Soviet Union, the world's first socialist state, which made a decisive contribution to the liberation of Europe from Hitler's yoke in the last war.

But it is because we care for the Soviet Union that we suffer when we feel that an error has been committed and when we find ourselves in disagreement on an important question.

Waldeck Rochet, *Ecrits Politiques* (Paris: Editions Sociales, 1976), pp. 261–7.

23 Georges Marchais' report to the Nineteenth Congress of the PCF, February 1970

Patriotism and Internationalism

We have always believed that, while each communist party is responsible to the working class and the people of its nation, that responsibility cannot allow it to neglect the interests of the workers' international revolutionary movement.

All the world's workers are linked by common interests. They have the same enemy – big capital. They have the same objective – the abolition of exploitation and of oppression, the arrival of a society without classes and without wars. The communists have made this objective solidarity of aims which unites them into an active force which is capable of bringing about the great social transformations called for in our times.

This is why there is no contradiction between our national responsibilities and our international responsibilities. On the contrary! These responsibilities are indissolubly bound together, as are the principles of the sovereignty of each party and of proletarian internationalism.

As the International Conference of Communist and Workers' Parties unequivocally emphasized, 'each party, starting from the principles of Marxism–Leninism and taking into account concrete national conditions, elaborates its policy in complete independence, defines the direction, the forms and the methods of its struggle, determines its road, peaceful or not peaceful, according to circumstances, as well as the forms and methods for building socialism within its nation' . . .

In its relations with brother parties, the French Communist Party will resolutely continue to draw its inspiration from the principles defined by the international communist movement: respect for the independence and equality of each party; non-interference in the internal affairs of brother parties; solidarity and mutual help; proletarian internationalism. These principles apply, as well, to the relations among socialist nations – as the declaration of the Moscow conference confirms.

At the same time, we believe that it is desirable that the communist parties engage together in common actions destined to mobilize the vast popular masses, in order to bring about one or another of the objectives defined by the conference of Moscow.

There are great possibilities in this area. Under present circumstances, when the deployment of the masses' political struggle constitutes a major factor in the evolution of the relations of those forces favoring peace, national independence and socialism – the communist parties' duty is to undertake together initiatives for common action which spring from their vanguard role in the battle against imperialism . . .

The French Communist Party is prepared to support all initiatives likely to demonstrate and strengthen the unity of action of the diverse anti-imperialist forces, notably by holding a great world congress of anti-imperialist forces.

Finally, it will continue to attach great importance to its ties with the democratic and revolutionary forces and movements in the former colonial countries and in different parts of the world. It will lend them its support in the struggle against exploitation and oppression.

The unity of the international communist movement – the strongest, most advanced, and most important anti-imperialist force – is the indispensable foundation for the wide and united anti-imperialist front that it is crucial to constitute.

'XIXe Congrès du Parti Communiste Français,' *Cahiers du Communisme* (February–March 1970), pp. 96–9.

24   Georges Marchais' report to the Twentieth Congress of the PCF, December 13–17, 1972

Our International Responsibilities
Our party's great national responsibilities do not make it at all neglect its international responsibilities. These are an integral part of its battle . . . Our party assumes them and will assume them in all circumstances with honor, for it is profoundly aware that the international solidarity of laborers and of the people in the struggle for their major objectives is a vital condition for the success of all and of each one.

A special importance was attached to this subject at the meeting which took place in July 1971 between our party and the Communist Party of the Soviet Union . . .

Making an identical judgement of the crisis of the capitalist world and of the new possibilities for the struggle against imperialism which have arisen, and extolling socialism and the success which it has already gained over a third of the globe, our two parties recalled: 'The irreplaceable experience accumulated by the socialist nations shows well that, in accordance with the teachings of Marxism–Leninism, the building of socialism obeys general universal principles and that, at the same time, they reveal their diverse forms in terms of the national peculiarities of each country, and of historical conditions. Each nation, in the future as well, will come to socialism in an original way, with its own variety of power of the working class and the laboring population, its own form of democracy, its own fashion of economic and social transformation.'

Our adversaries on all sides claim to set the proletarian internationalism which unites the communist parties in opposition to the independence of each one of them. As the joint declaration brought out, 'they have invented for that reason the so-called theory of "limited sovereignty" and the demagogic fable of two "superpowers" together deciding the fate of the world and the situation of the peoples. French and Soviet communists are fighting and will continue to fight these slanderous distortions. Far from denying or minimizing the independence, the sovereignty, the equality of rights, and the principles of non-interference in internal affairs, as much of nations as of communist parties, they forcefully confirm that the respect for and strict observance of these principles is a law for the communists precisely because, with solidarity and mutual help, they are an integral part of proletarian internationalism . . .'

On these grounds, to which it is very attached, our party endeavors to contribute to the strengthening of the unity of the international communist movement, to bring it to a higher level responding to the current possibilities and demands of the struggle against imperialism, and to develop joint actions among our parties. We welcome and always will welcome favorably initiatives going in this direction. In this manner we participated in the Conference of the Communist Parties of the Capitalist Countries on multinationals, which was due to the initiative of our British comrades. Likewise we were the source of the

Conference of All European Communist and Workers' Parties to intensify the action of mass solidarity with Vietnam and the other Indo–Chinese peoples, which met in Paris last July . . .

Our party is endeavoring, as well, to establish good relations with the democratic and revolutionary movements of the different parts of the world as well as with several socialist parties. On this matter we believe that there exists, especially in Europe, a 'lost opportunity for doing business,' detrimental to the European workers, in the relations among the communist and the socialist parties in this part of the world. We think that, beyond the differences which separate us, it is time to establish new relations between our parties, to begin exchanges of views, to consider joint actions on at least certain issues, such as the struggle against the policies of transnational monopolies or actions favoring collective European security . . .

'XXᵉ Congrès du Parti Communiste Français,' *Cahiers du Communisme* (January–February 1973), pp. 74–6.

25   Georges Marchais, 'The Communist Party "à coeur ouvert",' 1973

Solidarity has nothing in common, as can be seen, with any ties whatsoever of subordination between an imaginary 'center' of the communist movement and those which are labeled its various 'detachments.' There has been no communist international for more than a quarter-century. And, great as that organization's merits were in bringing help to the young communist parties, there can be no question of re-establishing one, in any form. We are excluding that possibility. The communist parties have come of age. When we exchange our views with other communist parties, or decide on great common international initiatives, we meet – at bilateral, regional, or world gatherings – and we freely and democratically discuss matters with mutual respect. There are no 'dominant' and 'subordinate' communist parties. All the communist parties have equal rights. For our part, in particular, we define our policy, our objectives and our methods of action with complete sovereignty and with full independence. And we could not tolerate any interference in our party's affairs, any more than in our nation's . . .

The reason is simple; here, in France, the task of building democracy and socialism belongs to the French working class, to the French people, guided in this fight by the French Communist Party. No one else could take their place. They will themselves choose the way of progress, success and grandeur for our nation.

Le Défi Démocratique (Paris: Grasset, 1973), pp. 213–14.

26   Jean Kanapa, interview with France-Inter, 1975

QUESTION: What do you think of the new developments in the Sakharov case?
ANSWER: . . . The Congress explains, in the chapter devoted to our vision of French society, that the society for which we are struggling in France is a French socialist society, in which everyone will, we hope, be able to travel freely, within and across the borders.

QUESTION: Do you believe that human rights are, as Sakharov says, not respected?
ANSWER: The draft of the document submitted for discussion at the Twenty-Second Congress elaborates, at length, all the human rights that we intend to see respected in our nation and in the whole world. They are indivisible and would certainly promote free circulation. So long as there is no free distribution of writings, there is no real creative freedom . . .

QUESTION: Does the Soviet Union's attitude – its refusal, for instance, to free a certain number of intellectuals from the places where they are now being held – doesn't this hinder your relations with Moscow?
ANSWER: When we have remarks or criticisms to make to our Soviet comrades on one aspect of their policy or another – especially concerning these questions – you know perfectly well that we don't hesitate at all to make them . . .

QUESTION: Does that mean that you think that they ought to live by the same rules, accept the same rights, in Moscow as in Paris, and vice versa?
ANSWER: You know that that is a more complex

question. Each has its own history, its own national conditions, also its own temperament, but there are a certain number of principles which are universal and about which we speak up as many times as we must.

L'Humanité, November 13, 1975, p. 2.

27 Georges Marchais' report to the Twenty-Second Congress of the PCF, February 1976

. . . The importance of our national tasks, our devotion to our country's interest and success, do not make us in the least neglect our internationalist duties . . .

We bring and we will bring an unflinching solidarity to all the peoples, to all the democratic and revolutionary forces struggling against imperialism and for independence, for peace as well as for democracy, socialism and communism. Fraternal ties unite us, first of all, to the communist parties. Together, with independence and equal rights, we constitute the powerful world communist movement, whose influence on the events of the universe is without precedent in the history of humanity.

There is nothing mysterious in this influence. It comes from the objectives for which the different communist parties have fought, in response to the interests and aspirations of each nation's workers. It springs from the effective struggle which the communists are leading in their respective nations to assure the triumph of these objectives.

But this influence is unquestionably strengthened by the solidarity in the struggle shown by the vanguard parties of the working class of all nations – capitalist nations, socialist nations, nations which have embarked on an original way of development. It is in this reciprocal solidarity that the proletarian internationalism which unites all the communist parties under the same heading is expressed. Proletarian internationalism is, by nature, indivisible. We know of no form of internationalism which is superior to it, any more than we can envisage it carved into regional slices. It is the reciprocal character of this solidarity, the universal character of our internationalism, which allows us to speak of a world communist movement.

Indeed, the communist movement is not and

cannot be a church of a centralized organization binding each party to its constraining decrees, to one uniform law. Further, the movement's progress, the growing responsibilities of the different communist parties, the fact that some are in power and others in opposition, the complexity of the international class struggle in the conditions of peaceful coexistence, can bring about differences in our points of view.

The international communist movement cannot fail to take this into account. In this situation one question assumes a particular importance for the cohesion of the world communist movement – that of united actions on large common objectives. United actions for peace, for collective security, for disarmament and for international co-operation. United acts of solidarity with the victims of reactionary repression and of imperialist aggression. Based on our experience, we are convinced that, if the communist parties play the vanguard role in this matter, the driving role which falls upon them, it is possible – especially in Europe – to gather the widest group of peaceful, democratic, anti-imperialist and labor forces to act for just causes. We intend to follow up our efforts in this direction . . .

'XXIIᵉ Congrès du Parti Communiste Français,' *Cahiers du Communisme* (February–March 1976), pp. 64–5.

28 Jean Kanapa, interview with *France-Nouvelle*, 1976

. . . One of the PCF's greatest attributes is that it has always manifested an internationalism as brisk as its patriotism. It had, for example, a duty particularly pressing for a communist party, but also particularly difficult to fulfill in a nation with an immense colonial empire: the duty of solidarity with the colonial peoples in their struggle for independence. We have always fulfilled all aspects of this duty, for a very long time entirely by ourselves, in France. And we did not do it merely by declaring our support, but by our acts. We did the same with respect to the Soviet Union which put socialism into effect for the first time in history, in the position of a besieged fortress; that position has fortunately changed. We have always been at the side of those peoples who, in turn, have started down the road to socialism, there when they encountered trials, difficulties. And today, at a time when imperialism, on the defensive, is multiplying its interference and repression, there is no communist party, democratic movement or patriot subject to this repression, no people which knows oppression or humiliation, for whom our party does not raise its voice and call for a show of workers' and democrats' solidarity in their behalf . . .

Proletarian internationalism in no way means uniformity. It implies the reciprocal solidarity of all the world's workers (to which Lenin justifiably added, for our times, the solidarity which must bind the laborers in capitalist nations and the peoples oppressed by imperialism). It therefore entails the solidarity of the revolutionary working-class parties, the communist parties. This solidarity naturally leaves intact each party's freedom of judgement and of action. It can no longer be said that it must be applied without exception, to all aspects of party activity. We ask that of no one, and no one can demand it of us . . .

France Nouvelle, March 29, 1976.

29　Georges Marchais, press conference, *L'Humanité*, 1976

A Great Solidarity

On the subject of relations among the communist and workers' parties, Georges Marchais recalled that the Twenty-Second Congress attempted to hide none of our differences with the CPSU and other parties on the problems of socialist democracy and of their appraisal of the French government's foreign policy. There are and, as we have said, it is normal to have, natural differences among our parties, which are the product of the working-class struggles. Each people has its own communist party, with its own traditions and peculiarities. We are, ourselves, no exception to that. That said, there is great solidarity among our parties. We are struggling for common ideals. We know that the solidarity of our battles is a necessary condition for progress toward peaceful coexistence, peace and socialism. Our Congress confirmed its devotion to proletarian internationalism, which is the solidarity of the world's laborers for socialism.

When a journalist asked him what he thought of 'eurocommunism,' Georges Marchais replied that it was a matter of a formula used by certain journals.

The truth is that there are affinities among French and Italian communists, there are affinities among communist parties – if not, the PCF would not be taking part in the preparations of the Conference of European Communist Parties. But there is absolutely no possibility of returning to an international organization of communist parties, at a worldwide or at a European or regional level. The nature of relations among communist and workers' parties is clearly defined. They are independent and their meetings, bilateral or multilateral, are arranged in the respect of this equality. There undoubtedly remains much to be done to make these occasions more spontaneous, more alive, but we have done much to make them what they are now . . .

L'Humanité, June 10, 1976, p. 6.

The Problem of Dissent

30　Remarks of Marchais in dialogue with Almarik, Antenne 2, 1977

The Twenty-Second Congress of the French Communist Party has very clearly recalled that for us liberty is indivisible and that we could not agree to arrest, imprisonment or apprehension of any form, that is carried out in any socialist country, the Soviet Union included, against dissenters. This is the reason why the PCF has participated in a meeting organized in Paris for the liberation of Plioutchtch. We consider socialism to be our business, to be the business of all communist and workers' parties and when, in any socialist countries, there are attitudes that wrong our ideal, we have a duty to act, which is what we are doing.

For us liberty is indivisible; it must not only be defended when it is threatened in socialist countries, it must also be defended in capitalist countries. I went to Vietnam and I saw a country crushed by bombs. The American leaders do not seem to me to be particularly qualified to defend liberty and the right of people to self-determination. Liberty must be everywhere defended, but without interference in domestic affairs. It is up to each people to give themselves the social regime of their choice. To defend the ideal of socialism everywhere is the business of everyone, but without interference in the domestic affairs of these people.

We are, therefore, for liberty, for democracy, for

the right of expression, but for us the fight for liberty of expression is hardly contradictory with the fight for détente, for peaceful coexistence. I consider that it would be dangerous to oppose the fight for liberty to the fight for détente and peaceful coexistence. We must not go back to the politics of cold war, and everything must be done to prevent war. We must lead the two struggles on an equal par. I must say that in so much as the problems of peaceful coexistence and international détente are concerned, we have no reproach against the policy of the Soviet Union.

Le Monde, February 24, 1977, p. 6.

SPANISH Communist Party: Diversity and Unity – the Frontiers of Internationalism

Titoism

1 Communiqué of the Political Bureau of the PCE, 1948

The Political Bureau of the Communist Party of Spain met on July 1 to examine the resolution by the Information Bureau of the Communist Parties on the situation of the Communist Party of Yugoslavia.

The Political Bureau has unanimously decided to approve the resolution and demonstrate its complete identification with the appraisal which it makes of the situation in the Communist Party of Yugoslavia, and with the critique of the grave mistakes committed by the Central Committee of this party.

The Political Bureau of the Communist Party of Spain, sure that it is interpreting the sentiment and will of all the members of the party, expresses its thanks to the brother parties in the resolution, for the considerable support which the resolution brings to the consolidation and development of an international communist front, the triumph of the cause of peace, democracy and socialism. These thanks are directed very particularly to the Bolshevik Communist Party of the USSR, the great party of Lenin and Stalin, which on this occasion, as on earlier occasions, has given the most conclusive evidence of its clarity of perception, its firmness and vigilance which fill its glorious history and life.

Nuestra Bandera, no. 28 (June–July 1948), p. 473.

2 Manuel Azcárate, 'Comrade Tito's trip to the USSR,' 1956

The results of comrade Tito's trip to the USSR, at the head of a delegation of the government and of the Union of Communists of Yugoslavia, have been received with satisfaction and enthusiasm by workers and progressive forces. These results have brought about manifestations of anger and discontent in more reactionary circles of the USA and other nations. Such attitudes can surprise nobody, for the trip constitutes an international event of great magnitude, which reinforces the cause of peace and progress in the world, and obstructs, in no small measure, the plans of monopolist groups interested in international tension and the Cold War.

Mundo Obrero (June 1956), p. 6.

3 Resolution of the Central Committee of the PCE, 1956

The Central Committee of the Communist Party expresses to the League of Yugoslavian Communists its regret for the rupture of the bonds which existed between them until 1948. It believes that it was a mistake to have formally accepted the resolution of the Cominform; unjust because of its content and incorrect in its reasoning. The Communist Party of Spain wishes to re-establish its fraternal bonds with the Yugoslavian communists.

Central Committee Plenum, Spanish Communist Party document, 1956, p. 65.

4 Dolores Ibarruri's speech at the Central Committee Plenum, 1958

We face a violent, ideological struggle against Marxism–Leninism, in which imperialism mobilizes its many agencies.

Imperialism has found a valuable reinforcement in the neo-revisionism represented by the positions of the Communist League of Yugoslavia.

Objectively the Communist League of Yugoslavia has placed itself, principally since its last Congress, in the front ranks of the ideological struggle against Marxism–Leninism.

Its positions are particularly obnoxious in as much as they are presented, not as an open rupture with Marxism–Leninism, but as its development and application in the unique conditions in Yugoslavia.

In reality that supposed development is nothing other than the negation of fundamental principles of Marxism–Leninism, whose correctness is confirmed by all the development of the Soviet Union and the socialist camp.

The starting point of the ideological aberrations of the Communist League of Yugoslavia is in the idea that an isolated country, small and economically backward, can construct socialism on the fringes of the socialist camp and even with the help of imperialism, in the idea that a socialist country can be neutral in the struggle between socialism and imperialism.

For us it is unquestionable that if Tito receives American aid, especially when Yugoslavia appears to be less bound to the socialist camp, it is because imperialism, in exchange for this aid, plans to be able to use it as a wedge against the unity of the socialist camp and the world communist movement. The imperialists do not fail to notice the fact that the Communist League of Yugoslavia, with its neo-revisionist positions, has become an important center of the struggle against Marxism–Leninism, against the communist and workers' parties, and primarily against the Communist Party of the Soviet Union, whose example and experience inspire the world communist movement. And this is, of course, what the imperialists aid and what they are prepared to pay for: not the construction of socialism, not Yugoslavia's neutrality and independence which is reasonable to assume; they would obliterate these with the greatest pleasure at the first opportunity.

The Soviet Union and the world communist movement corrected the errors committed in the past in relation to Yugoslavia. The leaders of the Communist Party of the Soviet Union, leaders of the Communist Party of China and, in general, of all the communist parties, did all they could do to improve relations, to facilitate the reincorporation of the Communist League of Yugoslavia to the bosom of the great family of the communist and socialist camp, to put an end to a division from which only imperialism could reap profit.

But the Yugoslavian leaders, instead of responding to the attitude of the rest of the communist parties, believed that the movement's attitude meant an acceptance of erroneous positions. The arrogance, vanity and pride of the leaders of the League of Communists of Yugoslavia grew to the point where, instead of examining and correcting their errors, they intensified their divisionist effort, making an effort to introduce their opinions in the communist movement with methods foreign to the character which relations between communist parties and socialist states should have. It is clear that their activity has been and is addressed toward weakening the unity of the socialist camp and of the communist movement . . .

Negating the necessity of a solid ideological and political unity of the socialist camp and the communist movement, the Yugoslavian leaders tend to weaken the international solidarity of the proletariat . . .

The Communist League of Yugoslavia takes as its own the old reformist conceptions of the spontaneous transformation of capitalism to socialism, without revolution and without the dictatorship of the proletariat. It is well known where those conceptions have led elsewhere, and what fruits they have given to the working class and the working masses. It will suffice to remember that, if the working class has acquired power in numerous countries, it has not been guided by social democratic reformism, but by the struggle against reformism and for the flag of Marxism–Leninism.

Spanish Communist Party document, 1958, pp. 82–4.

5   Manuel Delicado, 'Socialist Yugoslavia,' 1970

Yugoslavia has been and continues to be spoken of, although not always with justice. There was a time when the socialist character of its regime was denied, because its leaders, when the revolution had triumphed, adopted their own route in order to establish socialism, the route which in their judgement corresponded to the historic, political, economic and social peculiarities of their peoples. Those judgements ended, because they were fallacious, and the truth was seen. Yugoslavia is integrated into the fourteen states which today comprise the camp of socialist countries, as has been acknowledged by the Conference of Communist and Workers' Parties held in Moscow in June of 1969.

Yugoslavia moves forward in all spheres of life. And it does so with a rapid, firm and sure rhythm, overcoming the immense backwardness inherited from capitalism to be transformed, thanks to the socialist revolution, from a country which was predominantly agrarian to an industrialized one. Many Yugoslavian industrial enterprises can already be compared to their equivalents in the capitalist countries of Europe.

The Federal Socialist Republic of Yugoslavia is a state based on the power of the working people. All the riches and means of production are social property. The nation can consider itself as a managerial unity. The citizen's right to self-management in all economic, social, cultural, municipal activities, etc., is inalienable. Throughout the self-management system the citizens participate in the preservation of socialist legality, individual liberties, the correct working of municipal services, etc. The continuous development of direct democracy assures the political participation of the workers on all levels of the state organization, in the enterprises, municipalities, republics, and in the federation, where their respective representatives are those who are elected by secret vote.

The Yugoslavian system of self-management is an experience worthy of being studied deeply.

It is also worth while to explore other basic aspects of the political-social system of Yugoslavia and the application of the principle of socialist democracy. In Yugoslavia censorship of the press or of other means of information does not exist. The citizens have full liberty to expound their ideas without fear. And experience confirms that criticism which is constructive, public and at the heart of the organization is a positive factor in the construction of socialism.

Mundo Obrero, no. 12 (June 27, 1970), p. 7.

The Hungarian Rebellion

6 Santiago Carrillo, 'Following the latest international events. Redoubling the struggle in the ideological field,' 1957

The counter-revolutionary insurrection in Hungary and the imperialist military aggression against Egypt have shown the antagonism existing between imperialism and socialism, between imperialism and national liberation. In both conflicts the principal motive force has been this antagonism.

The errors of the old leadership of the Hungarian Communist Party are known. In essence they consist in not having taken into account the peculiarities of the development of socialism in Hungary, in having copied in a mechanical fashion certain aspects of the Soviet experience. This is more evident after 1948. It made the Hungarian leaders come into conflict with the situation existing in their country, and use bureaucratic and anti-democratic methods of rule . . .

And this is what happened in Hungary. One part of the militants of the Workers' Party led the opposition out of the limits of the party; to the public road, 'communist' opposition and counter-revolutionary opposition appearing confused (*confounding* one for the other) before the people. All enemies of the regime of popular democracy were able to criticize and systematically denigrate the regime and the party, taking cover behind the 'communist' opposition. The attitude of this 'communist' opposition gave a *legal* political center to the counter-revolution: the Pëtoefi circle, which uncovered other clandestine centers . . .

This is also a great lesson for the communists of all nations. He who – including, as a point of reference, partly justified criticisms – settles his differences outside the party loses all justification and authority: notwithstanding his intentions, from that moment he no longer fights these or those given errors, but the party itself, and he aids its enemies. In countries where there exists a dictatorship of the proletariat, such elements, as is proven by historical experiences, are themselves converted into points of convergence for all counter-revolutionary forces: into a most grave danger to the revolution. From that moment, weakness in dealing with them is weakness in the face of counter-revolution. One of the most inexplicable phenomena in Hungary has been the unexpected step from arbitrariness and bureaucratism to that *laissez-faire* enjoyed by those who confronted the party and the regime.

. . . Imperialist ideologies are trying to introduce into the workers' movement the concept of 'national communism.' The primary characteristic of this so-called 'national communism' is militant anti-Sovietism and struggle against proletarian internationalism and the communist parties that defend this principle. It is a weapon against the worldwide socialist system, to provoke its disintegration and its decomposition; a weapon to divide the worldwide communist and workers' movement.

The so-called 'national communism' does not materially exist in any place, because an anti-Soviet and anti-communist 'communism' cannot exist. But the imperialists thus baptize any manifestations of bourgeois chauvinism in the ranks of the revolutionary movement. Manifestations of chauvinism or other erroneous conceptions can be and have been produced. If in some party deviations from the ideology of Marxism—Leninism take form, develop and, instead of being corrected, eventually crystallize and characterize a policy, that party — if correction does not suddenly occur — can move away from communism; in no case can it form a *special* current within the communist movement.

The unity of the worldwide communist and workers' movement, whatever the forms it may take in each situation, must be made around the communist parties, which are realizing socialism, which for given historical reasons are found at the head of the worldwide workers' movement. And most particularly around the Communist Party of the Soviet Union which brings together extraordinary revolutionary, practical and theoretical experience. This role of the Communist Party of the Soviet Union in the international communist and workers' movement is based on the meaning of the struggle of the Bolshevik Party, the great socialist October Revolution, the construction of the first socialist state in the world, and the creation of the international socialist system, around the Soviet Union. This role is a historical reality. The fact that a dogmatic position should not be taken with respect to the opinions, attitudes and experiences of the Communist Party of the Soviet Union, considering anything coming from it as revealed truth, the fact that one is obliged to maintain a Marxist attitude, conscious and reasoning before facts and ideas, come from whom they may, does not alter that historic reality: the orienting, guiding role of the Communist Party of the Soviet Union, and, by its side, of the communist parties of the socialist countries which can be placed as an example of the application of Marxism—Leninism, in the heart of the international worker and communist movement. This role is exercised on a general, ideological level, and does not affect the autonomy of each communist party in the elaboration of its own national road toward socialism. Nor does it affect the right of each party, if it deems it necessary, to make friendly and constructive criticism with respect to any given aspects of the policy of the Communist Party of the Soviet Union or that of any of the other parties alluded to.

To go by another road, the road of negating the role of the USSR and the Communist Party of the Soviet Union, of negating the role of the communist parties of the socialist countries as guides and leaders of the international worker and communist movement, would be tantamount to moving away from the class position of the proletariat, of the positions of Marxism—Leninism . . .

Mundo Obrero (January 1957), pp. 3–4.

Stalinism and De-Stalinization

7   Editorial, 'Stalin is today's Lenin,' *Nuestra Bandera*, 1949

The twenty-first of December of this year is the seventieth anniversary of the birth of J. V. Stalin, leader, master and guide of the Communist Party of the Soviet people, of the revolutionary workers of all countries, of the progressive and democratic forces of the whole world. Around this memorable anniversary, there has surged forth in all corners of the earth a true clamor of admiration, respect and affection for comrade Stalin, for the profound leader, whose genius has been epoch-making in the history of the USSR and in the history of the international revolutionary movement . . .

In the course of this epoch, which extends from the establishment of socialism in the USSR to the step to communism, the gigantic figure of comrade Stalin raises itself as a banner in history, marking the road of liberation for the proletariat . . .

The objective conditions of the construction of socialism were complex and difficult. The agrarian and backward country was destroyed by the devastating fire of imperialist war, of civil war and of the first military aggression of international capitalism against socialism. It was necessary to build the socialist society under circumstances of the capitalist curtain and a bloody class struggle. And socialism has been gloriously constructed under the leadership of the great Stalin.

Following this Stalinist line of victory, the Soviet people understood the industrialization of the country, laying the economic bases of socialism in the USSR . . .

The great changes which occurred in the USSR were molded in the Stalinist constitution, the constitution of the most extensive democracy that history had ever known, the Soviet democracy, socialist democracy, based on the non-existence of antagonistic classes, on the obliteration of the exploitation of man by man. The constitution of the USSR, which the people call 'Stalin's Constitution,' is the battle flag of oppressed peoples, the triumphant standard of socialism.

In all of Stalin's work the importance of criticism and self-criticism in the party is highlighted . . .

The Stalinist doctrine of creative Marxism guides communists of all countries in the application of Marxism–Leninism–Stalinism, beginning with the concrete conditions of each country's situation . . .

Basing himself on the knowledge of the ways of war, comrade Stalin was able to foresee scientifically the defeat of Hitler's Germany and to establish the factors which contributed to the victory of the Soviet people.

More than once comrade Stalin warned the aggressors that in unleashing a new war against the USSR they would be defeated; that the war would result in the fragmentation of the links of the capitalist chain. The events of the Second World War fully confirmed Stalin's scientific predictions.

Comrade Stalin foretold the defeat of imperialism in China, the victory of the Chinese people and the character of the new regime . . .

Because of this, in their victorious march toward socialism the communist parties and the peoples of the people's democracies are inspired by the great work of comrade Stalin. Because of this, the workers of the whole world, the peoples oppressed by imperialism, the millions of democrats and progressive men who continue to fight against war, for peace and democracy, see in comrade Stalin the Lenin of our times, the leader and master, the guide of all of humanity, which inexorably moves forward on the trail of communism which the Stalinist genius illuminates.

Nuestra Bandera, no. 2 (December 1949).

8 Santiago Carrillo's speech at the Central Committee, August 1956

The Twentieth Congress of the CPSU has been an event of great importance, not only for the Soviet Union, but for all the communist parties of the world, for the whole socialist movement. The Twentieth Congress has made a very valuable theoretical contribution to the communist movement and the working world.

The Twentieth Congress has evaluated the extraordinary successes of socialist development in the USSR. The superiority of the socialist system over the capitalist system has been demonstrated, thanks to the experience of the first great socialist revolution in the world . . .

The resolution of June 30 of the CPSU elaborates the analysis of the historic circumstances in which such triumphs have been achieved: through a cruel class struggle against the Russian bourgeoisie, sustained by imperialism and world reaction, in which the dilemma 'who would defeat whom,' who would definitely dominate, was posed with extreme violence for many years . . .

The working class and the Soviet people have found themselves obliged to defend their revolution in a bloody struggle, without clemency, for long years . . .

The tragedy of Stalin has consisted in the fact that some features of his character and the disproportionate idea of his merits, which led him to be convinced of his infallibility, created a situation in which certain extreme measures, which were provisionally justified and were accepted by the people, were prolonged when they were no longer needed, and, instead of striking a blow against the counter-revolutionary forces, they struck a blow against the party and against Soviet democracy.

On the other hand, but with the same passion as the Russian worker, we communists of all the world have defended the great October Socialist Revolution, and defeat of Soviet power would have meant a step backwards in history, of catastrophic consequences for the working class and the popular masses. If the Russian revolution had been defeated, the workers' and democratic movement would have been literally crushed by the weight of world capitalism. The duty of the international proletariat and of all progressive men was to sustain and consolidate that great victory with all their efforts. Because of this, when faced with the enemies of the October Revolution and Soviet power, we engaged in an uncompromising battle. In the cause of this battle we have fallen into the error of confusing honest critics of good faith with simple enemies. For many years we identified the defense of Stalin, attacked since Lenin's death by all the enemies of the Russian revolution, with the defense of the revolution; and in large part, it was so in reality.

The characteristics of this recently ended period and the exceptional harshness of the struggle were able to create an objective climate propitious for the development of the cult of the personality of Stalin, as well as those same successes, precisely because those successes were achieved at a high price . . .

The cult of personality has had negative effects on the whole revolutionary movement. In general, the cult of personality led to exaggerating the role of personalities in the revolutionary movement and the lessening of the role of the masses, braking their activity; to employing non-collective leadership methods, to the weakening of criticism and self-criticism, to the introduction of dogmatism on questions of doctrine and to the stagnation of the evolution of communist theory precisely in a period of great change, in which such an evolution was of vital importance. For these reasons the attitude of the Soviet comrades constitutes a great aid to all the whole communist and workers' movement . . .

We did not realize that in the last part of his life Stalin, abusing the enormous powers which he possessed, had concentrated a disproportionate power in his hands, placing himself above the party and its leading agencies, above the agencies of the Soviet state, committing arbitrariness and injustices. We saw, above all, the great successes of the establishment of socialism in the USSR, successes which were submitted to their baptism of fire during the anti-Hitler war.

In our time it is the working class, it is the peoples, led by their communist parties, who are the authors of great social and political transformation, the creators of the new classless socialist society. No man, no matter how ingenious he may be, is capable of carrying out what only the people, with their immense energies, can realize. No man, no matter how great his knowledge may be, can replace the collective knowledge of the party, the vanguard of the ascendant classes . . .

The cult of personality cannot seriously be explained without taking into account the characteristics of the historic period in which it triumphed and the characteristics of the leadership of the dictatorship of the proletariat. Our leaders must counteract the tendencies to resolve state problems administratively and bureaucratically, in order to make the state in all cases an agency narrowly controlled by the masses. Neither the communists, nor any person who reasons objectively, can find it strange that in the course of the world's first socialist revolution errors and excesses have been committed. What is important is to correct them and to analyze their causes, in order to prevent them from being repeated . . .

Spanish Communist Party document, 1956, pp. 3–10.

9 Resolution of the Central Committee of the PCE, August 1956

The Plenum has examined the questions regarding the cult of the personality of Stalin and its serious consequences. The Central Committee of the Communist Party of Spain greets the brave self-criticism of the Central Committee of the Communist Party of the Soviet Union and makes clear its complete agreement with the Central Committee's resolution on the elimination of the cult of personality and its consequences. In this resolution the objective and subjective factors which have birth to this detour of Marxism are analyzed profoundly, demonstrating that it is not a product of the socialist system – as the enemies of communism maliciously claim – but a result of concrete historic conditions, in conjunction with certain personal characteristics of Stalin. With the Marxist criticism of the cult of personality, the Communist Party of the Soviet Union has performed an invaluable service for the world communist movement and all humanity.

The Central Committee of the Communist Party of Spain believes that with its self-criticism of the cult of the personality of Stalin and its consequences, the Communist Party of the Soviet Union has shown once again its faithfulness to Marxist–Leninist principles. This exemplary behavior fosters respect and confidence of Spanish communists toward the CPSU; it invigorates proletarian internationalism and accelerates the peoples' march toward socialism.

Spanish Communist Party document, 1956, cf. pp. 63–5.

The Sino-Soviet Dispute

10   Resolution of the Central Committee of the PCE, November 1963

11   'Defense of the USSR against Chinese attacks,' Mundo Obrero, 1967

Peaceful coexistence does not have anything to do with relations among antagonistic classes in the interior of a country; it refers to the relations among states of oppressive social systems; it concerns the antagonism of class in the sphere of the states.

The maintenance and consolidation of peaceful coexistence require, on the one hand, a broad mobilization of the masses of nations, the intensification of the fight for liberation and for peace; on the other hand, agreements and compromises among socialist states and capitalist states.

The Treaty of Moscow addresses simply the suspension of the nuclear tests in the atmosphere, in space and under water . . .

Our Chinese comrades are condemning the treaty because it prevents the countries of the socialist camp from carrying out nuclear tests, and consequently from manufacturing atomic weaponry. Until now all the nations of the socialist camp felt defended by the nuclear bombs of the Soviets.

But the leaders of the People's Republic of China would rather independently manufacture thermonuclear weapons. One can understand that in the imperialist camp different powers fight to have nuclear weapons without worrying about the dangers of the proliferation of such weapons. In that field antagonistic contradictions exist. But the question cannot be posed in the same terms among the socialist countries. The socialist camp uses nuclear weapons to demand the respect of imperialism and to force it to abandon any inclination toward aggression against the peoples who have attained national liberation, avoiding war and defending revolution.

By calling for internal subversion in the USSR against comrade Khrushchev, the Central Committee of the CPSU and the USSR government, the CCP attacks the direction of the world communist and workers' movement. Its attempt at secession indicates that its international policy signifies a moving away from the socialist camp and a break with it.

Nuestra Bandera, no. 38 (March 1964), pp. 50–1.

Taking the simplest reasoning to its ultimate consequences, it would seem that the USSR is guilty of all the revenges and of all the errors suffered by or committed by the revolutionary forces in any place; that the USSR has to make for each people that people's revolution or war of liberation; that any party or progressive group is in the embarrassing situation of enjoying the right to push the USSR to a thermonuclear war in order to conclude such a party's own negotiations.

The propaganda of the Chinese leaders feeds such attitudes with the most delirious extravagance.

That same propaganda attacks the Soviets because they do not respond to Yankee aggression in Vietnam with a military offensive in Europe, or because they have not sent their troops to the Middle East. In the meantime the Maoist leaders are the main obstacle to Soviet volunteers fighting in Vietnam directly against the USA, and they themselves assume that they will enter in a war with the USA when they directly attack the Chinese territory . . . The Chinese leaders proclaim terrific revolutionary phrases; but at the hour of practice they are of an exquisite prudence.

We do not reproach the Chinese leaders for the prudence in their acts, when they avoid war with the USA or Great Britain, because a nuclear world war would not represent any advance of revolution, but simply a catastrophe. What amazes and scandalizes us is their demagoguery, their verbal fierceness, their calumny against the USSR that, although making an effort to avoid world war, does nothing to help the people who fight against imperialism. In Vietnam the Yankees are met with Soviet weapons produced by Soviet machinery. In Egypt, Syria and Iraq the weapons are also Russian, as is the Aswan Dam. And the weapons which keep guard over the Cuban revolution are also Russian.

The world revolution is not a chain of uninterrupted and accelerated successes, an escalation without reverses. Each people has to make its own revolution, fight its own fights, pay the price of its own victory. The Soviets did theirs in conditions more difficult than anyone else's. They know how to fight and suffer. They paid for their victory and for the victories of other peoples. Let us congratulate ourselves that the USSR is in a position to help others today. But let us not ask that it does what only we – that is to say, each country, each party – must do.

Mundo Obrero, no. 16 (July 1–15, 1967), p. 8.

12 From *Nuestra Bandera*, 1969

The declaration of March 29 of the Soviet government represents the only way to face and resolve the frontier problems between China and the USSR: negotiation.

No island on the Usuri, no meter of land, is worth one drop of Soviet or Chinese blood.

The Soviet Union and China are two great socialist powers, and because of that we refuse to enter into the political quagmire that could signify the unfolding of a war in which there would only be one winner: imperialism, particularly US imperialism.

We have pursued a policy of coexistence to avoid the horror of thermonuclear war with imperialism, and we find ourselves at the beginnings of what could be – we fully believe it will not be – a war among socialist powers.

In fact, we have intervened in the polemic to defend the positions of our party in this area, positions which coincided with, in many aspects, those of the CPSU and the greater number of the other communist parties.

We believe that our criticism of the document of the twenty-five points which was the ideological base of the Chinese campaign was just. Our defense of the policy of coexistence, of the diversity of ways and forms of revolution; our criticism of the cult of personality and revindication of the Twentieth Congress, the opposition to the establishment of a political directing center of the communist international movement and of China's pretense that this center be in Peking; these are a defense of a new unity of our movement fit for the present times, for the condemnation of all divisive tendencies against our party. From the evidence of these positions and from the interpretation of the so-called cultural revolution, not as such, but as a fight for the direction and control of the party and the state between two groups, we do not feel the necessity of changing anything fundamental.

It can be said that surrounding certain Chinese actions there is an odor of chauvinism, and that is always dangerous. But even in judging these attitudes we must keep in mind that in the past China has been dismembered, occupied, sacked during long years by imperialist powers; that an old civilization, a large country, a great intelligent and hard-working people knew forages of foreign oppression. That even today the imperialist powers have managed to isolate China from the organs of international relations; that the policy of isolating a power of 700 million people can explain, to a certain extent, the chauvinist reaction. Life has shown us that no one is free of these grave aberrations and deformations and that in a socialist society these can be overcome, through difficult and complicated processes. The USSR showed us this in the Twentieth Congress by denouncing the monstrous deformations introduced by Stalin in the direction of the CPSU and the Soviet state . . .

Nuestra Bandera, no. 61 (March–April 1969), pp. 62–5.

13 Santiago Carrillo's statement upon his return from China, 1971

Some ill-intentioned people insinuate that the Communist Party of Spain has changed its party line: before it was that of the Communist Party of the Soviet Union, now it is that of the Chinese Communist Party.

In effect these are the stories of ill-intentioned people. They reflect the idea of a party line coming from a central directory of the communist movement. It is true that in other times the CPSU carried out this role and that lively reminders of this idea still exist . . . But this idea was categorically overcome in the resolutions of the 1969 international conference and the consequences of these resolutions should be pursued until the end.

It can also be said that for a certain time the Communist Party of China appeared as a new center or party line, attempting to group the movement around itself. But the Chinese comrades loudly affirmed that it is not their intention to play this role nor to dictate policies to other parties, and that they fully respected the independence of these parties and supported equal relations. This has been completely confirmed in continued conversations with them in Peking.

Consequently the re-establishment of relations with the Chinese Communist Party does not signify that we change our center or party line. For the Communist Party of Spain there is no center other than its own Congress and Central Committee. There is no other guide than Marxism and Leninism, and the positions implied by these. They are fully developed theories which must be elaborated and applied to the specific realities of the Spanish revolution. After returning from Peking, we are still internationalists and independent, maybe even more so than before we undertook the journey.

The so-called Cultural Revolution was a political revolution. Our theory and practice until then – I refer to that of Marxism–Leninism – had not envisaged the possibility of political revolutions within socialism. We thought that only counter-revolutionaries could rise up against socialism. Without a doubt this contributed to the confusion caused by the Cultural Revolution.

For all that we have seen and heard, the Cultural Revolution has consolidated socialism in China; it has incorporated youth and enormous numbers of women into revolutionary tasks; it has aroused the combativeness, enthusiasm and revolutionary romanticism of the masses; it has spurred production.

The Cultural Revolution has broken the crystallization of bureaucratic structures; in certain ways it has re-established the control of the masses, enhancing the possibility of a critique by the masses and an invigoration of mass initiatives. It has imposed forms of socialism which correspond more to the specific reality of China.

Mundo Obrero, no. 23 (December 10, 1971), pp. 4–5.

14 Manuel Azcárate, 'Great progress in China,' 1978

It is not an exaggeration to say that we are assisting in a new phase in the advance of the Chinese toward socialism, a phase open toward the future, which is followed with interest by all the revolutionary and progressive forces.

I would like to call attention to some of the traits that seem to be most characteristic of the decisions adopted recently by the representatives of the Chinese people.

First of all, singling out China's far-reaching economic plans, by the end of the century China seeks to convert itself into a modern nation, similar to those states which are most advanced culturally and industrially. It is significant to note the realistic attitude with which the Chinese comrades recognize the relatively low level from which they must begin with their plans of economic development, but at the same time it is evident that a people of 800 million women and men, which has demonstrated on many historical occasions its capacity for sacrifice and creation, can realize in the next decades a really gigantic work, altering some of the essential elements of the international power correlation.

One of the new preoccupations seen in the definition of economic problems is the achievement of an elevation of popular consumption, an improvement in the standard of living.

I believe that these traits demonstrate the profound evolution, in which the Congress of the CCP of last summer was undoubtedly a fundamental phase of China's determination to overcome the sectarian, dogmatic attitudes which earlier led China to a certain isolation from the progressive currents.

Mundo Obrero (March 16–22, 1978), p. 23.

The Prague Spring

15 From *Mundo Obrero*, 1970

We are very sorry, but in the face of the expulsion of comrade Dubček from the ranks of the Communist Party of Czechoslovakia we cannot remain silent. If the military intervention of August 1968 had not occurred, and if what is happening now were not a result of that, no one would feel the need to put forth a proclamation on what may be formally considered today an internal affair of a brother party.

After the intervention in August 1968, Dubček and his team continued in their charges. Later, through a well-known mechanism, they were slowly eliminated, one after another, expelled. At the same time a gigantic purge was already taking place in which thousands of functionaries and hundreds of thousands of party members have been affected. The criterion of this purge, as far as is known, is one's attitude toward the intervention.

Dubček has committed no wrong other than refusing to acknowledge the correctness and the necessity of the intervention. He has bowed to his successive dismissals with discipline; he has accepted with the same discipline his banishment to the Embassy of Ankara. He has returned to Prague when he has been called.

He is judged and condemned for a 'crime' of opinion. No one can reproach him for not having bowed down with discipline to the decisions of the superior agencies, throughout their successive reorganizations.

According to the status of the communist parties it is not possible to expel a member because he is not in agreement with one decision or another, so long as he bows down and submits himself to party discipline. If even we clandestine communist parties apply this rule, how and for what reasons should those who are in power violate it? . . .

The present Czech leaders say that there will be no pre-fabricated trials like those in the 1950s. None the less a very dangerous mechanism of political repression has been put into gear, which may make the division in the communist movement more acute. Under these conditions, no trial by the positions approved by the agencies of the party in the first half of 1968, or by documents published in the legal Czechoslovakian press in that period, would be justified. That would mean the return to the methods repeatedly condemned by the Twentieth Congress and by the international communist movement.

We all want the Czechoslovakian crisis to be resolved satisfactorily through the consolidation of socialism, but socialism without the decided support of the working masses is unimaginable. Because of this Dubček, expelled, continues to be a hope for the socialist future of Czechoslovakia.

The opinion of Spanish communists on this question coincides with that which has already been publicly expressed by Italian and English communists, among others.

Mundo Obrero, no. 13 (July 12, 1970), p. 3.

16 'Our reply to Enrique Lister,' *Mundo Obrero*, 1970

The party's attitude towards the military intervention in Czechoslovakia created the problems of Eduardo Garcia and Augustin Gomez. Lister, who had initially agreed with the party's position, now declares himself against it, and for intervention. If the party changed its attitude towards the problem of Czechoslovakia, then all the attacks and accusations of anti-societism, etc., would cease. However, the party's position cannot change because such a change would imply a betrayal of all its policies.

We want the state which will exist during the transition stage from capitalism to communism, the dictatorship of the proletariat, in our country to be a democracy 'a million times more democratic than the most democratic of the bourgeois republics,' as Lenin used to say. How could we support Novotny's regime, which politically was the dictatorship of a group over the party, over the proletariat and the whole of the people? . . .

We believe, in accordance with declarations of the CPSU and the government of the USSR, that the relationships among socialist countries should be carried out on the basis of fraternal equality, non-intervention in the internal affairs of another country, and effective respect for the integrity, independence and sovereignty of each people. How can we agree with the military intervention of one socialist country into another with the aim of making the latter party change a political line independently elaborated by its own communist party and the imposition of a new line upon it?

We acknowledge the political risks implied in the 'new way' stated in Czechoslovakia in January 1968. We did not, and we do not, agree with all its formulations and projects. However, such a disagreement is necessary and just. The direction of the Czechoslovakian Communist Party needed help from the other parties, which should have given it through fraternal criticism of its mistakes in the search for the correct way. But the military intervention was of extreme gravity and could cause much more serious diseases than those it sought to prevent. Experience has proven us right. Our party remains in opposition to the intervention.

Mundo Obrero, no. 19 (November 19, 1970), p. 11.

17 Manuel Azcárate, 'Czechoslovakia, yesterday and today,' 1978

This is the tenth anniversary of the change which occurred in Czechoslovakia and which then led to the blossoming of socialism, known as the 'Prague Spring.' ...

A significant aspect of the Czechoslovakian phenomenon of 1968 is that the change occurred from within the Communist Party; that the renewing current born in the party was molded in the bosom of its Central Committee and led to a change of leadership, as manifested in the naming of Dubček as secretary general.

Czechoslovakia was the only one of the countries which destroyed its capitalist structure at the end of the Second World War that had a modern industrial capacity. And it is impossible not to establish a relationship between that fact and the renovating process of socialism in the 'Prague Spring.' The industrially advanced economic basis, and its super-structural consequences, accentuated, much more than in other cases, the need for a democratic political structure in socialist society. Because of that, the events of the first half of 1968 in Czechoslovakia, brutally interrupted by the military intervention of the Soviet Union and other countries of the Warsaw Pact, represent perhaps one of the most important periods, on a historic level, of the process of the advance toward socialism.

But it does not suffice now to emphasize the value which we place on the Czechoslovakian experience of those times. Because the results of the military intervention continue to weigh tragically on the destinies of the country, the problem of Czechoslovakia remains open. The fact is that some of the best representatives of communism in Czechoslovakia are, at the least, radically eliminated from all political life and condemned to personal situations which are often intolerable.

Recently a 'white book' on the situation in Czechoslovakia was published which allows one to become acquainted with some of the most scandalous aspects of the persecution, such as that against people who signed the Letter of the 77.

Nuestra Bandera, no. 90 (1978), p.51.

The Problem of Dissent

18 Interview with Santiago Carrillo, *Nuestra Bandera*, **1966**

QUESTION: What do you think of the trial in the Soviet Union against Siniavski and Daniel?
ANSWER: One can be forever against that trial, without abandoning one's defense of the Soviet Union.

In all my training as a revolutionary militant, respect and love for the Soviet Union, admiration for the great October Socialist Revolution, have been an essential part. I belong to that generation which defended Madrid in 1936. By this I wish to indicate how much I feel inclined to make a defense of the Soviet Union; to what point I am repelled by criticisms of the Soviets when they are not well founded and serious.

But in the case of Siniavski and Daniel my impression is that the laws being applied are more in harmony with the period of the dictatorship of the proletariat than with that of the state of all the people. Thus the sentence gives the impression of a sharpening of the class struggle, of violence in domestic relations, which does not exist, which was overcome many years ago in the Soviet Union.

I will add that neither as persons nor as writers do they merit the fame which their trial has given them in the West.

To that end the worries of those who, sincerely or through manipulation, say that they are afraid that tomorrow in Spain we will do the same with those who do not feel the same way as the communists, lack sense.

Socialism has already triumphed in the Soviet Union, along a path of tests and difficulties, truly unique, which are very little like those which socialism will probably find in Spain.

The first socialist revolution in the world was victorious in a country with centuries of autocratic tradition, in struggle against all the powers of the earth, against all political parties, as a result of a very deep revolutionary crisis created by imperialist war, the collapse of the secular regime, misery and hunger, and the accumulation of inter-imperialist contradictions. The stubbornness, the implacability of the dictatorship of the proleteriat in Russia apart from the excesses of the Stalinist period, has to be necessarily much greater than in other countries.

The revolution will triumph in Spain with fewer enemies and more defenders, because the world has changed radically since 1917 and it has changed precisely because of the great Russian revolution, because of all the pains and sufferings which the Russian proletariat and people and their guide, the Communist Party, have borne while acting as the vanguard of the world revolution.

Socialism will surely triumph in Spain along other roads, without the necessity of resorting to such harsh methods, with a much broader and more positive consensus of the majority of the country, and, precisely, as a result of that consensus, with the collaboration and participation of many political groups...

These differences between the route to socialism which we foresee for Spain and those followed in other countries do not mean any condemnation of the others on our part. Those who, when speaking of new routes, criticize or condemn the CPSU's path, for example – I am not referring, naturally, to the negative phenomena related to Stalin – are charlatans and vulgar opportunists. Because of the fact that the CPSU successfully followed its route, is it the only one which is correct and possible? Because the USSR has sustained the revolutionary forces of the whole world, other revolutions have been able to triumph along different routes and today *we* may set ourselves the task of following that path which seems to us to be most fit for the concrete historic conditions of our country.

Nuestra Bandera (February–March 1966), pp.15–17.

19   From *Mundo Obrero*, 1978

The trials of Anatoly Schransky in Moscow and Alexander Ginsberg in Kaluga have still not ended. We do not know if a sentence has been handed down, or its gravity. Nevertheless there are already several aspects of those trials which cannot go without comment. The accused being held incommunicado for long months and the lack of publicity of the development of the judicial sessions (since the information from the news agency Tass does not make one forget that the Western press and the public in general have not had access to the rooms where the trials have been proceeding) are added in this case to even more serious facts, such as the fact that the

accused have not been able to freely choose their defense attorneys.

An accusation as serious as that of treason, which according to Soviet legislation can be punished by the death sentence, requires a trial with all, absolutely all, guarantees of respect for human rights. And this must be done not only in a generic form on the state level, but concretely on the level of individual rights which, aside from the commitment contracted by signing different international agreements, must constitute common practice in a socialist society.

To protest, as we have done, does not mean participation in any orchestrated campaign. It simply means that the Spanish workers have a concept of socialism in which socialism and democratic liberties are consubstantial. If they are absent, especially in something as serious as the judicial system, one cannot speak of true socialism.

Mundo Obrero (July 13–19, 1978), p.14.

20   'The inevitable transformation of Spain into a democratic country,' *Mundo Obrero*, 1974

. . . The experience of Portugal shows that it is possible for a change in regime to take place in a few hours and without serious disruptions. Of course in Spain the change could be even less convulsive than it has been in Portugal. We who fought the Civil War, as well as the present generation, have an experience which immunized us against any attempt to make a position extreme. On the other hand, the economic structures of Spain are more solid than Portugal's. Spain is also a country where, even underground, there are forces belonging to the left, the center and even the right. This is to say, there are possibilities of a change with broad participation, of a democratic change. There are in Spain possibilities which did not exist in Portugal.

Mundo Obrero, no. 11 (April 6, 1974), pp. 1–2.

21 Santiago Carrillo, 'Portugal's Spring and its echoes in Spain,' 1974

The fragrances of the Portuguese Spring enter Spain. In two weeks the press has carried out a legal campaign for freedom. The size of such a campaign would have never been possible with the means of our illegal media. It is easy to imagine that, when reading it, hundreds, thousands of Spanish people have rubbed their eyes with the surprise of one who awakens after a long sleep and understood that it is sunrise in Spain.

Those tens, those hundreds and thousands, are ready to join the workers' popular struggle if our organizations, if the platforms of the democratic forces, are capable of reaching them.

We have to understand immediately that new powerful forces lean toward our side, toward the side of liberty and democracy. It is not enough to welcome them with open arms. We must go towards them to join them and mobilize them with the vanguard which has already been fighting . . .

Those who do not understand that it is necessary to proceed with all the allies who appear are sometimes almost not authentic communists and authentic, conscious revolutionaries. We have no right to doubt the sincerity of the majority; and even if some of them are motivated by mere opportunism, it would be an enormous mistake not to offer them the possibility of helping us to expand the mass struggle, of making it more alert and decisive, of conquering new 'zones of liberty' to get closer to the elimination of the dictatorship.

War against sectarianism, against political insensibility and torpitude, against easy phrases, against the 'revolutionary aristocratism'! – this should be the attitude of every communist and conscious revolutionary.

We must go towards the masses; it is necessary to set up covenants with the people who can help us, in some way or another, to mobilize the masses without hesitation or fear!

Given the reality of Spain today, it is the working class, the people, who by means of general political and national strikes can play the leading role in bringing about change – under the condition of obtaining a broad national convergence on the primary democratic goals. Precisely such an element as the workers' and popular struggle against an oppressive regime, against misery and corruption, is what can make the army realize the need not to oppose the popular and national will and to coincide somehow with it . . .

The Portuguese Spring has opened the windows of our country to the air of liberty. We must use with courage the experience of our brother country, which modifies the face of the legal press. We must resolutely join with the new forces which such an example elicits and promotes. The party must grow, both politically and organically, and fulfill its vanguard role, precisely by its ability to understand and use what is new in the present situation.

In Spain, a country already taught by the horrors of a civil war, the change might be even more peaceful, if the Francoist policy of concentration of power does not impede it.

It is a step we must take immediately – toward the masses, toward the expansion of the struggle, toward covenant and convergence, with courage, boldness and flexibility. In doing so, freedom will triumph.

Mundo Obrero (May 23, 1974), pp. 1–3.

Proletarian Internationalism

22 From *Mundo Obrero*, 1954

Having established socialism, the Soviet people, guided by their great Communist Party, begin the gradual steps toward communism. And the steps toward communism require not only a gigantic development of production, not only the creation of the necessary material and technical base, but a cultural blossoming that will ensure for the citizens the full development of their physical and spiritual aptitudes . . .

Throughout our struggle, the aid of the USSR to our people, the Spanish democracy, has been enormous and permanent.

During our war they aided us with weapons and through various means to defend Spanish independence and liberty. After having undone the Hitlerian coalition, the USSR helped us to reclaim practical measures against Franco, which, had they been adopted (it was mainly the Yankee imperialists who impeded them), would have decisively helped the Spanish people to liberate itself from Francoism.

Today they aid us with their successes, each one of which weakens Francoism and Franco. They aid us with the triumphant achievement of the ideas of Marxism-Leninism which saturate the consciences of innumerable Spanish men and women, giving them direction and strength. The greater combativeness and confidence which is shown by the working class and the popular masses, the revolutionary zeal which manifests itself in them and in numerous intellectuals owes much – much more than it seems at first glance! – to the existence of the USSR and the instructive effect of its successes and teachings.

Because of this, upon saluting the October Socialist Revolution in its thirty-seventh anniversary, the workers and advanced men of Spain salute the highest pinnacle of history, a victory for all of humanity and a victory for themselves.

Mundo Obrero, no. 24 (November 15, 1954), p. 6.

23   Dolores Ibarruri's speech at the Central Committee of the PCE, 1958

The division of the world into two social systems and the inevitable struggle between them greatly influences the entire world situation, including that of Spain.

In this struggle the socialist camp is solidly united. Among the peoples that comprise it, there do not exist, nor is there reason for them to exist, antagonistic contradictions; their interests coincide, their relations are based on the principles of socialist internationalism.

At its side, closing the ranks, are the forces of the vanguard of the world proletariat, the communist and workers' parties, the progressive working masses.

The center and leader of the socialist camp is the Soviet Union, the Communist Party of the USSR, whose experience is the richest source of inspiration, not only for the communist parties and the peoples of the socialist camp, but also for the entire international communist movement.

There is something, however, about which the imperialists have always agreed. This is the savage hate toward the Soviet Union, the first country that put an end to capitalist exploitation and that broke the chains of imperialist oppression; the hate toward the socialist camp, whose successes are a strong stimulus for all peoples in the struggle for peace, democracy and national independence...

Spanish Communist Party document, 1958, pp. 80–1.

24   Central Committee declaration, 1959

...The cause of the working class in our country is a fundamentally national cause; but at the same time it is closely tied to the cause of the proletarians of all countries.

The Soviet Union and the socialist countries do not need bases in Spain, nor do they intend to create in our country, nor in any country, trusts or monopolies; the Soviet Union and the socialist countries do not at all try to interfere in the internal politics of Spain. The socialist nature of their regimes precludes a possibility of this sort.

We communists do not receive 'orders from Moscow' because Moscow does not give orders as do the imperialists of New York or London to their servants.

The policy of the Communist Party of Spain, as that of any communist party, is elaborated by its members, without any foreign intervention, which is not to say that the communist parties do not learn from the experience of the communist movement and of the world revolutionary movement and do not take advantage of it to abet their own struggle.

What all the comunist parties and the Communist Party of the Soviet Union have in common is our Marxist-Leninist theory, the struggle for the abolition of capitalist exploitation, for socialism and for peace. Proletarian internationalism is what there is in common.

No accusation, no slander, will make us deviate from the path of proletarian internationalism, of friendship and fraternal unity with the communist parties. Our internationalism is a guarantee of our national policy; it is a guarantee that the communist party will never sell Spain to the foreign capitalists, will not estrange national sovereignty of independence, will fight for the moral and material enhancement of our fatherland, freeing it from the domination of the reactionary classes that mortgage independence and sovereignty and hold back its development.

Spanish Communist Party document, 1959, p. 98.

25 'Proletarian internationalism, relations between communist parties, unity', *Nuestra Bandera*, 1963

. . . The defense of the socialist sphere is our first internationalist duty. But how is it possible to compare 'socialist sphere' and 'Soviet Union,' and not believe that the defense of the Soviet Union logically continues to be our first internationalist duty? It cannot be denied that within the socialist sphere the Soviet Union plays a particular vanguard role. The responsibility for the defense and reinforcement of the socialist sphere falls primarily on the Soviet Union. When it is necessary to defend Cuba, who is in the front line? The USSR. When it is necessary to stop aggression against Egypt, who takes the initiative to do so? The USSR. When it is necessary to crush counter-revolution in Hungary, who directly lends a hand to the Hungarian communists? The USSR. When it is necessary to block the German revanchists who dream of attacking the German Democratic Republic, who guarantees the failure of the plan of Adenauer and his consorts? The USSR. And the industrialization of the socialist countries is carried out essentially with the help of the USSR . . .

Recognition of the role and prestige of the Soviet Union is not an attitude of 'follow the leader'; it is a recognition of reality, an essential aspect of the attitude towards the problem of unity and the fortification of the socialist sphere and of the workers' and communist international movement.

Because of this, we reproach the call of the Chinese comrades to combat the policy of the CPSU and the USSR, and its unfounded accusations, as assaults upon the unity and strength of the forces of socialism.

There was a time – the time of the Communist International – in which relations between the parties were of another kind than they now are. The Communist International was an international party, guided by the principle of democratic centralism. Later the Communist Party triumphed in countries other than the Soviet Union, and the communist movement developed and extended itself to numerous countries which at the time of the International had no parties. With this there emerged a diversity of problems and situations; a process developed which has transformed the Communist International into an international communist and workers' movement. This change is not a simple change of form; it is a profound change in the structure, in the rules of the international communist movement. This change supposes that in the communist movement there is no longer a centralized command; there is no longer an executive committee which decides the tactics, the line, the direction of each communist party. This change supposes that upon a general and common political and ideological base, each party has great liberty of initiative. And no party has the possibility of imposing upon another its decision, its line! No party can impose its will upon the others. The truth is that today in the international communist movement each party develops, on its own, its line and is solely responsible to its own people and the international proletariat for its successes and its mistakes.

At the time of the Communist International there was a leading party within the movement: it was the Communist Party of the Soviet Union, the Bolshevik Party. It was the first party to have made a revolution; it was the party which had the most experience; it played the directing role. At the Twenty-Second Congress, and again at a meeting in 1957, Soviets themselves proposed that

> there is no leading party in the communist movement, there can be no leading party; the leadership is wholly of the communist movement. There may be prominence in the vanguard, those who have gone farther, but no leading party.

In these discussions who was it that insisted to the end in favor of a leading party, if not the Chinese comrades? The Chinese comrades, and Mao Tse-tung personally, were insisting upon a ruling party at the 1957 conference and upon the rule of the Communist Party of the Soviet Union. But we other parties accepted the Soviet proposal which corresponded with reality, and the new situation.

When, for example, we have elaborated our line of national reconciliation, we have not gone to ask 'directions' of our Soviet comrades, or the French, or the Italians. That policy has been elaborated by our party; we have elaborated it ourselves, the Spanish communists, and if it be proper or false, the responsibility is uniquely and exclusively ours. Nobody from the outside designates our leaders; we designate or appoint them ourselves, the Spanish communists. For this reason it is grotesque to read in the Spanish press these days that 'I am in disgrace' in Moscow and will be replaced. It may be that I may one day commit important errors, or no longer be in a condition to hold the position to which the party has appointed me, and so be replaced. But it will not be in Moscow that this affair will be dealt with; in any case, it will be for our party to take charge and resolve it in full autonomy...

In the declaration of the 81, the CPSU is characterized uniquely as the 'vanguard party,' that is to say, as the party which leads the way in the construction of socialism and communism. In this way the communist movement develops today. This is the reality.

And so it is that today, when it is said by our Chinese comrades that those who are in the minority can become a majority and impose their opinion, we are not in agreement, just as it does not appear correct to us to assert that the Chinese comrades need to submit to the 'rules of the majority.'

Today, within the communist movement, there can neither be the imposition of the majority nor the retaliation of the minority, because it is not a party. Within the communist movement today there may be, and indeed there are, accords on the fundamental questions of principle, ideological ones, about those tasks which are general and common to the international communist movement. But such accords cannot be imposed by the majority, nor can they be revoked by those who are today in the minority; such accords cannot be reached except through discussion, persuasion, analysis and study of experience, and the assimilation of the experience. Such accords cannot be reached today except through conviction. I say this to emphasize the fact that in relations among parties the peculiarities and the autonomy of each party must be respected. What should always remain a rule for all is suspect for the principles of Marxism-Leninism, the maintenance of discussion on a level of ideology and principle, a level of camaraderie and defense of unity in the socialist sphere and in the worldwide workers' and communist movement...

Nuestra Bandera, no. 37 (July–December 1963).

26 Communiqué of the PCE, 1965

The Executive Committee of the Communist Party of Spain, after having examined with the greatest interest the communiqué of the advisory meeting of the nineteen communist parties which was held in Moscow at the beginning of March, has approved the proposals it makes.

We believe that this meeting has been an important step in the search for the most adequate ways to reinforce the cohesion of the international communist movement upon the bases of Marxism-Leninism and proletarian internationalism...

The Communist Party of Spain believes that in a world where profound social transformations are taking place, in which the weight of the socialist camp increases day by day and in which the ideas of Marxism-Leninism inspire a large part of the working class and of peoples in the struggle for their social and national liberation, it is impossible that the forms of unity and collaboration among the communist parties remain invariable. Maintaining their internationalist content, these relations between the communist parties can be perfected and consolidated in the struggle for common objectives in the study of the new problems posed by social development and in the collective effort to find a solution to them, all this abiding by these two inseparable premises: in the national sector each communist party has the duty and the responsibility to elaborate its policies and tactics with complete autonomy and independence; in the international sector each communist party has the duty to maintain fraternal lines with the other communist parties for the defense of common interests, for the struggle against imperialism...

The complete equality between the communist parties has been proclaimed at the conferences that have been held by the international communist movement. There does not exist today, nor can there exist, any party whose decisions are obligatory for the rest. At the same time, no party has the right to become involved in the internal affairs of another. The first to proclaim these principles in both conferences was the Communist Party of the Soviet Union, correctly interpreting the characteristics which our movement should have at the present time. But this situation should not by any means be interpreted as the dispersion and absence of unity, but as an increased common desire to reach the maximum cohesion on a world scale, without prejudice to the greatest possible autonomy in the national sector. The absence of a directing party increases the responsibility of all the communist parties without exception, from the greatest to the smallest, for the maintenance of unity and cohesion.

Mundo Obrero, no. 8 (April 1–15, 1965), p. 8.

27 From *Mundo Obrero*, 1968

We look upon the fulfillment of our internationalist duties as something sacred. We are Marxist-Leninists and nothing will take us away from the chosen path. We will always proclaim with pride our commitment to the glorious October Socialist Revolution, our solidarity with the achievements of the Soviet people and the CPSU and our intimate friendship with the Soviet Union. We emphatically condemn any attempt to use the tragic error committed in Czechoslovakia to denigrate the glorious history of the CPSU and the Soviet people; their heroism and sacrifice in the war in order to save humanity from Hitlerian barbarity; their solidarity with the peoples who fight in Vietnam, the Arab countries and in Spain; their contribution to the establishment of socialism in other countries and to the development of nations liberated from colonialism. The defense of the Soviet Union, the defense of all socialist revolutions, without exception, is for our party an unavoidable duty. No obstacle, no danger will take us away from the fulfillment of this duty.

And today we continue that line of action with the position adopted by our party on the Czechoslovakian problem. In the international communist movement there is no longer a directing party, a leading party! All the parties are equally responsible for the orientation of our movement. All parties have the responsibility for making their own contribution to the evolution of Marxism-Leninism. Moreover all parties, all communists, have to think with their own minds. Marxism-Leninism is not a religion, deposited in a new proletarian Mecca, immutable, to which adoration must be rendered from the four cardinal points; it is a guide, a method and a process of continuing creation in which all participate...

It would be foolish to want to abolish the differences which exist between Soviet, Chinese, Cuban, Vietnamese, Rumanian and now Czechoslovakian development, 'decreeing' the 'nonexistence' of those differences to the point where we do not do away with imperialism; or to attempt to suppress them by force — because those differences are real, they cannot be ignored. And the use of force, which would not liquidate them, can only aggravate them, excite them, transform them into antagonists, which would be a tragedy for socialism. This is precisely what we communists have opposed in the case of Czechoslovakia.

'There is only one socialism,' some say. But this is only a relative truth. It is a truth when the affirmation is in opposition to the reformist experiences of certain countries in which social democracy presents itself as a 'model of socialism,' in which the real political and economic powers remain firmly in the hands of capitalism. It is a truth when it is in opposition to those who speak of 'socialism' without setting for themselves the task of changing the economic and political structures of imperialism without a radical transformation of society; when it is in opposition to those who deny the leading role of the proletariat and of their party in the struggle for socialism.

But it is no longer a truth — and because of this it is relative — if it is used to negate the reality of diverse paths in the march toward socialism, adapted to the characteristics and the development of each country. The diversity of the forms of socialism — of that which already exists today and that which may triumph tomorrow in other countries — is a real fact, an objective truth. The unity of the world communist and workers' movement will be reinforced if that diversity is admitted, understood and used as a point of departure; in the same way that such unity would continue to deteriorate if we were to persist in denying, either in words or in actions, such diversity.

We are in a time in which each party must think with its own mind and audaciously and creatively formulate its plan of action, the most appropriate form of socialism for its country. There was a time when we imagined that socialism would be the victory of the Soviets in all places. We have gone beyond this conception and today we know that the initiatives of the masses in each country with their own uniqueness and specific social structures give an original character and form to each revolution. And for each party to be able to conceive and achieve its revolution, the unity of the party must be respected and defended, so that no dispute of opinions can spawn a division. Let an end be put to any divisionist initiative.

The Soviet intervention in Czechoslovakia clashed with these conceptions of ours, as it has clashed with those of other communist parties. Could we have remained silent? There are those who think so. It is the thesis of unconditional support. If that thesis was admissible when the Soviet Union was the only socialist country, it has been surpassed today. It was the Twentieth Congress, the very same Soviet comrades who demolished it. And it does not involve burying the Twentieth Congress, but developing and completing it.

We disapprove of the intervention in Czechoslovakia and we plead for the fulfillment of the Moscow Accords, above all as they refer to the support of the program of the January Plenum of the Czechoslovakian Party and the recognition of the territorial integrity and independence of Czechoslovakia. We cannot conceive or admit the hypothesis – which our enemies formulate now – that the day on which our party comes to power in Spain, in alliance with the forces of labor and culture, another socialist power, whichever it may be, would dictate its policy to us, and, even less conceivably, would intervene militarily in our territory, without our most energetic resistance.

But in the same manner we affirm that, faced with imperialism, we will always be beside the Soviet Union, without the slightest vacillation. Just as we are and will be on the side of those other socialist states . . .

Mundo Obrero, no. 16 (September 1968), pp. 1, 4.

28 Resolution of the Executive Committee of the PCE, 1969

. . . Our party, as it concentrates all its strength in the struggle to end the Francoist dictatorship, to mark a path for democratic change in Spain, reaffirms with all its energy its proletarian internationalism. We reaffirm our solidarity with the Soviet Union and with all the peoples who, following the path marked by the great October Socialist Revolution, have ended capitalist exploitation, have established socialism in a third of the planet. Our struggle against imperialism is part of the great historic change that is being experienced by humanity: the step from capitalism to socialism.

Proletarian internationalism is part of the very substance of our politics, of our ideology, of our *raison d'être*. And it should be applied while recalling the new revolutionary possibilities, and the new situation which has been created in the international workers' and communist movement as a consequence, exactly, of the triumphs of socialism, of the formation of a worldwide socialist system, now composed of fourteen states.

In the communist movement great discrepancies have been produced lately which are impossible to ignore, and which spring up, to a very important degree, from the contradictions existing between socialist states.

The existence of contradictions between socialist states demands that our party adopt an attitude based on its own analysis and opinions, about the problems which are posed in the socialist countries about the contradictions which may divide them; an attitude that in certain cases will contain fraternal disagreements or criticisms. To refrain from such critical attitudes would mean that, while everyone argues about the problems of socialism, we communists could not participate in such discussions. It would be refraining from an essential aspect of our ideological and political struggle. Participating with our communist opinions in such discussions is how we can effectively combat the anti-Sovietism and anti-communism fomented by the class enemy, as well as the confusion which exists in certain sectors that form part of the anti-imperialist struggle, and that, in one way or another, favor a socialist perspective. When we express our opinions on the problems of the socialist world, even when they include critical judgements on this question or that one, we do not in the least diminish our complete solidarity with the socialist camp. On the contrary, we contribute to raising our internationalism, giving it greater combative and political effectiveness, and not reducing it to more verbal expressions.

Today an internationalist attitude cannot be 'unconditionality.' Proletarian internationalism cannot mean a position in favor of one party against another party; in favor of one socialist state against another socialist state; in favor of one proletariat against another proletariat. What is necessary is that the subjective factors, the conscious actions of the parties, far from aggravating contradictions between socialist states that originate in objective and historical roots, succeed, on the contrary, in reducing them, controlling them, overcoming them; prevent such contradictions from obstructing the unity which is so necessary against imperialism. For that reason the role of the international communist movement – in the presence of the contradictions arising between socialist states – is to contribute to their solution on the basis of Marxism-Leninism and proletarian internationalism.

This underscores the fact that the great choices of the Twentieth Congress of the CPSU are, in effect, that in this area they have overcome the notions of 'unconditionality,' 'guiding party' and 'executive group.'

New unity can only be based on the principles of Marxism-Leninism and proletarian internationalism. But these must be shaped in forms historically adequate to the situation which we have discussed.

This implies the acknowledgement of the diversity of situations in which the parties act and, as a result, of the necessity that each one of them be completely independent in the elaboration of its party line, applying the principles of Marxism-Leninism, and keeping in mind the concrete conditions of its country.

This independence should not only not diminish internationalism, but should give it greater vigor and greater reach. Today the criterion of internationalism is the capacity of a party to elaborate a national and international policy that will spur the revolution both in its country and in the world. Today, without independence, a party cannot be the directing force in the struggle, fulfilling its first internationalist duty: to carry out the revolution for its country.

The new unity also demands serious progress for our Marxist-Leninist theory. Loyalty to Marxism-Leninism means not to repeat static truths, but to develop them as scientific and revolutionary theory, boldly undertaking the enormous new problems that present themselves in the world today. No party has, nor can it have, the monopoly of the 'true doctrine.' We have to admit as a normal phenomenon the confrontation of theses and opinions that, parting from the principles that are common to us, may differ. In this way we will achieve a creative development of Marxism-Leninism, enriched by the theoretical elaborations and by the practical experiences of the various parties and by a discussion of ideas in the bosom of our movement . . .

Mundo Obrero, no. 17 (May 24, 1969), cf. pp. 6–8.

29 From *Mundo Obrero*, **1970**

What has happened during that period within the international communist movement?

The latent problems within it have exploded; sometimes with violence: Sino-Soviet conflict, the problem of Rumania, Yugoslavia, Cuba, etc., and the problem of Czechoslovakia. It has been a painful and sometimes tearing process, but it has been filled with experiences. Experience has told us that on many occasions, such as the 1948 condemnation of the Yugoslavian Communist Party, the cult of Stalin's personality and the condemnation of the Chinese Communist Party, we have been guided only by our faith in the Communist Party of the Soviet Union, without really knowing what was taking place in Yugoslavia in 1948, or in the USSR in the times of Stalin, or in China during all these past years. Conscious of its responsibility toward the working class and the people, the party has acknowledged such a painful experience by eliminating all the previous unconditional following which is so alien and incompatible with Marxism-Leninism and by looking for its own, revolutionary and internationalist, answer to our national problems and to those of the international communist movement. Only in this fashion will we be able to win the masses for the cause of socialism which constitutes our primary internationalist duty . . .

The Spanish communists have defended and will always defend the USSR. We have done so and we do so not only in publications and in international meetings but also when faced with the socio-politico brigade and the civil guard; in the prisons thousands of communists have died crying out their love for the USSR when facing their executioners. Others have written it with their blood in the cells where they were being tortured . . .

But our love for the USSR and for all socialist countries cannot lead us to abandon our freedom to criticize measures and decisions which their governments may make and which we believe are unjust or mistaken. Conformity, sheepish following, has nothing to do with Marxism-Leninism, which is *essentially* critical and nonconformist. We criticize what we feel is unjust or mistaken precisely because we are internationalists, because we love all socialist countries and we consider as ours their successes and failures, because we are profoundly interested in their development and strengthening. We do not allow any criticism to be considered as anti-Sovietism.

Mundo Obrero, no. 19 (November 19, 1970), pp. 10, 11.

30 From *Mundo Obrero,* 1971

31 Manuel Azcárate's speech at the Eighth Congress of the PCE, 1972

There have occurred events about which we, because of our often misunderstood concept of solidarity, cannot remain silent.

For example, the events in Poland, and the brutal repression of the Polish workers, which have facilitated the justified elimination of the Gomulka team, have served as criticisms of the struggle to save the youth of Burgos. Because as soon as those conflicts arose, the very broad front which had been created among world public opinion against the fascist terror of Franco was divided.

And then there was the Leningrad trial. To say that the Leningrad trial was one of the most inopportune things at the time in which the Burgos trial was taking place is to say much while saying nothing. It is to say much because that trial has hurt the campaign to save those of Burgos. And it is to say nothing because in its nature and form there are fundamental problems which call into question the justice of socialist society. At the same time that Carrero Blanco was speaking to the legislature about the 'international communist plot,' pawing at the disreputable topics of the worst times of fascism, and the Minister of Commerce of the conservative government of Her British Majesty was postponing his announced visit to Spain, the Vice-President of the socialist government of Bulgaria was arriving in Spain. What was the Vice-President of the Bulgarian government doing in the capital precisely during those days?

In this period there have also been several delegations from socialist countries. Why have they chosen the moment so inopportunely?

A few days after Carrero Blanco's speech on the 'international communist plot,' Franco addressed the country, speaking once more of the 'opening toward the East.' But the inconsistency of the regime's hierarchs worries us. What worries us and what we would like to see stop is the 'opening of the East' to the regime.

Mundo Obrero, no. 1 (January 1971), p. 4.

Socialism – whose essence is the collective ownership of the means of production and the winning of political power by the working class and its allies – today manifests a diversity of forms and models as a consequence of the uneven development of productive forces, historical and geographic conditions, ways of attaining power, traditions, etc.

Such a diversity will persist for a long time to come. Moreover it will enrich itself with the success of socialism in new countries, some underdeveloped, some industrialized, etc.

The respect for these diversities and specific models is one of the premises of internationalism and of the unity of all socialist countries against imperialism, the class enemy.

There is no one 'supreme judge' who can decide which 'models' are good and which are bad. The working class of each country, together with its vanguard, has the responsibility of deciding its own ways and of correcting errors and cutting off degenerations.

The respect for the uniqueness of the diversity of forms and models which socialism manifests today, together with a Marxist-Leninist discussion about such a plurality of life experiences, are, we believe, essential questions in the present stage of the communist movement...

Differences existed and still exist even among the parties present at the 1969 Moscow Congress. One of the most serious of these was the condemnation carried out by several parties, such as ours, of the Soviet troops' 1968 invasion of Czechoslovakia and other socialist countries. The problem has not disappeared. When faced with trials such as those that have taken place in Czechoslovakia, where workers and intellectuals have been tried as criminals because they support a form of socialism which differs from today's sad reality, many communist parties, such as the French, Italian, English, etc., have repeated their criticism and disapproval.

The 1969 Congress represented a step towards acknowledging diversity within the communist movement. In its principal document the Congress declared that 'there is no one directing center,' that all parties are equal and independent.

After the 1969 Congress, the events which took place in Poland tragically confirmed the gravity of the authoritarian methods, the degeneration which socialism suffers when it annihilates in practice the workers' democracy.

Several articles and speeches have restated the thesis that the Soviet Communist Party is the 'guiding force' of the communist movement, that the 'touchstone' of internationalism is one's attitude towards the CPSU, that it is necessary to re-establish in the communist movement an 'ideological coherence' around the positions of the CPSU and facing the Chinese Communist Party...

We reaffirm our decision to continue our resolute struggle to defend the sovereignty and independence of the party, its unity and its strength; to defend its capacity to be the guiding force of the Spanish revolution.

There is another formula which is sometimes presented as the 'middle-term' solution and which goes, more or less, as follows: (1) talk of the Soviet Union when one agrees with it in order to highlight something in it is positive, and (2) remain quiet when one disagrees. As to the first point, it is evident that we do it and that it must be done. As to the second point, it is also evident that we avoid agitation and excuses to create discord. But if we accepted being silent about the important problems which affect international politics and the nature of socialism, then we would be encouraging a new form of conformity and we would be giving up our revolutionary duties towards our working class and the world proletariat. We cannot do it, and we will not do it.

The trend to re-establish such 'conformity' is condemned to failure because it is against the most evident necessities of the revolutionary movement and the anti-imperialist struggle. We reject conformity because it closes the way towards the most cherished goal of communists: the furthering of the unity of action between China and the Soviet Union, among all the socialist countries, and among all the parties against imperialism.

Conformity means dogmatization both of texts and of past experience precisely when the communist movement needs a profound renovation which, continuing its glorious traditions, would allow it to incorporate into the revolutionary process the new contradictions which arise in the second half of the twentieth century. In this way the movement can win new revolutionary forces that manifest themselves (sometimes with mistakes and confusion) in order to carry out an offensive strategy against the disintegrating imperialism.

When we fight against the trend towards conformity, we do so totally convinced that we are defending the interests of our party, of the world revolution and of the Soviet Union and all socialist countries...

Our party has pointed out the necessity of creating a new unity of the communist movement, a *unity in diversity*. This unity, based on the respect for diversity, is an objective necessity of the present moment: the revolutionary process is characterized by growing differences among the situations that different parties have to face, because the movement itself grows and extends to the whole world. In the international communist movement there are parties which are heads of state, legal parties, illegal parties, parties which work in economically developed countries, parties which struggle against socio-political realities defined by ancient or feudal structures.

Diversity stems from each party's obligation to elaborate its own strategy and its own model of socialist construction if it truly intends to become the real and objective guide of the revolution in its country. Experience has demonstrated that, as Lenin had predicted, national differences persist strongly for a *very long* period even after the access of the working class to power.

It is sometimes said that it is not convenient to insist on specific traits, on diversity, because that would be conducive to nationalism. But the sin of many parties, and what becomes an obstacle to their influence on the masses, is precisely the excessive emphasis on the generality of common ideals. A more creative application is needed, more contact with reality, more diversity in the general ideas of Marxism, more courage and imagination in order to promote socialism and the way towards the diversity which it *must* have to be able to win the large masses and to succeed in varying national situations. Hence the insistence on *diversity* does not imply going away from unity or internationalism, but rather that, at the present moment, diversity is an indispensable condition for internationalism and communist unity if they are to acquire the offensive dynamism which is required by the emerging revolutionary potentialities.

In order to advance towards a unity of action in the struggle against imperialism, the present moment demands some *decentralization* of unity; that is, a period in which *bilateral relations* are the major form of relationships among the communist parties.

At the same time, the international meetings devoted to a common task, such as the one which took place to reassert solidarity with Vietnam, are very important both for the anti-imperialist struggle and for the unity of our movement.

With respect to Western Europe, where the different parties have both tasks and problems which are very similar, converge in their own elaboration, and face situations which are objectively interrelated. It is logical and necessary to establish regular and articulated relationships among parties, without creating any one center...

VIII Congreso del PCE, Spanish Communist Party document, 1972, cf. pp. 191–7.

32 Manuel Azcárate's report to the Central Committee of the PCE, 1973

One of the factors which impedes an offensive policy against imperialism is the division within the world revolutionary and communist movement. Primarily the conflict is between the USSR and China.

Such an aggravation of the Chinese–Russian conflict permits Yankee imperialism to maneuver, irritating both sides of the conflict between the two principal socialist powers...

The conflict is developing along routes more typical of the old policy; that they look for support even among imperialist states. Faced with this situation, we ask ourselves: what revolutionary consideration has led to the pursuit of such a path? In fact, it is the conflict of two great powers, of two states which are opposed to one another as states.

The source of this sad reality lies undoubtedly in the dominating role which the state plays today in socialist countries (at least in the most powerful ones), to the detriment of the proper role of the party, i.e. the vanguard of the working class, of the masses, the conscious vanguard of historic progress, a promoter of the process which must be brought in step with communism, with the world socialist revolution. We find ourselves faced with the phenomenon of a fusion of the party and the state as an instrument of power. Such a deformation of the essence of socialism, with the limitation or suppression of socialist democracy (at least with respect to fundamental political questions, which are resolved by a small nucleus of leaders), diminishes the role and weight of the working class, of the masses. On the other hand, the

state, with the characteristics *every* state (even when it is socialist) retains from pre-socialism, of capitalist residue (as Lenin has explained in great detail), is dominant. Steps backwards in revolutionary attitudes, externally, are added to an internal process of bureaucratization.

Within this framework there arise in the foreign policies of the great socialist powers aspects with which we disagree, because we believe that they run contrary to the demands of the revolutionary struggle.

We repeat our total support of the efforts of the USSR in favor of peace and coexistence. We also understand that the USSR, along with other socialist countries, makes agreements of commercial, economic, etc., co-operation with capitalist countries in order to raise the standard of living of their peoples, to accelerate their development, etc.

This disagreement is not there. It arises when, in the fulfillment of the policy, the perspective of a political and social *status quo* in the world is accepted as if it were a natural result of peaceful coexistence, while in our opinion, and as formulated by the 1969 Conference, they are two completely distinct things.

In the third point of the 'principles' of USSR–USA relations, signed by Brezhnev and Nixon in May of 1972 in Moscow, it is said that the two countries 'must do all that is within their power to prevent conflicts or situations which would aggravate international tensions,' a point which represents a serious step, in our opinion, toward a policy of political and social *status quo*.

With attitudes of this sort, in which revolution disappears from the foreign policy of the great socialist countries, together with those factors to which we have referred, one arrives at the following contradiction: in the presence of the increasingly obvious crisis of imperialism, the communist parties which are in power in the most influential countries take *defensive* attitudes which ignore the requirements of anti-imperialist combat.

When the principal leaders of those countries speak of international questions they generally do so only as statesmen. They do not express the combative thinking of the vanguard, for the world struggle against imperialism. Further, they use ideas, words, mediated almost always by diplomatic considerations, and which do not reach the revolutionaries. There is an enormous disparity between the potential of the material means and the potential of revolutionary thinking.

Nuestra Bandera, no. 72 (October–December 1973), pp. 21–3.

33 Manifesto program of the PCE, 1975

We are entering a decisive new phase in the world battle for socialism: the phase of the concrete struggle for socialist transformation in developed capitalist countries. The victorious culmination of this phase may be a fundamental aid for the socialist regimes which opened the triumphant road in less developed countries, under difficult and painful circumstances. In these countries the realization of developed socialism will be facilitated in a decisive manner by the movement of the most economically advanced capitalist countries to socialist regimes and for the subsequent cessation of imperialist oppression. Thus the Marxist idea that socialism is a *universal revolution* which will only triumph fully in a *universal environment* will become reality in all its true meaning.

The world revolutionary process has followed an eventful course which the founders of scientific socialism could not foresee in detail. Marx and Engels did not know capitalism in its highest, imperialist phase. Because of this they were not able to analyze exactly the role of inter-imperialist contradictions, the uneven development of imperialism and the possibilities of revolutionary ruptures which might derive from it. Afterwards Lenin, beginning with the analysis of these new phenomena, concluded that the socialist revolution could break through in countries which were not the most civilized, the most developed, as the founders of scientific socialism has foreseen; in countries which, at a given moment, due to diverse internal and external factors, were the *weakest link* in the imperialist chain.

That is how it took place. The socialist revolution triumphed first in countries where the productive forces had not matured sufficiently to achieve social change under the most favorable circumstances, but in those in which, nevertheless, at a given moment the conscientious revolutionary forces accumulated enough energy to overthrow the dominant classes and acquire power. For this reason the first socialist revolutions found themselves faced with a double task: to create an intensive accumulation in order to industrialize the country in a relatively short time and modernize agriculture – a question which, historically, pertained to capitalism – and to move toward political, social and cultural revolution. In addition, the first socialist revolutions – particularly the first, the socialist revolution in Russia – had to defend themselves against the military oppression of the developed imperialist powers and to concentrate great resources for defense, as much in military as in other aspects of national security...

The historic role of these countries in the new world civilization of the socialist future *has been and is decisive*. Their experiences have an undeniable value for all revolutions *even though they cannot be taken as a universal model*.

But the *double task* of those revolutions – to overcome underdevelopment and, at the same time, to raise the living conditions of the people – contained a contradiction which could only be resolved in a slow process and, as history has shown, an eventful one.

Because of this, revolutionaries, when criticizing the errors committed by revolutions which were beginning to build new societies in such difficult internal and external conditions of the deformations produced in one moment or another, cannot forget that these [deformations] have their objective roots, their origins, in good measure, in their backward starting points and the tremendous pressure of the imperialism of the most powerful capitalist countries, as well as in the persistence and the inertia of ideas and traditions of past societies.

In the specific historic experiences of the construction of socialism, these deformations were aggravated by certain subjective ideological and institutional factors, especially the tendency toward the fusion of party and state, authoritarianism, bureaucratism, and the solution of problems from above, reducing democracy.

This critical analysis would be incomplete if it were not to take into account the fact that the working classes of the developed capitalist countries, under the influence of reformism, were not able to undertake their socialist revolutions, which would have created a much more favorable context for the construction of socialism.

But in spite of these errors and the survival of the past, the existence of the socialist countries and their world weight, together with the struggle of the international working class and of the liberation movements, have made the ideas of socialism reach a formidable, expansive force, sharpening the general crisis of imperialism...

Spanish Communist Party document, 1975, pp. 15–18.

34 Santiago Carrillo, 'Old and new internationalism,' 1976

I support international proletarian solidarity. I believe that workers all over the world must maintain connections of solidarity and support.

However, I am (as I have said on other occasions) against the old internationalism. I mean that, when the Russian revolution created the first, and the unique, socialist state, we communists thought that it was our internationalist duty to defend the Soviet Union, because of the threats of the capitalist powers. The situation is different in today's world. The Soviet Union is a part of an international system; it is a gigantic power; it can maintain itself on its own. When the Soviet comrades want the communist parties of other countries to behave as if the Soviet Union were an emerging state, which is being surrounded and threatened, and to support the Soviet policies on all aspects, we say: the Spanish Communist Party disagrees. For us proletarian internationalism does not consist in always supporting the Soviet Union or any other country.

For us proletarian internationalism consists in understanding the richness and diversity of what we call the *international revolutionary* movement. Such a movement has many different manifestations which follow ways and orientations which are autonomous and independent. This internationalism has today a task, particularly in the developed capitalist countries, to transcend the schism produced in the workers' movement by the October Revolution and to create conditions for co-operation and understanding among all the socialist forces. This new internationalism has today a new component: the co-operation of the Christian forces which support a departure from capitalist society.

We are facing new problems and new situations. We cannot face today's reality with old conceptions.

When journalists and officers in the Soviet Union command us to obey and even accuse us of being heretics or deviants, I believe that we, heretics and deviants, are on the true road of internationalism as internationalism must be understood in our times. This opinion is not exclusively that of the Spanish communists, but is shared by an increasing number of communist parties...

Mundo Obrero, no. 16 (April 21, 1976).

35 Manuel Azcárate, 'We reject interference from wherever it comes', 1977

I believe that it is not only a personal attack against Santiago Carrillo, but also a political attack against the line of the Spanish Communist Party and, at a more general level, against the line of a group of Western European communist parties which defines them as eurocommunist. Nevertheless the personal aspect may stem from intentions of intervening in the internal affairs of the Spanish Communist Party. Many pressures have already been exerted on our party – they tended to question the secretary general. We reject these interventions, no matter whether they come from governments or reactionary information media or, as in this case, from the Soviets. The secretary general of the Spanish Communist Party is appointed by, and only by, the Spanish communists. Santiago Carrillo deserves the confidence of the whole Executive Committee, of all the Central Committee and of all the party, as it was recently demonstrated.

Eurocommunism has already become a great political force on our continent and, therefore, in the world. We are living in a period in which social democracy is in crisis and in which what could be called the Soviet model has ceased to be a source of hope and example for the revolutionary process. Another source was necessary, and that is what eurocommunism offers by presenting a concrete way of democratic progress towards the realization of the socialist transformations required by contemporary society.

The Berlin Congress stated very clearly each party's independence; each party's right to elaborate its own policies and to develop Marxist theory independently. The attack in *New Times* is a return to the period in which the Soviet Communist Party believed that it had the right to intervene in the affairs of other parties and to excommunicate, as if it were a communist Inquisition with the right of defining truth and error, orthodoxy and heterodoxy. The Berlin Congress had made it very clear that such attitudes have ended, and the article in *New Times* is a shameless violation of the agreements reached by the Congress...

I have said that the article reflects the Soviets' fear of carrying out a theoretical debate. Another area in which they show equal fear, and on to which they direct their major attacks, is the idea of a united

Europe. These attacks imply that, in international matters, the communist parties should be tools limited to approving and supporting the Soviet policies, that is, the policies of one of the big superpowers. However, if the communist parties followed that way, they would lose all touch with their countries' realities; they would cease to be true national parties and they would become a superpower's instruments. Such a fact, which would contradict the very nature of a communist party, would also deny the profound trend towards transcending a bi-polar world and towards the entry into an international life in which countries other than the United States and the Soviet Union would play an increasingly important role and would help to end some of the most negative aspects of today's world.

The article refers several times to the unity of the international workers' movement. I would say that it would be laughable if it were not sad. If the movement were to be as they conceive of it, it would do nothing but pay its respects and obey all the Soviet Union said. Such a conception of internationalism still exists in very influential circles within the direction of the Communist Party of the Soviet Union. There are still many documents of the CPSU and of the other parties connected to it in which the touchstone of internationalism is the attitude towards the Soviet Union. But such a conception is prehistory; all this has already happened, even if the article in *New Times* demonstrates how alive Stalinism remains, together with those prehistoric conceptions.

Mundo Obrero, no. 27 (July 6, 1977), p. 16.

PART FIVE

The Parties and the
International System

Introduction to Part Five

The eurocommunist parties' opening to the West in the last decade has represented a sharp reversal of their previous positions. A posture of *qualified acceptance* of the West's political, military and economic institutions has replaced the *a priori*, unconditional opposition of old. This is particularly the case with regard to the European Community which the parties have come to consider as an irreversible reality, as a political-economic phenomenon which cannot be dismissed as a mere concoction of European monopoly capitalism and/or as the spearhead of US economic penetration of Western Europe. Similarly the Italian and Spanish communists no longer call for the immediate withdrawal of US and NATO troops from their respective countries; the French communists, though still opposed to France's reintegration into NATO, have abandoned the request for France's complete disengagement from the Atlantic Alliance. Atlanticism itself, meaning the system of political, military and economic alliances established in the aftermath of the Second World War, is no longer regarded as necessarily implying the subordination of Western Europe to American economic and political interests.

Opening to the West is still a far cry, however, from wholehearted adherence to Western international institutions and to the principles behind them. The parties remain ideologically opposed to and critical of these institutions, aspiring to move them, especially the European Community, in directions more consonant with their ideological and political outlook. Here a distinction between short- and long-term interests on the one hand, and ideologically rooted goals on the other, is important. The interest of the parties in maintenance of the existing international *status quo* should not be confused with the aspiration to promote the establishment of a new set of power relations and a different political climate in the West. While in the short term the parties largely accept the framework of the Atlantic Alliance as it exists today, and are committed to the pursuit of their national strategies within it, their long-term goal is to bring about its transformation, especially with regard to American hegemony in the West.

Détente, perceived both as a process and as a policy goal, represents the driving force behind the eurocommunist parties' *Westpolitik*. The achievement of a condition of genuine peaceful coexistence in the international system is viewed as essential for the realization of their over-riding goal in international politics: the gradual and simultaneous dissolution of the existing military and political blocs. Because of this, they argue that no changes should occur in one of the two blocs unless matched by similar changes in the other bloc; otherwise the existing equilibrium of forces in the international system would be undermined, endangering the process of détente and increasing the likelihood of confrontation. Should this happen, detrimental consequences for the parties' domestic strategies, especially their efforts to achieve durable alliances with other political and social forces, would result. Moreover only the uninterrupted evolution of the international system towards a stage of peaceful coexistence can create conditions favorable to the achievement of the other fundamental international goals of the eurocommunist parties: the transformation of the European Community into an autonomous, regional force equally distant in its political orientation and behavior from the Soviet Union and the United States.

The parties' positive stand on détente is not, however, shaped only by strategic considerations. This stance reflects as well the eurocommunist leaders' recognition of the catastrophic consequences that a sharpening of conflict between the two super-powers might have in an era of nuclear weapons. Togliatti in the 1950s and Carrillo in recent years have been particularly vocal in stressing the concept that war can and must be avoided precisely because of the dangers that it poses in the present era. It is only in recent years, however, that the parties have drawn the full conclusions from this analysis, coming to recognize that what has prevented various confrontations between the two blocs from degenerating into open conflict has been the equilibrium of forces which emerged in the postwar period – an equilibrium which should be preserved in the years to come.

With regard to the international system, the positions of the eurocommunist parties are far from homogeneous. Many of the differences which exist among them are the result of the different positions and outlook of their respective countries in the international system. Equally important are, of course, the particular historical and ideological evolution of each party and the nature of their interaction with the international communist movement. The French communists continue to regard the European Community with suspicion, to advocate a 'Europe of states' as opposed to an integrated Europe, and to view the Atlantic Alliance as the creature of US imperialism. Similarly, they remain wary of the potential that détente, no matter what its advantages, might become a means to justify exclusion of communist parties from governments in the West. These positions reflect the party's historical and ideological development and the Gaullist heritage which permeates the foreign policy thinking of all French political forces. The Italian communists' more positive and constructive attitude towards European integration and their more conciliatory posture towards Atlanticism have, in turn, been shaped by the evolving foreign policy consensus which has in recent years developed in Italy. Finally, the positions of the Spanish communists have been subject to influences in many ways similar to those of the Italians. To these, however, a specifically Spanish national factor must be added: the realization that Spain's entrance into the European Community is necessary to remove the residues of old Francoist foreign policy and to facilitate the democratization of Spain's internal regime.

When one goes beyond these general principles to specific foreign policy issues, the parties continue to be consistently critical of American behavior in the international system. US policy in various areas has been the target of often vehement critiques. Examples range from Vietnam to Cuba to US policy in the Middle East, Africa and Latin America. Similarly the parties continue to demand that their respective countries give up their support for American foreign policy aims and take an independent stand on the major international issues. It remains to be seen whether criticism of American foreign policy is a proof of the eurocommunist parties' continued allegiance and subordination to the aims of Soviet foreign policy, as critics of eurocommunism maintain, or the attempt to develop independent foreign policies for their own countries and for Europe more generally which are consistent with their traditional values. What is beyond dispute is the fact that eurocommunist parties persist in their tendency to view American policy as the major cause of tension in the international arena.

Historically three major phases can be detected in the eurocommunist parties' foreign policy positions. The first, from 1947 to the early 1960s, was characterized by a posture of uncompromising opposition to the West. Throughout this period the convergence between the foreign policy positions of the parties and the positions of the Soviet Union was striking. The Marshall Plan, NATO, the building and subsequent rearmament of West Germany, the early plans for European integration, were attacked by the parties as manifestations of American expansionism. All conflicts which occurred in this period (Korea, Suez, etc.) were blamed on the United States. The responsibility for the outbreak of the Cold War itself was attributed solely to American behavior. 'Struggle against US imperialism' was the motto guiding the parties' positions and actions during this period.

As regards their respective countries' foreign policies, the parties also adopted a highly critical stance. French behavior in Vietnam, Algeria and Suez was, for instance, condemned by the PCF as outright colonialism. For their part, the Italian communists consistently requested that Italy assume a neutral stand in international affairs, while Spanish communists attacked what they regarded as Franco's subservience to American imperialism. The demand for the immediate break-up of NATO and other military institutions (see, for instance, the Western Communists' vehement opposition to the projected European Defense Community in the early 1950s), a posture of obstructionism towards all attempts to build a European Community, and the call for a popular mobilization against American foreign policy (of which the peace movement of the early 1950s represented the most concrete expression) were the chief traits of the parties' foreign policy posture in this period. With all its political, economic and military ramifications, the Atlantic Alliance was perceived as the instrument used by American-led international capitalism for repulsing working-class demands for change in the West and for combating the challenge posed by the emergence of the socialist systems in the East. As the section on the international communist movement of this casebook shows in greater detail, in this period the over-riding aim of the parties' foreign policy action was the defense of the socialist bloc in general, and of the Soviet Union in particular. Domestically grounded considerations were regularly subordinated to this goal.

The second phase of the parties' foreign policy evolution, covering the 1960s, was marked by a gradual and uneven reappraisal of earlier positions. Starting approximately at the time of the Cuban missile crisis, substantial changes occurred in the parties' foreign policy postures. First, peaceful coexistence became the *Leitmotif* of their pronouncements. Cold War themes began to be abandoned; an attitude of constructive criticism replaced the uncompromising obstructionism of the immediate postwar years. Conflicts between the two blocs were no longer considered inevitable. Although American foreign policy continued to be branded as imperialistic, especially with regard to the Vietnam War, Cuba and Berlin, the possibility of some form of understanding between the two camps was no longer excluded. The call for an agreement on nuclear arms limitation became one of the central themes of the parties' foreign policy positions. Secondly, they began to realize that the expanding European Community was an undeniable reality. It was acknowledged to have had some positive effects on EEC member-states' economic and social development, contributing to the prosperity which characterized Western Europe in the 1960s. The Italian communists were in the forefront of this process of reappraisal of the EEC. From the mid-1960s on they began requesting representation in Community institutions. The goal of transforming the European Community from within, that is, by working within and through its institutions, gradually replaced the previous demand for its dissolution. Likewise, although they continued to demand that Italy adopt a neutral foreign policy, Italian communists began to think of such a policy more and more in European terms, meaning an Italy fully integrated in (a democratized) European Community which would be neither pro-Soviet nor pro-American. The process of reappraisal of the French communists was slower and less thorough. As already mentioned, they have never fully accepted the principles behind the process of European integration and their foreign policy posture has continued to be marked by a pro-Sovietism which is less evident and consistent in Italian and Spanish communist positions. In the 1960s French communists seemed to respond more to the changes in France's foreign policy posture by De Gaulle than to the changes in the international system. In particular, they were content to echo some of the more anti-American themes of Gaullist foreign policy. The French communists responded positively to De Gaulle's decision to disentangle France from the military framework of the Atlantic Alliance, to his policy of opening to the East, and more generally to the promotion of national grandeur and a vision of a 'Europe of states.' Even De Gaulle's defense policy, with the possible exception of his program of nuclear build-up, was generally accepted, if not praised by the PCF. In the 1960s signs of change were also evident in the Spanish communists' foreign policy positions, especially with regard to the European Community. On the other hand, the PCE continued to oppose Spain's entry into the EEC on the ground that it would only lend legitimacy to the Franco regime. Common to all three eurocommunist parties in this period was the tendency to downplay their pro-Sovietism, that is, to pay increasingly less attention to the requirements of Soviet foreign policy. The national and European dimensions assumed a greater role in shaping their foreign policy orientations.

The third phase, shaped by an opening to the West, covers the last decade. As already mentioned, in the last few years the parties' positions have become increasingly conciliatory toward the West. With the exception of the French communists, who are still skeptical about the dynamics behind the process of European integration (they are, for instance, opposed to the enlargement of the Community and have been unenthusiastic about the usefulness of the recent direct elections for the European Parliament), eurocommunist parties have become committed to supporting and working within the existing Community institutions. The Spanish communists have declared themselves in favor of Spain's entry into the EEC. In recent years both Berlinguer and Carrillo have expressed their acceptance of the existing military institutions of the West, with the former going so far as stating that NATO might represent the shield behind which the Italian brand of socialism could be brought about. Carrillo has argued that it would be unrealistic and counter-productive to demand the dismantling of US military bases in Spain until a similar process of Spanish military withdrawal from Eastern European countries has occurred. The logic of maintaining the existing balance between the blocs has also led him to oppose Spain's full integration into NATO.

In general, domestic and European considerations seem now to be ever more determining considerations behind the eurocommunist parties' foreign policy postures. The tendency to subordinate their foreign policy pronouncements and stands to the needs and interests of Soviet positions has declined. The interaction between the domestic and the European dimensions in a context of international détente and interdependence is more than ever the frame of reference for the parties. As it has been articulated in recent years, the parties' positions on foreign policy are a delicate and unique mix of domestic, regional and international factors, of ideological and strategic considerations. While this mix is largely responsible for the incongruities which still pervade the parties' positions, it has also allowed them to transcend old constraints, to become more attuned to the realities and changes of the international system. And realism and a capacity to adapt to change are, in the final analysis, the two patterns which best capture the essence of the phenomenon of eurocommunism.

MAURIZIO VANNICELLI

DOCUMENTS FOR PART FIVE

ITALIAN Communist Party:
Realism and Activism – Seeking Autonomy in a Bi-Polar World

FRENCH Communist Party:
National Grandeur and the Quest for Autonomy

SPANISH Communist Party:
Legitimacy, Autonomy and the Search for International Linkages

ITALIAN Communist Party: Realism and Activism – Seeking Autonomy in a Bi-Polar World

The Evolution of the International System

1 Committee of the Directorate of the PCI, 1949

Gratitude of all democrats to Stalin
The fight against the entrance of Italy in war alliances
The leadership of the Communist Party has greatly concerned itself with the persistent maneuvers aimed at bringing about the membership in our country in international bodies like the London Union (so-called 'European') and the Atlantic Pact, which have the unmistakable characteristics of imperialistic alliances, formed with the intent of organizing a political and war coalition against the Soviet Union and against the new, democratic countries, and to subject the people of Europe to imperialistic Anglo-Saxon domination. The position of the Italian government and the parties of which it is comprised favors membership in these international imperialistic bodies, and is not only against the fundamental interests of Italy, but also constitutes a true betrayal of the solemn commitment which all the parties, without exception, made to the people in the electoral campaign on April 18. In fact, all parties in the course of this campaign promised solemnly that they would be opposed to Italy's membership of any international political coalition, believing that a position of freedom and independence from all international commitments is necessary to ensure peace and the democratic reconstruction of the country. The betrayal of this commitment, denounced even by some of the members of the present governing party, makes the political battle even more bitter and forces all those who are working for peace and for the future of the country to be more effective than ever.

The leadership of the party maintains that it is necessary that the Italian people manifest their desire for peace, a desire in opposition to every commitment Italy has made as a result of an imperialistic intrigue which opposes peace and threatens to cast the people in the abyss of war. It has been decided to contact the Socialist Party and all the other democratic and peaceful forces with the intention of studying the concrete forms of action necessary for this purpose.

L'Unità, February 4, 1949.

2 Palmiro Togliatti's speech to the Central Committee of the PCI, April 12, 1954

For an agreement between the communists and Catholics to save human civilization
A contradictory process is going on in the international situation. On the one hand, certain important steps have been taken towards a relaxing of international tensions and therefore towards achievement of one of the immediate objectives of our program for peace; on the other hand, however – and this is the contradictory element – we find ourselves facing the exasperating problems caused by the aggressive positions of American imperialism...

The most important fact in this area is the progress which has been made in the production of atomic explosives. Production has advanced well beyond the level of the first atomic bombs; it has continued on to the production of hydrogen bombs, the frightening effects of which have been established, and, from what they say, still more frightening explosive devices never before thought possible, with a capacity for destroying massive human, animal and plant populations, will be produced.

There is no doubt that the progress of man in conquering nuclear energy is to be commended. Man has made progress in his knowledge of the forces of nature and, after centuries, his efforts have finally borne fruit. These forces have been subdued and placed at man's disposition. However, today, these advancements, as far as the directors of American foreign policy are concerned, are used and employed in a way that opens a path leading to catastrophic prospects for humanity, not the sort of disasters which have been faced in the past, but rather total catastrophe.

Let us start with the fact that these instruments of massive destruction of life in all its forms are possessed by both sides and not just one. Therefore the policy of the leaders of American imperialism is not tenable. The position proclaimed by the President of the United States in his recent speech, which preceded an announcement by the Secretary of State, considers these weapons as a means of threatening and intimidating others. It is folly to think so. A policy which consists, I repeat, of using these weapons and the knowledge of destructive effects to modify the international situation is not, of itself, something which will help to achieve the end the Americans praise. This is true for all the states which are presently the object of this threat. It is true for the Soviet Union, which has never stooped to any haughty threat. It is true for China, which is probably already an 'atomic power.' . . .

It is evident that if by chance the policy which was formulated in the last two weeks by those responsible for American imperialistic policies were to be applied for a certain period of time, there would undoubtedly be an eventual confrontation of the powers, both of which have at their disposal a vast arsenal of nuclear weapons . . .

The threatened areas are the most heavily populated regions of the world, where civilization has advanced the most: the United States, Britain, Western Europe, the more advanced and populous parts of continental Asia, the Mediterranean, and so forth. In a word, it affects the centers of modern civilization.

The prospect offered to the world by those who propose the American policies of threats and atomic reprisals is therefore – and we must proclaim it openly – the prospect of the end of present-day civilization and the beginning of a new period about which we know nothing. It would be the total, or almost total, destruction of the results of a great work, of a material and spiritual development which has brought about the creation of the world, by man, that we live in today.

Luciano Gruppi (ed.), *Il compromesso storico* (Rome: Editori Riuniti, 1977), pp. 164–5.

3 Resolutions of the Eighth Congress of the PCI, December 1956

(1) The modifications in the economic and political structure of the world which emerge today are the result of the great victories won by the democratic peoples' and socialist movement, and within it by the communists, in less than four decades . . .

Socialism has today become a world system of states. On the partial ruins of the colonial system a new group of independent states has emerged. They represent a new area of peace, and among them the tendency to abandon the traditional ways of capitalist economy gains ground, and they are adopting some of the methods of economic management peculiar to socialism. Not only has the area of imperialism's domination been reduced, but the very prestige of capitalism has fallen low, its general crisis has worsened, and its internal contradictions have become deeper.

In these new conditions new perspectives in the struggle for peace are opened before the peoples. The attempt by the most aggressive imperialist groups to re-achieve an unassailable supremacy by pushing the world towards the abyss of a new world conflict has met with no success . . . The possibility and the necessity of peaceful coexistence and collaboration among states that are governed according to different economic and social principles, which was affirmed by the communists from the very first years after the conquest of power in the Soviet Union, can no longer be denied.

The real forces that are able to act in defense of peace have acquired such amplitude and economic and political weight that war no longer appears inevitable, notwithstanding the continued existence of the capitalist system.

(2) In this new phase capitalism and imperialism preserve their fundamental characteristics. The progress of technique and production is accompanied by an accentuated monopolist concentration and is not translated into social progress . . . Economic evolution continues to proceed in an unequal manner and in leaps, accompanied by a sharpening of class contrasts, social inequalities and rivalry among states, and with all the contradictions of the capitalist system manifesting themselves in an increasingly acute form . . .

The imperialist groups are resisting and

obstructing the advent of relaxed international tension. They have prevented the negotiations for the outlawing of atomic weapons and for disarmament from reaching a reasonable, even if only partial, conclusion. They have insisted on keeping open the German question, which is rendered insoluble not only by the rearming, unilaterally decided upon, of Western Germany, as part of an anti-Soviet plan, but also by the suppression of the German Communist Party, which demonstrates a return to fascist political methods. They have continued to nurture and to announce aggressive plans against the socialist countries, calling for the suppression of their independence and for intervention in their internal affairs, in order to restore capitalism. They impede the United Nations from assuming a universal character by excluding from it the great people of China.

The big imperialist countries do not intend to accept the end of colonialism as an accomplished fact. Wherever they are still in a position to do so they strive to maintain oppression over entire countries and peoples...

The crisis precipitated by the nationalization of the Suez Canal has brought to light how the end of the colonial system, having shaken the foundations of the whole edifice of imperialism, accentuates the contrasts among the capitalist countries, and can provoke sudden crises and hysterical convulsions, and render unexpectedly acute the danger of bloody military adventures and the threat of a new world conflict. But the Suez crisis has also shown that, faced with the will of the peoples and the mighty camp of peaceful forces which exist today, the big imperialist countries are no longer able to do just what they please. It has been confirmed that the perspective that new armed conflicts may be prevented and the people advance peacefully towards a better future is a real perspective ...

In this situation the imperialist bloc is trying to overcome or at least disguise its own contradictions, so as to find its unity once again in anti-communism and anti-Sovietism, to find the basis for a new aggressiveness and a return to the policy of opposing blocs and the Cold War, developing a threatening action to undermine the socialist world...

(3) The existence of a world system of socialist states is today the main guarantee for peace and progress for mankind.

In the Soviet Union a society now exists which is developing according to the economic laws of socialism, to translate the growth in production, which is incomparably more rapid than in the rest of the world, into an increasingly greater satisfaction of the economic, civil and cultural needs of all men. The other socialist countries are striving towards the same end. Freed or in the process of being freed from class antagonisms, economic crises, unemployment and mass poverty, these countries meet and resolve the heavy problems inherited from past regimes, overcoming the contradictions and the inequalities upon which these were founded. This advance is not made without difficulties, resistance and errors ...

PCI publication, Rome, 1957, pp. 27–30.

4 Palmiro Togliatti's report to the Ninth Congress of the PCI, January 30 to February 4, 1960

The establishment, through the beginning of a process of relaxation of tension, of a new international situation; the indisputable superiority of the socialist system and the constant strengthening of the Soviet Union in her march towards communism and of the other socialist countries in Asia and Europe; the continuous advance of new peoples towards their liberation from colonial rule; the possibility that the new international situation finds its expression, first of all, in the acceptance of the proposals for a general and controlled disarmament; all these are elements opening today a new historical perspective. Such a perspective is being opened to the working class, to the working people, to all peoples and men wanting freedom, progress and social justice...

The consciousness of the need to modify the course of what had been the foreign policy of the great capitalist powers in the last fifteen years has matured since 1956 even in large sections of the ruling classes. This process has been favored within the capitalist world by the economic developments themselves, giving rise to new and different problems; a new hierarchy of powers is being created, new contrasts and splits are taking place...

The changes in the foreign policy course of capitalist countries, the total elimination of the Cold War and the strengthening of a new international situation are linked to conflicts, and to a harsh struggle which is being waged today throughout the capitalist world...

General disarmament and the destruction of all mass extermination weapons set the real terms of the problem of the competition of the two systems, the socialist and the capitalist.

When all military blocs will be eliminated, together with all military foreign bases and occupation, all threats of intervention from outside and of constraint must disappear.

The democratic development and the march towards a new social regime becomes, then, the object of a free competition of classes and of a free choice of countries. Mankind can set itself the task and solve the problems of the present development of civilization, of a new powerful impulse of productive forces, of new, undreamt-of technological, scientific and research progress...

Italy is a country of 50 million inhabitants, having an industrial potential not fully developed yet but not negligible nevertheless. It occupies a geographic position of great importance in Europe. In spite of this I believe that nobody could maintain that Italian foreign policy in the last fifteen years has had its own objectives, its own course and characteristics, corresponding to the true interests, aspirations and original vocation of the Italian population. This correspondence could be found in the political line of the resistance, which did not neglect international problems. It was lost afterwards. In the Cold War alignment Italy was merely the fulcrum of actions carried out by other powers in their own interests and it gravely compromised its independence. Today the installation of American long-range extermination weapons of a purely aggressive nature and which will never be ours because we are not in a position to make them is making of Italy a stronghold, meant perhaps to protect other countries, but certainly doomed to be totally destroyed in the case of a catastrophe.

It is to be remembered, furthermore, that the strict allegiance of Italian foreign policy to the great imperialist and colonialist powers has seriously impaired our bonds and our prestige among the Arab countries in the Mediterranean and all the peoples who are freeing themselves from colonial domination.

The entire foreign policy of our country must be responsibly re-examined by all sides and revised...

When Europe, at the beginning of the Cold War period, divided itself up into two opposed military blocs, the Italian bourgeoisie thought it natural to associate itself with the ruling classes of other Western states in the so-called Atlantic Alliance...But what today is the meaning of this association? There is no unity within the Atlantic bloc over foreign policy issues, if not in the communiqués which are issued at the end of ministers' meetings and which usually do not mean anything. There are three or four differing and opposed views...Amidst such confusion, what is the Italian position? Should it not be necessary that someone within this camp acts coherently in order to lessen tensions, to achieve disarmament and to establish peaceful coexistence? We are firmly convinced that only by adopting such a position, inserting itself in the right future perspective, can Italy fulfill an outstanding role.

Our reply to those who ask us if we admit that Italy is part of the so-called Western world is that the question is meaningless, for this problem has been solved by nature and history, that is to say, by geography and by the development of our civilization...Today the real problem lies in seeing what position and what future is reserved for the countries of the European West at a time when two powerful centers of military strength exist at either extreme: the United States on one side and the Soviet Union on the other. Achieving an equal strength is impossible, and even if it were possible it is not to be wished, for it could only be achieved by sacrificing all civil progress. Agreeing to become the appendix of either of the two colossuses is the end of the principle of independence. The way out is not to be sought in a return to Metternich or to Bismarck; it must be found through an orientation towards the future, towards the general renunciation of a policy based on force or on the 'deterrent,' towards general disarmament and peaceful coexistence...

Only by moving along these lines can the European West again fulfill its function of progress and civilization...

We ask the Italian rulers to give a start to this movement and to take the first steps in this direction. And the first necessary step in this direction is the recognition of present-day European and world reality...

Foreign Bulletin (January 1960), pp. 22–30.

5   Theses for the Tenth Congress of the PCI, September 1962

. . . Our whole fight for peace is based on the conviction that war is no longer inevitable. This is the consequence of the present-day international situation; of the growing weight of the socialist world and of its determination to defend peace; of the existence of a large group of neutral countries opposed to the imperialists' war policy; of the will for peace of the masses.

Although it still retains its characteristic features, imperialism is rent by a deep crisis. For some time its ruling groups have no longer been in a position to dominate the international situation in their exclusive interests. The very differences arising among them make it more difficult for them to implement their plans. Moreover, as a consequence of these difficulties and of the threat of a destructive nuclear war, which menaces the capitalist countries too, there are hints that the need to avoid war is being admitted even amidst those groups . . .

Peaceful coexistence must be based on the refusal of force as a means to solve international differences, on the respect for the independence and sovereignty of each country and on non-interference in the internal problems of other states. It entails, therefore, the establishment of a system of international relations such as to consent that each people solve all the problems relating to their life, according to their aspirations and interests, decide freely on their own future, advance according to their interests, needs and forces on the road of economic and social progress. Thus a link is established between the fight for peace and peaceful coexistence and the fight for democracy and socialism and hence with the vital economic and political claims of the working class, of the working people, of the middle classes and intellectuals. Relaxation of tension in international relations and peaceful coexistence do not imply by any means that these claims should be given up. Similarly they do not mean that the prospect of the advent of new social groups to the leadership of the political and economic life is abandoned. They only mean that in the struggle for these aims both the prospect of a new world war and the possibility of a foreign intervention designed to 'export' either a counter-revolution or a revolution must be excluded . . .

In Italy the primary aim of a democratic foreign policy program must be the withdrawal from Italian soil of all American or NATO atomic bases. The program of the Italian resistance movement, to which all democratic parties pledged themselves, claimed that Italy should be kept strictly out of any military alliance or bloc. We must go back to that program. This is necessary also because of our economic development itself, which allows now much greater autonomy in all spheres, as well as to secure the full independence of our country, to develop Italian trade in all directions, and to establish normal relations with the neutral countries and the liberated ones, refusing the neo-colonialist policies adopted by the great capitalist countries. Even before Italy's neutrality is proclaimed, the Italian government should made a serious effort – within NATO, too – to propose practical initiatives and suggestions designed to lessen tension and to secure the ban of nuclear weapons, disarmament and a decisive improvement in the climate of international relations . . .

Foreign Bulletin (September 1962), pp. 7–10.

6   Palmiro Togliatti's speech in parliament, *L'Unità*, July 10 1963

No change in the Atlantic policy followed so far
What does Atlantic loyalty mean? It is the formula of the Cold War, the formula which for years hid the total absence of an Italian foreign policy, of any measures and proposals to ease up international tension and to pave the way for a world without wars.

The Atlantic Pact, it is said, is a guarantee of freedom and security. I reject this as one of the conventional lies of the Cold War propaganda. In the shadow of the Atlantic Pact we find Portugal and Greece, which are fascist regimes, and the military bases in Franco's Spain, which are hypocritically regarded as being merely American. Under the Atlantic Pact German militarism has raised its head again with its grim program of political and military revanchism openly advocated now by the most qualified representatives of Federal Germany. In the shadow of the Atlantic Pact the most deplorable exterminating wars were waged against colonial peoples struggling for their independence.

The Atlantic Pact has been and is nothing but one of the instruments of American foreign policy, and for all the respect I have for the American nation I cannot accept the affirmation that this nation as it is now represents a model of democratic political life.

The democratic inspiration comes to us first of all from the history of our country, from the struggles of the working class for its rights and social aspirations, from the anti-fascist experience, from the great collective experience of the resistance, and later from the action for the defense and development of democratic institutions that we conquered through the resistance movement.

We find neither inspiration nor a model of democracy in the anti-racial discrimination still existing in the United States; nor in the struggle waged by all means and violating all international laws to deny the right to self-determination to the people of Cuba; nor in the manifold initiatives directed to keep the majority of the peoples of Latin America in semi-colonial conditions, in poverty and subjected to tyrannical regimes; nor in the refusal to recognize the international sovereign rights of the Chinese People's Republic; nor in the military occupation and in the regime of terror to which the population of Taiwan and south Vietnam are subjected.

I repeat that all this provides neither democratic inspiration nor a model of democratic behavior . . .

We insist on asking this government and any future ones for a deep change in our foreign policy course. We are not interested nor satisfied with vaguely pacifist commonplace affirmations by means of which an attempt is made to induce those who should firmly reject the 'Atlantic loyalty' formula to accept it instead . . .

Our aim is to achieve the total disengagement of Italy from the policy of opposed military blocs. Even in the present situation there are vast possibilities for our country to contribute effectively to the creation of a new international set-up. We shall go on calling upon the Italian people to fight to reach both these aims . . .

Foreign Bulletin (July–August 1963), pp. 20–2.

7   Luigi Longo's report to the Central Committee of the PCI, *L'Unità*, April 22, 1965

We are holding this joint meeting of the Central Committee and of the Central Control Commission of our party in a particularly tense situation. American aggression in Vietnam is spreading every day and becoming more and more serious. It is following the so-called 'escalating' line, that is, the line of ascent to the steps which, one after the other, must lead to an always greater intervention in Vietnam, in South-East Asia and against the Chinese People's Republic. In those regions American aggression is kindling a fire which menaces the whole world. It is using, more and more, new, powerful, deadly arms against the southern partisans, against the northern populations, with no other right than that deriving from its strength.

The Vietnamese people are resisting with great courage. They know they are not alone, they know they can count on the solidarity of the people and on the concrete help of the socialist countries . . .

One admits that diplomatically and militarily Italy is not interested in South-East Asia as it does not belong to SEATO. Despite this, a whole right-wing chorus stresses the fact that Italy 'cannot remain indifferent' to the problems which concern the USA so directly down there. It cannot remain indifferent, not indifferent in a manner which our government men can clearly indicate to the leaders of the White House and the State Department, in the sense that Italy can in no way share in the war actions in South-East Asia. Instead, one demands 'a non-indifference' (in the sense that 'Italy should restate, at this moment, her sincere adhesion to an understanding' of the effort which the United States is facing down there; and in the sense that Italy should contribute to the preservation of American prestige in Vietnam . . .)

American aggression, owing to the international tension it causes, has produced and produces immediate consequences, not only because it rekindles the sparks of war which still exist, but because it pushes the right-wing and conservative forces to a more open action against international dissension and in favor of the consolidation of the power of the big monopolistic trusts . . . This is exactly what is happening in Italy with the press campaign in progress which aims not only at making our country more and more dependent on American imperialism but also at promoting a further shift to the right.

Hence the necessity to spread, strengthen and deepen the solidarity and sympathy of the Italian people for the national liberation struggle of the Vietnamese people. The Italy of the resistance is all with the resistance of the Vietnamese people. But a generic sense of solidarity is not enough: one must give it more precise and concrete forms. Our party delegation which is going to Vietnam under the leadership of comrade G. C. Pajetta is going also for this purpose. We are in the tradition of our people and our party. In the meanwhile, here in Italy, we must strengthen the action to impose a new trend to Italian foreign policy, a trend capable of annulling any responsibility on our part for the American aggression in Vietnam and which, by contributing to the maintenance of peace in the world, may also contribute to block the offensive of the conservative forces and to lead Italy on to a path of actual democratic renewal.

Foreign Bulletin (April–May–June 1965), pp. 5–8.

8 Draft theses for the Eleventh Congress of the PCI, *L'Unità*, November 7, 1965

. . . In the capitalist part of Europe the system on which the United States founded its predominance in the 'Cold War' years is being shaken by a major crisis. Capitalism, on the whole, has continued to develop within the limits of the big monopoly combines and increasingly under their control. This has accentuated the differences in the EEC and in EFTA, has created contradictions between the EEC and the EFTA countries which have so far proved insoluble, has brought out the critical state of social democracy and has liquidated the illusions about a 'third way.' In recent years the growing economic penetration of the United States has created new contradictions and new fissures. On the one hand, part of the leading circles have become subservient to US policy but, on the other hand, US penetration is arousing greater and greater resistance. A centrifugal force, represented by Gaullist France, has already emerged, with a new policy of active nationalism geared to making France the center of a new system in which Western Europe would establish different relations with the United States, with the socialist countries and with the Third

World. This is the reason for the crisis in NATO, which has been one of the factors which has so far prevented the atomic rearmament of West Germany through the so-called Multilateral Atomic Force. This is also the reason for the crisis in the EEC. Thus on several occasions most European countries with the exception of West Germany have shown a tendency to break away from the more aggressive aspects of US policy over Latin America, and to develop economic and cultural relations with the socialist countries, in spite of heightened international tension.

On the whole, however, the ruling circles in Western Europe have not yet managed to assert a position of their own on peaceful coexistence, they have merely endorsed the US one based on the division of the world into spheres of influence; nor have they come up with many new ideas on European security, or broken away from neo-colonialism in their dealings with newly independent countries – in fact, the EEC is itself a key instrument of neo-colonialism. The rebirth of German revanchism and militarism has been tolerated and supported by the West, which has also deliberately left open the question of Berlin and the Polish–German frontiers, which have contributed to the maintenance of international tension, and refused to recognize the German Democratic Republic. The West has also supported or tolerated fascist or openly reactionary regimes in several countries in NATO, the EEC and EFTA (Spain, Portugal, Greece)...

In Europe we must act to provide a positive solution to the crisis in NATO and the EEC, on the basis of the contradictions caused by the growing penetration of US capital and by the process of monopoly concentration which connects with it. This is the basis not only for a big anti-monopoly struggle – which must be co-ordinated on a European basis – but also for a common platform for the struggle against neo-colonialism, with the national liberation movements and the 'Third World' countries. This is the basis for fighting for a security system among all European states, transcending both NATO and the Warsaw Pact, and for initiating a process of economic and political collaboration embracing the whole continent. This is the basis on which the working classes in the European capitalist countries can fulfill the vanguard role which historically is theirs and confront the questions of the unity of the working class and enlarge its alliances with the classes hit by the advance of monopoly power.

The tasks facing our party today spring from this general line. Subordination to American foreign policy, acceptance of the spirit of NATO and 'Western solidarity,' have up till now been powerful weapons in the hands of the conservative and reactionary groups for opposing every policy for a real social change. This policy has never given Italy real security and allowed it to work for peace independently, least of all now, when events are moving so fast . . .

The essential aims of a new Italian foreign policy must, therefore, be to make Italy really independent, which must include independence from all military blocs; a refusal to any atomic agreement, non-renewal of the Atlantic Pact, and neutrality – these are the goals of our policy. Italy must make a contribution to relaxing tension and establishing peaceful coexistence.

We therefore demand that Italy openly dissociate itself from American aggression; we demand with regard to Vietnam the implementation of the decisions of the Geneva Conference; the recognition of the Chinese People's Republic; the immediate removal of American military bases disguised as NATO bases from our territory; a nuclear-free zone in central and southern Europe and the Mediterranean; opposition to every form of atomic rearmament, direct or indirect, of Federal Germany, and therefore to the Multilateral Atomic Force and any other NATO atomic force; recognition of the German Democratic Republic . . .

Our policy is not one of 'national isolation.' On the contrary we consider it inseparable from an active Europe-wide policy, which is the only democratic alternative we can and must put up against both 'Atlanticism' and Gaullist nationalism. We are for transcending the Atlantic Pact and for the neutrality of Italy, but we are also for the participation of Italy in a system of collective security embracing all European countries. We want the EEC changed and a new system in its stead, but we are resolutely against any form of autarchy. We are in favor of economic co-operation between the EEC and the socialist countries; we want new relations with the Third World and, in the first place, Africa and the Middle East; we want social progress and a more democratic Italy, not the rule of big industry and finance . . .

Foreign Bulletin (October–November–December 1965), pp. 80–6.

9 Luigi Longo's report to the Central Committee of the PCI, *L'Unità*, August 28, 1968

. . . We are convinced that on the basis of the general principles of solidarity, community of interests and respect for reciprocal independence, the socialist countries – all the socialist countries – will be able satisfactorily to work out the problem of their interrelations and eliminate the causes of friction that presently exist, even aside from the Czechoslovak crisis. Foundations for this solution already exist, among which are the Bucharest declaration of the Warsaw Pact nations of July 1966 and the Karlovy-Vary declaration of the Conference of European Communist and Working Class Parties of April 1967 . . .

Our party has followed and will continue to follow the spirit of this declaration in all its international action, in the firm conviction that only a policy aimed at overcoming the existing blocs – at the contemporary, if necessarily gradual, dissolution of the Atlantic Pact and the Warsaw Pact – can guarantee peace and at the same time permit the development, within each country, of new, more advanced equilibria and the demise of conservative conceptions which still today so greatly hinder the progress of both international and internal relations.

The division of Europe into blocs – imposed by imperialism with its policy of roll-back – has had deleterious consequences not only for international relations, creating a precarious peace founded on a balance of terror and the arms race, but also for the democratic development of the individual countries.

It is within the context of bloc politics that an increasingly intolerable inequality has emerged between the United States and all the other states of the Atlantic Alliance. It is within the context of bloc politics that we have witnessed massive American interference in the internal affairs of every Atlantic Pact country . . .

It is therefore this system that must be broken if we want to create in Europe and within each individual country new conditions for progress and democratic renewal. This is the real problem, which goes beyond the problems of existing relations between the various socialist states and within the single states . . .

The fact that not all parties have developed what we consider sufficient political initiative in this direction underlines, rather than detracting from, our commitment, which has been firmly developed, even in moments when there appeared in some of the socialist countries tendencies that seemed to work against a policy aimed at overcoming the blocs. Thus the meaning of the position taken by most of the communist parties of Western Europe on the Czechoslovak crisis, in this context, is all the more relevant . . .

Our political initiative with regard to relations in the international field with the other communist parties must, at the moment, be concentrated on the necessity to overcome the bloc system and on the general problems of the struggle against imperialism and for peace . . .

Foreign Bulletin (August–September 1968), pp. 27–32.

10   Luigi Longo's report to the Twelfth Congress of the PCI, February 1969

The military budget for the year that has just begun provides for an expenditure of almost 1,500 billion lire, twice what we spent seven years ago and about 10 per cent more than last year. But the exponents of Atlanticism are still not satisfied and go so far as to urge that 'the Italian territory in its entirety' be transformed into a NATO base. The military spending of the Atlantic Pact countries has already reached 100 million dollars a year, 65,000 billion lire, and plans are being made to increase it still further. We are caught up in a spiral with no end in sight, and we must get out as soon as possible. Italy's interest lies in safeguarding its own security and peace, in conserving its resources for its own renewal and progress. Its interest lies in working consistently for peace in the Mediterranean, in Europe and in the whole world. The line followed by past and present Italian governments instead moves in the direction of increasing subordination to the Atlantic military organizations and therefore to an increasing military commitment . . .

We know the objection raised by the right-wing and government exponents – now, they say, the Soviet fleet is in the Mediterranean. But what has drawn the Soviet ships, if not the American Sixth Fleet? And in what situation did they come, if not the crisis caused by the Israeli aggression against the Arab peoples? We are in no way glad to see this concentration of arms and armies in the Mediterranean. But precisely because we are aware of the grave dangers it involves for our country, we demand that the existing situation lead, not to passive acceptance, but to the adoption of a policy aimed at making the Mediterranean a denuclearized sea, a sea of peace.

Italy must not and cannot serve as a shield or a target for anyone. This goal can be reached only if all foreign and nuclear bases are removed from our soil, from Sicily, from Sardinia, from Naples and the Veneto, as soon as possible. It is not in belonging to a military bloc that Italy can find security. Italy can find real security only outside the blocs, only by gaining a status of neutrality, and by championing, both in the Mediterranean and in Europe, a new direction in international policy aimed at détente and a new system of peaceful coexistence. The signing of the anti-nuclear pact must not remain an isolated gesture; it must become the starting point for broader agreements on nuclear and conventional disarmament. We do not conceive of the conquest of neutral status for Italy as a sort of provincial isolationism. We are aware that today no country can shut itself up within its own borders. For Italy neutrality must be the first step in an active peaceful foreign policy for coexistence that contributes to overcoming the stalemate and even involution now reigning in international relations. For us the fundamental question is for the Italian people to have a guarantee that in no case will they be drawn into a new conflict, that our territory, our people, will never become the target for nuclear weapons. The Italian people do not want to fight a new war and they will not fight it. If any attempt is ever made to pull them into an aggressive war – through the mechanism of NATO, against their will and in violation of the constitution – they will use all their arms to overthrow the regime that intends to lead them to destruction.

It is this desire for peace and emancipation that leads us to ask that the NATO bases be removed from Italy and that Italy withdraw from NATO.

It is an old lie that Italy cannot be neutral. With this lie Italy has twice been led to massacre and disaster. This lie cannot and must not be repeated a third time. No one threatens Italy's borders . . .

The neutral Italy we desire will be an advanced and secure Italy. Advanced because the overthrow of the barriers raised between the popular, anti-fascist and democratic forces will free all the enormous democratic potential of our country. Secure because the foundation of national security lies in the democratic unity of the Italian people. The Italy we want is an Italy capable of playing a role of peace in Europe and in the world . . .

Foreign Bulletin (January–February–March 1969), pp. 45–9.

11 Enrico Berlinguer's report to the Central Committee of the PCI, February 7–9, 1973

With the conclusion of the Paris agreements, the struggle of the Vietnamese people – a long struggle fought with indomitable courage and at the cost of immense sacrifices – has been crowned with a great victory. The United States has been forced to end the war, to withdraw its armed forces, to dismantle its military bases and to openly commit itself, before the world at large, not to interfere in the internal affairs of that country. The basic national rights of the Vietnamese people – the right to freedom, independence and national unity – have been recognized and sanctioned.

The victory of the Vietnamese people is at the same time a victory for the socialist camp, for the worldwide revolutionary movement, for all the progressive forces, including the American democratic forces. It is also a victory for our people and our party and rewards all those in our country who have demonstrated their active solidarity with Vietnam in the most varied forms.

The conclusion of the agreement to end the war in Vietnam is an event of immense importance which will have positive consequences on the whole world situation. It will give new impetus to all the movements and struggles for independence and emancipation from all forms of national and social oppression, to all struggles for freedom and democracy being fought in all parts of the world, and therefore in our own country as well. It opens the way to new progress along the road to international détente, to the building of a world system based on peaceful coexistence and co-operation among all peoples on an equal footing . . .

In Vietnam we have had clear confirmation that imperialism, and US imperialism in particular, has retained its basic, intrinsic, aggressive nature: a confirmation for those of us who are communists, a truth grasped for the first time through direct experience for millions of men in every continent, and, above all, for the young masses in the capitalist countries. The war in Vietnam has shown what unheard-of crimes imperialism is willing to commit when the bases of its domination are threatened by the people's liberation movement – crimes not only against the sovereignty and freedom of nations, but also against the elementary factors of human life. We must not forget that in Vietnam almost all the most highly perfected weapons for the extermination of human life and the destruction of the natural environment have been used and experimented with on a vast scale, and that when even this destructive potential proved insufficient to bring the Vietnamese people to its knees authoritative figures in US political and military life repeatedly urged the use of nuclear weapons . . .

We must not nourish any illusions that imperialism will quietly resign itself, in Indochina and elsewhere, to the defeats it suffers; or that it will give up its practice of interfering with every possible means in the life of other countries to maintain, regain or expand its positions of domination.

At the same time, what has happened in Vietnam has confirmed that imperialism can no longer do what it wants. It can be beaten, or forced to retreat, led to negotiate and impelled to respect the rights of other peoples. Furthermore, in today's world, forces are at work that can restrain, limit and, in the end, reverse the most general catastrophic tendencies inherent in the logic of capitalism and imperialism. And, in fact, what has happened in Vietnam also stands as proof that the relationship of forces in the world has changed and continues to change, to the disadvantage of imperialism and to the advantage of the forces of socialism, democracy and peace.

Vietnam stands as an incomparable example of the coming together and merging of the struggle of an entire people for its own national salvation and a powerful action of international solidarity . . .

A totally new situation – indeed a situation in many essential ways the reversal of the situation existing during the Cold War period – has been created in the center of Europe: with the treaties between the FRG, the USSR and Poland; with the basic treaties between the two German states and recognition of the GDR by the FRG, Italy and over sixty other countries; with recognition by the FRG and the other Western powers of the frontiers created by the Second World War; with the affirmation of

Brandt's Ostpolitik, which has emerged clearly victorious from the recent political elections in Federal Germany. It is in this new European framework that the proceedings of the preparatory Conference on European Security (Helsinki) and the negotiations for arms reduction in Europe (Vienna) have opened – proceedings that are facilitated by the end of the war in Vietnam. Furthermore, after an initial, positive agreement, negotiations between the Soviet Union and the United States for a reduction in strategic weapons (missiles and anti-missiles systems) are continuing – negotiations of capital importance, not only to the end of saving mankind from nuclear catastrophe, but also to the end of reducing the tremendous and unbearable burden of military spending.

New important developments have also emerged in other areas and other continents.

In Latin America the rise to government responsibility of the united left in Chile and the emergence in other countries of increasing pressure for independence from the United States...

The overall meaning of these new elements can be summed up as follows: it is not true that the world is moving to the right; on the contrary, although the struggle is hard and the path difficult and complex, the world is moving to the left.

Naturally not all the important developments of these years have been positive. There have also been negative developments, which are still today far from being overcome; indeed the existence of negative factors has not only persisted, but in some cases actually worsened. It is enough to think of relations between China and the Soviet Union, or, on another level, of the fact that after so many years the conflict in the Middle East is still unsolved, along with the contradictions and crises gripping the Arab countries. But above all we must not forget the appalling problems peculiar to the modern era and the terrible threats hanging over mankind: the accumulation of new catastrophic weapons and the waste of endless resources being thrown away in the building of such arms; the persistent conditions of underdevelopment, poverty and hunger prevailing in vast regions of the world which are also subject to a population explosion; the processes of exhaustion of our energy resources and the increasingly serious problems of pollution and breakdown of the natural equilibria of the environment.

And yet, in conclusion, we feel that on the whole the developments we have here recalled indicate that many basic goals for which we communists, the socialist countries and the working-class, anti-imperialist and advanced democratic movement throughout the world have been fighting for years have been reached, and for others considerable progress has been made. We must remember, for example, developments such as the end of the Cold War, recognition of the GDR and the frontiers produced by the Second World War, recognition of People's China, its rights in the United Nations and its international function...

The Italian Communists, no. 1 (January–February 1973), pp. 5–18.

12 Agostino Novella's report to the Foreign Policy Commission of the Central Committee of the PCI, 1973

. . . The historical failure of the Cold War, the determined beginnings of a policy of détente, the search, the pressures, the attempts aimed at achieving a world policy of peaceful coexistence and co-operation among states with different social and political systems are real facts. Real, but obviously inseparable from many other facts denounced at the Central Committee that witness to the persistence of resistance, contradictions and counter-pressures, that continue to threaten peace in the world...

Within this general context the European situation is moving in the sense of détente, but not with the necessary decision and clarity. The conference on European security is continually threatened by conflicts and postponements, and the same can be said for the Vienna Conference on balanced force reductions in Europe.

Furthermore, in these very days we have had the proposal for an up-dating of the Atlantic Pact, dramatically advanced by Nixon through the mouth of his adviser Kissinger; a proposal that involves the whole Atlantic Alliance system and, in particular, Europe...

What emerges from the US proposals as they have so far been presented is the clear intention to continue Atlantic policy in new forms, extending it to include Japan, to reknit the fractures that have developed within the old alliances and, in any event, to stop the trend towards a greater unity and co-operation among the European states and the

298 THE COMMUNIST PARTIES OF ITALY, FRANCE AND SPAIN

assertion of an autonomous role for Europe in world politics, both with regard to US policy and in the establishment of a new type of inter-state relations with the socialist countries.

The most striking thing in Kissinger's statement is the fact that, while taking for granted the permanent nature of the division between the USSR and China, the general goal is obviously the formation of a new unity of the 'Western world,' founded on strengthened and renewed US hegemony, destined to become the pivot of a new phase of stepped-up competition – of a new type perhaps – with the socialist world in the political and economic fields, as well as in armaments.

The subdivision of the world into blocs, as politically reaffirmed in the substance of Kissinger's statements, is irreconcilable with a consistent development of the policy of peaceful coexistence. Nor can it in any way contribute to the rapid convocation of the conference on security and co-operation in Europe and the role this conference can play in overcoming the existing military blocs . . .

It is clear that on the basis of this stand we will sharply oppose any tendency on the part of Italy to underwrite the Nixon Plan.

Whatever the fate of this plan, our party must give more strength, more continuity and consistent development to its European policy.

In working for the progressive overcoming of the opposing military blocs, we reaffirm our policy for a peaceful, democratic and independent Europe. Within this framework our fight for rapid convocation of the conference on European security and co-operation assumes a fundamental importance . . .

In the present situation a declaration by all the European states on respect for existing borders, on the non-use of force in solving controversies among the states and on full respect for the autonomy, independence and equality of rights of all states would in itself be of the greatest importance.

Naturally such a declaration would not cover all the problems at hand, but in our opinion a conference on security and co-operation must necessarily start from these general principles.

For this reason we demand that the Italian government takes a clear stand on the primary and decisive value of these principles and therefore works for the rapid opening of the conference itself.

In line with these principles, and without in any way contradicting the urgency and importance of the Helsinki Conference, we hold that bilateral agreements can also be undertaken and that Italy must, as other countries are doing, take initiatives that work in this direction, toward the socialist countries in particular.

The comrades present are all undoubtedly aware that within the framework of preparations for the Helsinki Conference and the Vienna negotiations differences and conflicts have arisen not only on the substance of the individual problems to be dealt with but also on the geographical areas that these negotiations should cover and guarantee. Thus there has been and is a tendency on some sides to make a parallel process of Mediterranean security a condition for all progress in the realization of a system of European security. Similarly for the Vienna negotiations conflicting positions have emerged on the question of enlarging (or restricting) participation to the European countries more or less directly concerned. We must be very clear on this point: we are for a Europe from the Urals to the Atlantic, from the North Sea to the Sea of Sicily, but we do not consider that an all-or-nothing attitude is correct . . .

US efforts to keep Italy out of an eventual process of disarmament, with all this implies in terms of missile and naval bases directed against the socialist countries and in support of imperialist positions in the Mediterranean, will inevitably have the effect of limiting and slowing down balanced force reductions in Europe.

In failing to support consistently its request for full participation in the Vienna Conference, the Italian government is also failing to make a positive contribution to the policy of collective security in Europe and to efforts aimed at overcoming the military blocs.

Furthermore, to the extent that the Vienna negotiations are enlarged geographically, they would provide an indispensable completion to the SALT agreements. As is known, these talks do not cover the whole tactical nuclear arsenal spread about in Europe, and it is easy to foresee that the US may be tempted to make up in this area for the limitations it will be forced to accept on the strategic level under the SALT agreements. In this regard Nixon's recent assurance to Brandt that the 700 atomic bombers located in various parts of Europe will not be affected by the SALT negotiations is highly significant.

I have already mentioned that the problem of balanced arms reduction in Europe is closely related not only to the problem of the general force relationships between the military blocs, but also to the specific terms these relationships take in the

Mediterranean area, and therefore in a particularly acute manner, with the Middle East conflict...

Our initiative and struggle for the rapid convocation of the conference on European security obviously does not diminish our commitment towards Western Europe. Indeed, as I have already said, the US proposal for a new Atlantic Charter makes this commitment all the more immediate and important.

Our goal is a democratic Europe that plays an autonomous role and acts as a factor in détente, in promoting peace and in overcoming the blocs, a Europe marching towards the goals of co-operation among all peoples and peaceful coexistence.

We have already said that we are for a democratic Europe that is neither against the United States nor against the Soviet Union, a Europe that, on the contrary, develops good political, economic and cultural relations with all the capitalist, socialist and Third World countries.

This implies our determined opposition to all initiatives and tendencies, of whatever origin, aimed at turning Europe into a new political-military bloc, a sort of superstate that would openly or in practice contribute to consolidating bloc policy, rather than actively working to overcome it...

The Italian Communists, nos 2–3 (March–June 1973), pp. 62–8.

13   Enrico Berlinguer's report to the Central Committee in preparation for the Fourteenth Congress of the PCI, December 10, 1974

. . . Certain somewhat imprecise formulations circulated recently in the press have been taken to indicate a change in our basic assessment of the Atlantic Pact and, more generally, our position on the division of Europe and a part of the world into opposing blocs. This is not the case. The PCI still holds valid the judgement it expressed on the origins of the Atlantic Pact and on the way it was used by the USA and the governments of Western Europe.

The Atlantic Pact was one of the major instruments in the policy followed by the capitalist and imperialist forces to perpetuate the break in anti-fascist unity on a world scale and in individual countries. The purpose of this policy – which had as its prerequisite the monopoly then held over the atomic bomb by the two biggest capitalist powers (the USA and Great Britain) – was to compel the whole world, through force and blackmail (economic, military and political), to accept the so-called 'American way of life,' i.e. the capitalist-imperialist way of production and life, pushing, or as was then said, 'rolling' back the new reality of the socialist societies and the progressive democracies advancing towards socialism. The Atlantic Pact was an instrument for feeding the Cold War, for breaking off the processes of renewal begun with the great anti-fascist war and the victory over Nazi-fascism. Within the individual countries, as in Italy, it was an instrument for promoting and consolidating the break in unity among the anti-fascist and popular forces, thus making it possible to go ahead with capitalist restoration and monopoly development, by means of an all-out attack on the most advanced part of the working-class and popular movement. The Warsaw Pact was established shortly after the Atlantic Pact, in answer to it. But it is worth while to stress once again that the policy of force, the policy of Cold War – of which the Atlantic Pact was the culmination – was first announced by Churchill (his Fulton speech) in 1946, and immediately after begun by the USA, Britain and other capitalist powers, when there was no conceivable threat to fear from the Soviet Union, which had given every proof of following a firm, consistent peace policy and, among other things, did not even possess atomic weapons in those years. As a result of this policy Europe (together with Korea and part of South-East Asia) found itself divided into two opposing blocs: a division which had profound negative consequences of all kinds...

Over the past few years, with the failure to achieve some of its essential goals and the collapse of some of its underlying conditions, Cold War policy has entered into crisis. In practice, the Cold War has been attenuated, though it has not disappeared, and a process of détente has developed, which has already produced extremely important results, among which are recognition by all the European states of the boundaries sanctioned by the end of the Second World War, and recognition of the German Democratic Republic; creation of a positive climate, with the development of increasingly broad economic, cultural and political relations between the countries of East and West and negotiations for agreements on arms reductions; convocation of an international conference to work out a system of collective security in Europe...

It is evident that the goal of overcoming the blocs in Europe can only be reached if the process of détente advances in the political and military fields, together with an intensification of economic, scientific and cultural co-operation. Thus the goal of overcoming the blocs must be seen not as *a prius*, i.e. as a precondition necessary for détente and the establishment of an international set-up based on peace, peaceful coexistence and co-operation, but rather as an effect of détente, or better, as a concrete process going hand-in-hand with the process of détente: the one tied to the other by mutual relations of interdependence. Seen from this viewpoint, the complete dissolution of the blocs appears as one of the final consequences of the advance of détente and presumably not one that can be reached in the near future. To consider the goal of dissolution of the blocs as a precondition would instead mean relegating it to the realm of impossible things, and might indeed complicate and slow down the overall movement towards détente and co-operation.

It is clear, in fact, that in Europe and in other areas of the world there exists a strategic-military equilibrium between the two blocs and in particular between the USSR and the United States: an equilibrium that must be carefully and realistically taken into account by everyone, if we want to advance the process of détente and the creation of a new international set-up based on peace and full independence of all the peoples.

All the negotiations, both past and present, aimed at slowing down the arms race and arriving at arms reductions, have themselves been based on the condition of maintaining a balance of military power...For this reason as well, in all those areas such as Europe where the division into opposing blocs is clearly defined (despite the existence, which constitutes a highly important positive factor, of non-aligned countries, among which Yugoslavia plays a particular role, thanks to the foreign policy line it has consistently followed for years now), it is not realistic to think in terms of unilateral withdrawals by individual countries from one or the other alliance. In the present conditions the goal of gradually overcoming the blocs and their logic, down to their final elimination, depends on the general process of détente and therefore, also, on the efforts and initiative of each country, Italy included, in speeding up this process.

In fact, for the process of détente to advance, it is necessary for the individual countries, even within the context of the existing alliances − an idea repeatedly expressed by Togliatti many years ago − to develop an effective initiative and assert an autonomous peace and co-operation policy of their own...

The two processes (détente, on the one hand, and progressive assertion of the international autonomy of the individual countries and gradual overcoming of the blocs, on the other) are interwoven and mutually interdependent. Détente, correct peaceful solutions to existing conflicts, and measures for disarmament and international co-operation in all fields, all lead to overcoming the bloc logic, to gradually and concretely emptying the blocs themselves of their *raison d'être*, and thus towards their ultimate dissolution...

As concerns Italy specifically, we do not raise the problem of Italy's withdrawal from the Atlantic Pact as a prerequisite question. With the new, more advanced stage entered upon by the process of détente and the new prospects for European security concretely opening up, important signs have emerged of a less rigid conception of the blocs and relations between them. In the first place, the Soviet Union and the United States have agreed to work along this road, maintaining the strategic-military equilibrium existing in this crucial region and working together to reduce it to lower and lower levels of weapons, military bases and troops; and we believe that this is a road on which rapid, further and more substantial progress can be made, thanks also to mounting pressure from the European working-class and democratic forces.

The line we propose for Italy and Western Europe is not therefore one of simply accepting and working to favor the results of negotiations between the two biggest powers and the two blocs; it is a line of active intervention in the process of détente and co-operation. The Soviet−American dialogue remains an irreplaceable premiss for all policies aimed at maintaining world peace. But an Italian and European policy that is neither anti-Soviet nor anti-American can and must also be an increasingly autonomous, free policy, rich in initiatives both in promoting broad co-operation on the pan-European level to deal with problems of common interest and in the development of mutually advantageous relations with the non-European countries...

The Italian Communists, special issue, nos 5−6, 1974, pp. 58−64.

14 Enrico Berlinguer, interview with the *Corriere della Sera*, **June 15, 1976**

Q. There is something else that makes people uneasy about you: your ties with the USSR.

A. Our autonomy is total. The PCI decides its policies in absolute freedom. And it expresses completely autonomous judgements on the socialist experiences of other countries, also pointing out the aspects involving serious limitations of freedom. If we do not see everything black when we look to the East, as others do, this is simply a 'different' judgement, not a 'non-autonomous' judgement.

Q. Don't you fear that Moscow will bring Berlinguer and his eurocommunism to the same end as Dubček and his 'socialism with a human face'?

A. No. We are in another area of the world. There is not the slightest possibility that our road to socialism can be hindered or conditioned by the USSR, even presuming that it wants to. One can argue as to whether the USSR seeks to exert its hegemony over the countries that are its allies. But there is not one single act that indicates its intention to go beyond the boundaries set by Yalta.

Q. You therefore feel safer because you are in the West.

A. I feel that since Italy does not belong to the Warsaw Pact, from this point of view, there is absolute certainty that we can proceed along the Italian road to socialism without any constraints. But this does not mean that there are no problems within the Western bloc: indeed we find ourselves forced to defend Italy's right to decide its own future within the framework of the Atlantic Alliance, an alliance we do not question.

Q. In short, the Atlantic Alliance can also be a useful shield in order to build socialism with freedom.

A. I don't want Italy to withdraw from the Atlantic Pact, 'also' for this reason, and not only because our withdrawal would upset the international equilibrium. I feel safer over here, but I see that also over here there are serious attempts to limit our autonomy.

Q. Anyway, don't you think that socialism with freedom is more achievable in the Western system than in the Eastern one?

A. Yes, certainly, the Western system offers fewer constraints. However, be careful. Over there, in the East, they would perhaps like to see us build socialism as they like it. But over here, in the West, some people don't even want to let us start to build it, even if we do so with freedom. I realize that it is a little risky on our part to pursue a road that is not always appreciated either over here or over there. This is one reason why I hope the Italians will encourage us on June 20. Our road, which is different from those followed to date, is the one that most closely corresponds to the country's deepest interests. And we are convinced that the conditions exist to pursue it with confidence.

The Italian Communists, nos 2–3 (April–July 1976), cf. pp. 46–53.

15 **Enrico Berlinguer's preface to his book** *La politica internazionale dei comunisti Italiani*, **1975**

. . . The present crisis is not limited to the economic and productive mechanisms, structures and institutions of the individual countries and of Western Europe as a whole; it also affects – although in different ways – the political, social, civil, state and government set-ups in the various countries.

The morass now gripping the European West thus compromises the whole prospect of Europe's returning to play a full, vigorous, united, peaceful role of its own in the international forum, and threatens instead to push it to the sidelines, without replacing it with anything valid and fruitful for the purposes of a different type of world development that unfolds in conditions of détente, peaceful coexistence and co-operation.

It is no longer of any use, indeed it can only complicate and aggravate things, to try to reassert a European presence, pursuing the economic policies, productive orientations and consumption choices of the 1950s and 1960s, or dusting off political proposals and formulas that are dead and gone.

The old ideas, and the old forces that supported them and still support them, can no longer arouse any hope, much less offer Europe and the Europeans any prospect for solid, lasting recovery. This is true whether they present themselves in the bourgeois conservative variety or in the social democratic form: it is no accident that both the one and the other are in crisis.

Precisely because we have seen the Western Europe of the 'third force,' moderate, Christian democratic and social democratic schools fall into crisis, we have taken the initiative to take upon ourselves the cause of the recovery of a world function for Western Europe. And we have said that new ideas and forces must enter the European field and assert themselves within the individual countries and in their foreign policies: ideas capable, on the one hand, of safeguarding and developing the whole patrimony of values built up through centuries of European labor and genius, and, on the other, of constructively interpreting the demands for justice and change unleashed by the present crisis, the new levels of awareness that are maturing in the depths of European society and the widespread aspiration to break out of the capitalist system and move towards socialism.

Given the development and growing strength of the working-class, democratic and socialist movement, we believe that today it is possible, in Italy and in Western Europe, to open wider and wider passages for the advance of new forms of Italian and European social and political organization, while remaining firmly anchored to the democratic system and operating on this terrain; we are convinced, that is, that it is possible to build a socialist society in Italy and in Western Europe, without abandoning the democratic terrain, and indeed developing it . . .

The truth is that today, in Italy and in Western Europe, democracy can live, further develop and produce constructive and not disruptive effects, only if there is a change in the structures and the social and political framework in which democratic dialectics express themselves.

But this means doing something that the capitalist bourgeoisie is absolutely incapable of doing: it means thinking out and implementing a plan for the functioning of economic, political, social, cultural and moral life, guided by criteria, methods and ends different from and superior to those which have prevailed so far in Italy and in Western Europe; it means embarking on the building of a society that, to function, must incorporate elements of socialism . . .

Our interest is in the problems of the present world picture and, above all, in the problems involved in raising the underdeveloped countries and the vast areas of depression and hunger. This effort can no longer take the paternalistic form of 'aid' and 'assistance' – which has not only proven totally insufficient, but is also rejected, and quite correctly so, by the recipients – but must be pursued through wider collaboration, trade on 'equal terms' and, therefore, with full participation, which necessarily implies respect for the autonomy and independence of the peoples and new countries. Only if it strives towards these goals, only if it succeeds in pushing the Soviet–American dialogue (which is in any case essential to the conservation of world peace) to this same end, only if it is capable of realizing this comprehensive, yet diversified, political line of great breadth and scope, can Europe win back its world role. And it is precisely this that we are working and fighting for . . .

The Italian Communists, no. 6 (November–December 1976), cf. pp. 41–5.

16 Draft theses for the Fifteenth Congress of the PCI, December 1978

The Big Contradictions of the Present Time
More and more lacerating contradictions are piling up in the world situation. The capitalist system shows itself incapable of solving the problems generated by its own development, both in the individual countries and on the world level. The present phase brings to light the ills produced by the development of the 1950s and 1960s, compounded by the effects of the fall in the process of accumulation and investment of the 1970s. Unemployment has again become an acute problem in many countries. There are growing imbalances and spreading phenomena of malaise and break-up . . .

The answers to the drama of contemporary man tried to date, including those advanced by the workers' movement as a whole, have not as yet proved adequate to the gravity of the problems. The time has come for a fight to rediscover and realize the great socialist ideals of peace, freedom and equality. It is in this context that the Italian communists and the communists of other countries of the capitalist world have developed the idea of a new road of advance towards socialism and the building of a socialist society founded on democracy...

International Political Relations
Over the past years the process of international détente has achieved positive results, but now registers a worrisome stagnation with dangers of crisis.

The victory of the Vietnamese people ended a barbarous aggression and created new hopes for détente. In Europe the conclusion of the Helsinki Treaty defined and gave greater substance to peaceful relations on the continent.

Nevertheless new elements of deterioration in the international situation have emerged, first of all in relations between the two major powers: the United States and the Soviet Union. Understanding between these two powers is indispensable, although not in itself sufficient, for peaceful progress towards new international relations of co-operation. Without this the whole international situation worsens, as is happening today. The persistence of grave contention between the USSR and China constitutes a dangerous element. Acute disputes and in some cases military conflicts have broken out among certain of the newly independent and socialist-inspired countries. The conflicts between China and Vietnam and Vietnam and Cambodia are also a source of grave alarm.

Both in Africa and Asia there is growing competition and confrontation among various powers. Increasingly we can see trends towards the acquisition of strategic bases, trends constituting a source of serious concern for the prospects it implies. This situation also produces divisions among the non-aligned countries.

Notable changes and contradictory pressures can be seen in the international policy of the new US administration as it has emerged from the grave political crisis following the defeat in Vietnam and its internal repercussions. The confrontation with the Soviet Union on the ideological level and in various areas of the world has grown more marked. Open interference in the internal affairs of a number of countries, among which is Italy, continues. But other opposing tendencies are also at work in public opinion, in congress and within the government itself. These can be seen in the continuing negotiations for a limitation of strategic armaments and in the opposition to new military interventions abroad. In general what emerges is a policy marked by uncertainties and oscillations, but one that tends to avoid the more rigid schemes of the past and to work in more ductile forms.

The idea of bringing the entire developed capitalist world back together under a single line (the Trilateral) has proved difficult to apply.

Dialectics among the capitalist countries have grown more open as a consequence of the growing strength of some of them, in particular West Germany and Japan. Also emerging are new intermediate capitalist powers that tend to establish a supremacy of their own within a particular area, as in the case of Brazil or Iran...

Big responsibilities fall on the countries of Western Europe, the zone that prior to 1914 was the center of the world and in but a few decades has lost its century-old pre-eminence. Today, in a world shaken by a crisis of transition from one epoch to another, with the creation of new centers of power, from the United States to the Soviet Union and China, Western Europe finds itself in a position of relative political and, in part, also economic, weakness. The countries of Western Europe conserve important positions, but they have not succeeded in asserting an autonomous role of their own. Constraints stemming from US influence and the political and military division of the continent weigh on Western Europe.

The Situation of Western Europe
Thanks to productive expansion and the accumulation of wealth in the countries of Western Europe (in part secured, in the past, from colonial exploitation and, in the present, from persisting neo-colonialist practices), a part of the European populations enjoys high consumption levels. But these conditions are today jeopardized by the immediate consequences of the present economic crisis and by the advance of new peoples and countries.

Despite the bitter contentions of the past, the European countries have begun to seek forms of pluri-national unity, capable, through new relations of co-operation, of increasing Europe's weight on the world scene. The creation of the European Community in the 1950s was in answer to the need to promote new economic development and also to the US concern to give the Atlantic Alliance an economic base.

In the Cold War period the anti-Soviet function of the various attempts at European organization was clear. Nevertheless the process of integration has brought with it an objective factor of development induced by the new productive and economic dimension. In addition, in the course of the years, there has been growing awareness, even on the part of

European capitalist groups, that détente and the interests of Western Europe itself require more positive relations with the other part of Europe and a more autonomous policy with respect to the United States...

The communists have taken a stand for a gradual overcoming of the division of Europe into opposing military blocs, on the basis of clear-cut and mutual guarantees of security. In a world and in a Europe where peace still rests on the balance of power, this process can advance on the condition that unilateral breakings of the present equilibriums are avoided: such breaks would complicate, rather than facilitate, the process of détente. Hence the necessity for Italy to remain in the Atlantic Alliance, which must operate for exclusively defensive ends within the well-defined geographical area for which it was created. Within NATO Italy must not abandon the free and responsible exercise of its own autonomous initiative and the fight against die-hard, aggressive positions...

The Italian Communists, special issue, 1978, pp. 23–36.

The European Community

17 Political resolution of the Directorate of the PCI, August 1, 1959

... The development of disputes within the EEC and with the other capitalistic forces of the West is far from over. The very fate of the EEC is in discussion. The latest happenings have, however, clearly confirmed that what lies at the bottom of these convulsions and conflicts of the groups dominated by the West is the tendency to accentuate capitalistic concentration, to reinforce the domination of the great monopolies, by making the working class, the farmers and the intermediate class pay the expenses of the crisis which assails the capitalistic system as well as of the bitter fight for securing control of those markets which still remain under the control of capitalism. In the name of the economic war which they have unleashed and which they disguise under the name of free enterprise and private enterprise, in the name of the EEC and convertibility of currency, the monopolies, the strongest capitalistic groups, seek to liquidate the social conquests of the working class and of the people, by blocking and lowering salaries, and by absorbing the intermediate production forces.

The call for a return to the 'laws of the market' – during the era of imperialism laws were imposed on the market by the monopolies – reveal clearly that the reactionary attack is aimed at assuring maximum liberty for monopolistic capital and placing all the other sectors at its mercy...

Presented by its supporters as an instrument for the unification of Europe, for international economic liberalization and collaboration, the EEC is rapidly revealing itself as source of division, of breakage and of economic war, not only with regard to the socialist world, the new Afro-Asiatic countries and Latin America, but also within the capitalistic West. The decision for convertibility of currency, ending the European union of payments and making buying in one monetary area the same as any other, has destroyed even the illusion that the EEC could represent an incentive to intensify exchanges within Western Europe. In this situation, increasingly so today, the discriminatory barrier which the EEC has established against the rest of the world constitutes a particular and decisive reason for deviating from its sphere, towards other zones and important traffic currents.

The tinsel having thus fallen, the EEC is revealed as being what it has always been: the instrument of a reactionary political operation, aimed at accentuating the process of monopolistic concentration and at removing every obstacle to the expansion of monopolistic economic power...

For these reasons the leadership of the PCI condemns the policy of irresponsible and complete adhesion to the EEC which the Fanfani government has followed and the attitude which it has assumed regarding the latest economic and monetary happenings. First of all, the government has not even timidly protested about the fact that Italy has been practically excluded from the decisive phases of the international negotiations which have led to the present monetary and economic confusion. The parliament has been excluded from an ordinary examination of the problems and decisions which have presented themselves to Italy. It should also be noted that the legislative decrees announced by the government exceed the powers established in the EEC's rules of approval, posing a series of questions with regard to the legitimacy of the government action.

It should be emphasized that the government did not know how to follow guidelines calling for independence and prudent safeguards for the national interest. The actions which it has taken have clearly tended to support the role of monopolies and the strongest economic groups...

It is urgent that efforts be made to push back the reactionary attack and to orient our national economic and political life in a completely opposite direction. The present government is moving towards favoring the monopolistic concentration, the domination of the great capitalistic firms and even the penetration and supremacy of the giant international trusts. The communists instead hold that for a true modernization of the country, for true internal economic development which would permit peaceful competition with other nations, for an expansion of commerce and exchange, for effective European and international co-operation, it is necessary to limit and cut away at the power of the monopolies and the great capitalistic groups. This is the path of true 'modernization,' or, more exactly, of civil and social progress for our country and for humanity...

All this warrants the suspension of the EEC. The communists maintain that this political decision cannot be avoided. Rather, in view of the facts revealed this week, it is necessary. The communists are not simply asking for the suspension of the EEC, but suggest also a concrete alternative regarding the national economy and commerce among all countries, based on a plan of equity and reciprocal benefits. The communists, who have always considered a political autocracy absurd and ruinous, maintain that the suspension of the EEC is not in conflict with policies for customs reductions ending protectionism, and increasing non-discriminatory trade with all peoples. The customs reductions should be carried out in such a way so as to ensure that the relative weaknesses of the Italian economy are taken into consideration, as well as the necessities of development of certain sectors, so as to combat and not to reinforce the privileged positions of the monopolies...

L'Unità, August 2, 1959.

18   Document of the Political Bureau of the PCI, 'For a European democratic initiative and the revision of EEC treaties,' February 22, 1963.

Deep contrasts of economic political and military nature have recently arisen among capitalist countries and have been deepened by the creation of the Paris–Bonn axis and by De Gaulle's refusal to admit Great Britain to the EEC. These contrasts involve both the Atlantic Pact and the Common Market, and have the tendency to spread to the system of alliances and agreements which were concluded in this postwar period by imperialist countries in opposition to the socialist system and to the national liberation movement of the colonial and dependent countries... These contradictions are, also, a consequence of the unequal development registered in these years by the capitalist countries and of the strengthening of Western Europe in comparison with the United States. The EEC – created to meet the need, imposed by the development of productive forces, for overcoming the limited national markets – has greatly contributed to this consolidation, since, due to the manner in which it was conceived, it enabled the European monopolies to reach an unprecedented competitive power, and determined a new phase in the struggle between the imperialist states for a new division of markets and for their hegemony over the former colonial countries. For this reason, after having encouraged the creation of the European Common Market, because they considered it an instrument capable of strengthening the Atlantic front in the heart of Europe, the United States has tried to hinder the expansive impulse of 'Little Europe' by proposing to extend the process of integration and the creation of an economic, political and military system of interdependence between Western Europe and North America... It has been proved once again, thus, that the EEC is not only an obstacle to the development of economic co-operation between countries having different social regimes, but that – as the instrument of a new division of markets – it also represents a source of contrasts and antagonistic struggles among the capitalist countries of Europe and of other continents...

The 'Little Europe' created by the Rome treaties has not had any democratic life. Its power organs were created at the summit and have been dominated by a technocracy which has assumed an increasingly exclusive character. The national parliaments themselves have no control over the supranational organs and the appointment of national delegates is done with criteria of political discrimination, excluding the representatives of the working-class parties and of some important trade union organizations. Thus an abyss has been created between these supranational organs and the different national situations of the member countries.

Moreover an absolutist system, which is the denial of democracy, has been set up and tends to impose itself above the democratic and representative institutions of the member countries of the Community. This deformation of the need for a process of economic integration, in the interest of the monopolies, was also expressed, in addition to the increasing competition among the big monopoly groups, in a co-ordinated action of these groups against the conquests and aspirations of the workers and in an attempt to prevent even the slightest change in the political and economic life. If, on the one hand, the EEC favored the increase of production, employment and trade within 'Little Europe,' on the other hand, it contributed – even where employment and wages have increased – to emphasize the tendency towards a growing gap between earnings and labor productivity common to all capitalist countries. Not only working-class conditions but all the economic life of the EEC countries are more and more determined – directly or indirectly – by the will and decisions of the financial capital which increasingly conditions the very policy of the member states. 'Little Europe,' created through the EEC, has thus revealed itself in actual fact as an obstacle and menace to international relaxation of tension, democracy and social progress . . .

The Paris–Bonn axis threat to Europe must be warded off
Western Europe must change its course. It is at a crossroads. On one side there is the continuation of the course followed up to now. It has already led to deep crisis, to the decline of democracy in a whole series of countries, to the domination by authoritarian and reactionary forces, to the armaments race. On the other side there is a path, which, through the struggle for peaceful coexistence, leads to opposition and defeat of the reactionary forces and to securing a democratic renewal so as to transform Western Europe into a force for peace and progress. This alternative today requires a wide action directed to modify substantially the instruments and processes that permitted, through the Rome treaties, the monopoly domination within the Common Market. In view of the serious situation created now in Western Europe (fully confirming the repeated communist denunciations of the EEC as an instrument distorting the need for economic integration and tending by its own nature to deepen the economic and political division of Europe and to create new contrasts), it is now urgent to revise all the lines

followed up to the present, and to take an initiative of all the democratic forces to oppose to this type of Europe another Europe.

This alternative cannot be achieved by going back to the limited national markets nor to autarkical and protectionist positions. It can be achieved, instead, by the development of a unitarian initiative so as to lay the bases for European economic co-operation, also among states of differing social structure . . .

Foreign Bulletin (March–April 1963), pp. 45–51.

19 Giorgio Amendola's speech to the European Parliament, November 15, 1972

. . . I believe instead that only in Parliament, if all discrimination is dropped and it becomes truly representative of all the political and social forces active in the member-countries, and in the Commission, if it succeeds in incorporating and expressing the competence and capacity of the social, trade union, cultural and youth forces present within the Community, can the lines of development of the Community as a whole be established and present difficulties overcome. Only these organs, in other words, through a process of democratic transformation, can make the Community an open center of European and pan-European co-operation, of détente and peace.

As things now stand, the predominance of the Council of Ministers, as the motor-organ of the whole Community . . . subjects the Community to the perpetual oscillations of the shifting power balance among the states, creating a permanent state of uncertainty. Under the pretext of *Realpolitik*, all the political crises of the individual states, their emerging conflicts and evolving changes, are thrown off into the life of the Community, preventing it from moving forward.

In reality the Council, today the highest center of Community power, is, even more than the other organs, forced to operate on a day-to-day basis, given the daily pressures of national government activities . . .

What is needed is a political change of course, and

this cannot come from government summits, but rather from a new impetus to the Community process, which only the intervention of the democratic forces can give. Certainly the election of the European Parliament by direct, universal suffrage would be a central element in this change of course. We once more declare our will to work to see that this happens; without tricks, however. In fact, elections in a single country would count very little, i.e. the situation in this Assembly would not change just because the representation of a 'piece' of it changes (and the result would be something heterogeneous). What is needed, on the contrary, is an Assembly elected by all the European countries, regardless of what might be the political consequences of such a consultation. As far as we are concerned, I think we would still find ourselves in a minority, but a minority that rests assured on the soundness of its ideas and its capacity for argumentation. But I do not believe such elections will be held: at the most we can hope to find ways to make the European Parliament more representative of the forces actually existing in the individual national parliaments ...

The Italian Communists, no. 6 (November–December 1972), pp. 45–9.

20   Giorgio Amendola's speech to the Conference of Communist Parties of Capitalist Europe, January 27, 1974

... The EEC is a reality which should be judged for exactly what it is, but in its real weakness, aggravated by the world economic crisis. Set up in the Cold War years to play an openly anti-Soviet role, tied by an umbilical cord to the Atlantic Alliance, the Common Market has opened a space for undisturbed expansion by the monopolies and the multinational companies, but it has never become a supranational entity. Since 1970 a deep crisis has emerged in the EEC, which has been forced by the monetary crisis to recognize that its interests differ from those of the United States. On the other hand, despite the resistance of the inconsolable widows of the Cold War, it has been forced to discover the possibilities of co-operation with the Soviet Union and the socialist countries ...

In the face of the crisis brought on by the war in the Middle East, after the October 20 declaration, which had a meaning of autonomy and neutrality, the EEC member-states denied the use of NATO bases to US forces. And since then, in the face of the energy crisis, each state has followed its own road ...

In reality the EEC has shown itself to be powerless to give a united answer to the great problems raised by the world economic crisis, because of its own internal contradictions. The crisis of the EEC can only be overcome by means of a far-reaching democratic transformation. We are fighting for such a transformation, because we consider useful the presence of a democratic multinational organization capable of coping with problems which the individual national states have shown themselves unable to solve (currency, circulation of capital, control over the multinational companies, energy, pollution, etc.). Naturally the EEC cannot pretend to represent all Europe, but only a part of Europe − a part of Europe which must establish relations of co-operation with that part which is already socialist, which must aid the European peoples oppressed by fascism and establish new relations of co-operation with the developing countries, a Europe neither anti-Soviet nor anti-American. Italy, which has millions of emigrants present in the EEC countries, has a particular interest in building a united organization where Italians can enjoy secure rights of residence, circulation, social security, education and democratic participation.

In the struggle for democratic transformation of the EEC, we must overcome the resistance of those groups that have a vested interest in maintaining its present nature. The European Parliament has in fact only consultative powers. The Commission is a big secretariat without real powers of decision. All the power is concentrated in the Council of Ministers, where the ministers representing the various governments, after extenuating haggling, reach precarious agreements, on the basis of the variable interplay of a shifting relationship of forces.

These relationships must be overthrown. The representatives of the European trade union movement, of the agricultural associations, co-operatives and youth movements, must be brought into the Commission with responsible functions. Even if election of the European Parliament by direct, universal suffrage, under a common, proportional electoral law, is not a problem for today, we can nevertheless strengthen the authority of the parliament, working to make it more representative from a democratic standpoint and renewing and upgrading its composition...

The Italian Communists (January–February 1974), pp. 13–15.

21 Giorgio Amendola, interview with *L'Unità*, September 22, 1976

Q. After months of hesitation and postponements, what does the signing of the convention establishing direct elections actually mean?

A. The decision is certainly important. It represents the beginning of a process, which we Italian communists have always urged, of arriving at the election of a European Parliament with the power that a direct popular investiture can confer and therefore capable of becoming the working center of a real unity of Western Europe.

Q. In your opinion, in what direction should this process for an extension of the elected European Parliament move?

A. In the direction of creating a new multinational power, capable of fulfilling the tasks that the individual national states have shown they cannot tackle: the fight against the multinational companies, the control of capital movements, the elaboration of planned economic policies and, in other fields, the the fight against pollution, the search for new energy sources, and so forth. At the same time, in international policy, this power should succeed in reasserting a real autonomy for Europe in the process of détente and the over-coming of the blocs...

I do not share the overenthusiasm of certain Europeanists who think the difficulties in the operation of the European Community can be overcome by simply plunging ahead. If we want to work seriously to build European unity we must not hide the difficulties, but concentrate our energies and efforts for mobilization on overcoming them.

The first obstacle lies in the fact that today, because of the policies followed by the EEC and the very limited role assigned to the present European Parliament, the popular masses are not really interested in it. In particular, the working people are either hostile or indifferent. Italy, with its emigrants, is perhaps the country where the European cause is most widely understood. Therefore, preparing for the European elections does not mean just carrying out the necessary procedures; it also means creating the political conditions to make the elections a really democratic event...

I think there is a danger that the prospect of the elections will tend to cover up the present paralysis of the European institutions. The Community machinery is running out of gear and with increasing difficulty. The uncertainty concerning the institutions' future in connection with the elections is aggravated by the change in the Executive Commission due at the end of the year. While the designation of a strong personality like Roy Jenkins, former British Home Secretary, to head the new Commission undoubtedly represents a commitment on the part of the British Labor Party, everything else is still up in the air.

Among other things, there is the problem of selecting the Italian commissioners. Given the new situation in the Italian parliament, this choice cannot be left up to the discretion of the government or the frenetic activities of a few self-proclaimed 'candidates.' At least the criteria for the selection must be discussed by parliament, for example, in the Foreign Affairs Commission, in order to avoid yet another shameful division of the spoils and ensure the selection of the most competent people...

The Italian Communists, nos 4–5 (August–October 1976), cf. pp. 28–31.

22 Draft theses for the Fifteenth Congress of the PCI, December 1978

It is necessary to break out of the present situation in the European Community. The transformation of the Community into a democratic organism, founded on universal suffrage, is imperative. A pluri-national power is necessary to tackle effectively such problems as currency, capital movements, industrial re-

conversion, energy, agriculture and scientific research. The PCI has made and intends to continue
to make its contribution to the construction of a
democratically transformed European Community.
Parliament must be given the necessary powers of
initiative, political orientation and control over the
executive organs. In addition, the democratization
of the Community organs will be strengthened if
positive relations are established with the national
parliaments.

Proceeding along the road towards economic and
political unity, and with due consideration for the
alliances of the individual countries, the European
Economic Community must assert an autonomous
role of its own, with a policy of friendship towards
both the United States and the Soviet Union. Above
all, it must pursue a consistent policy of co-operation
with the developing countries. Western Europe
possesses a great potential of economic and cultural
forces. It can offer the developing countries the
products of industries supplying capital goods,
industrial plants, infrastructures and the resources
of an advanced technology. Western Europe can
immediately supply technical, educational and health
assistance. Naturally such a line of co-operation
requires abandonment not only of military intervention, but also of every other form of neo-
colonialist policy. It requires, on the contrary, a
policy inspired by democratic, socialist principles,
based on repudiation of the old practices of primacy
and dominion...

The PCI is in favor of the entry of Greece, Spain
and Portugal into the Community. Their entry must
be made the occasion for an extensive revision of
Community policies and orientations.

A united Europe resting on the will of the workers
and peoples and equipped with a democratic political
power can make an important contribution to the
solution of the problems raised by the world crisis.

In the epoch of renewal of Europe the Italian
communists will as always be advocates of the
broadest possible unity among the democratic forces.
It is totally senseless to seek to transfer mechanically
on to the European level the political divisions
existing within the individual countries...

The Italian Communists, special issue, 1978.

FRENCH Communist Party: National Grandeur and the Quest for Autonomy

The Evolution of the International System

1 Maurice Thorez, 'Essential declaration,' 1945

. . . The enemies of the people think to embarrass us by posing the following question: 'What would you do if the Red Army occupied Paris?' Here is our reply:
(1) The Soviet Union has never found itself, and cannot find itself, in the position of being an aggressor against any country whatsoever. The country of socialism by definition cannot practice a policy of aggression and war as do the imperialist powers. The Soviet Army, the army of the heroic defenders of Stalingrad, has never attacked any people. Against Hitlerian Germany it fulfilled its glorious mission as liberator of the people . . .
(2) We take our stand on facts and not on hypotheses. The crucial facts at the moment are these: the active collaboration of the French government with the aggressive policy of Anglo-Saxon imperialism, the presence of a foreign general staff at Fontainebleau, the transformation of our country and French territories overseas into bases for aggression against the USSR and the People's Democracies.
(3) Since the question has been put to us, let us say this clearly: if the common efforts of all the Frenchmen enamoured of freedom and peace did not succeed in bringing our country into the camp of democracy and peace, if, as a result, our people were forced, against their will, into an anti-Soviet war, and if under these conditions the Soviet army, defending the cause of the world's peoples, the cause of socialism, was led to pursue the aggressors even on to our soil, would the workers and the people of France be able to behave differently towards the Soviet army than the workers and the peoples of Poland, Rumania, Yugoslavia, etc?

L'Humanité, June 6, 1945, p. 1.

2 Marcel Cachin, commemoration of the twenty-eighth anniversary of the Russian revolution, November 6, 1945

. . . One has seen what has come of all these lies dealing with the settlement of the Polish, Rumanian, Bulgarian, Hungarian, Austrian and Czechoslovakian problems. It was the socialists of these very countries in question who have proclaimed that the USSR respected the political independence of their nations. They added to this that after having saved them from Hitlerian servitude, the USSR brought them important economic help and solid guarantees of peace . . .

What is true, is that the Soviet Union, throughout the course of its history, from its birth up to the present day, has practiced the most legal policies of peace . . .

'To Defend the USSR Is To Serve France'
. . . It is a fact that the French socialist and communist workers are carried towards union by a powerful current and the heads of the Socialist Party are opposed to this so necessary union for the one reason that we are, they pretend, too attached to defending the USSR. Would they want to require of us that we ask the people of France to renounce their admiration for a country and a regime that have just saved us from the worst destiny imaginable?

Popular France refuses such a perspective. And moreover is not the USSR, who saved our country, after all, *vis-à-vis* France, totally disinterested, economically and politically? What does it have to gain from us? Was it not the USSR who was the first to recognize the government of General De Gaulle the day after the liberation of the country?

No Frenchman can raise the smallest complaint against the USSR. The French people know this well and are grateful to the Communist Party for bearing witness to the Soviet Union for the services which it has rendered to our nation. Our people know that in defending the USSR it is, from the beginning, France's interest which guides our constant effort...

Cahiers du Communisme (October–November 1945), pp. 14–16.

3 Charles Tillon, 'The Marshall Plan: abandonment of French independence and national defense,' 1948

... We have been enlightened by the luminous and unerring analysis of Zhdanov at the Conference of the Nine, to which the men of our time have still to refer. And, as with all great texts, every event confirms this analysis. While those of the other camp have no other compass than the Marshall Plan...

But the Marshall Plan was primarily a plan which was supposed to ensure peace and make Wall Street a sort of relief committee for the new Europe!

It is easy now to establish with facts in our possession that the Marshall Plan as put into practice is a plan for war, but a bad war plan and bound to be a fiasco.

Zhdanov has shown that the Marshall Plan is supposed to create 'a bloc of states tied to the United States,' a bloc of states which would be placed 'in dependence on the economic power of Germany as it is being restored.' He also shows that the Marshall Plan is a weapon 'directed against the industrialization of the democratic countries of Europe, and consequently against the foundations of their independence.'

... The American party in France has abandoned the conception of national defense and everything related to it, to show that the war plans based on the negation of national defense are plans for a war lost in advance.

The European countries adhering to the Marshall Plan are considered bases of disembarkation and operation. West Germany becomes a protectorate and an arsenal for certain weapons.

With respect to Germany, has not General Marshall declared in a once confidential report that 'when the war is over, it is necessary above all to keep Germany, with its industrial and human capacity, from ever being at the side of the USSR, because no fight would ever be possible if a democratic Germany could one day join the USSR in an overwhelming bloc'?

All the positions which concern the United States have as focal points the center of Europe and the USSR. All these bases are necessary to permit, as the technology evolves, the utilization of new missiles and long-distance, large-capacity airplanes, and all combined operations.

Production in Europe will be organized as a complement to American and British industry. This is the moment to remember that General Marshall is the former Chief of Staff of the American Army.

One can thus sum it up with this: *the United States is preparing for war behind the screen of the Marshall Plan, but could not make it without forces of which it is not the master!*

The Marshall Plan, a military plan, foresees that manufacture in Europe will above all be oriented toward that material which is most difficult to transport by ship in wartime, or light material whose manufacture is suitable for countries which the Americans think can be evacuated before they are reconquered!...

All the facts which have just been cited show both the weakness of those who seek protection from the United States and the growing contradictions straining the Marshall Plan, presented as a plan for aid but in fact a plan for imperialist defense, and which constitutes a proof not of strength but of the weakness of the imperialist system.

The Conference of the Nine has shown that the noise made by the agents of imperialism about the danger of war had the basic goal 'of intimidating public opinion in order to obtain concessions to the aggressor by blackmail.' This blackmail did not succeed against the camp of democracy and peace.

But for France it is not concessions that the Americans are after, but delivery lock, stock and barrel.

Cahiers du Communisme (May 1948), pp. 476–84.

4 Declaration of the Political Bureau, 1949

. . . The Political Bureau raises a solemn protest against the government's decision to sign the Atlantic Pact − putting it before parliament and the country as a *faît accompli*.

The Atlantic Pact, which its organizers dare to present as a defensive pact, is in reality an instrument of aggression against our ally, the Soviet Union, and the popular People's Democracies. Indeed this is so clear that Norway, one of the countries preparing to sign the Atlantic Pact, refused the Soviet Union's offer of a non-aggression pact.

The criminal plans of the warmongers − if they are realized − would make France the atomic cushion of the American imperialists; the French would become the sacrificial army of the West to the greatest profit of the Anglo-Saxon and French capitalists.

The Political Bureau makes an appeal to all French men and women who, without regard to opinions or beliefs, want peace and are willing to unite and fight side by side against France's adherence to the war pact which the government is about to sign . . .

The Political Bureau claims as its own the declaration of the Combatants for Peace and Liberty in its letter to President Truman (a letter being signed all over France by men and women alike).

'We deny our government the right to sign the Atlantic Treaty which is contrary to the commitments made by the French people and to which they intend to remain faithful.

'We refuse to consider this treaty as equivalent to France's pledge. We refuse to accept this war.'

L'Humanité, March 18, 1949, p. 1.

5 The PCF's National Welfare Program, Twelfth Congress of the PCF, April 1950

The PCF demands:
(1) Denunciation of the Marshall Plan, of the Atlantic Pact and of all its satellite organizations. Active participation by France in all efforts tending towards the establishment of a democratic peace, just and lasting, based on a respect for the United Nations Charter. Reaffirmation of the Franco–Soviet alliance, the guarantee of peace and security for France.
(2) The absolute ban on atomic arms. The establishment of rigorous international control to ensure the adherence to this ban. All governments who first make use of the bomb shall be considered as war criminals. Conclusion of a peace treaty between France, the Soviet Union, England and the Republic of China.
(3) The application of the Potsdam Accords for the de-Nazification and de-militarization of Germany. Recognition of the German Democratic Republic which respects these accords. Denunciation of past accords with the fanatic government of West Germany; rupture with this government which is in the service of the accomplices of American war. The implementation *vis-à-vis* Germany of a policy conforming to the safeguarding of our security, the maintenance of our rights to reparations and to support the democratic and peaceful forces of Germany.
(4) An immediate stop to the Vietnam War and the repatriation of the expeditionary body. Recognition of the Democratic Republic of Vietnam. Support of colonial peoples in their fight for liberty and independence.

'Documents du XIIᵉ Congrès,' *Cahiers du Communisme* (May 1950), p. 49.

6 Central Committee report to the Thirteenth Congress of the PCF, June 1954

. . . Point One of our thesis project recalls that 'the Twelfth Congress has adopted a line of battle for peace and national independence.'

Following in the footsteps of the Marshall Plan, which Maurice Thorez had denounced from the beginning as a plan for Europe's economic and political servitude to the American imperialists and a plan for war preparation, the North Atlantic Treaty was settled under the high authority of the American imperialists. (And as indicated by Point Two of the thesis project, this treaty strangely resembles the 'Anticomintern' treaty of 1936 – which helped to unleash the last world war.)

The implementation of the Atlantic Treaty was intended to give a new breadth to the war policy which had already been expressed in the conclusion of the Brussels military alliance with Great Britain, France, Belgium, Holland and Luxembourg. The consequence of this military alliance was the installation of foreign headquarters in Fontainebleau.

That, however, was but a small step in comparison with what has been done with the Atlantic Treaty. In the months that followed the Twelfth Congress, a number of American military camps and depots were installed on our national territory, while France, Germany, Italy and the Benelux Countries joined the Schuman Plan.

Under the cover of the 'European Community of Steel and Coal,' this plan was intended to ensure the economic predominance of West Germany in Europe in the interest of US strategic aims. The American imperialists considered the adoption of the Schuman Plan to be a great victory, not only for themselves but also for their power in West Germany and, in the same spirit, this first victory called forth others.

Wishing to increase US advantages, John Foster Dulles demanded the rearmament of West Germany and Japan, while the national assembly approved the principle of incorporating German contingents into a European army.

As the thesis project stresses, the rearmament of West Germany was thus being prepared, a prospect denounced as early as 1947 by our party as a logical consequence of the Marshall Plan.

The reality of the war preparations denounced by Maurice Thorez at the Twelfth Congress was to become evident shortly thereafter when the Korean war broke out.

The American imperialists, attempting to remedy economic depression, carried along a number of countries belonging to the UN in the war against the Democratic Republic of Korea. Meanwhile the USSR continued to make efforts to re-establish peace, but the US leaders wanted the Korean War to continue.

American imperialists planned not to disarm, as the Soviet Union proposed, but, on the contrary, to rearm Japan on the one hand and West Germany on the other (with an eye to the creation of bases for anti-Soviet aggression in Europe and Asia). If the USA were alone in possession of atomic arms and the H-bomb, they could wield a terrible blackmailing power over the world... Luckily they are not alone; the USSR also possesses atomic arms and the H-bomb. But if the socialist country possesses such arms, it nevertheless declares itself in favor of prohibiting their use...

With the Paris and Bonn accords (which require French ratification), the American imperialists not only want to develop another Nazi army under European camouflage, but they also want to assure themselves of the possibility of bringing down France, if need be, to prevent it from rising up in one powerful, national leap against the political betrayal of our rulers.

The European Defense Community is a grave menace to peace in Europe. Concerning France, the EDC simply threatens its existence as a great independent nation.

The EDC tends to reduce our country to the rank of a satellite country of the USA and the Nazi revengers of West Germany.

The American imperialists, fearful that international détente will aggravate their economic difficulties, need war...

American plans are motivated both by political preoccupations (whose dominant trait is expansionism) and anxiety linked to symptoms of an economic crisis...

Economic relations between the USA and 'Marshallized' countries are developing under conditions which put these countries in economic danger.

Concerning France, American imperialist policy has, since 1947, with the aid and complicity of our leaders, managed to destroy the economic foundation of our national independence...

By accepting the Marshall Plan, French officials have effectively abdicated all sovereign power in commercial and monetary policy matters...

The prohibition from dealing with countries in the socialist camp has considerably aggravated commercial difficulties in France and has increased its dependence on the dollar . . .

In the interest of their own class, the ruling factions of the French bourgeoisie have embarked on the route toward submission to American imperialism, to the militarization of the economy and to fascism.

'XIIIᵉ Congrès du Parti Communiste Français,' *Cahiers du Communisme* (June–July 1954), pp. 633–46.

7   PCF declaration on the situation in Algeria, 1954

Each day the situation in Algeria becomes more serious... The French Communist Party stresses that the events which are unfolding in Algeria are the consequence of the French governors' refusal to consider the national demands made by the vast majority of Algerians. This refusal contributes to the widespread and growing misery which directly results from the harsh colonial regime.

By claiming to deny the existence of national political problems in Algeria and by persisting in camouflaging the colonial regime under the name of 'three French *départements*,' the government is turning its back upon the Algerian reality – notably, an entire people's desire to live in freedom and manage their own affairs democratically.

The French Communist Party denounces the violent measures taken in the attempt to break up the Algerian national movement, whether it be the actual war operations now taking place, or the arbitrary dissolution of the 'Movement of the Triumph of Democratic Liberties,' a pretext for an even greater repression. The government's policy of force will not resolve the problems in Algeria any more than it resolved those in Indochina, Tunisia or Morocco. As was the case in these different countries, the situation in Algeria will only be aggravated by such a policy. As a result, the problems will become more difficult to handle...

Cahiers du Communisme (November–December 1954), pp. 1406–7.

8   Central Committee resolution, 1956

The Central Committee of the French Communist Party met yesterday at Ivry and adopted the following resolution:

The brutal aggression against Egypt is added to the tragedy of the Algerian war.

The Egyptian people, already victims of Israel's attacks, witness the raging military power of two mighty nations, France and Great Britain...

The military intervention into which the government of Guy Mollet has thrown France has been premeditated and has been prepared since the day Egypt undertook the legitimate nationalization of the canal.

The Israeli aggression is the ace which permitted the French Minister of Foreign Affairs to affirm, several days ago, that 'the hand has not been played.' It is a contrived pretext to set in motion a war whose goal is to put the billionaires of Suez back in place, and, more generally, to oppose violently the national liberalization movements of all colonialized people. The people of Israel themselves, and their future, run the risk of being sacrificed in the adventure...

The interests of the country and of peace require the condemnation of the aggression, the immediate ending of the war in Egypt, the return to France of the expeditionary corps and the settling, by negotiation, of the Suez Canal question...

Once again the forces of peace and progress can triumph over the forces of reaction and war.

The condition is that the unique communist and socialist front, in spite of diversive maneuvers, develop in every country...

Aware of the gravity of the situation and the threats it brings, the Central Committee of the PCF appeals to all communists and socialists, all workers, all democrats, all partisans of peace, to unite to check the instigators of war who plunge the nation into mourning, who condemn it to isolation and debasement...

L'Humanité, November 2, 1956, p. 1.

9   Maurice Thorez' report to the Fifteenth Congress of the PCF, June 1959

The external policies of the Gaullist regime are in direct conflict with the aspirations of our people, who wish for peace. International détente, security and disarmament, these are the wishes of millions of common people in our country. The maintenance and the aggravation of tension, this is the objective of the government. It needs the Cold War to continue its military operations in Algeria, to better serve reactionary powers in France, and to organize the battle against democracy and socialism in Europe and around the world in the interest of the monopolies.

The facts have reaffirmed the government's loyalty to the aggressive Atlantic Pact. France has confined itself to this military bloc. Despite all the speeches about 'grandeur' and independence, national territory is still occupied by American troops who are preparing to set up dangerous atomic launchers there as well as in Italy.

The policies of our country, which was one of the first victims of Hitlerian aggression and remained under the heel of invaders for nearly five years, concentrate on entente with the Bonn militarists. While in Germany itself many Adenauer supporters are realizing that his unrealistic views have led to an impasse, the entire effort of our government is geared towards the strengthening of the Paris–Bonn axis and the development of the German war machine, already provided with atomic weapons...

The government remains tied to the imperialist bloc in South-East Asia. It continues to sabotage the decisions of the Geneva Conference on Vietnam. Against both the people of this country and the government of the Popular Republic it supports the puppet established by the Americans in Saigon. It persists in refusing to recognize the People's Republic of China, with its 600 million citizens.

Recently the government has opposed the solution of Europe's major problem: the improvement of the situation in the center of the continent and the disengagement of the armed forces facing each other there, the conclusion of peace with Germany, and the regulation of the situation in West Berlin, home of intrigues: and provocations in the heart of the German Democratic Republic...

The government has rejected the Polish proposal on the creation of a zone free of atomic weapons, hydrogen weapons, or missiles in central Europe...

Fortunately the adventurist policies of our country's leaders do not conform with the general tendency of the international situation, which is a tendency towards détente. The first results, the first indications of détente have been achieved. They are due to the politics of peace practiced with perseverance by the USSR, to the increasing power of the socialist camp and the international workers' movement, and to the actions taken by the international peace movement during the last ten years...

One must not forget that as long as capitalism survives, and as long as the monopolies are in control, there will be reactionary politicians who seek to maintain or intensify the Cold War, cultivate anti-Soviet sentiment, develop militarism, and oppose détente and disarmament. It is a great misfortune for France that its present leaders are in the top ranks of those who conspire against peace.

'XVᵉ Congrès du Parti Communiste Français,' *Cahiers du Communisme* (July–August 1959), pp. 38–42.

10 Waldeck Rochet's report to the Sixteenth Congress of the PCF, May 1961 (I)

The French capitalist monopolies are fighting stubbornly to retain and maintain a larger place in foreign markets, international cartels and alliances between capitalist countries.

However, they are not any less obliged to make way for American monopolies – as is evidenced by the progression of American investments made in Europe – including France.

American investments in France have practically doubled since the coming of the Gaullist regime – which has granted foreign capital and, especially to the Americans, advantages and privileges that no government has dared to grant before . . .

Therefore it seems that the Common Market, far from being a third, independent world force, is on the contrary facilitating positions in Europe...

That is why, despite the crises which shake the military blocs and imperialist policy, the imperialist camp – which was formed after the war – subsists with the USA at its head.

This is not contradictory with the fact that in capitalist countries, including France, there are strata within the bourgeoisie that are for a moderate policy and, under certain forms, favor peaceful coexistence, notably because they are aware of the danger that a new war would present to capitalism.

It is absurd to consider that De Gaulle would express the views of a supposed 'national inclination' of our great capital that would intend to liberate the countries in imperialism servitude.

This thesis, which tends to disarm the party and the working class in their fight against the reactionary policy of monopolies and Gaullist power, is contradicted by all the facts.

Central Committee Report, Sixteenth Congress, 1961, p. 37.

11 Waldeck Rochet's report to the Sixteenth Congress of the PCF, May 1961 (II)

One of the key events of the recent past was the fascist military rebellion of Algiers and its rapid collapse, thanks to the struggle of the working class and the people of France.

The authors and instigators of the new fascist conspiracy had as their objective the hindrance of peace negotiations in Algeria, and they dreamed of installing an openly fascist dictatorship in France.

The enormous mobilization of the French people, to which our party actively contributed, brought about the rapid collapse of the fascist rebellion, because the rebels had no support among the people and found themselves politically isolated.

In effect, if the rebel generals had been able to rely upon a substantial part of the army, on the extremists of Algiers and on the fascist politicians and groups in France, they would have had against them not only the immense mass of the French people, but also the mass of the continent and the Algerian people themselves, without mentioning international opinion, which was generally hostile or unfavorable to them.

The factious undertaking of the disloyal generals did none the less represent a grave danger, and not just an 'incident,' as De Gaulle said. It represented a grave danger in as much as the Gaullist power allowed the conspiracy to become organized without taking any measures to prevent or halt it. Because of the very nature of the Gaullist power, for the past three years De Gaulle and his government have not ceased to demonstrate their complacency and lack of sternness with regard to these factious elements.

But because of the fascist coup of May 13, 1958, the Gaullist power is, in part, a prisoner of its origins...

The Gaullist power is represented to be a strong power; in reality it is revealed to be a feeble power because of its complacency with regard to the fascist conspirators.

'XVIᵉ Congrès du Parti Communiste Français,' *Cahiers du Communisme* (June 1961), pp. 15–17.

12 Declaration of the Central Committee of the PCF, 1962

The aggressive measures that the American government has decided to take against Cuba are seriously imperiling world peace...

It is not that they cannot endure the American imperialist strategy which, after having severed all commercial relations with Cuba, seeks systematically to organize armed attacks and sabotage.

Rather, the Cuban people have repulsed these multiple attempts to enslave them once again; but the US government is moving on to another phase of its assault.

The US leaders have decided to blockade the heroic island people, in an effort to bring the Cubans to their knees. Who has given them the right to decide to blockade a sovereign state in this way, violating the UN Charter and all international law? The pretexts that Kennedy has invoked to mask the criminal nature of these acts are all lies. Everyone knows that the only foreign military base in Cuba at Guantanamo is an American base.

No one can forget, either, that military camps and refueling bases for planes carrying atomic bombs have been set up by the American government on all flanks of the socialist camp: in Japan and Turkey, in Pakistan and Iran, and in Norway, West Germany and in many other nations – including France.

What are these American arms and troops doing tens of thousands of kilometers from US territory?

The provocative, interventionist policy that the American government is practicing toward Cuba and nations supporting the valiant Cuban people could lead the world into thermonuclear war.

These American leaders are responsible for the appearance of a new source of tension in the world, and French men and women cannot ignore the fact that this criminal policy is supported by all governments belonging to NATO, including De Gaulle's.

The French Communist Party is calling on the people of France to profess their complete solidarity with the valiant Cuban people...

These latest aggressive actions show even more clearly the mortal danger which the existence of American bases on its soil entails for France.

The French people must insist that the French representatives to the UN condemn these measures of aggression and piracy against Cuba, and demand that they be immediately ended ...

L'Humanité, October 24, 1962, p. 1.

13 Waldeck Rochet's report to the Seventeenth Congress of the PCF, May 1964

With many misgivings we have approved the recognition of the People's Republic of China because it is harmful to international co-operation to ignore a country of 700 million inhabitants, as France has done for fourteen years.

Similarly we believe that the government's declarations about the neutrality of Laos, south Vietnam and Cambodia are positive because they take realities into account and can impede, to a certain extent, the aggressive policy carried out by the American imperialists in that part of the world.

However, a real French policy would require further attempts to apply the Geneva accords, to make the American troops leave Vietnam and to recognize the Democratic Republic of Vietnam.

However, in certain political milieux, speculation is now being made about a possible Franco–Soviet rapprochement ...

It is clear, though, that we would approve of a Franco–Soviet rapprochement, as we already approved of the rapprochement between the USA and the Soviet Union when the Moscow treaty on the control of nuclear testing was signed, because we believe that any rapprochement between the French and the Soviet peoples can only serve the cause of peace among all the peoples of the world ...

Analysis of Gaullist foreign policy shows that its fundamental aspects imply severe danger for France and for peace.

Gaullist foreign policy is based on membership in the Atlantic coalition and on a close understanding with the West German militarists and, consequently, on the presence of both German and American military bases in France ...

In the last few years De Gaulle has increased the interventions aimed at stopping or hindering the progress of international détente.

He has refused to adhere to the Moscow treaty on the control of nuclear testing.

He has systematically boycotted international negotiations on disarmament.

He has declared his opposition to a non-aggression pact between the Western NATO countries and the socialist Warsaw Pact countries . . .

It is not true that having *force de frappe* can secure French military independence, because American planes would have to carry our bombs and because guidance systems, without which no operation is possible, depend upon NATO, i.e. on the same alien power.

It is not true that a *force de frappe* can guarantee French security because such a force would push France to the fore of the arms race and would invite devastating attacks in the case of a nuclear conflict.

Finally, it is yet another lie to pretend that the creation of a *force de frappe* would promote the development of technical and scientific progress! ...

It is undeniable that the creation of a French *force de frappe* would increase the proliferation and dissemination of nuclear weapons throughout the world.

Already the revanchists of Bonn's Germany (who command the most powerful West European army) use the analysis of the French atomic argument insistently to claim access to nuclear armament, in one or another form, for themselves.

But the increasing number of countries possessing nuclear weapons can only heighten the danger of an accidental or provoked initiation of a thermonuclear war.

For France, as for all the other countries in the world, the only way which allows us to guarantee security in peace and independence is to promote détente and international co-operation, beginning with the banning of nuclear testing and through the promotion of the destruction of all the atomic weaponry in the world.

Those who presently possess power speak of France's 'role' and 'ranking' in the world.

But the time has passed when national grandeur could assert itself on the battlefields, because a thermonuclear war would be a catastrophe for everyone.

One does not work for French grandeur by sacrificing enormous moral and material resources to sterile production and against vital works ...

'XVIIᵉ Congrès du Parti Communiste Français,' *Cahiers du Communisme* (June–July 1964), pp. 36–40.

14   Central Committee report to the Eighteenth Congress of the PCF, January 1967

. . . The United States aggression in Vietnam is one of the most shameful manifestations of bellicose imperial policy.

American ground troops, fighting 12,000 kilometers from the US border, came to Vietnam in violation of international law and the United Nations Charter – which asserts all people's right to self-determination. They came in violation of the 1954 Geneva agreements, which prohibited the establishment of military bases in Vietnam as well as the entry of foreign troops.

Moreover the United States sought to enslave the other nations in the Indo–Chinese peninsula by continual brutal intervention in Laotian affairs and repeated provocations against Cambodia.

Thwarted by the heroic resistance of the Vietnamese people, bogged down in a war of aggression and meeting with popular reproach from peaceable forces within the United States, the American leaders are trying to mask their profound guilt by expounding on their alleged desire for peace.

But how could anyone believe their words of peace when, even as they pronounce them, they are intensifying the war, undertaking successive degrees of escalation at the risk of provoking a general conflict?

If the American leaders want to prove that they seek peace, they must commit themselves to a different path.

They must stop all bombing of the Democratic Republic of (north) Vietnam, and recognize the National Liberation Front as the only true representative of the south Vietnamese people.

Finally, they must decide to withdraw their troops, so that the Vietnamese people can conduct their own affairs, united freely without foreign interference, in peace and independence – in the south as in the north . . .

If these conditions were fulfilled by the US leaders, peace negotiations would then be possible – for no one can doubt the Vietnamese people's desire for peace, in the light of the terrible trials that they have endured for more than twenty years.

Unfortunately American imperialists have so far followed another course. The Johnson doctrine of brutal intervention in the internal affairs of sovereign peoples – in Vietnam, Santo Domingo, the Congo and elsewhere – is incompatible with the policy of peaceful coexistence and respect for people's rights to self-determination.

In attacking the sovereignty of these peoples, the American militarists are dealing a serious blow to the cause of world peace, and considerably aggravating the danger of a new world war.

'XVIIIᵉ Congrès du Parti Communiste Français,' *Cahiers du Communisme* (February–March 1967), pp. 23–6.

15   'They do not know the French Communist Party,' *L'Humanité*, 1967

Thanks to the policy of rapprochement between France and the Soviet Union outlined by De Gaulle, the French Communist Party is going to reduce, if not renounce, its struggle against the regime of personal power, and consequently the Gaullists will be able to win an important section of the communist vote.

We French communists congratulate ourselves on the amelioration of the relationship between France and the Soviet Union, because we have always believed that Franco–Soviet friendship and co-operation are in line with the interests of our two peoples and with peace, and in the interest of European and international security.

But we cannot forget that the Gaullist power is an anti-democratic power in the service of capitalist monopolies, a power practicing a deeply reactionary and anti-social economic policy.

Put simply, they do not understand the French Communist Party. As a result of repeating that the French Communist Party is dependent upon the Communist Party of the Soviet Union, the Gaullists have ended up actually believing it in such a way that when De Gaulle travelled to the Soviet Union they thought that such an action – positive in itself – would bring us to renounce the struggle which we have always waged against the monopolies' power in defense of the immediate interests and the future interests of the workers, for the future of French democracy . . .

The attitude of the Communist Party on matters of foreign policy is perfectly clear. We have not stopped fighting for peaceful coexistence between states, for the disengagement of the Atlantic Alliance and the dissolution of the military blocs created during the period of Cold War, and for international co-operation, arms reduction and for the safeguarding of world peace...

We have supported and will continue to support those who favor world peace among peoples regardless of their motives or nationalities because, for us communists, the interests of the working class and of France count above all else...

The French Communist Party determines with complete independence its policy on the vital needs of the working class and the French people.

L'Humanité, December 11, 1967, p. 1.

16   Georges Marchais' report to the Central Committee of the PCF, June 1969

In our struggle for peaceful coexistence, we attach primary importance to actions favoring European security.

American imperialism considers Western Europe as a keystone in its expansionist and dominating strategy. The Atlantic Treaty and its military organization, NATO, are the expressions of this strategy. This situation is further aggravated by the fact that American imperialism supports the demands of the Federal Republic of Germany – where neo-Nazism and militarism rear their heads – who are looking to begin anew the debate over the results of the Second World War and modify the frontiers of many European nations.

In this situation we must insist that the French people actively intervene in favor of the establishment of a system for the collective security of Europe, substituting itself for the antagonistic military blocs. The establishment of such a system requires the recognition and respect for actual frontiers in Europe; the recognition of the rights of the German Democratic Republic; and the rejection of German claims to nuclear arms, whatever their form.

In order to attain these objectives, our party is placing its total support behind the concrete proposals formulated by the Conference of Communist Parties and Workers of Karlovy-Vary of 1967 and those of the member states of the Treaty of Warsaw of Budapest in 1969 that call for a conference of all European states to deal with the problems of the security of the continent...

It is especially important to devote intense efforts to this subject, now that the administration proclaims its intention of proceeding towards a 'renewal of Europe,' that is to say, in fact, a renewal of tiny, monopolistic, Western Europe. But such a 'renewal of Europe signifies in reality an *accentuation of the division of Europe*. It favors the views of those who desire to give new vigor to the Atlantic Treaty, that is to say, the policy of alignment with American imperialism. This will result in the end of the policy of general co-operation, notably with the Soviet Union and other socialist countries, which the establishment claims to want to practice and which is imperative for the security, independence and economic needs of France.

We will continue to act equally in favor of general disarmament and measures which will favor accord on this question...

L'Humanité, June 30, 1969, pp. 3–4.

17   Georges Marchais' report to the Nineteenth Congress of the PCF, February 1970

National Independence and International Co-operation
Our program emphasizes that we desire a policy resolutely committed to national independence for our country.

The internationalization of production processes in our time is an objective phenomenon which renders all national isolation and autocracy impossible.

But this does not imply that it is consequently necessary to downgrade national independence or to believe that the national reality will disappear.

The nation has been a durable reality for a long period of history. The people are profoundly and legitimately attached to it. It is within the framework of the nation that the class struggles will take place and that the exploiting classes must be vanquished...

Moreover the nation is a modern reality and is far from having exhausted all its uses, precisely because the ruling classes have monopolized and oppressed it.

Hundreds of millions of men still struggle today to gain their national independence. They constitute an essential force in the anti-imperialist revolutionary movement. The battle for national independence is a crucial part of the fight against imperialism.

. . . The fight for the maintenance of national defense is a blemish which is profoundly necessary for us. The workers do not fight against the domination of French capitalists in France in order to accept the seizure of the essential branches of our economy, directly or through the expedience of 'integration' or 'supra-nationality' by American capitalists, West Germans or big city groups. They know that their exploitation is becoming more aggravated and their struggle more difficult. At a time when the large capitalists are tending more and more to lose their national attachment, the fight against monopolies and the battle for the national interest are indissolubly linked.

In striking out against the all-powerfulness of monopolies, a progressive democracy will be committed to the preservation of national independence and the service of France's interests. Independence is a vital condition for a democratic regime to be able to accomplish its plan for social progress and render ineffective the pressures and interference of the imperialism of the foreign monopolies . . .

'XIXᵉ Congrès du Parti Communiste Français,' *Cahiers du Communisme* (February–March 1970), pp. 65–7.

18   Georges Marchais' report to the Central Committee of the PCF, January 1972

In 1966 our country withdrew from NATO. We congratulated ourselves. We had, in effect, always come out against any French involvement in a military bloc. At the same time we stressed that it was dangerous for France to stay in the Atlantic Pact; membership of it would inevitably include the potential risk of a more or less pronounced political and military dependence. In fact, to take only one example, even today our air alert system is still integrated into that of NATO.

The facts are now well known: the entire press has confirmed them. The independent strategy 'at all costs' has been abandoned in favor of a strategy of 'close co-operation' with the Atlantic allies against a predesignated enemy situated 'in the East' with participation by high-ranking officers in NATO military committees and with participation by the French navy in NATO maneuvers.

Today we are brusquely told that the decision to increase the military budget again has been made, and that it is required by rising costs of production. But the military equipment plans include provisions for rising prices! The powers today would actually like to set up new projects, notably the development of tactical nuclear weapons, as M. Debré acknowledged last November. And, as if by accident, the use of tactical nuclear weapons is a corollary of the Atlantic strategy of 'graduated response.'

Of course the Pompidou government claims that one cannot speak of real French 'integration' into NATO. In sum, the current Atlanticism is not just like the old one. One must believe that these subtleties escape M. Maurice Schumann, Minister of Foreign Affairs, who crudely views the new form of French participation in NATO as being 'as effective and as dynamic as other forms of participation.'

In reality, for any Frenchman committed to national independence – and, I add, to the security of France – there is only one Atlanticism and it severely hinders the free determination of foreign policy, which should be inspired exclusively by national interest and the search for international détente and peace throughout the world . . .

The existing powers present the country with a factual situation which sees France increasingly engaged in intimate co-operation with NATO and its American leadership.

L'Humanité, January 22, 1972, pp. 6–7.

19   Georges Marchais' report to the Twentieth Congress of the PCF, December 13–17, 1972

The politics which democratic France will conduct outside our frontiers will be inspired by the spirit of our times.

Instead of staying in the wake of international

evolution, as does the present government, our politics will be of détente without reserve, and of co-operation with discrimination.

(1) The sole mission of the army will be national defense, and a military strategy will be defined to permit us face any aggressor. The leftist government will adopt a democratic statute for the soldier and staff.

The government will immediately stop nuclear testing and end the production of nuclear forces, signing treaties forbidding nuclear tests and the proliferation of nuclear armaments.

The government will actively participate in all negotiations on disarmament, notably on the balanced reduction of the forces and armaments in Europe.

(2) The leftist government will support the dissolution of blocs and will act to that end. Without hesitation it will manifest its will to launch the country on a road independent of all politico-military blocs. It is in this spirit that problems will be resolved which could result from France's belonging to the Atlantic alliance. Simultaneously France will take all initiatives to arrive at a European treaty for collective security, and it will contribute actively to the work of the conference for the security and co-operation of Europe.

(3) Democratic France will participate in the activities of the Common Market with the intention of liberating itself from the domination of big capital, democratizing its institutions and defending the interests of the workers. In all circumstances the French government will retain its liberty of action for the realization of the common program. Concurrently the government will develop its economic or social regimes.

(4) Democratic France, renewing its ties with the most beautiful moments of its history, will recognize the right of the overseas provinces and territories to self-determination. With the African states and with all Third World countries, France will establish new ties of co-operation, freely negotiated and excluding all colonial spirit.

This is the new policy, a great French policy, consonant with the role which France can legitimately seek to play in this world and with the hopes that the people put in us.

'XXᵉ Congrès du Parti Communiste Français,' *Cahiers du Communisme* (January–February 1973), pp. 56–7.

20   Paul Laurent, 'The political and social situation,' 1973

. . . The French people can only be deeply disturbed by the radical modification effected in our country's strategy by the present government. Abandoning the omni-directional strategy which General De Gaulle had outlined and which defined no particular adversary for France, the government of MM. Pompidou and Debré deploys the military means of our country exclusively against the East, that is, against the European socialist countries.

This orientation means an accelerated reinforcement of France's co-operation with NATO, and particularly with the power which controls this politico-military bloc, the United States. Our country's participation in NATO activities is at the present time so pushed that one can speak of a surreptitious reintegration of France into this organization. We see, further, that – under the aegis of the current majority – arrangements are being worked out with the Union of Western Europe with a view to setting up a new version of the 'European Defense Community' which constituted the military core of the Atlantic Alliance in Western Europe.

The policy of the current government in this domain, which plays to one gallery with statements in favor of co-operation with the Soviet Union and to the other with evocations of a 'threat from the East,' to put the security of our country in dependence on the American bloc, involves a disquieting duplicity . . .

An authentically national peaceful and realistic policy would start from recognition that the page of the Cold War has been turned. Our country's interest lies in doing all we can to strengthen and prolong the process of international détente. There is to be found the only true guarantee of security. It is in this perspective that the policy defined by the Common Program finds its place . . .

The tasks and means of national defense derive from principles on which the international policy of France will be based, that is: peaceful coexistence and co-operation with all countries, equality of rights, respect for the sovereignty and the territorial integrity of states, peaceful resolution of disputes, non-interference in the domestic affairs of other states, the refusal of all recourse to force.

Parallel to the diplomatic initiatives which it will take to strengthen dynamically all agreements on disarmament, collective security, the transcendence and dissolution of military blocs, the left government will immediately renounce the nuclear striking force, realize the industrial reconversion necessary to save the interests of the workers concerned, reduce the duration of military service, engage the country on the road of independence with respect to any and every politico-military bloc...

The nationalization of the armaments industries constitutes the indispensable condition for the utilization of these means. The same goes for the adoption of a new strategy, resting no longer on the arbitrary definition of a presumed enemy, but allowing for a stand against any aggressor whoever it may be; a strategy based on the fact that, as long as the risks of exterior interference, pressure or reprisals have not disappeared, our country must be in a position to safeguard its own security and the realization of the democratic objectives desired by its people...

The existence of a European collective security system obviously does not raise the question of the disappearance of the national armed forces, including France's, which will be the guarantor of the application of the foreign policy of the government of the left. This is the diametrical opposite of the perspective of MM. Pompidou and Messmer of a new military defense pact for Western Europe subordinated to the needs of American imperialism...

What we want to do is to have an active policy in favor of détente and collective security. We wish to base our national defense on a foreign policy of peace. Hence the issue we have made with the government for the negotiation with the USSR of a treaty of non-aggression and non-recourse to force.

'The German Federal Republic, which is part of the Atlantic organization, has signed such a treaty with the USSR. France could do as much. This would be an important political element of its national defense.'...

The Common Program does not foresee a freeze of nuclear weapons but the renunciation of the strike force in any form...

L'Humanité, February 23, 1973, p. 5.

21 Georges Marchais, 'France and Europe,' 1973

...An important problem must be solved: that of the existence of two military blocs which divide the continent. Shortly after the last war the Atlantic Pact was set up under the direction of the USA in order to organize an aggression against the Soviet Union and the other socialist countries. In response the socialist countries gathered under the Warsaw Pact, which contains a clause bringing about an automatic dissolution of this pact should the Atlantic Pact be dissolved.

The simultaneous dissolution of these two military blocs is today a realistic goal, as is replacing them with a system of collective security that would encompass all European countries without regard to their form of government. This system would be based on principles of peaceful coexistence and would rely on the recognition of all existing borders, on the renunciation of the use of force in relations between the states, on mutual aid, on the negotiated solution to all litigations, on the pursuit of disarmament, on the growth of economic, cultural and human exchanges. Such a system should be the goal of a general treaty available to all countries sharing the same rights and responsibilities.

This is one of the great goals that the Common Program of the left has for democratic France. It is in this spirit that the parties of the left affirm their support for the European conference in Helsinki for security and co-operation. It is in this same spirit that they have decided that the democratic power would not remain as expected, but would immediately take initiatives to demonstrate its intention to commit France to the pursuit of independence from any military-political bloc.

We communists think that France has little to gain and a great deal to lose by remaining tightly bound to the Atlantic bloc dominated by the USA. And in claiming this our goal is not to make France's withdrawal from the Atlantic Pact a first step to join the Warsaw Pact. We are totally opposed to this alternative. It is in the interest of our people, of our country, and also of peace that France should be free to play a new and active role in the peaceful organization of our continent. In that context France could exercise considerable influence.

Le Défi Démocratique (Paris: Grasset, 1973), cf. pp. 228–30.

22   Georges Marchais' report to the Twenty-First Congress of the PCF, October 1974

Giscard d'Estaing is absent from international negotiations on disarmament and has made himself the champion of arms sales, bringing attacks on the dignity of our country. He has stalled the progress of the European conference on security and co-operation by creating highly artificial obstacles. In this respect he appears as one of the governments which show the least willingness in international discussions.

He is increasingly putting our country in the Western European and Atlantic bloc. This willingness to link the destiny of France with that of countries in crisis is a dominant trait of the government's foreign policy. In effect this has only one goal: to give certain large French multinational firms their place in the imperialist circle. To defend these special interests the government has joined in the close-knit ranks of imperialist solidarity for reasons of class. In search of protection it has thus submitted itself to the general interests of the bloc dominated by the USA.

Even if the government is restrained by some prudence in the execution of this disastrous policy, it has already shown its readiness to abandon national imperatives.

It shows this by opting for a Bonn–Paris axis, which serves as a stepping-stone for the hegemonic intentions of imperialist West Germany in Western Europe.

It shows this by putting itself at the head of the return of the Little Europe of trusts, in which our country will consent to 'important abandonments of sovereignty.' . . .

It shows this by inspiring a campaign in favor of a European army, a new rehashing of the EDC of Cold War times. The constitution of this army would be a threat to peace, while signifying the liquidation of one of the essential attributes of national sovereignty . . .

Finally, the priority given to integration into 'the bloc of crisis' hinders the development of wider co-operation with socialist countries and with the developing countries, especially in Africa.

This policy of submission to monopoly interests is a policy of abandonment which is directly in line with the anti-nationalist tradition of the old French right.

The government is incapable of promoting a foreign policy which accounts for the significant trumps our country holds because of its history, its weight and its position. The only possible justification for this humble policy of M. Giscard d'Estaing is the depreciation of France. That is what he is striving for today . . .

'XXIᵉ Congrès extraordinaire du Parti Communiste Français,' *Cahiers du Communisme* (November 1974), pp. 27–8.

23   Mireille Nadaud, 'United States facing the contemporary challenge,' 1975

The main lines of force of the new American foreign policy can be determined as follows.

First of all, the need to come to terms with socialism even while intensifying the struggle against it, hence the faith in the maintenance of the political and social *status quo* and the attempt at a geo-political division of the world into 'spheres of influence.' In this framework belongs the wish to reinforce Atlantic integration, to enlarge NATO's role in such a way as to make it an instrument of economic integration, while maintaining its ideological struggle against the socialist system ('new Atlantic charter').

Then, the need – in the face of the crisis of the capitalist system – to maintain American leadership. It is thus that in the name of its national security . . . the United States reserves the right to intervene in the domestic affairs of the countries it still dominates. It is thus that it concedes to its allies only a 'limited sovereignty,' especially with regard to Western Europe and particularly the countries in which the communist parties can play an important role: we have had examples with the interference in the affairs of Portugal, of Italy, and quite recently of France.

And there we find NATO, an instrument of economic and political domination over the allies, with American imperialism's need to maneuver, for it cannot permit itself to ignore completely its partners' own interests. Hence the care to strengthen and accelerate European and Atlantic integration in order to attempt to overcome these contradictions rendered yet more acute by the brutal acceleration of the crisis of the capitalist system.

Finally, one must consider the preponderance of economic problems and of the ideological struggle. Its political and military setbacks do not prohibit American imperialism from seeing its ideological positions as strong. The 'champions of the free world' are certainly ready for ideological offensives in all directions against socialism, using any means, including those offered by détente and economic co-operation with the socialist countries...

It appears that the United States strategy is clearly shaped on two key concepts.
(1) 'World economic and political independence,' which brings with it the need for 'a new world economic order' and this, notably, through the redefinition of relations with the developing countries. This 'redefinition' is a very important event. In effect it is an admission of the defeat of the previous policy which consisted solely in exploiting the developing countries. It is an admission of the increasing importance assumed by these countries on the international stage, to the degree that their wish to recapture their national resources is affirmed. It is the proof that American imperialism has drawn lessons from what happened with the oil-producing countries. For even if the United States is the least dependent with regard to raw materials, it has strategic and political positions to protect and its leadership role to play, its most important allies (Europe, Japan) being themselves very dependent on raw material sources...
(2) 'The polycentrism of the communist world,' and the wish to exploit, especially on the ideological level, the problems which can appear within the international communist movement, is the second concept. If Helsinki incontestably marks a serious retreat for imperialism and great progress for peaceful coexistence, we are witnessing the attempt by Washington and its allies (notably France) to limit the consequences of the conference — this with the objective support of China.

To begin with, one can say that these possibilities, this margin for maneuver of American imperialism, fit into a double dialectic.
(a) Progress of détente and peaceful coexistence while the crisis of the capitalist system is deepening.
(b) Deepening of inter-capitalist contradictions accompanied by a need to strengthen solidarity against socialism...

In other words, aside from direct military conflict, any means are useful not only to try to stop socialism from progressing, but also to try to push it back . . .

But the great weakness of the American strategy is that it starts from the postulate that maintenance of the *status quo* is possible...

Cahiers du Communisme (December 1975), pp. 110–16.

24 Georges Marchais' report to the Twenty-Second Congress of the PCF, February 1976

For its part the international policy of Giscard d'Estaing scrupulously wedges itself into the world strategy inspired and directed by the United States. The flower of so-called 'mondialisme' cannot hide the fact that it represents a new Atlanticism.
– Industrial and technological Atlanticism with the seizure by American trusts of the French nuclear and informations industries, while expecting that tomorrow, perhaps, will come the turn of the aeronautic and telephone industries.
– Energetic Atlanticism, with the alignment to the Giscardian power with the theses of the International Energy Agency dominated by the cartel of the petroleum trusts and the USA.
– Commercial Atlanticism, with the accentuation of the deficit of our commercial exchanges *vis-à-vis* the USA and also West Germany.
– Monetary Atlanticism, with the dominance of the dollar in the international economy, the abandonment of the gold standard and fixed parities, and the submission to the mark in the West European sphere.
– Military Atlanticism, with the *de facto* reinsertion of France in NATO.
– Political Atlanticism, in the final analysis, with the new support given to American initiatives, co-operation in aggressive enterprises, as in Angola, and above all the eagerness to move towards a politically integrated Europe, for which election to a European Parliament by universal suffrage would constitute an important step.

The only ambition of the Giscard government is to obtain a spot for certain huge capitalist firms based in France at the banquet of the international giants of finance and industry. This preoccupation has ended up transforming ministers into the international couriers of the monopolies.

'XXIIᵉ Congrès du Parti Communiste Français,' *Cahiers du Communisme* (February–March 1976), pp. 29–30.

25   Marcel Trigon, 'Aspects of international politics,' 1977

The international situation reveals certain complex and sometimes contradictory evolutions which, far from invalidating our choices, on the contrary support them and show that we are right . . .

In the most recent period the international situation is essentially characterized by the aggravation of the crisis of capitalism. This deep and general crisis weakens imperialism. It exacerbates the contradictions within states as in their foreign affairs. It mobilizes the energies of imperialism. This is true on the economic level, and more so on the political . . .

The predominant tendency of the international situation remains détente. Following the American presidential election the new period ought to see new diplomatic initiatives, notably in the American–Soviet talks on the limitation of strategic arms, the Vienna Conference on the reduction of forces and armaments in central Europe, and the Belgrade meeting. This is an important aspect – one we have never neglected – of the struggle for peaceful coexistence . . .

But, faced with the rise of socialism, of working-class struggles, of the struggles of the peoples liberated from colonialism, the European capitalist states do their utmost to overcome their contradictions and form a bloc, to tighten their links. This bloc is becoming more and more Atlantic under the leadership of the United States. We are far from a Europe which could be an economic and political counterweight to the power of the United States. Today we are witnessing the attempt to create a true Atlantic community, in which Europe is no more than a region in which the global strategy of imperialism is to be applied. It is to the realization of this strategy that Giscard d'Estaing is lending himself, without caring for the national interest. In particular the dominating class interests demand our placement under German protection.

At the same time imperialism is striving to negotiate international problems from a position of power, between blocs, reducing the international dialogue to a face-to-face conflict between the USA and the USSR, in contempt of the positive role which every nation – and particularly ours – could play in the community of nations, and also in contempt of national interests and the independence of the world's peoples.

These efforts of imperialism to utilize all the means at its disposal in an attempt to restrain the advance of the world's peoples, to restrain détente, confirm the idea that the latter need not be irreversible. This is why our assertion remains true, that 'it is possible to maintain, consolidate and organize peace on the condition that the struggle to force imperialism to do so continues.'

It is to this end, in so far as it is our responsibility, that we exert ourselves. This responsibility is all the greater since Giscard's policy is totally opposed both to the deepening of détente and to the interests of France . . .

Giscard's foreign policy is entirely dictated by a class attitude, by the monopolies' fear of seeing France engaged in the democratic transformations of the Common Program . . .

One of the basic issues in our fight is in the area of national independence in the face of the government's desire for Atlantic and European integration.

Our battle to denounce the dangerous character of the election to the European Parliament on the basis of universal suffrage, because of the perils it poses for our national independence, has begun to alert larger sectors of public opinion for the dangers it represents. This coming to consciousness is encouraged by our denunciation of the realities of this Europe dominated by imperialism and West German militarism . . .

Another essential axis of our activity lies in the reinforcement of international détente and disarmament. There also we come up against the government's policy.

In this spirit the Giscardian policy of arms exports is dangerous. At the same time it damages the growth of the French economy and thus prevents full employment. It discredits France. How could the export of French nuclear material not be suspected of contributing to the proliferation of nuclear weapons, when this government refuses to sign the non-proliferation treaty and behaves as a regular cannon-merchant? . . .

Cahiers du Communisme (March 1977), pp. 85–8.

26 Jean Kanapa's speech to the Central Committee of the PCF, May 11, 1977

Reinsertion into NATO and the 'forward battle'

... Since February 1976 France has joined a group called the 'Eurogroup of NATO' in the middle of a European group of military programs. This group is bound to the military authorities of NATO and to the United States through the intermediary of the 'conference of national armament directors' in which France takes part. In the same way our country is integrated into an Atlantic Committee which is supposed to ensure the 'inter-operability' of armaments as a prelude to their standardization. But this alleged co-operation is only the disguise for a simple 'under-treaty' imposed by the United States on many European countries ...

At the same time American hegemony pushes Western Europe into co-operation in the production of weapons, including missiles, a co-operation behind which Germany puts all its weight. It is clear that, although it will be very expensive, we are directing ourselves to a 'European military community' which will give Germany access to nuclear weapons and make France a branch of NATO.

This orientation goes together with a new strategic doctrine ... We know it and have denounced it many times ... The doctrine of all directional defense has been replaced by the doctrine of the 'forward battle' at the sides of the 'Bundeswehr' against the socialist countries designated as the only potential adversary. This conception implies the transfer of nuclear weapons to West Germany, especially to its eastern border, where everything suggests that a battle is prepared for it ... This doctrine, particularly the mission assigned to the nuclear weapons, arises from an adventurous policy which could involve France in a conflict of interests which are not its own and could even degenerate into a nuclear conflict ...

Thus the French rightists have responded to their own class interests out of fear and hostility toward their own people, exposing our country to pressures, adventures and interventions from foreign imperialism – particularly West Germany – acting as the spine of the European imperialist system and following their own ambitions to dominate at the same time ...

Given the present state of national defense and the absence of a collective European security system, we favor keeping nuclear weapons, that is to say, keeping the weapons operational (implying the maintenance of technical and scientific progress) at the quantitative level dictated by the need for security and national independence.

This level will, therefore, be the lowest possible, evaluated in terms of range, strength and duration of operability. The present level, including the construction of a sixth submarine with programmed missiles, can be considered to be this threshold. The Mirage IVs will not be replaced at the end of their serviceability ... Democratic France will consider as the minimum threshold what we have just termed the limit, i.e. the maximum threshold.

Nuclear military doctrine will again become a strategy of dissuasion, in the strict sense. The adventurous theories of Giscard d'Estaing and Chirac, which would provoke a strategic conflict with tactical nuclear weapons, will be abandoned.

The nuclear strategy will be an all-directional defense system without designated adversaries. The targets will therefore depend upon the source of provocation ...

The present 'anti-city' strategy which is tantamount to taking the populations of big cities as nuclear hostages will also be abandoned. Tactical nuclear weapons cannot, in any case, be transferred except outside the boundaries of national territory.

We declare ourselves in favor of maintaining a nuclear force, considering France's great need for independence and taking into account a situation which we did not want but which has been created for our country. That said, the nuclear weapon is not *in itself* the weapon of independence. At this time it depends upon the Atlantic organization in order to be alerted – an essential element in the discussion. This dependence results at the level of radar detection because of the integration of the NADGE network of NATO and at the level of locating the ships of the national navy by resorting to American satellites. It is necessary, therefore, to make the nuclear force independent, which implies ensuring an independent system of detection in case of attack and an independent system of locating the French naval ships. We will not be told it is not possible. That is an objection bred by a spirit of resignation. Technically France has the possibility of acquiring these means, especially through the construction of surveillance radar planes (used only in times of crisis) and the launching into orbit of three satellites for observation, location and transmission. Political will is necessary.

Naturally, since it is expected to be at the exclusive service of national independence, the development of the nuclear weapon makes it necessary to put an immediate end to all the measures, as numerous as they are discreet, which have led to a *de facto* re-entry into NATO.

It goes without saying that any form of common European defense must be excluded. Such an organization would not only exacerbate the entry of France into the Atlantic strategy but would also make atomic arms available to West Germany. We declare categorically: we will never accept that West Germany have access to arms for mass destruction under any form or under any pretext . . .

Cahiers du Communisme (June 1977), pp. 11–22.

27   Jean Kanapa, interview with *L'Humanité,* 1977

. . . The Communist Party is always concerned with questions that touch on national defense. National defense is in effect one of the means − a prime means − of assuring the integrity of national independence, popular sovereignty, the integrity of the territory. We are passionately attached to our country's independence. It is known that the communists consented to great sacrifices in the struggle against Hitler's invaders. We say that the independence of France must be assured under *any circumstances*. It must be today − and it must be tomorrow, in order to allow the French people to implement, if they so decide in 1978, the great program of social progress and democratic reform of the Common Program. In the world as it now is and in the areas bordering France as they now are − for example, the ambitions for domination barely hidden by the Federal Republic of Germany − we want absolutely to assure the security of the country, and to put to flight every menace, every foreign intervention. For this, political means are necessary, as well as military means . . .

The absolute priority given to nuclear arms by the administration without our consent has resulted in a reduction in conventional forces. This reduction is catastrophic.

The actual state of our conventional forces does not guarantee an effective national defense.

On the other hand there is the nuclear force. We fought against it and, as Georges Marchais said, 'We have nothing to repudiate in this battle.'

But today it is a fact that it exists. It represents the only real means of dissuasion at the disposal of the country, for the time being, when faced with the menace of aggression. I say again, dissuasion. Because, as is evident, our country has no aggressive intentions! We want simply, but steadfastly, a national defense whose only mission is to signify clearly to the world: don't touch our country!

For this it is necessary for the country to rest upon a conscripted army, widely linked with the nation, democratic, modern and equipped with effective weapons.

This is the sense in which our Central Committee has spoken out for maintenance of nuclear arms. I say again: for maintenance. Nothing more. The current stockpile in France is sufficient. We are categorically opposed to France engaging itself in the arms race. On the contrary! We are taking into account the actual state of affairs, the state of things as they are, but we do not find much satisfaction in them. We are for the simultaneous ban on all nuclear arms and their liquidation, for disarmament: and we will act with this in mind . . .

Current French military policy aims exclusively at the socialist countries. It is a heavy responsibility which power exacts. Moreover nuclear power is dependent, in many ways, upon NATO, that is to say, the Americans.

We believe that the strategy of democratic France should be a strategy completely *of defense*, that is to say, that our military means shall be usable against all aggression, regardless of its source.

And we intend to become totally independent of NATO. Technically this is possible. It is what we desire . . . We, the communists, desire that the government of the left involve France immediately in all existing accords and arms limitations − because there are already such accords, and they are good. There is also a good American−Soviet accord for the prevention of nuclear war. France must involve itself in this.

France should propose non-aggression treaties, treaties of amity and co-operation with all willing countries, and, among others, the Soviet Union.

We are also going to propose next Wednesday a great policy initiative: that France demand to be allowed to join in the negotiations between the USA and the Soviet Union on the strategic arms limitation treaty.

This is a great policy for France. A policy which will help rediscover her world authority. A policy which guarantees her independence and security.

This is the grand policy we propose – not only to the left – but to all Frenchmen . . .

L'Humanité, May 16, 1977, p. 7.

The European Community

28 Central Committee report of the Thirteenth Congress of the PCF, June 1954

Our party, which over the years has struggled at the vanguard of the working class against the Marshall Plan, the Atlantic Pact, the Schuman Plan and against the EDC, has, thereby, helped to bring about profound changes in our nation . . .

The Atlantic Pact has already been accepted, albeit with certain misgivings, by the workers; but the disastrous consequences of the Schuman Plan have provoked an outcry of discontent, and have given rise to a current of hostility toward the EDC which, if ratified, will transform our nation into a sort of protectorate of the United States and West Germany.

By accepting the 'Marshallization' of France, by subscribing to the Atlantic Pact, by signing the Schuman Plan which is committed to the economic renewal of West Germany, and which is paving the way for the restoration of German militarism – in short, by putting their class interests before the national interest – the leaders of the French bourgeoisie have provoked great confusion within the nation, which is itself more tightly hitched each day to the American war machine.

In addition, the enslavement of France in a war economy and its economic subordination to the United States has brought about an aggravation of the internal tensions of capitalism.

Everyone knows, for example, that with the plan which bears his name Robert Schuman will closely tie the interests of certain very important French monopolies to the interests of the German monopolies.

He seeks in this way to quiet the opposition to this treasonable act, which will permit West Germany to reappear as a formidable competitor on the international capitalist market and, into the bargain, to prepare the necessary conditions for the rebirth of German militarism.

Further, because of the internal contradictions of capitalism, certain bourgeois circles have had their interests hindered by the policy of submission of the French economy to the United States, while other capitalists, although more and more detached from the nation, are even more closely tied to the American capitalists . . .

For a long time our party, in protest against the EEC, has denounced this policy, which aims at the liquidation of the French national army and the subordination of French officers and soldiers to Hitler's former generals.

Expressing these same sentiments – which have since been documented – our party said three years ago: 'French officers feel humiliated at being placed under foreign command, and are indignant to see French military tradition subordinated to foreign interests.' . . .

The assertion of our national political independence and the pursuit of peace by the working class and by even broader social strata, in the countryside as well as in the cities, has given rise to hesitation on the part of certain elements in the bourgeoisie and the governing classes . . .

'XIIIᵉ Congrès du Parti Communiste Français,' *Cahiers du Communisme* (June–July 1954), pp. 700–3.

29 Waldeck Rochet's report to the Central Committee of the PCF, February 14, 1957

. . . To begin with, it is not true that the partisans of the 'European comeback' want to unite Europe.

On the contrary, they seek to maintain the division of Europe by setting the 'Little Europe' of the Six against the socialist nations of the other part of Europe.

Further, far from constituting an independent third force, 'Little Europe' is destined to serve the imperialist designs of the United States . . .

For, in the final analysis, it is a fact that the six nations of 'Little Europe' all belong to the Atlantic Alliance, alongside and under the direction of the United States.

It is also a fact that the latter supports the European Common Market and Euratom as it yesterday supported the EDC.

And for what reason?

Not only for economic reasons, but especially because the 'Little Europe' forged by the Common Market and Euratom furnishes, in their eyes, a political framework for the aggressive military force that they intend to maintain and strengthen in Europe in order to struggle against the Soviet Union.

It is a fact openly acknowledged by its most zealous advocates that the European Common Market, with Euratom, would be an instrument of aggression, to be used against the Soviet Union and the socialist nations . . .

But if the Common Market serves simply as the economic infrastructure for the political and military coalition which we have denounced, it would still imply many serious dangers for the French economy and for the workers' standard of living.

We must expose these dangers, in order to mobilize the popular masses to struggle against the ratification of the treaty presently being negotiated . . .

First of all, if the Common Market were to come about, the firms of the five other nations, and especially those of Germany, could compete with our national production for our own market with no restrictions.

But experience has shown that, in such a system, it is necessarily the strongest economic power which is destined to dominate the others.

It is indisputable that West Germany is presently much better situated economically than France . . .

Capital would then desert France for West Germany – in any case, desert the regions of the Center, the Midi and the West.

. . . Contrary to the deceitful assertions of the propagandists of 'Little Europe,' it is not true that the European Common Market would permit Europe to act as a third force and to be independent of the United States . . .

Clearly the United States is counting on the European Common Market to facilitate its efforts to export American surpluses to Europe.

Actually, to obtain its objective, the United States will begin to benefit by the institution of the Common Market from a complementary unilateral lowering of French customs tariffs.

In effect, the planned Common Market treaty will ensure that the six European nations will apply a single customs tariff to nations like the United States, one based on the average of the current national tariffs.

For France the new tariff benefiting the United States represents a reduction of about half of our present duties.

In return the United States – which will in no way be required to reduce its customs duties – will maintain the present tariff, which is quite high, in order to keep French merchandise off the American market . . .

In truth, with the Common Market, whose rules will henceforth be applied to all our protectors, the French parliament will be stripped of all power on questions concerning the economic and political life of France.

French politics will no longer be decided in Paris, but by Germany at the headquarters of the Community . . .

By signing and ratifying the treaty, France will subscribe to the total liquidation of its sovereignty.

The advocates of 'Little Europe' do not disguise that their final goal is to begin creating a 'European Political Community' – a new state in which France would be reduced to the rank of a 'European' province, under German domination and American management.

Waldeck Rochet, *Ecrits politiques, 1956–1969* (Paris: Editions Sociales, 1976), pp. 26–34.

30 Theses of the Fifteenth Congress of the PCF, June 1959

'European' politics, with the Schuman Plan, the European Communities of Coal and Steel and the Common Market, voices the demands of the monopolies. De Gaulle has aligned himself with this policy.

In it the monopolies seek economic advantages: easy exportation; greater possibilities for concentration and centralization of capital; fixing high monopolist prices through agreements with foreign trusts; heightened pressure brought to bear on labor's wages, production and social rights, supposedly so as to be better able to resist competition by reducing production costs.

The Common Market is aggravating the domestic tensions within the nation: it is sharpening the competition between capitalist groups as is evident in the debates over the free exchange zone; it is impeding the development of its members' commerce with the rest of the world; it is increasing the dependence of the nations of 'Little Europe' on the

United States and French dependence on reactionary and vengeful West Germany. The French government is aligned with Bonn's aggressive anti-Sovietism, promoting its unwarranted intervention in Africa, and offering it a share of the imperialist spoils in the Sahara.

This policy is contrary to the interests of France, to its security and its independence.

'XVᵉ Congrès du Parti Communiste Français,' *Cahiers du Communisme* (July–August 1959), p. 521.

31 Waldeck Rochet's report to the Seventeenth Congress of the PCF, May 1964

The Common Market and its consequences

. . . Because it is dominated by capitalist monopolies, and because they use it as a forum for the struggle to divide up the capitalist market, and for the conquest of avenues for enormous profits, the Common Market can abolish neither the tensions nor the social discrepancies among the capitalist nations. On the contrary, it aggravates them by shifting them to a higher level.

Contrary to what was promised, the laborers of the Common Market nations have benefited from neither the growth of production nor the application of scientific and technical progress . . .

It is a fact that the industrialists in the Common Market nations make a pretext of the competition that they must endure as part of the Common Market, in order to push aside the workers' legitimate demands and to justify lay-offs and the closing of factories and mines.

The activation of the Common Market has also aggravated the underdevelopment of regions like the Center, South-West and West of France – which are far from the vital center, the Ruhr . . .

We hear the merits of the 'large units of production' on the European scale loudly praised, but we cannot ignore the fact that these giant firms are the property of the capitalist monopolies, not socialist enterprises.

And the facts show us that these monopolies do not use the Common Market to satisfy and alleviate the demands of the workers and the popular masses.

In truth, for them, the Common Market is at once a means of struggling in the economic sphere against the socialist nations – whose advance they dread – and, more especially, the means for realizing even greater profits and for strengthening their domination, politically as well as economically.

The reinforcement of the economic position of West Germany, to the detriment of France's own position, has had serious political consequences. Already the Bonn leaders are profiting by extending their political hegemony in Western Europe and increasing their military strength under the rubric of the Bonn–Paris axis, of which De Gaulle was the architect.

Perhaps the French bourgeoisie imagined that it could play the lead role in Europe by entering into a partnership with West Germany. In truth, it is the vengeful Germans who are strengthening their position at the expense of the interests of France and of peace. Again, the tensions between the trusts – who have no allegiance – and French interests is evident . . .

That is why we Communists – without modifying our position, but by taking into account the existence of the Common Market – hold that it is possible and necessary to establish a collaboration between our party, the Socialist Party and other advocates of European institutions, so as to struggle, together, against the anti-social and anti-democratic policy of the monopolies dominating the Common Market, and for an alternative policy which considers the workers' and people's interests.

For a long while already we have demanded that our party's candidate, like the others', be represented within institutions such as the Common Market, according to democratic practice – so that we can bring out our criticism there, and there defend the laborers' interests while defending the interests of our nation and of peace . . .

'XVIIᵉ Congrès du Parti Communiste Français,' *Cahiers du Communisme* (June–July 1964), pp. 14–19.

32 Jean Merot, 'Lost illusions (part 4),' 1969

. . . Confronted with ever sharper tensions within the world capitalist system, the EEC could be nothing other than an 'agreement to disagree' created to safeguard the monopolies and their ascendency in Europe. The ambition of dominant industries in each of the six nations is to make every effort to protect their own sectors and to gain access to the means needed to better negotiate with American industries. And all this goes on in the midst of the convulsions engendered by the ferocious battle in which the French oligarchy is vying with the West German for supremacy.

Germany possesses economic power which places it in second place in the rank of world capitalism and is strong by virtue of American support. It is already 'feeling cramped' in the EEC. France, however, still possesses political power, but is very unsettled by the foreign offensive abroad. What is not at all understood is that, in the long run, France cannot do what is in the national interest without renouncing the cosmopolitanism which is such an essential characteristic of monopolism.

Hence the Common Market is an arm of the imperialist policy of the big capitalist states. And it is precisely for that reason that it contains within itself all the tensions of the modern world and all the defects of the capitalist system.

Undoubtedly we cannot attribute to the EEC the invention of concentration and mergers. We know very well that these are the outcomes of the socialization and internationalization of production, of the laws of economic development, and the inventions of the capitalists themselves, they who claim to be powerless to stop it. Thus they are absolved of all obligation to justify or acknowledge the resultant reactionary operations.

If it has not invented capitalist concentration, the Common Market has none the less lent it greater momentum. The national interest – that of the people – is nothing more for them than an obstacle.

L'Humanité, January 31, 1969, p. 2.

33   Georges Marchais, 'France and the Common Market,' 1973

. . . We must acknowledge that the Common Market exists. It has woven economic and commercial ties among the member nations, ties which could not be cut without harming each individual member. For six years now our party has asserted that, in its eyes, the advent of a democratic France was compatible with the pursuit of the nation's activities within the Common Market, and we have unceasingly demanded our just representation in European bodies (which we have just this year obtained).

Obviously participation in the activities of the Common Market does not for us signify agreement with the line of those who currently control it.

To the contrary, we hold that France must have a double objective in all her actions. She must preserve, while in the Common Market, our nation's freedom to formulate its own policy – the opportunity for democratic government to work to bring about the economic, social and political transformation that the nation needs. For us the independence and freedom of action of France are inviolable principles.

For certain people, in a period in which economic development calls for the consolidation of forces and the intensification of international relations, France cannot by herself assure her independence. Hence she must, according to them, melt into a 'Little Europe' which could then be independent.

This deduction is strange. For the best means of being independent obviously cannot consist, for a nation, in renouncing its sovereignty to preserve the other aspects of its independence! . . .

Besides, we cannot allow our people's right to construct a political and social system, corresponding to its own wishes, to be given away to the capitalists of neighboring countries – under the pretext of a supranational 'European politics.'

Finally, Europe, under the domination of the big capitalists, could only be an appendage of the Atlantic bloc. Because they are in the service of the financial giants, the reactionary politicians would never oppose the penetration of American capital, the combination of multinational firms under American management, since they could not afford to renounce the class solidarity with the leader of world imperialism.

Only a democratic Europe of the workers and of the people could be an independent Europe, a Europe capable of establishing co-operative relations based on strict equality of rights in the people's interest, with the United States as well as with the socialist nations.

It is precisely to bring about this Europe of the workers and of the people, this independent Europe, that a democratic France will act – for our second objective – to democratize the institution of the Common Market, to liberate the Market from the domination of big capital, to support the demands of the urban and rural masses and to direct Community programs according to what these demands are . . .

Le Défi Démocratique (Paris: Grasset, 1973), cf. pp. 234–8.

34 'The Europe that we want,' *L'Humanité*, 1974

As is well known, since the decision to create the Common Market we have been the only ones to show that the Europe it would bring about would be a Europe of the big capitalists. Experience has amply confirmed a judgement which we are no longer the only ones to hold.

Yet ever since the Common Market became a reality and ties were woven between our nation and its partners which could not be unilaterally severed without damaging the national economy, the immediate task has been not to deny or to liquidate the Common Market, but to transform it. This is what we have asserted since 1967. Our party's program 'Changing Course' defines the major tenets of this necessary transformation. We are happy to see this become a part of the Common Program of the left.

I remind you that this document sets out a fundamental double objective with regard to the EEC, for a future government of the left:

– On the one hand, to participate in the construction of the European Economic Community, its institutions and common policies, combined with an effort to free it from the domination of big capital, to democratize its institutions, and to defend the workers therein.
– On the other hand, to preserve France's freedom of action while in the Common Market.

The current situation confirms the value of this position, while further emphasizing and clarifying the objectives and the necessary stages.

There are three essential reasons for this.

– First, it is urgent to oppose the actions of the multinational firms which are dominating the Common Market and who intend to make the workers and the people bear the consequences of the crisis which is upsetting the system.

– Secondly, it is urgent to block the attempts to create a politico-military bloc which will be a real bulwark for West European reactionaries and for which France would have to renounce the essential prerogatives on which her sovereignty is based in order to become integrated.
– Thirdly, it is a matter of urgency to form an opposition to the American attempts to profit from the current circumstances and to strengthen its role and its dominant position in a consolidated Atlantic bloc.

Far from responding to these imperatives – which express the interests of the workers as well as the national interest – the Pompidou government has turned its back on them. Its policy, even if it reflects the real contradictions between diverse capitalist nations, shows a general tendency towards compromise and towards capitulation in the face of American demands.

For us, in essence, the motive, objective and *raison d'être* of a new European policy must be to respond in all circumstances and in all areas to the real needs of our nation's workers and the majority of the people . . .

The Common Market cannot constitute a closed economic and commercial bloc. This would deprive other peoples of the immense possibility of international co-operation open to them today. Relations of all sorts must be established with the socialist nations and with developing countries. The establishment of new relations with the Organization of African States, respecting their sovereignty and equal rights, can serve as an example.

We have already said, but perhaps it must be repeated today, that for the Europe of the Nine, as for France, we cannot recommend disengagement from one bloc in order to join another. What we seek is a Europe free from any politico-military bloc, a Europe capable of establishing co-operative relations, based on complete equality and on the peoples' interests, with the socialist nations as well as with the United States . . .

L'Humanité, January 22, 1974, p. 6.

35   'EEC,' *L'Humanité*, 1975

There is a Common Market, mainly a customs union; a common agricultural market, and an effort by the state monopolies to consolidate economic and financial policies within the European Economic Community. We do not mean to raise the question of French membership of the Common Market or of the EEC.

That said, the shameful consequences of the EEC's current positions touch the laboring masses more and more directly. The peasants know that they must think twice about 'the Common Market, the hope of French agriculture.' In truth, it has brought about the ruin of our agriculture. We must consequently struggle against this trend. The Common Program satisfactorily defines what action must be taken in this area.

We must immediately add that the parties of the left in our nation can act together in this matter and promote a joint action of the Western European left forces. Our party hopes for this, and will do all it can to facilitate it.

If this action has any special importance, it is that the Giscardian government is precisely the one that is making the greatest efforts to go much farther, to bring about a sort of political union of the Little Europe of the Nine. That would naturally entail, as Giscard d'Estaing openly asserts, the abandonment of our national sovereignty.

We are resolutely opposed to this, now and for the future. We support the most active co-operation among all nations, notably in the EEC, but absolutely respecting the national independence of each. We do not at all exclude the possibility of a certain measure of economic integration, in so far as it would involve nations started down the road to economic democracy, or better still on the road to socialism – but, even then, with the most complete respect for national independence. Actually neither socialism nor even economic democracy has yet triumphed in any nation of the EEC.

For the present the struggle against the Giscard-Chirac government's attempt to forge a political Holy Alliance under West German hegemony, destined to enable the West European bourgeoisie better to resist the rise of the worker and democratic movements, is the pressing issue.

As we believe that it is possible to maintain French participation in the EEC, we also seek to avoid the construction of an economic bloc – still less, the creation of a political bloc – which would aggravate the division of Europe. This is also why we do not favor the concluding of agreements between the EEC and the Comecon. We suggest, rather, the development – the free development – of the widest possible number of co-operating nations acting as sovereign entities, on the basis of mutual interests . . .

There will be no European independence as long as it is part of the Atlantic bloc, under the direction of the United States.

Our party has come forward in support of a democratic Western Europe: that necessarily means a Europe independent of both the West and the East.

In addition, we support as we always have, French disengagement from any sort of political military bloc: the Atlantic Pact, the European Defense Community or the Warsaw Pact.

L'Humanité, May 29, 1975, p. 8.

36   Declaration of the Politburo of the PCF, July 14, 1976

Election of the European Assembly by universal suffrage
The heads of state of the Nine have just agreed on the election of the European Assembly by universal suffrage in 1978.

This decision holds serious consequences.

The French Communist Party is, on principle, in favor of universal suffrage with proportional representation.

But here something else is at stake.

Having the European Assembly elected by universal suffrage is intended to give it greater powers. French and multinational big capital need this democratic alibi to mask the failure of the Common Market and to try to impose austerity policies on everybody. The decision taken in this direction by the Giscardian government is thus one more manifestation of its policy of abandoning the nation. At the conclusion of this enterprise, a foreign majority – and in addition a reactionary one – would thus be able to dictate the law to the French people and to their elected representatives themselves.

Far from offering solutions to the distressing

problems faced by the workers and peasants (inflation, unemployment, ruin of agricultural operations), solutions in accordance with their interests, these would on the contrary further aggravate the difficulties which they have experienced since the European Community was created . . .

The French Communist Party fights and will fight every attempt to diminish our national sovereignty by extending the powers of the European Assembly.

It will use every means at its disposal, including action within the European Assembly, to make heard the voice of the French workers, to defend their interests, and those of the nation, to support constructive proposals which meet their needs, to advance the cause of a workers' Europe, democratic, independent and peace-loving.

It will defend, under all conditions, the right of our people, as of every people, to define with its sovereign power its national and international policy, the right freely to give itself the government of its choice.

Cahiers du Communisme (September 1976), pp. 155–6.

37 Declaration of the Politburo of the PCF, June 8, 1977

Communist initiative about the European Parliament
The Political Bureau of the French Communist Party

has adopted a position on the problems raised by the proposal to elect the European Assembly through universal suffrage . . .

The French Communist Party demands:

(1) that the ratification proposal and the draft electoral law be discussed at the same time;

(2) that the ratification law affirm the principle that national sovereignty cannot be alienated, in whole or in part, to any international organization whatsoever;

(3) that the electoral law specify that sovereignty can only be national and that only the representatives of the French people elected within the framework of the institutions of the republic can be regarded as participating in this sovereignty. The European Assembly will not belong to the institutional structure of the French republic and will not participate in the exercise of national sovereignty;

(4) that the method of proportional voting in a national framework be used for future elections, and not just for that scheduled for 1978.

These propositions, which are intended to keep the powers of the European Assembly within the limits fixed by the Treaty of Rome, correspond to our scrupulous respect for France's freedom of action. They are in conformity with the principles defined in the Common Program . . .

Cahiers du Communisme (July 1977), pp. 125–6.

SPANISH Communist Party: Legitimacy, Autonomy and the Search for International Linkages

The International System

1 PCE program, Fifth Congress, 1954 (published in 1955)

In the international order the Communist Party will fight for:

(1) A policy of peace and friendship with all peoples, re-establishing normal diplomatic relations with the Soviet Union, the People's Republic of China, countries with popular democracies and others. For the entry of the Spanish republic into the UN and all organs of international co-operation. It will actively support a policy of collective security, in which all European states, without distinction, will participate: it will oppose the creation or maintenance of aggressive military blocs and will fight participation in them; it will uphold all initiatives directed towards prohibition of atomic weapons and all weapons of mass destruction and work towards achieving progressive disarmament, to reach general disarmament. It will fight so that the Spanish republic defends in international relations a policy of strong and lasting peace, as willed by the people of Spain, and all peoples.

(2) Maintaining commercial and cultural relations with all nations, without distinction, based on the principle of mutual convenience.

V Congreso del PCE, Spanish Communist Party document, 1954, p. 19.

2 PCE international situation: Central Committee, 1956, 'Declaration . . . for reconciliation . . .'

Premises of a Spanish foreign policy
The actual international climate of coexistence and peaceful collaboration among states favors the possibility of peaceful changes in Spain, the national reconciliation of the Spanish.

Spain cannot remain isolated indefinitely from this powerful, universal course of events. It is not possible politically and economically for Spain to maintain herself on the margin of changes in the international situation.

We coexist on this planet with other countries and under penalty of the apocalyptic road of a thermonuclear war, something which our people, as do all peoples, reject . . .

General Franco's foreign policy is condemned to fail precisely because it begins with the denial of that reality.

The characteristic trait of our epoch is that socialism is not a 'Russian phenomenon' as certain people would like to characterize it. Today's socialism is a universal system which exercises powerful influence in international situations and politics. This is the most important aspect of this period.

Another of the changes which has broken the basis of imperialism is the collapse of the colonial system . . .

In a climate of universal condemnation of war and support for peaceful solutions to international problems, a conference of the heads of state of the Soviet Union, England, France and the United States was held in Geneva. What has been called the 'spirit of Geneva' was born there. The spirit of Geneva calls for discussion and negotiation in the conduct of relations among states, regardless of their political and social regimes, rather than war.

The imperialist policy of aggressive blocs, of Cold War, that the dominant circles in the United States formulate, is against the spirit of Geneva.

The profound contrast between the dangerous direction of North American policy and the policy of the Soviet Union and other states in favor of peaceful coexistence daily appears clearer to people, including the Spanish people. This, together with the success of the edification of socialism, explains the growing prestige and worldwide influence of the Soviet Union.

Evidence of the improvement in the international situation is the re-establishment of friendly relations between the Soviet Union and Yugoslavia . . .

To improve relations with all states which are disposed to do so, the USSR does not attempt to create enmity between those countries and the United States. Following the proposal of the Soviet government, the United States and the USSR signed a pact at the beginning of this year in support of peace and collaboration. It is authentic proof of the sincere intentions that guide the Soviet Union.

The vitality of the principle of peaceful coexistence has had one of its most eloquent confirmations in the normalization of relations between the Soviet Union and West Germany. The memory of the terrible war provoked by Hitlerism and its aggression against the USSR points to the necessity of peaceful coexistence between Germany and the Soviet Union.

The demobilization of 1,200,000 of the armed forces, and the proportional reduction of armaments and defense spending agreed to by the Soviet government, mark a new practical and effective road for the solution of the problem of disarmament. If the Western powers would follow the example of the USSR, the heavy burden that the arms race represents for all people will be alleviated.

The public positions of the Pope in favor of disarmament and the prohibition of nuclear arms, his change of tone with reference to certain problems of the contemporary world, are reflections of the powerful support of Catholics in all countries of peace and international collaboration.

In the past neutrality has been Spain's policy. Even during the Second World War Franco could not completely ignore it – although it was compromised with an active non-belligerence. The pact with the United States is a pact of war; it obliges Spain to abandon neutrality. The factors which suggested a policy of neutrality in the past continue to do so. In the new worldwide condition, neutrality could be the concrete form of the incorporation of Spain into the great movement toward peace and coexistence.

The forces which would benefit from warlike conflicts are not inactive and they intend to revive the Cold War with the hope of transforming it into a 'hot war.' They increase military bases in foreign countries. They do not cease in their campaigns against socialist and other peaceful countries. They provoke incidents in many places in the world and they resist every effective step toward disarmament, prolonging the arms race. They oppose the end of thermonuclear testing, in the face of the demands of universal public opinion and in spite of the support of the Pope, and they foment the creation of new aggressive blocs like the SEATO, the Bagdad Pact.

Today the forces of peace are sufficiently powerful – as events demonstrate – to prevent a new world war. The growing power of the socialist states is at the service of peace. In those capitalist countries whose leaders still have not taken steps toward forming a policy of peace, powerful forces are developing and are beginning to effect positive changes in the attitudes of the governments.

There are additional signs pointing to the change of world forces in favor of those who are for a policy of peace and coexistence. War has ceased to be inevitable. If the people do not weaken their efforts in the struggle for peace, humanity can free itself for ever from the terrible calamity of war.

The government of Franco, following the agreements with the United States, is pursuing a policy of rearmament. The construction of the military bases provided for in those agreements means a grave danger for Spain.

The pact with the United States compromised the security of Spain, and the national interest demands that it be denounced, and the relations between Spain and the United States established on the model of Spanish neutrality, which does not exclude collaboration or friendship founded on the respect of national sovereignty and of reciprocal interests.

North American policy tries to persuade Spain to enter NATO and the projected Mediterranean Pact. The national interest of our country does not advise Spain's entering such military combinations as attempt to establish security, but rather to leave those military combinations which even now compromise our security such as the pact of 1953 and the Iberian bloc, and place Spain on a course of neutrality, the great progression of peaceful coexistence and international collaboration. With disarmament, the burdens which weigh on the Spanish economy would be facilitated. The public opinion of our country should demand that Spain's representatives in the UN support all propositions and active initiatives to this end . . .

Spanish foreign policy is the only factor keeping Spain from trading with the Soviet Union and the socialist countries. Trade with the socialist countries does not mean the suppression or diminution of trade with the capitalist countries, including North America, but only that which is in the national interests of Spain and without dependence on anyone. It is unquestionable that the development of trade with socialist countries would help Spanish industries and agriculture to obtain better conditions in the capitalist countries.

But it is not possible to develop trade, to promote cultural, scientific, technical and athletic exchanges and at the same time practice a policy of hostility, of 'Holy War,' against the countries with whom the interest for relations exists.

For this reason the idea that important changes in foreign policy should be made, and that these should be a return to the policy of neutrality, gains support.

During the years of the Second World War Franco sacrificed Spain's foreign policy to the interests of Hitler and Mussolini. With the military defeat of the Axis, Franco passed to the service of the United States. Franco's onerous concessions to North American imperialism grew from year to year, until they culminated with the signing of the treaties of September 1953.

In this manner Franco has placed Spain in the humiliating role of appendage to the United States, an instrument of its warlike policy and a free zone for North American capital.

To justify this foreign policy which fails to take into account the national interest, Franco has always speculated on the absurd assumption of a threat of 'Soviet aggression' against Spain. Such a threat has never existed.

Such speculation has always been contradicted by the unvarying Soviet policy of peace. This disposition of the USSR to admit Spain to the collective security pact of Europe and its role in favor of Spain's entry into the UN demonstrate at the same time the falsehood of Franco's propaganda, and that the country of socialism is inspired by the best sentiments of friendship and collaboration toward Spain . . .

Spanish Communist Party document, 1956, pp. 6–14.

3 General assessment of US foreign policy, 1958, Dolores Ibarruri to the Central Committee

American imperialism is the profound and principal cause of the aggravation of the international situation. Faced with the eager efforts recently undertaken by the USSR and the rest of the socialist countries, supported by the non-aligned countries and the popular masses of the whole world, to diminish international tension and the threat of war, the USA has responded by accentuating its aggressive policy through armed intervention in the Middle East and aggressive actions against the People's Republic of China in Taiwan.

The launching of Soviet Sputniks has demonstrated Soviet superiority in the key realms of science and technology. It confirmed, moreover, even to the eyes of the most skeptical, that the USSR is the first nation – and to this day the only one – that has been able to construct intercontinental ballistic missiles capable of sending a nuclear bomb to any part of the globe.

The USSR immediately put this superiority in the service of peace, intensifying its efforts to achieve an international agreement prohibiting atomic weapons, initiating disarmament and guaranteeing peace to the people.

But the Yankee government answered with the meeting of NATO in December 1957, which repelled the Soviet initiatives, and increased the number of nuclear arms in Western Europe, especially those of medium and short range, the only ones which the USA presently possesses.

Despite the senselessness of the imperialists' attitudes, the USSR took new steps to diminish international tensions. The Supreme Soviet decided to suspend unilaterally its nuclear testing, and it addressed the parliaments of the USA and England, proposing that those nations adopt the same attitude.

In June of this year the countries of the Warsaw Pact decided on a new reduction of their armed forces, increasing to 2,477,000 the number of men taken out of active service since 1955.

. . . To each new pacifying effort of the USSR, Washington has answered with new measures, aggravating international tension, and taking the world, according to the tactic openly proclaimed by Dulles, 'to the brink of war.'

The US air force has been ordered to keep permanently aloft a great part of its airplanes packed with atom bombs. Any accident, any error of a pilot, could provoke an incalculable catastrophe and even unleash a general war. At the same time the Yankee airplanes undertake flights 'in the direction' of Soviet territory, and even try to penetrate into it, as was demonstrated by the forced landing of one of those airplanes in Soviet territory, many kilometers from the border between the USSR and Turkey.

The USA is accelerating the rearmament of militaristic West Germany and violating all the agreements contracted on this question, giving them atomic weapons, intensifying the realization of the plans of the Common Market, of Euratom, etc., in unquestionable efforts to create an economic base for the intensive militarization of Western Europe.

In assuming the direction of the capitalist world following the Second World War, the primary objective of US foreign policy was the blocking of socialism in the new nations of Europe and Asia where the working class had assumed power, and then to liquidate socialism in the USSR, re-establishing the world empire of capitalism under US hegemony . . .

The unity of the socialist camp, in which one-third of humanity lives, and the prestige of the USSR and of the CPSU as a center and guide of that camp, have been justified in this last period, as is demonstrated by the meeting last November in Moscow of the twelve worker and communist parties that direct the states in the socialist countries. The divisionist maneuvers of revisionism of Yugoslavia, on which imperialism had based so many hopes, have been crushed by the ideological unity and the Marxist–Leninist policy of the socialist camp.

So the primary objective of the policy of US imperialism has met the most complete failure.

A second great objective was to prevent the collapse of the colonial system of imperialism, without which it cannot subsist. For that the North American strategists developed a line which, although presented as anti-colonialist better to fool the people, intended in practice to inherit the colonial empire of England, France, Holland and other colonial powers . . .

The attempts to impose the 'new forms' of colonialism on liberated people have failed one after another because those peoples are no longer alone; they count on the economic aid, the technical aid and, when necessary, the military aid of the socialist countries.

. . . Thirdly, the USA had prepared to unite the capitalist world under its hegemony in order to concentrate its forces for the attainment of the objectives which we have outlined – the destruction of socialism, the maintenance of colonialism – and in order to place all other capitalist countries under the exploitation of US capital. The whole system of politico-military alliances, the axis of which is the Atlantic Alliance, as well as the diverse formulas of 'economic aid,' tended towards this end . . .

Neither the race for armaments, nor recourse to inflation or deflation, nor the theoretical constructions of bourgeois political economy have been able to avoid the cyclic crises predicted by the Marxists.

. . . The 'global strategy' of the USA – as its creators pompously call that policy – represented in reality a challenge to the objective laws of social development, to the historical fact that they have already developed more than sufficiently, and on a world scale, the objective conditions which make inevitable the passage of human society from capitalism to socialism.

With its 'global strategy,' first announced by the dropping of the atom bomb on Hiroshima, but directed against the USSR and the progressive forces of the world, the USA believed that it could pursue its conquest of the globe in conditions of 'absolute security,' protected by oceans and atomic primacy.

But atomic primacy was lost and oceans are not an obstacle, but a way cleared for ICBMs. 'Absolute security' has become 'absolute insecurity' . . .

The socialist camp directed by the USSR raises itself as an unbeatable fortress in the fight for peace, before the aggressiveness of imperialism, as a brake to aggression, as an invaluable support for the people who fight for their national and social independence.

Spanish Communist Party document, 1958, p. 57.

4 PCE program, Sixth Congress, 1960

The Communist Party will fight for peace and disarmament, for peaceful coexistence and fruitful relations between states irrespective of their political and social regimes, for the security and independence of Spain. It will mobilize the popular masses with these postulates and will develop them as the basis of the foreign policy of the state.

The Communist Party believes that the following tenets are fundamental to this general orientation.

– Spain's solemn renunciation of war as an instrument of foreign policy, and its refusal to participate in any military bloc or alliance.

– The consequent Spanish participation in international organizations and conferences which work toward general disarmament, backing every step in that direction, and in particular the prohibition of the testing of arms of mass destruction, or their abolition.

– The re-establishing of diplomatic, commercial and cultural relations with the socialist countries.

– The revision of the 1953 treaties with the United States to eliminate the North American bases in Spain, and the revocation of all military and other clauses which diminish Spain's sovereignty, endanger its security, or are detrimental to its economy, and the establishing of relations between both states on the basis of mutual respect for national sovereignty and independence, non-interference in internal affairs and mutual benefit. Opposition to the installing of launching devices for ballistic missiles on Spanish territory.

– Spain's faithful adherence to its agreements with Morocco, and the solution of remaining problems in a spirit of respect for the sovereignty and independence of the Moroccan state, of Morocco's territorial integrity in accordance with its historic past. The establishment of close friendly relations between both states and generally, with all the Maghreb states for a common defense against imperialism and the development of economic and cultural co-operation.

– Solidarity with all peoples who are free of the colonial yokes or who are struggling for liberation, and particularly full support for those peoples in various African territories who still suffer the oppression of Spanish colonialism, and who aspire to their independence.

– The annulment of the Iberian Pact and the development of close fraternal relations with the Portuguese people in the common struggle for democracy.

– The elimination of the last after-effects of the Second World War in Europe, through the conclusion of a peace treaty with the two German states, solution of the West Berlin problem, and struggle against the re-emergence of German militarism.

– A policy of close friendship and political, economic and cultural co-operation with our sister nations of Latin America, who struggle for national independence, democracy and progress.

– The development of foreign commerce without discrimination, and on the basis of mutual benefit. And in this context, the taking advantage of the great possibilities offered by commerce with the socialist countries, in whose markets Spain could sell a large part of its agricultural, textile, mineral, manufactured and other products, and in return acquire machinery, fuel and raw materials.

– With regard to the possibility of obtaining foreign aid to speed up national economic development, such loans, credits and technical aid as are free of political and military clauses and would be advantageous to Spain should be taken, regardless of the social or political regime of the country which may offer them. As for private capital investments, those which will not harm, but would rather contribute to, the development of national industry will be allowed. Efforts by private foreign monopoly capital to politically and economically subjugate our country will be opposed.

– That Spain not be integrated into organizations supported by European and American monopolies, such as the Common Market and the Association of Free Exchange, because such an integration would cause grave damage to the Spanish economy and would deepen its dependence. The Communist Party believes that the progress of West European peoples cannot be seen as opposed to that of the peoples of central and Eastern Europe, but rather within the general framework of a political, economic and cultural co-operation between all peoples on this continent.

VI Congreso del PCE, Spanish Communist Party document, 1960, pp. 13–14.

5   Santiago Carrillo, 'On some problems in the tactics of the fights against Francoism,' 1961

. . . It is true that the Kennedy election awakens no new hopes of the possibility of a miraculous disappearance of Franco . . .

Should we expect any changes in US policy? The strategy of global hegemony of the USA comes across ever greater difficulties. Dulles and Eisenhower, inspired by the most aggressive circles of monopolist capital, encountered these difficulties with their policies of Cold War, the armaments race, saving military bases abroad, and the power equilibrium 'at the brink of war.' Eisenhower's attitude towards Franco was integrated into all of this orientation. Kennedy finds himself with the grave political, economic and financial consequences of such an imprudent policy . . .

The policies of Cold War, bases abroad, the arms race, in short, the preparation for thermonuclear world war, has had a catastrophic effect on the economy of the USA without having provided the military supremacy that it sought. 'Our problems are critical,' the US President has confessed, 'the current of the tide is not favorable to us. In numerous regions of the world . . . the balance of power is inclined toward the side of our adversaries.'

If Kennedy were to take his analysis to its logical consequences, he would arrive at a radical revision of American foreign policy. Since practice has demonstrated that the arms race does not assure the expansion of the US economy and that military bases abroad provoke and aggravate the financial crisis, why not begin a policy of peaceful coexistence, of extended commercial exchange with socialist countries which would assure new markets for US production? Why not save the enormous costs that the foreign bases create and grant credits to under-developed countries which would assure their economic development and the possibility of increasing the commerce with them?

But logic does not guide the conduct of the great capitalist monopolies that dictate the policy of Yankee governments; their conduct is motivated by zeal for profit, for the achievement of maximum benefits. And though certain capitalist sectors seem to see the necessity – in their own interest – of revising the policy which has been followed until now, there are very influential groups which base their earnings on the arms race and the maintenance of bases abroad . . .

Spanish Communist Party document, 1961, pp. 5–6.

6 Executive Committee of the PCE, August 12, 1961

The problem of the signing of a peace treaty with the two Germanies and the establishment of West Berlin as a free city has become the crucial problem of the hour.

The maintenance of world peace and the prevention of a horrifying thermonuclear war depend upon the solution of this urgent problem.

The very existence of Spain, its political regime, its social structure, and even the lives of its inhabitants, rich and poor, depends upon finding a proper solution to the German problem . . .

Instead of demilitarizing Germany, the imperialists rearmed the Germans from the occupied zones and erected a new vengeful German state, Adenauer's Federal Germany, thus concretizing the country's division.

Because of its social structure, the composition of its leadership and its politics, the West German state is a reproduction of the Hitlerian Reich, differing only in so far as those who were called 'nationalists' yesterday are today self-made 'Western democrats.'

The Germans who were placed at the head of the new federal state continue Hitler's anti-Soviet and anti-communist crusade. And in just a few years the German Federal Republic has become the strongest capitalist state in West Europe.

Today West Germany participates in NATO, houses Yankee atomic weapons and sends its troops to train in the territories of countries which only yesterday were its enemies and occupiers. Hoping to make Spain and other countries into an enormous base for its atomic and military industries and for its army, Germany has become an immense danger to peace in the very heart of Europe.

The responsibility for this situation, which has returned Europe and the world to the 1930s, belongs exclusively to the United States and to the Western imperialist powers. Following its policy of peaceful coexistence, the Soviet Union has repeatedly pointed to the danger which such a situation poses to world peace and has taken every possible initiative to solve it through negotiation, without response from Western leaders.

In response to the creation of the vengeful federal state in complete violation of all the agreements among the allies, the Soviet Union gave its support to the creation and development of the German

Democratic Republic, the first state of the German workers and farmers.

The German Democratic Republic is a guarantee of peace; it represents a great obstacle to the aggressive vengeful plans of Adenauer and the imperialist powers.

The Soviet government and the government of democratic Germany, together with the support and sympathy of world public opinion, have been proposing to Adenauer and the Western powers the negotiation of a peace treaty which would end the state of war which has been arbitrarily extended during the past sixteen years, a peace treaty which would permit the establishment of paths leading toward a normalization of the situation, and the elimination of West German vengefulness and the solution of Berlin's critical problem. This would mean the end of the military occupation of Germany and would free Germany from the explosive burden which it now carries. This path would create the conditions for a reduction of international tension.

But the imperialist powers did not accept the signing of a treaty; they tried to keep Adenauer's Germany as a military vanguard against the socialist world.

In such conditions the Soviet government, supported by the whole socialist camp and world democratic opinion, has decided to invite Westerners for a last time to sign a peace treaty with the two Germanies and to normalize Berlin's situation.

Convinced of his correctness and of the extraordinary power of the Soviet Union and the socialist camp, comrade Khrushchev, in the name of the government of USSR, has declared that if Westerners refuse to participate in the conclusion of a peace treaty with the two Germanies, the Soviet Union and the socialist states which participated in the anti-Hitlerian war will sign a separate treaty with the German Democratic Republic.

Refusing to sign a treaty with the two Germanies, the Western powers plan to oppose the signing of a separate peace treaty among USSR, the socialist states and the German Democratic Republic, even threatening war!

The American imperialist leaders and the vengeful Germans would never dare to venture into war, if those countries on which they count on now, and those on which they have imposed military bases, inform the Americans of their decisions not to permit their territories to be used for such a criminal end. Already the mobilization of public opinion in countries such as England, demanding negotiation over the problem of Berlin, has led the Yankee leaders to declare that they are willing to negotiate, even though they are doing so with the intentions of gaining time and placating public opinion. However, in fact they continue with their preparations for aggression.

In Spain we can and should promote a great national mobilization against the use of our territory by the American military. Such a mobilization is in the interest of all the Spanish, the communists, socialists, democrats and liberals, the Catholics, monarchists, and even those who still feel linked to Francoism, the proprietors and capitalists, those who believe in God and those who are non-believers. Today's fights and differences would lose all meaning in case of a nuclear bombardment of our country . . .

Nuestra Bandera, no. 31 (September 1961), cf. pp. 5–6, 12.

7   Santiago Carrillo, *Después de Franco Que?*, 1965

The way toward an anti-feudal and anti-monopolist democracy will require an adaptation of the apparatus of the state to the modern and democratic characteristics of such a regime. A new military policy and a new national military doctrine will be necessary. Spain will not give up the army as long as the struggle for disarmament has not succeeded. We are not fond of a simplistic militarism. The official military doctrine is based on integration within the NATO bloc as a supplementary force and as imperialism's strategic base in the case of a war against the Soviet Union and the socialist and anti-imperialist countries; it also bases itself on the idea, characteristic of Francoism, of a police army, which occupies the country and maintains 'public order.'

There is no doubt that the starting point for a new national military doctrine must be different: a state nourished and supported by the nation, and whose only duty is the defense of the national territory and its independence, without any 'public order' function. Such an army would have, as much as possible, weaponry supplied by national industries; it should make use of foreign technology when necessary, but it should do so according to principles of efficiency and economy rather than by its membership in a certain military bloc.

The army should be restructured on the basis of its two fundamental parts: first, the permanent army, including the navy and the air force, whose high technical and professional level deserve particular attention and, secondly, a territorial militia, popular and voluntary, trained and armed to take part in combat with light and semi-heavy weapons, in case the country becomes the object of foreign aggression. The relevance of a territorial militia and its popular origins is great in the case of a war of independence, which would be the only sort of war in which the army should be necessary . . .

The army, the air force and the anti-aircraft forces should receive most of the attention, because of their duty to defend our territorial integrity.

In today's world Spain cannot aspire to be one of the great military powers. However, such a fact does not mean that Spain's military doctrine should be determined by any great power or power bloc. The criterion that small states must necessarily ally themselves and even integrate themselves into more powerful blocs is not justified. In the present situation, if a certain bloc attacked our country, and if Spain lacked sufficient defensive forces, our country would be guaranteed the help and collaboration of the no less powerful opposite bloc.

We know that the Warsaw Pact countries would never attack Spain, no matter what her political and social regime, and that they would support her in the case of a threat by aggressive imperialist powers. This is one of the reasons why we think that neutrality with respect to the military blocs is by no means a policy of isolation and defenselessness. However, even in the case of the absurd hypothesis of a socialist aggression, the same reasoning applies: the 'Atlantic bloc' would militarily intervene without any need for a prior engagement or treaty. The present division of the world into two blocs does not objectively constitute an obstacle, but rather the concrete basis for a policy of neutrality. Meanwhile Spain's interest from every point of view is to maintain herself independent of any bloc, not to limit her sovereignty or her economic capacity with any kind of engagement, such as the ones established in 1953 with the United States. Spain will find strength in a positive policy of neutrality, playing her role in the international effort towards peace and progress and benefiting from multilateral trade and relation.

In foreign policy the interest of a democratic state would be in diversifying and increasing its economic, cultural and political relations with socialist as well as capitalist and Third World countries, without any exception.

A democratic state in which the communists participated would not be, *motu proprio*, an 'anti-American' state. Rather, it would be a fully independent state, and it would clash with American (or any other) interest only when the other country attempted to intervene in Spain's internal affairs or threatened international peace and the principle of the self-determination of every people. Naturally a democratic state should negotiate diplomatically for the dismantling of existing bases and the annulment of the military accords with other powers . . .

An anti-feudal and anti-monopolist democracy, in which the state and the people would have the necessary tools to protect the national interest and negotiate on a level of real equality, could initiate the study of conditions for a possible association with the European economic organizations. We are aware of the complexity of the problem and the necessity of avoiding any improvisations which could harm our national interests. However, the new democracy would create new conditions and possibilities which it would be necessary to explore. At the same time there is no doubt that the conditions for exchange and access to the markets of socialist countries and of the Third World would be enormously enhanced by the existence of a democratic state.

Santiago Carrillo, *Después de Franco Que?* (Buenos Aires: Editorial Impulso, 1965), cf. pp. 127–33.

8 'NATO and Spain: European collective security,' *Nuestra Bandera*, 1966

. . . NATO's platform has provided fabulous benefits for the great armaments fellowships and great monopolies that thrive on military commissions.

The capitalists who joined together in 1949 under the leadership of the United States seemed to be tightly united. The countries of Western Europe accepted the bossism of the USA because they were weak, having recently ended a tiring war. To a certain extent it was convenient for the rulers of the capitalist countries of Europe to become associates of the 'Yankee' colossus, not only for economic reasons (the Marshall Plan, etc.), but to check the attempts of the masses to go beyond bourgeois democracy.

We experienced times characterized by tension generated by the Cold War, a mechanism which was supported by a gigantic apparatus exerting ideological pressure over public opinion. Nevertheless the democratic forces were developing and strengthening. In countries such as France and Italy the communist parties were gaining not only numerical force but an influence which was reflected in municipal and legislative elections. The pressure of the working class over monopolies, the establishment of social rights, the uncovering of schemes, etc., prevented the consolidation and advance of the most reactionary forces in support of Yankee imperialism.

In Spain the Communist Party never ceased to link the fight against Franco's dictatorship with the defense of peace, the suppression of the Yankee–Francoist military pacts, and the unmasking of the 'Atlantic' postulates against the people . . .

NATO's crisis, in reality, is an aspect of the crisis of imperialism in general. One cannot attribute to one man alone, not even one of the stature of General De Gaulle, a situation that has evolved in spite of General De Gaulle and the monopolies he represents in Europe . . .

In all these years – *and not despite his origin, but because of his origin* – Franco has been used by the United States in pursuit of its aggressive politics and the Cold War. The Hispanic–Yankee military agreements have permitted the Pentagon to install bases in Spain that not even countries belonging to NATO have allowed within their borders. The base on Rota for Polaris submarines is an example.

At present, when France is breaking away from NATO and when other countries in Western Europe can follow this example, Franco plays an important role in the plans of North American imperialism. Franco knows this. He will search to become 'marketable' and, in the process, Spain will once again be sacrificed. When Franco speaks of NATO he denies any particular interests, noting that his only concern is for bilateral agreements. In reality the only bilateral military agreements he has are those with Yankee imperialism. The commitments between Francoism and the USA are such that, with or without NATO, Francoist Spain will be used by the Pentagon, when and how the Pentagon sees fit, unless we Spanish prevent this by liberating ourselves from Franco.

Nuestra Bandera, nos 49–50 (May 1966), pp. 35–40.

9 'For the cancellation of the military accords with the USA,' *Mundo Obrero*, 1967

The military accords with the United States will end on September 1968. For fourteen years Spain has been an American aircraft carrier, a port for nuclear submarines and vessels, a gigantic base for the Pentagon's aggressive strategy.

What advantages have there been for Spain during these fourteen years of military submission to the USA? Those who signed the accords for Spain, as well as those who accepted them, justified them in the name of a necessary reaction to a supposed aggressiveness of the Eastern countries. The ghost of an 'aggression from the East' has vanished during these fourteen years. Even the most conservative European statesmen acknowledge today that the coexistence policy of the USSR and other socialist countries is a constant of the international situation. The broadest movements of opinion condemn the United States policy of aggression, its criminal escalation of the war against the Vietnamese people, its intervention in Santo Domingo, its threats against Cuba and its support of the aggression against the Arab countries.

The accords were immorally justified as a good economic business and as an excellent political and diplomatic operation. Dollars were going to rain on to our soil, coming from America's hand. Spain was going to enter the Western alliances through the front door. And the Spanish army, once modernized, was going to play an important role in those alliances. However, during these fourteen years, American capitalism has increased its economic colonization of Spain; Franco's regime remains in the leprosarium of its origin and sustains its fascist structures. Spain suffers the consequences. The armed forces, which consume a large part of the budget, are still waiting for their real modernization. In the American strategy they count only as the policemen who guarantee the security of American bases in Spain, only as an aid to American forces.

It was said that the accords were essential to Spain's security. Here are the results. Other North African and European countries (Morocco and France) have got rid of American bases in order to guarantee their own security, or have refused to lodge the most dangerous atomic submarines (Italy) or are negotiating for the departure of existing ones (Libya). The

Spanish government has accepted all of the Pentagon's initiatives (such as the Polaris base in Rota); the superatomic fortresses that have been rejected everywhere else have arrived in Torrejon, and the network of the American military does not cease to expand.

Henceforth we should speak out for a Spanish foreign policy of independence, neutrality and coexistence.

The first step, the primary condition for Spain to acquire a Spanish foreign policy, is the condemnation of the 1953 accords and the closure of the American bases on Spain's soil.

The danger for Spain is dramatically increased by the fact that the USA remains in Vietnam. The sacred interest of Spain necessitates the evacuation of the Yankee bases from our soil and the ending of the Vietnam War . . .

Mundo Obrero, no. 20 (October 1–15, 1967), p. 10.

10 'Anti-imperialist unity in the solidarity with Vietnam,' *Mundo Obrero*, 1971

More than two years ago, under international pressure and in light of the unhappiness of a great part of US public opinion, the government of the USA committed itself to end the bombing of north Vietnam; it announced the beginning of the withdrawal of its troops and the near end of the war. The opening of negotiations in Paris was saluted by the people with the hope that a peaceful solution would be achieved.

But what is the real policy of the USA? Nixon has just declared, unmasking himself to be an imperialist killer, that he believes he has the right to assassinate whomsoever he wants, that he would not put limits on the bombings of his armed forces. The air force has renewed its attacks against north Vietnam, Cambodia and Laos.

The USA invokes, with the utmost cynicism, the 'right of self-defense.' But what 'self-defense,' what right, allows the USA, tens of thousands of kilometers from its territory, to launch an attack with planes and cannons against people who want to be free and independent? How long is the USA going to continue

violating all the norms of international right, the minimum principles required for coexistence on a global scale?

The aggression of the USA is not only directed against the people of Indo–China. We are all affected by it. It threatens us all. The destiny of Vietnam – the necessity of victory – will be decisive for humanity . . .

The threat of direct aggression against north Vietnam lays bare the need for new measures, on an international scale, in support of the people of Indo–China. If today there is a cause to which the communists and revolutionaries of the world feel unconditionally linked, it is that of the Vietnamese people . . .

We salute the declaration of the government of the People's Republic of China, which declares that the aggression against Laos 'constitutes a grave menace for China as well' and that it will not remain indifferent.

In these declarations we see a basis for the overcoming of a factor that weighs very negatively: the division, the absence of a real unity of action in the face of the aggressions of the Yankee imperialism . . .

'An efficient unified action' to put an end to the Yankee aggression in Vietnam can be a stage in the world advance of the progressive revolutionary forces.

Mundo Obrero, no. 5 (March 5, 1971), p. 1.

11 Juan Calanda, 'No to NATO,' 1972

The regime is carrying out Spain's approach to NATO in several ways. One of them is to facilitate all kinds of military maneuvers on our territory. Among the tactical assumptions of NATO, should there be a Soviet attack on central Europe, is that Spain would be the ideal site for disembarkation and for beginning an advance of troops towards central Europe through the Pyrenees. Some maneuvers have already taken place under that assumption . . .

The American imperialists, who have a loyal servant for their policy of aggression in the Francoist regime, are most interested in the inclusion of Spain in NATO. For some time now they have been pressuring northern countries and Belgium, who are the major opponents of such an incorporation. The resistance of those governments is essentially based on their people's opposition to Franco's fascist regime, which is hated and scorned all over the world . . .

The inclusion of Spain in NATO would imply an immense growth of military expenditures and an even larger dependence – both political and military – on other powers. At the same time it would increase our country's risk and the eventual damage it would sustain in a war. The regime seeks such an inclusion because it wishes to stay in power at any price. But it is totally contrary to the interests of our country and of our people. Therefore it is against the true interests of the army, since inclusion in NATO would make it more dependent, more a servant of foreign strategies. Not even an increased military budget would make it a modern and effective army, because all resources would be directed in the interests of NATO.

Nuestra Bandera, no. 69 (October 1972), pp. 56–8.

12 Manuel Azcárate's report to the Eighth Congress of the PCE, 'On some problems of the international policies of the party,' 1972

As a consequence of the crisis of imperialism, there are today real revolutionary opportunities in places which resembled quiet waters during our last Congress.

In what condition is the international communist movement to face these approaching changes?

It would be inappropriate to respond in a Panglossian style, as if everything were fine, as if imperialism were already annihilated. Such a picture does not reflect reality, which is more complex and contradictory. What is true – and decisively so – is that the general trend in the world today is toward the growth of socialist and revolutionary forces and the deepening of the crisis of imperialism. However, even within this trend, we suffer reversals and defeats, and we have serious problems.

It is obvious that the revolution cannot be born of an international armed conflict between capitalism and socialism. Since such a conflict would be nuclear, it would be a holocaust, a cataclysm for most of humankind, regardless of one's political inclination.

Therefore *peaceful coexistence is an objective necessity* at the present moment of history.

The *raison d'être* of coexistence is the prevention of world war and nuclear conflict.

Various alternatives can exist within a context of coexistence: a policy aimed at maintaining the *status quo* and stopping the forces which oppose imperialism.

We must remember that capitalism rejected co-existence for many years.

Today its crisis obliges capitalism to accept, in a general sense, worldwide coexistence with socialism. But the nature of imperialism has not changed. It is still willing to commit the most monstrous crimes against people. It still commits genocide in Vietnam. When imperialism accepts coexistence as a framework, it does so with the aim of stopping the revolutionary process, of freezing the political and social *status quo* of our world.

This is why it is of enormous importance to determine *what type* of coexistence can exist between socialist and capitalist countries.

Generally the coexistence policies of socialist countries are advantageous to the revolutionary process, decreasing the dangers of war and atomic destruction. And such a fact has an importance which we cannot ever underestimate.

At the same time, however, we must acknowledge that there are contradictory moments within such policies, moments at which the foreign policies of certain socialist states also aim at 'freezing the *status quo.*'

When the socialist countries help Vietnam and other anti-imperialist movements, they contribute immensely to the international revolution. In other cases, however, the situation is more complex.

Coexistence cannot mean that imperialism accepts and promotes détente, or an 'improvement' of relations (mainly with socialist countries) at the same time as it carries out its crimes and aggressions – today against Vietnam, tomorrow against another people . . .

We find that there are some attitudes of socialist countries which confuse coexistence and *status quo* in relation to some international problems (such as a favorable attitude towards the participation of Francoism in the conference on European security).

In the area of international relations the socialist

states have inherited boundaries fixed during the capitalist or pre-capitalist periods; they have inherited economic and demographic structures; they have inherited habits and traditions which developed during centuries of national hatred, wars, conquests, etc.

The so-called 'interests of the state' are largely determined by those geographic and economic structures inherited from the past. Hence the contradictions among socialist states, which at times are of an acute and antagonistic nature.

Socialism, as an internationalist system created by the working class, is, due to its essential nature, in an infinitely better position than capitalism to create a new system of international relations, based on equality, independence and respect for each country's specificity. Such relations would aim at contributing to peace and to the international success of socialism. But such a trend is not automatic: it must struggle against the obstacles and brakes inherited from the past, from traditions which do not disappear . . .

Another aspect which must be taken into account in many cases is the degeneration of the democratic structure and the internal order of the socialist state which is, to a large extent, directed by a bureaucratic hierarchy and where the working class, the masses, are not the true and direct owners of the political power, even if they have destroyed exploitation.

Yet another problem is the relation of the party to the state. If the party merges with the state, rather than moving away from it, then it cannot play its critical role, it does not place itself at the renovative end of the dialectic between the past and the present . . .

The *new* problem which emerges is the following: for a long while the USSR was the only socialist state. The unity of all the workers and revolutionaries had to be centered and was centered on the Soviet Union.

Now there are many socialist countries. Moreover there is today *a new correlation of forces* which, together with the crisis of imperialism, demands a more offensive strategy from the revolutionary movement. In this new situation the politics of coexistence must (as we clearly established at the 1969 Moscow Conference) stimulate the struggle among classes, the struggle which liberates the peoples . . .

VIII Congreso del PCE, Spanish Communist Party document, 1972, pp. 185–9.

13 Santiago Carrillo's report to the Eighth Congress of the PCE, 1972

It is clear that as long as imperialism survives the danger of aggression and war will survive, and it is precisely against such a danger that we must always be vigilant. But we can be encouraged by the fact that in the historic competition between the two systems, the socialist and the capitalist, the specific importance of the socialist system is increasing, while the crisis of imperialism sharpens . . .

The situation of the Middle East is complicated. The expansionist Israelis, supported by the United States, refuse to comply with the accords of the UN Security Council and withdraw from the occupied Arab territories. Our position on this is clear: we support the Arab peoples, their revolutionary and progressive forces, and the people of Palestine.

One of the most important factors in this historic period of transition from capitalism to socialism are the movements of national liberation.

The Communist Party of Spain is in solidarity with the revolutionary struggles of liberation of . the peoples of Latin America, Asia and Africa.

The example of socialist Cuba has accelerated the revolutionary process on the whole continent. In Chile the government of Popular Unity, supporting itself by the mobilization of the masses, repulses the maneuvers of the counter-revolution and the plots of Yankee imperialism, deepens the socioeconomic transformation and offers an original example of advance and progress.

During this period in Europe important steps have been taken toward security and co-operation. Without a doubt the most far-reaching is the treaty between the Federal Republic of Germany and the Soviet Union, along with the one established between the Popular Republic of Poland and the Federal Republic of Germany, and the four-party accords concerning West Berlin. The European borders as they were established after the victory over Hitlerism remain sacred as they are. It represents a defeat of the revengeful thesis put forward for many years by the Christian democratic leaders of the Federal Republic of Germany, a consolidation of the positions of socialism in Eastern Europe and a success of Soviet diplomacy. Now it will be very difficult to continue to deny to the Democratic Republic of Germany the position which it legitimately holds in Europe and the world. As a consequence of this evolution it seems the project for a conference on security and co-operation in Europe, firmly defended by the Soviet Union and other states of the continent, will take place soon.

Through a contradictory process with its ups and downs and positive and negative aspects – one cannot forget that the war in Indo–China and the conflict in the Middle East can disrupt world peace at any moment – the time in which we live has known a progression of favorable currents of détente and coexistence.

The retreat of the North Americans from Vietnam and the solution of the conflict in the Middle East could be the confirmation of this process if they are brought about.

Then a situation could be created in which free competition between socialist and imperialist states would principally be in economic, political and ideological fields, which would be extraordinarily beneficial to all of humanity.

This would reduce international tension. Under these conditions the liquidation of military blocs, foreign military bases, and the cessation of the ruinous arms race would be easier; more effective aid to the underdeveloped countries and closer attention to the questions related to ecology, that is to say, the preservation of the human condition, would be conceived of.

The strengthening of coexistence is a great thing for the whole of humanity. However, peaceful coexistence does not signify peace between classes. Coexistence regulates the contradictions between states but not class contradictions and struggles . . .

It is not superfluous to insist that the relief of international tension does not imply the relief of tensions between social classes within capitalist countries. There can be both détente between states and sharpening of the class struggle and internal contradictions within each country. In general, it must be assumed that international détente as it diminishes the wars of international military conflicts will make internal contradictions and the need to overcome them even clearer.

In this order of things, the progress in the unity of the French working class is inspiring. The common program of the vanguard of democracy established between the French Communist Party and Socialist Party fuels the hope that in our neighboring country the working-class and progressive forces can pave the way for the conquest of political power, toward a radical change of the ruling policies and means of French government, and its short-sighted policy toward Spain, reactionary and hostile toward the rising

forces of the democratic opposition, and in mistaken co-operation with the Franco dictatorship . . .

VIII Congreso del PCE, Spanish Communist Party document, 1972, p. 5.

14 Declaration of the Executive Committee of the PCE, 1973

We have known through the Spanish press that, after secret negotiations which took place in Paris, the People's Republic of China has reached an agreement with Franco's government to establish diplomatic relations and exchange ambassadors. This news is a surprise for us: the Chinese comrades had not informed us about the negotiations they had initiated or about their conclusion.

We clearly and emphatically declare our disapproval and disgust at this step taken by the People's Republic of China, which damages the Spanish people's struggle against fascist oppression, goes against proletarian internationalism, and debases the People's Republic's prestige in the eyes of Spanish workers and revolutionaries, along with the many other international anti-imperialist forces.

The *People's Newspaper* of the Chinese Communist Party presents the establishment of relations with the Francoist regime as if the latter were just like any other capitalist country, as if such an establishment were a simple application of peaceful coexistence, and as if those diplomatic relations could, at present, contribute to the development of friendly relations between the Spanish and the Chinese peoples.

Historically and politically the establishment of relations with Francoism is a serious act, which has nothing to do with 'diplomatic routine.' Such a political act cannot be justified by means of vague references to coexistence or other historical situations.

The politics of coexistence – in its Leninist sense – does not tend to maintain the *status quo* in the world; its *raison d'être* is to prevent a world war from taking place and to stimulate the struggle of oppressed peoples. In practice several socialist states refuse to establish diplomatic relations with certain other states. Moreover several African states refuse to have relations with, for example, Portugal, etc. Such positions by no means imply a breach of coexistence. Therefore to have or not to have diplomatic relations with Franco depends upon a political decision and is not, by any means, a 'demand' of peaceful co-existence . . .

In this concrete political moment of Spain the People's Republic of China's decision to establish diplomatic relations with Franco implies the fulfillment of the most rotten fascist nucleus, that of the toughest 'ultras', the one in power.

The Francoist regime, as a consequence of its Hitlerian origins, is still in a certain international isolation. Capitalist institutions such as the EEC and the European Parliament do not open their doors to it, because of its fascist nature. This international isolation is an important factor in the struggle and for the convergence of the largest Spanish forces who work to end Franco's regime and its inability to effectively defend the national interest . . .

In such circumstances it seems obvious that it is in the interest of the People's Republic of China, of all socialist states and of all the anti-imperialist and progressive forces, to contribute to the increasing anti-fascist mobilization. It is incomprehensible for the People's Republic to do precisely the opposite, to establish (precisely now) diplomatic relations with Franco.

The Spanish Communist Party struggles firmly against the wall which imperialism had built around the People's Republic of China. We have celebrated the successes of the Chinese people when they achieved international recognition in the United Nations, in the Security Council and in other international institutions. Today imperialism's wall has collapsed. The People's Republic has relations with most countries.

The PCE has always supported the Chinese struggle to recover the province of Taiwan, which is an integral part of its territory. In the present situation, when the just positions of the People's Republic of China in that area command broad international support, relations with Franco cannot be of any importance to it. Therefore we believe that it is very grave that such a decision might be made in view of circumstantial considerations, state prestige, secondary advantages and the sacrifice of essential revolutionary positions . . .

Nuestra Bandera, no. 71 (April–June 1973), pp. 77–8.

15 Manuel Azcárate's report to the Central Committee of the PCE, 1973

Nixon today concentrates his efforts on Europe. His proposal of a new 'Atlantic Charter' represents a serious threat to the future of our continent. Why this special preoccupation with Europe? . . .

Initially the USA favored and supported the Common Market, seeing it above all as an economic infrastructure for the aggressive military bloc against socialist countries. Today all things are different or are changing: the Common Market appears to the USA as a competing economic bloc, in the most immediate sense. And, at the same time, as a zone where radical political changes can take place.

The 'new negotiations' which Nixon wants to initiate between the USA and Western Europe seek to obtain advantages for the Yankee economy in the face of European competence; and to that end to use the presence of 300,000 US soldiers in Germany (and other nations) not so much as a guarantee against aggression from the East (which almost nobody believes in) but as a supplementary bulwark in the light of the internal changes which are appearing on the European horizon. Nixon pretends in this way to keep the Yankee mortgage by adopting it to new conditions.

Condemned to a defensive strategy, Nixon none the less pretends within that framework to continue imposing a hegemonic imperialist position. As his spokesman Kissinger has explained, to the USA belongs a universal vision, to the European rulers only regional objectives. His general plan is to freeze the present division of the world between capitalism and socialism, with which he thinks that – in the long run – taking into account the actual level of productive capacity it will not be socialism that ultimately triumphs. Nixon wants to end the Cold War, to move towards détente, to bring about no change in present social regimes. With that end he looks for a certain acceptance – in the name of a 'peaceful coexistence' cut to his measure – on the part of the great socialist powers for this freezing of the actual division of the world; and, very concretely, he hopes that in Europe no radical changes will be produced. In the face of the bourgeois European rulers, he proposes a more flexible kind of Yankee mortgage to the survival of the capitalist regimes, while simultaneously calling for certain economic advantages.

Such plans, the 'new Atlanticism,' represent a serious threat to the working class and to all the revolutionary forces of Europe. And also to other sectors.

The future evolution of Europe will not progress as Nixon would desire.

As the 'dialectic of the blocs' moves to the margin (that has already begun to happen) other contradictions acquire greater strength and rise to the surface. The pretense of prolonging the US mortgage in a Europe which is much more powerful economically, and which is unthreatened by the supposed menace from outside, will make more acute the anti-Yankee sentiment even in sectors of European capitalism; it is reflected already in the attitudes of some governments and it will be a factor, not insignificant, in creating the conditions for an amplification of the alliances and support of the forces of the left.

In the face of this 'new Atlanticism' we communists, together with socialists, syndicalists, Christian progressivists, etc., must present a truly European alternative which guarantees the security of all the countries of our continent. We want a Europe which is not under the hegemony of any great power. That does not suffer the Atlantic mortgage, but that has good relations with the USA and with the USSR and China and with other nations. A Europe where the people are masters of their destinies, ending the yokes of the monopolies and of the systems of oppression and exploitation, of realizing the socialist revolution and edifying socialism, in accordance with their own wills. Faced with the Europe of today, dominated by monopolies (in great part multinational firms), we want an independent Europe, a Europe of the people and of the workers, a democratic and socialist Europe.

In the fight for this new Europe, we communists are presented with great common tasks. First of all, we must support and struggle for peace, coexistence, security, détente, and fight to overcome the systems of blocs and to end the Cold War. These are fundamental and decisive tasks. And to these ends the conference of security in Helsinki presents itself as a special phase. We cannot underestimate the contribution of the USSR with its gigantic military power and political influence, and of other socialist countries, to the advance of détente. It is enough to think where we would be if not already destroyed by a nuclear war, in a situation of a threatened world war. Supporting the policy of peace and coexistence of the socialist countries, fighting for peace and security, is

thus a key task, a *sine qua non* about which there can be neither doubt nor vacillation.

In the second place, we must fight against all tendencies, wherever they may come from, even on the part of our friends, to equate coexistence and *status quo* détente with the freezing of the actual social structure of the world. Our specific task as communist parties is precisely to push that objective dialectic through the advance of détente and the elimination of the systems of blocs, internal contradictions, the war of classes; and thus the revolutionary dynamic on a national scale will obtain a greater force in each nation . . .

Nuestra Bandera, no. 72 (October–December 1973), cf. pp. 18–21.

16 'Spain – Morocco: a national and anti-colonial policy,' *Mundo Obrero*, 1973

Parts of the Spanish population, particularly those of the coastal areas, have been seriously damaged as a consequence of the present state of the relations between Spain and Morocco: they are not able to fish in their traditional waters.

To conceal the profound cause of the problem, and to avoid responsibility for it, the government promotes an attitude of hatred against Morocco. At the same time its press has published gross distortions of the position of the Communist Party, which has even been described as 'traitorous' and accused of supporting Morocco 'against Spain.' We are not worried about such attacks. Because if there is someone who, in all respects and not only with regard to relations with Morocco, betrays Spain's interests, it is the government of Franco-Carrero.

Francoism is occupying areas which are not Spanish, such as Ceuta and Mililla, the wrongly called Spanish Sahara. It is a case of colonial occupation, based exclusively on the irrationality of force, with repression becoming increasingly brutal against a liberation movement which has manifested itself in some regions of the Sahara.

What right has Spain to occupy those areas? None. Let us say that it has the same 'right' as the English have to occupy Gibraltar. The Spanish do not accept such domination. It is only natural that the Moroccans do not accept the Spanish occupation of cities and lands which are not Spanish.

The large capitalist monopolies, particularly those which exploit the rich phosphate mines of the Sahara, thereby obtaining enormous profits, are the ones who are interested in such an occupation.

Therefore the colonial policy of military occupation of the Sahara serves the large multinational monopolies. It is an anti-Spanish policy.

We believe that Spain should unilaterally abandon its colonial policy, returning Ceuta and Mililla to Morocco, and leaving the Sahara. These decisions would create very favorable conditions for the peaceful resolution of the conflicts of interest which are common to the populations of both Spain and Morocco . . .

Mundo Obrero, no. 18 (October 17, 1973), p. 8.

17 Leonor Bornao, 'Spain and the socialist countries,' 1977

Rumania, Yugoslavia, Bulgaria, Czechoslovakia, Hungary and the Soviet Union have established diplomatic relations with Spain. This is a fact of historical relevance, if one takes into account that for thirty-eight years the existence of Franco's regime made impossible any normal relations between Spain and the socialist countries, which constitute much of our continent.

During all these years the Spanish Communist Party has manifested its opposition to the re-establishment of those relations because it believed that they would not have favored our people's struggle against dictatorship and for democracy.

As is known, at the press conference on December 10, comrade Santiago Carrillo announced that, from that moment onwards, and given the new political situation of our country, the PCE would end its opposition to the re-establishment of diplomatic relations with all socialist countries. We see with satisfaction that our opinion has been taken into account.

The growth of commercial exchange will benefit everyone. In the concrete case of Spain the opening of Eastern European markets may contribute to the relief of the economic crisis our country is undergoing.

It is an aspiration of our party and of all the democratic forces that Spain play the role which is fitting for it both in Europe and in the world, abandoning the ghetto where the Francoist regime has imprisoned us, and giving our country and our people the reciprocal and varied enrichment implicit in normal inter-state relations with all other countries . . .

Mundo Obrero, no. 7 (February 16, 1977), p. 12.

18 Manuel Azcárate, 'Spain must recognize the Polisario,' 1978

A policy, which I would call not merely sympathetic but realistic, should transcend and end the shame implicit in the Madrid Agreements, whereby Spain abandoned the Saharan people and betrayed its decolonization engagements, opening the Sahara to Morocco and Mauritania. I have noted among the heads of the Polisario an energetic, firm reaction, filled with anger against the Spanish foreign policy. I do not understand how the Spanish government has been able to force parliament to vote for a fishing accord which implies a violation of Saharan sovereignty over its territorial waters, and how it has been able to carry out such scandalous actions as the expulsion of the delegates of the Polisario from Spain. It seems that the government is not acting as a functionary of the interests of Spain but as a functionary of the interests of the Moroccan invaders; in this way Spain is being detrimental to herself. We should not forget that our democratic institutions have come only after the horrors of Spanish colonialism, which constructed practically nothing and committed shameful crimes. The only legacy of Spanish colonialism is that the Saharan population speaks Spanish.

The Spanish state should be interested in ending Moroccan expansionism, which could direct itself against the Canary Islands. An independent Sahara could be an agent of co-operation with Spain, and would give us very positive possibilities in the area of international commercial policy, in contrast with the results of the fishing arrangement which has been signed with Morocco and which implies a political turn that might bring about very serious confrontations. It would be necessary to recognize the Polisario Front in order to support a solution of self-determination for the Saharan people and to put an end to a policy of submission, which would be transformed into a policy of real independence for Spanish policy.

Mundo Obrero (March 9–16, 1978), p. 3.

19 Resolution of the Ninth Congress of the PCE, 1978

NATO – the PCE firmly and clearly pronounces itself against the projected entry of our country into NATO. Such an entry would stimulate a dialectic of reinforcing military blocs and accelerate the arms race in Europe, both of which are negative influences upon security and peace. Such an entry would have cumbersome consequences for the economy of the nation, and would adversely affect the Spanish armed forces. Further, such an entry would lead to the inclusion of the whole of Spain, and particularly the Canaries and Balneares, in the strategic scheme of the North Atlantic Alliance, dominated by the United States. Finally, such an entry would introduce external constraints, whose consequences upon the democratic process would obviously be unfavorable . . .

We recognize a Spanish policy of non-alignment, and pronounce ourselves in favor of the elimination of the existing military blocs, and for the simultaneous dissolution of NATO and the Warsaw Pacts. In the SALT negotiations important steps have been made. In reality today's 'equilibrium' between the two superpowers does not rest on bases established in one country or another, but rather on long-range nuclear weapons, existing in the United States as well as in the Soviet Union. The different historic factors from which they originate notwithstanding, the two blocs are more instruments of hegemony than organizations which respond to military requirements. And strong objective factors are pressing in the direction of eliminating the division into blocs.

On the other hand, the refusal to integrate Spain into NATO, affirming a policy of active neutrality, of non-alignment, will contribute to the conversion of the Mediterranean into a sea of peace and collaboration.

With respect to the problem of American bases on Spanish territory, we assert that it is a situation which derives from the existence of the two military blocs. It is our firm intention to attain a Spain free of foreign military bases, without any accords which threaten national sovereignty. In the present situation the most feasible means of removing foreign bases and troops, in the West with the Americans, as well as in the East with the Soviet Union, is to advance towards the dissolution of blocs.

IX Congreso del PCE, Spanish Communist Party document, 1978, pp. 146–8.

20 Santiago Carrillo's speech at the Ninth Congress of the PCE, 1978

Aside from the other significant new characteristics of the phase of imperialism in which we are living, nuclear weapons have appeared as a consequence of the development of productive forces. This has come to break the cycle of worldwide imperialist wars. A war of this type would not be 'the continuation of politics by other means' but the *suicide* of both contenders. That is to say, the redistribution of colonies and markets by means of war, which we Marxists considered *inevitable* during the earlier phase of imperialism, is no longer an inevitability. The same policy of coexistence which earlier sought only to postpone war now serves to prevent war.

It is certain that as long as imperialism and the military blocs exist and the arms race continues, and as long as the revolutionary forces which guide certain states are incapable of resisting the hegemonic pressures of international interests, the danger of world war cannot be completely eliminated. But this will not open the way to revolutionary crises, as in Russia in 1917 or in Europe and Asia in 1945. On the contrary, it would represent humanity's brutal regression, a massacre in which the forces both of conservatism and of progress would be destroyed.

Even without world war the tension between the two systems begins to affect the ecological equilibrium, the quality of life and the conservation of the planet itself.

Not only the communists, but all conscious people, work for peace, the suppression of military blocs, disarmament and for co-operation among all countries and states. The SALT talks, the conferences on European security in Helsinki and Belgrade and that which will take place in Madrid in 1980, if Spain remains outside of NATO, should continue until today's threat of world war is eliminated. In reality the struggle for peace has been transformed into the struggle for human survival and for the defense of civilization.

IX Congreso del PCE, Spanish Communist Party document, 1978, cf. pp. 22–3.

The European Community

21   Juan Gomez, 'The negotiation with the Common Market: myths and realities,' 1970

Once again, on January 29 when the government's delegation, led by Ullastres, was singing victory, the Brussels negotiations tripped over a rock; this time the 'cheese' of Holland . . .

Even after having received the blow, the government spokesmen are trying to give credit to the idea that the 'differences are merely technical.' Here we find the first myth. The EEC's political repudiations of Franco's regime have been proclaimed and consecrated by the course of the negotiations themselves.

In February 1962 the Franco government presented its demand for 'association, in view of integration into the Common Market.' Five years of rebuffs. Why? The incompatibility of Spain's 'organic democracy' and the parliamentary democracies of the European Six, as is stated in the protocol of the Treaty of Rome. The governments of the Community are sensitive to the reluctance the people of Europe feel towards associating themselves in any way with the Franco regime.

In 1967 negotiations oriented themselves towards the conclusion of a preferential commercial agreement which would not need to be discussed or approved by the parliaments of the countries of the Six. The Franco government, obsessed with presenting its discussion with the Community as an 'opening toward Europe' and as a back-up for its

pretended liberalization, proposed that the commercial agreement, whose duration is six years, be considered as the first phase of the process of association. Another rebuff. The Community decided that, after the six years, the problem will be discussed anew. There will be no organic link between the commercial agreement and the future association. The Francoist delegation took a beating. The political repudiation is consecrated by the actual course of the negotiations.

In this way, through 'merely technical' obstacles, political resistance continues to manifest itself. It is no coincidence that hours before the 'technical' incident of January 29 in Brussels, one of the most distinguished personalities of the Community, its Vice-President, Sacco Mansholt, declared again his opposition to discussions with the Franco regime.

Mundo Obrero, no. 4 (February 21, 1970).

22   Santiago Carrillo's speech at the Eighth Congress of the PCE, 1972

In the present world context the Common Market has reaffirmed its existence and is about to open itself to the entrance of new countries. It has become an economic monopolist–capitalist group which is impossible to ignore, and which almost inevitably attracts other countries of the continent, including our own . . .

At its creation the Common Market seemed to be a political and economic creation of the Cold War, a bloc hardened essentially against the USSR and socialist countries, of which the vengeful Germany of Adenauer could become the leader. The Common Market acted as an auxiliary of NATO . . .

One must say, however, that the Common Market was created and is consolidating itself as more than a consequence of subjective factors, limited to the interests of capitalist monopolies. At its base there is an objective factor: the tendency for the internationalization of productive forces, an economic law which operates in capitalism as well as in socialism. It is this law which is knocking over many of the walls raised by reactionary rulers against commerce and economic co-operation with socialist countries.

Having overcome the politics of the Cold War, the

Common Market underwent a certain evolution. It became more of a capitalist economic enclave, defending its markets with common customs barriers and fighting against its competitors for world markets. American imperialism, by exporting capital and technology, penetrated into the firms of the Common Market, and participated in the Market's benefits. But at the same time it clashed with the rivalry and competence of these firms and with the customs duties of the Common Market . . .

Today the Common Market is a fact, a reality. The real possibility of fighting the Common Market, as a monopolist superstructure helping the policy of domination, lies essentially in changing the character of the powerful classes in those countries which make up the Common Market. And the communist parties of these countries orient themselves more towards avoiding its transformation into a Holy Alliance of capitalist states than towards changing its structure by making its members more democratic. Such parties increasingly conceive of their action not as a fight against European economic integration *per se* – since that is inevitable – but rather for a socialist democratic Europe as opposed to the Europe of monopolies, and meanwhile for peace and economic co-operation with socialist countries, a fight which is evident within each country as well as on the European scale . . .

On the other hand, among the problems of the fight, within the context of this new situation, there arises an even greater need – and without its being in contradiction with the forms of European articulation – for each party to elaborate a revolutionary strategy capable of transforming the socio-political structures of its country, which as we have said is the real way to end the capitalist-monopolist character of the Common Market.

The class position, confirmed by the experience of these years, does not consist so much in opposition to the ever greater internationalization of the economic structures, but more in changing the political-social regime of each country, in harmonizing the struggle of the workers across the frontiers of Europe, in impeding the conversion of the Common Market into a new Holy Alliance, and in fighting all class discrimination in trade and relations with socialist countries.

From its creation the Common Market has provoked great discussions in Spain. In 1962 the Franco regime, without considering the state of the Spanish economy, made a demand for admission which was received very coldly. The motivations of the regime were fundamentally political. The Spanish economy did not find itself in a position to compete on equal grounds with the economies of other Common Market countries; in that situation integration would have signified the ruin of a large number of Spanish firms, a total subordination of our country. But the regime hoped that European capitalism, alarmed by the contagiousness of a possible revolutionary crisis in Spain, would grant Franco all sorts of economic and political concessions. It believed that it could overcome the illegitimacy that has plagued the regime even in its moments of greatest triumph, by obtaining the benediction of Europe . . .

At that time our party opposed immediate integration because it would have been catastrophic for the national economy; and, when it was signed, we denounced the preferential agreement since it was against the interests of Spain.

The entry of new countries, in particular Great Britain, into the Common Market has created new and greater difficulties for Spain's external commerce; our country will find itself seriously prejudiced by the extension of the Common Market customs barrier to its new members . . .

The Common Market is a competitive reality which surrounds us and before which one must lay the foundations of a policy which would seriously defend the national interest.

Basing itself on the national interest, the Communist Party believes that Spain first needs to rid itself of the dictatorial regime. This regime has neither the authority nor the force nor the will to start negotiations with the Common Market which would guarantee the national interest. Any agreement the dictatorship could negotiate would be harmful, as is the preferential agreement. Moreover if the rules of the Treaty of Rome are applied – and at the heart of the Common Market there are decisive forces which will act so that they are applied – the dictatorship would be unable to achieve any agreement of association. Some alteration of the present preferential agreement, which is what Ullastres is attempting to do in Brussels, will not change the situation in the least.

What is most urgent, then, is to end the dictatorship and to establish a democratic regime which can treat with authority, making itself respected in the name of Spain.

Upon the creation of such conditions, the Communist Party will pronounce itself in favor of an agreement of association with the Common Market which would allow for progress in co-operation among the European nations, as our economic structures are renewed and reach the necessary competitiveness. A democratic state would have to undertake this task of modernization, leaning preferably on the public sector of the economy . . .

The Communist Party and the forces of progress of Spain, should we arrive at an agreement of association with the Common Market, following the liquidation of the dictatorship, will unite their efforts, together with the efforts of the communist parties and the progressive and socialist forces of Europe who seek to democratize the Common Market and transform monopolistic Europe into socialist Europe . . .

The most convenient solution for the nation with regard to the problems of the European markets and economic co-operation with Europe is not in the hands of the dictatorship of Franco, nor in the hands of centrism, but rather in the articulation of the democratic alternative, in the pact for liberty that the Communist Party proposes. A strong national democratic government, with ample popular backing, is urgently needed in order to deal with the Common Market today and throughout any negotiations for association. One must not forget that the Common Market is a capitalist institution, with which we must deal, but in which each step of the negotiations will be a real battle to defend the national interests in the face of the other capitalist countries. The Common Market must be seen and dealt with in this way. An authentically democratic government could go into association with the Common Market, diversifying external commerce and considerably expanding economic relations with socialist countries and with the countries of the Third World . . .

First, I find it convenient to state precisely that for the moment the issue we are speaking of is association. The question of integration must remain until after the creation of a new economic competitive structure and the creation of a political democratic superstructure.

Secondly, we speak of an association on the condition that it gives guarantees to the national interests and class interests. That is to say, to the existence of a democratic government in Spain. And this is not only a declaration in favor of the association; it is also a form of opposition to whatever type of association which would be detrimental to the national interests of the country. This gives us great latitude for the implementation of our tactic and it distances us from the chorus of voices which now present the Common Market as the miraculous panacea for the solution of all the problems of Spain . . .

. . . if we understand our national interest with a dogmatic attitude concerning the Common Market, we will be politically devastated. The national interest, the interest of the development of the nation, by one or another path, will have its way. Whoever opposes it – and this is the destiny which awaits Blas Pinar – will be overrun. If we obfuscate ourselves and oppose a democratic solution to this problem, we give the oligarchy an opportunity for demagogic agitation. For its own exclusive benefit the oligarchy will isolate us. In this case we will have conserved political virginity, but at the cost of revolutionary sterility. And I do not think it is for our party to choose sterility . . .

VIII Congreso del PCE, Spanish Communist Party document, 1972, pp. 16–20, 89–91.

23 Juan Gomez' speech at the Eighth Congress of the PCE, 1972

Integration, it has been pointed out, rides on the objective current of the internationalization of the productive forces. From there it derives its power; from there, by overcoming the many obstacles born fundamentally out of the existing contradictions among the actual nations involved, it moves forward, achieving important results with regard to the objectives and the interests of the oligarchies.

But the objective tendency toward the internationalization of the productive forces of the market is not a global trend. It is blocked by the regional character of economic integration, which leads to a common regional tariff.

The problems derived from the internationalization of the productive forces and of markets, on what we can call the historic level, affect every nation, and each nation must face their consequences. These are specific problems which each country has to confront by questioning its own structure and economic development.

But the regional capitalist integration carries with it another level of consequence. The common external tariff institutionalizes discrimination against third nations. In this way the problems inherent in regional capitalist integration do not affect only the countries included in it; they decisively and directly affect third countries, most of all those situated geographically and historically in its zone of influence . . .

Remembering that Greece and Turkey are already associated with the Common Market, the only country in all of capitalist Europe that still remains at the margin is Spain.

If one adds that the countries of North Africa – Morocco and Tunisia – are already related in more advantageous conditions than Spain: that Algeria which now enjoys some advantages is already negotiating for more; that African countries, old colonies of France and, from now on, the countries of the Commonwealth, are entrenched in the Community – one can measure the depth of our isolation.

One must assess the consequences for Spain not only by the greatest obstacles that our exports are going to find, but by the advantages and preferences that countries which are our most direct competitors will receive . . .

We are very familiar with the true character of the Common Market. It is a regional association of monopolist states, the heart of European imperialism . . .

But, as we cannot abandon Spain because of its oligarchic domination and dictatorial government, so we cannot turn our back on Europe because of the domination of the Common Market of monopolist states.

Confronted with such realities, what is decisive is our struggle, and what is important is to free it, in order to change and improve it more rapidly.

Is it that we have at hand some alternative with which to replace it?

First of all, contemporary Spain is not prewar Spain, nor even the Spain of two decades ago. Before, we would survive and hibernate under the autarky; today the dependence of our economy on the exterior sector is not merely important, but determinant . . .

An integrated Europe today is essentially a complete customs union for industrial products, equipped with a common external tariff and an arrangement and regulation of production and of agricultural markets which is autarkic, protectionist and fiercely discriminatory against third countries. It is this integrated Europe, such as it is today, which creates a situation which forces us to take a position to adjust the aim of our policy.

The supranational Europe, the European government, even a parliament with legislative functions which are supranational, are for now mere projects, declaimed objectives which are beyond the foreseeable future and need not be taken into consideration when evaluating the problems in the present state. In any case integrated Europe will find in us, the communist parties of Europe, and the other revolutionary forces, the only real program in concordance with the development and internationalization of the productive forces: the program for a socialist Europe.

The imperialists' support of our oligarchy, as well as the obstacles that they can raise to block the will of the people, occur in the framework of the fundamental contradictions of the contemporary world and with all the conditions that these problems represent, rather than as a function of being or not being associated with the Common Market.

On the other hand, the position that party takes today is unambiguous with regard both to the oligarchic imperialist nature of the Common Market and to the historic rsponsibility of our oligarchy.

Responsibility for the situation in which Spain finds itself, confronted with the challenging objective of European integration, lies in our level of development and our degree of competitiveness.

And responsibility for this imbalance, for the last ten years of no progress, lies with the regime.

Responsibility because, by isolating with violence the destinies of Spain, the regime places Spain in a situation in which it can neither remain at the margin nor negotiate with the Common Market. And when the regime signs a preferential commercial agreement, it does so under such conditions of inferiority and abandonment of sovereignty that today not even the regime can defend its own policy . . .

VIII Congreso del PCE, Spanish Communist Party document, 1972, pp. 209–14.

24 Strasbourg declaration on the Democratic Jaunta, 1975

The Democratic Junta of Spain, which joins together the most representative democratic sectors of the country, and which remains open to all the Spanish democrats, presents itself today before the institutions of the European Community and before public opinion to repeat its conviction that a European democratic basis constitutes the only alternative for the future of Spain.

The Democratic Junta of Spain declares its will to participate in the task of the construction of Europe, with all the rights and responsibilities that are necessary. Only the integration of Spain into the Community will put an end to the isolation and international discrimination of which our country is a victim in every area: social, economic, cultural and political. That will mean, in time, that Spain assumes the responsibilities and obligations derived from full membership in the Community.

The Democratic Junta of Spain recognizes that the political situation in Spain is a problem which concerns only the Spanish, that the re-establishment of political liberties necessarily occurs by a definitive change of our present political institutions which are decrepit and inefficient, a peaceful change in the interest of which the European Community and the Democratic Junta of Spain ask the participation of all the democratic, political and social forces of the country.

Mundo Obrero (March 19, 1975), p. 1.

25 Resolution of the Ninth Congress of the PCE, 1978

The PCE supports the integration of Spain into the European Community. It is an economic and political necessity that arises out of the development of the productive forces, out of the structure of the Spanish economy and of its external commerce. The economic integration will require a relatively long and complicated process which will not take place without tensions or fights. On the other hand, it is important to be sure that Spain can participate as soon as possible in the organs of the Community . . . We call for the participation of the Spanish people (including the *émigré* workers in Europe) in the election by universal suffrage of the European Parliament in May 1979. We believe that those who oppose Spain's entry into the EEC turn their backs on the conveniences of a democratic, progressive process in the heart of the Community; to a construction of a balanced Europe, in which southern Europe has the weight that belongs to it.

The PCE, in proclaiming the entry of Spain into the EEC, affirms its will to transform, together with the rest of the forces of the left in Europe, the actual character of the Community, dominated by the great monopolies. We aspire to a Europe of workers, to a Europe of peoples: a Europe united on the economic and political planes, that has its own independent policy, not subordinated to either the United States or the Soviet Union but which maintains positive relations with both powers; a Europe that will be an autonomous factor of world politics, contributing in this way to overcome the military blocs and bi-polarism, to democratize international life, facilitating to all the peoples greater liberty to be masters of their own destinies. Détente and co-existence will in this way have more effective and profound meanings. And the problem of disarmament will be confronted with new possibilities for progress . . .

IX Congreso del PCE, Spanish Communist Party document, 1978, pp. 140–1.

APPENDIX:
Joint Declarations of the Eurocommunist Parties

1 Joint declaration by the Italian Communist Party and the Spanish Communist Party
(Leghorn, July 12, 1975)

At a moment when the fall of the fascist dictatorships in Portugal and Greece and the lacerating crisis gripping the Franco regime in Spain concretely raise the possibility of making Europe a continent without fascist regimes, and for Spain as well the outlook is for a regime of democracy and freedom, there is a more pressing need for the working-class and democratic forces – both on the level of the individual countries and on the West European level, in the new conditions created by the positive advances made in the process of international détente – to indicate new orientations capable of promoting a coming together of all the democratic forces for a policy of democratic and social renewal and for a positive way out of the deep crisis gripping the capitalist countries of Europe.

This crisis reveals the inability of capitalism to solve the general needs of development of society and the problems it is now facing, and to implement in all fields those deep-reaching structural reforms that alone can guarantee the progress of nations. It renders increasingly strident the conflict between a policy imposed by the monopoly groups and the big multinational companies and the need to find positive answers to the requirements of the broad popular masses for freedom, participation and economic, social and cultural progress. It is necessary and possible to find a positive way out of this crisis, developing the broadest possible convergence and agreements among the forces with which the working-class and democratic movement on the continent today identifies. This is also indispensable to defeat the attempts by certain capitalist groups to steer the crisis towards an openly reactionary, authoritarian outcome.

Conscious of this responsibility, and moved by the will to do everything possible to promote such convergence and coming together, the Italian and Spanish communists solemnly declare that their conception of democratic advance to socialism, in peace and freedom, is not a tactical attitude, but a strategic conviction rising out of reflection on the experiences of the working-class movement as a whole and on the specific historical conditions of their respective countries, in the West European situation. The common task facing communists and all the democratic forces is to work for the solution of the problems facing the broad popular masses and society as a whole in such a way as to give real satisfaction to those social needs and human values of freedom, justice and civilization which capitalism increasingly sacrifices and restricts.

The prospect of a socialist society today rises out of the reality of things and has as its premiss the conviction that socialism can only be built in our countries by means of the development and full implementation of democracy. Underlying this is full recognition of the value of the individual and collective freedoms and their guarantee, the principles of the lay nature of the state and its democratic organization, the plurality of political parties in a system of free dialectics, autonomy of the trade unions, religious freedom, freedom of speech, culture, art and science. In the economic field a socialist solution must ensure a high level of productive development, by means of a policy of democratic planning that makes use of the coexistence of various forms of enterprise and public and private management.

On the basis of these convictions, which are a fundamental part of their political and theoretical conceptions, the Italian and Spanish communists are working to achieve the broadest coming together of all democratic political forces – the restoration of democracy in Spain and its development in Italy. This coming together, with full respect for the personality and autonomy of each force, is the only road capable of opening a prospect of progress and freedom, of advancing the interests of the working class, peasant masses, middle classes and intellectuals, and creating a national unity of the forces of democracy and progress capable of isolating the forces of social conservatism and reaction. New political prospects, a new way of governing, based on the broadest possible participation by the popular and youth masses and their organizations, have become imperative.

On these issues, both in the individual countries and at the West European level – as already indicated by the Brussels Conference of the Communist Parties of the Capitalist Countries of Europe in January 1974 – it is necessary and urgent to promote the broadest possible comparison of opinions and responsible search for points of convergence and agreement among all the political forces – socialists, social democrats, Christian democrats, Catholics, democrats and progressives – who want to find a common meeting ground for the great democratic potentialities of Western Europe in a policy of renewal and progress.

The development of international détente – which will shortly find new expression in the conference on security and co-operation in Europe, for whose achievement a fundamental factor has been the meeting between the peace-oriented foreign policy of the Soviet Union and the other socialist countries and the new realistic trends that have emerged in the Western capitals – eliminates old impediments and obstacles along this road. The problem is to grasp all the new possibilities, to ensure, also, that the countries of Western Europe and Western Europe as a whole will be capable of making their own original contribution to the building of an international society based on respect for the right of each individual people freely to choose the road of their own future, on the elimination of imbalances, on justice, progress, development and peace. A new West European policy, based on relations of friendship and co-operation, on a basis of equality, with all countries of the world, beginning with the United States and the Soviet Union, and on new relations with the developing countries, can make an irreplaceable contribution to the achievement of these great goals.

The Italian and Spanish communists intend to intensify their efforts and initiatives in this direction, both in continental Europe and in the Mediterranean area. Restoration of democracy in Spain and development of democracy in Italy, together with the new processes characterizing life in many European countries, can give Western Europe new impetus in solving the problems facing it, with a prospect of freedom, democracy, progress and peace.

The Italian and Spanish communist parties, which elaborate their internal and international policies in full autonomy and independence, are fully aware of their great national and European responsibilities. On the basis of these common visions, they will further develop in the future their fraternal relations, which are marked by a long, solid friendship.

The Italian Communists, no. 4 (June–August 1975), pp. 39–42.

2 Joint declaration by the Italian Communist Party and the French Communist Party (Rome, November 15, 1975)

The situation in France and Italy is characterized by the worsening of a crisis affecting all aspects of economic, social, political, moral and cultural life.

In its economic aspects this crisis – which is an integral part of the crisis gripping the capitalist system as a whole and affecting all economic relations on the world scale – has heavy consequences for the working people and popular masses, hard hit by unemployment and rising prices. At the same time the peasantry, artisans and small and medium-sized businesses are struggling against serious difficulties.

The institutions of civil life are encountering increasingly severe problems. The political crisis is deepening, and social and moral relations are affected by phenomena of degeneration.

This crisis reveals the inability of the capitalist system to answer the need for development of the productive forces, including science and technology; the need to ensure the right to work, a rising standard of living, the development of culture and the affirmation of all human values. In the two countries, as, in different forms, in other countries of Western Europe, the threat of a serious regression of society as a whole is emerging.

The forces of big capital and imperialism are attempting to take advantage of this situation to undermine the economic, social and political gains of the working people. But through their struggle the working class and popular masses can defeat these attempts, making new gains and opening the road to further social and democratic advance.

To this end the PCI and the PCF, while fighting for the immediate interests of the working people, are working at the same time for a policy of far-reaching democratic reforms, capable of solving the grave economic, social and political problems of their countries.

For France and Italy the present crisis has more clearly than ever revealed the need to develop democracy and advance it towards socialism.

The two parties conduct their action in concretely different conditions, and, for this reason, each follows a policy suited to the needs and characteristics of its own country. At the same time, since they both fight in developed capitalist countries, they observe that the essential problems facing them present common characteristics and require similar solutions.

The Italian and French communists hold that the march towards socialism and the building of a socialist society, which they propose as the prospect for their countries, must be achieved within the framework of a continuous democratization of economic, social and political life. Socialism will constitute a higher phase of democracy and freedom: democracy realized in the most complete manner.

In this spirit all the freedoms – which are a product both of the great democratic-bourgeois revolutions and of the great popular struggles of this century, headed by the working class – will have to be guaranteed and developed. This holds true for freedom of thought and expression, for freedom of the press, of assembly, association and demonstration, for free movement of persons inside and outside their country, for the inviolability of private life, for religious freedom and total freedom of expression for currents of thought and every philosophical, cultural and artistic opinion. The French and Italian communists declare themselves for the plurality of political parties, for the right to existence and activity of opposition parties, for the free formation of majorities and minorities and the possibility of their alternating democratically, for the lay nature and democratic functioning of the state, for independence of the judiciary. In the same way they declare themselves for the freedom of activity and the autonomy of the trade unions. They attribute essential importance to the development of democracy in the workplace, allowing the workers to participate in the running of their firms, with real rights and extensive decision-making powers. Democratic decentralization of the state must give an increasingly important role to regional and local governments, which must enjoy broad autonomy in the exercise of their powers.

A socialist transformation of society presupposes public control over the principal means of production and exchange, their progressive socialization and implementation of democratic economic planning at the national level. The sector of small and medium-sized peasant farms, artisan industry and small and medium-sized industrial and commercial enterprises can and must fulfil a specific, positive role in the building of socialism.

This transformation can only be the result of great, powerful struggles and broad mass movements, uniting the majority of the people around the working class. It requires the existence, guarantee and development of democratic institutions fully representative of popular sovereignty and the free exercise of direct, proportional universal suffrage. It is in this framework that the two parties – which have always respected and will always respect the verdict of universal suffrage – conceive the rise of the working people to leadership of the state.

The Italian Communist Party and the French Communist Party attribute a value of principle to all these conditions of democratic life. Their position is not tactical, but derived from their analysis of the specific objective and historical conditions of their countries and from their reflection on international experiences as a whole.

The two parties hold that in relations among all states – which must be characterized by increasingly close co-operation, within the framework of a new international division of labor – the right of every people to decide in sovereignty their own political and social system must be guaranteed. They therefore stress the necessity to fight against the presumption of US imperialism to interfere in the life of other peoples, and declare themselves against all foreign interference.

The two parties hold that to guarantee success in the fight against the principal enemy of the working class and popular masses – monopoly capitalism – it is essential to achieve a free understanding among different social and political forces, within which the united working class must succeed in establishing its capacity for leadership. These broad alliances are necessary both in the present phase and for the building of socialism.

The development of solid, lasting co-operation

among communists and socialists constitutes the basis for this broad alliance. Furthermore today broad strata of the Catholic world are becoming increasingly aware of the contradiction existing between the reality of imperialism and capitalism and their deepest aspirations to brotherhood among men, social justice, the affirmation of higher moral values and the fulfillment of every personality. This fact creates growing possibilities for a coming together among communists, the whole of the working-class movement and the popular forces of Catholic inspiration. These forces can and must play an important role in the creation of a new society.

In this situation of crisis, with the big tasks it implies, the two parties are fully conscious of their growing responsibilities and their irreplaceable function.

In conformity with the conclusions of the Conference of Communist Parties of Capitalist Europe, held in Brussels in January 1974, the two parties reaffirm their will to work to promote common action among the communist and socialist parties and all the democratic and progressive forces of Europe against fascism and all attacks on freedom, in defense of the interests of the working class and popular masses and for far-reaching democratic transformations in the economic and social structures.

In the face of the orientation, deeply hostile to popular interests, of the multinational and national monopolies and those ruling groups whose policies are aggravating unemployment and social imbalances in Common Market Europe, the two parties attribute great importance to the development of united initiatives by the popular forces and the left forces – within the framework of the European Parliament as well – for democratization of the orientations and modes of operation of the European Economic Community and for the progressive building of a democratic, peaceful and independent Europe.

In the same spirit, in this crucial hour for Spain, the two parties condemn all attempts to perpetuate the Franco regime, in one form or another, certain that in this regard they are interpreting the conviction of all democrats. They reconfirm their militant solidarity with the working class and all the anti-fascists of Spain, who are fighting to save and free the political prisoners and establish a system of full political freedom.

They express, moreover, their concern for the difficulties encountered by the young democracy in Portugal and their hope that all the working-class and democratic forces will again succeed in finding unity in the struggle to bar the road to all reactionary threats and to guarantee the democratic and social progress of that country.

The Helsinki Conference of European States – to whose convening and success the Soviet Union made an outstanding contribution – marked an important step forward along the road of international détente and towards the creation of a system of collective security in Europe. Peaceful coexistence is the only alternative to a war of extermination; it is a condition for solving conflicts among states and developing the broadest international co-operation in all fields. Peaceful coexistence, which does not mean the social and political *status quo*, offers the most favorable terrain for struggle against imperialism and for democracy and socialism. While pursuing this struggle, the two parties develop their action in favor of new progress for peace, for gradual mutual arms reduction – with the final goal of total disarmament – and for a gradual overcoming and dissolution of the military blocs. They express their will to contribute to union among all forces interested in halting the arms race.

In reconfirming the principle of the autonomy of each party, of respect, non-interference and internationalism, the PCF and the PCI intend to pursue and strengthen their fraternal co-operation.

The Italian Communists, nos 5–6 (September–December, 1975), pp. 74–9.

3 Joint declaration by the PCE, PCF and PCI (Madrid, March 3, 1977)

On March 2 and 3, 1977, a meeting took place in Madrid between comrades Santiago Carrillo, General Secretary of the Communist Party of Spain; Enrico Berlinguer, General Secretary of the Italian Communist Party; and Georges Marchais, General Secretary of the French Communist Party. Accepting Santiago Carrillo's invitation, comrades Marchais and Berlinguer thus intended to reconfirm to the Communist Party of Spain and to all the Spanish democratic forces the solidarity of French and Italian communists with their action for democracy and to build a free Spain.

In this spirit the French Communist Party and the Italian Communist Party express their conviction that the Spanish people will achieve the full re-establishment of democracy, an essential criterion for which is today the legalization of the Communist Party and all the parties, as this is indispensable for the holding of genuinely free elections. They express their solidarity with all those who are working in Spain to obtain the release of the political prisoners and to halt the fascist crimes and provocations which seek to place obstacles on the road to democracy.

The end of the Franco dictatorship, after that of fascism in Portugal and Greece, represents an important and positive change in the situation in Europe.

Democratic progress in Spain is of special interest for the French and Italian people.

The three countries are now experiencing a crisis that is at one and the same time economic, political, social and moral. This crisis underlines the need for new solutions for the development of society. Above and beyond the differences in conditions existing in each of the three countries, the Italian, French and Spanish communists affirm the need to provide a positive alternative to the crisis and to defeat the reactionary orientations by realizing the broadest agreement among the political and social forces which are ready to contribute to a policy of progress and renewal. This requires the presence of the workers and their parties in the leadership of political life. At the same time as they defend the immediate interests of the workers on a daily basis, the communists advocate profound democratic reforms.

The crisis of the capitalist system requires ever more forcefully the development of democracy and advance towards socialism.

The communists of Spain, France and Italy intend to work for the construction of a new society, respecting the pluralism of political and social forces and the guarantee and development of all individual and collective freedoms: freedom of thought and expression, of the press, of association, assembly and demonstration, of the free circulation of people inside their country and abroad, trade union freedom, autonomy of the trade unions and the right to strike, the inviolability of private life, respect for universal suffrage and the possibility of the democratic alternation of majorities, religious freedom, freedom of culture, freedom of expression of the various philosophical, cultural and artistic currents and opinions. This determination to build socialism in democracy and freedom inspires the conceptions elaborated in full autonomy by each of the three parties. The three parties intend to develop in the future as well their internationalist solidarity and friendship, on the basis of the independence of each party, equal rights, non-interference, and respect for the free choice of roads and original solutions for the construction of socialist societies corresponding to the conditions of each country.

On the occasion of this meeting in Madrid, the Spanish, Italian and French communists also want to reaffirm the essential importance they attach to new steps forward on the road to détente and peaceful coexistence, to real progress in arms reduction, to the integral application by all the states of all the provisions of the Final Act of the Helsinki Conference and a positive holding of the Belgrade meeting, to action for overcoming the division of Europe into antagonistic military blocs, to the establishment of new relations between the developed countries and the developing countries and the creation of a new international economic order.

This is how the three parties envisage the prospect for a peaceful, democratic, independent Europe, without foreign bases or the arms race, and for a Mediterranean of peace and co-operation among all the bordering states.

The free Spain for which the communists and all the Spanish democratic forces are fighting will be an important factor for democracy, progress and peace in Europe. To achieve these goals it is necessary and possible that, above and beyond the diversity of ideas and traditions, dialogue and the search for points of convergence and united understandings should prevail among communists, socialists, Christian forces and all the democratic forces. Often in the course of these years the cause of freedom for Spain has offered a terrain for common actions. From the capital of a Spain that is starting down the road to democratic rebirth, the communists of the three countries today call for union of all the forces that want democracy and progress.

The Italian Communists, no. 1 (January–March 1977), pp. 123–4.

Bibliography of Secondary Sources

Italian Communist Party

English

Allum, Percy A., *The Italian Communist Party Since 1945* (University of Reading Graduate School of Contemporary European Studies Occasional Papers, no. 2, 1970).

Are, Giuseppe, 'Italy's Communists: foreign and defence policies,' *Survival*, vol. XVIII, no. 5 (September–October 1976), pp. 210–16.

Are, Giuseppe, 'Italy's Communists: foreign and defence policies,' *Atlantic Community Quarterly* (Winter 1976–7), pp. 508–18.

Ball, George W., 'Communism in Italy?,' *Atlantic Community Quarterly* (Summer 1976), pp. 178–87.

Barnett, V. M., Jr, 'Competitive coexistence and the communist challenge in Italy,' *Political Science Quarterly*, 70 (June 1955), pp. 230–57.

Bartoli, Edgardo, 'The road to power: the Italian Communist Party and the church,' *Survey*, vol. 21, no. 4 (Autumn 1975), pp. 90–106.

Blackmer, Donald L. M., 'Continuity and change in postwar Italian communism,' in *Communism in Italy and France*, eds Donald L. M. Blackmer and Sidney Tarrow (Princeton: Princeton University Press, 1975), pp. 21–68.

Blackmer, Donald L. M., 'International strategy of the Italian Communist Party,' in *The International Role of the Communist Parties of Italy and France*, eds Donald L. M. Blackmer and Annie Kriegel (Cambridge, MA: Harvard Center for International Affairs, 1975), pp. 1–33.

Blackmer, Donald L. M., 'Introducton,' *Communism in Italy and France*, eds Donald L. M. Blackmer and Sidney Tarrow (Princeton: Princeton University Press, 1975), pp. 3–17.

Blackmer, Donald L. M., 'Italian communism and the international movement, 1956–1964', PhD dissertation (Harvard University, 1967).

Blackmer, Donald L. M., 'Italian communism: strategy for the 1970s,' *Problems of Communism* (May–June 1972), pp. 41–56.

Blackmer, Donald L. M., 'Notes on the foreign policy of the Italian Communist Party,' ms.

Blackmer, Donald L. M., *Unity in Diversity: Italian Communism and the Communist World* (Cambridge, MA: MIT Press, 1968).

Blackmer, Donald L. M., and Tarrow, Sidney (eds), *Communism in Italy and France* (Princeton: Princeton University Press, 1975).

Boggs, Carl Elwood, Jr, 'The transformation of Italian communism,' PhD dissertation (University of California at Berkeley, 1970).

Broadhead, H. S., 'Togliatti and the church, 1921–1948,' *Australian Journal of Politics and History*, vol. V, no. 1 (April 1972), pp. 76–91.

Cammett, John M., *Antonio Gramsci and the Origins of Italian Communism* (Stanford: Stanford University Press, 1964).

Cantril, Hedley, *The Politics of Despair* (New York: Basic Books, 1968).

Casale, Frank Louis, 'Subculture, ideology and protest: the nature of mass support for the Italian Communist Party,' PhD dissertation (University of Michigan, 1971).

Croci, Osvaldo, 'The international policies of the Italian Communist Party: some implications for the European Economic Community and the Atlantic Alliance,' MA thesis (The Norman Paterson School of International Affairs, Carleton University, Ottawa, Ontario, 1977).

Davidson, A. B., 'Varying seasons of Gramscian studies,' *Political Studies*, vol. 20, no. 4 (December 1972), pp. 448–61.

De Luca, John Anthony, 'The challenge of Italian communism to Soviet world strategy,' *Italian Quarterly*, vol. 7, nos 27–8 (Fall–Winter 1963), pp. 53–92.

Devlin, K., 'Moscow and the Italian Communist Party,' *Problems of Communism*, vol. 14, no. 5 (September 1965), pp. 1–10.

Ducoli, John, 'The new face of Italian communism,' *Problems of Communism*, vol. XIII, no. 2 (March–April 1964), pp. 82–90.

Edelman, Murray, 'Causes and fluctuations in popular support for the Italian Communist Party since 1946,' *Journal of Politics*, vol. XX, no. 3 (August 1958), pp. 535–52.

Evans, Robert H., 'The changing role of the Communist Party in Italy,' in *Democracy in Crisis*, ed. E. A. Goerner (Notre Dame, Ind.: University of Notre Dame Press, 1971), pp. 89–109.

Evans, Robert H., *Coexistence: Communism and Its Practice in Bologna, 1945–1965* (Notre Dame, Ind.: University of Notre Dame Press, 1967).

Fried, R. C., 'Communism, urban budgets and the two Italies: a case study in comparative urban government,' *Journal of Politics*, vol. 33, no. 4 (November 1971), pp. 1008–51.

Galli, Giorgio, 'The Italian CP: conservatism in disguise,' *Problems of Communism*, vol. VII, no. 3 (May–June 1969), pp. 26–34.

Garosci, Aldo, 'The Italian Communist Party,' in *Communism in Western Europe*, eds Mario Einaudi *et al.* (Ithaca, NY: Cornell University Press, 1951), pp. 154–218.

Hamrin, Harald, *Between Bolshevism and Revisionism: The Italian Communist Party 1944–47* (Stockholm: Swedish Institute in International Relations, 1975).

Hellman, Stephen, 'Generational differences in the bureaucratic elite of Italian Communist Party provincial federations,' *Canadian Journal of Political Science*, vol. VIII, no. 1 (March 1975), pp. 82–106.

Hellman, Stephen, 'Organization and ideology in four Italian communist federations,' PhD dissertation (Yale University, 1973).

Hellman, Stephen, 'The PCI's alliance strategy and the case of the middle classes,' in *Communism in Italy and France*, eds Donald L. M. Blackmer and Sidney Tarrow (Princeton: Princeton University Press, 1975), pp. 373–419

Hellman, Stephen, 'PCI strategy and the question of revolution in the West,' in *Varieties of Marxism*, ed. Shlomo Avineri (The Hague: Nijhoff, 1977), pp. 195–225.

Hine, David, 'Socialists and communists in Italy – reversing roles?,' *West European Politics* (May 1978), pp. 144–60.

Hobsbawm, Eric, *The Italian Road to Socialism: An Interview with Giorgio Napolitano of the Italian Communist Party*, trs. John Cammett and Victoria De Grazia (Westport, CT: Lawrence Hill, 1977).

Jacoviello, Alberto, 'The Italian situation and NATO,' *Survival* (July–August 1976), pp. 166–7.

Kertzer, D. I., 'Participation of Italian communists in Catholic rituals – a case study,' *Journal for the Scientific Study of Religion*, vol. XIV, no. 1 (1975), pp. 1–11.

Kertzer, D. I., 'Politics and ritual: communist festa in Italy,' *Anthropological Quarterly*, vol. 47, no. 4 (October 1974), pp. 374–89.

Kertzer, D. I., 'The two worlds of Albora: Catholic-communist conflict in an Italian working-class quartiere,' PhD dissertation (Brandeis University, 1974).

Kogan, Norman, 'Italian communism: the working class, and organized Catholicism,' *Journal of Politics*, vol. 28, no. 3 (August 1966), pp. 531–55.

Kogan, Norman, 'National communism *vs.* the national way to communism – an Italian interpretation,' *Western Political Quarterly*, vol. XI, no. 3 (September 1958), pp. 660–72.

Kohak, E., 'Italian sinistra: a report from Rome,' *Dissent* (Fall 1976), pp. 328–32.

Lange, Peter M., 'Change and choice in the Italian Communist Party: strategy and organization in the postwar period,' PhD dissertation (MIT, 1974).

Lange, Peter M., 'The PCI and the local level: a study of strategic performance,' in *Communism in Italy and France*, eds Donald L. M. Blackmer and Sidney Tarrow (Princeton: Princeton University Press, 1975), pp. 259–304.

Lange, Peter M., 'What is to be done – about Italian communism,' *Foreign Policy*, vol. 21, no. 2 (1975), pp. 224–40.

Lange, Peter M. and Vannicelli, Maurizio, 'Carter in the Italian maze,' *Foreign Policy*, no. 11 (Winter 1978–9), pp. 161–173

Lange, Peter M., 'Crisis and consent, change and compromise: dilemmas of Italian communism in the 1970s', in *Italy in Transition*, eds Peter Lange and Sidney Tarrow (London: Frank Cass, 1980), pp. 110–32.

La Palombara, Joseph, 'Left-wing trade unionism – the matrix of communist power in Italy,' *Western Political Quarterly*, vol. 7, no. 3 (June 1954), pp. 202–26.

Leich, J. F., 'The Italian communists and the European Parliament,' *Journal of Common Market Studies*, vol. IX, no. 4 (June 1971), pp. 271–81.

Levi, Arrigo, 'Italy's new communism,' *Foreign Policy*, vol. 23, no. 1 (1977), pp. 28–42.

Magri, Lucio, 'Problems of the Marxist theory of a revolutionary party,' *New Left Review* (March–April 1970), pp. 96–128.

Martinelli, Alberto, 'The economic policy of the Italian Communist Party,' *Challenge* (September–October 1976), pp. 35–40.

Napolitano, Giorgio, 'The Italian crisis: a communist perspective,' *Foreign Affairs* (July 1978), pp. 790–9.

Pasquino, Gianfranco, 'Before and after the Italian national elections of 1976,' *Government and Opposition* (Winter 1977), pp. 60–87.

Penniman, Howard R. (ed.), *Italy at the Polls: The Parliamentary Elections of 1976* (Washington, DC: American Enterprise Institute for Public Policy Research, 1977).

Platt, Alan A., and Leonardi, Robert, 'American foreign policy and the postwar Italian left,' *Political Science Quarterly* (Summer 1978), pp. 197–215.

Putnam, Robert, 'The Italian communist politician,' in *Communism in Italy and France*, eds Donald L. M. Blackmer and Sidney Tarrow (Princeton: Princeton University Press, 1975), pp. 173–220.

Rossi, Angelo, *A Communist Party in Action* (New Haven: Yale University Press, 1949).

Sani, Giacomo, 'Mass-level response to party strategy: the Italian electorate and the Communist Party,' in *Communism in Italy and France*, eds Donald L. M. Blackmer and Sidney Tarrow (Princeton: Princeton University Press, 1975), pp. 456–503.

Sani, Giacomo, 'The PCI on the threshold,' *Problems of Communism*, vol. XXV, no. 6 (November–December 1976), pp. 27–51.

Sassoon, Donald, 'The Italian Communist Party's European strategy,' *Political Quarterly*, vol. 47, no. 3 (July–September 1976), pp. 253–75.

Segre, Sergio, 'The "communist question" in Italy,' *Foreign Affairs*, vol. 54, no. 4 (July 1976), pp. 691–707.

Serfaty, Simon, 'The Italian Communist Party and Europe: historically compromised?,' *Atlantic Community Quarterly* (Fall 1977), pp. 275–87.

Sours, Keith J., 'Italy and NATO: the policy of the Italian Communist Party,' in *Columbia Essays in International Affairs: The Dean's Papers*, vol. VI, ed. A. W. Cordier (New York: Columbia University Press, 1971), pp. 134–50.

Sprigge, S., 'De-Stalinization in the Italian Communist

Party,' *World Today*, vol. 18, no. 1 (January 1962), pp. 23–9.

Stehle, Hansjakob, 'The Italian experiment and the Communists: could political and economic pragmatism bridge the gap between today's emergency collaboration of communists and Christian democrats and a "historic compromise" of the future?,' *World Today* (January 1977), pp. 7–16.

Stern, A. J., 'Italian Communist Party at the grass roots,' *Problems of Communism*, vol. 23, no. 2 (March 1974), pp. 42–54.

Stern, A. J., 'Political legitimacy in local politics: the Italian Communist Party in north-east Italy,' in *Communism in Italy and France*, eds Donald L. M. Blackmer and Sidney Tarrow (Princeton: Princeton University Press, 1975), pp. 221–58.

Tarrow, Sidney, 'Italian communism: the new and the old,' *Dissent* (Winter 1977), pp. 54–60.

Tarrow, Sidney, 'Peasant communism in Southern Italy,' PhD dissertation (University of California at Berkeley, 1965).

Tarrow, Sidney, 'Peasant communism in Southern Italy,' in *Yale Studies in Political Science*, vol. 21 (New Haven: Yale University Press, 1967).

Tarrow, Sidney, 'Political dualism and Italian communism,' *American Political Science Review*, vol. LVI, no. 1 (March 1967), pp. 39–53.

Tarrow, Sidney, 'The political economy of stagnation: communism in Southern Italy, 1960–1970,' *Journal of Politics*, vol. XXXIV, no. 1 (February 1972), pp. 93–123.

Tiberti, Enzo, 'The Italian ex-communists,' *Problems of Communism*, vol. VIII, no. 1 (January–February 1959), pp. 52–6.

Urban, G., 'Dante, the Italians and the PCI; a conversation with Luigi Barzini,' *Survey*, vol. XXII, no. 2 (Spring 1976), pp. 118–39.

Urban, Joan Barth, 'Italian communism and the "opportunism of conciliation", 1927–1929,' *Studies in Comparative Communism*, vol. VI, no. 4 (Winter 1973), pp. 362–96.

Urban, Joan Barth, 'The Italian Communist Party and Moscow, 1926–1945,' PhD dissertation (Harvard University, 1967).

Urban, Joan Barth, 'Moscow and the PCI: KTO KVO?,' paper, APS Annual Meeting, Washington, DC, September 2, 1977.

Urban, Joan Barth, 'Socialist pluralism in Soviet and Italian communist perspectives: the Chilean catalyst,' *Orbis*, vol. XVIII, no. 2 (Summer 1974), pp. 482–509.

Weitz, Peter, 'The CGIL and the PCI strategy, 1944–1972,' paper, Conference on French and Italian Communism, MIT, October 12–15, 1972.

White, S., 'Gramsci and the Italian Communist Party (today),' *Government and Opposition*, vol. VII, no. 2 (Spring 1972), pp. 186–205.

Wiskemann, Elizabeth, 'Italy's "red" zone,' *Twentieth Century*, no. 150 (October 1951), pp. 297–306.

Zanotti-Karp, Angela, 'Left-wing intellectuals and the Italian Communist Party (from 1944 to 1956),' PhD dissertation (New School for Social Research, 1973).

Zoppo, Ciro, 'The defense and military policies of the Italian Communist Party,' *Rand Paper Series* (October 1977).

Non-English

Alberoni, Francesco (ed.), *L'attivista di partito, Una indagine sui militanti di base nel PCI e nella DC* (Bologna: Il Mulino, 1967).

Galli, G. (ed.), *Il comportamento elettorale in Italia* (Bologna: Il Mulino, 1968).

Lange, Peter M. and Vannicelli, Maurizio, 'L'America e il PCI: I principi della politica estera americana e la "questione comunista",' Il Mulino, no. 257 (maggio-giugno 1978), pp. 343–69.

Macciocchi, M. A., *Lettere dall' interno del Partito a Louis Althusser* (Milano: Feltrinelli, 1969).

Magri, L., and Maone, F., 'L'organizzazione comunista,' *Il Manifesto*, vol. 1, no. 4 (1969), pp. 28–40.

Mammarella, Giuseppe, *Il Partito Comunista Italiano, 1945–1975* (Firenze: Valsecchi editore, 1976).

Poggi, Gianfranco (ed.), *L'organizzazione partitica del PCI et della DC* (Bologna: Il Mulino, 1968).

Sivini, Giordano, 'Gli iscritti alla Democrazia cristiana a al partito comunista,' *Rassegna italiana di sociologia*, vol. VIII, no. 3 (1967), pp. 429–70.

French Communist Party

English

Althusser, Louis, 'On the 22nd Congress of the French Communist party,' *New Left Review* (July 1977), pp. 3–22.

Campbell, Ian, 'French communists and the union of the left: 1974–1976,' *Parliamentary Affairs* (Summer 1976), pp. 246–63.

Collinet, Michel, 'The French CP: signs of crisis,' *Problems of Communism*, vol. VIII, no. 3 (May–June 1959), pp. 22–7.

Cortieu, Paul, 'France's future socialism,' *World Marxist Review* (June 1976), pp. 28–37.

Domenach, Jean-Marie, 'The French Communist Party,' in *Communism in Western Europe*, eds Mario Einaudi et al. (Ithaca, NY: Cornell University Press, 1951), pp. 60–151.

Fejtö, François, *The French Communist Party and the Crisis of International Communism* (Cambridge, MA: MIT Press, 1967).

Friend, Julius, 'The French Communist Party: where now?,' CSIS Monograph, Georgetown University, 1978.

Jenson, Jane and Ross, George, 'Strategies in conflict: the XXIIIrd Congress of the French Communist Party,' *Socialist Review*, no. 47 (September-October 1979), pp. 71-99

Jenson, Jane and Ross, George, 'The uncharted waters of de-Stalinization: the uneven evolution of the Parti Communiste Française,' in *Politics and Society*, vol. IX no. 3, 1979, pp. 263–298.

Jenson, Jane, 'The French Communist Party and feminism,' in *The Socialist Register, 1980*, eds Ralph Miliband and John Saville (London: Merlin Press, 1980).

Jenson, Jane, 'Strategic Divisions within the French Left: the case of the first elections to the European Parliament,' *Journal of European Integration*, vol. IV, no. 1 (forthcoming).

Johnson, Richard, *The French Communist Party Versus the Students: Revolutionary Politics in May–June 1968* (New Haven: Yale University Press, 1972).

Kanapa, Jean, 'A "new policy" of the French Communist Party,' *Foreign Affairs* (January 1977), pp. 280–94.

Kriegel, Annie, *The French Communists: Profile of a People* (Chicago: University of Chicago Press, 1972).

Leduc, Victor, 'The French Communist Party: between Stalinism and Eurocommunism,' *Political Quarterly* (October–December 1978), pp. 400–10.

Libbey, Kenneth R., 'The French Communist Party in the 1960s: an ideological profile,' *Journal of Contemporary History*, vol. XI, no. 1 (January 1976), pp. 145–65.

Machin, Howard, and Wright, Vincent, 'The French left under the Fifth Republic: the search for identity in unity,' *Comparative Politics* (October 1977), pp. 35–67.

Macridis, Roy, 'The French CP's many faces,' *Problems of Communism*, vol. XXV, no. 3 (May–June 1975), pp. 59–64.

Macridis, Roy, 'The immobility of the French Communist Party,' *Journal of Politics*, vol. XX, no. 4 (November 1958), pp. 613–34.

Mendel, Arthur P., 'Why the French communists stopped the revolution,' *Review of Politics*, vol. XXXI, no. 1 (January 1969), pp. 3–27.

Micaud, Charles, *Communism and the French Left* (New York: Praeger, 1963).

Milhau, Jacques, 'Theoretical activity of the French Communist Party,' *World Marxist Review* (September 1975), pp. 96–105.

Nugent, Neill, and Lowe, David, 'The French Communist Party: the road to democratic government?,' *Political Quarterly* (July–September 1977), pp. 270–87.

Rieber, Alfred J., *Stalin and the French Communist Party, 1941–1947* (New York: Columbia University Press, 1962).

Ross, George, 'The PCF and the end of the Bolshevik dream,' in *Politics of Eurocommunism*, eds Carl Boggs and David Plotke (Boston: South End Press, 1979), pp. 15–47.

Ross George, 'The Confédération Général du Travail in Eurocommunism,' *Politics and Society*, vol. IX, no. 1 (1979), pp. 33–60.

Ross, George, *Workers and Communists in France* (Berkeley: University of California Press, 1981).

Stiefbold, Annette Eisenberg, *The French Communist Party in Transition: PCF–CPSU Relations and the Challenge to Soviet Authority* (New York: Praeger, 1978).

Tiersky, Ronald, *French Communism, 1920–1972* (New York: Columbia University Press, 1974).

Tiersky, Ronald, 'French communism in 1976,' *Problems of Communism*, vol. XXV, no. 1 (January–February 1976), pp. 20–47.

Tiersky, Ronald, 'The French Communist Party and détente,' *Journal of International Affairs*, vol. XXVIII, no. 2 (1974), pp. 188–205.

Tiersky, Ronald, 'Western policy towards the French left,' *Survival* (September–October 1977), pp. 194–201.

Wilson, Frank L., 'The French CP's dilemma,' *Problems of Communism* (July–August 1978), pp. 1–14.

Wilson, Frank L., *The French Democratic Left, 1963–69: Toward a Modern Party System* (Stanford: Stanford University Press, 1971).

Wohl, Robert, *French Communism in the Making, 1914–1924* (Stanford: Stanford University Press, 1966).

Non-English

Bon, Frédéric, *et al.*, *Le communisme en France* (Paris: A. Colin, 1969).

Duhamel, Alain, 'Le parti communiste et l'élection présidentielle,' *Revue française de science politique*, vol. XVI, no. 3 (June 1966), pp. 539–47.

Fauvet, Jacques, *Histoire du Parti communiste français*, 2 vols (Paris: Fayard, 1964 and 1965).

Gross, Babette, *Frankreichs Weg Zum Kommunismus* (Zürich: Neptun Verlag, 1971).

Kriegel, Annie, *Les communistes français*, 2nd edn (Paris: Editions du Seuil, 1970).

Kriegel, Annie, *Aux origines du communisme français: 1914–1920*, 2 vols (Paris: Mouton, 1964).

Timmermann, Heinz, 'Zur aussenpolitischen konzeption der franzoesischen KP,' *Berichte*, no. 17 (1972).

Spanish Communist Party

English

Carrillo, Santiago, *Dialogue on Spain*, with Régis Debray and Max Gallo (London: Lawrence & Wishart, 1976).

Hermet, Guy, *The Communists in Spain: Study of an Underground Political Movement*, trs. S. Seago and H. Fox (Lexington, MA: Lexington Books, 1974).

Linz, Juan, 'An authoritarian regime: Spain,' in *Cleavages, Ideologies and Party Systems*, eds Erik Allardt and Yryö Littunen (Helsinki: The Academic Bookstore, 1964), pp. 291–341.

Linz, Juan, 'The party system of Spain: past and future,' in *Party Systems and Voter Alignments*, eds Seymour Martin Lipset and Stein Rokkan (New York: The Free Press, 1967), pp. 197–282.

Mujal-Leon, Eusebio M., 'The domestic and international evolution of the Spanish Communist Party,' in *European Communism in the Age of Détente*, ed. Rudolf L. Tökes

(New York: New York University Press, 1978), ch. 4.

Mujal-Leon, Eusebio M., 'The PCE in Spanish politics,' *Problems of Communism* (July–August 1978), pp. 15–37.

Mujal-Leon, Eusebio M., 'Portuguese and Spanish communism in contemporary perspective,' in *The Many Faces of Communism*, ed. Morton Kaplan (New York: The Free Press, 1978).

Mujal-Leon, Eusebio M., Spanish communism in the 1970s,' *Problems of Communism*, vol. XXIV, no. 2 (March–April 1975), pp. 43–55.

Preston, Paul, 'The dilemma of credibility: the Spanish Communist Party, the Franco regime and after,' *Government and Opposition*, vol. XI, no. 1 (winter 1976), pp. 65–83.

Rabinovitz, Daniel, 'The evolution of the Spanish Communist Party,' senior thesis (Harvard College, 1978).

Non-English

Colombo, Cesare, *Storia del partito comunista spagnolo* (Milano: Teti editore, 1972).

Linz, Juan, 'L'opposizione in un regime autoritario: il caso della Spagna,' *Storia Contemporanea*, vol. I, nos 1 and 2 (March and June 1970), pp. 63–102 and 219.

Eurocommunism

English

Almond, Gabriel, *The Appeals of Communism* (Princeton: Princeton University Press, 1954).

Arkes, Hadley, 'Democracy and European communism,' *Commentary* (May 1976), pp. 38–47.

Aron, Raymond, 'My defence of our decadent Europe,' *Encounter* (September 1977), pp. 7–50.

Asher, William, and Tarrow, Sidney, 'The stability of communist electorates,' *American Journal of Political Science* (August 1975), pp. 475–99.

Atlantic Community Quarterly, 'Eurocommunism: does it exist?,' *Atlantic Community Quarterly* (Fall 1978), pp. 259–98.

Blackmer, Donald L. M., and Kriegel, Annie, *The International Role of the Communist Parties of Italy and France* (Cambridge, MA: Harvard University Center for International Affairs, no. 33, 1975).

Blackmer, Donald L. M., and Tarrow, Sidney (eds), *Communism in Italy and France* (Princeton: Princeton University Press, 1975).

Brown, Bernard E., (ed.), *The European Left Confronts Modernity* (New York: Cyrco Press, 1978).

Caroe, Olaf, 'Communism in the EEC,' *Round Table*, vol. LX, no. 238 (April 1970), pp. 172–6.

Denitch, Bogdan, 'The rebirth of spontaneity: Il Manifesto and West European Communism,' *Politics and Society*, vol. 1, no. 4 (August 1971), pp. 463–77.

Devlin, Kevin, 'The challenge of Eurocommunism,' *Problems of Communism*, no. 1 (January–February 1977), pp. 1–20.

Devlin, Kevin, 'The interparty drama,' *Problems of Communism* (July 1975), pp. 18–34.

DiPalma, Giuseppe, 'Eurocommunism?,' *Comparative Politics* (April 1977), pp. 357–75.

Dougherty, James E., and Pfaltzgraff, Diane K., 'Eurocommunism and the Atlantic Alliance,' Special Report, Institute for Foreign Policy Analysis, Cambridge, MA, 1977.

Einaudi, Mario, Domenach, Jean-Marie, and Garosci, Aldo, *Communism in Western Europe* (Ithaca, NY: Cornell University Press, 1951).

Feld, W., 'The French and Italian communists and the Common Market: requests for representation in the Community institutions,' *Journal of Common Market Studies*, vol. VI, no. 3 (March 1968), pp. 250–66.

Frank, André Gunder, 'Eurocommunism: left and right variants,' *New Left Review* (March–April 1978), pp. 88–92.

Gati, Charles, 'The "Europeanization" of communism,' *Foreign Affairs*, vol. LV, no. 3 (April 1977), pp. 539–53.

Godson, R., and Haseler, S., *'Eurocommunism': Implications for East and West* (London: Macmillan, 1978).

Goldsborough, James O., 'Communism in Western Europe,' *European Community* (April–May 1976), pp. 3–6.

Goldsborough, James O., 'Eurocommunism after Madrid,' *Foreign Affairs*, vol. LV, no. 4 (July 1977), pp. 800–14.

Greene, Thomas H., 'The communist parties of Italy and France: a study in comparative communism,' *World Politics*, vol. XXI, no. 1 (October 1968), pp. 1–38.

Greene, Thomas H., 'The electorates of non-ruling communist parties,' *Studies in Comparative Communism* (July–October 1971), pp. 68–103.

Greene, Thomas H., 'Non-ruling communist parties and political adaptation,' *Studies in Comparative Communism*, vol. VI, no. 4 (Winter 1973), pp. 331–61.

Griffith, William E., 'The communist and socialist parties in Italy, Spain and France – "Eurocommunism," "Eurosocialism" and Soviet Policy,' ms, MIT, Cambridge, MA.

Hassner, Pierre, 'Eurocommunism and détente,' *Survival* (November–December 1977), pp. 251–4.

Holt, R. T., 'Age as a factor in the recruitment of communist leadership,' *American Political Science Review*, vol. XLVIII, no. 2 (June 1954), pp. 486–99.

Ionescu, G., 'Chile, France and Italy: a discussion,' *Government and Opposition*, vol. VII, no. 3 (Summer 1972), pp. 389–408.

Irving, R. E. M., 'European policy of the French and Italian communists,' *International Affairs* (July 1977), pp. 405–21.

Kissinger, Henry A., 'Communist parties in Western Europe: challenge to the West,' *Atlantic Community Quarterly* (Fall 1977), pp. 261–74.

Kissinger, Henry A., 'Eurocommunism: a new test for the West,' *The New Leader* (July 18, 1978), pp. 8–14. (Adapted from a paper delivered at the Conference on

Italy and Eurocommunism, sponsored by the American Enterprise Institute for Public Policy Research and the Hoover Institution.)

Kogan, Norman, 'The French communists and their Italian comrades,' *Studies in Comparative Communism*, vol. VI, nos 1–2 (Spring–Summer 1973), pp. 184–95.

Kohak, E., 'European communists and European defense,' *Dissent* (Summer 1976), pp. 273–8.

Kolakowski, Leszek, 'The Euro-communist schism,' *Encounter* (August 1977), pp. 14–19.

Kusin, Vladimir V., 'An overview of East European reformism,' *Soviet Studies* (July 1976), pp. 338–61.

Lange, Peter M., 'The French and Italian communist parties: postwar strategy and domestic society,' in *The Age of Radicalism*, ed. Severin Bialer (NY: Praeger, 1976), vol. III, pp. 159–99.

Laqueur, Walter, 'Eurocommunism and its friends,' *Commentary* (August 1976), pp. 25–30.

Ledeen, Michael, 'Europe breaks apart,' *Commentary* (May 1977), pp. 53–7.

Ledeen, Michael, 'The "news" about Eurocommunism,' *Commentary* (October 1977), pp. 53–7.

Leonardi, Robert, 'The United States and the historic compromise: an end to the Cold War?,' paper, APS Annual Meeting, Washington, DC, September 1–4, 1977.

Levi, Arrigo, 'Eurocommunism and East–West relations,' *Survey* (Summer–Autumn, 1976), pp. 91–4.

Löwenthal, Richard, 'Moscow and the "Eurocommunists",' *Problems of Communism* (July–August 1978), pp. 38–49.

Luchsinger, Fred, 'Communists: Euro and otherwise,' *Swiss Review of World Affairs* (April 1977), pp. 4–5.

McInnes, Neil, *The Communist Parties of Western Europe* (London: OUP, 1975).

McInnes, Neil, 'Eurocommunism,' *The Washington Papers*, vol. IV, no. 37 (Beverly Hills, CA: Sage Publications, 1976).

McLellan, Robert, 'Eurocommunism and US Foreign Policy,' paper, Harvard University Center for International Affairs, April 1978.

Mettler, Eric, 'Eurocommunists past and present,' *Swiss Review of World Affairs* (June 1977), pp. 4–5.

Morris, B. S., 'Some perspectives on the nature and role of the West European communist parties,' *Review of Politics*, vol. XVIII, no. 2 (April 1956), pp. 157–69.

Moss, Robert, 'The specter of Eurocommunism,' *Policy Review* (Summer 1977), pp. 7–26.

Pipes, Richard, 'Liberal communism in Western Europe?,' *Orbis* (Fall 1976), pp. 595–600.

Report on West European Communist Parties, submitted by Senator Edward W. Brooke to the Committee on Appropriations, US Senate, June 1977 (Washington, DC: US Government Printing Office, 1977).

Revel, Jean-François, 'The myths of Eurocommunism,' *Foreign Affairs* (January 1978), pp. 295–305.

Ross, George, 'Toward a new Popular Front,' in *The Socialist Register, 1977*, eds Ralph Miliband and John Saville (London: Merlin Press, 1977), pp. 188–208.

Ross, George, 'Crisis in Eurocommunism: the French case,' in *The Socialist Register, 1978*, eds Ralph Miliband and John Saville (London: Merlin Press, 1978), pp. 172–93.

Ross, George and Jenson, Jane, 'Conflicting currents in the PCF,' in *The Socialist Register, 1979*, eds Ralph Miliband and John Saville (London: Merlin Press, 1979), pp. 139–171.

Schlesinger, Arthur, Jr, 'Eurocommunism and détente,' *Current* (October 1977), pp. 42–5.

Serfaty, Simon, 'An international anomaly: the United States and the communist parties in France and Italy, 1945–1947', *Studies in Comparative Communism*, vol. VIII, nos 1–2 (Spring–Summer 1975), pp. 123–46.

Starobin, Joseph R., 'Communism in Western Europe,' *Foreign Affairs*, vol. XLIV, no. 1 (October 1965), pp. 62–77.

Starobin, Joseph R., 'The identity crisis of West European Communists,' *Dissent* (Summer 1975), pp. 251–60.

Steinkühler, Manfred, 'Eurocommunism: myth and reality,' *Aussenpolitik* (October–December 1977), pp. 375–402.

Tannahill, Roy Neal, 'A comparative study of communist parties in Western European democracies,' PhD dissertation (Rice University, 1975).

Tannahill, Roy Neal, 'The future of the communist parties of Western Europe,' *World Affairs* (Fall 1976), pp. 141–54.

Tannahill, Roy Neal, 'Leadership as a determinant of diversity in Western European communism,' *Studies in Comparative Communism* (Winter 1976), pp. 349–68.

Tarrow, Sidney, 'Communism in Italy and France: adaptation and change,' in *Communism in Italy and France*, eds Donald L. M. Blackmer and Sidney Tarrow (Princeton: Princeton University Press, 1975), pp. 575–640.

Tarrow, Sidney, 'From Cold War to historic compromise: approaches to French and Italian radicalism,' in *The Age of Radicalism*, ed. Severin Bialer (NY: Praeger, 1976), vol. I, pp. 213–35.

Tarrow, Sidney, 'Party activists in public office: comparison at the local level in Italy and France,' in *Communism in Italy and France*, eds Donald L. M. Blackmer and Sidney Tarrow (Princeton: Princeton University Press, 1975), pp. 143–72.

Timmermann, Heinz, 'Eurocommunism: Moscow's reaction and the implications for Eastern Europe,' *World Today* (October 1977), pp. 376–85.

Timmermann, Heinz, 'National strategy and international autonomy: the Italian and French communist parties,' *Studies in Comparative Communism*, vol. V, nos. 2–3 (Summer, August 1972), pp. 258–76.

Timmermann, Heinz, 'West European Communism in flux,' *Problems of Communism* (November 1976), pp. 74–8.

Tokes, Rudolph L. (ed.), *European Communism in the Age of Détente* (NY: New York University Press, 1978).

Uliassi, Pio, 'Communism in Western Europe,' in *The New Communisms*, ed. Dan N. Jacobs (NY: Harper & Row, 1969), ch. 10.

Uliassi, Pio, and Willenz, Eric, 'Origins and limits of communist pluralism,' in *The New Communisms*, ed. Dan N. Jacobs (NY: Harper & Row, 1968), pp. 74–102.

Urban, G. R. (ed.), *Eurocommunism: Its Roots and Future in Italy and Elsewhere* (London: Temple Smith, 1978).

Urban, Joan Barth, 'Contemporary Soviet perspectives on revolution in the West,' *Orbis* (Winter 1976), pp. 1359–402.

Valenta, Jiri, 'Eurocommunism and Eastern Europe,' *Problems of Communism* (March–April 1978), pp. 41–54.

Vree, Dale, 'Coalition politics on the left in France and Italy,' *Review of Politics*, vol. XXXVII, no. 3 (July 1975), pp. 340–56.

Non-English

Cesarini-Sforza, Marco, and Nassi, Enrico, *L'Eurocomunismo* (Milano: Rizzoli, 1977).

Timmermann, Heinz, 'Die entspannungskonzepte der Eurokommunisten,' *Berichte*, no. 48 (1977).

Timmermann, Heinz, 'Eurokommunismus – eine herausforderung für Ost und West,' *Deutschland Archiv*, vol. IX, no. 12 (December 1976), pp. 1276–97.

Timmermann, Heinz, 'Die Krise der französischen Linken: Zur kommunistischen Einheitsfront-Strategie vor und während der Praesidentschaftswahlen 1969,' *Berichte*, no. 15 (1970).

Timmermann, Heinz, 'Westeuropas kommunisten und die politik der Entspannung,' *Berichte des Bundesintituts für Gewissenschaftliche und Internationale Studien*, no. 19 (1975).

Wagner, Wolfgang, 'Kommunisten im westlichen Bündnis? Atlantische Allianz und Europaeische Gemeinschaft vor einem neuen Problem,' *Europa-Archiv*, vol. XXXI, no. 10 (May 25, 1976), pp. 315–24.

Index of Documents

Part One   National Roads to Socialism

Part Two   Alliance Policy

2 Palmiro Togliatti's report to the Eighth Congress of the PCI, December 1956

3 Communiqué of the Central Committee delegations of the PCI and CLY on the talks carried on in Belgrade (January 15–21, 1964)

4 Communiqué of the Directorate of the PCI, November 3, 1956

5 Palmiro Togliatti's speech at the eighth regional congress of the Bologna Federation of the PCI, November 18, 1956

6 Palmiro Togliatti's editorial, *Rinascita*, 1949

7 Palmiro Togliatti's report to the Eighth Congress of the PCI, December 1956

8 Luigi Longo's interview with *Stern*, in *L'Unità*, November 10, 1964

9 Giancarlo Pajetta, 'On the relations among communist parties,' 1972

10 Palmiro Togliatti's memorandum, *Rinascita*, September 5, 1964

11 Luigi Longo's report to the Central Committee of the PCI, *L'Unità*, October 12, 1966

12 Enrico Berlinguer's speech at the national *L'Unità* festival, September 19, 1976

13 Communiqué of the Political Bureau of the PCI (August 21, 1968), *L'Unità*, August 22, 1968

14 Communiqué of the Directorate of the PCI (August 23, 1968), *L'Unità*, August 24, 1968

15 Luigi Longo's report to the Central Committee of the PCI, *L'Unità*, August 28, 1968

16 'Eight years since the intervention in Czechoslovakia,' *L'Unità*, September 7, 1976

17 'An unacceptable measure,' *L'Unità*, November 20, 1976

18 'Unresolved problems,' *L'Unità*, December 20, 1976

19 'Arrested in Prague – the signatories of "Charter 77",' *L'Unità*, January 12, 1977

20 Palmiro Togliatti's interview with *Nuovi Argomenti*, May–June 1956

21 Palmiro Togliatti's report to the Central Committee in preparation for the Eighth Congress of the PCI, June 24, 1956

22 Palmiro Togliatti's report to the Eighth Congress of the PCI, December 1956

23 Palmiro Togliatti's report to the Tenth Congress of the PCI, December 1962

24 Palmiro Togliatti's memorandum, *Rinascita*, September 5, 1964

25 Luigi Longo's interview with *Stern*, in *L'Unità*, November 10, 1964

26 Order of the day approved by the Central Committee of the PCI, *Rinascita*, June 12, 1965

27 Luigi Longo's speech to the Central Committee of the PCI, February 25, 1967

28 Draft theses for the Twelfth Congress of the PCI, October 1968

29 Luigi Longo's report to the Twelfth Congress of the PCI, February 1969

30 Enrico Berlinguer, 'Internationalism and autonomy,' 1971

31 Giancarlo Pajetta, interview with *L'Unità*, November 23, 1975

32 Enrico Berlinguer's speech at the Twenty-Fifth Congress of the CPSU, February 27, 1976

33 Editorial comment, *L'Unità*, June 28, 1977

French Communist Party: Diversity in Unity – Proletarian Internationalism and the Strains of Allegiance

1 Maurice Thorez, 'Homage to Stalin,' 1950

2 Theses of the Fourteenth Congress of the PCF, July 1956

3 Maurice Thorez' report to the Fifteenth Congress of the PCF, June 1959

4 Marcel Veyrier, 'Yugoslavia: The Tenth Congress of the Communists' League,' 1974

5 Etienne Fajon's report of the Central Committee, 1956

6 Declaration of the Politburo of the PCF, 1956

7 Jacques Duclos, 'Long live socialist Hungary,' 1956

8 Declaration of the Politburo of the PCF, 1948

9 Waldeck Rochet's speech to the Central Committee of the PCF, April 18, 1968

10 Declaration of the Central Committee of the PCF, 1968

11 PCF Central Committee resolution, 1968

12 Georges Marchais' interview with Europe 1, 1968

13 Editorial, 'Blows to freedom in Czechoslovakia,' *L'Humanité*, January 25, 1977

14 Waldeck Rochet's report to the Central Committee of the PCF, October 6, 1963

15 Waldeck Rochet's report to the Eighteenth Congress of the PCF, January 1967

16 Georges Marchais' report to the Central Committee of the PCF, June 28, 1969

17 Central Committee of the PCF, 1976

18 Declaration of the Politburo of the PCF, 1956

19 Maurice Thorez' report to the Fourteenth Congress of the PCF, July 1956

20 Maurice Thorez' report to the Twelfth Congress of the PCF, April 1950

21 Resolution of the Central Committee of the PCF, October 10, 1964

22 Waldeck Rochet's report to the Central Committee of the PCF, October 20–1, 1968

23 Georges Marchais' report to the Nineteenth Congress of the PCF, February 1970

24 Georges Marchais' report to the Twentieth Congress of the PCF, December 13–17, 1972

25 Georges Marchais, 'The Communist Party "à coeur ouvert",' 1973

26 Jean Kanapa, interview with France-Inter, 1975

27 Georges Marchais' report to the Twenty-Second Congress of the PCF, February 1976

28 Jean Kanapa, interview with *France-Nouvelle*, 1976

29 Georges Marchais, press conference, *L'Humanité*, 1976

Part Five The Parties and the International System

French Communist Party: National Grandeur and the Quest for Autonomy

1 Maurice Thorez, 'Essential declaration,' 1945
2 Marcel Cachin, commemoration of the twenty-eighth anniversary of the Russian revolution, November 6, 1945
3 Charles Tillon, 'The Marshall Plan: abandonment of French independence and national defense,' 1948
4 Declaration of the Political Bureau, 1949
5 The PCF's National Welfare Program, Twelfth Congress of the PCF, April 1950
6 Central Committee report to the Thirteenth Congress of the PCF, June 1954
7 PCF declaration on the situation in Algeria, 1954
8 Central Committee resolution, 1956
9 Maurice Thorez' report to the Fifteenth Congress of the PCF, June 1959
10 Waldeck Rochet's report to the Sixteenth Congress of the PCF, May 1961 (I)
11 Waldeck Rochet's report to the Sixteenth Congress of the PCF, May 1961 (II)
12 Declaration of the Central Committee of the PCF, 1962
13 Waldeck Rochet's report to the Seventeenth Congress of the PCF, May 1964
14 Central Committee report to the Eighteenth Congress of the PCF, January 1967
15 'They do not know the French Communist Party,' *L'Humanité*, 1967
16 Georges Marchais' report to the Central Committee of the PCF, June 1969
17 Georges Marchais' report to the Nineteenth Congress of the PCF, February 1970
18 Georges Marchais' report to the Central Committee of the PCF, January 1972
19 Georges Marchais' report to the Twentieth Congress of the PCF, December 13–17, 1972
20 Paul Laurent, 'The political and social situation,' 1973
21 Georges Marchais, 'France and Europe,' 1973
22 Georges Marchais' report to the Twenty-First Congress of the PCF, October 1974
23 Mireille Nadaud, 'United States facing the contemporary challenge,' 1975
24 Georges Marchais' report to the Twenty-Second Congress of the PCF, February 1976
25 Marcel Trigon, 'Aspects of international politics,' 1977
26 Jean Kanapa's speech to the Central Committee of the PCF, May 11, 1977
27 Jean Kanapa, interview with *L'Humanité*, 1977
28 Central Committee report of the Thirteenth Congress of the PCF, June 1954
29 Waldeck Rochet's report to the Central Committee of the PCF, February 14, 1957
30 Theses of the Fifteenth Congress of the PCF, June 1959
31 Waldeck Rochet's report to the Seventeenth Congress of the PCF, May 1964

32 Jean Merot, 'Lost illusions (part 4),' 1969
33 Georges Marchais, 'France and the Common Market,' 1973
34 'The Europe that we want,' *L'Humanité*, 1974
35 'EEC,' *L'Humanité*, 1975
36 Declaration of the Politburo of the PCF, July 14, 1976
37 Declaration of the Politburo of the PCF, June 8, 1977

Spanish Communist Party: Legitimacy, Autonomy and the Search for International Linkages

1 PCE program, Fifth Congress, 1954 (published in 1955)
2 PCE international situation: Central Committee, 1956, 'Declaration . . . for reconciliation . . .'
3 General assessment of US foreign policy, 1958, Dolores Ibarruri to the Central Committee
4 PCE program, Sixth Congress, 1960
5 Santiago Carrillo, 'On some problems in the tactics of the fights against Francoism,' 1961
6 Executive Committee of the PCE, August 12, 1961
7 Santiago Carrillo, *Después de Franco Que?*, 1965
8 'NATO and Spain: European collective security,' *Nuestra Bandera*, 1966
9 'For the cancellation of the military accords with the USA,' *Mundo Obrero*, 1967.
10 'Anti-Imperialist Unity in the Solidarity with Vietnam,' *Mundo Obrero*, 1971
11 Juan Calanda, 'No to NATO,' 1972
12 Manuel Azcárate's report to the Eighth Congress of the PCE, 'On some problems of the international policies of the party,' 1972
13 Santiago Carrillo's report to the Eighth Congress of the PCE, 1972
14 Declaration of the Executive Committee of the PCE, 1973
15 Manuel Azcárate's report to the Central Committee of the PCE, 1973
16 'Spain–Morocco: a national and anti-colonial policy,' *Mundo Obrero*, 1973
17 Leonor Bornao, 'Spain and the socialist countries,' 1977
18 Manuel Azcárate, 'Spain must recognize the Polisario,' 1978
19 Resolution of the Ninth Congress of the PCE, 1978
20 Santiago Carrillo's speech at the Ninth Congress of the PCE, 1978
21 Juan Gomez, 'The negotiation with the Common Market: myths and realities,' 1970
22 Santiago Carrillo's speech at the Eighth Congress of the PCE, 1972
23 Juan Gomez' speech at the Eighth Congress of the PCE, 1972
24 Strasbourg declaration on the Democratic Junta, 1975
25 Resolution of the Ninth Congress of the PCE, 1978

APPENDIX: Joint Declarations of the Eurocommunist Parties

1 Joint Declaration by the Italian Communist Party and the Spanish Communist Party (Leghorn, July 12, 1975)

2 Joint declaration by the Italian Communist Party and the French Communist Party (Rome, November 15, 1975)

3 Joint declaration by the PCE, PCF and PCI (Madrid, March 3, 1977)

Glossary of Terms

ACLI (Associazione Cattolica dei Lavoratori Italiani) See *Catholic Workers' Associations.*

Alvarez, Santiago Secretary general of the PCG (Communist Party of Galicia) and member of the Central Committee of the PCE. He is known as a PCE theorist and a specialist on agricultural problems.

Amendola, Giorgio Member of the Central Directorate and Central Committee of the PCI. He has been a major intellectual force in the party, often taking positions which opened major debates. In general, he has been moderate on domestic matters and more hard-line on international issues.

Anti-latifundist One who opposes latifundism, the system of landownership in which a few landowners own most of the land. This is the system of landownership in the south of Spain. The PCE opposes it and advocates redistribution of land.

Article 18 One of the seven fundamental laws that were the 'constitution' of the Francoist regime, it refers to the right of 'habeas corpus' (a person should be sent before a judge within seventy-two hours following arrest). This article was frequently suspended by the declaration of the State of Exception established in Article 35 of the same law.

Atlantic Alliance The organization created to implement the North Atlantic Treaty of 1949, which engaged the United States and Western European democracies in a collective defense and security system (also known as NATO). The agreement provided a framework for the integration of German military strength into that system under international control, and the counterweight to an otherwise overwhelming Soviet military capability in Europe.

Azcárate, Manuel A member of the Executive Committee of the PCE with principal responsibility for foreign affairs, Azcárate is noted for his radical opposition to the foreign policy of the USSR. An intense anti-Stalinist, Azcárate also opposes any connection of the PCE with the Soviets.

Beneš, Eduard Former and first President of Czechoslovakia, Beneš, together with Thomas G. Masaryk, led Czechoslovakia to independence during the First World War; that independence lasted until 1938 when it was destroyed after the Munich agreement. Beneš headed the Czechoslovakian government in exile during the Second World War. In June 1948 he resigned from the presidency after the communist coup.

Berlin Conference of European Communist and Workers' Parties (June 29–30, 1976) Twenty-nine communist and workers' parties met at a consultative conference in East Berlin which underlined the autonomy of each party to pursue its own way to socialism. The final declaration of the conference (which was non-binding) did not make any reference to the dictatorship of the proletariat or proletarian internationalism. Instead, by way of compromise, the document referred to proletarian internationalism. The conference is considered to be the high point of the eurocommunist movement towards independence from Moscow.

Berlinguer, Enrico Secretary general of the PCI (1972–) and a member of the Chamber of Deputies (1968–). Berlinguer authored the policy of historic compromise.

Biermann, Wolf Biermann, a poet-performer, was born in 1936. He moved to East Germany in 1953 and worked as an assistant director at the Berliner Ensemble with Bertolt Brecht and Hans Eisler until he made a name as a performer in his own right. On November 16, 1976, while he was performing in West Germany, he was stripped of his citizenship by the GDR.

Brandt, Willy Federal Chancellor (SPD) of the Federal Republic of Germany, 1969–74, and today a major international socialist and social democratic leader. Brandt was the author and leader of the 'Ostpolitik' of the FRG which led in the late 1960s and early 1970s to a normalization of West German relations with Eastern Europe and the Soviet Union.

Bucharest declaration (July 1966) Called for an all-European security conference meeting.

Bukovsky, Vladimir Leading Soviet dissident released on Brezhnev's birthday in 1976 in exchange for Luis Corvalan, the Chilean Communist leader imprisoned by the military junta in Chile.

Burgos trial A trial in December 1970 against some members of the ETA, a Basque separatist terrorist group, who were sentenced to death for the murder of Melitón Manzanas, Chief of Police of Bilbao, who used torture in interrogation. Later put in prison for life, the 'Youth of Burgos' were freed by amnesty in 1977.

Cahiers du Communisme Academic and theoretical journal of the PCF. Published bi-monthly in Paris.

Carlist Party A monarchic party, it has its origins in the Wars of Succession that took place in nineteenth-century Spain. Opposed to the liberal tendencies of the Isabelline monarchy, it used to be a very traditionalist and Catholic party. It fought on Franco's side in the Civil War. Now, with no claims to the Crown at all, it considers itself as an independent, socialist and federalist party.

Carrero Blanco, Luis Prime Minister of Spain from 1967 to December 20, 1973, when he was killed by the ETA, a Basque separatist terrorist group.

Carrillo, Santiago Secretary general of the PCE, Carrillo has gradually separated the PCE from the tutelage of Moscow. Carrillo led the PCE to legalization in 1977, and had an important role in the establishment of democracy in Spain after the death of Franco. He has been perhaps the most outspoken of Communist Party secretaries general in criticizing the USSR.

Catholic Workers' Associations (ACLI; Associazione Cattolica dei Lavoratori Italiani) Associations of Catholic workers organized by the Catholic Church after the Second World War when all unionized Italian workers were part of a single unified trade union. After the formation of the CISL (the Catholic trade union federation), the ACLI remained an important organizational support for the Christian Democratic Party. In the late 1960s the ACLI moved significantly to the left, breaking many of its ties with the DC and espousing socialist values.

Caudillo Means 'leader' – a title used by Franco as leader of the *movimiento nacional.*

CC (Central Committee) The committee of a communist party composed of regional, local leaders and administrative cadres. It is the highest deliberative body of a communist party, charged with establishing the major lines of policy between party congresses. It is the Central Committee which chooses the members of the party's executive organs.

CC OO (Comisiones Obreras) Workers' commissions were founded in Spain in 1962 by Catholics, socialists and communists and some falangist workers. Initially a unitary, non-bureaucratic syndical movement of anti-Franco workers, after Franco's death the organization split into several independent syndical organizations. Nowadays CC OO is the largest Spanish syndical organization.

CCP (Chinese Communist Party) Known in Europe as ChCC.

CD See *Democratic Co-ordination.*

CGT Confédération Général du Travail, the trade union confederation linked to the French Communist Party.

Champigny Manifesto (December 1968) A reiteration of party platform calling for 'democratization' which would lead automatically to a transformation of the nature and goals of the state; stressed role of working-class participation in party and in government.

'Charter '77' A letter written in 1977 by a group of Czech intellectuals and artists criticizing the Czech regime. It was published by the PCE's mouthpiece, *Mundo Obrero.*

Chiaromonte, Gerardo A major figure in the new generation of PCI leaders. Former editor of *Rinascita*, he is currently a member of the secretariat and director of PCI economic policy.

Christian Democratic Party (DC) Formed at the end of the Second World War as the political party of Italian Catholicism, the DC has been a partner in all postwar governments and has dominated postwar Italian politics. Composed of a number of disparate components – peasants and workers, landholders and industrial entrepreneurs, shopkeepers and white collar employees – the DC has been the most successful party in all postwar elections, winning a little more or less than 40 per cent of the votes. The DC has promoted Italy's presence in the Atlantic Alliance and the Common Market. Closely tied to the church, it has also sought to defend the role of Catholic values in Italian politics and society. In the 1970s the DC suffered a number of internal crises and lost ground to the PCI. It had, furthermore, to come to terms with the communists' proposal for

a historic compromise, including a governmental alliance. To date the DC has become more conciliatory toward the PCI but has refused to allow the communists to enter the Cabinet.

Cierna and Bratislava Cities in Czechoslovakia.

Claudín, Fernando A former close friend of Santiago Carrillo and an important theorist of eurocommunism, Claudín wrote about the liberation of communism from Stalinism in the late 1950s and early 1960s, but he was expelled from the PCE for his opposition to collaboration with the Soviets.

CLY See *League of Communists of Yugoslavia.*

Common Program (Programme Commun) An agreement signed in 1972 by the PCF and PSF to work together for shared goals and national power. Among the proposals for social reform were a forty-hour week, retirement at age 60, nationalization of major industries, including banking and greater control over industry. The program was less defined on international questions. Always subject to internal tensions, the coalition behind the Common Program divided sharply in 1977, leading to a defeat for the parties in the 1978 legislative elections. The Common Program has subsequently been abandoned, with the PCF moving back toward some of its more traditional positions.

Conference of Communist and Workers' Parties (June 1969) An international conference of all communist parties willing to attend a meeting organized by the Soviet Union. It was the first such meeting after the Soviet invasion of Czechoslovakia, and several parties, including the PCI and PCE, refused fully to endorse the conference document and the Brezhnev doctrine which the Soviet leader sought to assert.

Cortes Traditional name for the Spanish parliament. The Cortes were unicameral under Franco, but now are a bicameral body.

Corvalan, Luis Chilean communist leader imprisoned by the military junta in Chile after the coup in 1973 who was released in exchange for the USSR's release of Soviet dissident Vladimir Bukovsky on Brezhnev's birthday in 1976.

CPC Communist Party of Czechoslovakia.

CPSU Communist Party of the Soviet Union.

Cultural Revolution (Chinese) Inaugurated in 1966 by Mao Tse-tung's call to 'bombard all the headquarters,' the Chinese Cultural Revolution mobilized socialist forces against supposedly pro-capitalist initiatives in education and the economy. Although sometimes violent, the Chinese Cultural Revolution was also characterized by intensive persuasion and discussion, and a collective social effort to root out bourgeois ideology and implant Maoist socialist ideology.

Daniel, Yuri See *Siniavski, Andrei.*

DC See *Cristian Democratic Party.*

Delicado, Manuel A member of the PCE since the 1930s, he became an important figure in the party. He has recently died.

'Democratic centralism' The organizational principle employed by communist parties to reconcile the divergence of individual preferences with the united will of the Communist Party. Debate among party members in formulation of policy constitutes the 'democratic' element of decision-making, while mandatory allegiance to final decisions and implemented policy constitutes the 'centralism' aspect of the principle.

Democratic Co-ordination (DC) Clandestine unitary platform formed in March 1976 by the political forces opposed to the reformist Francoism, mainly socialists, communists and other democratic parties. It was the result of the unification of the previous unitary platforms, Junta Democrática and Plataforma de Convergencia Democrática.

Despuẽs de Franco Que? A book written by Santiago Carrillo in 1965 on the future of Spain after Franco's death.

Diaz, José Secretary general of the PCE in the 1930s.

Dien Bien Phu At the meeting of the Big Four foreign ministers in Berlin in February 1954, the French succeeded in having the Indo–China problem placed on the agenda of a forthcoming international conference at Geneva which was to discuss a settlement of the Korean War. In anticipation of this conference the Viet Minh launched a major effort to turn the tide of battle in their favor. On March 13, 1954, forces under the command of General Vo Nguyen Giap began an assault upon the French fortress of Dien Bien Phu where General Henri Navarre had concentrated 10,000 troops. Navarre had hoped that French superior firepower would enable him to smash such an attack and score a decisive victory. Instead the Viet Minh, greatly helped by a substantial increase in Chinese aid, including artillery and radar, showed themselves the stronger by far and by early April the fortress was in serious danger of falling. President Eisenhower was unwilling to intervene militarily without the support of Britain and congressional approval. Attempts on the part of Secretary of State Dulles to obtain British and French commitments for a program of collective military action failed, and on May 7, 1954, Dien Bien Phu fell. The French military effort in Indo–China, for all practical purposes, had collapsed.

Doriot, Jacques Former communist leader of the 'red' district of St Denis in Paris from 1920 to 1934 and contender for the position of secretary general in the early 1930s, Doriot was expelled from the PCF in 1934 after he declined an invitation from the Comintern. In 1936 Doriot organized the French Popular Party (PPF) in opposition to the Popular Front. The PPF stood for 'an awakened nationalism,' which entailed support for fascist leaders Franco and Mussolini, and the promotion of negotiations with Hitler.

Dubçek, Alexander Inaugurated as first secretary of the Communist Party of Czechoslovakia in 1968, Dubçek succeeded Stalinist Antonin Novotny. His rise signaled a potential for the emergence of a more autonomous Czechoslovakian state and the creation of democracy in a communist framework. The Soviet invasion of Czechoslovakia in 1968, however, foreclosed these possibilities.

Duclos, Jacques A member of the PCF since its founding, he was party secretary in 1931, a vice-president of the Assembly in 1936, vice-president of the Director's Office of the PCF during its clandestinity (1936–9) and a resistance leader. Considered to be second man in the party's leadership after Maurice Thorez, Duclos died in 1975.

EEC (European Economic Community) An international organization established in 1958 in the Treaty of Rome by France, Germany, Italy, Belgium, the Netherlands and Luxembourg to improve standards of living, unite the economies and avoid disequilibrium in their balance of payments. The countries accepted a long-term plan to reduce tariffs, abolish import quotas, and to establish a common investment bank to finance under-capitalized projects of individual states and developmental projects among the countries, both in Europe and abroad. Subsequently Britain, Denmark and Ireland have joined the EEC and new memberships for Portugal, Spain and Greece are today under consideration.

EFTA (European Free Trade Area) In June 1959 Austria, Great Britain, Denmark, Norway, Portugal, Sweden and Switzerland established the European Free Trade Area as a means to introduce free trade among themselves incrementally as long as the EEC continued to resist expansion. The initial aims of EFTA were the liberation of foreign trade from tariffs and quotas, the formulation of common rules of competition and anti-dumping provisions.

Engels, Friedrich A socialist philosopher, Engels collaborated with Karl Marx in writing *The German Ideology* and the 'Communist Manifesto.' After Marx's death Engels edited Volumes 2 and 3 of *Capital* as well as many other of Marx's incompleted writings.

Fajon, Etienne Director of *L'Humanité* since 1958, Fajon has also acted as president of the PCF Central Committee for Political Control. The Committee is the PCF's internal intelligence mechanism employed to maintain complete autobiographical information on party leaders at all levels and to maintain principled conduct by party members.

France-Inter One of France's radio stations.

France-Nouvelle French socialist intellectual journal, published weekly in Paris.

Franco, Francisco Bahamonde Dictator of Spain, 1936 until his death in 1977.

French Socialist Party (PSF) Dominant party of the non-communist left in France. Rooted in the indigenous Jacobin tradition, the PSF aims towards the creation of a socialism based upon a new humanism rather than economic materialism. In contradistinction from the PCF, the French socialists have traditionally been committed to the institutions of liberal democracy such as elections, universal suffrage and legislative dominance. During the late 1960s the PSF acquired new members and a more open posture towards the PCF, although the two parties have always coexisted uneasily. The new alliance was formalized by the Programme Commun of 1972 and the Socialist Party gained in electoral support, becoming for a time the largest party on the left with around a quarter of the electorate. The collapse of the Common Program in 1978 led to sharp internal party divisions about future party strategy.

FRG (Federal Republic of Germany) West Germany.

Garaudy, Roger Member of the PCF from 1945 to 1970, and former director of the Centre d'Etudes et de Recherches Marxistes (CERM) (Institute of Party History), Garaudy was expelled from the party in 1970 due to his vigorous criticism of the Soviet invasion of Czechoslovakia, the internal organization of the PCF and the party's general strategy. In the 1950s, by contrast, Garaudy had been a major hard-line critic of the Italian Communist Party's strategy.

García, Eduardo, and Gómez, Augustin García and Gómez defected from the PCE in opposition to the anti-Soviet position the party took on the invasion of Czechoslovakia. García and Gómez organized the PCI, a small communist party which followed Moscow's directions.

GDR (German Democratic Republic) East Germany.

General Workers' Union (UGT; Unión General de Trabajadores) A socialist syndical confederation, the UGT was founded in 1886. It was the largest confederation until the Civil War, now is second after the CC OO.

Geneva Conference (April 26 to July 21, 1954) This conference officially registered France's defeat by the Viet Minh and provided it with a face-saving means of disengagement. Two agreements on Vietnam were reached at Geneva: the bilateral armistice agreement between France and the Viet Minh and the later and more publicized multilateral Final Declaration.

Ginsberg, Alexander A Soviet dissident author, Ginsberg was sentenced to eight years in a hard labor camp for anti-Soviet propaganda in 1978 after a trial which aroused great international discontent. Ginsberg was allowed to leave for the West in 1979.

Giscard d'Estaing, Valéry President of the Fifth Republic of France since May 1974. Giscard d'Estaing, an economist, was Minister of Finance and the principal architect of France's austerity program in the 1960s, and of economic growth in the 1970s. As the most prominent member of the Independent Republicans, Giscard d'Estaing has provided leadership for the non-Gaullist conservative forces and has sought to develop policies which will maintain France's international prestige without being anti-American.

Gomulka, Wladyslaw First secretary of the Central Committee of the Polish Communist Party from 1956 to 1970, Gomulka is noted for his initiation of armed opposition against the Germans and as organizer of the National Council of Poland during the Second World War. He was imprisoned in the postwar period but triumphantly returned to power after the riots in Poland in 1956.

Gonzalez, Felipe Secretary general of the PSOE, the Spanish Socialist Party, since October 1974.

Gottwald, Klement A founder of the Czechoslovakian Communist Party, Gottwald became Premier of Czechoslovakia in 1946, led the communist coup of 1948 and replaced Beneš as President in June 1948. He held that office until 1951, during which time he consolidated his power through a series of state and party purges. He died in 1953.

Gramsci, Antonio One of the founders of the Italian Communist Party in 1921, Gramsci was its recognized leader at the time of his arrest by the fascists in November 1926. Gramsci spent the last eleven years of his life in prison writing. Between 1948 and 1951 Gramsci's 'Prison Notebooks' were published. These notebooks reveal, among other things, Gramsci's ultimate views on two major problems of political theory and modern Italian history that had engaged him from the beginning, namely, the nature and tasks of the political party, and the historical role of Italian intellectuals. In prison Gramsci argued that bourgeois rule depended ultimately on maintaining bourgeois cultural 'hegemony,' i.e. the received ideas of a self-confident bourgeoisie, transmitted via control of the media, education, advertising, the churches, and so forth. Hence Gramsci's constant interest in 'communist education' and in the training of working-class 'organic intellectuals.' Moreover Gramsci continued to believe that cultural propaganda was not enough by itself. If 'bourgeois hegemony' were to be overcome, workers would have to develop their own 'authentic' ideas, in line with their own social experience, and this could only be done through 'practical political activity' – mass participation.

HOAC (Hermandades Obreras de Accion Catolica; Workers' Fraternities of Catholic Action) Catholic workers' organization often used as a platform against the official unions by the workers opposed to the Francoist regime.

Horthy De Nagybanya, Nicholas Regent and dictator of Hungary from 1920 to 1944, Horthy led a counter-revolution against Bela Kun, a communist, and aided Hitler in the Second World War.

Ibarruri, Dolores Former secretary general of the PCE, she is now its president. She had an important role during the Second Republic and the Civil War, but at the time of writing is purely a symbolic figure, though very respected, within the PCE. She is popularly called 'Pasionaria.'

Il Manifesto The title of a journal and of the group of PCI dissidents who founded it. They objected to the overly moderate and pro-Soviet orientation of the party in the late 1960s. This group was sympathetic both to the

Chinese Cultural Revolution and to dual power strategies in Italy based on factory councils. They were 'radiated' (expelled with the possibility of re-entry) after a major party debate in 1969 and have gone on to lead part of the movement to the left of the PCI in the 1970s. (See *'Manifesto' debate.*)

Italian Socialist Party (PSI) Formed at the end of the nineteenth century, the PSI became the largest party in the Italian parliament after the First World War but refused to join a government, in part because of a deep division between reformist and maximalist factions. Outlawed during fascism, it allied with the PCI in the 1930s, played an active role in the resistance and maintained its links with the communists after the war. After the events of 1956, however, the PSI broke its ties to the PCI and began to move toward a coalitional role with the Christian Democrats which was solidified in the center-left governments of the 1960s. The party remained divided between more and less reformist factions, suffered a scission in 1964 and in the 1970s began to move back toward the left. The PSI was the largest party on the left in 1946 with 20 per cent of the vote, but has gradually lost ground to the communists subsequently and has seen its vote percentage fall to around 10 per cent.

Juan Carlos, Prince In 1969 named by General Franco to be the future King of Spain; became King of Spain in 1975. In July 1976 the king named Adolfo Suarez to lead Spain to a democratic order. In June 1977 voting took place in a completely orderly fashion, and Suarez was confirmed by Juan Carlos as head of the government.

Junta Democratica Unitary platform created in July 1974 by the PCE and other democratic parties and independent public personalities to oppose the Francoist regime.

Juquin, Pierre A professor and, since 1964, a member of the Central Committee of the PCF, responsible for questions of teaching and research.

Kadar, Janos First secretary of the Central Committee of the Hungarian Socialist Workers' Party and head of the Hungarian Communist Party from 1956 until the time of writing. He was Prime Minister of Hungary from 1956 to 1958 and 1961 to 1965, Minister of State from 1958 to 1961, and was an organizer of the resistance movement in the Second World War.

Karlovy-Vary declaration A Moscow-convened meeting of all European communist and workers' parties in the spring of 1967 at Karlovy-Vary, Czechoslovakia, at which Brezhnev devoted his attention to the threat posed by NATO to Soviet aims in Europe, in an unsuccessful effort to reconcile the differences between nationalist communist parties and the Soviet Union on the issue of how much autonomy Eastern European communist parties could maintain without jeopardizing Soviet interests. The declaration confirmed the strategy of a 'peaceful road to socialism' initiated by Khrushchev and called for a broad, popular-front-type collaboration of progressive forces and communist parties in Western Europe.

Khrushchev, Nikita Secretary of the CPSU from 1953 to 1964, and Premier and Chair of the Council of Ministers of the USSR, 1958 to 1964. Khrushchev instituted de-Stalinization policies after denouncing the excesses of the Stalin regime in 1956. Forced to resign from his state and party duties in 1964, Khrushchev lived in retirement until his death in 1971.

Labor Party of Spain (Partido del Trabajo de España; PTE) A communist, Marxist-Leninist party. Small, but very militant, it is, perhaps, the second communist party of Spain, but very far from the PCE (from which it split).

La Croix Roman Catholic journal published daily in Paris.

Laurent, Paul Secretary general of the PCF Young Communists from 1954 to 1962. Since 1973 Laurent has performed the role of secretary of the Central Committee of the PCF.

League of Communists of Yugoslavia (CLY) Tito's communist party in Yugoslavia, which attempted to claim a 'national road' to socialism, but which was criticized in 1956 by the Soviet Union for not being an entirely Marxist–Leninist organization. The Soviet leadership thereby discouraged other national communist parties from modelling themselves on the domestic Yugoslavian experience.

Le Défi Démocratique (1973) Book written by Georges Marchais, secretary general of the PCF.

Lenin, Vladimir Ilich Ulyanov Founder of the Russian Communist Party, Lenin led the Bolshevik Revolution in Russia (1917) and became the architect, builder and first head of the Soviet state.

L'Humanité Daily newspaper of the PCF, published in Paris.

Lin Piao Former Defense Minister of the People's Republic of China, Lin Piao served as a guerilla, together with Mao Tse-tung, against Chiang Kai-shek in the 1920s. Lin Piao was designated as Mao's successor in 1969, but he disappeared in September 1971 and was reported dead in a plane crash in July 1972.

Lister, Enrique Secretary general of the PCOE, the Spanish Communist Workers' Party, a small communist party opposed to eurocommunism and loyal to the CPSU. Lister, a famous commander of the Army of the Republic in the Spanish Civil War and a former member of the Central Committee of the PCE, led a split of the PCE in 1970 over the anti-Soviet position the PCE took with reference to the invasion of Czechoslovakia, and founded the PCOE.

Longo, Luigi Member of the group which founded the PCI in 1921, Longo was an active partisan in the Spanish Civil War and a leader in the Italian resistance. He became PCI secretary general after Togliatti's death in 1964, and remained in that position until 1972. He is now president of the PCI.

Lubljana Congress (1959) The Twenty-First Congress of the Soviet Communist Party which ended in agreement for common opposition to the Tito-led 'revisionist' movement. At the Congress Khrushchev emphasized the absolute inadmissibility of nuclear war and spoke warmly of the need for an East–West détente.

L'Unità The daily newspaper of the Italian Communist Party, published in Rome.

L'Unité The daily newspaper of the French Socialist Party, published in Paris.

Manifesto **debate** A debate within the PCI over positions advanced in *Il Manifesto*: the major contention was whether a dissident journal headed by major party members was appropriate. *Il Manifesto* was deemed to have subverted the ideology and procedures of democratic centralism; *Il Manifesto* members were eventually radiated (expelled but with the possibility of re-entry into the party). (See *Il Manifesto*.)

'Maoism' This philosophy requires that, henceforth, Marxist–Leninist theory must be tested in action, applied to rural China's concrete realities. As the new CCP constitution of 1945 put it, 'the ideas of Mao Tse-tung, the combined principles derived from the practical experience of the Chinese revolution,' were now added to Marxism–Leninism as the party's guiding principles. The growth of Maoism represented the sinification of communism in China. Henceforth it was no longer an alien creed. Its principal achievement had been to build a Leninist party on a peasant base, demonstrating (contrary to its own theory) that the communist order is in fact independent of the proletariat. The inversion of Marxism implied that a man's ideological tendencies did not come from his class affiliation, as posited by historical materialism. His class was now determined by his ideology. This was a triumph of subjective and political considerations over the influence of the economic mode of production.

Mao Zedung (Mao Tse-Tung) Co-founder of the Chinese Communist Party in 1921, Mao was a key figure of the Chinese revolution and became head of state of the People's Republic of China from its establishment in 1949 until his death in 1976.

Marchais, Georges From December 1972 to the time of writing, secretary general of the PCF. Marchais was responsible for the formulation and formation of the Common Program with Mitterrand in 1972, and remained a critical actor in the break-up of the communist–socialist alliance in 1977–8.

Marx, Karl The nineteenth-century political philosopher who formulated the communist revolutionary theory of social transformation. With Friedrich Engels, Marx co-authored *The German Ideology* and the 'Communist Manifesto.' In the 'Communist Manifesto' Marx argues that while the bourgeoisie created an economic revolution, only the nascent working class will achieve a social revolution. In *Capital* Marx analyzes capitalism and explains the nature of its instability. Marx was the leading theorist of the International Working Men's Association, subsequently known as the First International.

'Matesa' scandal A scandal in 1969 in Franco's government over money given to the Matesa Company. Official funds were used, not for improvement of the company, but for investment in foreign companies. Some ministers belonging to the Opus Dei were involved in the affair.

'Maximalists' Refers to the ideology of supporters of 'all or nothing' forms of revolution as opposed to the reformism of the 1920s. (In Spain in the 1920s the 'maximalists' were the supporters of the Soviet revolution. Not only the radical socialists, or the communists, but the anarchosyndicalists were in this group as well.)

Mindzenty, Cardinal Josef Former Roman Prelate of Hungary, Mindzenty was noted for his vigorous resistance to totalitarian regimes. Tried and jailed for treason by both fascists in 1944 and communists in 1949, Mindzenty was freed from custody by Hungarian insurrectionists in 1956. He was given asylum in the American Embassy in Budapest until President Richard Nixon persuaded him to leave. He died in 1975 during exile in Vienna.

Mitterrand, François Chief secretary of the French Socialist Party since 1971, vice-president of the Socialist International, and co-author with Georges Marchais (PCF) and Robert Fabre (leader of the center-left Mouvement des Radicaux de Gauche) of the Common Program in 1972. Mitterrand was the candidate of the united left for the presidency of the French republic in 1974. He has sought to promote the alliance with the communists while maintaining the Socialist Party's particular identity as an agent for decentralizing workers' control and participation policies.

MLF See *Multilateral Atomic Force*.

Moch, Jules Socialist party leader, former socialist Minister of the Interior who repressed the 1947 Confédération Général du Travail strikes, deputy from 1928 to 1958, and author of *Peace in Algeria*, *La Folie des Hommes* and *History of German Rearmament since 1950*.

Mollet, Guy Secretary general of the French Socialist Party from 1946 to 1948, and Prime Minister of the socialist-radical coalition government of the Fourth Republic which was in power from January 1956 to May 1957. He was also a Minister of State in De Gaulle's emergency government which prepared the Fifth Republic after June 1958. He had more recently been critical of much of the policy of the united left led by François Mitterrand. He died in 1975.

Montero, Simon Sanchez A member of the Central Committee of the PCE, Montero reorganized the PCE in Madrid in the 1950s and was imprisoned for twenty years by the regime.

Multilateral Atomic Force (MLF) In December 1960 the Eisenhower administration proposed giving NATO five ballistic missile submarines with eighty Polaris missiles before 1963 if a system of multilateral control could be established. Although the proposal attracted only mild attention, it represented a first step in the direction of nuclear sharing. The Kennedy administration decided to continue along these lines. It proposed in 1961 an allied force of surface vessels with jointly owned nuclear weapons. The ships would have been manned by mixed crews of personnel from the NATO countries. US agreement would have been required before bombs or missiles were used. The British and French vehemently opposed this joint force; the Italians were divided; the initially enthusiastic Germans concluded that the political costs exceeded the possible advantages.

Mundo Obrero The daily newspaper of the PCE, published in Madrid. Prior to 1978 it was a weekly.

Nagy, Imre Hungarian Communist who was Premier of Hungary from 1953 to 1955, when he was expelled from the Politburo, the Central Committee, and removed from the premiership under Soviet pressure. Nagy's attempt to create an alternative economic and cultural policy within the existing framework, called the 'new course,' was an effort to show that communism could exist without Stalinism. Nagy died in mysterious circumstances subsequent to the Soviet invasion of Hungary in 1956.

National Council The supreme body of Spain's only political party under Franco, the National Movement. The National Council consisted of members appointed by Franco.

NATO See *Atlantic Alliance*.

Natta, Alessandro A major postwar leader of the PCI, Natta was active during the resistance, presented the introductory speech for the party debate on *Il Manifesto*, which led to the radiation of party members who belonged to the dissident journal. Today Natta is a member of the Secretariat of the PCI. (See *Il Manifesto* and *'Manifesto' debate*.)

Nenni, Pietro Former president of the Italian Socialist Party (PSI) from 1978) until his death in 1980, Nenni was noted for his negotiations between the left and right of the PSI. He served as secretary general of the PSI from 1944 to 1963, Vice-Premier and Minister of the Constituent Assembly in the De Gasperi Cabinet, 1945–6, and as Deputy Prime Minister from 1963 to 1968. He was responsible for the socialists' commitment to 'unity of the left' with the PCI after the Second World War until 1956. He then broke that policy and led the PSI into the center-left governments of the 1960s.

New Times A Soviet political journal often used to criticize European communist parties.

1947 Peace Treaty Agreement signed in February 1947 by Britain, the United States and the Soviet Union to dismantle the Allied Control Commissions in Rumania, Bulgaria and Hungary. The Commissions were originally established by the United States in conformance with the Yalta Agreement, to ensure free elections in these Eastern European countries.

1960 declaration Refers to the 'December manifesto,' a statement of international communist policy adopted on December 6, 1960, by representatives of eighty-one communist parties, which reaffirmed the USSR as the vanguard of socialist development and the United States as the bulwark of capitalist imperialism, but endorsed negotiations with the West as preferable to world war in the struggle for socialism.

Novella, Agostino Former secretary general of the General Confederation of Italian Workers. Novella was a union organizer and member of the Directorate of the Central Committee of the Politburo of the PCI until his death in 1974.

Novotny, Antonin President of Czechoslovakia from 1957 to 1968, Novotny's election in 1957 was perceived as a departure from the post-Stalin collective leadership principle because he united the office of the president and secretary general of the Communist Party for the first time since the death of Gottwald. Novotny pursued the rigid policies to which the Czech 'experiment' of 1968 was a reaction.

Nuclear Test Ban Treaty (1963) A British–Soviet–American agreement not to test nuclear weapons; it would not ban their further manufacture or, if the powers should so decide, their endowing other states with the armaments, but the treaty could be and was open to ratification by other states which, in signing it, would *practically* forsake their right to produce atom and hydrogen bombs. Furthermore the Soviets hoped that the treaty would be expanded into a rigorous non-proliferation agreement banning the nuclear powers from sharing their weapons and know-how with third parties, and imposing upon the latter an obligation not to develop nuclear weapons of their own.

Nuestra Bandera Theoretical organ of the PCE, published monthly in Madrid.

Nuovi Argomenti A small Italian journal in which Togliatti published his important personal analysis of the future of the international communist movement after the Soviet Twentieth Congress and the Hungarian and Polish events of 1956.

October Revolution Refers to the overthrow of the provisional government of Premier A. F. Kerensky by Russian soldiers and workers on October 25–6, 1917. Led by the Military Revolutionary Committee, which was largely controlled by Bolsheviks, the overthrow was followed by the assumption and proclamation of power by the Second All-Russian Congress of Soviets of Workers', Soldiers' and Peasants' Deputies. Finally, a provisional workers' and peasants' government, the Council of People's Commissars, was formed under Lenin.

Opus Dei A religious organization, popularly termed the 'White Mafia,' founded by Josemaría Escrivá de Balaguer in the 1930s. Opus Dei members were very influential and became chief officials in Franco's regime in the 1960s; since the late 1970s, however, the organization has weakened.

Ostpolitik West German foreign policy towards Eastern Europe. Designed by Chancellor Brandt, Ostpolitik aimed to create stability and détente between West Germany and Eastern Europe without, however, the transformation of fundamental political oppositions.

Pact for Liberty Refers to the PCE's adoption of the

notion of alliance with all the social forces opposed to the Francoist regime, with no consideration of their social origin, as the only way to defeat the dictatorship. This new strategy was adopted in 1956.

Pact of the Moncloa Agreement of all Spanish parliamentary parties after the general election of June 1977 to construct democracy. It included political, economic and labor clauses. The constitutional process and the new Spanish constitution itself could be considered the result of this pact. It opened a period in the Spanish political life, which ended with the second general election in March 1979, known as the 'consensus period.'

Pajetta, Giancarlo A prominent resistance and postwar leader of the PCI, Pajetta has in recent years headed the Office of International Affairs of the party and was, until 1979, a member of the Secretariat of the PCI. He remains a member of the Directorate at the time of writing.

Pinochet, Augusto Chief of State of Chile since 1973. Pinochet was the leader of the four-man military junta which led the coup in which Marxist President Salvador Allende was killed.

Platform of the Democratic Organs Formed in October 1976, before the legalization of the political parties, the Platform of Democratic Organs replaced the Democratic Co-ordination as the unitary organization representative of the opposition to the Francoist regime, including other political parties that were not included in the Democratic Co-ordination, from the far left to the democratic right.

Platforma de Convergencia Democratica Unitary platform created in July 1975 by the PSOE and other social democratic, Christian democratic and nationalist forces, to oppose the Francoist regime.

Pliotchtch (French translation); Plyushch (Russian name) A Russian mathematician, Plyushch voiced his opposition to the Soviet invasion of Czechoslovakia by writing letters, attending trials and contributing reports to uncensored journals. Fired from his job and blacklisted from other work, he became a professional dissident. Arrested in January 1972 and singled out for 'special treatment,' he was committed to a psychiatric institution. After a protracted and intense campaign to win his release, he was allowed to leave for the West in 1976.

Political Bureau From the 1930s to the 1950s the political bureau, or 'politburo,' was the name used for the secretariat of a communist party. Decisions of the political bureau were considered political rather than administrative.

Popular Democratic Party Small Christian democratic party, it is one of the several small parties that founded the Unión de Centro Democratico in Spain.

Potsdam Agreements The agreements established at the Potsdam Conference (July 17 to August 2, 1945), the third meeting of the heads of state from Britain, Russia and the United States to address the major problems facing the Second World War allies in the postwar era. They included: (1) establishment of a council of foreign ministers; (2) formulation of measures to preclude further attempts by Germany to threaten world peace; (3) German military equipment was to be divided equally and the United States and Britain agreed to contribute to reparations claimed by Germany against Russia; (4) the German territories east of the Oder and Neisse were placed under Polish administration until the final demarcation of Poland's border; and (5) the three powers welcomed the intention of the Polish government to hold free elections.

'Principles' signed by Brezhnev/Nixon (May 1972) Refers to the Strategic Arms Limitation Treaty (SALT I) signed by Nixon and Brezhnev in which they agreed to limit the United States and the Soviet Union to 200 defensive anti-ballistic missiles each. Agreements about co-operation in space, trade and protection of the environment were also made.

Programme Commun See *Common Program*.

PSF See *French Socialist Party*.

PSI See *Italian Socialist Party*.

PSOE See *Spanish Socialist Party*.

'Red Guards' During the Chinese Cultural Revolution Mao Zedung moved against outspoken critics in the fall of 1965. Because the widespread opposition was largely within the party, Mao responded with a vast new effort to mobilize support from outside the party. As part of his effort he went outside the party apparatus to field groups of teenagers as Red Guards, calling upon them to 'sweep aside all masters' and 'bombard all the headquarters.' They were to 'learn revolution by making revolution.' In the fall of 1966, 13 million Red Guards came to Peking for a succession of nine mass rallies and then dispersed over the country to carry out their own 'long marches' and to attack the four 'olds' (old ideology, thought, habits and customs).

Revanchist A reactionary.

Rinascita PCI party policy and news journal. Published weekly, the journal is read primarily by party activists and non-party sympathizers and intellectuals.

Rochet, Waldeck Secretary general of the French Communist Party, 1964 to 1972, honorary president of the French Communist Party since 1972, and author of *L'Avenir du parti communiste français* (1969) and *Ecrits politiques* (1976).

Rossanda's letter Letter to PCI defending *Il Manifesto* by Rosanna Rossanda, one of the leaders of *Il Manifesto*. She was radiated (expelled with the possibility of re-entry) in 1968.

Rude Pravo Official journal of the Czechoslovakian Communist Party, published in Prague.

Schcharansky, Anatoly Leading figure of the Soviet Jewish community who was arrested in March 1977, found guilty of treason and sentenced to three years in prison and the rest in a corrective labor camp in July 1978.

Schmidt, Helmut Chancellor of the Federal Republic of Germany from 1974 to the time of writing; Minister of Finance, 1972–4; Minister of Defense, 1969–72.

Secretariat The executive committee of a communist party, responsible for day-to-day policy-making.

Secretary general The leader of a communist party.

Section The local, primarily territorial, organizational unit of a communist party.

SFIO (Section française de l'Internationale Ouvrière) French section of the Socialist International, founded in 1905 through a unification of other left-wing parties. In 1969 the SFIO evolved into the PSF, the French Socialist Party.

Siniavski, Andrei, and Daniel, Yuri Two Soviet writers tried and convicted in 1966 of charges that they had slandered the Soviet state in their writings. The first trial of a Russian writer expressly for his or her writings, the event precipitated a struggle for artistic freedom in the USSR. Soviet dissidents rallied against the conviction. Daniel, Siniavski's translator, was freed in 1970; Siniavski has been living in Paris since 1973.

Smrkowski, Josef Former Czechoslovakian party and government official, Smrkowski initiated the Prague Rising in May 1945. He was arrested in 1951, and sentenced to life imprisonment, but was released on probation in 1955. A close associate of Dubček, he died in 1974.

Spanish Social Democratic Union A social democratic party founded in the last years of Franco's dictatorship.

Spanish Socialist Party (PSOE; Partido Socialista Obrero Español) One of the oldest socialist parties and co-founder of the Second International. The party was founded in 1879 by Pablo Inglesias. It had a decisive role in the Second Republic and today is the second electoral force in Spain.

Stalin, Josef Secretary general of the Communist Party and government of the USSR from 1924 until he died in 1953. A dictator, he transformed the Soviet Union into a major world power.

'State of exception' During the Franco period a legal situation in which the Spaniards were deprived of their legal guarantees. It was used on many occasions.

Stern West German newsweekly.

Swindle law In 1953 a coalition led by Italian Christian democrats attempted to give a bonus of parliamentry seats to the winning party in the national elections. The proposal failed by a small number of votes. The left labeled the measure the 'swindle law.'

The Italian Communists PCI publication in English of major party documents.

Third International An organization of national communist parties founded by Lenin and the Soviet Communist Party in 1919. During the 1920s it became increasingly dominated by the CPSU, which imposed policy directives on individual members. It was dissolved in the 1930s.

Thorez, Maurice Secretary general of the French Communist Party from 1930 to 1964. Thorez was the undisputed master of the French communists, and able to manage the intrigue and dissent within the party through

absolute adherence to the Moscow line of democratic centralism. He spent the years 1939–44 in Moscow, but returned after the war to work with De Gaulle in order to rebuild France. He held the position of Minister of State and then the Vice-Premiership in three governments. He had a stroke which left him partially paralyzed in 1950; he died in 1964.

Tito President of Yugoslavia from 1953 until his death in 1980. Tito is noted for his defense of independence for communist regimes in Eastern Europe from the tutelage of the USSR. 'Titoism' refers to the attempts of other communist leaders to imitate Tito's defense of state autonomy and to the Yugoslav decentralized, workers' control system of economic policy management.

Togliatti, Palmiro Secretary general of the PCI from 1926 until his death in 1964, Togliatti was one of the founders of the party in 1921 and was active in the Third International. In 1935 he was made secretary of the Comintern and was chief of the Comintern in Spain during the Spanish Civil War from 1935 until 1939. In the postwar period he worked to build the largest communist party in the West and the second largest political party in Italy. Togliatti was acclaimed at his death as the most eminent communist leader outside the Russian or Chinese leadership.

Trotskyites Self-styled supporters of the political doctrines of Leon Trotsky, who fled the Soviet Union when Stalin consolidated his power, and was killed by Stalinist agents in 1940. The Trotskyites denounce the bureaucratic centralism of the Soviet Union and support spontaneous workers' revolution. The term 'Trotskyite' is often used by communist parties to stigmatize their left critics.

Twentieth Congress of the CPSU The Twentieth Congress of the Soviet Union met in February 1956, in Moscow, and marked the conclusion of the Stalinist period. Soviet Communist Party leader Nikita Khrushchev denounced in graphic terms the repression employed by Stalin, reintroduced Lenin's ideas as the model of Soviet socialism, and reopened relations with the independent communist state of Yugoslavia, a form of communism denounced by Stalin. At the same time Khrushchev developed the idea of the possibility and necessity of peaceful coexistence between the capitalist and socialist countries in light of the possibility of nuclear annihilation.

UGT See *General Workers' Union*.

'Vertical Trade Unions.' Refers to the Confederación Nacional de Sindicatos, the rigidly hierarchical official trade unions of the Francoist period. All the Spanish workers were obligatory members of the CNS.

Warsaw Pact (Warsaw Treaty Organization) A mutual defense organization composed of the Soviet Union and its satellites – Bulgaria, Czechoslovakia, East Germany, Hungary, Poland and Rumania – established by the Warsaw Treaty. Signed on May 14, 1955, the Warsaw Pact provided for unified military command and also for the maintenance of Soviet army units on the territory of the other participating states. The Warsaw Pact was one means the Soviet Union employed to consolidate control over its satellites.

Workers' Commissions See *CC OO (Comisiones Obreros).*

Zaccagnini, Benigno Italian Christian Democratic Party notable and a close associate of the late Aldo Moro, Zaccagnini became party secretary in 1975 as part of the effort to renew the image of the DC after the political scandals of the mid-1970s and the electoral losses suffered in 1974 and the 1975 regional and local elections. Zaccagnini has been seen as possibly sympathetic to an eventual compromise between the DC and the PCI.